Socio(onto)logy

Socio(onto)logy

A Disciplinary Reading

Ben Agger

University of Illinois Press
Urbana and Chicago

This book is printed on acid-free paper.

Library of Congress Cataloging-in-Publication Data

Agger, Ben.
  Socio(onto)logy, a disciplinary reading.

  Bibliography: p.
  Includes index.
  1. Sociology. I. Title. II. Title: Socioontology,
a disciplinary reading.
HM24.A38 1989   301   88-10697
ISBN 0-252-01558-4 (cloth: alk. paper)
ISBN 0-252-06019-9 (paper: alk. paper)

For Buddy

Contents

Acknowledgments   ix

Introduction. Social Fact, Social Fate, Social Text   1

SECTION ONE
Sociology, Pedagogy, Ideology

1. Writing/Science   21

2. Reading/Politics   45

SECTION TWO
Text/Book/Discipline

3. Durkheim's Discipline   71

4. Method's Reason   103

SECTION THREE
Marginalia I

5. Centering Dissent   137

6. Disciplining the Dialectical Imagination   161

7. Mainstream Marxism   193

SECTION FOUR
Marginalia II

8. Straight Feminism   229

9. Androgyny: "Beyond" Misogyny and Patriarchy   264

SECTION FIVE

Sociology as a Literary Production

10. The Argument Revisited   303

11. Open Text, Open World   335

Notes   373

Bibliography   397

Index   417

Acknowledgments

Beth Anne Shelton and Bill Warner read the entire original manuscript and provided many useful comments as well as encouragement. Paul Diesing read six chapters closely and helped me rethink some crucial issues. Rob Moore, Jr., read two chapters and gave me my first enthusiastic response.

I gave versions of this book at the Sociologists for Women in Society annual meeting in Washington, D.C., 1985, Southern Sociological Society annual meeting in Atlanta, 1987, and American Sociological Association annual meeting in Chicago, 1987. I enjoyed the opportunity to discuss the book at a talk I gave to the Literature and Society group in the Department of English in 1986.

Ann Beutel was extraordinarily helpful in the preparation of the final draft. Professor Robert Edwards, Chair of the Department of English, generously supported this project at a crucial time. Lisa Nowak Jerry patiently and skillfully edited this book.

Publication of the book was supported by the Research Foundation of the State University of New York at Buffalo.

Larry Malley, editor-in-chief at Illinois, is a gem of an editor: intellectually broad-minded, encouraging, constructive. I hope I justify his faith in my work.

Introduction:
Social Fact, Social Fate, Social Text

American positivist sociology disciplines dialectical imagination, reflecting and reproducing other types of discipline today. One way to undo this disciplining is to investigate the literary nature of mainstream sociology—how and why it suppresses its own narrative in order to close off radical reformulations of history. This is not to say that sociology matters; that is a conceit of discipline in the age of academe. Yet every discourse strengthening positivist culture bears reading. In reading sociology as what a Marxist might call an ideologizing discourse, I want to exhibit a textual-critical method appropriate to all sorts of discourses in fast capitalism—a capitalism in which texts and their objects blur so that prose rushing by cannot be read as an authored act.

This overall aim requires me to consider at the outset whether people today *can* dent the massive structure of thought, language, and action—history—so powerfully constraining political imagination. Our desire is diverted and disciplined into a managed everyday life—drugs, money, power, science. At root this is an empirical question. Although I am not particularly optimistic in these times when administration penetrates the deepest core of our bodies and psyches as well as the furthest reaches of the extensive world, answering it necessarily shifts the balance of power just a little. The negation of disciplinary discourse, critique refuses its subordination to alleged "social facts" compelling writing simply to reproduce them by reflecting them as unalterable pieces of social nature. I mean for text as a model of all free communication to wriggle out its own self-imposed methodism sublimating authorial constitution to the disciplinary representation of an obdurately awful world. In this, I hope to demonstrate writing as a generically self-expressive practice—Marx's labor, discourse, action—both models productive freedom and opposes the apparent indubitability of domination.

Socio(onto)logy: A Disciplinary Reading demarginalizes a variety of intellectual currents either ignored or oppressed by mainstream social science, particularly sociology, my "home" discipline. Sociologists in leading journals typically evaluate those of us who work within these marginalized traditions with respect to dominant criteria of scientificity as well as political conformity. They inevitably find us wanting—methodology, objectivity, reasonableness. I want to reverse the direction of this attention in reformulating the texts of mainstream sociology as discourses both reflecting and reproducing domination. In this I am not investing more political weight in sociology than is its due. However, ideology in the traditional Marxist sense is *everywhere*—that is precisely its newfound efficacy: It hides itself and thus insinuates itself into unthinking practice. It must be addressed by those most familiar with its entwining grip on the minds and bodies who otherwise follow it slavishly. Discipline is perhaps best undone from within.

This book is not directly about my favorite theorists; instead, I address the way the dominant discipline distorts or altogether ignores them. Nonscience becomes nonsense. In this I hope to understand more about the empirical process—academic life—through which mind is disciplined into dull submission. While some of the leading modernist and postmodernist theorists such as Habermas, Adorno, and Foucault provoke my reading, there is no single or simple Habermas. Habermas arises in contest between a dominant discipline that would ignore or manipulate him and my own rebellious reading looking to Habermas to get me out of the mainstream but necessarily daring me to challenge him. As I will suggest by both example and thesis, good reading creates a peaceful community in which writers recognize their bond to other writers whose versions stimulate response. The nonrepresentationality of truth fortuitously makes way for what Habermas calls an ideal speech situation—or Marx, simply socialism.

In what follows I do not mechanically apply one or another critical theorist to my critique of disciplinary sociology. I read Habermas but reject him as a slogan replacing thought; he and others I cite raise but do not resolve the important questions. This is not an account reductively trading on great names for its pedigree, for we all try to make our name by reformulating diverse sources into a new text. As such, reading affords the freedom to reread and rethink. Nevertheless I will probably be read by insiders to work under the auspices of, not with, my favorite theorists. This is acceptable as long as one's relationship to authority is not hierarchical but provides for new versions not simply branded Habermasian or feminist or postmodernist. Concepts help do the work of remembering the community from which a version emerges; yet overreliance on authority robs that version of authority. Authority stems from author-ity, thus suggesting its heterogeneity.

Readings that exhume affiliation at best help educate one to one's own debts. A reader of this book in manuscript called the argument a mix of Marcuse and Derrida—this by way of praise. I had not thought about it exactly that way. I preferred to see Adorno as a major player and perhaps did not acknowledge fully the Derridean (and Foucaultdian) character of the argument; at least I know that Derridean deconstruction needs to be policitized—to become social theory—before I can call myself a Derridean; here I politicize deconstruction with the Marxist insights of the Frankfurt School. I would prefer to be read as Adornoian—if there is such a thing given Adorno's utter resistance to methodologization as an aversion to mindlessness. Naming is best considered an exercise in autobibliography. Of course, writing cannot control its reception; it can only anticipate and thus head off its reduction to clichés. I want to say this at the beginning to assure readers at this early stage that they will not find cookbook versions of my favorite theorists any more than they will find a proposal for a new sociology. We scarcely need more discipline today. I do no more than confront mystification with historicizing imagination: CRITIQUE. If writing strains unsuccessfully to posit a new world, at least we can reduce the intellectual and institutional impediments to imagination—a substantial agenda today.

I address the empirical plausibility of hope by reading mainstream sociology for ironic if unintended insights into the nature of discipline; taxonomists might call my version of method the critical sociology of knowledge or simply critical theory. Mainstream sociology is not only an intellectual discipline but suggests and thus provokes an entire social world disciplined by discipline. Intellect in the age of academe is merely scholarship—thought minus the Dionysian; as such, it affirms. I pursue sociology as a political narrative. No matter how desireless in tone, positivism desires the present world. Disciplinary discourse mirrors a contradictory social order and at the same time creates and recreates it; positivist writing complements the lawfulness of dominations—capitalism, racism, patriarchy—it claims neutrally to describe. As a discourse of the power of the social, sociology imparts discipline to history.

Disciplinary sociology adds its fatalizing account to a world it secretly realizes it must complete; its textual representation socially reproduces existing hierarchies. In this way, sociology disciplines by concealing its authorship as a version subject to both revisions and different versions; instead, it presents the world implacably as a nest of "social facts" whose depiction occupies everyday journal science. In this way, the discipline devolves from Durkheim where in the first thirteen pages of his *Rules of Sociological Method* (1950) he charted sociology as the discourse of subordination, endlessly reflecting—and thus fatefully reproducing—the power of the social. *Fact*—capitalism, patriarchy, racism, the domination of nature—thus becomes *fate* through readings enacting what the naturelike text represents as ontologically frozen, and thus freezes. Sociology dehistoricizes domination by posturing a distance from the world it secretly would make whole. As such, the fact that positivist disciplines discipline discloses the world's historicity, provoking new orders of being.

My analysis borrows from and necessarily transcends a complex intellectual and political inheritance spanning western Marxism and various strands of phenomenological, existentialist, feminist, and poststructuralist thought, all conspicuously absent in mainstream sociology and its own account of its origins in the Industrial Revolution. My project draws on the tradition of ideological analysis and criticism developed by key figures in the tradition of western Marxism, particularly affiliates of the Frankfurt School on whom I rely most directly. Belonging in an ambivalent way to Hegelian Marxism developed by Georg Lukacs and Karl Korsch in the early 1920s, critical theory explains the surprising resilience of capitalism; a system-serving "everyday life"—culture, family, education, sexuality—deceives people that the real is not only rational but also inevitable. Capitalism requires discipline—alienation that we do to ourselves in addition to what is done "to" us. Positivist discourse in particular disciplines by organizing thought into academic departments each responsible for a version of necessity.

False consciousness since Marx has deepened. Virtually all of our experience is permeated by the injunction to accept, and thus enact, the world in the spirit of what Nietzsche called the love of fate, *amor fati,* all the more entrapping for its perversity; people seemingly enjoy and reproduce their own domination. Ideologizing texts like sociology defy readings deconstructing them as authored acts. Their naturelike existence implies that the world cannot be changed in fundamental ways. As such, people are to take solace from the opportunities for self-betterment and entertainment, even eventual salvation, that do exist; capitalism balances between the freedom of the market and its state and cultural management keeping it off the shoals of implosive economic and psychic crises. Disciplines reduce imagination into acquiescence.

As the door of social change is slammed shut by the silent discourse of positivism in this way, a door cracks opens on the prospect of limited personal mobility, modest reward in return for renunciation; the good becomes goods.[1] In its version of this hopeful text, western sociology supplements the imagery of an economic invisible hand with the reflection of essentially binding social laws of hierarchy, patriarchy, and the division of labor.[2] Positivist sociology defies readings strongly showing the irony of versions pretending not to be texts at all; we can learn from this deconstructively where the world's textuality provokes reformulations (including reformulations of the constitutional nature of writing itself).

Comte, Durkheim, and Weber struggled to justify and thus reproduce a bourgeoning early entrepreneurial capitalism undergoing birth pains associated with declining religion, deepening anomie amidst a rapidly growing industrial division of labor, the resulting demise of community, and spreading tentacles of bureaucratic stagnation and amorality.[3] Western sociology from this beginning theorized these and other social problems as largely unavoidable externalities of a fundamentally progressive society governed by laws of internal differentiation and stratification—division of labor plus bureaucratic hierarchy in the context of privately owned capital—as well as by laws of overall societal evolution; sociology kindled the legacy of the Enlightenment as freedom within necessity.

But while Europeans like Weber, Simmel, Toennies, and Mannheim retained Nietzsche's pessimism about the ironic irrationality of instrumental reason, Parsons's Americanization of sociology as structural functionalism smoothed out the ironies of "modernization," collapsing self and the social system entrapping it. The overarching theoretical articulation of subsequent American sociology, his *Social System* (1951) became a veritable metaphysic of the Eisenhower years; it promised a postindustrial order beyond scarcity —and thus ideological contention. Parsons gilds Weber's iron cage in his persuasive version of sociological positivism.

With Parsons American sociology turns away from the anxiety expressed by Weber in his metaphor of the iron cage or by Durkheim in anomie. Although Weber and Durkheim did not sufficiently understand social irrationality as endemic and not only episodic to bureaucratic capitalism, Parsons altogether silences Weber's foreboding,[4] shared by Freud and Wittgenstein among others, in his version of what Adorno called an identity theory. Heralding the facile reconciliation of personal subject and social object, Parsons suppresses the historical tension between individual and societal interest; the original irony of self and socialization disappears from postwar American sociology. Parsons's pattern variables in linking self and society express and thus expedite the rational reality of late capitalism. Adorno (1973a) directs his critique against Hegel's expression of the Enlightenment. In trying to dominate the external world enlightenment driven by a mindless technical reason only invites the "revolt" of objectivity—capital, nature, human nature[5]—and thus perpetuates domination; Adorno's "negative dialectics" can equally well be applied to Parsons's functionalism. Buttressed by positivism, functionalism subordinates the individual to "laws"—the dominion of capital and patriarchy. History becomes ontology through discipline.

Critical theory reads science as secret political theory. Like science, all sorts of discourses from Marx's religious opiate to popular culture assign the person a fixed place in the social system essentially characterized by powerlessness; this is justified in the name of supposedly higher developmental imperatives, an imputed naturelike necessity transcending history. With Comte's "social physics," the first sociology, positivist social science is especially persuasive where its "laws" of social motion provoke duty in the name of empirical necessity, whether obeisance to the division of labor, bureaucratic coordination, or patriarchal family; it narrates these laws in a way that conceals narration, the literary ruse of positivism. Deconstructive readings show invariant patterns of duty and domination to be episodic stages. The deconstructive narration of science reveals data to be frozen chunks of history; in melting them critique suggests their reformulation—ontology proposing new history. Thus, sociology as a text reflecting discipline disciplines. In this book I narrate discipline, unleashing text's secret desire to bring about a world in which writing is not limited to mute representationality, the ultimate abdication of power.

This is not to say that we should continue to use the name sociology to describe our writing. Sociology means what Durkheim meant it to mean. It can flourish in numerous iterative ways—social psychology, status attainment research, ethnomethodology, conflict theory. Yet sociology as a disciplinary activity requires a commitment to Durkheim's first thirteen pages of *Method* (1950) where he froze social structure's—history's—power over people's desires. Thus, in freeing sociology to be itself I mean only that we allow writing to live peaceably and playfully with other versions; epistemology suggests substantive social relationships. No amount of methodology will cancel the driving urge of sociology's version to shed these conformist constraints. All writing wants community, especially the kind that does not show it.

Evoking and thus provoking domination, sociology repeats Durkheim's dreary ontology; "social facts" turn history into ontology. Freedom is equivalent to obedience; laws govern the advance of hierarchy, patriarchy, capital. Following Durkheim, sociology freezes powerless subjectivity into ontology, thus freezing it politically. I trace this discursive strategy in order to overcome it, showing the aporetic shadow of an author behind science's chimerical text. In so doing, deconstruction reformulates and thus opposes discipline as a narrative accomplishment.

Seen in this way, the anticipated charge that my disciplinary reading overdetermines its ideological content depends on one's version of the relationship among writing, discipline, and history. I want to say more than that. Not only do the concepts—social fact, bureaucracy, causality—serve certain political functions and thus close the open horizon of the future; they are so imbedded in the real that they become part of it. The text is virtually impossible to disentangle from a world that would negate its difference from it as a sign of intellectual advance. Sociologists of knowledge and students of the professions who suggest that sociology is a "social institution" only know the half of it. Sociology and society are inseparable where text has become an institution concealing its political purpose—to bring about the world it reflects in its postured sufficiency. Science in lying tells the truth to those who read underneath chilly text to molten desire at the core of every version. Ideologies have sunk so deep and extended so far into routine practice, sociology's (Garfinkel 1967) dehistoricized "everyday life," that, as Marcuse (1964) suggests in *One-Dimensional Man*, it is nearly impossible to separate appearance and reality, concept and referent, signifier and signified.[6] The Durkheimian language of external determination or causality lies at the heart of our thoughtlessly commonplace adaptation to a world we only suffer, the self-consciousness of eternal victimhood entering discourse as a result of overarching "laws" somehow making the bad bearable. In the mien of the reasonable person enlightenment spells adjustment.

I analyze society backward through the sociology that provokes by reflecting it, concealing its own constitutional contribution to the world it dumbly makes present. I read an assortment of sociology textbooks as they represent and reproduce a discipline, as such both signifying and signified by intractable forms of life under sway of discipline. If this is overdetermining, drawing large conclusions about both the discipline and then the social order at large from the examination of mere textual fragments, it is because the world is already overdetermined; meaning is merely fragmentary, and yet the fragments can be made to say a lot. Concepts allegedly reflecting an intractable social object sink so deep into psyche that through them we experience a positivist world; texts suggesting the experience of fate seal it. The intractability of the world is only intensified by texts that efface their own difference from the world they in part constitute, suppressing the appearance of their own literary artifice in order to preclude the possibility of *any* artifice. In disciplining, positivism reproduces discipline.

The anticipated charge that I risk simplification along with overinterpretation rests on a model of interpretation that would rescue authorial intention from its own opacity; textual explication pretends to solve philosophical problems. A positivist model of interpretation augurs definitive exegesis establishing monological certainty; once read, books can be shelved and forgotten. Nonpositivist literary critics (Culler 1982) accept, even celebrate, permeable boundaries between text and world, giving rise to the concept of a genuinely social text riddled with historicity and anchored in a social scene that it both reflects and creates. Deconstructive reading is properly both interpretation and constitution, a version of writing itself. As such, reading bears responsibility for history.

Developments in phenomenology, hermeneutics, reception theory, structuralism, and poststructuralism (Eagleton 1983) suggest that writing is not simply a means of communication, ideas clearly present to the author's mind and thus easily communicable, but is instead fraught with contradictions, lapses, and contingency. The feminist poststructuralist Julia Kristeva (1980) writes of "intertextuality" as the inherent relationships between a text and others in its tradition that inhabit it, providing it with silent interlocutors. Harold Bloom (1975) observes that the poet is locked in struggle with earlier poems and can be read as trying to surpass them interconstitutively. The positivist version of sheer reading (e.g., the New Criticism) obscures the textual politics surrounding the struggle over meaning.

Because the Frankfurt School's critical theory is for me the most important empirical version of classical Marxism, grasping the "colonization" (Haber-

mas 1984, 1987) of psyche and body by the simultaneously exteriorizing and
interiorizing imperatives of capital, poststructuralist deconstruction powerfully
proposes an imaginative versions of versions; texts refer not only to the established literary canon, even popular books, but to heterogeneous discourses—
MTV, soap opera, and sociology as well as Mozart and Shakespeare.[7] Indeed
the most telling "texts" are those that elude their ready readings, instead dis-
persing themselves as text-objects into the inert landscape of fast capitalism
and thus defying other versions of themselves. Although I do not overdeter-
mine sociology's contribution to domination's totality—for sociology is only
one among a thousand self-reproducing discourses of occlusion—I refuse, with
certain Marxists, to ignore the local contexts of power's fateful reproduction,
especially where these have become con-texts.

It is not a question of misinterpretation in my disciplinary reading but
of an appropriate social-textual analysis revealing the permeable boundaries
between sociological concepts and society. They reproduce each other through
the language games (Wittgenstein 1953) of everyday life; communicative in-
competence and unequal dialogue chances frozen in ethnomethodology and
social phenomenology are readily incorporated as humanism, Blumer's "loyal
opposition," by a neofunctionalism celebrating its difference from Marxism.
Concepts have been tailored to describe "reality" in limiting imagination and
innovative action, evoking certain lived responses that ironically prove the
concepts to have been correct in the first place; the reproduction of hierarchy
validates its chill in the text of bourgeois social science. Mainstream sociology
as a discipline disciplines; it is one among many language games that through
a disinterested representationality only reproduces the world it aims validly to
reproduce, playing on the tellingly double sense of the notion of reproduction
here—both artifact and copy, the one through the other. Legitimated by their
citation of authority and display of methodology, positivist texts tell a world
read and thus lived incontrovertibly.

Positivist writing claims legitimacy as a reflection of the indubitably present
and—thus—unalterable, the here-and-now and close-at-hand. In the course of
this book I argue for a different concept of science eschewing an ontologizing representationality; a nonpositivist version of versions foregrounds its own
political desire to live peaceably with other versions and other writers—a variant of Habermas's own notion of the ideal speech situation as a contemporary
metaphor of earlier socialism. I reveal to sociology its occluded narrativeness
as a way of opening it to dialogues constituting good community. Here my
standard of validity is not correspondence to an inert reality, an epistemological principle destining us only to relive the dominant social arrangements of
our time; instead good discourse acknowledges its own literary desire and then
argues for that desire in undecidably allowing for—no, requiring—other versions. The literary undecidability of truth makes community possible as text

amplifies desire. Writing liberates by revealing its own ontological contribution to history.

A nonpositivist version of science acknowledges its own drivenness by authorial desire in eschewing a deauthorizing methodology cleansing text of literary traces; after all, science tells a story, too. Positivism disinterestedly disengages from the world it describes and thus freezes, reproduction reproducing its own subordination to the real it reifies. Good science denies presuppositionless representationality not only as bad politics, prolonging a fatefully historical present, but as sheer impossibility; text is inextricably bound up with the world it mutely imitates—noisily. Dialectical prose in this way constructs a world only to give these constructions the lie, or to modify them, showing their limitations in literary imagination. Adorno wrote that the only way out of what he called the objective context of delusion is "from within," giving text play so that it might negate its false claim to universality.[8]

As I understand it, the deconstructive program is virtually identical to this, working with(in) texts so as to allow their instructive contradictions, inherent openness, and resistance to closure to show through, *to break out,* thus modeling a textual practice generalizing itself as an ideal speech situation in Habermas's terms. Text is practice; yet practice does not always employ discourse. In this acknowledgment, I avoid apolitical versions of deconstruction that overvalue "talk" as a counterpoint to a talklessly reductive materialism— typical Marxism. As discourse, good politics is alert to its own aporias and artifice; its literary corrigibility opens to other versions in the gentle practice of dialogue, echoing Habermas's notion that every speech act intends consensus but adding to him that good talk recognizes its own provocative undecidability in Derrida's terms. Socialism here is simply a book that in listening to itself and others write never closes, rejoicing in the noisiness of intertextuality as the essence of genuine democracy.

The difference between my appropriation of Adorno's critical theory and an apolitical version of deconstruction is this: whereas Adorno as a Marxist of sorts advanced dialectical writing as a constitutive medium of a dialectical society, Derridean deconstruction is inscribed in Nietzschean transvaluation and thus foreswears its own inherently political nature. Relativism risks undoing itself absolutely, thus providing no basis for what Adorno called nonidentity —no critical standard against which to measure the insufficiency of history. Deconstruction intends to be an ontology pure and simple where critical theory as negative dialectics uses ontology to make a better world, indeed, a world in which ontology suffuses all human interaction through discourse making thematic its own mortality and contingency. Dialectical discourse liberates language from discourse keeping us powerless, notably positivism. Marxist discourse critique turns positivist practice against itself by revealing its constitutional nature—thus in reformulating it, reformulating its world. Here I open the more political insights of deconstruction to the neo-Marxism of the Frankfurt School by trading on the transition from Adorno, Horkheimer, and Marcuse to Habermas's communication theory via various discourse theories and feminism.

That positivist discourse does not acknowledge its own nonidentity to reality and thus its own openness to reformulation—presuppositionlessly mirroring a frozen world—already reveals its enmeshedness in the social fabric it would make only denser. Science's disinterestedly representational account conceals a subtext in which desire burns to reproduce the given and, aporetically, its own subordination to it. Oppositional writing by its very nature begs interpretation and thus constitution. Reading animates the text's hidden possibilities as well as empowers the reader not only to read but also to write—and thus to live; strong reading is both literary and political artifice.

In this sense, science is only a fragment of literature constituting what Marcuse (1964) called a Great Refusal,[9] echoing the Frankfurt School's view of art as critique and imagination. Rooted in a simple base-superstructure model of the relationship between economy and culture, Zhdanovism and other mechanical tendencies of Marxism crudely tried to disclose the ideological reflection of social contradictions in art; yet art by its very difference preserves the possibility of radical otherness, both a refusal of the present and the figure of a different, better world.[10]

Scientific prose crafted under the sign of a fraudulently disinterested representationality refuses to acknowledge its immersion in society precisely to further it, the goal of the Enlightenment since Condorcet. Positivism suppresses its inherent difference from what it describes in order to reproduce its object by provoking its thoughtless representation, its repetition by positivist readers. Writing that recognizes its simultaneous autonomy and historicity, "*écriture*," points beyond itself by involving the reader quite directly in the process of imaginative reconstruction. Positivism suppresses the continuum of reception, criticism, and construction in order to conceal its own constitutional efficacy as mere reflection. Supported by insights from deconstruction, critical theory reverses this concealment in bringing to light the traces of busy authorial work. This is the undoing of positivism; its frozen representations—the power of the social—are thawed in a text refusing to suppress its desire to bring about a certain order of being.

Sociology in its grounding Durkheimian version promulgates a language game—a positivist world—disqualifying any but the most meager freedoms. Weber was no different. Although he lamented the runaway rationality of bureaucratic organization, depicting it as a soulless world drained of cultural meaning and community, he reflected and helped freeze that world in his theory of technical reason. Weber disliked history yet gave it the imprimatur of ontology—the iron cage. This capitulation to seeming necessity stretches from the Greeks and Paul to Luther and Hegel; Comte, Durkheim, and Weber merely recast domination in supposedly invariant principles of social differentiation and hierarchy, thus contributing the discourse of sociology to overall disciplining. In reinterpreting American functionalism more broadly as a sociology of order linking "laws" of evolutionary progress (Durkheim's division of labor) with "laws" of social process (Weber's bureaucracy), I can trace it to Judeo-Christian beginnings. If not an unwitting celebrant of a godless instrumental reason in its original European formulations, sociology with every idealism sharply divides the realms of necessity and freedom. Discipline thus begets more discipline.

Sociology in seeking to describe immanent laws thus chills history into a social fate that its account would bring into being simply by being read and then lived. Intending a certain world, texts ironically become that world. Durkheim and Weber flatten the abundant human misery of early capitalism into an inexorable tableau of modernization; thus, they help bring it about. Sociology dehistoricizes exploitation into a disciplinary discourse centered around the axiom that advanced society necessarily diminishes autonomy. Sociology accepts a mindless reader as an accurate account of all possible readers, freezing powerless subjectivity into all possible subjectivity. Research finds what it knew always existed, thus reproducing it. The positivist account of "fate" reproduces itself as an accurate account, Hegel's ruse of reason taking methodological form. Fate begins where science's social text ends; by appearing ontologically exhaustive, science exhausts ontological possibility. Of course, in the present historical situation the text of mainstream sociology makes surface sense as an accurate account; life-chances are not distributed equally and never were.

Born of reality, science bears reality by ensuring its reproduction on grounds of metaphysical necessity. The positivist text describes certain modest compensations in return for adaptation, suggesting a bearable fate; otherwise legitimation in state-managed capitalism plummets too far. A vast productive infrastructure smoothes if not eliminates the contradictions of class, race, and gender. As Marx saw, capitalism has been a progressive force. Domination is not ontologically without interruption or amelioration.

And yet the appearance of science's neutrality strengthens its hand. The well-adjusted personality "knows" that life is compromise, with costs balanced against benefits; thus a rigorous science, beginning with Durkheim's (1966) study of suicide, appears to tell the truth beyond morality. A form of popular culture in its visceral knowledge of "fate," sociology leaves room for social reform in response to the inequities of the time. Ventilating a certain moral passion, sociology's desire to change the world is circumscribed by disciplinary commitment; freezing if not loving a preponderant objectivity—history thus far —sociology disciplines its temptation to oppose history with a fuller ontology refusing domination in the name of the modern. Durkheim's concepts of social facts—the notion that behavior is willy-nilly *caused*—drives the sociological discipline. Positivism reflects and thus reproduces these "facts" as our fate; the power of the social is frozen by the discourse of the power of the social —sociology. At the same time, sociology's liberalism wants to reduce suicide, ameliorate poverty, and cure drug addiction as regrettable by-products of modernization. The former precludes the latter; positivism redoubles misery. The historical totality would have to be undone if we are to address the real causes of suicide and poverty—an unequal social system strengthened by texts converting fact into fate, history into ontology. Sociology condemns us to an eternal present by concealing its deep roots in the past. However much sociology "calls" us to mitigate suffering by explaining it as a social product, positivism silences that calling. It offers no solutions to history reflected timelessly.

The preponderant experience of the modern cannot be transcended because, as Weber and Durkheim believed, technical rationalization is a juggernaut. Institutions today strangle us by virtue of their very size and complexity. Undoubtedly this is true. But must they? Mainstream sociology conceals a philosophy of history taken over by the first sociologists from Condorcet. Society moves forward, compelled by an institutionalized rationality joining capitalism and democracy in the mastery of both inner and outer nature. Yet as Weber and Freud lamented and Marx denounced, the mastery of inanimate nature is bound up with regimentation of social nature; the master principle of enlightened civilization is an urge to control. Where this urge backfires, we make war, commit organizations to immoral purposes, and exploit our intimates. Freud in his *Civilization and its Discontents* said that progress requires increasing psychic repression to prevent the revolt of inner nature increasingly bottled up by both the organizational and libidinal requirements of an industrial civilization.[11] Rationality is the ability to adapt, to cut one's losses, to censure onself before preponderant authority. At its limit rationality is silence.

Sociology reflects our own powerlessness back to us as a fate leavened by certain rewards, the emoluments of the oppressed. This concept of equity at the heart of a capitalist order infiltrates a whole range of the human sciences from economics and psychology to structural linguistics and sociology. As Marx, Adorno, and poststructuralists tell us, however, the binary opposition of subject-object is rarely an equal exchange. Difference deconstructs itself as the likelihood of inequality; equality is only defined by its frequent absence. Likewise, although "fate" for many today is less brutal than it was a thousand years ago, it is still enacted as unavoidable necessity, as ontology—recompense for freedoms renounced in the name of science. Sociology is the liberal *cri de conscience* asking for *more*, but not for the end of fate as such, which is the only true solution. Yet in asking for "more"—power, prestige, wealth—

Weber developed his classic trinity to show that Marx was wrong to reduce all social efficacy to economic issues, a construction of Marx proposed by most "conflict theorists"; sociologists accept this version of the realm of necessity, disqualifying radical social change on metaphysical grounds. From that point on, reform within the context of the capitalist welfare-state can be only piecemeal, quantitative not qualitative.

The standard neo-Kantian argument for free will as a regulative concept of social science fares no better in its ability to surmount the binary oppositions —freedom/necessity, reward/duty—driving the discourse of the power of the social. There is neither only free will, the domain of the human sciences according to Dilthey, Windelband, and Rickert, nor only causation. Nor does Parsons's identity theory transcend the silent oppressions of dualism where he simply collapses freedom and necessity in positing a cosmic harmony between self-interest and societal requisites and thus occludes the tension—the domination—between person and system in any exploitative society. Free will and causation are contingent categories describing various historical relationships between people and the enveloping social environment. Their duality captures the essential historicity of what are often thought to be ahistorically philosophical categories of possible social experience. No will is ever entirely free of social context, and behavior is never simply imprinted by external conditioning forces, Durkheim's social facts. But social science and neo-Kantian philosophy hypostatize causation as a transcendental category and thereby obscure its very historicity—the open possibility of *making* history. The one regards social facts as fate, the other as mere externalities of mind that can be transcended.

The mastery of history would end the mainstream sociology we know; it would end heteronomy that Durkheim and others after him scientize as the incontrovertible human condition. Sociology is parasitic on domination. The prospect of revolution revolts it. This scandalizes academic sociologists because it violates a disciplinary self-consciousness deriving its own literary possibility from the generalized existence of "social problems" seemingly crying out for analysis and, subsequently, redress. Comte constructed sociology to deal with the excrescences of a burgeoning economic system quite advanced of the political, social, and cultural systems of the time (e.g., factory work preceding labor laws and unions). Conflict sociology correctly reminds us of the roots of sociology in social problems analysis lest we forget that the canon's founders leavened *la science pour la science* with moral verve. Social fact—history—blocks any but the most modest reform agenda because its text frames, and thus helps to reproduce, an existence experienced as unalterably perverse, obdurate.

In spite of its original reconstructive program, sociology entrenches the domination it seems to oppose morally; positivism strengthens capitalism. While sociological discourse acknowledges less than complete identity between personal subject and social object—social problems—it conceals its own interest in perpetuating a misbegotten history in the account it weaves out of the cloth of scientism. Oppression is softened into "social problems." Division of labor, bureaucracy, inequality, and patriarchy become preconditions of modern civilization even though *they* are the problems. Sociology freezes history into a text more metaphysical than metaphysics—science. Methodically the reflection in text of social determination bled dry of any constitutive trace and thus rendered generic, *dehistoricized,* the positivist version of science overpowers liberating desire. The tension between a superficially animated liberalism and the apodictic aim of science is utterly eliminated as the apparatus of representation becomes sheer technique and is fetishized. Methodology effectively blocks Marxism.

As even a casual perusal of the leading journals and monographs will indicate, current American sociology as methodological, statistical, and figural display thus drives out mediating prose, even the hypothesis testing of Merton's middle range. It is thought that philosophical and political problems can be resolved technically, especially through better measurement. The original engagement of the European founders with the crisis of the modern, resurrected briefly in the 1960s, has been eclipsed in a discipline committed more to professionalism than politics; the text's political surface was never more than a thin veneer. In this light, because they are simultaneously introductions to the discipline and to American "society" written for neophytes, introductory textbooks are both more problem-oriented and more proseful than much of journal science whose methodologism has become utterly morbid. Thus, far from worrying that my disciplinary reading focusing on textbooks needlessly simplifies a pluralistic discipline, I submit that the texts are much more direct versions of disciplinary ontology, thus politics, than is journal science; the figural displays of the journals virtually defy reading even though, as such, they are powerful metaphysical accounts. I narrate journal science for its part in my forthcoming *Reading Science: A Literary and Political Analysis.*

Some will object that science can valuably upgrade the stature of a young discipline struggling for respectability alongside the less self-conscious hard sciences as well as point the way to social reform. But this dehistoricizes what has actually happened to political passion in the discipline since the 1960s: two steps backward for every one forward. Indeed, the sociological 1960s are widely entombed in the retrospection of intellectual history as an infantile disorder now happily replaced by mature science. The paradigm of conflict flourishing in the 1960s now becomes a strike *against* Marxism from the point of view of Weber, and a potentially critical phenomenology is reduced to ethnomethodism.

Science deludes as it both opens and closes the door of fundamental social change; impervious social laws are to be softened by the prospect of self-betterment, spiritual plenitude, leisure time, believed to lie beyond the realm of necessity, a neo-Kantianism animating the discipline. Where sociology arose in the crucible of the Industrial Revolution as a way of addressing the dysfunctions of urbanization, the factory system, and the decline of religion as an integrative force, the idealist-identitarian thrust of later American sociology virtually equating self-interest and social interest drops out the anxiety of Durkheim and Weber about the possibility of happiness in the iron cage of industrialism. This falsifies intellectual as political history in the defense of scientific disinterestedness, a fatal mistake for later sociologists who do not share Parsons's equanimity about Comte's vision of "order with progress" or about Durkheim's first thirteen pages. Critical sociology unable to shed its investment in Durkheim's account of generic domination as the essence of group life fails because it does not address the roots of discipline in discipline; in explaining domination empirically, positivist sociology reinforces it. However small its contribution, disciplinary positivism is part of the problem.

Social problem-oriented scientism is still scientism, unable to understand its own constitution of, as well as its constitution by, the impermanent present. Freedom requires the lived experience of free thought as seeming social determinism is undone historically, not only in "humanist" method—idealism. An emancipatory text refuses to reproduce domination in the name of scientific representationality, thereby only reproducing it as a fate to be suffered, even occasionally enjoyed.

The long tradition of idealism can only seek liberation in transcendence, the ethereal beyond of spirit. From Paul and Parsons to postindustrialism,[12] idealism retreats from practice to the City of God in the mistaken belief that God's cards have all been played. Western thought locates freedom on the far side of necessity, after life itself or simply after work; subordination is only reinforced by foreshortening imagination and agency, the present enacted as the possible. This is not to say that domination is simply a construct; tell that to political prisoners, welfare recipients, victims of genocide. But it is neither simply an external reality, *imposed*. Domination is rarely only what "happens" to us; it is also something we do mindfully to ourselves and to others. The metaphysical location of subordination outside history obscures the dialectical character of oppression, the capacity for self-negation negated by the closing, freezing text of science.

That is all Marx meant when he criticized capitalism as historical artifice, subject to new versions the dialogical writing of which itself constitutes good community. The so-called tendential laws of crisis—underconsumption, rising organic composition of capital, unemployment—are only tendencies and thus must be unfolded in practice. Marx unmasked bourgeois economic theory as a text enacted in people's capitulation to the apocryphal laws of the market. His critique of ideology was a different text that tried to evoke the self-contradictory tendencies of market "laws" in the possibility and imagery of a different life called communism. Marx meant for the *Manifesto* to burst into the streets as a meditation on and mediation of existing social contradictions working themselves out in the space between necessity and freedom, text a reproduction that in turn produces.

Moving back and forth between contingency and agency, transformative action is therefore neither wholly one nor the other; it is thus, perhaps, the truest freedom.[13] Compare this notion of socialism as text to Engels's static and statist image of the "administration of things." The notion of a productive text captures the processuality and historicity of socialism, seen and lived both as process and product at once. A textual version of socialism opposes the portrayal of socialism as a discrete event that arrives punctually and then endures unalterably, thus inhumanly.

Socialism ruptures the apparent continuum of domination, the false necessity of science's "necessity"; positivism construes and thus deepens domination as ontology, not history. Ideology today lives as life itself, the single point of agreement between Althusser and the Frankfurt School who would demechanize Marx's sense of ideology as what Marx and Engels in *German Ideology* called a "*camera obscura*," the representational inversion of an unambiguous reality. Positivism transforms history into ontology—bureaucratic division of labor, patriarchal family, religion, possessive individualism compensated by accumulation and desublimation, the inauthenticities of late capitalism that recycle desire and profit by sating it. This positivist order of being is itself a social text written into the multifarious cultural discourses of our time, from fast-food advertising to sociology textbooks.[14] We no longer read writing that stands at a critical remove from the world; nor does writing oppose that world. Instead the texts are dispersed into the built and figural environment and thus occlude the appearance of their artifice, an issue to which I will return in my concluding chapter. As such, writing is meant to relive itself without the contemplative mediation of readerly interpretation and critique. Speculative reason reduces into routine via the methodology figuring it.

Fast capitalism requires *both* the release of pent-up frustrations, domination having been conveniently psychologized and thus rendered harmless, and mounting resistance to a technological *promesse de bonheur* that could virtually end scarcity and thereby toil. It is the task of social texts both to reinforce superego restraints in an era when they could be eased and to appease desire by leavening a harsh version of necessity—the perverse simultaneity of progress and repression. Where the Keynesian state since FDR has managed the economy and thus kept its crisis tendencies temporarily in check, today culture administers (by suppressing) desire, keeping it busy in the supermarkets, classrooms, bedrooms, bars, and churches in order to deflect the terrible realization that we are doing this to ourselves.

Sociology lightens domination by promising modest social reform, self-betterment, and meaning—increasingly scarce in a Nietzschean capitalism perpetually eroding its own bedrock legitimacy in the relentless transvaluation of (use-) values. This liberal text addresses material misery, legitimates careerism, and restores tradition as a way of establishing a privatized "public" sphere, the system saved by efflorescent subjectivity. A professed humanism within scientism in a neo-Kantian way employs science for human betterment, Condorcet's original faith in progress. It elicits adaptation by suggesting the possibility of certain socially and psychologically ameliorating strategies, the penumbra around the dark cloud of necessity. Adaptation is then derived from Durkheim's version of the power of the social just as it is softened, made acceptable and accessible to the middle-class sensibility by the promise of "creative" work, an "authentic" lifestyle, "community," "faith,"—all characteristics of civil religion in contemporary America. Ideology must mollify just as it forecloses, both opening and shutting doors. Otherwise, if the social text simply rendered a reality without exit, democratic legitimacy in a capitalist society would dangerously erode, leading to all sorts of "irrational" outcomes; Habermas as a Marxist addresses this issue differently in his *Legitimation Crisis* (1975).

Liberal American sociology by equating the modern and the power of the social on the deep level of its concealed assumptions about the world not only fuels a generalized accommodation but also *is* that capitulation, without prepositions. Ideology is practice, not only thought; indeed, it is often practiced without being thought, the peculiar character of its unconsciousness. Quiescence is not a rational choice, in Weberian terms, but a complex outcome of a disempowering history that removes the traces of authorship from everything originally written, wrought, made. Nietzsche's *amor fati* twisted into a Marxist framework both explains that history (e.g., the Davis-Moore thesis functionally justifying economic inequality)[15] and gilds the iron cage of the present, making it bearable and thereby bearing it. Positivism in foreshortening expectations also meets them.

This is an age where stress is quickly overtaking alienation, injustice, and oppression as the major social complaints, leading us further to privatize and psychologize[16] what C. Wright Mills (1959) called our personal troubles.[17] A liberal sociology comforts by discomforting, allowing the expression of concerned moral sentiment. As well, it holds open doors of self-betterment in adapting itself to a powerlessness utterly dehistoricized, flattened into the linear topic of a representational version of the world.

In the rest of this book I want to dig deeper into the various levels of sociology's positivist narrative that by concealing its own interest in reproducing the dominant social order thereby reproduces it. Positivism constitutes by appearing merely representational. Most sociologists are animated less by an ideological self-consciousness forbidden by science—brazen advocacy of capitalism, racism, sexism—than by disciplinary commitment; to be a sociologist circularly means to do sociology. Durkheim inspires sociology where he suggests the irreversibility of domination, the power of the social. The study of "social facts" reproduces them. Ironically, sociology's ontology is more metaphysical than traditional speculative reason. In suppressing its own literary nature, science exhausts history with its mere reflection. *This* industrial society becomes all possible industrial societies. History swallows its tail.

A philosophy of history subsists in the social texts, even if it is an absent presence; no position is a position after all, indeed the most impregnable one as it turns out. Socioontology excavated from surface sociology only deepens it. Our seeming destiny in late capitalism is reinforced by being written, read, and thus enacted; the difference between text and world narrows under the sway of a deauthored version that by inviting a natural life. Unless critique uncovers the literary production of these disempowering texts, we utterly forget that authority is rooted in author-ity, thus vitiating the possibility of other versions. I read sociology as a discourse of domination, a discipline that in disciplining dominates; the power of writing lies in the power it conceals. In reading sociology I model a version of discourse, hence society, that eschews presuppositionless representationality; good writing builds good community in the multiplicity of versions it unashamedly provokes. I would be content if this was read as another way to name socialism, although I am wary of namings that get in the way of autonomous critique and thus become slogans.

I narrate positivist sociology as a modal example of discipline in a way that shows the busy work of authorship beneath it. That will strain the text against itself; sociology's subtext—the world whose recommendation it conceals in mere reflection—methodologically suppresses authorial presence. Positivist pretends authorlessness in order to author a world. Although positivist sociology was drafted in the busy work of authorial artifice, a poetry of the social putting an end to poetry, it endures as the suppression of its literariness. Thus, a new version will not best call itself sociology. Yet it will have the taint of the sociological if only because it engages with it. This is the irony of all critique. The irony cannot be escaped through agenda-setting—a better sociology would —but must be met squarely, as I will try to do in the following chapters.

PART ONE

Sociology, Pedagogy, Ideology

1

Writing/Science

Text as a Political Universe

Positivist writing is both more and less than literature, more in the way it presents an unalterable world, less in the way that the reader by design is to be less involved in reading science than in, say, Dickens or Updike. Not only is science not superior to fiction; it is also a version of literary imagination fundamentally similar to literature except in the single sense that it methodically claims validity for itself, a claim only implied in the fictive portrayal of a generic human experience. Following a distorted model of natural science's allegedly presuppositionless representation of the world, sociology suppresses its narrative imagination precisely to have its reflection of invariant social patterns acted out uncritically. I want to open science's text to literary readings in order to challenge the *unmade* truth claims of credentialed expertise. As literature, positivism makes truth of the fictive world it provokes. Positivist reading is political (in)action.

Owing much to a Marxist poststructuralism, the most advanced voices in literary theory today recognize that there can be no criticism proper without the simultaneous exercise of a social theory regarding the text in question as one among a number of discursive practices having a variety of social forms, contexts, and outcomes. I am more interested here in discourse theory as a reading of cultural and ideological practices than in internal or immanent modes of interpretation per se, a discipline on the verge of imploding anyway under siege by people like Barthes (1977), Derrida (1976), Kristeva (1980), and Eagleton (1983) who show texts' imbeddedness in symbolic and material worlds of which they are dialectical productions. In this, I abandon the distinction between science and fiction that surreptitiously privileges a positivist —and thus a political—version of science.

My concern here is both to elaborate a strategy of disciplinary reading and as such to understand how the positivist world is narrated; I read a single discipline to illuminate discipline generally. A version of sociology suggests a version of all versions, reversing the tendency for history to chill into ontology.

I write reading in order to read writing as a central political relationship fatefully reproducing the topic of its own representationality. As the author of a book about books, I recognize that the social world saturates and is in turn saturated by writing, making what Marxists call base/superstructure distinctions virtually impossible. Writing is a material practice where labor is a textual practice, both presentations and (re)productions of the dominant world. Indeed, discourse theory as I intend the term is the most relevant metamorphosis of what in the early history of Marxism might have been called the critique of ideology, inspired largely by Hegelian Marxism and then taking off in different directions (critical theory, feminism, state analysis, and so on).

With Adorno, Marcuse, and Derrida among others I view ideology not as external to production, a mere representation of the existent and thus only epiphenomenal, but as a lived relationship between textuality and society, the one reproduced in and through the other. In this way, I develop a critical theory of the text as a more empirically and politically relevant version of a total critical theory; a version of versions suggests a version of the world itself in its literary and political overdetermination. Call this a new Marxism as long as we remember that Marxism is a particular version of an overarching critical theory and not the other way around. I read disciplinary sociology in much the way that Marx read disciplinary political economy in *Capital;* critique in uncovering falsehood suggests a more adequate social theory. Critical theory mires in the mud of hagiographical disputation if it avoids the challenge to rewrite historical materialism in sweeping terms. Since Derrida, it is clear that rewriting must proceed through rereadings that treat other versions ironically as unwitting sources of validity; in this case, disciplinary sociology tells a world it would occlude but aporetically fails to do so completely.

Habermas (1984, 1987) is among the only recent Marxists to have attempted such a sweeping rewriting, and I want my book to be read as a response of sorts to his own version of disciplinary sociology (Parsons, Weber, Durkheim). In his terms, I too contribute to the reformulation of Marxism as communication theory albeit in ways that more explicitly draw from poststructuralism and feminism. His version makes way for mine, which I conceive largely as a response, not "better" according to a pregiven standard of validity nor simply "different" in a relativizing Derridean sense—perhaps more politically cogent. Perhaps. In any case, Habermas opens the discussion in his reformulation of historical materialism.

In the introduction I characterized the dominant ideology today as a social text drawing from various discourses comprising what anthropologists call "culture" or Marxists "ideology." This hegemonizing discourse inculcates an *amor fati,* Nietzsche's love of fate, enacting text in the language games of diverse lifeworlds, thereby reproducing both fatalist resignation and "self"-oriented desublimation utilized in modern capitalism to keep people in tow.

Where for Marx religion was the opiate postponing liberation or salvation until the judgment day, today people engage in a range of culturally and economically desublimating activities diverting them from their powerlessness and thus only deepening that powerlessness read in fatalizing texts. And the texts fatalize by appearing to have no author, and thus to still imagination; instead, they present themselves as historyless pieces of nature—the literary ruse of all positivist representationality.

As such, ideology today is a textual practice provoking adaptation to the frozen world, thus keeping it frozen. People seek the few available blandishments like money, status, power, salvation, and even opium as meaningful texts ameliorating the pain of an insufficient existence. The metaphysical nature of Marx's religious opiate as a paradigm of ideology is undone, corporealized and routinized. Metaphysics is no longer contained in mystifying books that have to be read interpretively; metaphysics is the lifestyle of thoughtlessness provoked by "books" less read than experienced. Religious bliss is now paralleled by blissed-out Yuppies who drink, smoke, and snort their "ideology" in the various lifeworlds into which texts are dispersed and then quickly read as obdurate entreaties to consume, divert, withdraw, and go along. Fast capitalism disperses discourse into things taking on a figural significance overdetermining their meaning. Today reading is not the contemplative reconstruction of arguments but quick assimilation of an encoded metaphysics of adjustment, even celebration. Sociology as a local version of scientism is one among a number of these dispersed texts figurally dictating a whole ontology—the love of fate: hierarchy, private capital, bureaucracy, patriarchy, racism, domination of nature.

An adequate analysis of self-reproducing discourses today must array together a decentered range of practices from sociology, television, and revivalism to careerism, cocaine, and pornography. The asceticism and economism of the Old Left represses theoretical innovation in fear of being contaminated by what mechanical Marxists have traditionally dismissed as cultural analysis. Yet it is nearly impossible today to discern where production ends and reproduction begins. Although "everyday life" may one day be an oxymoron, deritualizing the possible exuberance and intelligence of daily human existence, it neatly captures what is happening now to reproduce domination in psyche, body, culture, and community, topics ignored by old-age Marxists only at their peril. This does not restore idealism by privileging textuality over the economic. The personal and political interweave, a key theme of feminism, [1] converging with the postmodern Marxism I am writing here. Text and/as labor also blur, albeit without losing their nonidentity. In spite of Marx's *Grundrisse*, orthodox Marxism for too long has missed the crucial relationship between production and reproduction, labor on the one hand and culture, psyche, sexuality, family —*text*—on the other. As Horkheimer recognized in 1937 when he demarcated what he called traditional from critical theory, positivism from Marxism, [2] base and superstructure in emerging state capitalism are increasingly inseparable; this locates "contradictions" not simply in the economy (*if* that is what Marx, enticed by bourgeois physics and mechanics, really did in his own work) but over the length and breadth of modern capitalism, from side to side and surface to depth.

This does not so relativize domination that we abandon empiricism[3] in favor of discourse analysis to the exclusion of everything else; indeed, I propose theory as a self-conscious and dialogical version of science. Positivism has invented the duality of philosophy and science to claim value for itself. My version of the world only recognizes the relative invulnerability of capitalism to the economic and sociocultural strains that Marx reasonably expected in the mid-nineteenth century. I am supplementing Marx's metaphor of labor as the most generic human activity with that of writing, mindful that this could be read as an untoward act of idealism. Yet if we understood human practice as the imaginative transformation of the world, then text is as good a metaphor as product or commodity especially where the metaphor can do a lot of analytical work in fast capitalism. Discourse reproduces a productivist world; like housework, it is valuable but unvalued labor.

It is widely agreed among western Marxists that crisis tendencies have extended from the economy per se to the cultural, political, and psychosexual spheres in which economic contradictions are seemingly defused; Habermas (1984, 1987) has called this process "colonization." State intervention in the economic realm manages volatile domestic and global crises of state debt and underconsumption while textual/sexual intervention manages cultural crises of legitimation and meaning. As such, the most propitious battleground today may be the terrain of an increasingly manipulated "everyday life," the struggle to liberate mind and body from the system's colonization as both preparatory to, and part of, economic transformation; the so-called productive and reproductive blur together analytically as they blur in practice. Thus, the topic of a contemporary critical theory is the complex cycle between production and reproduction or public and private that involves reproduction in its own self-subordination to the more highly valued realm of remunerated labor. Positivist discourse accelerates the self-reproduction of reproduction's (text's, women's, labor's) devalorization; a different version of the world deconstructively explodes the texts, freezing history into the cement of ontology. Critique constructs by showing the occluded traces of busy authorial labor—how disciplines increase discipline by suggesting a world they only pretend to imitate.

The binary oppositions of Enlightenment rationalism—either/or—fail to capture the subtle circuitry from the personal and cultural to the political and economic, a failure reinforced from within Marxism by those who mechanically derive ideology from economic interest in deference to Marx. Indeed, dualism conceals both the hierarchy of its terms and their relationship. Here production is valued only in comparison to the "nonproductive" activity surrounding it. Texts are imbued with the social as they are part of this circuitry among mind, body, culture, and political economy. A sociology of literature reducing meaning to authorial intention, mediated by lifeworld or genre, fails to understand the constitutional nature of discourse, especially where that constitutionality is supressed, as in positivism.

Textuality in Derrida's terms is never "decidable," meaning unproblematically prised from yielding text. As words decode meaning they raise new problems of decoding in their own right; interpretation ambiguously begs interpretation. Meaning is structured by the axial principles of civilization, sex, class, language. One might say that the goal of socialism is to free meaning to *mean,* an aim achieved only by demolishing these structures oppressing language in its role as a fatalizing representation, notably science's text. As well, the text is inherently open because the reader can throw over or deconstructively reverse authorial meaning just as interlocutors disagree both about putative states of affairs and issues of morality, truth, and beauty. Austin's speech act theory (1962) shows that speech is action; writing and reading open "mind" to a public world in a variety of illocutionary and constative ways that make textuality a vital political process, an authorizing exchange of influences, significances, and currencies. In appearing unconstitutional, positivism constitutes.

Habermas's work on communication theory (1979, 1984, 1987) further elaborates the political nature of discourse. Albeit more involved with problematics of interpersonal communication than reading and writing, Habermas suggests a broader approach to discourse addressing their heterogeneous contribution to domination—what he understands as "the colonization of the lifeworld." Similarly, I want my disciplinary reading here to do the work of a theory of ideology yet broadening the category of ideology beyond orthodox-Marxist usage. As such, I suggest a wider perspective on the tableau of what I call fast capitalism (1989), in which texts quickly dispersed into social nature create a positivist world simply by concealing their own narrative and constitutive nature.

The claim that texts are inevitably, unavoidably undecidable is, to be sure, a regulative idea in this historical period of culturally enslaved and overdetermined discourse in which meaning is made out to be indisputably transparent, clear for all to see. Words lose their ability to mean where meaning can be demonstrated easily with regard to its topics; the names given to things become things themselves. Positivist meaning is decided circularly with respect to technical criteria; for example, "social class" is its measurement, not a deeper theoretical construction. Why? Poststructuralists might understand the methodologization of meaning as a false solution imposed by a science concealing its literary nature. Once opened deconstructively, science's narrative cannot be stilled with technical and figural suppressions. Science eviscerates meaning the more in Saussure's terms it signifies, reflects, or represents a preexisting world. This is not at all to suggest that evocative writing cannot have the world as its topic—think of poetry—but to understand the way that positivist narrative, silencing its narrativeness, *excludes the reader* from the hermeneutic process, thereby making the reader an empty vessel or blank slate; Locke's epistemological metaphor is perversely undone by being realized. Positivism: a world of blank readers whose imaginative competence has been drummed out of them by their reception/enactment of texts impervious to their narrative constitution of meaning. The critique of positivism narrates texts as genuinely unconstrained language games.

The contrast between science and nonscience is constructed by science itself; yet science as scientism does not exhaust all possible playful knowledges.[4] The presuppositionlessly representational positivist text is written in a way requiring little interpretive work apart from sheer technical reception. Although this is often hard won, it privileges science against other validity claims including "ordinary language" and thus empowers it. This is because the methodical practice of science, the cognition of seemingly natural processes, is seen to be decided in terms of science's capacity for both knowing and then controlling a mute region of objects. Positivism suppresses its authorial subjectivity precisely to entice a certain objectivity out of dulled subjects. Concealing its own desire, positivism manipulates the desires of others. In the meantime, other versions of science are disqualified as nonsense—polemic, passion, perspective.

The representational text is not a conversation in which author signifies and reader fills in gaps, questions, disagrees, and goes on to write anew. Science closes off dialogue[5] as it presents a world inevitably driven by laws, virtually geological forces pushing up from the deep core to shape surface formations. Positivist prose removes history from a world that even natural scientists now agree is characterized by undecidability and historicity. The revolution wrought by Einstein and Heisenberg in nuclear physics (relativity, indeterminacy) once and for all gives the lie to the Newtonian construct of a timeless nature that has only to be reflected, not (also) constructed—the construction *changing* its topic, "nature" thus blurring with history. And if nature is undecidable and historical, at least at its margins, then the social world utterly defies a positivist version banishing historicity—"controlling" for it, as the methodologists would say. Positivism's version of history's nature itself belongs to history—changing it.

A positivist version of itself disempowers readers by removing them from all but passive participation in textuality, the paradigm of which might be the reception of technical definitions and the taxonomic presentation of a conceptual apparatus: methodology. Where science would seem to dehistoricize, it also in effect cancels the constitutive powers of readership by assuming that the reader is to be a receptacle of terminology and a technical apparatus, the model of which has been criticized from Illich to Freire. The literary practice of methodology parallels and thus reinforces epistemological disempowering in the Cartesian-Lockean model of a subject inactively copying an external world, an overarching disempowering that also takes place *through text* in the economy and polity. The reader's role shrinks nearly to nothing when presented with a representational fait accompli; a world that has already been dissected simply awaits its transmission as information. This version of writing assumes that clear reception is unproblematic once a certain technical competence in reading has been acquired, presumably a combination of basic literacy and disciplinary apprenticeship.

Analytic philosophy in its approach to "ordinary language" dominates Anglo-American philosophy, as a positivist functionalism dominates sociology. It is assumed that words used clearly in descriptive statements can be checked, verified, falsified[6] in a grounding community of science. In assuming that the world can be communicated in a technically relevant way, science narratively buttresses the existing canon or "literature" authorizing disciplinary practice; research circularly finds what has always been known anyway. As critics of ordinary language philosophy from Gellner to Derrida have shown, this reliance on convention to establish convention only perpetuates the prevailing conception of the world—thus the world itself. Capitalism requires science to suggest it historylessly; the dominant world comes into being by being lived. As discourse suppressing its discursiveness, ideology secretly conceals its own political agenda—the perpetuation of the given. In this way disciplinary sociology endlessly repeats Durkheim's founding notion that to do sociology is to map—to re-search—the terrain of domination, thus only provoking people's repetition of it. The discourse of the power of the social, sociology empowers discipline. *For Durkheim's discipline to be human is to succumb to the structuring imperatives of social forces.* Thus, positivist text so powerfully reproduces the world by suppressing the appearance of its own authorial desire—to bring about a certain order of being.

Garfinkel's ethnomethodology is an ingenious twist on the premises of positivism only superficially disempowering its postured representationality. Garfinkel reports that language is not lucid; yet people nevertheless manage to make themselves understood, even Garfinkel himself. This paradoxically strengthens the authority of science just as it appears to de-authorize science by giving the lie to the distinctiveness of its discourse as against the discourses of art and philosophy. In showing that science itself is an everyday accomplishment, Garfinkel undercuts its claimed transcendental privilege. Yet at the same time he suggests a communicative rationalism, an optimism, regarding distorted, interrupted, even silenced conversation as exceptional cases. Another pluralism, ethnomethodology in this way presumes that people usually make themselves heard and understood by interlocutors, a constitutional, not contextual, claim. In hoping history were different, he freezes the present by falsifying it.

A critical phenomenology would take the ethnomethodological disempowering of positivist prose one step beyond Garfinkel, as Habermas has begun to do, in arguing that communication itself is a deeply political process wherein power relations between and among speakers are played out. It would thereby avoid Garfinkel's protofunctionalist premise that conversational order is the rule not the exception in this society, a question of historicity the ahistorical ethnomethodologist does not confront. Thus, a critical phenomenology could elaborate a more adequately historicist account of the aporetic modalities of discourse of the kind I am offering here. As social theory itself, science interrogates its desire to bring about a certain state of affairs through its own prose. Its version of the world becomes a world itself. Thus, disciplinary talk can help deconstruct discipline when it is understood as the agenda it is. Description conceals recommendation.

I draw from some of the work of Marxist existential phenomenologists like Merleau-Ponty, Sartre, and O'Neill[7] as well as from Frankfurt critical theory; the difference between these two traditions is perhaps only the gap between French and German intellectual and political cultures, reflected today in the strangely symptomatic silence between Derrideans and second-generation critical theorists like Habermas, who nonetheless converge on certain issues of substance (Jay 1984b). They all rethink the nature of ideology or what Lukacs called reification, the tendency of language to become a thing. And in so doing they intend politically to refresh oppositional movements and resistances run aground both strategically and intellectually. Yet there is divergence, too; Derrida in his opposition to programmatic construction does not offer an explicit social theory whereas Adorno moved effortlessly between philosophical and cultural critique on the one hand and social theorizing on the other largely because he kept the political requirements of intellectual life clearly in mind (even if Adorno was a Marxist patently heterodox by most "Marxists' " standards).

The reader's eclipse by a positivist version of science reflects and reproduces the institutional authority of science today. The reader reads only to accumulate technical information, an ideological practice precisely because it appears neutral with regard to political choice. *There is no merely or purely technical information,* as Marcuse (1964) and others have argued against Weber, especially against Habermas's (1971) Weberianization and neo-Kantianization of historical materialism. Like the assumption of unproblematically lucid "ordinary language" available to all, disinterestedness is a construct masking interest and thereby enhancing the patina of a universal reason, a standard move in the social text of science. Science and technique, like language that encodes them, are never value-neutral but inevitably imbedded in what Marx (1973) called social relations of production and reproduction that give them (and are given) their meaning. Just as there is no "airplane" apart from its historical context—the reading and writing practices getting it off the drawing board—so there can be no transcendental text apart from what Habermas calls the "interests" of readers and writers.[8] Science profits precisely in portraying itself as a discourse needing no readerly work to be understood; it thus masks its drive to control through the silencing of other voices, other claims to know, write, and live the world.

This discussion originally resonated in the neo-Kantianism that split science into lawful and interpretive texts and still authorizes methodological humanisms like ethnomethodology (Mehan and Wood 1975) and symbolic interactionism within sociology; these nonpositivist versions of science eschew nomothetic description in favor of ideographic intuition and understanding.[9] But the construction of two sciences capitulates to the deauthored text of positivist representationality by ceding it to the realm of the unproblematically objective in return for a plenitude of subjective meaning, the virtually inaccessible, evocative realm of sensibility resisting generalization and thus intersubjective analysis. This construction of two sciences[10] gives up a lot to science's representationality, even as it is counterposed to the enrichment of poetry and art, the ungeneralizably particular. But this misses science's imperial urge to control the entire cognitive map, to banish the nonquantitative as, literally, nonsense. When I say science here I refer to positivism—a special version of science claiming exemption from the requirements of epistemological grounding, that is from argument. I say science, implying the posture of antiscience, because positivism says science, too, claiming for itself the right to be all objective knowledges. Thus, I want to diminish positivism's claimed apodicticity by at least initially taking it on its own terms. By the end of this book, I hope to have made possible an alternative version of science— disciplined knowledge that does not suppress authorial voice or preclude its encounters with other versions. Indeed, new science requires dialogue in order to bring about the community it recommends.

Science cannot simply coexist with poetry because it disempowers readers, leaving poetry (and the human sciences generally) with no autonomous audience capable of writing poetry or doing science themselves. Readers become writers only when they can make qualitative distinctions and enter into imaginative conversation with authors, transcending readership in order to write yet without losing the ability to read—to hear others' arguments. Science outlasts the nonscientific because it comes to define a culture in which ordinary language, disinterestedness, unproblematic lucidity, and the assumption of readerly competence hold sway; these are propped by the founding assumption that science presuppositionlessly reflects a world imprinted on readers' brains and thus enacted in resignation to the metaphysical constraints implied in the descriptive account.

Science is not a project of transcendental egos living outside or above institutions but a powerful force in a social world in which the authority of science is a replica and prop of the authority of capital, patriarchy, and political elites. Science shelters the powers by describing—thus prescribing—an unalterable world to which the only reasonable response is adaptation, albeit leavened by the various poetries of goods and spirit. Science's text encodes power by having the power in effect *to read itself;* the figural and quantitative rhetorics of conventional science dictate precritical readings that *enact themselves* in their own imitation of the world imitated, hence constituted, by science. Science in its own representational terms does not simply get the world wrong; it suppresses its own worldliness precisely to move the world forward—completing it as the text of necessity it pretends to be.

Deauthorization and Hegemony

Reading is so severely disempowered by science that it slips quickly under the spell of the text; positivist writing pretends a universality and decidability that it cannot have and thereby degrades poetry to a pastime. The ability to read imaginatively and intersubjectively, along *with* and sometimes *against* the writer, is reduced under sway of representation. The spell of passive complicity is cast by a version taking elaborate pains to conceal its own narrative nature, having been written by a human hand and thus subject to rewriting, redoing. As such, a nonpositivist version of versions opens to a genuinely nonauthoritarian intersubjectivity—community brought about by writing itself as a communitarian language game. A nonpositivist version of the world need not renounce objectivity at all as long as we view the subject as an object in its own right (and the object a subject, a text).

In contemporary publishing this kind of cleansed textuality with profound self-understanding is called the "managed" text, written, as it were, by committee. A book is assembled on the basis of readers' reports and market research, reducing authorial caprice in order to standardize the project. Science claims authority by purging itself of author-ity—personal, poetic, pespectival, evaluative, and political tones, any nonrepresentationality. Science thus suggests itself as an accurate account of external/eternal objectivity, virtually a piece of nature itself. As such, it brings it about—suppressed constitution thereby constituting. Scientificity is thought to be enhanced as literary traces are removed from the text or at most relegated to acknowledgments, preface, or footnotes. Derrida and Benjamin might look first to this front matter and back matter, as I almost always do, and then to the writing's symptomatic silences for evidence *the book has actually been written,* before—better, as a way of—reading the explicit text itself. Without knowing the con-text of the author's desire to change the world via a text, meaning disperses into the figural objectifications of writing seemingly unconnected to an originary hand that crafted prose into an argument.

Deauthorized texts mean nothing more or less than their self-reproducing performances—in sociology, for instance, family's claimed universality "meaning" only that people are being encouraged to family. Here "text" is not only message or meaning but the ensemble of social practices imbedding familied reading practices in this particular history. I regard what science means by family here as a kind of text itself, an ensemble of discursive practices guaranteeing family's reenactment as a fact of social nature. Sociology's text includes more than the pages reflecting family as a human universal; text is stretched to collect all of the discourse-driven activities that reenact their own subordination to the valorized realm of male production and to the science reproducing the reproduction of that subordination.

The sociology textbooks are exemplars of what passes for scientific discourse in this sense. After all, there can and should be different versions of science, of systematic knowledge, blending the acknowledgment of authorial presence with the author's account of objectivity; subtext informs text of its own drivenness by an elemental desire to change the world through its own version of the world. Truth here includes not only objective accounts but a reflexivity and advocacy of a secret desire to provoke a certain state of affairs. Desire is the objectivity of subjectivity that understands itself in these terms, forcing the writer to plumb his or her own depths of interest *as a directly thematic topic of the writing itself.* The literary suppression of authorial motive can be prised free deconstructively.

The managed textbooks are cleansed of the traces of literary work that made them what they have become between covers—crisp, clean print leaving no authorial fingerprints or traces. Ontological constitution is hidden in the figural, technical gestures of the science text. The literary work of science includes revision through various drafts best heard as anticipated conversations with readers who would respond in certain ways, thus requiring writing to head in unforeseen directions. Science flaunts its scientificity as a naturelike object reflecting nature, not as the objectified subjectivity of sweaty writing. The metaphor often used by copy editors and others responsible for bringing the manuscript into publishable form is clean copy, connoting the removal of evidence that the text had actually been written compulsively, perspectively, politically. Editing is to efface the mark of authorial work inviting rewritings as the circuitry of gentle community in which all writing opens itself to different versions of itself. Indeed, to be publishable, science writing conventionally must be cleaned of the tones and traces of subtext that spill out in tawdry advocacy, emotion, and self-reflection; untoward excrescences of authorial vantage contaminate the text's surface validity by violating its methodical suppression of its own desire—to bring about a certain readerly response and thus a certain world. Text is cleaned with methodology—the replacement of sweaty prose with technical writing, citation, figure, and number.

Fiction purposely reveals its own rough-hewn literariness in refusing to clean its surface before publication, recognizing that writing is not only product but process: a good text reflects itself as *having been written* and thus opens itself to new writing and, thus, to the community of other readers, writers, and versions. This is not necessarily to urge first-person signatures on the text but to require writing to acknowledge, and then advocate, the upsurge of its desire politically to remake the world—and this not in a marginal way, as in footnotes or appendices, but in the body of the text itself. Although inevitably nonidentical, for words can never fully convey the origin or extent of their passion without utterly abandoning prepositions, subtext and text fade into each other; the more authorial presence is foregrounded as a requirement of democratic speech, the more difficult it is to separate writing and its marginal embellishments. Margins become central.

Science washes its text by privileging its meaning above the merely contextual. Words become inscriptions read from a transcendental perspective; having been disciplined clean by reviewers, editorial committees, and copy editors, writing is read as if written from a god's-eye view, the validity posture of both religion and science. In turn, this removal of authorial signature inspires the accompanying awesome obeisance that plays itself out in the irony of a text discouraging readerly work; reporting information, science vitiates intelligence. Where Walter Benjamin (1969) argued that the deauratization of art in an age of mechanical reproduction could have a liberating effect by democratizing the great works of art, Adorno (1978b) felt that the erasure of an authorial signature or "aura" would dispel the powerful rupture between the auratized work and an administered, banalized reality. This horizon later came to be called everyday life; an ironically deconstructed Beethoven is piped into elevators and offices or, alternatively, everyone is to be famous for a scant fifteen minutes.[11] Mechanical reproduction too frequently does not popularize a tabooed truth (the romantic idealism of Beethoven, for example) that once unleashed prods consciousness to reformulate the world along with its enmeshing texts; instead, expressive insight becomes Muzak, commodified and coopted.

It is crucial to recognize that deauratization, resulting in clean copy effacing the author's trace, is driven by both economic and discursive interests. Formerly conceptualized as ideology, class standpoint, unconsciousness is now dispersed among millions of seemingly unconnected social atoms, their class and gender position as obscure to them as ever. The economic rationale, so obvious it might be missed, is to standardize "product" and prepare it for mass production and consumption via publishing, radio, television, taping, VCR. The standardized product is both homogenized and cheapened; it is thus made available to a much wider public than could otherwise consume culture before the age of mechanical reproduction. Mechanical reproduction creates a mass market and thereby mass culture. Aura is exchanged for accessibility; liberalism's general availability here converges with liberal capitalism, a veritable orgy of abundance.

Removing the aura of the text, evidence of its artifice by a person who worked at it, disempowers readers by affording them no imaginary interlocutors, no intertextual community, with reference to whom to phrase their own responses. As well, mechanical texts inhibit the reader's engagement with their version; they are prohibited from interpreting or rewriting them. Positivist writing in concealing its own narrativeness prevents others from offering different narratives—thus, different worlds. The cleaner, more deauratized the text, the less role the reader can play in decoding it. In turn, this forestalls the possibility that the reader might otherwise resist, refuse, or rewrite a text that by appearing to have been written could equally well have been written *differently*.

Deauratization at the same time paradoxically deifies the author whose trace has been removed from it, elevating the disembodied author above mortal subjectivity; a crucial consequence of mechanical reproduction is to make way for instant celebrity. Where the author is not simply invisible, as in most middle-range science, s/he is to be cultivated hagiographically. This allows disciplines like sociology to rely on an original literature—so-called Grand Theory including Durkheim, Weber, Spencer, Comte, and a sociologized version of Marx— to establish their object domain *and thereby settle accounts with troubling epistemological and metaphysical questions.* Indeed it is arguable that an established discipline like sociology even needs theorists except as archivists, custodians of a lifeless legacy.

Texts whose artifice has been scraped off them by the busy hands of readers, editors, and even the author who willingly revises a number of times before going to press, demand an obeisance from readers who can only accept or infer that they are utter works of genius (as in art) or unmuddied representations of timeless nature (as in science). Such versions require no crafting mediation by a constitutive, questioning reader. The concealment of a work's authorial aura not only stills responses that would become versions in their own right. In addition, the author's absent presence intimidates readers into genuflection; retaining enough of a palimpsest of authorial divinity, published writing in its own slick deauratization is instantly more credible than is writing that is to be read in carbon copy, smudged with the author's unerased fingerprints and dog-eared. In high art or pathbreaking science the author may still be faintly visible. If not, the appearance of a literature's originary founding might be purposely conjured to protect the subsequent canon from willful decentering; the author-ity of Durkheim, for example, gives subsequent disciplinary work in his fashion the imprimatur of verisimilitude. Deauratization tends to induce obedience through the cultivation of "taste" or a minimal professional competence. And where the mechanical text not only denies the imaginary interlocutors present within it whose meaning they have to produce, readers are also led to accept the work's validity as an adequate reflection of the external world.

Validity or iterability is enhanced as texts appear not to have been mediated or constructed at all by an authorial subject who left traces of construction in the body of the text but perhaps only in footnotes. Even footnotes as traces are increasingly expunged as the dominant editorial style in social science publishing is the one favored by the American Psychological Association reducing footnotes to the parenthetical citation of author and publication date, to be exhumed from the bibliography at the end. This further reduces talk between text and subtext, enhancing text's seeming validity by removing the subjective hand of the author as a nonidentifying mediator between prose and world. The trace of constitution is nettlesome to professional science; it preserves the power of the author to make judgments and thus undercuts the scientificity of a version shunning mediation as a betrayal of methodological competence.

Removing the literary aura of the work suggests a noncontradictory world in the text's cleanliness. Words or concepts serve as adequate accounts of an external world that, it is presumed, can be discursively reconstructed. Science brackets out the nonidentical, the undesirable, the disciplinarily irrelevant, and the dialectically contradictory exactly as Husserl's pure phenomenology, essentially a version of positivism, intended to do. This bracketing supports the illusion that science can give a straightforward account of natural processes devoid of historicity and thus an essential noniterability. Advanced disciplines reject metaphor as indeterminate because the authority (*not* author-ity) of science is thought to derive from a logic of adequation empowering words and figure to disclose a world. Metaphors mediate where mediation is a trace of authorial presence threatening the scientificity of texts. Concepts are not allowed to "play" lest the determinacy of science—describing *this* world in static, ontological terms—come unraveled, thus courting Nietzsche's transvaluation of all values or simply nihilism.

The postulate of a noncontradictory world that can in a sense be swallowed by the text and then displayed captive under laboratory glass or in smooth print is central to the imperial self-understanding of positivism. This version of science tolerates apostasy no more than did the Roman Catholic church during the Inquisition or Senathor McCarthy a few decades ago, now resurrected as Accuracy in Academia. Words are power because through them the "given" world is given its imprimatur, its sanction as a piece of necessity. And necessity can contain no trace of its own discursive nature, its narrative nonidentity evoked by a version making its own constitutiveness thematic, the most dangerous political resistance today—undoing necessity as the unnecessarily oppressive.

Science's text strongly tries to rip the world free from its mooring, paste it into the text and thus give it an indubitability, an obdurate, naturelike facticity; readers then live science's world *and thereby ironically prove it*, (constructed) laws reconstructed by weak readers. The (image of) the world's noncontradictoriness must be maintained by science so that the world's essential ambiguity and indeterminacy do not erode the appearance and thus reality of the world's ever-the-sameness, its imperviousness to history. Clean texts that do not contain ellipses, tension, or outright contradiction, nearly inevitable traces of dirty writing, shore up the world's identity to itself, a crucial defense against critical thought eschewing representation as an inadequate model of science.

The positivist version of itself as authorless writing pays little attention to the echoes it sets off in readers that move them to engage text in dialogue or move beyond it altogether; a nonpositivist version of science recommends its version's relations to other texts, times, people, and nature. Self-sufficient once it reduces its difference from the world it imitates, positivism is impatient to resolve its initial circumspection about having-been-written as the author rushes through acknowledgments, preface, and introductory chapter in order to get to the world itself. The world is then unproblematically represented —named, numbered, figured—as an invariant tableau of the noncontradictorily present, freezing history into nature and thus redoubling discipline. Even "conflict" on this version of writing can be built into the text as inexorable Darwinian, Weberian, even Marxian "laws" of competition and struggle, thus helping to make it so on the basis of the version's claimed authority to know what it is talking about. Presuppositionlessly undistorting representation thus smoothes conflict into ontology, hence nature.

Finally, science would write exhaustive texts, a crucial selling point of books that try to wrest away readers from their competitors. A noncontradictory version of science aspires to an encyclopedism even if authors add what Garfinkel calls an "et cetera" clause, premising a future that can never be entirely foretold or exhausted in present constructions. While the positivist social sciences ape what they take to be the natural sciences, they differently exist because elusive sociological causality can only be approximated by a writing cunningly shy about its own constitutional nature. In stepping down from causal to correlational explanation, from seeming ontology to empirical description, science is the deepest ontology precisely because it hides its constitutiveness behind the claim of mute representationality. It does so in order to intrude in a world that admits of openness to, indeed *requires*, the fine-tuning measures of social welfare, macroeconomics, and cultural manipulation keeping capitalism off the rocky shoals of crisis—its inability to reproduce itself.

Sociology developed as a discipline in Comte, Durkheim, and Weber because the social turbulence of industrializing Europe needed to be addressed by steering agents who could in effect make on-course corrections to the evolutionary unfolding of modernizing societies toward its ultimate telos of common values, market equilibrium, familism, domesticated nature, eventually postindustrialism. The absence of causality requires a version palliating the power of the social with the prospect of a middle-class life, truncating the good into goods. So-called free will survives as a trace and makes possible, indeed requires, late capitalist social engineering, including its version of a whole world that defies revisions.[12] So science intends closure and yet stops short of causality; thus, it entices the readerly enactment of constructs, for example "law," represented as binding. The text accepts its own constraint by allegedly invariant socio-ontological patterns; and yet in reflecting, hence defending, the world's nature it justifies its existence as a discipline that in Weber's sense applies scientific findings for purposes of social advance.

No matter how validly noncontradictory its text, social science necessarily accepts the distance between itself and the world it copies as its motive force. Science flattens the world ahistorically *because* it understands the world's inherent historicity that its version aims eventually to overcome, a last-text swallowed in the lawful world it has provoked. In this sense, science would outlast its nonidentity to things calling it forth in the meantime as a disciplinary complement, the ruse of all representation that does not admit its aesthetic— thus political—impulse. Sociology tries to be physics and fails, *must fail*, if it is successfully to close a world it already deems fundamentally closed, the cunning of all ideology. Text cannot hermetically seal itself off from politics precisely because it covertly opens science to practice. Positivism intends reading as a form of life ironically validating its premature closure of a world it secretly knows is incomplete. Legitimated by its own claimed scientificity, sociology enters the fray as an agent of discipline; allowing for modest social reform, sociology, like Weber, Mannheim, Bell, and Galbraith, preclude a radically different order of being.

Ultimately, quite against its nature, science fails to achieve metaphysical closure in cleansing itself of all worldly influences. There can be no totally administered text, even in natural science; such an account would utterly lose its nonidentity to, thus its independence from, the world it interrogates even if only descriptively. Physicists have known this at least since relativity theory overtook Newton's model of a timeless nature. In pursuit of disciplinary legitimacy, American sociology is yet decades behind the most advanced philosophy of science in failing to recognize this about itself—it needs to *avoid* exhausting the world whose ultimate mystery it wants to lay bare on the page in pure number and figure. The representational text intends to undo itself as science approaches its limit in the absence of an absolute correspondence between signs and things. Positivism's aim of identity can only arise as a goal in a heterogeneous world in which nonidentity characterizes most social relationships and thus provokes text as a way of being human in face of our ineluctable mortality; writing expresses our protest against our destiny to be mute, eventually identical to the world from which we were born.

As such, science always risks becoming, if not poetry, at least a text that at the margins (footnotes, introduction, epilogue: *subtext*) unravels itself as a human artifact whose author-ity is not metaphysical but in a sense physical; text is the objectification of voice. For science to realize this about itself would open it to other versions of the truth that in their own obdurate facticity—the reality of *many books*—are inherently political challenges, echoing, indeed encouraging, different motives and desires. This reformulates democratic socialism as an undecidable babel of tongues, many books suggesting the rights of many speakers to speak as long as they do not decidably enforce a monolithic version —whether The Book, *ASR*, or *Capital*.

I am not arguing from aestheticism against silence as adequate politics but for writing that talks about, and thus lives, the imponderables and blockages riddling existence. Writing reformulates the world to which it relates as topic without losing sight of the corrigibility of language standing in the way of our attempt to engulf the world. This does not cede the realm of necessity to science in neo-Kantian fashion. I reject altogether a frozen dualism dividing the realms of spirit and nature, freedom and necessity; dualism conceals the hierarchical and constitutional relations between its terms. Nor is privatized language an adequate response to the causalities littering history and which no text by itself can dissolve. The prospect of a different version of the world suggests the possibility of a different world (to which it makes a small contribution). Today that world can only be characterized by what it is *not* and yet might become, a gentle community of speakers embracing the sentiment that the good is talk itself—recognizing the requirement of its own endlessness.

Literariness and Liberation

Writing that tries to be clean, exhaustive, noncontradictory, valid, and amoral ultimately fails because it will always bear some trace of its artifice as a piece of *dirty work*.[13] Science at the limits shows its narrativeness and thus deconstructs its own postured presuppositionlessness. In sociology particularly, the tension between claimed science and a certain social progressivism and reformism— Vienna Circle plus Mannheim equals Popper—cannot be resolved short of disciplinary self-destruction. Sociology's purchase on disciplinary power is value-freedom, a representational virtuosity provoking a seamless world that would make sociology's text unnecessary, ever the aporia of scientism.

But for us to recognize, via a politicizing deconstruction, the limits to closure in science's pretended representationality does not require social analysis to be read its last rites, as Derrideans sometimes intend through their critique of metaphysical logocentrism. Ideology critique, of which this book is a local example, works at the margins of the social totality, uncovering the world's artificiality as a way of empowering different versions of it. It would not redraw the boundaries of disciplines so much as show their attempt to discipline readers who write and thus live against their hidden ontology. Disciplinary sociologists require a Durkheimian world of powerlessness; other conceptions of the world imperil discipline. A critique that works through disciplines does not, as Derrida hopes, simply reposition margins at the center for that only creates new margins, new oppressions; instead, my reading of discipline traces the *connection* between center—discipline, logics of capital, race, sex, and ideology—and the margins it creates imperially—artificiality, subjectivity, resistance. Derrida's reading strategy is only that; he fails to offer a critical social theory that locates discursive practice as constitutive activity within a larger conception of the nature and possibilities of social history.

The reader is not the only casualty of a version of science that is metaphysical because it tries to be clean of metaphysics. Where the reader is all too quickly disempowered by a version pretending a totalizing accumulation of the existent's particulars, thus freezing them into a social nature whose unproblematic lucidity is already encoded within it as a world that can read itself, the writer is too easily eliminated by a text that writes itself—through committee, compromise, collegiality, all of the ways disciplines discipline rebellious thought. Science's repository of accredited knowledge, its "literature" comprises books and articles written by different people that in effect has the same author and reflects the same chilly world; in addition, these averaged writers do not write the text but are written by it, disciplined by the discipline that would discern a single logos, in Durkheim's case subordination to the social. Where intertextuality is the irreducible web of dialogues inhabiting a single piece of writing, linking author with other authors as well as with readers and thus self-consciously locating the text in a nest of intersubjectivity, science silences dialogue in the establishment of an originary master text, canon, literature to which all writers pay professional deference.

The disciplinary establishment of canons is different from biblical exegesis to which it otherwise bears resemblance in that Bible study at least preserves the critical distance between text and reader required for decoding and thus for the demonstration of faith. Science deceives itself that it comprises different versions; instead disciplines are singular versions of the power of the social that they only deepen. Durkheim wrote sociology's book in the first thirteen pages of *Rules of Sociological Method* where he names ("social facts") our generic subordination to the naturelike monolith of the social. The traces of dialogue among texts and the other texts animating them, as well as the dialogue between author and readers, are suppressed not in the name of faithful exegesis but in service to a logic of accumulation disciplining all concrete particulars into a single version. Ironically, with Hegel's absolute idealism, science claims the whole truth; yet, unlike Hegel, science comprises a totality of disintegrated flotsam and jotsam—merely *data*.

The books and articles comprising the disciplinary version ground and bound scientific research, describing limits beyond which disciplined writing cannot go lest it be read as marginal, disputatious, *nonscience*. But obeisance to science's disciplined literature precludes difference between author and authority; at least in biblical hermeneutics interpretation was an expression of faith, indeed, exegesis a way of life (if not a democratic one). Science requires no such faith enhanced or evoked through hermeneutic digging but instead participates in the disciplinary norms of objectivity disinterestedly searching for nomothetic explanation—faith replaced by sheer obedience to a historyless nature, the clean text enacted as the clean life. This only makes idiots of authors; authority is not to be an object of disputation but an inert accumulation only guiding research as a distant landmark guides explorers.

Disempowered disciplinary scribes are constrained circularly by discipline; they are unable to put critical distance between themselves and authority, which is given in the official history of the discipline. This was harmful even to natural scientists who regarded the possibility of a non-Ptolemaic universe literally as nonsense. For social scientists, obedience to a disciplinary master text containing and thus consuming all attempts to rewrite it reproduces an intellectual conformity stifling intellectual and political innovation. The discipline's literature becomes an author in its own right, inscribing the particular texts with a self-sameness showing up in studies such as mine. This is the sense of Foucault's claim that historians make history where it has become a written text. At first blush the numerous journal articles and monographs seem "different" in the obvious sense of having different authors, topics, lengths, forms of presentation, and findings; yet this superficial heterogeneity conceals a deeper sameness—a centering—drowning out both writers and readers with the numbing coda of the discipline's self-understanding as one version but not others. It is virtually impossible to publish, get tenure, and survive if one does not give one's work a disciplinary name, thus reproducing it—sociology, economics, chemistry.

Sociologists to be sociologists must publish sociology in sociology journals—Durkheim's discipline disciplining. As such, sociology reflects, hence perpetuates, people's subordination to the social. Otherwise one's writing as nonscience neither leads to the establishment of an academic career nor

addresses academic readers. But deinstitutionalization is not truth, only unemployment. The discipline tolerates eccentricity as long as it can establish
that eccentrics are interlopers from other disciplines, ideologies, planets. Even
the most ostensibly critical (e.g., Giddens in his recent *Social Theory and
Modern Sociology*, 1987) still hold out for what they call "good sociology" as
if that were a possibility in its own terms. Paying lip service to the disciplines
housing us, we forget the worlds they recommend.

Undisciplined writing rejecting discipline as an intellectual and methodological aegis is rejected by the reviewers, editors, and publishers who manage
publishing and thus disciplines. It is rejected as nonscience and thus nonsense; yet rejection is couched in a variety of more specific claims having to
do with a work's quality or appropriateness as if these standards are unconstructed in their own right. Thus, a seeming professionalism conceals a deep
particularism vested in discipline; discipline constructs the standards by which
work is judged disciplinary or not, thus authorizing what is to be published as
legitimate.

This self-referencing defense of professionalism begs the question about
what it means to advance a discipline. It is assumed that we (on the inside)
know and do not have to be told. Advance, quality, and appropriateness do not
define themselves but are powerful, proseful constructs compelling scholarly
conformity by drawing boundaries around disciplines as well as regulating
them internally, excluding work that is "not good sociology" or "even" sociology at all. But as a dense weave of unacknowledged constructions of this
sort, discipline cannot be derived without, or beyond, writing interrogating
and then advocating its own authorial desire, the way that—and *why*—writing
intends to change the world. Not-good-enough, a typical reader's response
to a piece of scholarly writing, is not irreducible but calls on other sorts of
con-textual claims author-izing it. The hyphens I am using here want to connote the activity of ontological concealment that science does to itself in the
name of science in order to be read as a report of nature, the disinterested
truth of things; science differentiates itself from fiction by claiming to overcome the literary nature of undisciplined writing. Science does not engage
in the reflexivity necessary to penetrate its suppression of authorial construct
lest it confront its own undecidably narrative character not as an occasion of
despair but of further joyous self-expression touching, even promoting, other
scribbling.[14]

If the notion of a disciplinary literature—indeed, a single text—written by
no one and everyone at once seems mystical, the monolithic imperviousness of
discipline is the real mystique of the seemingly demythified. Like any scientific
literature, sociology embodies a subtext, methodology, enjoining imagination.
It is not enough to reduce this subtext to norms of a community of science, thus
sociologizing its ideological impetus and impact. The bourgeois sociology

of knowledge suppresses the fact that disciplines exist *to discipline*; in the human sciences disciplines advance a deauthorized version of the world only reproducing that world through its eclipse of authorial intentionality.

Disciplines are concrete forms of life, social texts enmeshing readers and writers in a historyless view of the world. American sociology identifies this world and all possible worlds as a way of both enforcing and leavening eternal discipline, people's reputed lot in every society. This is the deepest metaphysic of a discipline inspired by Durkheim's disquisition on the nature of the social's dominance. The politics of its science lie in its suppression of the political character of any writing intending a version of the world *that would become that world*. The narrative nature of writing refers to the way authors intend not only consensus (Habermas) but to change the world (through readers) in a way that prevents writing from thinking of itself as mere copy—thus merely copying. At once a prefigurative form of good community, good writing accepts this spiral within itself between text and subtext: intellectual work on one hand and the desire to do that work on the other. In undoing discipline, other versions of the world help bring it about.

An understanding of the institutional basis of knowledge explains how the same text gets written over and over again as it writes its writers, the discipline disciplining mind by limiting it to replication—the re-search of the already-said, precisely the nature of reproduction in capitalism. A notion of a disciplinary version thus explains the intertextuality of all writings done under its logos; my version of sociology is an example of a disciplinary reading. Sociology's representation of the generic power of society over the individual reproduces itself in people's acquiescence to the social. Thus, a disciplinary text becomes a subtext informing most "everyday lives" in late capitalism. Although sociology is only a single disciplinary discourse, it alone grounds the *amor fati* in disciplined representation. As historians make history (Foucault), so sociologists chill domination into "society."

Sociology only repeats as re-search what most of us have already discovered in our dealings with the dominant institutions of the time; Durkheim was right: we *are* powerless, and at best we can expect modest compensations for our enactment of the power of the social. By getting the text right we will be rewarded with the emoluments virtue brings forth, close reading (Kant's duty) matched with material and spiritual attainment. A more traditional Marxist would doubtless call sociology's disciplining text an ideology, failing to see it not as a simple reflex of the production process but mediatedly as part of that base already, reproduction including the host of fatalizing, reifying, commodifying processes blinding us to its own discursive subordination in the more highly valued realm of production.[15] Writing thus accepts its own seeming epiphenomenality precisely to reproduce the order to which text is allegedly subordinate, just as women performing unwaged expressive labor in the so-called "private" sphere and underpaid labor in the workforce reinforce the primacy of public over private, male over female, and capital over labor.

A version of disciplinary power informed by and informing critical theory and left feminism interrogates the subordination of reproduction to production as a means of understanding the manifold ways in which we have ceded primacy to the public realm of waged, valued activity. This alternative version of power thus makes our own constitutive competences thematic. After all, the fact that production needs to subordinate reproduction only shows that subordination can be reversed once its reproductiveness is adequately valued. Discipline is another name for ideology lived out in subservience to particular interests described and thus defended generally, the pernicious character of scientism today. This extends the original Frankfurt School's notion that positivism is no longer only a theory of knowledge, if it ever was, but only a mode of everyday life reproducing its disempowering in a suggestively representational text. Science disempowers itself before the compelling power of the social; it only reflects, thus doing more than that.

Marcuse's one-dimensionality (1964) describes the introjection of an epistemology of representation played out in the various modes of unnecessary accomodation to the social—capitalism, sexism, racism. Reason is thus reduced to reasonableness—all that a sensible person could hope for. Disciplines only academicize these common sense adaptations through their perpetuation of positivist language games; they do not create one dimensionality *de novo* but contribute to its preexisting momentum by disciplining the readerly imagination, especially crucial in late capitalism where nearly the majority of Americans attend college. It is difficult to fix disciplinary texts enduring primarily in absent presence—what they do not say about the historicity of the social and thus about their own discursiveness. The books and articles in their seeming heterogeneity imply a disciplinary openness belying a deeper oneness of ontological assumptions and ontologizing practices. Less explicit construction than a combination of innuendo and what is excluded or suppressed, these deconstructive traces haunt sociology, belonging to neither surface as such nor the inaccessible substratum that Jameson (1981) calls the "political unconscious." Text's subtext exists in force more as a signifier in an encyclopedic version of the world than as a piece of ontological doctrine accessible directly.

The text of the discipline does not tell us very much in itself but takes on significance as it participates in authority whose authorship is hidden from writers "in" the tradition; academic professionals are taught to eschew reflexivity as an unprofessional indulgence to be shed through the disciplining apprenticeship of graduate education. Thus, subtextual traces are less intended meanings than signifiers feeding off the whole disciplinary text and at once animating it, creating a region of normal science above it, closer to the surface, that saturates readers and writers with obtrusive, taken-for-granted facticity—

the realm of necessity. Science's driving desire to bring about a certain world is everywhere and nowhere at once; as such it resists substantial critique in a version containing virtually every author except traitors and poets.

In this sense the disciplinary text kills the author, who becomes merely a cipher through whom the discipline's preponderance flows. If the books and articles are all the same, writing and rewriting the same ontological subtext driving representationality in a political way—reflection of inequality intending its perpetuation—authorship becomes only an act of fealty, echoing but not thinking holy words. At least biblical exegetes had to sweat to unlock the sacred codes, thus inherently preserving their own politically apostate nonidentity to the texts and traditions in question. And exegetes were ever at risk, inviting the harsh inquisitorial repression of apostasy that looms as a real possibility when people are encouraged, indeed required, to make sense of the mythic.

Admittedly, the image of the disciplinary text as a force field electrocuting writers on its fences either coming out or going in risks the postulate of a *deus ex machina*. It is important to trace discipline to disciplining texts, and then rewrite them—in particular, injecting history into sheer description, really ontology. Science takes form in the institutional and intellectual process of social reproduction; the ever-the-sameness of research imitates necessity and thereby suppresses its own unnecessary acquiescence to it. Textuality cedes its freedom to a world in which text is always ontologically free to affirm or oppose.

American sociology narratively conjoins social fact and fate; its representation of the power of the social reproduces it through discipline. To resist such a seductively seamless web of concepts, constructions, and findings is only to *escape*, for discipline does not turn on the voice of its next prime mover introducing a new and better paradigm. Foucault reminds us that power is everywhere; Marx reminds us that power accumulates. The model of an unconstrained intellectual competition assumes an openness to discourse that has long been a regulative fiction in bourgeois science, using a phony universalism (the putative "power of the strongest argument," whether Mill or Habermas) to conceal a particularism every bit as mythic as the most dogmatic religion and, by virtue of its fetish character, a good deal less penetrable by external critique.

It is a hard truth that the discipline's one version vitiates authorial responsibility; intellectual work portrayed by Weber as a "calling" possessing intrinsic satisfactions is eclipsed in the era of disciplined writing. By the late 1980s it is hubris to pretend that the discipline needs writers anymore than it needs readers; it disempowers both equally, putting words and thus practices in their mouths. The text *becomes* an "everyday life"; its postulate of generic subordination to the social—really, capitalism, sexism, racism—is continually reproduced by people who live as they read. Reading and writing in late capitalism become sheer repetition, *re-search*, defanged by the remarkable self-management of academic practice that reproduces discipline out of a willful professionalism—academicism. What Adorno called total administration and Marcuse one-dimensionality takes place from within academic texts and lives.

2

Reading/Politics

The Problem of Archimedean Subjectivity

If reader and writer are both eclipsed by a monolithic science researching itself through suitably acculturated academics and various publishers and editors, how is any defiant reading possible? Asserting the possibility of defiance does not defy; it only exercises bravado. This is the familiar problem of educating the educator, an irony continuing to haunt the intellectual life that would dangerously end elitism in an elitist way. How are reading and writing even possible in an era of the text's and the world's thoroughgoing disciplining? Readers will ask and want answered whether *this* is "really sociology." If not, what? Theory, philosophy, criticism? *How* can I write in light of science's seeming centering of all external standpoints that are either disciplined and thus domesticated (sociology, anthropology, chemistry, etc.) or marginalized as nonscience?

Adorno continues to be interrogated by readers who want him to say how he can write, indeed how he can suggest a mode of free discourse and thus of freedom generally, when he has already said that poetry is impossible after Auschwitz. Surely he does not intend negative dialectics as a poem. But can poetry theorize? It is not that he is wrong; the center swallows oppositions it produces to feign an openness that unplanned society requires in the form of risk taking. We must return here to the foundational problem of a search for unambiguous standards of reason in an unreasonable, defeating world, a problem of a transcendental vantage of knowledge that accounts for its own groundedness—indeed, as I will say in my concluding chapter, celebrates that ground as the occasion of its poetry and passion.[1]

The postulate of an Archimedean point from which truth claims can be evaluated is devilish to ideology critics: it is simultaneously a necessary principle that makes ideological unmasking or "reading" possible and thus overcomes relativism as a secret absolutism; and it threatens an elitism that seems unreasoned against its own emancipatory intent to install reasoning as the central ordering principle of a moral polity. If indeed there is a transcendental vantage beyond the sullying gravitational pull of the preponderant object world, a grasp of esoteric insight, then how can it be generalized, democratized, indeed methodologized, in a stupid world under sway of disciplinary discourses compelling self-defeating reading practices? I have many questions but few answers; critique must move ahead anyway. The possibility of a transcendental reading of texts, then, is as much as anything a matter of the relationship between true and false consciousness, ever a Marxian problematic whose irony is not reduced by being thought this way.

Marxists have traditionally resolved what I understand to be the irony of all interpretation with reference to an indubitable history whose riddle is available to historical materialism. Who interprets the interpreter? The Archimedean vantage of apodictic knowledge, then, makes history itself accessible to a theoretical practice representing a certain class standpoint, only a variation on the notion of a transcendental subjectivity. False consciousness inverts itself in the electric moment when workers realize a history written into their possibility as universal subjects heretofore enchained to the false necessities of capital.

This historicist account of the dynamic relationship between true and false consciousness is adequate if history bears within it an incipient qualitative break with itself, a *coupure politique* to paraphrase Althusser's version (1969) of Bachelard. But Marx missed the very real possibility that the prolongation of false consciousness would deepen it. His optimism turned on his Hegelian assumption that truth resides in a history of which the proletariat is unproblematically the world-historical agent.

But if this grandiose history is reduced to a merely contingent history as the moment to change the world is either missed or indefinitely delayed (Adorno 1973a), the problem of an Archimedean point from which to evaluate truth claims and thus to read and write new science remains a fundamental epistemological, thus political, problem for critical theory, especially as Lenin has demonstrated the likely relationship between esoteric science and political tyranny. We are thus challenged to find a vantage for criticism without reintroducing the concept of a groundless transcendental or collective subjective justifying our privilege in an a priori way and not contextually, as *argument*. This version of criticism hears its own subtext of transformative desire—why it writes "what" it does—and incorporates it narratively, as a topic equally as important as the one it thought it was talking about in the first place.

The risk of failing to educate the educator is greater than the risk of elitist education as a progenitor of political authoritarianism. The first is the risk of liberal capitalism disguised as the open marketplace of ideas while the second involves both political elitism and a certain self-contradictoriness in one's claim both to stand outside the contingent world and yet to reject one's own Archimedean status as politically audacious. But a Derridean might say that the dichotomy of epistemological privilege and relativism is false, virtually always resolved in favor of the powers. Disciplinary sociology in reproducing both its own and thereby, it hopes, universal heteronomy swallows dissension by subverting its self-proclaimed openness formulated in terms of the allegedly universalistic norms of science. Thus, it seems to have met all challengers when in fact it places contesting versions outside the parameters of normal science, either untoward passion or poetry.

If other knowledges were compelling, they would already have been integrated into discipline or have overcome it, a knowledge even more certain than that of science. But representationality does not admit the constitutive contribution of authorship to the object-world precisely to deflect knowledges that not only admit but also enhance authorial agency *as a prefiguration and paradigm of a more general empowering of constitutive subjects.* This epistemological relativism grounding scientific apodicticity in the normative practice of the professional community of science ends up as authoritarian as the posture of transcendental subjectivity or an Archimedeanism that rejects intersubjective validity as a ruse. From critique's point of view, epistemological relativism is riskier than an Archimedean elitism, not because transcendentalism avoids Prometheanism but because liberalism (if not real laissez faire) dominates today.

The more the myth of a transparent writing and reading is purveyed, the more impermeable scientism becomes in service of the managed metamorphosis of capitalism. Liberalism is elitism by default, defining the given by "giving" it an equal right to be a text, as if reality were only prose and the given needed equal time. Liberalism champions the margins where, in Habermas's regulative terms, the strongest truth claim can actually emerge victorious, his Marxization of John Stuart Mill; but it betrays them in a relativism that suicidally tries to protect illiberal forces in the name of fairness.

Following Walter Benjamin, who suggested that every monument of culture is a monument to barbarism, Adorno historicized the end of poetry after Auschwitz by attaching the guilt of survivorship to it. Derrida declares meaning dead with reference to the inherent metaphysicality of language of which deconstruction is the subversion. But where Adorno against Lenin wanted to break out "from within," poststructuralism considers escape hubris; it condemns language to eternal irony and opacity. Thus, poststructuralism as a Nietzschean version of relativism does not think the concept of utopia.[2] Although Adorno, a left-wing intellectual Jew adrift in postwar America and western Europe, lived and wrote marginally, Derrida flaunts his marginality as a chic cynicism whose truth is eclipsed by his antimethodical method, the deconstructability of every text. Where Adorno uses irony as a basic resource of a dialectical theory that makes falsehood speak the truth in spite of itself, Derrida capitulates to irony, disqualifying attempts to break through it as typical western hubris.

Deconstruction misses the dialectic that would extract the non-negative (if not the cheerfully unalloyed positive) from historical negativity just as it recognizes the reactionary implications of an idealist dialectic. The dialectic contains a moment of construction as well as deconstruction, writing as well as its subversion—negation of negation, albeit an indeterminate one. The demarcation point between the two is either the possibility or impossibility of a final reconciliation of opposites, avoiding the vanguard outcome by warning against the tendency of every canon to swallow other knowledges, and lives.

Adorno, Horkheimer, and Marcuse's negative dialectic preserves discourse against both its Soviet silencing and the disciplinary text whose reading and writing are reduced to representation—science swallowing history. But with Derrida, the theorists of the Frankfurt School do not privilege discourse itself as an adequate form of life; they dialectically preserve both the possibility of writing and the impossibility of full or total versions capable of capturing all the world's particulars in an omnibus account, thus wending their way between the absolutism of the Archimedean transcendental subject and sheer relativism. It is an act of intellectual will to oppose both relativism and idealist identity theory—John Stuart Mill and Stalin—in the name of a writing that is neither writing degree zero (Barthes 1967) nor undistorted ideal speech (Habermas 1979, 1984, 1987). Sartre (1965b) calls it committed literature. The committed author can live with(in) his or her own insufficient historicity without becoming so cynical that the writing fails to see beyond its own pages toward other pages and, indeed, the world of which it is born and to which it inevitably returns as a useless passion.

Cynicism is not a political strategy, at least not a good one, in spite of the realization that the text's totalizing force field into which minds are almost inexorably absorbed and thus reduced to sheer powerlessness makes defeatism a virtually unavoidable conclusion. But defeatism derived from empirical defeat is as false a conclusion as the derivation of social law from social fact. The historicity of defeat does not necessarily lead to millenarian conclusions about the impossibility of social change. Indeed, defeat as a central tendency of world history only throws into starker relief the marginal possibility of a qualitatively different otherness.

Yet no text is impervious to active readings rewriting and thus reliving it. That people must write in order to plug the cracks around the edges of history indicates an inherent nonidentity of subject and object to be prised open further through the imaginative struggles and deconstructive work of critique. Texts are not totally administered because liberalism and its relativity on the one hand and absolutist idealism and Archimedeanism on the other can be debunked and reworked. In spite of science's apodictic pretensions, the very fact that science must write, must ideologize, spells the insufficiency of the world it would portray so inertly. Marx did not adequately explain how the fact of ideology ought to be energizing in its own right, superstructure's functional contribution to base evidence of their very difference—hence the possibility of their reformulation.

This is crucially not an argument for a new metaphysic or theory of knowledge "grounding" the stance of negative dialectics in its own apodictic system, an absolute mode of the nonabsolute where the nonidentical ultimately identifies. The thinly political Derrida agrees with Merleau-Ponty, Sartre, and the Frankfurt School that systems tending toward totality are inherently authoritarian because they seek closure and thus violate marginalia necessarily inhabiting all intellectual as well as political and economic practices. The block to totalizing "reason," the obdurateness of limit promises freedom from tyranny just as it is the splinter in the scientific eye; a text purporting to swallow the world only gets swallowed itself. Claiming unchallenged authority, science's authority diminishes under the withering gaze of deconstructive critique refusing science its posture of absolute objectivity. The susceptibility of the world to reformulation is inherent in the dialectic of particular and general, mortality and world history, animating existence to think about itself as a mode of existence. That this usually fails is of little consequence for people must still endure their brief passage; the alternative is misery and boredom. It is the conviction of any writing, even if it cannot admit it, that suffering can be reduced if not abolished altogether. We reach beyond ourselves in our various acts of self-externalization, working over things—pages, fields, metal—that then take on the enduring facticity of history. Otherwise we are stilled.

The particular and general are mediated by the various processes of production and reproduction that keep us going in the meantime. Lives and texts are variably less and more self-determining as people are less and more able to control the metabolism with nature through economy, politics, culture, and sexuality. The irreducible perspectivity of writing and reading as generic acts of self-expression make it impossible for a literary version of science fully to remove its imbeddedness in subjectivity even if only as traces suppressed methodologically. Discourse solicits its playful transcendence, refusing monologue as well as monopoly. One version inevitably solicits another—even if unaware. And yet discipline is also powerfully defined today by social relations of production and reproduction requiring obedience; this obedience is engendered by social texts enacted by the vast majority of readers who otherwise, in their right minds, would choose against servitude to the Word or Law or Logos. Everyone wants to write—that is, for Marx, to labor—even if text plays out in different tableaus.

People are both free and unfree at once, free *to be* unfree and yet unfree where that "choice" is often not self-understood as a choice at all; disciplines provoke naturelike adaptation through texts read not as authored acts (that could be different) but as pieces of an unalterable history—nature. Power reproduces itself. Western dualism falsifies the mediate character of human existence—limit, nonidentity, differance, ambiguity. Dualism oppressively reinforces itself; a history deepened by dehistoricizing texts of religion and science is only trivially ameliorated by leisure, culture, spirit. Dualism is not only a superstructure but also a base, a form of life—*production not just reproduction;* it overwhelms subject with the object world that it only imagines it controls. Dualism conceals and thus reproduces the inequality of its terms.

Once we relinquish the ideal of a purely disinterested reading, the epitome of an objectivism leaving the world unchanged as liberalism methodologizes itself in *amor fati,* our interpretive strategy becomes more aggressive. The texts love their precious status as cultural "treasures"; yet they are read as discourses little different from television, telephone, conversation, or journalism. Meaning is not the oyster's pearl but an interrogative process, a *practice,* shattering textuality just as it begins with writing. A strong writing aggressively breaks through its own self-enclosed marginality in refusing to be patronized by critics who mute it just as they shelter it from stronger, reconstituting dialogue. Language otherwise becomes a museum piece as it submits to its own objectification in print, to reverse one of Derrida's main attacks on logocentrism. Although he is right to reject the western rationalist's priority of talk over writing, he fails to go far enough. Writing is a practice enmeshed in certain social relations of production and reproduction, a connection among writers/ readers and readers/writers constituting a material form of human community.

The meaning of textuality in this sense is written into the human relations constituting the text's "society," its intertextuality inseparable from itself. A text in this sense is truly its readers; in a post-Kantian world they would not be confined to interpretation or appreciation but would themselves write—rebut, affirm, and elaborate text's logic and life. So to understand any text one needs a whole social theory that relates writing to other modes of material practice, avoiding reductionism by showing the dialectical connections between production and reproduction. Indeed, a utopian theory argues for a world in which textual and sexual "re"production would be as highly valued as economic production.

Such a version of postmodernist criticism would endorse a Habermasian communicative ethics, unashamedly. Socialists need a regulative and constitutive image of nonauthoritarian intersubjectivity, almost a Marxist social psychology,[3] to work through individual-society mediations or what Habermas (1984, 1987) calls problematics of lifeworld and system. In other words they need a version of socialism as an intertextual practice where reading and writing become vitally productive practices not relegated either analytically or empirically to the subordinated realm of superstructure. This could be called a communicative rationalism as long as "communication" contains writing and representational art and "reason" includes a notion of its own materialism.

Communicative rationalism is another term for historical materialism, albeit one grounding a new Marxism in sources strictly outside the textual ambit of Marx. Or perhaps better said, dialectical materialism would become dialogical materialism.

Socialists need a notion of nonauthoritarian discourse practices *as political theory* in order to model a dialogical socialism in light of its intertextual mediations, a politics of everyday life drawing together authorial subjects and their "texts" of a large social order. Writing can comprehend its own imbeddedness in a community of writers to whom one's desire reaches out for recognition and gentle correction. Thus, intertextuality can be a substantive political theory of socialism as it resolves problems of subject and object—problems of *mediation*—that have plagued Marxists since the Second International. This is possible largely because authority, the epochal problem of political theory since the *Republic* (and essentially bypassed by Marx), can be seen to lie in author-ity, the corrigibility and undecidability of social order grounded in reciprocating discursive practices.

This is not to suggest that socialist text objects will always be approached violently by readers and writers; we must respect nonauthoritarian discourse as a form of praxis in its own terms. Yet to take writing on its own terms, whether immanently, hermeneutically, or New Critically, risks capitulating to a preponderant object—Shakespeare, the Bible, Adam Smith, Parsons—carrying with it the tremendous momentum of "tradition," precluding new versions and thus different lives. Tradition must be transvalued out of respect for the idea of interpersonal and intergenerational continuity that today it betrays. Good talk only respects respectful talk encouraging its interlocutors to give different versions. Preponderant canons that would enforce monologue must be silenced before they silence.

The dominant methodology of criticism, textual analysis, yields an interpolated meaning and makes sense of symptomatic silences and gaps. Whether in the realm of literature or film, interpretation concentrates on the text as a sufficiency. This is not to suggest that text is unimportant or that the analysis of reader response, a corrective to textual immanence, can proceed without an anchor in the text. It is only to view "close reading" alongside the epistemology of ordinary language analysis predominating in Anglo-American philosophy as a form of textual scientism, where philosophy only clarifies the muddled meaning of talk, a kind of positivist auxiliary to common sense, and criticism reconstructs the homely rationality of text.

Close reading is an aestheticism operating remarkably like the scientism of ordinary language philosophy in treating language as an adequational vehicle for expressing and thus secretly completing the world. Textual aestheticism like scientism probes the lacunae of language in order to extract "meaning" from garbled authorial intentionality. In this way, aestheticism pursues immanent meaning through a close reading of texts in the same way that science presuppositionlessly seeks to freeze the object world. Aestheticism is a closet objectivism in this sense, almost a Platonism, evaluating artful texts against internal standards of Meaning, as scientism measures description against the described world. "Meaning" is the irreducible fundament of this approach to interpretation ceding the world to science in return for the inner life—or so it seemed in the romanticism of the eighteenth and nineteenth centuries that created aestheticism and its concepts of beauty, the sublime, and meaning.

Textual analysis is to yield the treasure trove of the author's coherent voice striving to evoke the Beautiful. But this textualism is equally easily borrowed by nonaesthetic disciplines like history, philosophy, and even sociology where science is founded by certain classic texts that are to be endlessly explicated. Science actually has a double structure in this sense, containing both a substantive research literature (DNA, deviance research, monetarist economics) that is continually revised in light of its emerging conceptual and technical status and at once an originary literature demarcating the discipline from other disciplines in the first place—Smith, Darwin, Marx, Comte, Pythagoras. The discipline's book must be persistently reflexive on its founding version to think itself as science. Thus, the introductory textbooks in sociology virtually all contain a chapter on theoretical first principles, with pictures and dates of the founders along with brief biographical synopses of their work, just as many empirical journal articles begin with "literature reviews." Sociology contains a subfield called "theory" in which this a priori foundation is consistently revised through historiographical "survey" writings as well as through an interpretive reading intended, as in the study of literature, to yield immanent meanings—cultivating original genius, notably that of Durkheim and Weber.

This is not to say that theorizing is always reduced to textual analysis but that theory is usually seen as a domain whose problematics are already essentially settled, leaving the field open only to revisionists and elaborators.[4] Durkheim, Weber, and Parsons define American theoretical sociology even if few read them anymore. *The textual analysis has already taken place;* the definitive second readings and disciplinary meaning are sufficiently extracted. Indeed, the main theoretical reader in American sociology has been Parsons; in his *Structure of Social Action* (1937) he developed a rudimentary structural functionalism, not to receive explicit form until 1951, out of his readings of earlier European sociology. Parsons did not extract testable propositions out of the European founders any more than neo-Parsonians verify or falsify Parsons's own propositional functionalism. After all, in spite of a certain naive theory-constructionist bias in recent American sociology that subordinates theory/thought almost entirely to the humdrum daily routines of normal science, that is not to be the province of theory.

Theory methodically carves out a domain of investigation—really, research

—that can be plowed over and over by a research corps deepening the discipline by accumulating factual detail. Theorists in this sense are the readers who make writing possible, linking the original framing of the discipline to its latter day empirical analyses. It is futile to approach the sociological corpus immanently or intersubjectively precisely because a derivative version has essentially settled its score with the first sociologies. The chapters on deviance or demography yield their meanings, findings, unproblematically, without the requirement of readerly intervention and mediation. And the "theory" chapters are third-order readings, readings of readings (Parsons) of readings (Comte, Durkheim, Weber). Theorizing becomes the practice of canonizing great names as author-ities in the writing of local journal science occupying most professional careers. As everyday scientists ask each other: Which theoretical perspective are you using?

Yet historiography or biography is not strong writing making thematic its own narrative interest, presenting the author to the community of readers and thus inviting rejoinders. Although theory is *said* to be the conceptual armamentarium from which researchable hypotheses are derived, thus giving "meaning" to the everyday business of Durkheim's documentation of the power of the social, the distance between grand theory and actual research if anything seems to be growing, especially under sway of quantification replacing prose with figure *for its own sake*. Theory really operates to sanction disciplinary production as this is thought to flow from the early works of "pioneers" who first demarcated sociology from psychology and philosophy. Thus, immanent analysis of Durkheim, Weber, and Parsons is iconic restoration, the veneration of early strong writing long since forgotten except as historical symbolism deemed important in the early growth phases of science; theory is a discipline's rite of passage from literature to science, pen to computer.

Science has no immanent meaning apart from its discursive practice as a social text. Science enters history by denying it. Thus, I read discipline as a political language game suggesting the world it only describes. Inhering in the concatenation of institutional publishing, academics, readers, writers, and society, sociology embodies and enacts a text that would have us deepen our submission to the social by living it. This freezes our historical powerlessness as a metaphysical outcome of an unalterable social nature. The interrogative work devoted to Milton is thought inappropriate in reading science because the texts seemingly participate in an intellectual culture in which *anyone* could have written the deviance or demography analyses. Text is washed of evidence of its authorial construction lest authoriality—*political desire*—seem to evidence political possibility in a world science would close *to itself*.

Meaning in sociology is unproblematic where the text refuses to poetize a reality instead rendered proselessly in figure and number. Authorial voice is silenced by equations, tables, graphs, and figures bearing the text's meaning and thus replacing prosefulness as science's mode of signification. One of my colleagues chided me for writing a book about social problems and the texts of their diagnosis without "tables." These tables ostensibly would have provided an adequate reference against which the diagnostic claims of functionalism and Marxism could be assessed. But he was really saying that science demands figure and number as signifiers of scientificity, circularly arguing for a natural science logic of presentation simply because physicists and chemists favor figure and number. The verisimilitude of my text is to be decided by its willingness to *look* like natural science.

Textual interpretation in the old-fashioned sense of the immanent or close analysis of prose is increasingly scuttled as it gives way to the use of inferential statistics and acquaintance with research design—methodology. Therefore, I read the discipline in textbooks intended for an audience yet unsophisticated in statistical and figural cabalism. Although it is widely, if only ritualistically, recognized that "data" are not phenomenologically immediate and have to be constructed and interpreted and that interpretation presupposes the possibility of its own error, this is lip service. The valorization of number and figure is not a mere "prejudice" for mathematical elegance imbedded in a mathematizing culture teaching us to value math as well as to eat meat. It is a way of *circumventing the prosefulness of knowledge* in terms that do not seem to trade on rhetorical construction—speculative philosophy, armchair sociology, grand theory, journalism, all banes of scientificity.

But the further we get away from writerly textuality—fiction as writing's attention to its own literariness—the less constitutive writing appears. Numbers sound mute in the same way that domination is often silence; marginalized groups have neither the powers' ear nor their own coherent voice. Mathematized "texts" possess no trace of how they became the way they are or appear to be. Their figure constitutes behind the back of constitution. Their seeming imperviousness to interpretation trades off their originless, ahistorical character; after all, positivism would disenchant the world, overcoming the mythic caprice of literary hubris. Arithmetic is to resolve the babel of tongues not as mere cultural prejudice or preference but as the indubitability of the authorially silent. Utopia cannot be thought through mathematics.

Committed Literature

Thus, false consciousness may teach us as much as true, especially where the dominant ideological practices are encoded in claims that can be deconstructed against themselves, always Adorno's goal of escape "from within." Ideology is falsehood that knows it distorts; its secret understanding can reveal a treasure trove of truths—against itself. The powers understand the world better than the most perspicacious critic looking in from the outside; at least, their perspectivity is profoundly revealing, for it is dominant. The sociologizing critique of ideology reducing text to circumstantial "influence" fails to learn from ideology about how it manages to perpetuate itself as the love of fate. It is not enough to denounce religion as working-class opium but also to read the Bible and go to church; Marx epitomized this practice during his hard years reading bourgeois economics to understand the world ironically understood in the mystified "world" of political economy. Underneath ideology lies both knowledge and interest; knowledge can be used against itself to think and live prefiguratively. Critique unhinges the weakest links in domination's chain while making new connections among pacifist socialist versions—each requiring every other where talk is community itself. Social texts once understood to be authored lies promise new texts that lose their subordinate status as mere reproductions; instead, they are valorized work in themselves, indeed metaphors of free human activity. But writing cannot simply take wing in an originary becoming where it is burdened by the suppressions and silencings disciplining all valueless activity in a productivist world assigning value differentially.

Marx read bourgeois society in its scientific texts. Discourse and production do not relate crudely as knowledge and interest (Mannheim, Weber, mechanical Marx, the *German Ideology* against *Capital*); instead science both reflects and thereby reproduces the larger world. Positivist reflection is constitution, chilling history into ontology. We can only transcend the present by authorizing the hidden self-consciousness of texts grasping its contradictoriness and as such ameliorating it. Positivism's falsehood ironically tells the truth—if not about all being then at least about this particular stage of social being. Reading not only uncovers concealed textual commitment but learns from the text itself as it manages to hold in mind the nonidentical relationship between text's cleansed "world" and the contingent, historical world to which it is an ontologizing address. In these terms, the historical world containing the written "world" is thereby completed by it. The task of critique is precisely to learn from the deceptions of the written "world" about the encompassing world, thus leveraging it toward a different future—not completed but undone (as a way of being rebuilt).

History's promise remains after the text's "world" is read deconstructively; the fact that disciplines dehistoricize and thus ontologize tells us something: today the world needs discipline lest it unravel. This promise is to be realized not least through textual practices that rehabilitate intelligent authorship and readership as a way of taking back the culture. If this appears a marginal strategy, an intellectualizing abstraction, then I can only suggest that truth is presently at the margins. Even worse than "doing nothing" for the left is to reproduce identity theories only entrenching the Promethean logocentrism that results in the domination of all otherness by the imperial subject of western reason. Thus, Marxists and feminists must resist centerings that install new axial principles, whether dictatorship of the proletariat, deconstructive text play, or matriarchy, and thus only reproduce hierarchy. At the moment, anyway, critique is the truest construction, an issue to which I return in my concluding chapter.

Sartre offers a name for the interpretive practice working outward from the inside in thawing the frozen "world" found in texts today. Committed literature combines writing and reading in a new social practice that breaks the spell of texts to which we too frequently capitulate unthinkingly. Reading itself is a kind of rewriting, negation negating itself toward a new but necessarily impermanent synthesis. As a life only reproducing text's own subordination to the world it would presuppositionlessly represent, positivist prose keeps us stuck in ontological flypaper from which *we think* there is no escape—the timeworn purpose of ontology as discourse suggesting a truth it knows is false, thus making it true. [5] This is reading *against* the author who especially in science limits the "world" so that we give in and give up. Reading is a political struggle with the work's "world"; yet paradoxically we must work through and out of that "world" to the world itself as we confront its falsely generic depiction—for sociology, the power of the social. Ontologically closing history with a version of necessity, ideology recognizes the difference [6] between its own claims and a world completed by its discourse. If people did not embrace their plights suggested as just desserts, iron cage, duty, then the positivist account of an unalterable world would be false on the very evidence of history's indeterminacy, *freedom* giving the lie to texts' closure. Reading opens writing to lives that refuse the agendas encoded in them.

Sociology explains away our adjustment to the social as the invariant human condition of life with others. Yet existence would not be experienced in this way as an unavoidably bad fate if various discourses creating the social by naming it did not hem us in, completing discipline with the anticipation of its own enactment by readers—text's ingress into the world it presumes only to describe. Reading completes social texts, proving them by living them. We can learn from deconstructed discourse what we as readers unthinkingly do to complete their narrative version of the world, thus reformulating it. Read backwards, or better down to (and up from) their concealed desires to bring about a certain world, the texts release us from their spell. In a peculiar sense deconstructive reading recoups their dehistoricizing fiction as the truth: where science ontologizes, we historicize, thus opening the possibility of new history. Bourgeois sociology cannot be falsified by a supposedly nonbourgeois representationality freezing Marxist truth into a new ice age; that only restores the positivist world. The only way around discipline is through it, making text —fiction—of what appears to be the dumb reflection of nature itself. While a fact today, the power of the social reproduces itself discursively in the billion lives one might call readings, if we recognized the power of the social as a text.

In this way a practice throwing off the numerous mutilations of bourgeois existence transcends the text. Rewriting is political practice if the reformulated texts are lived politically. I submit that positivism is the central discourse in capitalist and state-socialist societies today at least judging by the aporetic evidence of unconsciousness admist what passes for enlightenment. The point is not only to grasp competently disciplinary discourses but also to reformulate them by reformulating their chilly "world" as formulation itself. This formulation of formulation, transvaluation, necessarily reads technical and figural representation to have been authored. Committed writing in this sense always regards tradition skeptically as a literary accomplishment; critique prises free the freedom disciplinary texts deny by their surreptitious promotion of a certain order of being. This is not to say that committed writing is always superficially polemical; yet in these times most versions of the world take the side of the world, even in spite of their "radical" intentions. As ontology named differently, they occlude and thus oppress.

Committed reading as a writing resisting its disempowering takes the critical analysis of authorial partisanship one step further than a radicalized sociology of knowledge; Friedrichs (1970) called Gouldner's (1970) and Mills's (1959) books "sociologies of sociology." Such reading recognizes that *writing reproduces itself as society;* presuppositionless representation adds the conviction of its own constitutionlessness to a nonidentical world requiring readings to prove the truth of writing—the power of the social named by sociologists reproducing itself not on multiple-choice exams but in "everyday life."

As political acts in this sense, texts can be read ironically as interventions precisely where they reveal their own necessity as a stabilizing complement to a perilously incomplete world. A constitutionless positivism constitutes an insufficiently constituted world. Discourse speaks a certain truth about the world's need where it can itself be read as a necessity; indeed, by denying its constitutional nature, positivism constitutes social nature—thus telling us something about the historicity of that nature. Mainstream sociology can thus be reformulated against itself as a telling account both of late capitalism's relatively monolithic imperviousness, whose discipline is described in minute and encyclopedic detail, and the inherent self-contradictoriness of a system requiring surreptitious science to seal its marginal cracks and leaks. Text by concealing its desire to complete the world only admits the world's need, and thus its historicity. And *that* is a part of the truth revealed deconstructively when we read science ontologically.

This reading historicizes the power of the social as a cogent description of the social today. The iron laws of capital, bureaucracy, sexism, and racism are not laws at all but texts that (science hopes) are real in their consequences. Although Parsons (1951) is wrong about the blissful eternity of advanced capitalism seamlessly knitted together by pattern variables mediating social and personality "systems"—wrong because the pattern variables seemingly reflecting the social system are not nature but artifact, pieces of history—he captures a nearly totally administered postwar capitalism in an accurate if ultimately undecidable way. Parsons goes wrong where he freezes the Eisenhower years into the social nature of the modern, gilding Weber's iron cage with an identity theory ambitiously equating self and society, subject and object, freedom and necessity. He conceals the fact that the seemingly equal exchange between subject and object is deeply skewed; the object's preponderance, a particular capitalism, is not only missed but also propped by a disciplinary version of the world. Parsons purposely fails to explicate the system's own ideological deficit thought to make a version of discipline necessary in the first place.

This deficit is another topic of a disciplinary reading of discipline. It can be shown deconstructively that science's suppression of normative claims in its representation of the ephemeral world helps constitute that world in turn, freezing the imprimatur of necessity onto it. Texts can be read not only in pursuit of the "world" that, once historicized as an insufficient horizon of social possibilities, can be seen in its last detail; their own traces and symptomatic silences can be read and thus reformulated as the possibility of lives lived beyond ontology. Freedom dispenses with ontology because it can bear the indeterminacy of history—of course, an ontological claim in its own right. Social science self-contradictorily suggests a self-sufficient world in a way subverting its disciplinary formulation of that sufficiency. Having to tell the truth means that there was no truth to tell in the first place. People write because the world runs a certain deficit, in the case of sociology an insufficiency of capitulation; too much noise around the edges threatens to become the concerted voice of defiance. Reading suppressing its own constitutionality as the missing truth of science ironically only completes a world prematurely depicted as complete. The descriptive competence of science solicits a certain self-neutralizing reading, an enactment of writing vitiating the reader's possible autonomy from the spell of a text constraining imaginative transformation.

The written is constructed by a version that plugs the gaps of nonidentity, nonconformity, undecidability, and inexhaustible desire forever existing as traces, as otherness, at the margins of the dominant world. The text's apparent centeredness comes only at the expense of the margins on which it relies for its own identity in a kind of literary imperialism. If opposition did not exist already, positivism would invent it as an example of inferior being. A nonidealist dialectics emphasizes that the world has no metaphysical center disclosed to fundamental ontology. Instead centeredness is a literary achievement of readers who perversely accept their own chilling subordination to a center they have constitutively established. Text dominates, constructs, creates —against its own falsely representational self-presentation. Adorno's metaphor of the concentration camp self-consciously embraces the guilt of survivors as a sign that the ultimate identity of fascism—mass extermination of subjects by subjects—is never exactly achieved but leaves the traces of memory and guilt that then serve survivors as a dialectical resource toward reconstruction: it shall never happen again, the ultimate political morality.[7]

Where a Marxist version of deconstruction suggests that positivist discourse itself reveals the world's deficit, and thus hope, the orthodox Marxist and liberal populist alike view skeptically the practicability of what appears only a textual politics. After all, neither Adorno's negative dialectics nor Derrida's deconstruction is a political strategy in the ordinary sense of providing blueprints. They do not instrumentally link analysis to action anymore than they reduce knowledge to interest. Instead they write as refusal, adding to the momentum of vestigial resistance in writing that relentlessly historicizes the mistakenly ontologized. The textual paradox of incomplete completeness fortuitously calls forth writing as a counter to the world's deficit. A nonpositivist version of writing need not make up this deficit socio-ontologically; rather writing can celebrate the nonidentity of the world as the crack in history opening to a world made up of coexisting margins, all centering denied as political myth.

That the powers require the world to be postured discursively is a sign of hope inhering and expanding in deconstructive reading; texts turned against themselves break their spell over readers muted by their seemingly implacable impenetrability. Breaking out from within, Adorno's leitmotif, critique as a textual-political strategy pierces the shell of science by historicizing scientificity as the suppression of the literary; at the same time such a reading leaps forward to new versions, thus new worlds, in reformulating the world concealed—hence congealed—by positivism. Reading writes the positivist world discouraging versions essayed outside discipline, the problem of academicization. What reading's writing can say programmatically, if anything in these times, is that de(con)struction necessarily opens the prospect of new artifice, the topic of my concluding chapter. Meanwhile a committed reading learns the *(un)truth* of the present by undoing its putatively generic explication of the power of the social in a disciplining discourse; where sociology writes "society," I write history.

Bourgeois discourse contains the key to understanding the bourgeois world whose historicity it conceals. Representation reflects it precisely as what it is not but only claims to be, the rational real. We decenter the bourgeois order by learning the desperate secrets of its insufficiency from its version of itself freezing a postured "world" into ontological sufficiency—being into Being. Yet the positivist version of a versionless world betrays, hence deconstructs, itself in *needing to be written in the first place*. Sociology in its disciplinary existence shows that the teleological order announced by Comte, Durkheim,

Weber, and Parsons—bourgeois modernity—is insufficient; in requiring texts to empower the concept of the power of the social, thus inducing it, sociology suggests historical irreversibility. Complicity, adjustment, adaptation bear the affordable price of mobility, goods, leisure, and spiritual plenitude.

This is what Marx meant by opiate when he talked about the dulling effects of religion. Yet science, a deeper, more intraveneous text, refuses to cede spiritual matters to a church for fear of circumscribing its own territoriality, thus admitting the possibility of apostasy, even atheism. But as a version of totality only achieved through its discourse science undoes itself. Intervening historically, science undermines its own lack of historicity; its deconstructed narrativeness, its thoroughly ontological agenda, augurs less oppressive versions of the social. In thawing the world frozen timelessly by science, reading reformulates the world as a discursive accomplishment, ever the promise of liberation. Parsons discloses not "society's" lawfulness but the world he tries to provoke through the casuistry of the pattern variables. The essay of Parsons's world suggests other possible formulations of the social. The historicity of the social suggests new formulations of the relationship between discourse and social life. If sociology is not allowed to exhaust exciting social possibility, prematurely closed to an indeterminate future, discourses about the social can be rewritten.

Derrida suggests that reading meets the resistance of aporias that cannot be skirted but must be dealt with squarely, Adorno's "from within." Sociology as a textless text is haunted by the fundamental irony of having-been-written at all; where science purports to reflect, its version of reflection discloses its narrative nature—suggesting the possibility of new narratives. Reading confronts the self-undoing implications of a version that must both ignore and address *a deficit that is history itself;* the gulf between lawful and lawless versions of the world suggests discourses rerouting, not simply repeating, history. Discourse is history's midwife. Here I want to exploit the aporias as well as the telling silences of disciplinary sociology, both to show the possibility of different versions of discourse and to learn from sociology's aporias and silences (a Marxist would call them contradictions) about sociology's history unnecessarily frozen into nature. Once a deconstructive reading exhumes the suppressed literariness of disciplinary versions, we pierce the deceptions of versions harmonizing the cries of pain and the stunned silence of the miserable along with the hearty self-congratulation of the powers. The discipline's ahistorical version of itself conceals a disciplined world to which it contributes its own soundless voice.

Entering the public world in an act of protean subjectivity, positivist discourse undercuts its own claim to reflect by having had to be written at all. Ideology deconstructs its own reflection of a harmonious social order; the fact of its discourse suggests otherwise. I concentrate my critique on the identification of history with the power of the social, sociology's modernism. Whereas sociology's version of the modern is marked by domination—Weber's iron cage—it is also leavened by certain compensations in the cheerful liberalism of scientism. Discipline constitutes the modern in naming its "necessity" in an advanced industrial age. Recognizing the deficit of obedience continuing to haunt popular capitalism, science describes just as it secretly recommends, thereby hoping to secure political reproduction through the intellectual reproduction of its topic—the power of the social.

I refuse to read this version of science in its own terms, simply engaging with its "world" at what it hopes will be face value, the fate of readers habituated to their own constitutional irrelevance. Instead I examine its lapses, inconsistencies, and silences in a way that excavates history underneath its purported "world." In my concluding chapter, having deconstructed sociology as a piece of fiction, I essay other versions of versions undoing science's posturings of a privileged presuppositionlessness. These are neither discontinuous nor discrete processes; the glimpse of a different version of the world will already show through my deconstruction of the disciplinary version. Dedisciplining liberates. Deconstruction is unavoidably reconstruction. Yet as positive takes its bearings from the implied not-negative, I do not want to offer blueprints for fear of deepening cheerfully idiotic optimism in the face of imminent darkness. It is incredibly difficult to negate, let alone essay, a positive world. Yet, unavoidably, the one inhabits the other if only as an absent presence, as possibility. Nor am I marshalling evidence to be spoken against science at its eventual tribunal; I cannot resolve its aporias without already addressing its role in perpetuating a world it claims only to copy. There is no balance sheet but only a version in its totality, a version of versions. Sociology is already an institution, and thus we cannot pretend to read or write *de novo,* as if ours were not answers to questions already asked and tentatively answered. It is enough to hear science as ontological discussion in the first place.

I uncover history beneath the text's "world" in an aporetic reading reformulating science's chilled laws *as if* they were narrative constituting a certain political intent. This is less a search for the interest "behind" knowledge than a deconstructive version showing how authors formulate a "world" behind the back of literary, hence political, constitution. Textuality discloses the truth of its falsehood when read narratively. Sociology would realize its account of a patterned world through its account itself. Although a ruse, ruse deconstructs itself into a version of reason—if not the most rational one. Disciplinary reading functionally uncovers its textual spell woven to disempower readers insinuated into the disciplinary world frozen in historical time and thereby disciplined by it. Dialectical thought cannot separate cause and effect: the world is narrated, hence constituted, by discourses that are themselves (re)productions.

Positivist reading positively enacts its own constraint by the social. Neither a simple effect of material interest nor a single disempowering cause, this discourse both suggests and is suggested by a positivist world. To the extent to which domination is self-inflicted—ultimately, it *all* is—we can overcome the compulsion to repeat it in the name of necessity, at best a minimalist political strategy. Yet overcoming self-defeating behavior is no mean accomplishment in a world crushing down on most of us, limiting imagination to the next meal. Mechanical Marxism for too long has trivialized oppositional practices simply because they threatened the primacy of white male labor along with its self-explication as economism. Not every opposition "counts" equally, and radical social change does not always average into the arithmetic of numerous angry voices and groups, all margins equalling a center. Radical strategy cannot be decided transcendentally, outside history, but only in the ebb and flow of texts made thematic between and among writers inevitably imbedded in the local regions of Wittgenstein's forms of life.

Blank Pages: Domination as Silence

In this chatty, conversational age we tend to vest more constitutiveness in language, text, and talk than is really found there, a paradoxical claim by a writer interested in political textuality. I am wary of the self-methodologizing trends in recent literary criticism and communication theory from deconstruction and semiotics to Habermas and Garfinkel.[8] Poststructuralist discourse theory risks reducing oppression to language, a problem that can be made good only through relentless historicization locating text in the webs of power and resistance. Freud profoundly recognized that silences are often as meaningful as utterances, suggesting a psychoanalytic perspective on discourse enduring as one of his most important legacies. The theory of repression underwrites the poststructuralist analysis of the subtext as objective subject; the silent dialogues and desires beneath the surface of writing give it a certain dialectical spin. Again, I submit that reflection constitutes. Subtext is the realm of the text's engagement with itself and other texts opening the writer to other writers in the give-and-take of unencumbered argument or, better, simply *rewriting*— a version of Habermas's ideal speech situation secured in the undecidability of discourse.

Intertextuality is an ideal text and therefore the ideal society it prefigures; in it arguments are never closed, and no one owns or controls the truth. The footnote, a standard apparatus of bourgeois scholarship serving to acknowledge the copyright of ideas as well as adding value to the disciplinary literature, is brought back into the text, not to ignore the authority of diverse intellectual sources but to engage those sources dialogically. Naming makes way for a plurality of names and thus a plurality of power. This decanonizing approach to authority creates a real community where before there was only a single dominant version, citation constituting deference not communicative reason. My version of the public acknowledgment of authority provokes many versions as the basis of genuine solidarity. Slavish authority citation deceptively suggests that ideas have a divine origin to be revealed, thus reconstituted, in a genealogy of sources. This conservative doctrine suggests the myth of original representation, positivism's unexamined premise. This only inhibits our search for a qualitative break in the continuum of domination that will, as Marx said, catapult us from prehistory to real history. It also vests "tradition" (Gadamer 1975) with a contingent continuity and richness, unassumable as an essential property of a merely temporal past. By no means does intertextual writing ignore past or present authorship or reject the possibility of "creativity," subjectivity become solipsism; rather it treats tradition not as a dead weight to be born ritualistically, but as a lively body of writing privileged only to the extent to which it makes any sense for us and, as such, becomes the topic of our reformulation. Positivism conceals the fact that citation is construction, a text in its own right.

Subtext is the writer's desire to bring about a certain world through writing itself. The closer subtext is to the surface, the more open to other voices the writing—hence, world—will be. This is a balancing act of sorts; just as subtext can be relegated to citation and thus ritualized, albeit at the risk of its own revolt, so it can overwhelm the text with a surfeit of voices, embellishments having little internal coherence—merely autobiographical signifiers indicating "where" the author has been before in text and life. The subtext can be heard as the author's struggle to trace the links between self and text, an internal process of clarification and thus publication resembling the psychoanalytic dialogue, albeit without the monologizing skew of power between analyst and analysand on the model of medical psychotherapy. Subtext undoes the repression of sources, readings, and interests that led the author to essay a certain version; as such, the thematization of these contingent but unavoidable circumstances of authoriality gives the writing a reflexivity and self-consciousness—a literariness—inviting other concatenations and transvaluations of the same sources. A book on Marx would present both "my" Marx *and* at the same time, as subtext, a guide to how my Marx (compared to the Marx of others) came to be mine.[9] The more these levels of discourse are integrated the more "ideal," in Habermas's sense, the writing will be; the less monologizing, monopolizing, scientizing, *the more text will be a gentle community*.

The more the subtext covers itself in the deceptions of disinterestedness, thus inhibiting its excavation as thematic literary work, the more signifying it becomes. The suppressed subtext, authorial desire, casts an unacknowledged spell on the text's surface and thus overdetermines it, giving it surprising meaning from the outside—here, the inside. Although science's text appears to harbor no discernible subjectivity other than footnotes, bibliography, index, and maybe a glossary of terms, this seeming objectivity makes all the more certain its animation by repressed desire powerfully shapes the writing, often in spite of itself. Derridean reading locates the repressed subtext in a methodological deconstruction of methodology itself; disciplinary reading inspired by Derrida turns text against itself, showing where its smoothly diachronic linearity is really interruption and synchronicity, what Adorno called nonidentity.[10] Broadening a poststructuralist literary criticism already inured to social theorizing, deconstruction lacks an historicizing moment of utopian imagination that would allow it to formulate a less dualistic, more heterogeneous, thus more fully human world. Its own text fails to shorten the very distance between its surface and its subtext, writing itself in light of what it takes to be its inheritances from and entwinements with its own desire and those of others. By suppressing its inherent politicality out of the correct view that all previous political orders have been excrescences of various perversions of desire, deconstruction joins the chorus of affirmation, if only in silence.

Recognizing and thus enacting itself as a form of social life, a different discourse avoids closure by being open to its own worldly imbeddedness in self, society, history. An essentially non-Marxist, even anti-Marxist, poststructuralism, whether in Lacan, Derrida, or Foucault, shades so much toward Nietzschean cynicism that it fails to account for, and thus project, its own *different writing* as a utopian possibility. By inviting self-deconstruction, deconstructors like Derrida trivialize by methodologizing their own argument and make of language a prison house only to be escaped by flaunting its most bizarre extravagances. Although good text is playful in its attitude toward its own imbeddedness in a preexisting world and in its own perspectival and passionate embodiment, it also takes seriously its world-constitutive responsibility, a notion Habermas captures when he suggests that every speech act intends consensus; in my terms, it intends to change the world. The Derridean refusal to be read as constructive, as political, is more an inability; Derrida is not an optimist. Critical discourse theory must contain as it exemplifies a utopian image of writing and reading, however nuanced by the sobering awareness of every text's subordination in these times; writing in refusing also kindles hope—the harbinger of imagination.

Derrideans criticize the metaphysics of neat binary oppositions. Yet this critique methodologically bypasses politics and history; cynicism becomes a worldview, thus a world itself. Deconstruction shortcircuits the dialectical alternation of enlightenment and myth, a vestige of a Nietzschean attack on the Enlightenment so devastating that the prospect of a universal reason is abandoned as untoward Promethean pretense, a new will to power. But criticism always discloses an alternative world—here one in which criticism loses its derivative status altogether. Deconstruction exhumes only to put to rites a subtext of pretentious metaphysics underlying Descartes, Rousseau, Husserl, and

Hegel (among Derrida's critical targets); Derrida then rejects all metaphysics, hence political imagination. He feels that a different metaphysics would court all the prior problems of a logocentric Cartesian rationalism. Thus, he conceals the metaphysical nature of deconstructive methodology, turning it away from history and toward ironically self-enclosed literary texts—ironic because poststructuralists believe that the text has no outside. The issue of the metaphysical nature of the critique of metaphysics can be recast in a way that enacts a nonlogocentric concept of reason, whether socialism (Marx), the new sensibility (Marcuse), or ideal speech (Habermas).

Idealism in the garden variety sense of *hope* is not exhausted by metaphysics, although surely they trade off each other. Idealism, as hope, is given the lie by the unworldliness of Idealism, as metaphysics; idealism only reinforces the empirical truism that the world today betrays optimism. This negation of metaphysics has the patina of sophistication but the falsehood of capitulation: it is only a metaphysic itself, perspectivity absolutized and thus losing perspective.

Here I explicate the simultaneously positivist and liberal subtext of American sociology as a metaphysical compromise between hope and heteronomy. But prehistory does not decide the future if only because writing is inexhaustible; the power of the social describes but does not exhaust the modern. This does not mean that the play of texts is a total politics, a position as fractured as one that endorses economism, feminism, antiracism, or parliamentarism in and of themselves. Rather writing is prioritized here because texts bear, and betray, what Marx called ideology and thus reproduce themselves and the world they seem only to reflect—keeping capitalism off the shoals of a legitimation crisis (Habermas 1975). Without the psychic emoluments of the culture industry, the imbedded contradictions of capitalist production and reproduction would surface volcanically; only discourse can pacify, integrate, and coopt—science no less than television.

Marxism has not outlived its original subordination of cultural, sexual, and psychic reproduction to value-bearing activity controlled by capital, men, and science. This is largely because, at least since Engels, Marxism has modeled itself on positivism, reflecting value only in what is currently valuable—an issue decided discursively. Thus, issues of productive contradictions addressed centrally in the elegant artifice of *Capital* seem "harder," more ontologically prior and thus more politically engaging than oppressions in the realms of the cultural, sexual, ideational. But where the state manages economic crisis, culture today palliates psychic crisis—legitimation deficit, surplus repression, hegemony, misogyny. Discursive practices blind/bind people to their oppression and thus reduce their socio-ontological opportunities as playful writers —bearers and authors of value. To deny a theory of the culture industry on Marxist grounds is to miss what Horkheimer (1972) in his 1937 essay on "Traditional and Critical Theory" noted as the increasingly tight linkage, indeed inseparability, of so-called base and superstructure in an emergent managed capitalism.

The easy either/or of orthodox Marxism, indeed of all western dualism—economics "or" ideology—is unable to understand a world so interrelatedly complex that CBS owns the news, books, and entertainment in one fell swoop. A Marxism so canonical and puritanical that it ignores the inseparability of base and superstructure, and perhaps even the reversal of their structural priority with culture or text now being "determinative in the last instance," was already decried by Marx when he said he was not a Marxist. Perhaps it is better to say that Marxism is critical theory (and always was) than the other way around. This understands Marxism as an open text alive to its own historical imbeddedness in (a) desire (to change the world), foregrounding its literary nature as critique and utopian imagination. This is not simply a technical device serving a certain reader-response theory stressing authorial presence as the basis of a good review but a way of acknowledging and creatively preserving the tension between particular and general—self and society/history.

This version of versions recognizes that desire and knowledge do not necessarily collide, with perspective or "bias" reducing validity, as methodologists would worry; they must be allowed to coexist as a complex weave of author, history, other texts, and topics soliciting a genuinely democratic community of versions. Subtext moves up to meet and inform, if not identify with, surface text that then dialectically/dialogically incorporates it; authorial desire ought not be celebrated as such. After all, positivist writers would create a desireless world. First-person prose and poetry in themselves fail to liberate; the defense of desire is not an argument against objectivity. Disciplinary critique restores an authorial subjectivity kept down and out, *mute,* by the strictures of positivist representation. Yet subjectivity is not an end in itself; desire desires a different order of being—in which subjectivity and objectivity are not opposite terms.

The sociology texts constituting one encyclopedic version as such contain all sorts of indicative silences about tabooed material. What is said is signified by what remains unsaid; the books contain invisible pages that by being blank constitute the surface text living off its claimed scientificity—freedom from the contaminants of desire, motive, interest. Just so, a text's subtext is often found between the lines, *under* them, not only in the notes pasted in at the end for the sake of "scholarship" but also in the substantive ellipses and omissions in the text's body.

American sociology silences authorial presence, ideology, its articulation of other disciplines, and ontology. Sociology's oppression of the nonidentical is rooted in Comte's invention of sociology as a separate science as well as in Durkheim's characterization of sociology's differentiation from psychology, the founding articulation of disciplinary distinctiveness remaining virtually unchanged. As the expositor of the power of the social, Durkheim first charged sociology with the suppression of the historically utopian, relegating it to inferior knowledges like art and philosophy. Thus, sociology's symptomatic silences concern the nonsociological, the other disciplinary perspectives on social things bracketed for the sake of the autonomous development of sociology.[11] In this sense, monologue is the hallmark of disciplinary maturity.

PART TWO

Text/Book/Discipline

3

Durkheim's Discipline

Constructing Nonscience

Every discourse differentiates itself from other discourses and thus implicitly suppresses undisciplined talk. Are blank pages—unexamined problems—not inevitable inasmuch as language constrains some meaning in making other meaning possible? This is very much the Derridean argument for a relativism that deconstructs all writing in skewering its self-contradicting absolutism. But just as language necessarily excludes the unspoken, so the unspoken, the repressed, shadows text in giving it what Merleau-Ponty called its *sens*.

This book is about disciplinary sociology, and thus about all discipline—and not about Russian formalism or baseball, even though I could legitimately refer to Jakobsen in passing. Yet because the silences and suppressions in my text *as silences* do not tell us much about my subtext, I need to bring desire closer to the surface as a way of writing and living intertextual connections making way for other versions—hence community. One might say that this is a way of reforming the discipline; I would prefer to think of it as a way of building good community. The silences have to be "heard" as they are placed in a certain relationship to what is said. That I do not write about Russian formalism or baseball only indicates the infinity of topics and says little about how ecumenism or downright silence about other topics underwrites "this" text (and not texts on literary criticism or sports). The silences must be heard as the imagined interlocutors informing this version of my text; as such, they must be understood as symptoms of some sort of suppression, a topic in its own right. In disciplining, the discipline decides who can speak.

A truly intertextual version may be silent on topics utterly beyond its ken (e.g., sociology in a book about baseball) but omits little else that constitutes its problematic, its discussion with itself and others. Indeed a narratively reflexive writing of the kind I aim to be doing here is a vehicle for counterhegemonizing my way through a discipline, hence discipline in general. In the spirit of my own agenda, I interrogate my version's own silences as a way of making them present—*listening to itself listening as a way of giving everyone the possibility of a hearing*. This is a foolishly liberal desideratum only if liberalism is allowed to claim a dialogic ethics as its own and then subvert dialogue in monopoly/ monologue capitalism. This book at the end will have exhausted its topic in the sense that it will have written not only the apodictic text (of which I am "certain") but also to the ambiguous text that could have been written instead or differently; my silence about this other text—every one but this—is as much as possible made a topic itself. Objections are anticipated, my own indecision about what to include registered, and my account opened to the inscription of other names and possible arguments.

My text is self-conscious of its own territoriality, its difference from other possible versions of itself. This version of my version discloses not only my artifice but also *why* it was written, in light of what topic—the closed book of American sociology I try to open. Continuous with its topic, deconstructive writing keeps it forever in sight, refusing to abandon it after the opening chapter only to rejoin it once again at the end in a concluding reprise; authorial circumspection is not only an embellishment but also text itself as it listens to itself write writing. Thus, reading is a version (of writing). How could it be otherwise? Discipline is as territorial as an account of discipline, laying claim to a topic whose treatment it arrogates to itself (e.g., the power of the social and the discourse producing the power of the social). In suppressing why it was written, it leaves pages blank that must be filled in a genuinely dedisciplining version. A nondisciplinary account of discipline writes itself everywhere, anticipating not only rejoinders but, even more important, excavating authorial intentionality as a resource of its comprehension, not a muddying excrescence. Science's text appears ontologically uncommitted because it suppresses the subjectivity necessary for any commitment; its interest is disinterestedness, one of the strongest interests of all. A less encumbered writing in thinking why it writes suffuses its version with a sense of effective, unblocked intentionality, thus precluding altogether the problem of immanent meaning. I will *tell* you what I mean, allowing for the likelihood that you and others will mean differently.

Although rarely silent in the sense of suppressing the text's reason for being, writing may fail to "cover" the subject. Commitment as a state of mind is insufficient without publicity; the best text, warts and all, risks everything in going public. Discipline discourages essay—the attempt to write unbidden to authority. As the pen beneath text, authorial desire to write "this" account falls on its face without developing an argument making good on commitment. Each version must not only acknowledge its worldliness but also argue for a world; merely to write straightahead, heedless of the possibility of other versions, reneges on the promise of one's own reformulation—hence, community. In anticipating, even encouraging, other versions of itself, nonpositivist writing opposes discipline with dialogue, always the best antidote. Commitment is never enough in itself to accomplish writing; yet the apparent lack of literary investment in a version of the world will result in a weak text going nowhere, least of all toward other readers.[1]

Its net will not be cast widely enough to take in otherness, alterity, difference, and contradiction. It will dwell so much within its own homogeneous problematic that it will fall short of readers themselves in pursuit of a more worldly writing addressing text to its driving desire to bring about a new state of affairs (an intent laid bare in Habermas's universal pragmatics). The sociological discussion of women's issues (see Section 4) is a striking example of how the numerous silences drown out a thin text in self-referential, banalized observations epitomizing disciplinary differentiation. The silences are significant when they repair a faulty text so out of touch with its authorial subjectivity that it becomes a frozen object, almost a part of nature; science ultimately wants itself to be nature's mimesis. What the text suppresses matters most to its (lack of) sense of itself; its territoriality would reproduce a territorial world. Ultimately, science suggests a world without subjects or subtexts, excluding even itself from the constructed world it mirrors; disciplinary reading includes itself in its account of discipline. While risking infinite regress it gains a textured world that promotes a real intersubjectivity, real community.

Science silences because it leaves its own voice out of its account. This inherently falsifies its claim to capture the world in its web, instead being captured by it. De-authored writing represents, hence secretly recommends, a world in which people are not empowered with a curiosity to intervene in the world interpretively, authorially, politically. Positivism self-contradictorily excludes itself from its account by repressing its own desire to be a purely technical account, thus bringing about a purely technical, figural world.

Sociology is silent about the nonsociological, the huge realm of human studies beyond the discipline charged by Durkheim with the study of the power of the social—its discourse ironically bringing it about. As I unfold an argument about the world argued for silently by positivist analysis, notably in what it does *not* say, I will register these silences as they exclude a host of knowledges falling beyond the disciplinary purview. Sociology names and thus provokes the power of the social, freezing our subordination to social structure —capitalism, sexism, racism. The nonsociological is a tautology; sociology by exclusion creates the nonsociological as that about which nothing is spoken, including ideology, authorial presence, other disciplines and ontology generally. Yet Durkheim's original differentiation of sociology from psychology remains the centerpiece of sociology's suppression of marginal voices; Durkheim's discipline creates the power of the social as the essence of modernity. Before sociology constituted the power of the social in incontrovertible principles of societal differentiation and stratification, the power of the social was not recognized as such. Discipline helped create the experience of discipline, criminology the experience of criminality (Foucault 1977), sociology the experience of the power of the social.

Durkheim rejected psychology as psychologism, an insufficient grasp of the conditioning effects of the social environment on subjectivity. Psychology to Durkheim was an idealism that failed to address social structure as a "variable" intervening between personality and history. In this, of course, he was right. The ultimate identity theory, psychology does not even raise the question of an obdurate objectivity's nonidentity to the subject; instead, it situates the rational agent in an irresistible world of potential "satisfactions." Only as psychology becomes variously social psychology, neo-Freudian psychoanalysis, and third-force psychology does the easy self-sufficiency of the mindful subject confront its recognition by other subjects and, frequently, its blockage by "society" as psychologism slips into sociologism: intersubjectivity is scientized, frozen, and thereby reproduced in the disciplinary discourse of the power of the social (to which one might read psychology simply as an antidote).

Durkheim forged sociology not in an emboldened optimism about the seamless integration of self and society but in acknowledgment first and foremost of the historical amnesia of a psychology "explaining" behavior with reference only to internal mental states. Durkheim introduced determination simply because determination appeared an ineluctable universal of all previous, and therefore projected, social history. This way of reading Durkheim (and, as much, Weber) counters Parsons's gloss of their thought as functionalist, merely upsurges of *angst* in the patterned order of lawful capitalism. Durkheim demarcated sociology from the nonsociological because he saw in it a realistic skepticism about our powerlessness before the division of labor and bureaucratic hierarchy, only trivially ameliorated with collective consciousness —later, Parsons's American common values. Durkheim's *Division of Labor in Society* (1964) both extols alienation and indicts it; he seeks solace in our subordination to the power of the social, suggesting a "religion of society," collective self-consciousness of common bondage. Psychology was false because it failed to recognize the ample but ontological impediments to free self-determination in social structure, sociology's generic idea of domination drained of the historicity making it so (and thereby potentially undoing it).

This demarcation of sociology and psychology enduring in American sociology inures the discipline to psychological accounts. But the original reason for Durkheim's suppression of the psychological is itself suppressed. He is misunderstood by those who read *Rules of Sociological Method* not as social criticism, a dismal philosophy of history freezing our powerlessness in cement, but as an invigorating call to a world guaranteeing its own discursive reformulation. Moreover, Adorno and Horkheimer (1972) understood sociology as a perverse celebration of powerlessness and psychology as an idealism overlooking the historical tension between self and society in a time when all inwardness (*Innerlichkeit*) is subject to the social object's preponderance.

Sociology reflects the virtually unmediated, self-reproducing power of the social in turn making representation of the here-and-now ironically come true. Adorno reads the difference between psychology and sociology as the struggle of subjectivity against the preponderant objectivity of administered capitalism; psyche is a myth driven (against itself) by introjected systemic imperatives, an increasingly ineffective bulwark against the revolt of its own inner nature. Administration thus reproduces itself.

Sociology suppresses the psychological out of disciplinary territoriality; it thus ignores the truth of its own analysis of a powerlessness itself suppressed by psychology. There is truth and error here, even if truth in a way is unintended, as deconstruction (through psychoanalysis) always shows it to be. Psychologism glosses the "fact" of society; yet in suppressing psychological accounts sociology paradoxically loses a possible way out of its own prison house of the social, an account only fulfilling itself in the world it provokes. The truth of psychology is the desideratum of freedom, if not yet its actuality; psychology posits a life unconstrained by domination.[2] Psychology for its part "finds" this freedom already to hand, abundant in the agency it thinks it finds in the world; sociology rejects the prospect of freedom as metaphysically impossible in light of (its) necessity—factories, hierarchy, scarcity, family. It intends to surpass psychology with the sobriety of a science whose time has come in a world in which free "space" is increasingly precious.

In time disciplinary divisions harden, and we largely forget why they arose in the first place. Psychology abounds today as a celebration of selfhood increasingly at risk in administered society. As the subject succumbs to its "patterning" by discipline, Parsons's (1951) prescient term intended as the fateful logic of every social order, it must be rehabilitated by discipline; freedom is forced out of the meat grinder of a nearly total socialization. People inwardly cultivate the region of the "personal" (Lasch 1979, 1984) as compensation for the rigors of a socialized/sociologized existence.[3] Sociology originally broke with psychology's untimely individualism as capitalism intensely socialized production and administered everyday life generally; today psychology appeals where sociology offers few reprieves from a colonized, patterned existence. This is not to say that more sustaining gratifications can be derived from a psychologism that in effect invents subjectivity in face of its demise; upward mobility (e.g., the text "success is the best revenge") appears to give way to self-attention in est, aerobics, evangelism, volunteerism, and the like.

Marxism reminds us that the public/private split is never resolved in favor of the private constructed as a mythic enticement or apologia to placate people's wounded souls.[4] Psychology continues to delude because it reduces the imposing object world to manageable contingencies that can be circumnavigated by the resourceful, interpersonally skilled subject armed with late twentieth-century coping mechanisms—not least a sense of one's needy selfhood. Sociology today fights a rear-guard action against a psychologism waxing and waning with the tide of total administration. The less promising the public sphere as a ground of real satisfactions—politics, community, social movements, culture—the more psychology takes hold. Sociology preaches to the converted today; our subordination is no longer a mystery as we are all-too-familiar with the bureaucratic machineries of late capitalism hemming us in at every turn. Sociology tells us old news when it documents the sway of giant institutions over us, yet it does not stop telling us that news. By contrast, psychology fascinates in offering us respite from the power of the social, if only "inside," in selfhood.

Sociology and psychology endure in a relationship of first- and second-order discourses; the psychologistic escapes of the needful subject are essentially derived from sociology's portrayal of bureaucratic administration only ameliorated by career advancement, status attainment, and spiritual plenitude. Psychology in a sense takes up where sociology leaves off, plotting the beatified, bourgeois personal space allegedly uninvaded by the socio-organizational imperatives of total administration—no space left unwritten in a fast capitalism. In fact, bourgeois sociology contains a subjective moment just as psychology's subtext is itself a social theory: as social texts they presuppose each other, with psychology and its offer of authentic existence leavening domination that sociology names but as a structural version cannot really explain. Sociology's nostrums of self-help can only be implied.

Sociology's symptomatic silence about psychology since Durkheim is less an opposition than a hint of their inherent mutuality. Psychological explanation is more disdained the more sociology senses its own inability to provide adequate compensation for the rigors of subordination it constructs as fate. They are united by their common commitment to the rationalization of a social order that runs a deficit of obedience only to be made good through discourses disqualifying any but the most constrained satisfactions as ontologically impossible. Where sociology relegates freedom to private life, psychology elaborates the possibility of an authentic existence within subjectivity; as such it supplements sociology's nearly unrelieved colonization of the world with the depiction of characterological traits—insight, priorities, care, honesty, intimacy—necessary for psychic survival today, even "happiness."

Here sociology rejects psychology as a breach of discipline, even a freedom theory. Psychology promises an abundant interior life in a deadening external world. Total administration is driven by an imperial logic of domination assaulting psyche as a condition of its own reproduction. Like philosophical idealism and romantic high culture before it, psychology promises to ease discipline in the reprise of consciousness represented by the ideal of "self-hood." Although psychology so often trivializes itself as a virtual metaphysic of adjustment, "coping," and in this aligns with sociology in its promise of leisure as the best revenge, its hidden desire is general freedom. Freud is an exemplar here (as Marcuse has shown[5]) especially in his later work (e.g., *Civilization and its Discontents*) where he criticizes the oppressive degree of renunciation in late capitalism; the dialectic of happiness and progress usually sacrifices the former to the latter.

Marcuse (1955) radicalized psychoanalysis as a critical theory, eloquently denouncing "surplus repression," an excess of discipline in late capitalism beyond the minimum required for civilized life (Horowitz 1977; Agger 1982) Surplus repression routinizes obedience, hence surplus value, by diverting people from the stunning prospect of worldwide liberation in a technologically advanced age when all basic needs could be met. Marcuse's (1969) critical theory argues for the possibility of immediate transformative prefiguration through the organon of the "new sensibility,"[6] issuing in the end of capital, patriarchy, racism, and the domination of nature. A playful science and technology would gently express the life instincts and blur the false division between production and reproduction, valued and valueless activity.

Although Marcuse ends in Adornoian despair, his reading of Freud gives western Marxism a powerful toehold in an emancipatory politics rejecting the orthodox Marxist "long road" as well as Lenin's vanguardism as a betrayal of Marx's original radical humanism and his image of *autogestion* (Agger 1977b, 1979b). Rejecting the clinical Freud—sexism, harsh repression, mechanism, and biologism—Marcuse distinguishes between psychoanalysis as critical theory and psychoanalysis as a medicalized clinical practice.[7] The inspiring Freud here wrote a "negative psychoanalysis" (Jacoby 1975) confronting the psychic scars of excessive renunciation; at the same time he posits an indomitable core or trace of deep subjectivity valiantly resisting its total administration, even *in extremis* continuing to struggle and hope. Marxism is never completely resigned because the trace of the subject imbued with Freud's indomitable "life instincts" is irreducible to the colonizing forces of capitalist administration ironically mobilizing the subject (against itself) in the name of the object's allegedly ontological preponderance. The irony is that ever-more-effective self-alienation requires a "self" at all.

The concept of an indomitable subjectivity nonidentical to historical social structure issues in emancipatory hope where the subject resists its own patterning. An insurgent desire fostered by a negative psychology neither succumbs to the subject's total absorption by an external world nor pretends that the subject can simply dissipate its own unfreedom through the heroic effort of disembodied but thereby disempowered mind. A negative psychology preserves a dialectical concept of subjectivity that in Adorno's terms is capable of sending out SOSs cast into the vast ocean perhaps to be recovered some day as both the victims' cry for help and expression of hope.[8]

Critical theory's "politics" are unabashedly negative, criticizing the nearly total eradication of subjectivity as a way of keeping alive the memory of hope in an age reducing it to the clichés of the Protestant ethic, third-force psychology, or weight-loss clinics. Sociology rejects this negative psychology as a betrayal of its complicity in the reproduction of the power of the social; negative psychoanalysis abdicates value-freedom and, worst of all, a "positive" attitude. Of course, mainstream psychology, whether behaviorist or humanist, has already relegated theoretical, and hence political, psychoanalysis to the scrap pile; Freud's psychoanalysis surviving as medical psychotherapy contributes to the patterning of subjectivity wracked by the traumas and terrors of contradictory existence today, just as a version of Marx contributes to the Soviet police state. American psychology is positive (and positivist) like sociology where it imbues the damaged subject with a sense of efficacy and coping skills, relieving the deficit of subjectivity with more subjectivity packaged in the numerous forms of psychic relief abounding today.

Habermas (1984, 1987) in his reformulation of critical theory calls for an interdisciplinary materialism uniting intellectual work across disciplines falsely isolated from each other. Whatever one might say about his truncation of Marx's original sweeping utopianism in his essentially neo-Kantian bifurcation of emancipatory and purely technical interests (1971), he smashes disciplinary barriers in the interest of theoretical and thereby practical totalization. This continues the original thrust of Adorno, Horkheimer, and Marcuse, all of whom understood that the complexly mediated world of administered capitalism, once fragmented in disciplinary specialization, had to be reassembled intellectually to be understood as the totality that it is—a reversal of deconstruction on the level of interdisciplinary merger.

The assemblage of interdisciplinary knowledge is crucial in order to address a world fragmenting knowledge not only to comply with the alleged inexorability of endless differentiation, an especially problematic assumption when it comes to knowledge, but also to *decenter its object* so that it cannot be seen and thereby addressed. This is not simply a conspiracy of university administrations, although they surely marginalize truly interdisciplinary work as illegitimate by disqualifying knowledge lacking a seeming "home." The disciplinary differentiation of knowledge is also an outcome of the evolution of human studies, now "social sciences," modeled on a version of science dealing descriptively with a billion natural phenomena. Once regarded naturalistically, human society and human beings are inevitably disassembled by specialized disciplines that then exalt their own perspectivity for the sake of legitimacy; intellectual fragmentation both mirrors, and thereby reproduces, social fragmentation.

Not only do things connect, especially in the social world, but fragmentation also serves the interest of domination by destructuring the totality and thereby preventing us from knowing and opposing it as the structured whole it has become. From Hegel through Marx, people like Althusser and Adorno agree: "The whole is the false." Disciplinary isolation is more important the more that disciplinary object domains overlap in a nearly totally administered society. Disciplinary connection would liberate knowledge from its isolation and thus delegitimate disciplinary specialization; in turn, this would enable us to understand a world ironically portrayed in its complex difference as an object defying a singularly totalizing reading, albeit continuing to pose the notion of an encyclopedic text at least as a regulative idea.

Here science parrots Derrida without believing him, disclaiming totalization on epistemological grounds *as a way of* working toward it politically— naming a world so concatenated that few can even begin to think its totality. It is a sociological truism today, if not a historical universal, that specialization is to be defended as expedient, a chapter in "progress"; Durkheim first valorized division of labor as a sign of societal maturity as well as, ironically, a cement to replace demystified religions as a source of integration. A blow against disciplinary specialization is thus a blow against the differentiation and fragmentation of the social world. A genuinely intertextual materialism would both understand the world as complexly mediated and criticize its mediations as oppressive in their discursive portrayal as unalterable pieces of nature, not the constructions—*texts*—they really are.

Not only, then, do disciplines exist apart; they are also mediated in distinctly hierarchical ways, reflecting both their deep intellectual content and their location in the technocratic division of labor. Economics dominates sociology, for example, by its degree of scientificity as well as in its engagement with seemingly more fundamental human concerns, *homo faber* above *homo sociologicus*. Sociology accedes to economics by taking over its sense of determinateness, whether through Weber's analysis of class, status, and power or Marx's notion of economics as determinate "in the last instance." Economics refuses to engage with sociology except in the trivial sense that society and polity are background assumptions contextualizing the economic marketplace. In a more general way, a neo-Kantianism allowing *Geisteswissenschaften* to coexist with *Naturwissenschaften* as separate-but-equal intellectual object domains is undermined by elevating natural and "harder" social sciences, economics and psychology, above the cultural and hermeneutic disciplines.

It is impossible to separate intellectual from institutional dynamics here; economics bests literary criticism precisely to the extent to which jobs are more plentiful for economics graduates, and, as such, economics is thought a higher calling. This is in large part the old story for sociology of the relative weights attached to jobs in terms of their degree of functional importance, a backbone of the Davis-Moore defense of structured inequality (1945). Doctors are "worth" more than garbage collectors, let alone poets, because they are *worth* more; accordingly, the ex post facto defense of vocational privilege in terms of a transcendental hierarchy of less and more functionally important jobs is a fraud. The abstraction "society" grinds to a halt either way, although allegedly more quickly without doctors.

The sociology textbooks are ensconced within disciplinary specialization, its attendant intellectual isolation, and hierarchically mediate disciplinary relationships privileging hard, marketable, fundamental disciplines over soft unmarketable, marginal ones. The worst of both worlds, this cuts off disciplines from a grasp of the existing totality (totalized *by* disciplinary fragmentation) as well as mediates them through their prioritization as central or marginal. Sociology neither learns from outside its field nor contests the hegemony of the hard sciences and professional schools turning it into a training ground of human capital. As such, ironically, it instructs the middle-level white-collar workers of the future in both their essential powerlessness and interpersonal and managerial strategies for coping with an otherwise recalcitrant world. Thus, sociology further empowers the power of the social.

With most other disciplines, sociology accepts its seeming fate, treating its specialized isolation as an occasion for the legitimation of its own intellectual territoriality, even self-celebration. American sociology is administered through a national association boasting 14,000 members, whose main activities are the publication of the *soi-disant* mainstream journal literature and organization of the annual meeting at which sociologists and graduate students present papers, order and sell books, get jobs, and otherwise "socialize" (with) each other. There is little if any articulation between the discipline as an institution and other disciplines, nor is there much cross-fertilization between academic sociology departments and other departments or programs (outside of some of the "applied" specialty areas like demography and criminal justice, which sometimes articulate with medical, law, or social work faculties). The discipline deepens its sociologism as it expands a literature couched in a territorial vernacular further and further removed from the interdisciplinary materialism exemplified by Habermas. Sociology since Durkheim suppresses the voices of other disciplines because it has staked out the *socially heteronomous* as its object domain, sociologizing and thus reproducing—as "fate"—lives already alienated from themselves.

Although sociology in institutional terms is often a poor relation to economics and psychology because they are more quantitative and thus seem more fundamental, sociology uniquely constructs the power of the social, taking its disciplinary leave from Durkheim's original demarcation of sociology from psychology. As the most general social science in the sense that generic domination is a precondition for the unfolding of the other disciplines, sociology has the most to gain by suppressing other disciplinary voices; if heard, they might decenter sociology by raising questions about the specificity of sociology's version of the power of the social. Sociology might dangerously confront the thought and thus practice of freedom in disciplines like negative psychology, linguistics, philosophy, and history, deconstructing its logos of the social. The discipline of history, after all, vitiates the notion of total administration simply by showing that world-historical obedience often occasions resistance, the upsurge of the nonidentical thus refusing the seeming "fate" sociology encodes in its notion of its own subject matter—the power of the social. Sociology zealously girds itself against the humanities, philosophy, and critical psychology in bald imitation of what it takes to be the natural sciences because it fears their evidence (and, sometimes, open advocacy) of human resistance. Durkheim's study of the social correlates of suicide,[9] the enduring exemplar of sociological research as the study of impinging social structure (in this case, religion over psyche), unravels if suicide is *also* seen as existential choice, moral passion, the only way out, or even as a dreadful mistake.

So sensibly applied to the numerous other false dichotomies conveyed in language, Derridean methodology runs up against either nonrelativity (I hesitate to say "absoluteness") of human freedom or simply subjectivity. In stigmatizing humanism as vain anthropomorphism, deconstructionists invite the relativity of their own relativism, Hegel's negation of the negation becoming permanently positive (e.g., a state withered away always threatens to return as a trace, a new horizon of oppression). Subjectivity scandalizes deconstruction as well as Adorno's critical theory because it is so false today, an absent presence remaining after objectivity has been subtracted.

But freedom haunts domination as a moment that resists totalization; as Marx understood, capital collapses just as it triumphs over living labor, the dialectical reversal threatening all oppressive social orders as their permanent crisis. The reconstruction of a properly sobered "negative" ontology (Derrida, Adorno, Nietzsche) is presupposed by any writing. To write is to live, no matter how aporetic the text. That is, Derrida rejects the concept of an original writing, recognizing that writing in some sense is always rewriting or criticism, but eventually criticism edges into construction, shamelessly risking its own scandalous credibility by giving in to the ontological construction it would become. Text seems to flow almost serendipitously ("cunningly," according to Hegel) from an authorial subtext holding it in its sway, but authorial desire never replaces its mediated writing this side of silence, thoughtlessness, *Dasein*. Deconstruction reflects the desubjectified world of sociology; it does not work through it to a human universe, rejecting construction as sheer Promethean metaphysics attempting to organize history into a seamless narrative. But this reluctance only kills the messenger who brings the bad news about the subject's historical eclipse.

As a narrative embarrassed by its own narrativeness, sociology deconstructively reveals a subtext problematically struggling to actualize negative psychology's premise/promise of freedom. In this sense, the authorial subtext animating any writing is not simply ideology, relativized into unavoidable perspective, that occludes truth but ontology seen as a questioning about the possible. Other disciplines such as philosophy and negative psychology threaten sociology's metaphysic of the social with the glimpse of past and future freedom. Sociology suppresses speculation about utopia tautologically as nonsociological. This intellectual isolation turning sociology into an apologist of power is less autonomy than subordination. Sociology does not portray graven images because the realization of those images would put it out of business. As the Soviets under Stalin realized, a nonantagonistic society does not require, in fact cannot bear, a sociology existing only to complete it; Soviet positivism is nonetheless positivism. Since then, Soviet sociology has flourished, aping American methodological advancement albeit under the name *diamat,* a minor difference at most. Against and beyond the disciplinary inculcation of discipline, undisciplined discourse frees the human faculties to be themselves; this is the possibility of a new science.

In the rest of this book I move from the surface of American sociology's disciplinary version to its suppressed subtext—the methodologically silent writer. I excavate the fossils of author, argument, ontology, and epistemology that, buried, give sociology its pernicious motive force as a voice of necessity, the power of the social, thus further empowering the social. I am decidedly not writing another version of sociology, to compete on the shelf with the many extant versions; I deconstruct discipline as disciplining, freezing the social into being itself. Deconstruction negates the negation, if impermanently, and thus opens versions to their artifice of a better world. If I move hesitantly toward an image of the positive—perhaps simply fiction, reflexive writing— it is not so much to rewrite the book of a discipline undoing critical intelligence as to rethink writing in general. Or to rewrite thinking. I take seriously Adorno's admonition that we must escape the objective context of delusion "from within," a politico-methodological route also taken by Derrida *in the name of antimethod.*

Sociology's Human

I have said that sociology demarcates itself from the disciplines of psychology, economics, and political science as well as from the nonscientific, the tabooed territory of the personal, subjective, common sense, and ideology. Sociology in this way defends its own claim to be a science, ensuring its discipline the indubitability of the natural sciences and thus discipline; a positivist version of science reflects the world's rationality as it becomes a social text, reproducing history thoughtlessly as ontology. Science produces a common "world" that in turn contains science as its disinterested description; science's account of so-called social facts freezes a world that otherwise would melt and leak all over the place. Without a disciplinary center, the world decenters. As intended, disciplines discipline. Science adheres to the norms of communitarian knowledge—professionalism—enhancing its claim to public legitimacy; without self-discipline discipline would be just one among many competing voices, enjoying no privilege over art and politics. If science allows itself to be relativized epistemologically, hence institutionally, it loses its special authority to name the world, a danger even greater for a discipline historically associated with the study and even advocacy of social change. Nonscience threatens sociology now more than ever as universities contract, pinching the qualitative, engaged disciplines. Like all liberalism, sociology turns tail at the first hint of opposition, retreating to the validation procedures of Kuhn's normal science. The bravado of scientificity is a defense against the dissipating effects of sociology's eroding institutional position and deepening conservatism generally; as such, it tenaciously defends itself against the suspicion of nonscience.

Remember also that American sociology is trying to live down its reputation as an enfant terrible of the 1960s; the legacy of the New Left on campus further erodes its legitimacy today as political officials and university administrators exact a certain price from what is reconstructed as a historical indulgence. Never mind that most sociology departments were riven by conflict then, the most politically engaged faculty usually being an embattled rump, or that antiwar activism is in no way discontinuous with sociology's scientificity. The reality counts for less than the stigma of radical activism borne more heavily by sociology than physics simply because sociology alliterates with socialism, a tiresome line in the stand-up routine of sociology teachers who on opening day try to dispel the caricatures of the discipline: not-socialism, not-psychology, not-common sense, not-speculation. If the 1960s were not real, disciplines would invent them as an infantile disorder—"the sixties."

Science's institutional being in the university has always defined its theory of being, giving the lie to teleological and romantic-Luddist hypostatizations of an enduring essence of science; Marcuse's (1969) possible "new science" (Agger 1976b) here vies against Weber and Habermas's (1971) unalterably instrumental science and techne.[10] As such, in spite of the cavils of bourgeois philosophers of science who are really its metaphysicians, science's nature has always been historically affected by its uses and its users; thus, "science" cannot be taken on its own terms lest the critique of scientism (Hayek) dwindle into a romantic protest against all conceptualization—read romantic as foolishly utopian. Otherwise this slots the critique of science into a convenient neo-Kantianism fighting science with "humanism" and inevitably losing.[11]

The science/humanism contrast characteristic of the neo-Kantian response

to what it took to be the illegitimate encroachment of an imperial natural science's apodicticity and methodology into the human studies cedes to science
the understanding of system, pattern, and structure; for these humanists, systematic knowledge as such, any abstraction from experience, violates people's
unique essences. Indeed, much of American microsociology, and symbolic
interactionism and ethnomethodology in particular, opposes functionalism on
the ground that its heavy structural concepts—the very notion of the power
of the social—are alienations in themselves; distortions of mind's synergis-
tic processuality, abstract concepts do not reflect intuitive, lifeworld-grounded
thought and experience. Although true, this drops out the truth content of
idealism—freedom from external determination; however mistaken its solution, mere thought, at least humanism protests the inhuman. Antipositivists
too frequently make idealism a methodology, thus losing its ideas. As such,
microsociology becomes a constructivist backdrop to functionalism, linking
micro and macro, constitution and constituted structure, in a balanced way.
The addition of the so-called human factor holds out against its conceptual
reification; yet precisely for that reason it fails to resist history.

> Above all, sociology studies the human factor, and the human factor is at work
> within bureaucracies, just as it is in every other aspect of social life. (Goode
> 1984, 176)

Humanism tries to restore humanity by fighting its reification in concepts, a
resistance to a representational text mirroring the frozen world—*a mirroring
contributing to its freeze*. This raises the empirical question of how and why the
world is frozen, the power of the social routinizing history into destiny. This
concern has animated western Marxism since Lukacs, bifurcating neo-Kantian
humanism—antiscience—and the Hegelian Marxism of Lukacs, Korsch, and
the Frankfurt School. Whereas neo-Kantian humanism cedes abstract conceptualization to science, retaining only the intuitive and expressive as its topic
domain, western Marxism opposes imperial scientism as well as humanism,
equally contemplative epistemologies leaving history unchallenged. Instead,
critical theory understands the evisceration of subjectivity as an objective
process repeated by a dormant, stupefied subjectivity itself. The subject experiences and thus relives the world as fate, where fatalism is reinforced by the
discursive practices bridging the objective and subjective, reflecting one in the
other. Alienation is deepened by passive reading strategies; the reader is neutralized by seemingly unreadable science thus having the status of ontology.
Technique and figure representationally disclose unalterable being.

Science's historicity clearly makes way for a critique of science. There is
no single science (positivism or Engels's dialectics of nature), nor are there
only two sciences (neo-Kantianism); instead, *historical science* constitutes an
object-world as it postures toward that world in different ways. The humanism

of ethnomethodology restores humanity by banishing the concept of social structure. Yet thereby it fails to restore the human factor politically; idealism seeks an autonomy from the power of the social solely in autonomous ideas.

There is no merely rhetorical escape from imperious science; yet escape proceeds through rhetoric. History adds discourse to itself, producing ontology; discipline constitutes fact, history, into fate, ontology. Sociology adds power to the power of the social. Thus, sociology's portrayal of itself as a presuppositionless portrayal of the world recommends that world. Sociology claims scientificity, its postured presuppositionless representationality rising supremely above the din of many voices—art, humanism, rhetoric, religion. It surveys the frozen landscape of a world captured in time, adjudged unattainable because existent. *There can be other nonscientistic sciences,* other literary versions of knowledge, posturing differently toward a world neither unalterably frozen nor inexorably advancing. These versions regard the history of domination and barbarism as insufficient, not as a fortunate fate where others have perished to save us; the myth of progress glosses the Christian myth that Christ died to save sinners, ever the world-historical excuse for victims. Sociology's cleansed text is desperate, fearing other sciences, other knowledges, as erosions of its own version—the world's buttress in secular times.

Sociology claims science to discredit other writings as nonscience, from which it advances as enlightenment. But as any knowledge, science need not acquiesce to the world, suppressing its authorial presence as a blemish on its rigor, precision, predictiveness. Instead, it can celebrate its authorship as the possibility of committed textuality, where texts join us to others intertextually, constitutively. Sociology's claim to be science fails to exhaust other formulations of the world, especially ones interrogating their own constitutive nature as narrative.

> Perhaps we are all puppets on strings, but if we can neither see those strings, nor feel them directly with our fingers, nor demonstrate their existence via some indirect means—such as casting a light to see if they leave a shadow—we do not concern ourselves with them. (Orenstein 1985, 3)

Because sociology down deep recognizes the literary myth of its scientificity as a worldly text blurring "fact" and fate, it claims science with such adamant piety. Here a note of irony shows through: "Perhaps we are all puppets on strings." The "perhaps" is a ruse, posturing an agnosticism already decided by the founders of the discipline—Comte, Durkheim, and Weber—who believed our fate was heteronomy. A middle-range sociology captures the ontology of the social in the frozen frame of the photographic lens, presuppositionlessly.

> To stray beyond the boundary of the empirical is possibly to lose onself in a land covered by a forest of confusion and contradiction. It is to find oneself in

an intellectual forest in which it is difficult to assert that one idea is more true or
probably true than another. (Orenstein 1985, 3)

Against scientism, this "forest of confusion and contradiction," is *the world,*
not to be cleared away simply with intellectual defoliation. Science so fears
nonscience that its narrative makes history into a completed story. Science
represses the very undecidability of its version of the world and thus the
undecidability of a world that will melt if not chilled narratively. The perspectival, everyday, psychological, idealism, myth, faith, and intuition, nonscience
weakens sociology's claim to science not so much because it is a better account
of the world but because it *also* in its way claims science; nonscience claiming
objectivity dangerously essays a world that can be essayed in any number of
ways. The point is that history never entirely freezes over into being itself.
As Horkheimer and Adorno (1972) wrote in *Dialectic of Enlightenment*, "all
reification is a forgetting," cleansing mind of the horrors it has perpetuated and
suffered in the happy illusion that history is going forward. The past is detritus,
science's prehistory; faith and belief are entrenched as stagnant customs.

The Enlightenment freed knowledge for precisely the constitutive role denied it by scientism today so that it would gain a vast worldly dominion. Ideas
are no longer true or false because truth has been decided by the totality, albeit
in Adorno's reading falsely; ideas are reduced to empirical operations now that
the Idea of Science has been common currency for the last two centuries. Yet
science's Idea is only the suppression of nonscience. In itself it is a shamelessly
passionless version inscribing the historyless world in the pages as quantity,
the graphic and figure; methodology pretends to solve philosophical problems
through "objective inquiry," the jigsaw puzzles of career academics.

> The science of sociology moves such issues as sexual inequality out of the
> muddy waters of philosophical or common-sense debate onto the solid ground of
> objective inquiry. (Bassis, Gelles, and Levine 1984, 30)

Science intends epistemological closure here, moving from "muddy waters"
to "solid ground." The grounds of solidity are to be provided first and foremost by objectivity which, like scientificity, is the indubitability claimed for
itself by science, exorcising the trace of the nondisciplinary. Both philosophy and common sense are thought to evade clarity ("muddiness") as well as
terra firma; they have neither precision nor much epistemological endurance.
Nonscience is particularism, courting too much perspectivity and thus failing
to *defuse* the study of hot topics that burn of the political. Here the subtext
drives to avoid the political, politically occluding the historicity of the present
in order to freeze it; for example, inequality is unnecessarily derived from
patent biological-sexual differentiation, Durkheim's power of the social given

the imprimatur of generic social being. Yet authorial desire passionately suppressing the passion of its own account deconstructs its own suppression; the text reopens itself as an open horizon of workable possibilities—abolishing the sexual division of labor, sharing nurturance, ending misogyny. Nonscience is denied essentially on grounds of its *partisanship,* perspectivity inevitably turning into a platform. Yet the denial of partisanship is partisan itself, denying the narrativeness of writing on surreptitiously ontological grounds. This partisanship is an overt taboo of scientism that wants to, but cannot, leave the examined world untouched, affixing to it the methodological seal of metaphysical permanence.

As particularism nonscience erodes the logos of the disciplinary, the power of the social.

Whatever theoretical perspective sociologists may prefer, their task is always the same: to understand and interpret events and problems that transcend particular individuals. (Light and Keller 1985, 19)

Frozen by the text provoking its ritual enactment, sociology's social being cannot admit either philosophical or common sense partisanship. Science aims to clean the "muddy" world methodologically, refusing to see that methodology itself raises philosophical and literary questions it cannot answer. Science also opposes writing eschewing so-called nomothetic explanation for empathetic understanding and interpretation, a distinction central to neo-Kantians. Scientism endorses the science/humanism contrast so that nonscience can be blocked from engaging in generalizing explanation of the cause/effect variety. Explanation surpasses mere understanding ("understanding refers to what might be called gut level acquaintance") as methodology and verifiability outstrip mere ("personal") argument:

Expressing a theory as an "If/then" statement allows scientists to test it in a systematic manner (assuming, of course, that the phenomena in question can be adequately measured). It is such systematic testing that differentiates scientific research from personal opinion and mere common sense. Testable theories are therefore crucial to science. (Light and Keller 1985, 14)

In this sense, sociology's construction of nonscience as inferior discourse involves the stigmatization of nonscience's partisanship. In these times the world seems to need no overt cheerleading on its behalf, only subtle buttressing by discipline fine-tuning discipline. As well, nonscience is constructed in a way that makes it inevitably inferior to science's methodology and falsifiability. Sociology accomplishes the contextualization of itself as an alternative or corrective to banalized barroom populism by showing its data, tables, and regression equations as patent evidence of its own epistemological authority.

The apparently necessary presence of quantification in the disciplinary text reflects and in turn constitutes the methodological injunction that "claims" have to be "adequately measured" for science's indubitability to differentiate itself sufficiently as a superior knowledge from the speculatively nonscientific, the domain of rank opinion and perspective. But science's committed lack of speculative commitment, seemingly breaking with the distorted commonplaces of the everyday, is usually savvy enough to coopt the "humanities" (human effort, intentionality, practical reason, etc.) by swallowing the various constructivist microsociologies as buttresses of a dominant macrosociology.

> Microtheoretical orientations are intellectual maps that guide sociological quests that are concerned with micro, or small-scale, social processes such as how individuals learn social rules, how they make decisions in terms of their jobs and other roles, and how they react on the personal level to inequality and the frustrations of discrimination. (Orenstein 1985, 49)

These microsociologies support the usual "macro" research on social structure by showing (e.g., Berger and Luckmann 1967) the human nature of social institutions. These accounts confuse the evident (arti)fact of social constitution on the so-called micro level with the inference (Jameson 1981, 76) that people rationally accept their subordination to the social as duty. Yet nothing suggests that the social construction of reality proceeds without coercion and unconsciousness. The millennial idealism making a virtue of necessity understands the satisfaction of subjective wants as a prop of the larger boundary maintenance processes of the social system as a whole, the essence of Parsonianism. The various microsociologies add a constitutional basis to the power of the social in a stupified "everyday life." This links microconstitutional voluntarism with Hobbesian order not through Parsons's magic pattern variables, a sociological invisible hand, but through the more palpable media of interaction, small groups and sense-making talk that have been thematic for humanist microsociology (Mehan and Wood 1975) since Garfinkel's (1967) *Studies in Ethnomethodology*.

Happily, as Collins [12] and others have pointed out, the humanism of microsociological constructivism—Mead, Garfinkel, Cicourel, Blumer, Schutz—can be used to discipline the "just" exchange of duty for compensation; it usefully buttresses a Parsonian version claiming that order flows up from the freely joined intersubjective constitution of the everyday lifeworld as well as down from the disciplining imperatives of social structure. As such, in integrating the nonscientific science defuses nonscience with the appearance of theoretical eclecticism, a crucial subtext of explicit sociology. A discipline that can fend off critics by showing its own humanistic underside, a "soft" concern with the lifeworld processes constituting an orderly society, does itself a favor by ostensibly healing the micro/macro schism as if that were a legitimate problem in the first place. The so-called micro/macro problem is only a reflection of the troubled imperialism of science that rides roughshod over nonscience as muddy, unsystematic, and speculative. Science appears to solve the micro/macro problem by admitting methodological humanism to the fold; it thereby coopts the epistemological opposition. Humanist methodology names the benign everyday resolution of the Hobbesian problem of social order.

This seeming ecumenism works wonders for sociology as it offers something for nearly everyone: hard science and art, rigor and empathy. But microsociology is not nonscience in the same way philosophy is. In appropriating Husserl for the discipline of sociology—now, ethnomethodology—Garfinkel like Schutz affords little critical resistance to the hegemony of scientism. Garfinkel posits a sociological invisible hand ethnographically disclosed in the successful sense making of middle-class Americans; later Husserl hints at a critical theory seeking to empower by historicizing a disempowered subjectivity at sea in the world of institutional gigantism. The constructivist microsociologies do not eschew scientificity at all, only traditional science's Parsonian avoidance of the constitutive processes of the lifeworld as props of Hobbesian order.[13] Sociology thus integrates what it passes off as strong science but what is really weak scientism in the first place. The jubilation about the emergent diversity of American sociology, putative room for both micro and macro methodology, puts us off the scent of versions effectively challenging sociology's hegemony as the modal text of adjustment and amelioration.

Science has not only integrated microsociology as a phenomenological solution to the Hobbesian problem of order; it has also denatured Marxism and feminism into versions of conflict theory and liberal social psychology, respectively. Sociology protects its claim to be a discipline the more it can swallow spuriously different epistemological and methodological voices. Ethnomethodology is not at all the barroom gossip that science abhors as pedestrian speculativeness but a methodologization of gossip as constitutive of micrological order—barroom subculture's emergent norms typifying the constitution of larger societal values. Constructivism is critical theory only if its focus on the intersubjective constitution of lifeworlds is *historicized* in such a way that constitution is seen as a competence nearly suppressed under capitalism.

A dulled subjectivity—puppets on strings simply acting out roles—is disempowered by the discourse of the power of the social. Estrangement is not the nature of science except as science converts estrangement into the order of all things. By bringing subjectivity back in, getting down in the gutters with the winos and taking to the streets with pimps and pushers, sociology does nothing more than *say* "humanism"; like every idealism before it, humanistic sociology is enfeebled as long as it is robbed of its historical and political specificity—its ability to rupture the continuum of domination. Instead, today, it is just another affirmative metaphysic.

Epistemology as Political Theory

Sociology pastes conceptual photographs of the frozen world ruled by the power of the social directly into its text, suggesting the world's ontological presence, hence unalterability. In reflecting the power of the social sociology adds value to it; this narrative presentation took methodological form in Durkheim's notion of social facts. Dehistoricized as generic pieces of domination, the subordination of subject to social object, data become an ideology recommending capitulation as *amor fati*. Sociology as postured nature tries to become the "world" it tells, and hence reproduces. Scientificity is the ability of science narratively to portray the world without narrating it. Discipline exhausts ontological possibilities, silently recommending a world governed by indubitable laws leading people to do what they *already do*—give in and give up. Indeed, the "social construction of reality" is itself ironically named as an invariant socio-ontological pattern, grounding other "laws" like eternal inequality, bureaucracy, patriarchy.

Science is authored by sociology as an unmediated translation of the world into words silently recommending it. While not an advocate of suicide, Durkheim suggested the eternity of a world that makes people want to kill themselves. Discipline hardens social existence into social essence; it demonstrates the eternity of discipline (and hence the unreasonableness of defiance) with reference to the abundant discipline of our history. Only fools and zealots demur.

> The task of sociology is to reveal the underlying patterns and meanings of all varieties of social structure, from the abstract macrosystems of society to the fragile microsystems of everyday life. (Hess, Markson, and Stein 1985, 24)

Sociology announces the logos of "society"—all social orders and disorders, past, present, and future; thus, it duplicates the present. Objectivity, science's regulative idea, is construed as unmediated reflection of the "patterns and meanings" of the power of the social—Durkheim's suicidal world, Weber's iron cage. Social facts representationally impinge on science's eye as *presence;* the data allegedly speak for themselves in figure and number as episodes of social determination, the purported essence of the modern. Although the notion that sociology is to excavate the "underlying" patterns of social structure would seem to afford the writer some room for imagination, indeed require it, structure is essentially reduced to epiphenomenality. Society is the hegemonic social, the concatenation of our suffering. Thus, science mediately pretends not to mediate. Writing wrongly chooses not to make its own subtext a topic—its desire to reproduce the social in its own version of it.

Representation discloses the world on the page, completing it by provoking its enactment as the invariant order of things. "Underlying patterns," the socio-logos, are to be *made* true by hapless subjects, a deconstructive irony. The mass readers of current social texts really write them—sociology, religion, popular culture. Reflection reconstitutes itself in "everyday" life, a telling sociological banality. Positivism disqualifies the absent, the utopian, where scientificity claims the world's presence as a plenitude of being. As Adorno wrote in *Negative Dialectics*:

> In fact no philosophy, not even extreme empiricism, can drag in the *facta bruta* and present them like cases in anatomy or experiments in physics; no philosophy can paste the particulars into the text, as seductive paintings would hoodwink it into believing. (Adorno 1973a, 11)

The texts counter this way:

> Sociology is an *empirical* science. Sociologists work only with information that can be verified through direct experience or observation, as dictated by scientific method. . . . They demand proof. (Bassis, Gelles, and Levine 1980, 21)

The empiricist objectivity of sociology seeming to cut through the thicket of metaphysical anxieties about the deep relationship between subject and world renders ontology useless by eclipsing subjectivity altogether; science is modeled photographically on photographic realism. The world's presence is to be entered into the book of science as data, "information," that are indubitable because—the great ontological leap—they are available to readers who can check them. The representational indubitability of the disciplinary world provokes the enactment of that world in turn. If Durkheim does not cause readers to take their own lives, he reinforces the assumption that modern life is somehow less than a full life.

Adorno (1973a) elaborates critical theory on the basis of theory's own non-identical irreducibility to reality, concept neatly equalling its object. Science professes to exhaust the world it would make present in a text thus (re)producing that presence. History becomes ontology in history—through discipline, a more comprehensive version of Marx's ideology. In this telling way, Adorno like Derrida challenges the disciplinary narration of the power of the social; science deconstructs into ontology, supposedly producing an ontological world.[14] There can be no sheer presence; the world must be crafted by validity claims reaching beneath themselves for buttress in their desire to bring about a certain state of affairs, a certain order of being. These tentacles in desire must be argued for. Hence the political outcome of a literary version of science is not the final adjudication of truth claims, the world finally apprehended, thus completed, in its seamless totality; a narrated narrativeness constitutes what Habermas calls the "ideal speech situation" into which all speakers may enter. Thus, science is merely a rhetoric, a version of versions bringing writers together in nonviolent construction.[15]

Deconstructive prose eschews the postulate of its presuppositionlessness; the historical object-world always resists its conceptual identification and thus depletion. Good text chooses instead to create liveable communities through the dialogues of science and art in which committed writing, recognizing its solitary insufficiency, is a *performance* opening itself to other versions as the essential circuitry of social solidarity. This is not to reject the so-called advancement of science but to interrogate the concept of advance. For positivists this represents a useless exercise in light of the obviousness of progress's actuality today—more journals, books, grants. Yet busy intellectuality conceals the emptiness of the tasks at hand. We only assume that writings proceed linearly. The narration of science's seeming narrativelessness brings to light what Habermas calls the "interests" of scientific validity claims, namely—today—discipline. A deconstructive version of critical theory does not extirpate interest as a blur of objectivity but celebrates interested writing as a constitutively narrative performance, what Marx called praxis.

This version of versions contests the denigration of alleged nonscience by the disciplinarily legitimated—white coats, Ph.D.'s, academic jobs, fancy methods, and state-of-the-art equipment. A nonpositivist science does battle *over* the right by a text to claim science in differentiating itself from the literary. The deconstruction of scientificity reveals science's fear of its own insufficiency, opinionatedness, perspectivity, ground in so-called common sense and metaphysical/political partisanship. Marcuse through Nietzsche reformulates a "new science" (1969) not in terms of its technical capacity to exhaust mystery through methodology, but as a mode of nonalienated self-expression—free labor. This scandalizes Marxists who since Engels and Lenin have swallowed the bourgeois ideal of scientificity as a goal of Marxist method, albeit a science defined by "dialectical" laws of contradiction and not the linear laws of natural and social evolution—different endpoints, same guaranteed teleology. New science in expressing cognition's playful desire does not relinquish objectivity but only recognizes that the truth is a kind of practice, indeed a text.

> Research findings are social facts in the everyday sense of the term: they are facts about social life. (Bassis, Gelles, and Levine 1980, 18)

Sociology claims science circularly, seemingly without reference to ontology. The world is what it "is"; our words mean what we intend. Elaborately described by Durkheim in the first thirteen pages of his *Rules of Sociological Method* as subordination—the strings that play the puppets—the social is reduced, banalized, by contemporary sociology as bare facts. Facts enter text as discrete phenomena to be made present—annual income, party affiliation, measures of intimacy. Science would illusorily paste untheorized particulars into the text; "world" becomes the essential world of the social (that those particulars' representation elicits). Mediately, science refuses to admit that it mediates not only in selecting a research topic but also in the whole process of writing a version materially intervening in the history it methodologically shuns as a contaminant.

Derrida is Adornoian *minus* a critical social theory and politics—although to make this stick one would have to interrogate "social theory" and "politics" just as I interrogate facticity, objectivity, science here. Nevertheless Derrida offers insights into the politics of language informing a positivist Marxism. Like science, politics is a matter of argument. This is not to say that all the world is a text but that the text is a world, a political language game circuited through dialogue opportunities—the more so the more it appears *not* to be. Although all life is not a text, all text is a life, an ensemble of social relationships between writer and reader. In this sense, empirical research is often more theoretical than theory named as "theory construction," the disciplinary assemblage of confirmed and disconfirmed hypotheses, really Lévi-Strauss's *bricolage* or the text of myth.

Science's name for thought, theory is frequently only textual interpretation gilding disciplinary founders or the assemblage of data in prose, prototypically a first chapter of a doctoral dissertation and monographs or a section of journal articles in which the author relates the research problem and findings to a "literature" as a way of establishing the topic's context. Disciplinary theory fatefully truncates theory. The editor of the *American Sociological Review* recently relegated theory to this:

> Most of all, I want *ASR* to be read. To entice people to read it, my first suggestion is that you write simply and clearly. The more tortured the prose, the more critical the reviewers. We will try to improve the writing of accepted articles to make them more understandable to more readers. But even the best-written articles may appear trivial if their messages are narrow. The narrower they are, the smaller the potential readership. So you should try to relate your work to broad issues of sociology and social psychology. This pleases both the reviewers and the editor because it tends to improve the theory section of the paper. (Form 1987, *v*)

Although every paper has a "theory section," no paper presumably is only theory, in spite of the editor's later promise that "*ASR's* editors are equally attracted to long . . . theoretical and historical pieces." Theory is truncated precisely as it is seen to belong to any empirical writing, ecumenism belied by the relegation of speculative concerns to a "section" of each writing. Seemingly better than nothing, this is worse than nothing for it harnesses theory to the merely representational project of empirical research; the words "literature review" are dressed up as "theory section," thus disqualifying real theorizing—speculative reason. Theory is thought that mediates, not thought minus mediation.

> All ideas must be put to the empirical test before they are accepted as true. (Bassis, Gelles, and Levine 1980, 21)

In a telling reduction of science to technique, method seemingly replacing metaphysics, "ideas" are reduced to factual instances of the power of the social, to be "tested" against an unalterable world. Facts circularly reflect, and thus reproduce, a world driving people to suicide—Durkheim's exemplary social fact. Thought is divested of the constitutive work that even Kant's idealism once assigned to it (for positivism is notoriously anti- and post-Kantian). In this, positivism supports its self-differentiation from the nonscientific. It is notable that the text does not restrict itself here to theory in its insistence that truth is "in" the world, only to be excavated; far from being a misstep, the text is saying what it wants to say in dismissing all constitutive ideation essentially as superfluous to a rigorous version of science.

Science is haunted by the absent, occluded world threateningly disclosed by nonscience, whether fiction or myth. Presence textually overrides absence by filling the pages with good, solid "observations" or "information." This precludes a version describing the world not only in its surface actuality but also in its deficiencies and silences, paradoxically absent or "untestable" symptoms of domination. The silent admission that statements somehow can go unsupported by "observations" shows science's secret suspicion—subtext— that there can be a writing (like *itself*) that portrays the world in terms of what it is not and could be as well as what it contingently "is." The text deconstructively admits its duplicity in cloaking its self-consciously constitutional prose with "observations" it already admits are extraneous to the text; it is just "backing," giving the lie to the unavoidably metaphysical notion that the world can be made forcefully present on the page. Science identifies concept or utterance with the world at hand and thus exhausts its socioontological and thus political opportunities to stand apart—nonidentity the vital spark of revolt.

Only "facts," science banalizes itself; it enhances social power emerging from its reflection of the irreversibility of power. Method quiets intellect, fearing the speculative resistance of mind to a mode of existence, scientism, reducing mind to a mirror—or *less*. Science's secretly constructive disqualification of construction pivotally represses what it really wants—in the case of science to write discipline as narrative, thus opposing it unashamedly in narrative opening itself to other versions. Representational writing is still praxis, albeit one stifling other praxes. The methodological suppression of the narrativeness of method is imposed by science on itself; method is a defense mechanism checking its dangerous desire to write and live joyfully. Otherwise, without the apodicticity afforded by method, science blurs with literature and becomes rhetoric, even politics. Scholarship today is thought minus the Dionysian; its institutionalization in a normative community of science disciplines imagination, replacing speculative reason with technical reason. In challenging science to exhume its desire and then argue for it, we do not necessarily change its mind but at least open textuality, and thus the social world it occludes and thereby reproduces, to other versions.

Science's self-confidence as a veritable tool of power (Bacon) is belied by the constraints it places on its own intelligence, "backing" ideas with information and observation and thus ensuring they hug the near shore of terra firma. Science represses an abundant intellectuality, nonscience (or, potentially, new science), as the ego represses libidinal desire—to produce a version of the world. Discipline fears imagination, even what science calls theory, as ego resists its tabooed polymorphous gratification. Facticity is the safe route, keeping the discipline on the straight and narrow, out of court or off the administrative carpet. Intellect is thus methodically reduced, removing its constitutive responsibility for its own commitment to a certain state of affairs. Mind does not refuse the world as an untruth that a version of textual representationality would only reproduce. A new science would not so much debate the explicit partisanship of bad science; it would surface as science's suppressed political desire into the light of day. At that point debate could ensue. Even more, perhaps, bad science might be playfully alerted to its own literary corrigibility, thus refusing the deconstructively self-contradictory representationality cancelling its own narrativeness. Like labor, all writing wants to be free even if it suppresses that longing methodologically. The suppression itself is a narrative choice; discipline fatefully redoubles discipline.

Methodology assuages science's anxieties about its own context, perspectivity, mortality, and commitment, its ironic existence as *nonscience*. In forcefully claiming its own scientificity through the cleansing procedures of method, science may keep the nightmares at bay. Yet it does not properly learn from them. Like history badly lived and the unconscious forgetfully repressed, the subtext haunts science with the prospect of its author-izing return. The positivist text allows this fear of its own presence deconstructively to surface, either by mistake (where deconstruction seizes the opportunity to exhume its entirety) or as evidence of science's humanity, only a ruse to highlight the genuinely apodictic.

This emergence of the subtext at science's surface is marginal at best, appearing to be only a limiting case of science's claimed indubitability. But as deconstruction suggests, the margins are at the center in the sense that repressions cannot be submerged indefinitely; once free from the center's centrifugal pull, the repressions reverse the priority of center over margin, revealing centeredness (e.g., science's claimed scientificity as objectivity) to be riddled with the marginality it so fears as its own demystification. Undoing science's seemingly whole text reveals that science knew all along that its world is fatally incomplete—a piece of writing that importantly educates, indeed *politicizes*.

This deconstructive concentration on the marginal as signifying, paralleled in Adorno and Benjamin's critical theories,[16] is authorized by a version of psychoanalysis addressing reading as a telling act of self-expression and self-creation. Science's desire to be something other than what it is—poetry, philosophy—is repressed lest science confront its anchor in libidinal and historical context, thus relinquishing its claim to be science—a problem from the perspective of its political intent to hide intention. Text never completely represses its authorial defiance of method; desire drives text to poetize its account of the world as an antidote to methodological mindlessness. In spite of its self-understanding as scientism, positivism wants to enjoy the pleasure of the text for its own sake; new science is a version of Marx's original praxis refusing to choose between poetry and objectivity.

Seen in this way, science's parenthetical reservation about the roadblocks to scientificity is not parenthetical at all; disciplinary self-doubt acknowledges discipline's imbeddedness in nonscience, its validity claims secretly self-understood as constructions. Science tellingly evidences awareness of its own foundational insufficiency in light of the immense task it sets for itself —once and for all to freeze being in a writing. Moreover, it *desires* to be insufficient, requiring the undecidability of the world as an occasion of its intervention in it. If not unabashedly celebrating its contamination by the mythic properties of the speculative and self-expressive, science recognizes the political deficit calling it forth as textual healing. Science opens itself to the revolt of its repressed desire; its subtext inevitably shines through, blurring the text's mechanical, monologic quality with a constitutional indecisiveness. This inability to suppress evidence of its authoriality shows the text to be an act of artifice full of human echoes and fingerprints that in Habermas's terms intend consensus—more so, to change the world. Text needs the seeming contamination of the subtext in order to be what it is, but only in possibility—a full-blooded literary version soliciting its own reading as re-search. Only as fiction can science claim the truth, suggesting deconstructively the untruth of that distinction in the first place.

If they have even read this far, most sociologists probably shrink at the notion that not only can they not suppress their narrative desire but also that they secretly do not *want* to. Subtext inevitably surfaces, if only parenthetically, as a presage of the transvaluation of textuality; frequently this is never attained because, alas, science's institution is too powerful, marginalizing the marginal yet again—but, perhaps, not eternally. Derrida's point is that logocentric writing, especially positivist science, inescapably deconstructs itself. We have only to read it, and thus rewrite it, as the narrative it suppresses narrativelessly.

Let me begin with a self-confident text and show how it begins to open up under its own deconstructive internal pressure, like a spring seed trying to force its way to the surface.

In their research sociologists strive to be as objective as possible and to adhere to the facts. (Bassis, Gelles, and Levine 1980, 26)

This text could have easily been read in the preceding sections on sociology's fetish of the social-factual. But the key words here, "as possible," suggest the inherently problematic relationship between science and the world that, against science's claim, has to be mediated by text's self-conscious construction of its own scientificity; strong writing inherently opens itself to other versions as responses and corrections, thus undermining its own postured sufficiency.

Just as objectivity is elusive, threatening scientificity with (what science regards as) the blur of nonscience, the "facts" defy science's adherence to them. Objectivity is something to be "approached" ("objectivity can be approached by"), never entirely gained; science runs up against the world's opacity (facts that cannot be adhered to) and it bears the mask of subjectivity within it. Nonscience frivolously flaunts its defiance of rigor and thus refuses objectivity on the epistemological and therefore also social level. Respecting being, science brings it into being. Science struggles to constrain the Dionysian it always bears within it as the threat of its self-deconstruction into literature— the threatening caprice of sweaty, passionate perspective. Objectivity would still both art and politics.

Sociologists, like other scientists, try to be rigorously objective in their investigations. (Sullivan and Thompson 1984, 16)

Rigor is another unexplicated goal of science, echoing its pretended objectivity. But rigor is only an *attempt*, a heuristic or ideal-typical posturing —science claimed but not achieved. Rigor wilts in the face of the world's indubitability and, as such, reveals science's repressed desire to be something it claims it is not—speculative reason. Rigor sublimates science's gratifying impulse, diverting its play into work. A critical psychoanalysis has no quarrel with either repression or sublimation as both ontogenetic and civilizational requisites; the growth of ego replaces infantile insatiability with the civilizing conscience of mature adulthood. But as Marcuse argued in *Eros and Civilization* (1955), a central text of Freudian Marxism, late capitalism induces "surplus" repression beyond the amount required for self-preservation as well as species survival precisely to divert people from the unprecedently immediate prospect of their technological liberation.

People are led to enact extra repression lest they taste the forbidden fruits of an utterly new reality principle not riven between play and work, the central dualism of western rationality. Thus, Marcuse imagines liberation to be contingent on undoing and reliving the false distinctions (subject-object, freedom-necessity, play-work, margin-center, unuseful-useful) that are textu-

ally transposed from history into nature, unnecessarily. Disciplinary sociology
dispersed into the impenetrable books and articles suggests its own reading as
a piece of nature. Discipline disciplines constitutional reading into mere interpretation, reception. In a fast capitalism textuality is frequently dispersed into
things themselves—books not meant to be read but simply lived. Similarly,
science surplus represses the cognitive impulse to play with words and things,
inducing positivist scientificity as a bulwark (e.g., rigor) against Nietzsche's
and Marcuse's happy science. The prospect of a nondominating science is
denied on socioontological grounds in favor of the inert order of the present,
positivist representationality helping to bring it forth.

Psychoanalysis cunningly shows that basic repression necessary for on-
togeny and phylogeny is all too easily supplemented with its surplus, repression becoming a tool of *oppression*. Disciplining all desire and not just the
self-defeating component of it, surplus repression risks its possible upsurge in
the various personality disorders of the age—narcissism, neurosis, psychosis,
schizophrenia, and sado-masochism. Neo-Freudian and third-force psychologies attempt to bleed off this potentially destructive repression through clinical
means, provoking, if successful, what Marcuse calls repressive desublimation,
the futile expressions of "self" that "work through" the calamities befalling the
contemporary person in privatized, nondangerous ways.[17] Repression is thus
harmlessly reduced and diverted—therapy, "process" groups, religion, entertainment, sports; otherwise, badly repressed, it sinks so deep into the unconscious as unavailable material—amnesia—it loses touch with ego altogether,
erupting in the various psychopathologies of the times. Science suggests its
own version of this repressive desublimation, letting subtext occasionally touch
text without allowing the subtext's inherent emancipatory desire fully to be
played out. Discipline takes a day off now and then. Occasionally science
acknowledges that the world's absolute presence eludes it; while powerful, the
social is disorderly, too. Nonetheless, to be science, writing tries to bracket
its own desire; it then disingenuously reconstructs this submerged desire as
the politically modest quest for greater understanding or human betterment,
reasonable subversions of substantive reason—revolution.

Science thus accommodates its own repression of nonscience, acknowledging nonscience as a pathological possibility. Rigor and objectivity are valued
more as inherently unreachable end states than as pragmatic accomplishments
of everyday research. Science might chalk up its epochal advances simply to
genius. Or it might preach a daily methodism that has to be deconstructed,
as I am doing, in order to reveal any hint of self-doubt. The sentence, "Sociologists, like other scientists, try to be rigorously objective in their interpretations," is a desublimation once both "try" and "rigorously" are read as key
words.

Attempts fail, and science becomes jaundiced. Similarly, objectivity, such as it is, may lack rigor, especially where rigor is defined and defended as quantitative in nature. Science's claim to be science deconstructs itself; repressed authorial hubris returns as unashamed narrative when methodology reformulates itself as metaphysics—worse (for science), as literature, sheer make-believe. In confessing its own insufficiency, science strengthens its case to be a total writing. Yet I deconstruct science's own strategic acknowledgment of authorial perspectivity (value, interest, investment) as its desire to be *nonscience*, at least to be a literary version intending a dialogical community of coequal readers and writers—ideal speech encoded in writing's own undecidability.

> The loss of objectivity can occur in any social scientific study. (Doob 1985, 40)

The text quickly regains scientificity on the methodological high road—including replication, better instruments, and more rigorous bracketing of value judgments by the scientist. But in spite of the confidence with which science conquers its lapse of confidence, the truth is plain that science comes undone when, albeit strategically, it parades its weaknesses in order to underline its strengths—rigor, apodicticity, objectivity. Adept at public relations, science cleverly brackets its desire in this way. It captures an audience by appearing all-too-human, as susceptible to perspective and even sentiment as the next version, even common sense.

But these are also clues demonstrating science's desire to be nonscience as well as the sheer impossibility of a version completely suppressing its desire to change the world. It simply will not do for science to deny its marginal infection with the nonscientific, with desire, for the "proof" is everywhere —disputes over virtually every single issue in (and beyond) the sociological purview as well as low disciplinary status in the pantheon of knowledges. Disciplinary desublimation is a rear-guard action designed to dispel doubts about its scientificity. However, in the long run it only strengthens the case against science by showing it to be under sway of its explosively deconstructive subtext. Deconstruction takes place against the self-suppressing will of the writer.

As sociology becomes increasingly insecure about its disciplinary respectability, haunted by the memory of campus tear gas, fractious department meetings, and even a Marxism itself claiming to be sociology, as well as by its low profile in public and in the university (with the retrenchment of the "soft" social sciences and humanities), the more volatile its bracketed desire becomes. Science's descent into perspectivity is the occasion for a ban on research accepting its authoriality and contingency shamelessly, even gladly:

> The loss of objectivity can occur for several reasons. One source of the problem is the characteristics of investigators themselves. As an extreme case, it would

be unreasonable to expect a black or Jewish sociologist to do an objective study
of the Ku Klux Klan, which had a history of terrorizing both ethnic groups,
especially blacks. (Doob 1984, 39)

This addresses science's seeming perspectivity with the decommissioning of
research on hot topics by scientists belonging to groups suffering from the
problem or issue in question, a novel way of enhancing rigor. But far from
cleansing science, this only admits the ontological nature of research, thus
sealing the illegitimacy of science's claim to be above perspective or beyond
construction. This repression of subtext at its harshest only serves to call the
text further into question.

A more extravagant desublimation of science occurs where it is argued
that "value-free sociology is an impossible ideal," seemingly giving the lie
to science's claim to scientificity, although not for the reasons it intends;
science exudes a corrigible humanness just as it silently holds out hope of
objectivity, if not total value-freedom. This version drops out an unqualified
value-freedom as a goal of science; yet it does not abandon the other methodological desiderata of objectivity, rigor, and indubitability, claiming objectivity
by acknowledging the role of so-called values in the choice of research topic
and the like. Indeed, the admission of this degree of perspectivity makes its
other validity claims all the more believable.

In a time of public skepticism about whether it earns its keep, sociology
carefully lets the subtext of research perspectivity come to the surface as a
parameter of its indubitability. Where the text does not urge blacks and Jews
to abandon the study of racism and anti-Semitism (as above), it asserts the
impossibility of value-freedom as a way of scoring points for honesty where it
can be acknowledged that "value judgments" do indeed "enter into" research,
for example in the "choice" of topic and methodology. The abandonment of
value-freedom does not give up much at all—science's origin in the human
community and in history; it only strategically buttresses science's claim to the
other desiderata of scientificity like objectivity and rigor. Science's "value"
commitment to scientificity is not a basis of shame at all but a prop of science's
disinterestedness in the meantime. Sociology defends the power of the social
with its textual production of "fate" just as it elaborately opposes impediments
to a world without racism and sexism. Science gives up little in standing against
the Ku Klux Klan, especially where the acknowledgment of its committedness
buttresses its larger claims to stancelessness itself. Discipline in empowering
the social chills capitalism into a teleological version of the modern.

But a strong reading of the impossibility of value-freedom *extends* to science's other desiderata like objectivity, rigor, and closure. Seemingly allowing
authorial presence as an evaluative actor whose own political druthers emerge
in topic choice and the like, science's capitulation on this score does not

strengthen science's overall claim to scientificity as a kind of phenomenological bracketing of "values" once acknowledged. Where the text admits the
traces of its desire, it does so strategically in order to confront nonscience and
defeat it, controlling for its contaminating influences. But it cannot escape
a deeper infection by a self-deconstructing subtext no matter what it does,
especially where subtext is the energy, however deeply repressed, of all science
that wants to write.

I doubt that I am alone in opening books claiming science first to preface,
acknowledgments, footnotes, bibliography, and indexes as I pursue the author's veiled presence wherever I can find it—where he or she comes from
intellectually and politically, why they say they wrote the book, their collegial networks, and the acknowledgments of their personal lives, dedications,
debt to mentors. However strategic this efflorescence of humanity, whether
discursively in front matter or parenthetically in the circumspection about objectivity's possibility (e.g., "value-freedom is impossible"; sociologists only
"try" to be objective), it signals the heartbeat beneath the books. The marginal traces of literary intelligence demonstrate that authorial subjectivity has
not been silenced, no matter how ineffectual or muted its humanist desublimation is. Ironically, science's claim to be human is belied by its intended
inhumanity. The occasional use of first-person voice would drown out narrative
voice altogether; luckily, science fails to extirpate its constitutional nature.

The deconstruction of scientificity shows that science's confidence is shaky
and that in this sense science's oxymoronic self-understanding as authorless
writing is revealingly ironic. One might say that as long as books are written
(as opposed to being merely compendia of graphs, figures, and tables) the
author will struggle autobiographically to get out from beneath the weight of
the explicit text's suppressions; positivist writing attempts but fails to disclose
the world's inert presence beyond any narration. The world's presence erodes
under pressure of authorial subjectivity. Thus scientificity cannot remain un-
informed by its secret desire to be other—rhetoric.

Sociology blurts out what it wants to be when it claims objectivity, hoping
that this self-limiting posturing will persuade readers that it is indeed a science,
albeit one not fully mature. This is thought to require further re-search in
order to squeeze out the marginal once and for all, the world fully illuminated
in an unmediating version. The subtext's irresistible revolt is the undoing of
science. Once unleashed, the text's desire to be poetry and politics cannot be
stilled on the whim of the text. Science wants to unleash methodology from
sheer representation; science knows itself to be exhortation, too. To paraphrase
the quote above, the impossibility of scientificity is *already* demonstrated in
science's inability to "clean" the text of the haunting subtext, ever the revolt of
authorial subjectivity against its surplus repression. Although the text cannot
just chat, as episodic and allusive as any talk, neither can it replace argument,

perspectival and passionate, with the mirror of pure description. Even mirrors distort, especially when we forget we are seeing ourselves backwards in the silent glass. It is possible for us permanently to imagine that our left ear is where the mirror tells us it is. As falsely promised, science *cannot* inscribe the world in its pages without turning history into a story.

The more science attempts to conceal its own subtext, as in sociology's argument that racism should not be studied by members of its victimized groups, the more the writer's presence will be sacrificed to the world's historical immediacy, only increasing his or her propensity to surface. An increasingly disciplined sociology only produces longer front matter, dedications, explanations of authorial purpose, and footnotes along with the caveats intended to buttress science's hubris by acknowledging its humanness. But this also signifies deconstructively the authorial equivocation about being rendered superfluous by a text that, once rigorous, no longer bears the touch of the human hand. In mirroring the world, we forget what is text and what is history.

4

Method's Reason

Rigor as Ontology

Most of the time science keeps out the dark night thoughts of its permeation by the mythic, by nonscience; it insists methodologically on its ability to swallow the world whole, text becoming the world it exhorts stancelessly. The text's claim of science rests on the premise that facticity can be brought into the text not only as an adequate reflection of the world (Locke) but as the world itself, ever the protocol of positivism.[1] Science's strong claim to reproduce the world figurally is undone by the revolt of a poetic objectivity always pushing to the surface as traces of sweaty authorial work. No writing can contain the concrete particulars of social facticity embodying alleged laws of social nature; writing cannot fully bridge the nonidentity of text and the world it would secretly reproduce.

> The *scientific method* is a way of investigating the world that relies on the careful collection of facts and logical explanations of them. (Light and Keller 1985, 27–28)

Science's accumulation of the world's minutiae, data, aims to reveal the data's *logic,* immanent in their representation. This logic is the eternity of the power of the social. Facts "carefully collected" and inscribed in the text are not thought to require construction; they lie obdurately on the page directly as being itself, if still frequently rendered proseful by theory *this* side of text's thoroughgoing dispersal into figure and number. This assumes that the logic of textual presentation is equivalent to the world's logic, a feature of identity theory attacked by Adorno as an obfuscation of the world already frozen *in history.* Transparent positivist text is to reflect the transparent world—figure suggesting figure.

Marginality or nonidentity—otherness—is extirpated. It is extraneous to the logic of science properly refusing to address contradiction in its own linear terms—although, as I will show, science ingests what *it* constructs as "other" in an effort to vitiate more threatening discourses like Marxism and feminism.

Scientificity is the equation of textual and metaphysical logic, text aiming only to reflect what is decidable, testable, measurable. Measurement most strongly links the allegedly distinct logics of text and world through the nondiscursive medium of sheer figure; as such, measurement is widely thought to distinguish science from nonscience. By figuring and numbering the world, science intends to display its superiority to speculative reason. But the outcome is a more figured and numbered world.

> The investigator may perceive this world as an artist, but he or she must describe it in an orderly and rigorous manner as a scientist. (Smith and Preston 1979, 11)

The text's categorical imperative "must describe it in an orderly and rigorous manner" tautologically defines what it means to be a scientist; science's rigor contrasts with speculative nonscience. This is like saying, with neo-Kantians, that art and science can coexist as long as they do not get in each other's way, admixing the speculative and indubitable, myth and certainty. This badly glosses the original neo-Kantian debate over two sciences; the substance of that debate was largely forgotten by the time sociology entrenched itself as a discipline. Today the texts simply assert the criteria of figural and numerical presentation as irreducible fundaments of science.

As the science/humanism contrast is duplicated unwittingly by a science claiming to make a place for humanists, the implied identity of history and ontology is submerged so deep under method that it can only be excavated with difficulty. After all, the problematic status of sociology's claim to science is basically a dead issue in the disciplinary mainstream. Functionalists, "loyal" microsociologists, and even conflict theorists rarely resist their disciplinary status as scientists. The identity of textual and ontological logic is submerged so deep that it can only be excavated by turning method into a text itself (a task I pursue in my forthcoming *Reading Science: A Literary and Political Analysis*).

> Sociologists prefer to be thought of as social scientists for many reasons. Americans have traditionally placed great faith in "experts." They tend to find numbers more compelling than ideas. Advertisers have long recognized the instant authority of a figure in a white coat reading statistics from a clipboard. Even though the "authority" is actually an actor, the scientific impression leads buyers to choose one toothpaste over another.
>
> However, there is science in sociology. The standards of objectivity, precision, and disclosure that should govern sociological work will become clearer as we follow the research process from its origin in history to its ultimate presentation to colleagues. Nonscientific factors will also be considered. (Hess, Markson, and Stein 1985, 31)

Even the ironic acknowledgment of phony scientific expertise, the toothpaste huckster dressed up as a savant, fails to deter sociology's claim to be science—

"objectivity, precision and disclosure." This is an example of textual repressive desublimation, floating the telling, if explicitly marginal, self-understanding of science's fraudulence as a way of further repressing the really dangerous material contained in its deconstruction: A science susceptible to willful distortion by the artist or zealot is narrative pure and simple. Once a construction, always a construction.

The acknowledgment of science's ability to benefit from the American public's gullibility where experts in white coats are concerned does not undercut science but only strengthens science's case for the authority of its level-headed objectivity. This is especially true in a time when the voice of reason (or, now, reason-ableness—the most that can be hoped for) has been virtually silenced, at least in nonwestern "terrorist" countries. What appears to be a kind of mea culpa turns out to be a textual ruse; science admits weakness only to claim strength, bringing the logic of being into harmony with the logic of science. Again, in my earlier terms, the world portrayed as a naturelike object becomes nature; text elicits a role-playing only making it *so*.

> Sociologists speak of *methodology,* the principles and procedures that guide sociological research. The use of methodology permits sociologists to do research that produces systematic, convincing results. (Doob 1985, 24)

Completing a world reflected lawfully, method ontologically premises its rationality. The master principles of mechanical production are required of science circularly in order for it to *be science;* figure and number both reflect and reproduce a world in their images. This methodical reason valorized as the essence of science insists on what are essentially pregiven criteria of scientificity *in terms of which* to judge its own claim to be science. Sporting the accoutrements of method, the science text is science.

Here science becomes identical to what passes normatively for science. Rigor as a methodological desideratum is only copied from the rigor of factory and office bureaucracy, Weber's instrumental reason animated in time-and-motion principles of generic bureaucratic hierarchy. Science organizes itself like any industrial age bureaucracy in order to chill a world that must be textually overdetermined in order to live up to its own hypostatized rationality. Science freezes history into being using history's own methodical principles of hierarchy. In this case the historical conflation of the logics of science and history reproduces itself. This is quite a stunning achievement; science defines itself in terms of itself, notably in counterpoint to what its convention excludes as nonscience in order to license its version of the world in a self-sufficient text.

Subtext surfaces where, almost parenthetically, the purpose of rigor promoted methodically is said to be one of "correction," again admitting that scientificity is hype cashing in on public gullibility about expert pronouncements. Rigor is ontologized circularly by making science the measure of science.

Methodology is just an excuse for the confidence trick cleansing science of authorial motive; method is just another name for text's denial of its energizing desire. Methodology replaces speculative reason with technical, figural, and numerical "text"—yet no less text than words especially where they promise an unmediated world. The texts invoke methodology as a boundary principle connecting textual and socio-ontological logic; rigor is simply the degree of science's imitation of the given world—methodology a means of mimesis. But science's text is not content with simple repetition, as if *that* were ever possible, for it would add something to the world portrayed deceptively as closed to interventions. Text would intervene to guarantee a history it has already frozen on the page.

A logic of textual form turns into political substance; method provokes political obedience. In this way, writing ironically writes to end writing, withering away once reproduction has become automatic. Method justifies science's representation of the world as the principle of its own production. Through it science intervenes in history where scientificity explicitly disallows this intervention as "interest" or "value." Without method, bridging text and world through productive principles of knowledge constitution freezing history's contingencies into icelike necessity, science lacks an excuse for intervention. It cannot risk being seen and thus practiced as only another inherently transformative text, the bane of its postured disinterestedness. *Science tries to transcend the rhetorical through a worldly productivity* called methodology that collects its "results" of science in reports, data, tables, graphs, statistics, journals, and books.

> Perhaps the most important part of a research report is the presentation of data
> in tables, charts, graphs or diagrams. (Hess, Markson, and Stein 1985, 44)

Science's machine hands over knowledge as "output," putting further distance between readers and texts. Writing is now dispersed into its own figure in a fast capitalism replacing mind with matter. The emphasis on rigor, precision, quantification as constitutive features of science is an effort to purge the text of human fingerprints, apparent authorial commitment risking other versions —*political action.*

Science's chosen form of life makes thoughtlessness its first principle, an argument, in effect, against argument. Thought, an archaic subjectivity, gives way to technical method. The valorization of method is a counterweight to the vagaries of text—yet method is not the more text for all that. Imagine Aristotle, Condorcet, or Kant chalking up knowledge to the "presentation of data in tables," leaving argumentation to the philosophers and fancy to the poets. It is telling that when the sociological text elaborates its constitutive principle of scientificity it elevates the stylistic over the substantial, replacing epistemology and ontology with the mere furnishings of the professional office —from computer to file cabinets.

[S]ociology is able to employ the same general methods of investigation that all sciences do, and to use its findings to make reasonably reliable generalizations. Like natural scientists, sociologists construct theories, collect and analyze data, conduct experiments and make observations, keep careful records, and try to arrive at precise and accurate conclusions. (Robertson 1983, 7)

Methodology is here reduced to "keep[ing] careful records" and "conduct[ing] experiments," a chemistry set caricature of scientific practice. The role of authorial construction originally reserved for theory gives way to the busyness of record keeping. Rigor intrudes again as a manifestation of precision and accuracy ("and"—are they different?), a leitmotif in sociology's discourse on method. Consider this elaboration of precision as metaphysic.

Sociological concepts, too, must be measured and indicated, or operationalized. Sociologists try to move beyond vague feelings about the social world and make precise and specific assessments of it. (Goode 1984, 29)

"Feelings" are "vague"; measurements are "precise," conflating a variety of echoes from the subtext. The usual science/humanism contrast here is expressed in the contradiction between precision and vagueness; humanism or nonscience is now reduced from "art," above, to "feelings," where art formerly retained at least a little neo-Kantian respectability as a legitimate epistemological perspective. "Feelings" connote not only vagueness, a liability for science's methodologizing rigor, but even the feminine, transforming the science/humanism contrast into the proverbial contrast of hard and soft writing, even male and female; this becomes a central topic of feminists who attack patriarchy as heterotextuality, maleness made methodical in the hegemony of the productive and analytical over the reproductive and emotive.

It is unclear why science "must" consist of computer readouts, sharp cornered filing cabinets, test-tube experiments, tables, and graphs except inasmuch as science decides itself with reference to itself and its contingent folkways today. What is this *about*? The text plumbs its subtext for an answer, although not a conclusive one.

Obviously one must use such [quantitative] data or be rather much at the whim of personal experience—what we may call the "my Aunt Gretta theory" of human behavior. (Smith and Preston 1979, 13)

The text goes on to reject sheer scientificity unleavened by the alternative perspective of "art," although this is a standard attempt to keep the embers of subjectivity lit while methodologizing it out of existence as a superfluous, distorting trace. In any case, it is telling that the "whimsical" relative who brandishes opinions unsupported by the numbers is an aunt and not an uncle. This is not simply to argue that methodology is patriarchal; that would reduce Enlightenment's imperialism to the subtext of gender and thus both miss domination's totality and idealize feminized whim as superior to the science marginalizing it with the cruel innuendo of misogyny. The alternative to science's "reason" is not (female) unreason (whim, intuition, fancy) but a writing that refuses science's imperious claim to be disinterestedly free of the constraints characterizing every discourse; peaceful talk and text prefigure community. Like humanism and liberalism generally, mainstream feminism is the cry of the victim, inverting but only negating oppression.[2] Feminist method ironically accepts the superiority of allegedly male method by claiming to be different. Feminist humanism differentiates itself from "male" science on grounds of biological differentiation and not history, thus only reproducing women's relegation to the realm of spirit, intuition, and sensibility. Feminist method confuses the marginality it presently suffers with the hoped-for dominance of new sciences that do not exist only parasitically on the fringes (nonscience, feminism, Marxism, etc.).

Mainstream science supports feminism where feminism accedes to positivist standards of representation. Yet nonpositivist feminism is too frequently a self-isolating aestheticism, failing to stand and fight for the right to write, and thus live, a new objectivity. Science wins the contest with poetry; it is no contest where poetry renounces objectivity. A better version of science contains both analysis and art. It might be said that to "stand and fight" is just another sign of the male will to power. But nonsocialist feminism misreads male supremacy simply as the will to power and thereby, in the name of difference, abandons control as a viable political goal in favor of a doomed evocativeness. The opposite of heteronomy is *not* hegemony, however; the cry of the victim is not an adequate alternative to science, the will-to-power abandoned for quietistic nurturance, female *over* (and thus under) male. Rather a better version of science collapses the constraining dualisms of capitalism, sexism, racism, and ethnocentrism in reformulating the subject-object relationship anew.

In this vein, scientism must not be allowed to define its opposite as nonscience, pitting rigor against the whimsy of Aunt Gretta. This is why I claim a different science and oppose the renunciation of science. Feminist methodologists reproduce their own relegation to the realm of the cosmic, the historically feminine. In this, mainstream sociology smoothly integrates feminist method as another version of the other microsociological constructivisms. Quantification, neat filing cabinets, methodology are only pernicious when identified with being. Science today does have certain habits of method—cycletrons, laboratories, control groups, reliability tests; but these are not science's essence anymore than canvas is the essence of art or the fountain pen of poetry.

Rigor is the empty set filled by whatever science wants to put in it. In itself it is nothing more than a certain interrogative disposition toward the world, hardly unique to high-tech science but the opening of mind to world since the Greeks. Method is not an adequate logos for science; procedures of research cannot impose a logic on a recalcitrant world ever witholding its mystery.

Sociology harbors the conceit that rigorous research will produce a rigorous world devoid of the nonidentical marginality remaining today as the detritus of otherness—that which the system cannot integrate. Positivist method assails this otherness with the concerted tools of high science and high technology; yet the method succeeds only in annihilating, not understanding, it, neither wiser nor sadder for having really *thought* the marginality of the people and groups discipline silences.

The criticism often leveled by humanists that sociology paints a conformist world—socialization, role taking, social control, imitation—and thereby endorses it is not far off the mark. Yet this observation does not go far enough toward a literary reformulation of historical materialism. Conformity is built deep into the organon of positivist science as methodology, an imitation of the natural sciences drawing heavily on the principle of mechanical fungibility —standardized parts and products spewed out by the assembly line. Methodology not only objectifies knowledge in a palpable form—output, filing cabinets, data tapes, floppy discs—but it also sets up *rules* for its reproduction in a capitalist economy sustained by consumption, biological reproduction, and acculturation to subordination.

Method is the connection between intellectual production and reproduction reducing knowledge to the proceduralism of early logical positivism. Conformity is vested in the so-called community of science; this construction of the marketplace of ideas functions essentially as a transcendental intersubjectivity appealed to as a final epistemological arbiter in the methodological fetish of replicability.

> The distinction between knowledge and understanding is a major difference between sociology as science and sociology as art. In addition, there are important differences in method. Sociologists as scientists are more concerned with certain criteria of formal scientific inquiry. In particular, they feel they must conduct their investigation in such a manner that another person could exactly duplicate, or *replicate,* the process. In other words, if the study were repeated, the results would be similar, just as certain chemical experiments consistently yield the same results. (Smith and Preston 1979, 11)

Science measures itself against itself in the tautology of self-definition. "Sociologists as scientists are more concerned with certain criteria of formal scientific inquiry." This tells what they do, but not why, presumably fulfilling the role obligations of a discipline founded by Durkheim. Nor does it explicate the adjective "formal" that, like rigor, tantalizes with its seeming indubitability ("rational," "reasonable," "efficient," "cost-effective," and the like). Subtext surfaces where in the next sentence sociologists' penchant for ensuring the replicability of research results is ascribed to their "feelings," a remarkable acknowledgment of authorial presence in the midst of all the talk about science's break with sentiment.

Finally, these "feelings," perhaps simply remnants of a progressively eroding subjectivity, are justified by the replicability of "chemical experiments"
ceaselessly "yield[ing] the same results." Here chemistry affords a model of
constancy to be attained by scientific sociology. Although sociologists are
"also" human beings imbued with affect and daunted by perspective and thus
they (only) "feel" that this pursuit of replicability is good, their judgment
is confirmed if and when sociological research duplicates the replicability of
chemistry. Circularity entwines circularity as science seeks a ground outside
authorial constitution altogether, in this case in what other circularly self-
defined sciences do.

> Because methods of observation and the language of description became more
> precise, scholars could reproduce each other's results by repeating, or *replicating,*
> the steps of observation or experimentation. Because a scientist's claims were no
> longer acceptable on the basis of authority the methods *had* to be repeatable.
> This also enabled later experimenters to discover the shortcomings or oversights
> in the original method that affected the accuracy of the results. (Rose, Glazer,
> and Glazer 1986, 15)

Shamelessly traced to technological advances and not a more speculative
concept of reason, conformist science confirms its scientificity on specious
grounds. "Because" methods become "more precise," replicability of research is possible and—thus?—desirable. Mediating the newfound technological availability of "precise" methods and the conclusion that replication is
a constitutive hallmark of scientificity, science no longer relies on a dubious
textual authority but achieves validity through method, making a virtue, replicability, of necessity, a deauthorizing methodology. Lucky for science that
"methods of observation and the language of description" became more precise in the wake of secularization, thus hinging scientific advance on technical
innovation, a standard phrase of the Enlightenment. Although this technological optimism and determinism seem inoffensive at first reading (after all, since
technology virtually cancels polio, why should it not reduce scientific vagueness and speculativeness as well?), it is intellectually disabling at a deeper
level. Science reduces the contribution of mind to the constitution of knowledge the more it cedes constitution to a technology/methodology enhancing
"precision"—valued circularly as the epitome of science.

   This exchanges what the neo-Kantian text above called understanding for indubitable knowledge, a standard construction reserving *Verstehen* and whimsy
for Aunt Gretta—intuitive, nurturant, story-telling. Meanwhile "male" science
possesses the "tools" with which to dispel uncertainty and ensure accuracy,
Bacon's equation of knowledge and power. While a healthy disobedience is
allowed within the confines of the poetic, subjective, female, supposedly healing the split between reason and passion, it is clear that science is hard science
—circularly defined by what "science" does.

Technology advances science not only through the enhancing power of the microscope and the speed of computers but also by means of what Walter Benjamin called "mechanical reproduction," including printing and publishing.

> One major goal [of publishings results] is to link one's own study to an existing body of theory and research. Most research reports also point to gaps in the knowledge base, thus generating new questions for other sociologists to explore. In this way, social science becomes cumulative, building a base of data over time. (Hess, Markson, and Stein 1985, 43–44)

The dissemination of research findings made possible by publishing is an advance over subjectivism inasmuch as knowledge gathers a momentum of its own. Discipline transpires above the heads of its fungible writers; the journals will always be filled. The cumulative model of what Kuhn called normal science entices us with its intellectual forward movement. Yet deconstruction suggests that this advance is constructed circularly in terms of advances in the technology of scientific presentation like computer and xerography.

Text, now "research reports," intertextually connects with and is corrected by other texts where before writing advanced only through monastic discipline. Before the Enlightenment the written reproduction of texts was dominated by a biblical model of exegesis. It is second nature that the monk in the Xerox advertisement, who looks heavenward in thanks for this miraculous technology, understood the enormous opportunities opened up by mechanical reproduction. Today the office shelves of American sociologists filled neatly with issues of the *American Sociological Review* arranged in chronological order hold icons of modern science, ensuring forward disciplinary movement made possible largely through technological reason. This puts truth in the hands of mechanical reproduction, in effect authorizing the versions already published as legitimate disciplinary work—*good sociology* in the case of the *ASR*. The legitimate stock of knowledge, ironically called "the literature," is exactly what has already been published under the Durkheimian rubric of sociology. Thus, the power of the social is produced through the circuitries of disciplinary reproduction.

Quite unsociologically in its own terms, this brackets out the intermediate constitutions by authors, readers, editors, and publishers; these people constitute what is to become "literature" in the first place. In turn, this leads to the confusion of what has been published and what ought to be published, between literature or books and a literature—norms governing the publishing of books. This is an especially ironic confusion where science (as "a" literature) denies its own literary self-awareness as a narratively driven authorial accomplishment. This stifles intellectual imagination where in reproducing the dominant discourse of the discipline it adds value to existing knowledge *that has authority simply because it exists.* Sociology claims the right to decide what is legitimate disciplinary work and what is not simply on the basis of what has appeared as "sociology" before. Thus, discipline reproduces disciplined writers.

As disciplinary writing becomes an institution it gains an ontological authority much deeper than that of the feudal church, which was constantly afraid of apostasy. Today heretics are not burned at the stake but rather have their writing "rejected" by journals and publishers. As a result they are either denied academic jobs in the first place or eventually turned down for tenure. The implacable presence of "the literature"—*ASRs* on academic bookshelves —squeezes out alternative writings that do not accept the discipline's terms of discourse; this literature swallows or disqualifies all other versions. In particular, authors who eschew a disciplinary rule of scientificity are disqualified simply because they do not acknowledge the established disciplinary canon and instead write rhetorically, playfully, argumentatively in defiance of disciplining strictures.

This raises some deeper questions about the nature of writing and reading that I will rejoin in my concluding chapter, particularly those about the inherently sociopolitical relationship among readers, text, and tradition, an issue raised in Habermas's idealization of a communicative ethics as the basis for critical theory. The typical stance of hermeneutics—e.g., Gadamer (1975) and Shils (1981) in American sociology is to engage and thus restore "tradition" as a silent interlocutor in the endless versions characterizing intellectual activity. Thus, in a certain sense hermeneutics accepts its own marginality compared to the obdurate centrality, the sheer force of presence, of the established canon as its dialogue partner. Although all writing necessarily writes with reference to other texts, thus, in effect, to the past, I am questioning the subtle, indeed subtextual, translation of technological *into* intellectual reproduction without the critical dialogical mediation of a radicalized hermeneutics recognizing the undecidable nature of "tradition." My version of a radical hermeneutics regards other texts contingently rather than accumulatively, as partial answers to an unfolding riddle of history.[3] I want to model a writing that is both analytically and politically adequate, at once a theory and a critique of ideology.

Although acknowledging tradition as a force of its own, whether in Marx's image of the past as a nightmare or in Sartre's (1976) notion of the inescapable practico-inert, I resist a conservative version of reading modeled on biblical exegesis. Such a version inherently disempowers reading as against the sheer authority of the tradition setting the intellectual/political agenda, thus requiring any reading of it to speak its own language *that then becomes the only legitimate tongue.* Instead I would raise writing to the level of dialogic equality with tradition, indeed its necessary enlivening, in opposition to an accumulative model routinizing writing as simple addition.

> A scientific claim is not valid until proven so. Like other scientific communities, sociologists carry out this norm by having panels of anonymous readers review research proposals and research papers submitted to scientific journals such as *American Sociological Review* or the *American Journal of Sociology*. The work of faculty members who are being considered for promotion or applying for a position also gets reviewed by anonymous colleagues. At scientific meetings and in the journals, people openly challenge one another's work—a pattern not commonly found in the business community or the clinical professions. (Light and Keller 1985, 46)

Finally, the text baldly invokes a consensus theory of truth to ground its own claim to be science. The intersubjective community of science or literature operates less as an enabling reference point of intellectual work than as an epistemological arbiter or institution of validation. This only obscures the hermeneutic understanding that truth is talk; instead, it chooses the monologic outcome of a single "correct" version processed through the various methodologies, editorial boards, and conferences of the discipline. The mainstream sociology journals, as such exemplars of "good" sociology, claim scientificity as disciplinary journals of record in order to differentiate themselves from the political, philosophical, and journalistic collections of writing either beyond the disciplinary purview or rampant with the intertextual subjectivities of both author and editor.

Although disputation is disciplined, the text by its own admission uses disputation as a means of achieving intellectual closure from which an original normative consensus can then ground the textual practices of middle-range, methodologized science. *This assumes that closure is even possible,* to be approached through the dispassionate desubjectivized anonymity hiding reader and writer from each other. A positivist version of reading construes reading as a valid correspondence of text to the world taken as given by the normative community of science. Thus, ironically, reading reconstitutes those norms of adequacy. The consensus theory of truth uses anonymity to cleanse writing of its subjective traces, defusing the status-systems that might prejudice readings by famous, as opposed to obscure, names as well as protecting readers against either authorial wrath or emolument. This presupposes the contamination of readings that make author and reader known to each other ("bias") and encourages clean writings that do not make reference to the writer's identity and prior work. Anonymity brackets authorial presence as a way of strengthening the text's claimed objectivity. The splitting of text and subtext thus enforces a posited generic lawfulness chased by an authorless, readerless version. This extirpates authorship as an impediment to presuppositionless representation and thus the provocation of an inert world.

Authors' and readers' names, work, perspective, passion, subtext are seen to muddy text with the silt of desire, requiring its methodological repression in order for science to advance beyond speculativeness. This assumes that the world can be inscribed in writing as mute presence, keeping reader and writer apart lest they talk to each other in light of the intertextual, interested perspectivity of their mutual accounts. Otherwise their subtexts become the central topic of their peaceful talk, disqualifying the search for a final apodictic writing administering subjectivity by burying it in footnotes or deeper. A consensus theory of truth disembodies writing as a way of countering the gravitational pull of worldly commitment. An allegedly decidable truth would be attained through the intersubjective circuitries of validation. Indubitable knowledge is reduced to a disciplinary norm; consensus emerges as a result of the methodical production and reproduction of science, the regulative principle of a disciplinary master text anchored in the scholarly community. Through the referee process and the assurance of texts' replicability, method reproduces the *original literature* of a discipline, giving the editorial gate keepers of science standards with which to evaluate the next writings as disciplinarily legitimate.[4]

This concept of an original literature that science never entirely outgrows disciplines science territorially by tracing its "mature" contemporary phase back to its prehistorical constitution by Grand Theorists, the Edisons, Newtons, or Durkheims who set its parameters in the first place. Discipline reproduces itself through the various mediations of the intellectual reproduction process —referee, replicability, literature review—thus invariably only reproducing what has always been known. The literature only swallows itself; it does not overthrow its beginnings and set new tasks or standards for itself. Thus, the authority of a disciplinary literature only tyrannizes later versions with the acculturating strictures of science's emergent consensus, domesticating and even disqualifying wild writing breaking the hold of tradition altogether.

In this era of epistemological relativism it is entirely credible that the general will *can* be tyrannical (Rousseau) and falsely conscious (Marx), poisoning consensus with interested perspective. It is harder to accept that the very concept of epistemological consensus or a community of scholarship is authoritarian. Methodical science is the epochal attempt to answer nihilist critics who despair of any truth by providing an institutional basis for intellectual reproduction as dispassionate, replicable writing tested against a sacrosanct original literature. But in its very nature, writing that tries to suppress authorial identity and intentionality by submitting it to the disciplining forces of tradition vested in the community of science is bound merely to repeat the original literature, thus unduly empowering its academic gate-keepers. As long as writing is neutralized as perspectival, otherwise erupting from depth to surface in a way that text can check its original desire, the covert perspectivity of scientific conformity will haunt mainstream science as its unexamined subtext, kept at bay by the screening, cleansing procedures of methodology.

The price of intellectual reproduction, then, will be the fool's gold of distortionless representation, secured by the thoughtless duplication of an original literature that never seems to quit. Where writing orients to the sequence of *ASRs* arranged on the bookshelf as evidence of disciplinary advance, it loses the potential to transform literature into a different mode of intellectual inter-rogation, blocked by its very difference from the methodical constitution of sociology as a provocative text of a frozen fate. Science establishes a disciplinary literature by robbing it of its literariness.

A "sociological" writing, thus, is one that trades off the founding sociologies of Durkheim, Weber, and later Parsons without examining its reason for doing so, thus buttressing them. Argument that counters this socio-logos—the power of the social representing a fate that it hopes to bring about—is, truistically, not-sociology, to be published and read *elsewhere,* outside of the discipline's vouchsafed journals and monographs. This only silences voices arguing against this logos of a generic "society" described on the plane of Durkheim's social-factual, dismissing them as discontinuous with the discipline's original literature or, strictly speaking, as nonreplicable with respect to the operative standards of the prevailing community of science. After all, if Marcuse's Nietzsche is a rhetorical basis for developing my version of Marxist/poststructuralist argument, and if neither Marcuse nor Nietzsche were employed or wrote as "sociologists," the disciplinary community, traced in Durkheim, cannot evaluate the truth content of my writing except to say that it is not sociology. It refuses to write under his aegis or the numerous iterations of him in the meantime.

Science's community is not a transcendental subject but a lifeworld infiltrated by historicity. Like most sociology department chairs across the country, the editor of the *ASR* both reads and writes within the ambit of sociology's constitutive literature, deviation from which is rejected not as false but simply as nonsociological. Thus, other versions are not heard in the discipline. "Consensus" does damage simply by understanding itself as disciplinarily framed, inculcated through professional socialization in graduate schools embracing Simmel but not Schopenhauer, Durkheim but not Derrida. Sociology is a reading list of books, articles, and methodology suggesting legitimate discourse by what it excludes. Science in this way repeats itself by defining itself in a way that now as before regards scientificity as the iteration of an original boundary-setting literature, denying not simply sociologists' concealed "values" or "biases" but, deeper, their identities as artisans of society's logos. This in turn excludes the panorama of texts that write of social things only mediately, without license by an original socioontologizing literature. Disciplinary allegiance is the ultimate intellectual conformity, filling the journals (albeit in the promise of advance) with the elaboration of what has always been known—*disciplinarily.* Sociology is (and can only be) what sociology does.

Thoughtless Theory

The recent infusion of constructivism into sociology as a "loyal opposition" grounds Hobbesian order in the micrological practical reasoning of an "everyday life." Historicized, this mode of routine existence is only the engendered stupidity of a powerless existence raised to the level of ontology as a sociological topic—is there a life which is not "everyday?" This constructivism is celebrated by a range of recent theorists from Giddens to Collins in softening the unreconstructed positivism of Durkheim's empiricism.

Science thus employs theory in the strong sense to explain data, covering descriptive particulars in a discursive language only to freeze them again into generalized patterns of hypotheses, theories, laws. Its subtext is repressively desublimated in the interest of giving science "meaning" from the outside as if science's text was not already a literary production, simultaneously authored, intended, and signifying. Atlhough this is an evisceration of theory conceived differently, as I do here, as any writing that makes its own writing a topic —text's self-consciousness as narrative practice refusing to truncate history into ontology—at least it leaves theory something to do in the way of textual constitution. A weaker, less apologetic version of theory shamelessly reduces thought to an instrument ("map," "guide"), no longer serving even the role of proseful embellishment.

This regresses behind so-called theory construction subordinating thought to the larger research enterprise. At least theory construction makes theory both the beginning and end of research, the assemblage of which is to be accomplished with the fragments of a world science brings into the text as, in effect, raw material. But weak theory is not even allowed to be circumspect about science as it is reduced mainly to a provocation of science's subsequent method. This is truly "grounded theory"; unlike Hegel's idealism, it never gets off the ground.

> As a kind of map, a theory guides the investigations of an individual on a sociological quest. (Orenstein 1985, 48)

> The more immediate purpose of theory is to lead researchers to ask good questions, to formulate interesting problems, and to pose intelligent hypotheses. (Bassis, Gelles, and Levine 1984, 31–32)

The distinction between the seemingly strong and weak versions of theory at work here is not at all absolute; by restricting theory to explanation and tying its validity to data (and not to other writings) the strong version is really weak after all. The explicit reduction of theory to a tool (map, guide, source of insight) in the weak version has already taken place covertly in the strong version inasmuch as explanation is a woefully inadequate role for theory conceived differently as writing (about) writing—the preposition getting in the way here.

Theory in the best sense is speculative reason open to its own narrativeness—its fictive imagination. Theorizing is writing that recommends a world in its own literary example.

The sociological text often endorses theory's utility as a research "tool" in the same breath that theory is offered as data's embellishment, usually in the first couple of chapters, to which the history of theory and then its role in scientific methodology are usually restricted. The seeming contrast here is not a disjunctive alternative; on one hand, a buried subtext exists in the case of theory's role in explanation (even though, ironically, this seems to desublimate the subtext as constitutive explanation—a sham, as I have said); and on the other, science admits that theory is "useful" primarily as a "guide" to research, acknowledging theory's utter marginality to the research process, to science's fictions. Between these two textual levels the transition that addresses the place of theory in sociology reads like this:

> Quite simply, a *theory* is a systematic explanation of how two or more phenomena are related. In this sense, theory is a tool. It allows sociologists to bind together a good many facts so that they may work with and comprehend them all at once. (Light and Keller 1985, 14)

> Sociology then, like any science, looks for theoretical explanations. A *theory* is a logical and scientifically acceptable principle to explain the relationships between known facts. (Stewart and Glynn 1985, 19)

> A good theory should be stated in abstract terms and allow predictions to be made. Theories also serve as important sources of new hypotheses. (Eshleman and Cashion 1985, 54)

If science is photography, then theory is the album in which the photos are kept, unifying the construction "known facts." What seems like an egregious tautology at first, "known facts" stifles writing addressing the unknown and particularly the future. How can this be? Theory's data stand or fall on its ability to predict the future; yet now theory's explanation is restricted to the known facts, the past and present from which the future is projected as a simple evolutionary extrapolation—*more* of the same. This tellingly opposes both an explicit text claiming to know the future in advance through the thawing/freezing of prose framing the many particulars of data and subtext ("known facts"). This prevents science from knowing what it does not yet know, the essential character of dialogue and dialectic that playfully recognizes their own world-constitutive nature as fictive imagination. In resolving the seeming contradiction between its own text and subtext, science delegates to theory as a "tool" of research the responsibility of bridging present and future—"a logical basis for further investigation"—to be accomplished, presumably, by theory's translation of data into universal patterns of necessity, "laws."

This seems to give theory free rein to probe an unwritten future; yet it really deprives theory of the capacity to presage a future discontinuous with the present. In the strict methodism of science, theory's prognostication is to be linked to the "knowable," that is, what has already *happened*. Dialectical thought would suggest no single demarcation of past and future, known and unknown; the one makes way for the other through a historical imagination both spiked by Kant's sense of what is possible and conveyed in versions suggested prefiguratively as new world themselves. The nonidentity between past and future is played out in the existential freedom of writing that accepts the past, nature, and other people as both a constraint (the accumulated objectifications called "society" by sociology or the practico-inert by Sartre) and an open horizon along which we create ourselves. Writing bears the past as the possibility of new versions of it. This demolishes the teleological/technological linearity of progress, final synthesis, end-of-time. Positivism's suppression of its own disciplinary narrative suggests a *last text,* the death knell of thought hastened by its own capitulation to a language game of representationality— another name for domination.

Science posits this last writing, disciplinary denouement, in restricting itself to the "known facts," the particulars dumbly ingested by science's versionless version of history stalled at ontology. Theory is the mechanism through which science leaps from one project to another, eventually conquering the whole terrain of the potentially knowable—although potential is defined, thus constrained, by discipline itself. A totalizing text that, by having to be written at all as the solicitation of its enactment in "fact" by disempowered readers, the positivist version of theory only underscores the historicity of theory and science. One day there will be nothing else to write.

In the meantime, the piecemeal displays of journal science stitched together loosely by "theory"—literature reviews—keep science on the straight vector of intellectual advance. In turn, this is thought to engender social progress, closing the book of known facts at the instant a teleological history adds up to the necessity of the power of the social, the City of God becoming just a city. In this sense, the surge forward from science's accumulating version to the cumulative advance of a science intending one day to write the last book is to be effected by a theory drawing in prose the map of the "world" as science progressively conquers *terra incognito*. The metaphor of the map or guide presupposes an *end* to map making once the data are in and assembled, a metaphor taking its original if literal subterranean form in Plato's image of the cave; the emergence from falsehood, for Plato, ironically required the exercise of what he called "dialectic" but what today we call science.

> Sociological theories can be considered maps that guide sociological quests.
> Theories are written works "drawn" by arranging concepts and propositions in
> terms of underlying assumptions. (Orenstein 1985, 56)

One might inquire whether the drawing of the map itself is the quest or whether "map" should be replaced by "text"; although a map seemingly can be exhaustive, it is less credible to imagine a last text. Nonetheless, science holds out hope for the end of text—absolute identity between sign and thing —as a regulative idea legitimizing its busy iteration in the meantime. This is not to argue for a version of systematic knowledge eschewing methodology, a construction whose subtext holds science to exclude theory from the beginning. It is rather to hear theory as science's echo of itself in an unavoidable interrogation and advocacy of its own validity claims. As a special case of generic fiction, science in claiming validity for itself is confronted with the problem of addressing its animating literary/libidinal nether text. Other types of literature, whether *King Lear* or Graham Greene's demythified world in which no one is innocent, have no subtext problem because they do not claim a freedom from it as a condition of their veracity. Where fiction and science both literarily intend a world, only science has to claim validity for itself; its aim is explicitly to represent and thus bring about a given order of being within its own self-excavated concept of what is possible.

As such, every empiricism is also necessarily deeply ontological as well as narrative. Only science has this problem. And it can either suppress its inner desire methodologically (positivism) or, as I do here, make subtext a lively topic of writing itself, celebrating the text's endlessly spiraling literariness as an opening to other readers and writers in a constructively deconstructive politics. In turn, this prefigures a dialogical/democratic political community— the institutionalization of Habermas's ideal speech situation broadened through Marcuse's Freudian Marxism plus a political version of deconstruction into a new world in which we no longer distinguish categorically, thus hierarchically, between text and social being. Text's reflexive recognition that the text is a world and as such could be narrated differently vitiates science's derogation of nonscience as the impossibility of a version immediately inscribing the world's presence. The positivist denial of positivist constitutionality is belied by the fact that positivism must discursively reconstitute itself as a principled text governing its methodological practice. In conjuring its own programmatic practice imaginatively, positivism betrays its own ontologizing representation of a world without an imagination.

Good science is a writing linking the possibility of new versions to the possibility of new worlds, rejecting the preoccupation with "research" that truncates theory into explanation, logic, map, or tool. Theory cannot be useful, only used. Theory is speculative reason essaying a version of the world that takes account of the difference it makes to that world.

Science constructs theory's expediency in images of its ability to focus on "significant" questions; its superego disciplines the exuberant, unruly child that wants to engulf the world, Freud's oceanic feeling.

Theories provide scientists with a general explanation of how the world works. This perspective aids researchers in distinguishing significant from trivial questions, relevant from irrelevant problems, and meaningful from meaningless facts. (Bassis, Gelles, and Levine 1980, 32)

This is a very real problem for a version of science which lusts after a world from which one day it wants to be indistinguishable, the telos of original Viennese positivism that wrote both science and philosophy as the *principia mathematica* of their logos.[5] Psychoanalytic theory rightly plots a developmental path for children that requires some repression and sublimation of this insatiety as a condition of well-organized personality as well as, thus, well-integrated society. As a constitutive moment of phylogenesis, western progress, science curbs its own lust for the world ingested by the accumulating text with a reprobatory theory focusing it on the task at hand. Positivism suggests a reading of itself as map making to end all maps, writing to end all writing. Having swallowed the world, the last text cumulates in a dissolution of "text" itself, merging with a world it has completed in its addition to it of writing that via misreadings only reproduces a love of fate enacting its own postured seamlessness. I explore this topic more fully in *Fast Capitalism* (1989) by elaborating a general theory of text's constitutional dispersal into the reality it only presumes to describe, thus—fatally—eclipsing book culture altogether.

Once positivist readers act out their reading of the power of the social, the text loses its reason for being. The text allegedly will have been engulfed by a world it originally wanted to ingest through its imperial version of itself as science. Whether in hubris or simply lack of development, the subject that originally wanted to master/map the mute object world ends up being mastered/mapped by it; science's "success" is undone by a social object whose preponderance it helps constitute. Theory keeps science repressed for sufficiently long that it can accomplish the provisional mapping of the world; once frozen into eternal being, the world devours science as the last nonidentical version of it, a perverse deconstruction of a volatile subject. Science's deathwish is ironically contained in its pleasure principle, consumption tends to be consumed by the data themselves, the "last" book being one without words— nearly approached today in journal science.

If this account is held in mind, theory turns out to be inimical to science in the long run, something that science on the level of its subtext *already knows*. Positivist discourse aims to exhaust both words and things. Whether or not science really desires its own death is immaterial; in the end, it will get what it deserves—the eclipse of its textuality making it simply a fief in the totally administered world.

In the end, theories are to be judged and selected like methods in terms of their use in increasing knowledge. A good theory is the theory which aids one in finding out what one seeks to know. All other criteria are, at best, of secondary importance. Sectarian squabbles about the one "true" theory do not belong in sociology. (Orenstein 1985, 83)

Being "well suited to the quest upon which one is entering" (has *already* entered, the "quest" being the subject's immersion in open history), theory already knows what will be found. This self-referential quality does not make science incorrigible, stuck in the groove of endless iteration; it is the occasion of its openness both to desire and to the future desire seeks, its literariness neither shed nor shunned. Instead theory acknowledges its own constitution of the world it represents; representation dialectically constitutes, thus ensuring its validity. Text's echo made narratively thematic, theory thus produces a fuller version of a version that longer seeks to repress part of *itself,* its authorial desire making it a version at all.

Theories should be judged in terms of their fruitfulness in guiding research and increasing sociological knowledge—any other criteria are of secondary importance. (Orenstein 1985, 57)

In this way, theories of the middle range provide links between grand schemes and research. They guide sociologists in framing specific questions, in deciding what is needed to answer those questions, and in understanding the facts that their research produces. (Bassis, Gelles, and Levine 1984, 45)

Incorrigible, however, is the deceit that findings, unexplained by theory, are not somehow inscribed already in the "theory" that *both* "frames specific questions" and "understands the facts that their research produces." As a mere tool, guide, or map, theory's utility is much greater than typically thought; far from being marginal, theory is central to science, connecting text and subtext (or findings and search) in a simultaneously open and closed relationship— open in its essential nonidentity to the world making disciplinary discourse necessary, and closed in the inescapable gravity between mind and pen. Text —theory—gives sense to a text straining to follow a thread of meaning.

Science, however, disables theory as a mere instrumentality and then uses theory to close the circle of its version, ensuring that what is sought is found *and* what is found is not seen to be inscribed in the search itself; a kind of textual profiteering extracts a surplus value from theory that it then sinks into the bank account of scientificity. This only further conceals theory's priority as lively, marginal writing—writing that *goes somewhere*—while wringing it dry of constitutive efficacy: explanation, map, store of insights to guide future research. Theory would otherwise endanger science's closed text as the liberation of thought from mechanical reproduction, giving back to the people what has been (self-)alienated as writerly competence. The ability to theorize is no more or less than the writing of writing's desire, the endless self-correction

of free text in charge of history but itself historical—the difference of which is
fiction or, better, freedom.

> The previous discussion of contemporary sociological theories suggests that
> there is no such thing as the best sociological theory. . . . No theory is inherently
> correct or incorrect. In some situations a particular theory is more appropriate or
> is well-matched with a sociologist's personal tastes. (Doob 1985, 19)

> Overall, no theory is "best" or most valid; each theory is adequate for some
> issues, but not others. No single theoretical perspective will dominate this book.
> (Goode 1984, 23)

In the end, science relativizes theory as a matter of perspective, covertly
using theory to complete the big chill and overtly denying it the constitutive
efficacy already covertly imposed on it; weak theory writes with strength but is
seemingly kept weak so that theory—thought, writing—does not revolt against
the text's version of the world enchaining it. In denying theory epistemological
validity—"no . . . best theory"—science not only overlooks, really occludes,
the heavy burden of constitutive explanation that it assigns theory (weak theory
really being strong); it also, quite purposely, cuts off theory from the sort
of truth claims that, given the essential contemplativeness of *theoria* (Arendt
1960), would challenge science's hegemony over speculation.

Where theory is simply a matter of "personal taste," it is denied the strong
universality that would extend beyond the small tasks science desires for it,
becoming much more than just the harbinger of research. The text denies
theory any "inherent" correctness, as if there were any other kind. But science
instrumentalizes theory *as* a methodology that is simply another station on the
intellectual assembly line—like surveys, coding, statistical analysis, literature
reviews. Theory is a method of explanation putting words to what science
knew all along but wants to present as a surprise, the "findings" of a presuppositionless mirroring text, reproduction tellingly reproducing. "Adequate
for some issues, but not others," theory provides a powerful subtext denying
theory any epistemological validity; "inherent" correctness is opposed to an
unexplicated "explicit" type that only constructs theory as the methodology of
writing itself, turning number into validated concepts. This utterly undercuts
the textual call for theory as explanation, map, store of further hypotheses,
and the like.

If one theory is as good as another, depending on "situation" or "personal
taste," theory's alleged primacy in scientific methodology is suppressed once
and for all by the same text that earlier valorized theory's utility for science.
Thought is dangerous both because its contemplativeness troubles science's
daily busyness and because it inherently claims an "inherent" correctness,
more universalistic than mere taste or situational appropriateness. Science fears
thought's transcendence as an undoing of the object world giving science life

in return for completing it. Although science utilizes thought ("theory") as its own immanent textuality, putting words, the imprimatur of supposed necessity, to numbers, it wants thought decided at the outset. Thought that strays from the data, turning them upside down as it writes the possibility of their self-negation (e.g., "necessary" inequality producing a classless society through its active deconstruction), reveals science's apparently linear noncontradictoriness and closure to be self-contradictory at root.

This sort of version emerging from its own subtext of my disciplinarily implosive motives excavating all data as pieces of history thaws the world frozen by science's own theory as apologia, the objective preponderance of the social-factual over subjects disabled by their own discourses. The Husserlian admonition to trace all phenomena back to their constitutive roots in the lifeworld can be made political where the phenomenal world is insufficient, a totality wanting to be totalized. Yet totalization never attains eternity; the rapprochement of subject and object always leaves a remainder, the nonidentical forever blocking imperial thought. The world's insufficiency is recognized both by science and a committed writing that one might call theory or, acknowledging the inherent literariness of science, *fiction*. History is concealed by the one only to be completed surreptitiously by science's conceptualization of the unalterable social through "explanation" and revealed by the other as the possibility of different versions (of history). In effect, there are two different theoretical practices designed to complete the world: one represents the world's putative rationality so as to reinforce the perception and practice of the world's governance by imperious laws of subjugation and adaptation; the other shows the irrationality of the social as an occasion for its reformulation.

Science avers a reason to the world that it knows it must make good by chilling the particulars already frozen in the generic exigencies of duty, adjustment, psychic amelioration. Alternatively, critical theory addresses the world's insufficiency as an occasion to transform it in textual-political practices prefiguring new writer-reader—thus human—relationships. Its deconstruction extracts history's opportunity from the false semblance of necessity holding sway, uncovering its authorial desire as evidence that the text is never clean of the imprint of its artifice *and thus can always be reformulated.*

In this sense, a critical theory of the text reads positivist "theory" to thaw and then freeze the world's deficient reason as a deeply constitutive practice chafing against its own denigration by a science disciplining this deficiency. Science fears its revolt as the protest of thought against its duplicative/duplicitous use. As soon as science's theory thinks for itself, beyond the ambit of science's accumulating busyness, it becomes dangerous to the world requiring science as the text engendering fate. The critique of middle-range theory seemingly hunched over its workbench in support of the discipline's assembly line is not so much an interrogation of functionalism's inherent partisanship or ethnomethodology's humanistic irrelevance to the brutality of history as an attempt to reveal the powerfully constitutive role of thought. Theory thinks the world; it is also *in the world* that requires a mystifying, ontologizing version of itself—"explanation."

The protest against theory's instrumentalization challenges the denaturing of theory/thought by a text assigning theory the enormous task of completing the world's discipline and thus the world itself. In addition, by protecting the world from its own reformulation, its subversion by the constructive processes—*fiction*—that created it in the first place, science denies theory the claim of "validity": "Overall, no theory is best or more valid." Although science secretly believes that the best theory is the one best reproducing the world, it cannot admit it for fear of unmasking its "world" as the contingent accomplishment of generationally and interpersonally cross-cutting, layering, overlapping, and mutually reinforcing versions. Text is always an irremediably institutionalized intertextuality, not simply a molten blob cooled by the simple negative entropy of chronological history and its teleo-textualization. Theory challenges writing by writing itself, no longer content to accept, and thus to effect, the work place imperatives of science's high command.

The Politics of Representation

Theory is admissible only where it can be enlisted in naming the invariant power of the social, putting words to a represented "necessity" that is not called necessary but, subtly, frozen into the pages *as such*. Disciplinary figure suggests, thus provokes, a figured world. Thought outside the circle of the reasonable and researchable is rejected as undisciplined; thus, it deconstructively reveals the seemingly open synthesis promoting nondoctrinal research to be rigidly constrained by a deeply ontological partisanship. Positivist discourse advocates the present world by presenting it stancelessly. Of course, stancelessness is a stance—it is advocacy. Theory in the larger sense in which I intend it as writing committed to exhuming its narrative validity claims clashes with the so-called "sociological theory" valorized by the text and then seemingly centered in the name of theory's utility. This centering assigns functionalism dominance simply because functionalism as sociology's alleged original literature has been dominant, the auspices of most subsequent research. Synthesis omits science's otherness as nonscience, guaranteeing that intellectual averaging will eschew thought defying its reduction to an instrument as one research tool among many. The original protocol of logical positivism continues to echo in the offices and labs of sociology: ideas are only as good as the work they do. And ideas that resist their pillage by an operationist eclecticism are excluded from the common ground of disciplinary disputation in the beginning; science recognizes its mutual enemy in thought that is irreducible, nonidentical, indefatigably insistent on its autonomy.

Theoretical ecumenism, then, is a protective strategy designed to neutralize nonsociological thought, defying the productivist imperative of science inasmuch as it demarcates useful thought from what remains outside the scope of intellectual fungibility. The quest for sociological legitimation animates theory's commitment to its own adaptability within the common project of science, thought's self-transcending death-wish. Nonscience resists its operationalism as science precisely because it claims (to be) a totality that is intellectually autonomous if not inexorably isolated from other writing with which it can build community through the back-and-forth of gentle talk. Genuine theory boldly claims internal coherence—totality—as a way of confronting a world it knows it can never exhaust. It adds its own nonidentity to the world as it claims a basis for writing in its own intelligibility, better its susceptibility to deconstruction.

Science in the opposite way acquiesces to, even promotes, its cross-fertilization with "other" models or schools while proclaiming to reflect, and thus exhaust, the world in its sufficiency, albeit as a way of completing a world it secretly knows to be incomplete; contingency is not yet necessity. Theory's audacious resistance to its banalization as "perspective" or "interest" arises out of its humility; science's imperial arrogance allows for its dismantling at the hands of those who would build a bionic science out of the various "bits and pieces" plundered from the separate schools or models. Science gives in to its own compartmentalization as a way of actualizing thought that does *not:* all for one and one for all. It does this by denying validity to any one theory, perspective, model, or school; yet its secreted subtext reveals that the averaging procedures of intellectual "synthesis" will inevitably leave the center centered and the dominating perspective dominant. Original literature is thus canonized as the aegis for subsequent quantification; it is only peripherally "enhanced" by other sociological theories joining the cause of scientificity and thereby relinquishing their autonomy as nonidentical, nonidentifying thought. Yet no writing can really renounce its autonomy; methodology suppresses authorial autonomy autonomously.

Science gains an encyclopedic momentum by creating the artificial negativity[6] of real intellectual debate that it then defuses by edging difference toward the center; only later is marginalia swallowed up by the center that disciplines it, the identified world like the proverbial alien from outer space devouring everything it meets. The text is cleaned, thus neutralized, by denying any one theory the constitutive efficacy retained by science itself depending on theory for its reason and, in turn, on the appearance of epistemological, theoretical, political pluralism calming the ideological water.

The hidden absolutism of relativism assimilating conflict theory and interactionism to the posttheoretical parody of quantitative busyness propped by the original literature of reconstituted functionalism both creates and extirpates an artificial negativity evidencing science's regulative openness. It also ignores undisciplined theory as nonscience so it does not even have to deal with thought insisting on its independence from the grist mill of iterative research. Theory is bent to data's needs and thereby eviscerated as independently constitutive thought.

> Adherents of each theory can select an example, conduct a case study, and find the influence of business is great or small, just as they please. It seems that each of these perspectives is incomplete or flawed, though each has something to offer. (Goode 1984, 444)

Science tames the seeming opposition it constructs by denying each "theory" closure; yet it acknowledges that "each has something to offer." Truth is way-laid by a relativism secretly collaborating with a text collapsing all distinctions; discipline disciplines a world that would otherwise fissure under the pressure of nonidentity driving to be free of the entrapping illusion of identity—only another name for hierarchy. The reflected world dissolves if not propped by the seeming assemblage of the "bits and pieces" of partial truths into a master version; the world itself is mirrored in the text, its reproduction reproducing. The distinction between society and sociology ultimately dissolves into the sheer imitation of the one by the other, the extirpation of nonidentity in the mastery of nature matched, and accelerated, by textual accumulation of the world's contingent particulars.

> Some of the theories that attempt to explain social change are clearly unsatisfactory, and no single theory seems able to account for all social change. (Robertson 1983, 612)

The text fends off different versions that are not only peripheral with respect to the dominant consensus but that reject altogether the logos of the timeless social; it matters that "some" versions "are clearly unsatisfactory." Sometimes this refers to "accounts" merely invalid, committed to science but unable to deliver validity promised by method. But at other times discipline disciplines versions seeming to reject validity as a legitimate aim of science, the hallmark of identity theory.

Writing is neutralized if truth claims ultimately conciliate, shown to be complementary perspectives on different topics. Text becomes almost heuristic, a demonstrative exercise but not a commitment to a deeper subtext whence commitment comes in the first place. Science comfortably smoothes over the rifts among versions whose difference it constructs precisely in order to disable any singular validity; the impression of textual openness and competitiveness ensures their secret betrayal. Science out of the babel of tongues establishes a singular validity reposing in the text's and world's center; it orchestrates the three theoretical versions—functionalism, conflict theory, symbolic interactionism—in a version straining against language toward a page in sheer reflection of a lawful world that it would provoke.

Science denatures textuality even as it uses it to propositionalize the introjected unalterability of the here-and-now in "meaningful" ways. Text suffers disputation within itself only in the short run; eventually science must grow up, quieting doctrinal differences over what to name the prison house of the socialfactual. As before, theory is a heuristic device reflecting the subjectivity and perspectivity of immature discipline. Eventually science congeals into lawful propositions provoking the power of the social by naming it—order, necessity, role taking, hierarchy, rationalization. But theory's historicity is equivalent to the time it takes science to lay waste to the doubt plaguing old-age readers in the emerging new age of science's luminosity. Words and text are increasingly nostalgic residues of the speculative reason heretofore accompanying the social as its supposed transcendence—writing now cheerfully reduced to "word processing," prose collapsing into figure and particularly number.

This escape from reality, thought holding out against its replacement by the protocol statements of mathematics, is a metaphysical poetry touching the soul of the humanist as it seals humanism's fate in the text of the unalterable. Words matter as episodes of humanity in an increasingly frozen world, having a virtually sublime value; fiction is escape, *l'art pour l'art*. However, it is ironic that theory subordinated to data does the chilling, mediating—*explaining*. As speculative reason, this version of theory self-contradictorily drowns out whatever poetry it might salvage as the nostalgic expression of great suffering. The unwitting inmates chat on the way to the gas chamber, perhaps sharing the guards' taste in Wagner.

With Adorno, Derrida argues that seeming dualisms whose extremes play off against each other in apparent market equivalence are always resolved in favor of one or the other polarity, the stronger and more central. As discourse, difference hierarchizes. The three official sociological theories are never intertwined equivalently; they are subordinated to the whim of a text that invents artificial opposition within itself. Differences constructed similarly are averaged, thus propping discipline's postured ecumenism while removing the sting of their critique. Theories' pluralist reconciliation in this sense is only the hegemony of one over others it constructs, strengthened by a seeming rapprochement placating the various readerly constituencies, pork-barrel politics made metaphysical. But the concept of theoretical integration boldly assumes that texts can confine internal oppositions without imploding or, as is more often the case, exercising overt authoritarianism in order to delimit the scope of legitimate science. Theoretical integration fails to integrate where it has already constructed difference similarly. As we will see, sociology's Marxism is *sociology's* Marxism.

Sociology resolves this dilemma by posing false, toothless oppositions (e.g., order/conflict) that it then resolves in a functional division of intellectual labor: Parsons's students address periods of systemic harmony like the Eisenhower years or today's me-decade, and more disenchanted Weberians are responsible for "explaining" male/female and white/black income gaps, the deindustrialization of the urban northeast, and, perhaps too, religious wars in the middle East. Microsociology for its part is to describe, and thereby render generic, the coping strategies of minimal selves struggling to get and keep good jobs, maintain intimate domestic lives, and raise perfect children, tracing the palimpsest of ongoing interpersonal harmony in the frenetic "everyday lives" of yuppies.

This is not to say that a more genuine intermediation is possible; the meeting of theories and findings does not result in a new and better overall version but only a provisional intertextuality that is science's own existential connection to past and future versions with which it is inevitably, inextricably engaged. American sociology dreams the dream of the Enlightenment; eventually science could contain all oppositions joined in unequivocal mutuality, plural perspectives meshed together nonantagonistically. But intertextuality differs from this aim of intermediation precisely in the sense that it never rests with a resolved writing, sublating negative and positive towards a higher, neutralized glimpse of cosmic order only preserving hierarchy by seeming to have transcended it, the desideratum of idealism from Paul, Luther, and Hegel to western science.

The drive for closure is so irresistible that we deeply assume, and then repress, that a resolution of the dualisms deafening us with the cacaphony of dissent can be effected through intellectual architecture; pluralist synthesis reduces debate to selective perception and thus localizes versions in a way that preserves them all, if only in their contribution to the well-being of the whole. The analogy of the economic marketplace here joins Mill's marketplace of ideas in which liberal truth is the mediation of diverse "interests" into a populist version summing modes of understanding into a pluralist totality. Thus, writing that suppresses its own literariness out of political motives would contradictorily eliminate writing and the writer altogether as the permeable boundary between itself and the world. Reason is eclipsed in favor of a mute logic of control through which the instrumental goal of the manipulation of nature—in this case, data—replaces reflected meaning as the goal of science.

Once sociology is reduced to the world's naming, text aping the given as if it were the necessary, writing remains simply a crazy-quilt of names and numbers assembled to reflect and thus reproduce lawfulness. All else of substance follows from the text's reduction to mirror, tool, instrument seeking a power over things through representation. The text's subsumption under the logos called society might be seen instead as things' power over writing reducing it to cut-and-paste, no longer constitutive thought.

Scientificity is the text's claim faithfully to reproduce the world; the subtext here tellingly suggests "reproduction" in both senses of the word—copy and perpetuation. Positivism is the commitment of writing to this double reproduction, devaluing the nonproductive. *The central desire of modern sociology conceived under the sign of scientificity is to reproduce the given order by mirroring it;* textual work immobilizes the historical world by inducing obedience to what is depicted as the power of the social, thus producing reproduction *through* reproduction, a tautology only if the double meaning of reproduction as copy and completion is silenced.

I read sociology's claim to be science as a double reproduction of historicity, albeit leavened with the exterior "humanism" of micrological interpretation (*Verstehen*) plus, or instead of, liberal politics. This reading is a plunge off the deep end only if floating on the surface, buoyed by "evidence," is preferred to deconstructive excavation as political interrogation. I respond that depth and surface shade into each other, one opening to the other and both interesting places to be. Illuminating thought continually plumbs the depths of desire out of which it emerges as the self-referential activity I earlier called committed literature, devoted to its own undecidable possibility as both *of* and *not* the world that bears it. Good writing is fiction, a sustained self-reflection as text that listens to the echoes as well as silences in writing's clarification of "what" is (being) said and thus making formerly unconscious activity, why writing writes what it does, the focus of literary consciousness—writing's topic. Science differs from art only in that science claims validity where art unproblematically intends it without having to play out text/subtext dynamics in a topical way.[7] Both are fiction; both imaginatively construct a world whose narration recommends it.

This risks a hermeneutic circle or spiral in which the requirement simultaneously to understand the whole as well as every single line within it cannot be met; thus writing peters out as a fruitless, willful attempt to catch sunlight or dodge raindrops. But this is a risk only if the end-of-text—all writings swallowed by a disciplining version and thus decided—is held out as an epistemological desideratum. Although few scientists deny the awesome mystery of the unknown, few doubt that science legitimately aims at closure and therefore acts *as if* a last text could be written; in the meantime science represses authorial desire in a methodologically contained subtext and thus ontologizes a world that science wants only to reproduce—*politically.* This version of writing acquiesces to the present as the untranscendable horizon of all possible futures, an eclipse of imagination relating to objects as the possibility of their transformation, that is, in terms of their historicity—seen by science to be a devilish distortion. Science views the world as insufficient and therefore chills it in order to provoke its enactment by disempowered readers, but thereby science chills itself; sheer representation seeks, but fails, to still the pen. A nonpositivist version of writing, theory recognizes its insufficiency as the perpetual question asked of its own answer: why did I write that?

This might only lead to further writing, the simultaneity of the production of objective knowledge and self-creation (early Marx's and Marcuse's conjoined work and play). This is a scandal from the point of view of scientificity that represses authorial gratification as well as the fingerprints connoting authorial presence. Science expects its frieze of the episodic one day to add up to the world, meanwhile denigrating nonscience as aimlessly nihilistic. Discipline constructs undisciplined writing as willful violence to the official tradition. Nihilism threatens science by debunking the philosophy of history imbedded in the myth of progress: history, the collection of the past, is going somewhere. Science rejects the purposely artificelike writing of fiction as nihilism because it does not point toward a last-text or last-time, even if only as a regulative idea, as such violating the productivism of science elevating knowledge on the shoulders of past giants.[8] Nihilism as an antisystem refuses to produce what it knows is both impossible and, as such, oppressive—text eclipsing thought with a merely technical accumulation of the world's particulars. The world inscribed in the text as all possible worlds perversely becomes so.

The text in using methodology as supposedly value-neutral resolves nothing in the way of intellectual disagreements; it only reduces writing to the figural inscription of the world. Thought gives way to technique. *There is no such thing as unmediated writing,* no neutrality allowing one to choose between or among different writings as indubitable versions; every version *already* changes the world it claims to reproduce, following Heisenberg's principle of indeterminacy as the basis of a critical theory of text. Interestingly, science acknowledges this fragment from its subtext where it says that theoretical differences are "to a large extent . . . based on values and tastes," wavering between accepting the difference of differences as one of committed argument or simply predilection, even whim ("taste"). By appearing to admit irreducible difference, the text cuts out the legs from under its forthcoming attempt to "resolve" difference with a supposedly neutral methodology. Method is always and only the principle of science's iterative work, the logos of text itself is the logos of the power of the social, and methodology is a mode of (re)production.

But the text does not go as deconstructively deep into itself as it might; the alternative perspectives between or among which one supposedly chooses on grounds of "values and tastes" are not stretched between science and nonscience but merely between different official versions of science, two decidedly complementary namings of the social. Taste here distinguishes between two different Durkheimian versions and not between or among really heterogeneous writings, encompassing Marxism and feminism as well as the official versions of the world. As ever, the text's seeming catholicity is a fraud invoked to create the false impression of openness where it is neither openly heterogeneous nor synthetic, resolving issues of "taste" with the disciplinary apparatus of science—precision, clarity, and the proscriptive community of scholarship.

This forces me to be more explicit about the notion of heterogeneity in my opposition to the false catholicity of the disciplinary text claiming to have room for difference. I keep in mind as a future topic the question, What is sociology? In my critique of discipline I presuppose a standard of textual heterogeneity introducing real diversity into writing and thus exposing the false diversity of a seemingly synthetic version authorizing sociological versions committed, albeit surreptitiously, to the exhaustion of history. I have to explicate the adjective "real" (in real heterogeneity), suggesting that a different version of writing is possible as writing itself; this is exemplified by my own version that tries to be self-conscious "about" what it is saying—better, that makes self-consciousness directly a topic.

It is not enough to claim difference on the grounds of validity in the long run, as oppressively disciplining as representationality, indubitability, and lawfulness. The argument "for" argumentativeness can avoid being monologic only by regarding itself as a corrigible expression of what it purports to argue for, thus requiring its own reformulation as a condition of its version of the world. In a way that is disturbingly paradoxical for garden variety scientism, I can only demonstrate the sense of my argument by interrogating its openness to gentle correction in the self-determination of a written or writerly community. By writing the world I change it in a way that makes my account originally false; I can only anticipate the difference my version made to the world.

Professional sociology is not a self-referencing community in this sense but rather a bureaucratic institution in which an official writing is imposed from the top down through the canons of disciplinary accumulation and scholastic mediation. Bureaucratic community tries to "resolve . . . points of disagreement" between and among contesting writings using the "scientific method" to derive "testable propositions" against which texts can be measured. As constituted in the capitalist and state-socialist blocs, science is impatient with truth claims, the adjudication of which must await a future *that we author*. Heidegger tell us that since Plato we have mistakenly thought of the truth as timeless, failing to recognize mortality's own impact on knowledge. We freeze a world in its process of becoming, a process hastened or delayed by writing itself.

Science vitiates hope metaphysically by restricting itself to the empirical present subtly broadened into all social being. This restriction is rejected by a version that *by writing* lives a different, better world, delivering knowledge-constitution from the large bureaucratic institutions producing official versions of the truth to the dialogic community, Habermas's ideal speech situation and Marx's socialism. The truth of writing is made true by having a certain relationship to its topic and audience. It is is not adequate in terms of its "fit" to a pregiven world; rather it is a deeply imbedded feature of the world it would create through its own version, instituting and continually renewing a nonauthoritarian relation among writer, reader, and topic as an alternative to disciplinary hegemony. This is inherently a political writing if politics is understood as partisanship; such writing *advocates* a certain relation to its topic as an exemplar and prefiguration of the world it discloses in its essay of its possibility. All writing on this view is political—the mute, disabled writing of scientism as much as the kind I am doing here. Yet science does not understand itself in these terms; instead it aims to end politics by striking a relationship to the world similar to Christian witnessing, stifling its own voice in awe of the world's immutable logos, here the power of the social. It is not hard to see that positivism is religion in this sense. This is bad politics because it necessarily defeats all resistance to history. And if one witness is good, more would be better, leading to the enshrinement of a disciplinary community of the faithful harmonizing the witnesses' voices and thus allowing the world to appear to us in its ineluctable presence. Both religious and academic communities are founded on a univocal account of the timeless world—the book. Faith is demonstrated in its iteration.

A better version of science would recognize the writer's responsibility for the world, even if we add that others bear responsibility, too. Description is inevitably a form of partisanship made present in the text and thus made available to others' inspection, response, and commentary; *the dialogic community is created in committed but self-consciously undecidable versions of the world.*[9] This politics recognizes and actualizes the nonidentity of text and world; their difference is not at all a hindrance to truth but an occasion of a self-limiting confidence about the indeterminate openness of the future. Writing intending to exhaust history in a book only subdues the writer. History moves on nonetheless, the fewer writers the better. Recognizing the world-making opportunities available in a protean version, positivism suppresses them methodologically. Before long, disciplinary workers believe they are only witnesses, not poets, too. At the same time, representation arrogantly tries to end all argument with the hidden argument of methodology. The scientist is installed as an authority but stilled as an author. On the basis of privileged access to the recondite mysteries of a world science freezes technically and figurally, hence politically.

Writing is politics as the writer posits and enacts a certain relationship to the world under account. A presuppositionless version of science strikes the worst possible relationship in its duality of dominance and false humility, trying to control nature with text and then pretending that science is only a voiceless witness unbounded by worldly interest in one version over another. In this, the world's reproduction as a self-evident reason to be buries its will to power deep in subtext. The writer who supposedly sacrifices intellect to the overarching mission of science does so in full knowledge that this is not a sacrifice at all "because"—the reasoning of those who live power vicariously, parading their Izod labels and IBM microcomputers as the equivalent of the real thing (whatever *that* might be)—science closes a world that yet remains marginally open. Thus, science is on the side of the powers; as discipline it is power.

The so-called end of ideology favors those closest to ideology, who meanwhile keep their hands clean by disavowing an interest in it. Synthesis can be dusted off and displayed (in the introductory textbooks, for example) as evidence of science's universalism. Meanwhile science keeps busy propping a world to which it enjoys only a supposedly disinterested relationship, "objectivity" concealing the subtext of objectivity as objectification of the as-yet-fluid; description becomes reproduction.

Science must consume the intellectual otherness that, if unchecked, would force it to take sides and thus abandon its pretended disinterestedness; disabling science's transcendentalism with all sides averaged toward the center as just another version, science is defrocked as willful subjectivity. Committed writing embodies a political telos of an alternative community, challenging the bureaucratic community of science to give reasons for its existence apart from the tautological appeal to a vouchsafed literature as meaning itself. This is a challenge that by definition—to be science—science must refuse, as the queen of England does not answer questions put directly to her lest she lose the concomitant edge that constitutes royalty. The disclaimer of politics offered by science's explicit text, all differences collapsed into an amorphous center and thus defused simply as taste, hides its own politics—skewed subject-object relations—behind the superficial textual politics of liberal Christian moralism, "making the world a better place to live." Thus, with Kant, science carefully distances itself from its carnal desire to end textuality, the world fatefully enacted by readers convinced of this truth.

It takes little these days to convince people that political perspectivity, all too quickly becoming naked self-interest—Reagan, Politburo—is to be avoided at all costs, assuming a definition of the political (who gets what, when, and how) owed to Weber. The political lives on as its disavowal, shaming partisan writings either into compliance with the norms of objective science (Marxism-become-conflict theory, feminism-become-the-sociology of gender, topics for the next two sections), and thus becoming official versions, or marginalizing partisanship as incorrigible nonscience, the remotest otherness of official otherness.

> However, the importance of Marx's sociological contribution has not been acknowledged by American sociologists until recently. His ideas were initially dismissed because they were highly political, which seemed to be inappropriate for the science of sociology. (Ritzer, Kammeyer, and Yetman 1982, 82)

The marginal is mainstreamed by finding official epistemology in it, in this case its contribution to a concerted disciplinary voice. In the next two sections

I will discuss this process of the marginalization and then centering of deviant intellectual/political "perspectives" in greater detail. It only appears an irony that mainstream sociology claims these dissident voices for itself. As we shall see, sociology's Marxism and feminism are not only distortions but opposites of themselves, disciplined as iterations of that which they explicitly oppose.

PART THREE

Marginalia I

5

Centering Dissent

Rehabilitation, Truncation, Conformity

American sociology defeats the political intent of two sorts of intellectual marginalia by swallowing them in its oceanic text, distorting them while extracting safe meaning from them as pluralist components of the official disciplinary canon. The text saddles Marxism with both theoretical and historical responsibility for the Soviet gulag, rehabilitating safe Marxism, properly depoliticized, as an official conflict theory, a safe denizen of the mainstream discipline. For its part feminism is narrowed to its so-called liberal variant that, like centered Marxism, is reduced to a single-minded economism and psychologism and thus politically neutralized. In general, the social text does not simply ignore what is initially renegade writing but assimilates it to science in order to preempt its writers, Marxists and feminists. In turn, oppositions become respectable "sociologies" harnessing the fervor of 1960s rebels safely ensconsed in the academy to a liberal textual politics opposing conflict, sexism, racism if only as persistent "social problems" that can be addressed piecemeal.

The marginalia of radical dissent are *disqualified;* radicalism is modulated by liberal reasonableness suggesting the inevitability of some degree of hierarchy, inequality, and heterosexist family. They are then *rehabilitated* as disciplining vehicles for liberal sentiment. "Research" on "social problems" of poverty, gender inequality, and the like are guided by the "paradigm" of these captured writings, conflict theory along with the sociology of gender and family. Margins are relocated at the center as legitimate accumulations of data in their own right, complementing functionalist state intervention and allowing the text seemingly to transcend perspectivity altogether, margins seemingly as central as the center. I borrow from Derrida in treating the marginal as a telling signifier of the center that constructs marginality as its empowering otherness, the not-I that, like Hegel's slave, has the power to recognize the master and thus give his or her existence meaning. Yet Derrida, like Hegel, idealizes marginality as a self-sufficient, even desirable, status; its nonidentity to the center expresses a kind of freedom from the material altogether. But margin is still margin, dominated by the center requiring it for its own recognition, as Marx saw in trying to reverse the master-slave relation in the slave's favor through its and others' historical practice.

Thus, a nonidentical otherness dialectically survives its distance from the mainspring of power pushing relentlessly to administer everything, ingesting all otherness and thus metabolizing it. The danger in a totally administered society is not simply that the margin will revolt, claiming its own centrality, for the forces of social control are immense: a few radical intellectuals trying to defeat Exxon, Pentagon, and KGB armed with copies of the *Dialectic of Enlightenment*? As Gramsci saw, the Russian revolution was a revolution against *Capital*, and the next revolution—if such apocalyptic imagery makes any sense today—will have to be a revolution "against" critical theory in the sense that it would demonstrate the ability of the masses to free themselves from canons, even left-wing ones.

The textual law of contradiction, paralleling those of political economy that Marx originally described, is played out in the text's need to suggest marginalia as the text's own inner otherness—signifier, completion, cooptation. This meets head on the text's drive to consume what it has produced, marginalia given the imprimatur of official writing and thus losing the very otherness that the text needs to support its own claimed ecumenism. No less than the inexorable clash of capital and labor—capital needing labor to sustain itself both as value producer and consumer but in that tending to destroy labor through its immiseration—this tension of contradiction cannot easily be resolved on its own terms.

Text needs an official version of its other, whether conflict theory or the sociology of gender; yet it consumes that otherness in its drive to identify everything with itself. Science's text is the demiurge first unleashed by the Enlightenment as the "power" of knowledge bent on territorial expansion, mystery beaten back by the advance guard of science. This deprives science, given its nature, of what it needs to sustain its momentum. Eventually text runs out of external material, the desideratum of a closed writing achieving symbiotic identity with the frozen world iterated in the image of its own projected logos. Otherness, then, is consumed as soon as it is produced, with production implying consumption inasmuch as the "marginal" is already constructed. This conflict theory derives from Marxism; Marxism is disqualified and then rehabilitated as sociology, a version of the power of the social. In spite of text's promise to finish off the recalcitrant world by ingesting it, science discovers that there is always an outside, regions of nonscience yet to be assimilated. Constructed by the center, these margins are centered as they are officially disciplined in science's "advances"—today Marxism and feminism, tomorrow, perhaps, deconstruction and critical theory.[1]

Discipline contradictorily needs a margin as it drives toward the last, luminous version of history containing all differences. The exhaustion of history in a single version of it is now a regulative principle of thought's domestication as stanceless inscription. In fact, no writing is ever the last, at least *this* side of mutually assured de(con)struction; meanwhile its ideal subdues the intermediating versions that the world needs as evidence of its chatty plurality. Disciplinary work in the meantime drives writers from rethinking the alleged requirement of scientistic iteration and thus the possibility of other texts and lives. Endlessly duplicative of the power of the social, sociology derives its political function less from what it says than from what it fails to say; writing is itself a political way of life and the world is thus susceptible to being rewritten. *Text sidesteps its own logic of contradiction, needing marginality while driving to center it in the inexhaustibility of the written word.* Writing is always able to count on another version to which to oppose itself (text's manufactured but phony ecumenism) and yet devours that opposition as its seeming completion. Although this seems to postpone the resolution of contradiction, it cannot do so permanently; in spite of itself disciplinary writing will never transcend its *own* need for the pseudomarginality it must construct out of various sources of nonscience available. If difference does not exist, it must be invented.

If text were somehow really to end, having announced the final world in its expressive multifariousness, swallowing Derrida and Marx as well as Parsons, the power of the social would be here to stay. Text freezes over into the social nature it prematurely posits. The regime of necessity would reveal flawless freedom—no work, no politics, no problems; writing, struggle of any kind, would be unnecessary. But ingesting the world as its own self-transcendence, the last text is never written. Social reproduction must continue, for texts do not exhaust lives. *Writing is both protest and gratification.* It addresses domination as the possibility of its naming (what Marx, but not positivism, meant by "science"), hence reformulation. In its own constitutive activity, writing exemplifies the untotalizable totality of the particular life. Writing's own undecidability echoes the possibility of undecidable worlds.

The logic of the text's linear advance promises one day to have charted the entire territory of the unknown. Yet the last text is indefinitely delayed, allowing discipline in the meantime to sate itself on the feast of integrated, ecumenized writings holding out against the text's rapaciousness. Were it not for new writings to be disqualified and then rehabilitated under the sign of discipline, the text would run out of things to say, thus losing epistemological authority. Without marginalia to swallow, to center, the text's accumulating logic would be shown to be just another excuse for playful discourse. In its revealed perspectivity it loses the capacity it now enjoys to order lives as it orders the world. The power of the social is frozen by a concatenation of theories putting their names virtually to everything, "explaining" and thus reproducing them.

This is not to say that science understands its capacity to make all differences similar as the self-contradicting logic that it is; "progress" destroys the nonidentity, the *terra incognito,* science needs in order to keep busy and thus keep going. The alleged last text is postponed inasmuch as the center needs a margin that, once disciplined—digested—loses its marginality and must be surpassed; intellectual synthesis relentlessly pushes back the frontiers of knowledge. Instead science plods along, getting nowhere in the way of an approach to the final version it constructs as the aegis of its own relentless integration of alternative perspectives. But getting nowhere (more data sets, research money, accredited graduates) protects science from the realization that there is no ultimate version; the worldly is gradually pasted into the pages completed by the obedient role playing it prompts as the unavoidable enactment of a disempowered "fate."

Cumulation is denied not, as science would have it, because its instruments and support troops are yet insufficient and because political opposition to it is too strong but because the marginality of nonscience, indeed of protest, proliferates under the harsh regime of textual necessity. Text's authoritarian edicts are met with resistance. If not self-consciously political, aware of its literarily self-referential character as an alternative language game and thus life, writing protests against its subsumption under the sign of a totally administered world bending it to the mindless ritual of disciplinary representation.

The Frankfurt School's theory of art (Adorno 1982; Marcuse 1978) locates an innate politics in representation that surpasses a superficially neo-Kantian cultivation of the sublime soul, instead in its very otherness prefiguring the otherness of a redeemed future. Although the power of the social is never total as long as there needs to be a text at all reproducing it in the blur of fact and fate, ironically—the faithful might say dialectically—history resists closure. Certain versions of the world defy science's integration, being marginalia that stay that way. Contradictorily, the disciplinary text that seeks to ontologize the power of the social *cannot* because each textual advance only sparks new resistance that the text then tries to engulf, ceaselessly alternating between text and those whom it tries to put under its spell. Discipline tries but ultimately fails to induce them to live their reading as the stupid role-players premised by Durkheimian sociology. Curiously, text's need for marginalia is invariably met as resistance rises to meet it. Discipline fails to discipline every version, especially those it provokes.

Indeed, there need not be discipline at all were it not for a certain recalcitrance in the body politic that innately resists its disempowering.[2] The text needs an otherness against which to play off its dominant center, thus centering even the margins it officially constructs as an otherness—conflict theory, the Democratic party, prochoice feminists, the Soviet Union. Yet some margins are more difficult to integrate than others, the world in its inherent multidimensionality calls forth discipline precisely *because* resistance is difficult to contain, setting up a seemingly undecidable chain of text integrating margins and then finding new defiant margins which it curiously needs as a topic for "further research."

The process of integration simultaneously disqualifying and then rehabilitating dissent is always inherently problematic, for it takes place in a world that necessarily fissures.[3] Margin resists its ingestion by center just as labor resists absorption into capital. The fractured world calls forth the disciplinary text in the first place. For this reason, because the world provokes its opposition as well as its textual healing, the center will always have to engage with an opposition it only constructs in the first place. The text as the world's purported reproduction is a battleground on which center and margins struggle for survival. The supremacy of the center that depends on the validating otherness of margins is continually threatened by new versions claiming that there can be text and life beyond the pale of the constraining present. *Writing defies.* Even positivism in its volcanic desire to recommend the present world resists its self-transcendence by its own account; even science resists a writerless world.

As the theorists of the Frankfurt School recognized, rarely are the most overtly political versions the most successfully defiant in an administered society; rather those texts, representations, and music that by their very otherness, their autonomous aloofness, refuse to be sucked into a disciplinary text reconciling all differences, whether Beethoven or Muzak, Marx as a scientific sociologist or feminism as an affirmation of American "family," are most effectively oppositional. This remains an unpopular position among soi-disant Marxists who accuse critical theorists of having no "strategy" of political struggle other than an indulgently elitist art, the disingenuous stance of pampered intellectuals who fiddle while Rome burns or, to use Lukacs's metaphor, who take rooms in "Grand Hotel Abyss."[4] This criticism feeds off both the guilt of the Marxist intellectual about apparently "doing" nothing to expedite the revolution and the pragmatist aversion to theory, abstraction, strange literature, unpopular music. By listening to itself and its animating desire and then by arguing passionately for its version in light of that desire, recognizing its simultaneous contingency and aloofness, writing prefigures the form and content of a new society defying the hegemony of production over reproduction, man over woman, capital over labor, and science over fiction. Adorno found Beckett and Schoenberg radical because their work reflexively distanced itself from other work acquiescing to the prevailing order of being. In centering autonomous work, blunting it with other writings as their completion or correction thus stilling their voice of negation, discipline robs them of their nonidentity, their protest against identification.

This does not license any gibberish because gibberish is supremely easy to accommodate, whether television, profound literature and metaphysics, some

rock lyrics, too much of Heidegger (Adorno 1970). Rather writing that accepts, even celebrates, its nonidentity to the world and its master version holds
out *not* for identity, ever the idealist panacea, but for a different version replacing the self-confident principle of integration with a principle of dialogical
difference; radical humility recognizes its simultaneous constitutiveness and
contextuality—new world fostered by defiant writing and yet never identical
to it. At root, the nonidentity between text and world can be amplified as
the possibility of a version that accepts its unconsciousness and yet does not
thereby capitulate to the comfortable version only pretending to identify, thus
auguring a world in which all closure is politically vitiated.

Adorno's (1973b) Schoenberg accepts the difference between his music and
the world that bears it as the possibility of a different music and, through it,
a different world that does not need texts to complete it, ontologizing identity
as fate and thereby making it come to pass. This offers only one example
as purposely remote from the text of sociology as possible, hearing Schoenberg perhaps as a theorist of small-group disharmony. It does not matter that
Schoenberg protested Adorno's "political" version of his music; he thought he
wanted only different music, immanently self-articulating, and not a different
world. Like most artists, he was trained as a neo-Kantian to separate private
from public, art from politics. Adorno politicizes Schoenberg where he recognizes in his oeuvre the genuine practice of nonidentity, refusing totality as the
deadly cessation of all art, writing, politics—thought—and instead installing
disharmony as the marginalized center of a new music that Adorno begins to
broaden into the discourse of a new world.

Self-conscious of its own nonidentity to the world, marginality regards
margin as center and center as margin, reversing the traditional tendency of
idealism and scientism to move outward from the known to the unknown in
brutal conquest. Subtext/text, text/world, reader/writer, person/community,
present/history, nonidentity constitutively accepts its marginality. Yet it struggles to free other disciplined margins as well, recognizing their false identity
with the central principle of domination in western civilization, namely accumulation. Writing that resists its integration will also try to liberate other
versions usurped by the disciplinary text and rehabilitated as official oppositions only reflecting the center's glory, even adding a certain cosmopolitanism
to it. Here I want to explore the integration of the two most notable marginalia
confronting recent scientific sociology—Marxism and feminism—and then to
try to disintegrate them in order to let them live and breathe on their own. This
is not a task that should inspire much more optimism than Adorno does in
rewriting Schoenberg or Marcuse Freud, for neither the left nor the women's
movement, even if liberated from the text's deforming tentacles, will likely
restore itself on only one writing. How could it? Can ads in *The New York
Times* and spots on network television trumpet their liberation from a text that

has made them slavish idolators or simply nothings? How do texts take life? Opposition faces the responsibility to make vivid its imagery of a different life, the text of freedom dialogically becoming a version of freedom itself. I have no better programmatic answer; freedom defies method.

In disqualifying by centering the radical vision of the marginal, the writers who live and write the nonidentical are dazzled by Hollywood and Harvard; they do not simply "sell" out (as if everything had its price, a pernicious version today—thoroughgoing monetarization). Instead they simply forget what it is to live a wild life, having been conventionalized, commodified, and academicized by the omnipotent mainstream. *Radicalism almost invariably finds its niche in bourgeois society,* or else it is drowned out altogether in the hum and chatter of television talk shows, newspapers, gossip, what passes for common sense—discipline turning negation into affirmation. This is not to suggest a radicalism so ungrounded in the topical[5] that it is absolved of betrayal simply by having never committed itself to the world, an impossibility anyway as idealism knows.

The idealism/realism split plays into the hands of "realists" who would use idealism as the repressive desublimation of radical imagination, keeping its rebels busy with thought projects so transcendental that they never come down to earth.[6] Adorno's reading of Schoenberg, for example, is radicalizing only because it is a rewriting, adding a de- and reconstitutive intentionality to Schoenberg's musical project. "As such," uninterpreted and thereby unpoliticized, Schoenberg's music has little value for the bourgeois other than, perhaps, delightfully to scandalize and thus further integrate a stratum of cultivated listeners, music consumers. Adorno had to theorize Schoenberg (to write him, literally) in order to materialize his implicit negation of bourgeois identity theory and practice, recouping it as *opposition;* while Schoenberg opposed bourgeois harmony, his opposition was not theorized, relived self-consciously in a political way.

Theory in this sense adds politics to rebellion by raising rebellion to a reconstructive level, twisting negation toward the light of positive possibility. It understands oppositional writing as the project of a different world, the essence of politics. Writing raises protest to the level of articulate advocacy even if advocacy is not spelled out in instrumental and operational terms; the "blueprint" of socialism called for by skeptics as a way of discrediting it piece by piece in light of the common sense intractability of the present. Protest in advocating surpasses simple resignation that is so enticing in a mad world seemingly getting worse. It is a prefigurative and constitutive example of *difference,* "reality" thawed, if not refrozen, by an image of socialist necessity —the pitfall of most Marxism. It is easy to misunderstand the advocacy of writing that defies by thinking freedom, thus opening its prospect of an undecidably nonauthoritarian community. Our training in instrumental reason is so deep we often miss the practical side of supposed abstraction, the charge leveled at critical theory joining neither the mechanical left nor mechanical feminism.

Most Marxists sold on the pragmatic immediacy of revolutionary practice disdain the subtle advocacy of theory—writing as fiction intending to persuade —just as much as do those who would discipline Marxism, making protest into science and thus repressing its anger and desire. Eventually the passion that moved Marx to study, write, and organize is simply banished from memory by a text that would smoothly integrate Marxism, and thus pacify it, by affording it a slot in the pantheon of official university knowledge.

Protest is so deeply suppressed that discipline reads the marginalia as if they celebrated the very object of their original protest, *naming it* (e.g., "conflict") *and thereby ontologizing it.* The text of American sociology crudely mitigates Marxism in an act of intellectual damage control where it preposterously ascribes the postulate of eternal conflict to Karl Marx, a construction utterly collapsing the argument between Marx and bourgeois sociologists like Durkheim and Weber about the nature of history. Marginality is recentered by repressing its passion in favor of its implacable absoluteness, *easier when the marginal already claims a scientificity of its own,* albeit not the chilling scientificity of the bourgeois text. As we shall see shortly, Marxism is more seamlessly marginalized where it claims to be a science itself, a version of Marxism that has predominated from Engels through Althusser.

Protest's advocacy is repressed by sociology where passion can be disqualified out of hand by the rigor of protest's seeming scientism, a case made to order especially where protest writing claims its own scientificity and thus invites its dispassionate verification or falsification "on evidence." Marxism is easily convicted on the trumped up charge of failed historical prophecy. That inequality persists is evidence read against wild Marxism at its disciplinary tribunal.

Its patent advocacy of a better world stilled as undisciplined, the marginal is divested of its otherness that more subtly advocates by standing apart and against, opposing its absorption by a center that engulfs, but now ecumenically. It is easy to vitiate the hortatory advocacy of the *Manifesto* on grounds of its patent disavowal of a representational version of science and thus to rehabilitate its supposedly "scholarly" content—a favorite adjective of promotion-and-tenure committees trying to decide whether a person's writing is safe or wild, Marxology or Marxism, women's studies or feminism. It is more difficult to dislodge marginalia itself as protest. Nonscience prefiguratively lives a nonadministered life by defying its scientization, truncation, rehabilitation as the official opposition the text antinomiously engulfs and thus absorbs. For this reason, the disciplinary version disciplines marginal writing in order to make it conform to the scholarly apparatus—deference to a literature, suppression of authorial presence, and commitment to middle-range research instead of speculativeness. Methodology makes Marxism mouth the words of the power of the social. Technical obfuscation limits the audience to trained specialists who tolerate science, not politics, as a vocation.

Where the margin does not conform, where it theorizes against and above the oceanic text of totally administered science, it is simply ignored and thus doomed to obscurity. The discipline ignores esoteric Marxisms, feminisms, and philosophies because it wants to rehabilitate official Marxism, feminism, and philosophy that neither preach politics nor theorize about their otherness *as* prefiguratively negative politics. Wild writing *escapes,* a thoroughly truthful term in spite of macho caricatures of it as unmanly capitulation claiming ill-deserved intellectual conscientious objector status, too wimpish to go to war on the side of the pragmatically positive. The prefigurative otherness of autonomous writing is a way of life joining commitment and circumspection in the institution of a dialogic community, text/practice constantly aware of its own insufficiency and thus overcoming the arrogance of a version attempting speciously to make good the world's insufficiency. Margins convinced of the indeterminacy of history recognize that there will be no teleological endpoint; thus they lend themselves to the task of deconstruction loosening us from the chilling hold of icelike necessity, exploding the arrogant concept of necessity's deficit *as if* it—text—could supply it.

In this way, by picking and choosing among the scraps of the marginal, the text invariably domesticates radical thought, denying it utility, validity, and realism, *rehabilitating only its safest passages that can be read as the world's iteration thus ontologizing the object of its opposition.* Marx and Engels's ringing sentence from the 1848 *Communist Manifesto*, "The history of all hitherto existing society is the history of class struggles," is thus easily turned into the verity that conflict will be everlasting, just as their first sentence, "A specter is haunting Europe—the specter of communism," is made grounds for the failure of Marxist prophecy over the long term. This strongly rewrites what can only be understood hermeneutically in relation to the writing's totality as isolable "claims" turned into "evidence" by the text and thus used for proof of ontological arguments. That all history has seen class-struggle becomes the basis for reducing Marxism to a so-called conflict theory that not only ontologizes conflict as endemic to all society; conflict is positive, even healthy (e.g., Coser 1966), fulfilling certain functions in a dynamic society.[7]

There is nothing inherently wrong with a reading enlightening author with his or her forgotten desire, text with subtext, the classic mode of a psychoanalytic literary criticism passing through both Derrida and Adorno. Yet science's text does not deconstruct Marx as much as disciplines his criticism originally intended dialectically with the spin of a writing reaching beyond and behind itself but not flattened into literal description. Scientism addresses Marx as if he were part of the same story. Any criticism runs the risk of distortion. But science purposely distorts in order to sustain itself with the addenda, "corrections," of marginalia translated from a type of nonscience, *theory,* committed to its own historicity, hence openness, into science. Its passages are ripped from the page and entered into discipline as evidence of the unavoidable power of the social.

While at first blush this may appear generous, giving the margins their due —a special issue of the *American Journal of Sociology* devoted to "Marxist sociology," the "application" of conflict to various social problems, a few Marxists hired and perhaps even tenured—it is only a deceptive tolerance, what Marcuse (1966) so aptly called "repressive tolerance." The literal accumulation of marginalia's constructions oppose the theoreticity of the intended marginal totality. In Marxism's case, this utterly obliterates the *politics of otherness* holding out for a different world by refusing to freeze the present and thereby exhaust the future, instead moving back and forth between the two as the possibility of a discontinuous history. Opposing science as the depoliticization of writing, Marxism's theoreticity is rejected by an interpretive accumulation process that takes Marx's dialectical descriptions to be frozen "fact," either invalidating Marxism as failed prophecy ("specter of communism") or ontologizing it by reading his description of capitalism literally and not, properly, in a way that treats Marxism as an inexhaustible textual practice the truth of which can only be gauged in its practice.[8]

It is crucial for the discipline to sanitize the names the marginalia give to themselves, ensuring that their politics is subordinated to their science and thus taming them. Their names are often then assigned to existing political practices that do not deserve them at all in order to play them off against their own constructed versions; Marxism becomes Soviet ideology, doubly distorting the reality of Soviet practice, which has already been falsified by the Soviets as "communism" when in fact it is nothing of the sort; feminism inhabits the lesbian separatist lunatic fringes. In this way, the rehabilitation of the margins requires new margins to be constructed utterly beyond the pale of middle-class, middle-range respectability, repugnant to the liberal/familist/capitalist textual politics of a sociology cheerfully opposed to nettlesome "social problems." Sociology could not integrate a safe Marxism without counterposing it to, indeed rehabilitating it from, the wild Marxism of either the Frankfurt School or Stalinism.

Where Stalin is disqualified on surface grounds of his abundant illiberalism in a way that locates that illiberalism in Marx's texts, read as recommendations for terror, the discipline dismisses Frankfurt on grounds of its alleged inability to write clear positivist sentences; occasionally it conflates critical theory with any "critical sociology" lamenting the eternity of inhumanity—thus making a place even for me in a sociology department as its moral philosopher. This reversal of names from the original margin, now sanitized and made safe for democracy, to a new margin that is the Janus face of original Marxism confuses the issue entirely. It allows the center to negate oppositional versions simply by unnaming and then renaming them, Marx become a Weberian and Lenin a Marxist. This prevents marginal writing from defining itself as oppositional, as an alternative, *by splitting the text into good and bad versions of itself.* Good safe Marxism is what Marx allegedly had in common with Weber, notably a bureaucratic version of the power of the social; bad wild Marxism is Leninist vanguardism and Party hegemony. On the evidence, only fools are Marxists. Better to call oneself a Weberian—as sociology says, a conflict theorist.

This makes headway because non-Marxists rarely know the difference. Anyway, the splitting of oppositional writing allows protest in its centering to be politically engulfed, leaving only crack-pot authoritarianisms to guide dissent under their name. Feminism is similarly split between the liberal sociology of gender ontologizing sex roles and bourgeois family and departmentalizing women's studies on the one hand and a notoriously antimale and antifamily lesbian separatism on the other. This splitting as it opens wide allows other versions of Marxism and feminism to drop out of sight altogether. We are left with their disciplinary version, protest turned miraculously into science on the one hand—determination replacing dissent—and incorrigibly authoritarian practices on the other. This shows what "happens" when Marxists and feminists get into power: the first in politics produce the gulag; the second in the family wreck it by displacing men and children altogether. Resisting its bifurcation into good and bad versions of itself, science versus politics, protest writing defies this good/bad construction of itself in a discourse of otherness insisting on its own legitimacy without installing itself as a new center.

The text fears communism or lesbian separatism per se inasmuch as non-science challenges science's textual-political strategy as an account of the power of the social. Ironically a construction of the positivism marginalizing it, nonscience defuses the authority of science over muted readers in prose unencumbered by science's self-imposed straitjacket as iteration/apologia. Denaturing by splitting the opposition simultaneously shows the sanitized version of dissent—Marxist sociology, women's studies—to best advantage when contrasted with the authoritarian practices of what are renamed "Marxism" and "feminism" and at once exhausts marginalia with their unnamed versions. In turn, this precludes a Marxism that is neither scientific nor Soviet and a feminism that is neither scholastic nor separatist. The text by renaming the left— (Soviet) Marxism, (separatist) feminism—brings the discussion of politics to a close and succeeds in silencing theory.

The appeal of the text's deceptive ecumenism that really distorts in the service of disqualification lies in its apparent graciousness toward margins that in this seemingly postmodern, postideological era are given their due by mainstream sociology. Even if they are kept in disciplinary cages earmarked for the weirdest, scariest species, left versions of the power of the social affirm discipline. The text profits simply by doing the textual work of splitting opposition into safe and wild versions of itself. Marxism and feminism are "heard" merely by giving their names a place in the disciplinary text, even if it is only denunciation followed by rehabilitation; Marxism is held responsible for the gulag and then, depoliticized, made safe for sociology.

To appear truly inclusive, the text follows its disqualification of the margins with their splitting into safe and wild versions, suggesting a rehabilitated version of one of them as official knowledge. Splitting mediates between disqualification and rehabilitation, ensuring both that the centered margins will be "central" (that is, non-Marxist, nonfeminist) enough and that the text will be able to unname the centered margin, sanitizing it, by giving that name to emphatically repugnant practices both discrediting the writing and precluding other versions under that name. Margin is centered only by being *re*marginalized, affording the text full control over the disposition of protest and thus silencing real opposition as nonscience.

Science's arrogance is revealed perhaps most dramatically in the license it takes both in centering the margins, disqualifying their politics under the aegis of science, and affixing its name to authoritarian practices that scandalize the western sensibility with its highly visible inequality—prison camps, hatred of men, and so on. In this sense margins' disciplining is not so much temporally segmented as simultaneously overlapping moments in the reformulation of writing's protest. The depoliticization of marginalia is reinforced by and reinforces the equation of Marxism and Soviet practice; utopia is revealed to be a nightmare. The text mitigates the margins in its audacious decision to split the opposition between good and bad versions—science and authoritarian politics. This only further marginalizes the marginal, thus making the center safe for the disciplined opposition that completes and corrects it while scandalizing what is made to pass for "Marxism" and "feminism" in the eyes of unwitting readers.

In constructing a split between the two versions of opposition, engulfing one and excluding the other, the text chooses to overlook the fact that an important version of Marxism (and, less clearly, feminism) defies its centering just as it refuses to equate itself with a singular blueprint of social change or regime, holding out for a universalism that, while far from being realized, is no less valid for that. It is not simply that the text gets Marxism "wrong" but that its standard of validity—representation—is foreign to a Marxist version vesting truth in truthful practice, thus in history.

Marxism cannot be disassembled and then plundered for its "insights" any more than it can be evaluated as science. The text distorts Marxism *in opposition to itself* because it opposes the unity of truth and politics argued for by Marx as a corruption of its representational version of knowledge—that of claimed science. The bourgeois text does not accept that Marx's so-called "science" is not a mirror of the world at all but a reconstruction of its deepest structural dynamic, its historicity or susceptibility to becoming something *other* than what it "is" in the present. Marx's critique of the alienation of labor assumes that alienation alienates precisely because it is nearly inaccessible to the untheorizing eye (that he tries to make good in his own theoretical practice).

Marx constructed concepts like "surplus value" to address the labor contract in terms of its dialectical potential for exploding on the basis of its imbedded contradictoriness that no text can contain. Capitalism deconstructs where discipline fails to contain desire. The emergent outcome of an unjust labor contract, surplus value is a construction of what *appears* to be fair exchange through which both capitalist and worker derive something of value from their relationship. Bourgeois science in pursuit of certain naturelike socioeconomic laws "sees" only a flattened world of surface appearances reflected by a seemingly presuppositionless text. It thereby reproduces the power of the social, here the wage nexus, by in effect naturalizing it; economism is a prototype of self-reproducing discourse at one with the world it reflects, hence constitutes. A literary version of writing recognizing the constructed character of the apparently unconstructed listens to itself write as a construction, no more incontrovertible than other versions. As such, in providing a different account of accounts it keeps in mind, even celebrates, its own worldly desire. This fiction recognizes that there is no directly accessible generic world; by understanding its worldliness in this sense writing does not refuse to construct a complex world using concepts like surplus value, sexual division of labor, or patriarchy but makes their historicity—their artifice—thematic as a way of developing them.

Conceptlessness as epistemological relativism or nihilism, a tendency of poststructuralism and so-called feminist method, secretly capitulates to the flattened, frozen horizon reflected and thus reproduced by science. Difficulty is not an indictment if it interrogates its own dialectical relation to the world under view. To eschew abstraction in the name of existential freedom from abstracting social forces is the impasse of every idealism. Marx, differently, modeled a science that could think the complexly overdetermined nature of domination in order to address this complexity politically, although I would add here that this rethinking—science—is also a political transformation in its own right. Refusing to be merely poetry, although recognizing its poetic moment, theory confounds the scientific text by offering accounts of actual and possible worlds without adequately inscribing them as a way of completing them. This alternative concept of science deals in "facts" *knowing all the while that there are no obdurate facts*. Nonpositivist and positivist versions of science thus share the premise that facts do not exist apart from the words we use to cover them. They differ in that in concealing its constitution as mere reflection positivism embraces the power of its constitutiveness, submerging in its worldly interest the supposed authority of presuppositionless objectivity —discipline.

A nonidentical, literarily emboldened text derives a different kind of authority, admitting its constitutiveness as a way of generalizing the constitutive powers of the poor as well as the rich, women as well as men, people of color as well as white, third world as well as first and second worlds. This is not the authority of science embarrassed by its own authored nature, constructing the world conceptually in spite of its pretense of presuppositionlessness. It is the appeal of a self-confident writing that shamelessly inserts itself in history as a wedge between present and future, the headlong drive toward a new version of the world *exemplified by its own literary exuberance*.

Literariness is simply writing's awareness that it is being written from an inexorable depth of authorial desire. It then must choose itself in the defiant act of advocacy *for* itself, recognition of one's driving subtext incomplete without the prose that puts words to it—that *reasons for* it. In the eleventh of his "Theses on Feuerbach" Marx announces that philosophy exists to change the world "as well as" to understand it; he says more than he is conventionally read to mean. For Marx to philosophize is *already* a prefiguration of liberation and not just a map (strategy, guide, tool) leading us toward the buried treasure. Thus he turns upside down the priority of technical and figural iteration over speculation in opening the way for a life that listens to itself live, a theoretical life, one might say, if that did not immediately conjure the image of its own passivity and elitism—theory as *against* practice.[9] For Marx, theorizing as thought's thought of itself in relation to the big world would join socialist community intertextually without abolishing people's individuated nonidentity to it.

The person unashamed to write takes back cognition and expression and thereby begins to take control politically. Bad science fears theory as a version of the literary that, unlike fiction, claims validity explicitly and therefore arrogantly rewrites it as official science (e.g., "surplus value" tested: economism; misogyny reduced to gender differentiation and women's "role strain"). Yet good science is unafraid to announce the power of word over world not simply as a semiotic medium but as a form of intelligible life itself, our expressive connection to others, nature, and ourselves.[10] Habermas's recent (1984, 1987) argument for a shift from what he calls the "paradigm of consciousness" to the "paradigm of communication" grasps the constitutiveness of talk in overthrowing the model of the reflective subject enshrined in western idealist philosophy. The western model of the subject cuts people off from public life in the worst alienation of all: isolation.

In this light, science's text fights marginalia by assimilating it to the paradigm of consciousness, banalizing it merely as disciplinary knowledge reflective and thus duplicative of the existing state of affairs. The margins resist the center most effectively by writing in a way that explicitly sheds the paradigm of consciousness, celebrating its difference from discipline without abandoning its effort to expose representation as a construction that, once written, only reproduces a heteronomous world heteronomizing *it*. Writing read through a paradigm of communication is infected with worldliness as well as its own subconsciousness, on the one hand constrained by its topic and on the other by its subtext. "Communication" in this light is not only person-person exchanges but the numerous concatenated, layered articulations between and among word, text, and subtext constituting any version. Literature is "communication" sensitive to the simultaneous influences of the one on the other; writing commits itself to bringing about a certain worldly state of affairs— here, peaceful writer-reader relationships—out of its various embodiments and interests issuing in "this" particular text. The more subtext is able to "communicate" with its surface text, the more writing will accept itself as intentional activity engaging with other people in a way that extends textual to societal openness.

The more marginal theory is, the more self-consciously literary, the more threatening it will be to a mode of science that eschews communication for representation, alternatively understanding communication, whether person-person or subtext-text, as the electricity of revolt—imploding the paradigm of consciousness imprisoning subjectivity in its own privacy. Ultimately, the difference between Habermas's paradigms of consciousness and communication is simply the difference between representation and literary artifice, science and fiction; it is no surprise that the disciplinary text wants to prevent people from writing, indeed from believing that they can write, lest they also believe that they can take control of the totality of relations comprising production and reproduction—thus continually reinventing the world as an artifact, a piece of fiction playfully and transformatively intended.

Prophecy Failed: Testing/Taming the Left

The main text aims to disqualify and then rehabilitate Marxism by splitting it into good and bad versions of itself simply because Marxism is the most systematic challenge to the hegemony of bourgeois science and the bourgeois world; bourgeois *text* is the circuitry between the two. This is not at all to say that there is a single prepotent Marxism or that extant Marxisms manage effectively to be marginal in their self-understanding as a textual practice but only to recognize the persistent dialogue between sociology and Marxist oppositions. The text tames the renegade left by evaluating it in terms of its supposedly indubitable criterion of validity, the conclusion that Marx's "predictions" were wrong opening the way for the centering of Marxism as conflict theory or Marxist sociology.

For itself Marxism has often been only too willing to have itself evaluated in terms of adequate criteria of proof and prophecy in its own unfortunate claim to be science; Engels played the game of the bourgeois text and *lost*, the failure of an "inevitable" socialist revolution vitiating the Marxist project altogether. Evaluated purely with reference to criteria of adequate to the apparent present, that is *outside of (the) history* to which it would contribute as its radical rupture, Marxism is an epistemological failure. No revolution yet, no revolution ever.

The first move of the text is to bring home the idea that Marxism is a relic, no longer fitting the facts of postindustrial America.

> Marx did not foresee how capitalism itself would change. Capitalism is no longer a system of family-owned firms but one of huge corporations owned by millions of people. You may own some shares yourself but that doesn't make you a "capitalist." . . . Then who are the capitalists whom Marx hated so bitterly? They might be the top executives in the corporation who actually manage the firm. But if so Marx's theory is still wrong, because executives are not owners but salaried employees. Marx considered ownership the only standard for determining who is a capitalist. He thought salaried managers would not be driven to exploit workers. After all, the profits don't go directly to *them*. . . . Rather than exploiting workers, the ordinary stockholder today does not control the corporation at all. The capitalist that Marx had in mind was the entrepreneur who set up a business and managed it himself—the typical "robber baron." In Marx's day that was a fair picture of a capitalist. But not today. The modern capitalist doesn't own the company, but only a small part of it. And the workers, since they are doing very well themselves, have little reason to hate the owners. (Spencer and Inkeles 1979, 444–45)

The text here follows its proto-Weberian analysis of the decentered corporation (Berle and Means 1933) in which no one dominates with the ringing declaration that the workers "are doing very well themselves" and thus "have little reason to hate the bosses." Affluence coupled with bureaucratic differentiation, and particularly the separation of ownership and control, prove Marx wrong.

At a deeper level, it is suggested that rebellion must spring from "hatred [of] the owners," a highly problematic assumption from Marx's essentially metapsychological point of view. He sought to expunge this sort of emotional or moral reductionism—hate/love—from his critique of capitalism by instead suggesting that the final cataclysm of the economic order will be a virtually natural product of immiseration triggered by the rise in unemployment as capitalism staggers from crisis to crisis. Poverty occasioned by the gargantuan excesses of one-sided capital accumulation would prepare the structural ground for the intervention of enlivening text into the flux of an indeterminate history. Whether or not the poor had to "hate" their masters was irrelevant to Marx because he understood that consciousness could all too easily be manipulated with utter disregard to the subordinating reality, provoking what Marcuse (1964) called "euphoria in unhappiness."

The text paints a picture of generalized contentment on the basis of which it announces Marx "wrong."

> Contrary to Marx's predictions, communism is not very attractive to workers in the advanced capitalist societies, who are actually quite well off. Most European societies have strong socialist labor parties but weak communist parties. (Spencer and Inkeles 1979, 444)

The euphorically happy working-class, "doing very well themselves," even "quite well off," shun what the text calls "communism." This small textual fragment conceals and thus reveals many explosive constructions of the kind I mentioned in the preceding section on marginalia. First, the text echoes the standard observation that the western working class has become bourgeois as a ground for rejecting Marxism and its prophetic mistakes. But the notion that basically powerless people are "doing very well themselves" and are "well off" misses Marx's notion of the alienation of labor, a virtually universal trait of the disciplinary text relentlessly taking encouragement from rising per capita incomes in the West and an attendant consumerism. The near absence of massive unemployment in the United States is thought to vitiate Marx's prophecy of an inexorably falling rate of profit. The status seekers and conspicuous consumers attest to the muting of class contradiction; in 1867, the year the first volume of *Capital* was published, capitalist contradictions seemed unavoidably to be sharpening, leading in short order, it was expected, to the final "expropriation of the expropriators"—the end of prehistory and beginning of socialist history.

But Marx misunderstood the crime of capital against labor not simply as economic imbalance—Rolls Royces versus Chevettes—but in structural terms as the differential ownership and control of the means of production (and now, left-wing feminists add, of reproduction), poverty being a thoroughly mediated moment of capitalist hegemony over labor's product. Marx (1961) makes clear in the *Economic and Philosophical Manuscripts* that the alienation of labor is a totality of powerlessness in which the working class is denied not only a decent wage but also job security, control over the working process, humane relations with bosses, fellow workers, and even with nature, indeed *all* constitutive efficacy—the ability to think, write, paint, make love. And the discourse of the power of the social only deepens labor's powerlessness.

Rooted in the mitigated Marxism of so-called "conflict theory," the neo-Weberian sociology of stratification substitutes a narrow economistic "measure" of alienation—annual income, level of education, occupational prestige, so-called SES or socioeconomic status—for Marx's broader criterion of powerlessness. This is partly to demonstrate in quantitative terms that workers are now "quite well off" and therefore do not need socialism and partly to further the text's verve for quantification per se, beginning in 1967 with Blau and Duncan's *The American Occupational Structure* and now extending through the quantified Marxism of Erik Olin Wright (1979). The disqualification of Marxism on grounds of failed prophecy turns on the thesis of working-class *embourgeoisement;* capitalism survives Marx's expectation of its collapse by in effect paying off the structurally alienated. The two-car garage, "even" for those who carry lunch pails, undercuts the Marxist "prediction" of sharpening class conflict on seeming empirical grounds along with the "hatred" of capitalists by workers that, according to the canonical text, must be present for socialist revolution. This replaces Marx's notion of the totalizing alienation of labor—dehumanization—with a narrow Weberian measure of attainment, an accumulative index of well-being including both objective and subjective "dimensions" (Centers 1949), number of cars and VCRs as well as reported "happiness." That the majority of Americans may report satisfaction with their jobs, and even find them creative and fulfilling, gives the lie to a dinosaurlike Marxism wedded to a simplistic, even mythic binomial structuralism: center against margin, the zero-sum game construing your gain as my loss.

As contemporary sociology reduces alienation to personal accumulation, from cars to joy, "proof" abounds that the western industrial countries are veering away from the apocalyptic scenario written for them by Marx in the mid-nineteenth century; they have managed to create a world in which virtually everyone seems to get *something* in the way of allocative spoils. Absolute deprivation is supposedly supplanted by the relative deprivation of keeping up with the Joneses. The text links the *embourgeoisement* of the working class explicitly with their rejection of "communism," although it is acknowledged that "strong socialist labor parties" abound in western Europe. This is triply distorting. It truncates Marx's concept of alienation into a simple measure of attainment along Weber's three axes of conjoined socioeconomic status; it vitiates Marxist prophecy and therefore Marxism; and it splits marginalia into good, social democratic, scientific and bad, communist versions of itself.

This inaugurates a systematic textual politics blaming Marx for the gulag and thus converging with the neoconservative "new philosophers" in France and a host of less erudite right-wing groups from the John Birch Society to the Republican party today advancing politically by ridiculing the socialist/ Soviet "evil empire." The text suggests that people do not favor communism as Stalinism while conceding that they may nonetheless legitimately support what are called "strong socialist labor parties." Presumably this includes the Labour party in England but not the Socialist party in France under Mitterand and

Greece under Papandreou. This misses the fact that the communist parties of Europe are the for the most part modeled on the centralist lines of the Communist party of the Soviet Union under Lenin and Stalin, in crucial respects violating Marx's central stress on the importance of democratic, self-organizing socialism. The name "communism" was taken over by Soviet leaders and theorists since 1917 to describe the immature statist or command socialism of the early Russian revolution, ripping it out of the context of Marx's own work which itself was frequently ambiguous about the seeming developmental trinity of capitalism, socialism, and communism—the last being presumably the final stage of development characterized by the withering away of the state among other things.

The text accepts at face value that the communist party of France embodies Marx's meaning of communism, thus implying that its lack of popular support indicates deficiencies in original Marxism, notably in Marx's overexuberant prophecy of increasing polarization between the classes along with deepening immiseration. But the various communist parties of western Europe are so authoritarian they do little to warrant the support of people who desire an end to all hegemony, refusing to exchange the "communist" kind for those of capitalism, sexism, and racism. And the "fact" that the "socialist labor parties" are "strong" in Europe should give apologists little additional comfort for in many respects the established socialist parties are more radical—that is, less accomodational and more administratively decentralized—than the Communist Parties, making them that much more threatening to the interests of capital.

Where the communist party is often the establishment party, socialist parties are frequently more militant in their opposition to international capital and both American and Soviet imperialism. The text's inference of working-class contentment from two-car garages and a disinclination among workers to support western communist parties is made to order. It disqualifies Marxism as bad politics—official communist Party policy and practice—as if the Kremlin honchos and their western and eastern henchmen really pay attention to Marx's theory of alienated labor and his attendant vision of a humane socialism returning the person to herself and himself.

> Another reason [why Marx has been neglected by American sociologists] is that his predictions about the future of industrial capitalism were hopelessly wrong. He did not foresee that individual capitalists would be largely replaced by corporations. He did not anticipate that the wealth of industrialism would create a much larger middle class or that the poor would be better off, both relatively and absolutely, than they were in his own time. He was even wrong in predicting that socialist revolutions would take place in highly industrialized societies. Without exception, the uprisings have taken place in such countries as

Russia, China and Cuba when they were advanced agricultural societies. Very few western sociologists accept Marx's view that historical forces will lead us inevitably to a classless society. (Robertson 1983, 250)

Marx is rendered archaic by his inability to "predict" both the growth of the so-called middle class and the ascendance of the working class out of the depths of grinding poverty. The main text retrospectively hinges its disqualification of Marxism on this alleged historical twist of fate detouring western capitalism around the apocalypse "predicted" by Marx on the basis of his mid-19th-century projection of the iron laws of capital. The text to clinch the argument states that there have been no "exceptions" to the rule that socialist "uprisings"—a Marxist concept at all?—have taken place only in "advanced agricultural societies" like Russia and China and not in the industrialized countries of Marx's prophecy. This strains credibility where, like the version above, it categorizes the "uprisings" in Russia and China (is *that* all they were?) as socialist ones, imbued with Marx's galvanizing vision. This both discredits Marxism for being patently authoritarian, as the Soviet Union and China certainly are, and, as well, for misreading history as a teleology toward socialism. If it was, why does the "end" occur in backward societies?

Marxism is wrong because, at the very least, "socialist uprisings" broke out where he least expected them, to be explained by a sociology that understands their detour around advanced capitalist countries in light of the economy's ability to mute, and through the welfare state even resolve, what Marx called its contradictions. Finally, on this basis, much of the "evidence" being in, "few" sociologists in the West accept Marx's deterministic view of history announcing an inevitable socialism, a "classless" society. This only deepens the fatalizing fiction of science enshrining some classfulness—inequality—as a socio-ontological necessity, the usually authoritarian revolution having occurred, against Marx's prophecy, in relatively backward societies.

"Many" (all minus very "few") sociologists cannot be wrong inasmuch as the text tries to heal the split between an incomplete world and the literary practice completing it; the preponderance of professional judgment like that of expert court testimony defines a certain unequivocal reasonableness subtly hemming in dissenting opinion. The sentence beginning "very few sociologists" comes at the end of a vigorous denunciation of Marx's philosophy of history, exuding most sociologists' contempt for Marx's teleological fanaticism, his "dialectical" certainty that capitalism would close prehistory with its demise.

Although as we shall see, Marxism's frequent claim to scientificity eases the burden of disqualification inasmuch as it allows Marx's prophecies to be read simply as "predictions" and thus to be tested out of existence—two-car garages and mass contentment—it also challenges the authority of bourgeois sociology claiming a monopoly of "validity." Professional sociologists rejoice that "Marx was wrong" because, otherwise, they would be out of jobs, presumably as in the Soviet Union where until recently sociology has been banned as unnecessary in a contradiction-free society. The Soviets have something there, although they inhabit the wrong society in which it could happen; Marx's audacity to predict that communism will bury "us" is matched by the matter-of-fact dismissal of Marxism as failed prophecy reflected in the statistical consensus—all minus "very few"—that, as such, as stated, becomes invariably a normative one.

Only fools can look facts in the face and still cling to their fantasies. And Marxism hastens its own disqualification by too frequently blustering with bravado about its own scientificity, thus only opening itself to bourgeois "falsification" in face of an evidently recalcitrant, even improving history. Once "disproven," Marxian prophecy is permanently laid to rest.

> The fact that communist revolutions have come in backward, rural nations rather than advanced, industrial countries is an embarrassment to Marxist theorists. Also, the omission of peasants from his class concepts was probably a serious flaw in Marx's work. (Stark 1985, 203)

The temptation is almost overwhelming to reject Marxism "because" the revolution did not occur when and where it should have; text takes comfort in the distorted meteorology of original Marxism as a subtext using any excuse to falsify the original theory it conceals. The charge of false forecast is confused with what was to have been predicted in the first place, the "communist revolution." A different, better version would defend Marxism on the grounds that the so-called communist revolution, said to be communist both by the "communists" and their vigorous western opponents, is not really communist at all. Communism requires the self-destruction of state power, a crucial component of Marx's original version of a postcapitalist society (and, circularly, of my version of him).

This confusion of communism is so easily made (even Susan Sontag, who should know better, called communism—presumably all versions of it—"fascism with a human face") because since 1917 we have used the state-socialists' name for themselves, "communists," thus rejecting Marx's vision on unacceptably nominalist grounds. But communism is a life devoted to the interrogation of itself as an endless literary practice; no one owns or can exhaust the word. That, as the text proclaims, "Marxist theorists" are "embarrassed" by left-wing agrarian revolutions (earlier the text called them "advanced agricultural" countries, but no matter) is not to be taken at face value. Certainly, from the first hints of the Show Trials in the 1930s to Stalin's death in 1953 with the subsequent horrifying revelations of the full extent of his terror, Sontag and many others before her who grew disillusioned with the Soviet Union are

embarrassed that they clung faithfully to the Soviet experience shrewdly calling itself Marxist and communist. The Soviets in monopolizing the discourse
of Marxist eschatology sought left-wing legitimacy and protected themselves
against internal challenges (just as sociology today claims science for itself).

Yet the text is wrong to think that "Marxist theorists" have given up on every
version of communism, commune-ism after all, simply because the name was
once used to cover the gulag, anymore than one might believe after the fact
that the slogan "Work Will Set You Free" over the gate at Auschwitz really
reflected what was going on inside or because in Reagan's America the poor
have ketchup, a "vegetable," they are well-nourished. Indeed, to many of us
the Communist version of the name communism is only a further incentive
to resist its sovietization in support of a more dialogical version of a good
society, whether or not we continue to draw self-consciously on the Marxist
tradition as a resource for our utopian imagery: if not (the name) communism,
then ideal speech situation, rationality of gratification or pleasure of the text.
Does it matter? It *does not* if we recognize that these names are all versions of
a better form of life in which the peaceful dialogical proliferation of versions is
itself what we mean, and live, by a new society—epistemological democracy
becoming a substantive principle of social organization.

"Communism" accepted as communism, Sontag's fascism with a human
face, allows Marx's version of a new life to be discredited; if he was wrong
about that, surely he was wrong about other things. The text's response to
Marxism is that Marx has not met the test of time, history having laid waste to
his original prophecies, indeed turning them virtually upside down—affluence
in the West, what passes for communism in the East. The text as presuppositionless copy (hence a discourse of the power of the social) tellingly never
raises, let alone systematically pursues, the issue of communism's desirability.
This is both because science does not advocate anything and, contradictorily, because the answer is intended to be self-evident. Who would not prefer
the Golden Arches to gruel in the gulag? Science assails Marxism for its
misbegotten developmental scenario, with communism springing virtually full
blown from the brow of exhausted capitalism. Most disturbing to science is
not Marx's communal imagery (for that appeals to most of us, I suspect, on
all sorts of levels) but his code to unlock the riddle of history phrased in the
tone of science, albeit the mystical science of dialectics. Ironically enough,
science rejoices in Marx's failure to have advanced his science as long as that
advancement would have jeopardized, indeed demolished, the world to which
the social text clings like a remora on a shark.

Marxism is politically incorrect not so much for its Sisyphean communism,
more remote today than ever in a time when official Communism is an utter
negation of the spontaneously organized communism of Marx and the Paris
Commune. In its opposition of science by science, positivist and linear by

dialectical, Marxism gives the lie to science's ideal of a single engulfing text accounting for conflict as well as order, nature as well as history. Where bourgeois science wants to end history by writing the last text, obedience acted out identically as freedom, Marx's science wants to *begin* history by writing a text to negate, not complete, the world, shattering the power of words—labor contract, religion, bourgeois economic theory. Marxism blasphemes where it understands even scientific prose as "ideology," as a source of worldly oppression, thereby in science's eyes weakening its own validity by disempowering the covert constitutiveness of writing, representation read to be ontology. Unlike science, Marx's writing shrieks with the pain of the damaged life, disturbing the reverie of the disinterested text only reflecting a dreary, dreamless world.

The text portrays such a pleasant, uncontradictory order that, set against the brutal images of Afghanistan, Albania, allegedly socialist elements in the Middle East, and of course the Soviet Union, there is little reason to salvage Marx's image of commune-ism from the dustbin of history. Alleged communist facts "disprove" his prophecy of communism, thereby discrediting his whole glimpse of a new life. It is not only a case of blaming the messenger but of despising the message's form, a text self-consciously enjoining action to validate the truth of its own version. Science eases the pain with the balm of its contemplativeness idealized as the regulatively peaceful stance of the scientist who, by his or her own example, would have world peace modeled on peaceful writer-reader relations that become a universal rule.

> To be sure, there is poverty in capitalist societies, but most of the poor are unemployable. The workers have done well. The current high rate of unemployment in North America has caused some hardship, it's true, but with unemployment insurance and other benefits it is by no means as severe as Marx predicted. (Spencer and Inkeles 1979, 445)

The text disqualifies Marxism for inverting progress and regress and then explains—away—the remnants of regress (Merton's dysfunctions) in a shamelessly reactionary defense of freedom's ring. The poor are excluded from progress's center simply by being "unemployable," matching Reagan's rationalizing nominalism—ketchup equals vegetable—with a version of his scholastic distinction between the needy and "truly" needy, only the second of which deserve state assistance.[11] The text dismisses the poor, the unemployed, as "unemployable," telling us nothing and thereby everything; a neoconservative text if ever there was one, this not only blames the victim but also rewrites victimhood as a generic disability defying social engineering.

It is announced shamelessly, against Marxist science, that workers have "done well" and therefore that Marx was wrong in his "prediction," capitalism's social problems being merely quantitative—"by no means so severe"—

and not qualitative. Science proceeds with appropriate sobriety in counterpoint to Marx's Dionysian passion, truncating the usual liberal textual politics—science plus a modicum of compassion—into the cynical apology that passes for social philosophy and morality today (Nozick, Friedman, Bloom, sociology), no free lunch but, no matter, most people can pay to eat.

6

Disciplining the Dialectical Imagination

Lawless Marxism

The Soviet Union's political system is based on the ideas of Karl Marx and Friedrich Engels. (Eshleman and Cashion 1985, 425)

That the so-called communist revolution, said to be owed to Marx, occurred in Russia and not in the more industrialized West demonstrates the failure of Marxism as science to predict where and when the revolution would happen, resonating his failure to foresee the internal reform and thus salvation of capitalism (e.g., the welfare state's minimally redistributive mechanisms protecting legitimacy by keeping the poor alive and thus in check). In addition, having taken place in "Russia," the so-called communist revolution was pinned on Marxism as its just dessert, the inevitable outcome of its failed prophecy (contradictorily, yes, but also convincingly since the Cold War endures). The text has jumped at the chance to blame Marx for Stalin; at the same time it has vitiated the credibility of his politicized science on the basis of his failure to "predict" the site and date of the revolution.

Never mind that the unforeseen upsurge in St. Petersburg might have been unforeseen precisely because it was not "Marxist," not a product of mature contradictions of the kind described in the *Manifesto* and *Capital*, for hay can be made of the Soviet pride in Lenin's having been a Marxist of one sort of another. The year 1917 punctually split the left into good and bad versions of itself, the "tools" of Marx's scientific analysis of presumably generic conflict versus the gulag Marxism called Communism by the Soviets themselves; the analysis pieced together with those of Weber will emerge below as so-called conflict theory.

Sociology's Marxism fails, then, both because it reads history incorrectly, failing to understand capitalism as the positive finality it is, and because it gives rise to a politics bypassing modernization by skipping political democracy and free labor en route to industrialization, the Soviet police state. *Because* Marx got history wrong, Lenin had to intervene to turn it around, thus changing the timetable—capitalism, socialism, then communism—that Marx had originally laid out for the unfolding of dialectical laws. Instead the dialectic was to come out of the barrel of a gun, not strictly because Marx "predicted" it but because his inferred blueprint of the workers' state could be actualized in no other way, industrialized societies moving rapidly away from socialist possibility as they continued to mature. Lenin and Stalin were all that remained once history was subtracted from Marx, the providential handmaidens of teleological politics.

The text discredits Marxist science as bad prediction, deriving a license for Lenin and Stalin's "violence" from the rump of Marx's writing. It then recenters the thin remainder as the addition of economism and generic conflict analysis to mainstream sociology, a textual pastiche that has become second nature. The recentering of the mitigated margin splits Marxism into good bourgeois science and bad Soviet politics, both factored out of Marx's original account of a dialectical history—capitalism-socialism-communism. Ironically, virtually alone in reading Marx's original developmental scenario as the indeterminate construction it was, Lenin moved to start the revolution from the battleship Aurora, hurrying what otherwise may not have happened at all.

Marx's writings thus go the way of the other millennial prophecies that get the eschatological calendar wrong and acquire simply a minor scholarly significance, usually a place in the so-called history of ideas. The Russian revolution gave Marxism credibility as a text that *matters,* even if, in the process, it disproved him. Sociology would have us believe that the teeming hordes outside the Winter Palace all clutched copies of *Capital* or, at least, the *Manifesto.* Lenin represented a "Marxist" necessity (at least Marxist to its bourgeois critics and Lenin) that challenged liberal scientism not in its positivist account of the relation between text and world but only in its version of who should be the writers—Party epigones instead of the business and state elites along with their academic underworkers.

Today the specter haunting western countries is the official Communism of Zinoviev and the original Third or Communist International passed off as the authentic correction of Marx's prophetic version.[1] Russia having missed the stage of capital and instead hurtling directly from agrarian Czarism to Soviet industry under the imprimatur of Lenin's vanguard version of Marx, Marxism-Leninism survives the challenge of the western welfare state largely unforeseen by Marx. The state saved capital by mediating between capital and labor, albeit on the side of capital. Leninism is Marxism today "because" in western eyes Lenin succeeded where Marx did not, effecting the textual politics of *Capital* by, in Gramsci's terms, leading a revolution "against" *Capital.* Ontologized as truth's bottom line in a world making reason an instrument, success becomes the criterion of political truth. Lenin's Marx is thus an improvement over the defeated Marx of western Marxism not least in the sense that it has something to show for itself, the palpable infrastructure of the Soviet empire—wedding-cake Stalinist architecture, Red Square, Soviet ICBMs, where Marx is objectified only in his theoretical treatises and by his gravestone in London.

Marxism needs a national hockey team that periodically plays the teams fielded by the free west for us easily to understand their opposition in concrete terms. Marxism threatens because soi-disant "Marxists" do, and thus a kind of double identification takes place in which the Soviet claim to be Marxist matches our need to concretize, personalize, and nationalize a discernible ideological opponent. This opponent is found at the Olympics as well as at superpower summit meetings adjudicating the political and economic problems of their respective client states. The Soviet version of Lenin Russifies Marxism and paves the way for the western identification of Soviet Marxism as the real thing; all others are academic, obscurantist pretenders. The Russification of Marxism simplifies matters considerably for sociology. It affords a visible opponent; it splits Marxism by marginalizing the already marginal, thus leaving the non-Soviet "insights" of Marx available for sociologization; and, perhaps most important, it exhausts possible Marxism by being the second better version of the only two possible ones—the "sociological" Marx, he who can be read to have produced testable "hypotheses."

The disciplinary text in this way supports the neoconservative conflation of Marxism and the gulag in the name of science, fueling the attack on all social and philosophical programs aiming to end inequality categorically. The gulag is heard as eloquent testimony to the power of the social: the Soviets have tragically failed to abolish "stratification," as if the original Bolsheviks really believed in Marx's vision of communism as the fundamental leveling of inequalities but in face of the exigencies of "building socialism" could not do without them as transitional expedients. According to the text, an implacable necessity intervened to prevent the Stalinist architects of the Soviet new person from dispensing with bureaucracy, hierarchy, and an imperatively coordinated division of labor, offering perverse evidence that classlessness is a utopian fiction, as such even counterrevolutionary. The Soviet experience is treated almost as the Soviet experiment, methodically "testing" the Marxian hypothesis that socialism would abolish inequality once and for all, Lenin's euphemistic democratic centralism constructed as an honest empirical comparison between democracy and centralism.

In this way, many western opponents of Marxism are less critical of what is passed off by the Soviets as Lenin's faithful version of Marx than are other Marxists who virtually from the beginning recognized the continuity between Czarism and so-called Communism and, then, the continuity among communist state socialism, fascism, and capitalism. The left history of the left is much tougher on apparatchik Marxism than are western liberals who want to believe what they see; their burden is eased considerably if the Soviet "experiment" is rejected (on "evidence") as the definitive Marxist test/text. Indeed, the various freezes and thaws in Cold War politics—Stalin, Stalin's death, detente, the Helsinki Accord, Olympic boycotts, Afghanistan, now the trendy Gorbachevs—indicate a far less realistic appraisal of the Soviet elite by western scholars and journalists than found within the Marxist critique of the Soviet Union as a police state and nothing more.[2] Even Reagan's "evil empire" gives them more credit than they deserve, imputing more rationality to internal and external politics than is really warranted. Once Soviet Marxism is taken to be all Marxism, undeniably constructed to be the major opponent of the disciplinary text, Soviet practice takes on an episodic importance unwarranted on theoretical grounds, that is, as anything more or less than a writing defending the police state as revolutionary exigency.

It is inevitable that the Russification of Marxism by the American press and academics leads to a contest mentality reflecting our goodness off Soviet badness. After all, liberals still celebrate the Soviet Union "because" they opposed the war in Vietnam, the Reaganization of poverty, Central American policy, American truculence guaranteeing Soviet virtue. In any case, the daily rapportage from Moscow mistakenly comes to represent the "status" of Marxism today, one day Marxism/Moscow as evil empire, the next day a promising society led by the buoyant husband-wife team of the Gorbachevs. Couturier Marxism is absurdly traced back to Marx.

The text in rehabilitating the left's center and further marginalizing its illiberal component—in effect, Marxist sociology versus the gulag—establishes Marx's responsibility for Marxism and particularly Communism, the Marxism of the Soviet Union. This is in spite of Marx's admonition that he was not a Marxist, fearing perversions of his thought as well as recognizing that Marxism is only another version that falsely aims to become an inclusive, thus oppressive, system. The text has to forge a strong analytical link between Marx and subsequent Soviet practice if it is going to divide Marxism into good science and bad politics, neither capable of thinking through and beyond the so-called Marxist categories. In other words, Marxism is a textual practice and not simply a body of knowledge or blueprint to be prised out of the canon and then "applied" to the world after Marx.

> He died in 1883 but his works became official doctrine shaping the policies of many nations throughout the following century. (Spencer and Inkeles 1979, 9)

The word "but" at second glance is not an equivocation about the "official" use of his writings to justify and prohibit certain subsequent practices (as one might have hoped in defending the possibility of unofficial, even oppositional, Marxism). It is only a transitional signifier setting up a counterpoint between Marxism then and now that is *resolved* in the implied continuity between original writing and subsequent interpolation. This is a deft way of pinning the gulag on Marx himself, indeed showing the efficacy of Marx's pen—"many nations"—in translating itself into guns, distinctly shortening the distance between the 1880s and 1980s in the claim that Marxism lives today in Moscow. This constructs the difference between the Marxism about to be disqualified—Russified Marxism "as" the obviously illiberal police state it is—and the safe Marxism of the academy—economism, conflict theory, and the like.

> The writings of Karl Marx, along with those of the Soviet leader Lenin . . . form the basis of a secular ideology called *Marxism,* which gives its believers the same certainty that Christianity or Judaism brings to others. (Hess, Markson, and Stein 1985, 358)

The next step is to construct Marxism as a confluence of Marx's original writings (usually the *Manifesto*, his advocacy document, plus the "economic determinism" of *Capital*, never the *Economic and Philosophical Manuscripts* or *Grundrisse*, rarely the historical-political writings) and those of Lenin. This establishes that Marxism is animated in the particulars of Soviet practice from Politburo to samizdat to hockey team. Further, this couplet of science and politics that the text eventually wants to sever is neither strict science nor politics but *religion,* the standard Enlightenment concept of myth directed at Communist practice. This twists the claim in *German Ideology* about the dominance of "ruling class" ideas over subjugated people as "false consciousness" back upon Marxism itself, now seen to be even more powerful in its appeal than either "Christianity or Judaism."

The unity of Marxian science and politics is dismissed as "ideology," the object of disciplinary rehabilitation saving the ideas in ideology by divesting them of their mythic—that is, transformative—overtone. As "secular ideology," Marxism is automatically disqualified as nonscience, a path of least resistance for a text that wants to Russify Marxism as a hell on earth, *which is then construed as the original aim of Marx's communism.* Marx is read as an apologist for the latter-day Soviet Union in closing the case on "political" Marxism.

> In Marx's vision . . . [the desirable socialist economy] would be what economists have come to call a *command economy,* meaning that economic decision making would not be left to the vagaries of the market but would be placed in the hands of a central planning board. This board would have the enormous task of determining what goods society would produce and in what quantities, and where and how it would produce them. (Light and Keller 1985, 268)

> Socialism also differs from capitalism in that it is not controlled by the marketplace. It has a *planned economy*—the government controls what will be produced and consumed, sets prices for goods, decides what goods the society needs, what are luxuries, and what can be done without altogether. Thus, there is no free market. (Eshleman and Cashion 1985, 446)

The text combines sarcasm couched in irony ("left to the vagaries of the market") with caricature ("enormous task of determining") in tracing Soviet economic centralization and statism back to Marx. This is not to preclude such a reading simply on grounds of interpretive inauthenticity; virtually anything can be found (or lost) in reading that strongly rewrites. But the Russification of Marxism intended as scientific iteration of his work obscures the heterogeneity of possible readings in light of Marx's persistent reluctance to architecture socialism.

The supposed "central planning board" that the text finds in Marx's version is not there *if only* because Marx did not pause to draw up the policies and procedures of incipient socialism, preferring to let the substance of socialism emerge out of the intertextual practices both exemplifying and defining it. Marx may have preferred "central planning boards" or at least believed that they were inevitable. Yet he refrained from the sort of specificity to which the text descends in its version of Marxism as a Soviet practice for which it has *already* made him responsible. He did not advocate a "command economy" simply because he did not spell out any definitive economic model beyond vague but crucial principles of socialist ownership and control, a reluctance instructive in its own right. What is important here is not the supposedly lousy scholarship that does not cite chapter and verse—the point being to interrogate one's *own* reading in light of the desire it reflects and not establish an official version whose reading is reduced to dumb iteration. More revealing is the extraordinary investment of the text in a Russifying version disqualifying Marxist political practice.

The text's conflation of Marxism and Marxism-Leninism is virtually impenetrable on a casual reading in light of the preponderance of existing "common sense" about the identity of Marx, Lenin, and Stalin. That Marx authorized both the command economy and gulag is brought home by the wide variety of illiberal Second and Third World countries calling themselves Marxist or socialist and butchering opponents in their names. "Marxists" from Lenin to Ho and Castro have operationalized their Marxism as economic and political hegemony, only entrenching the conflation of Marx and massacres. The text is half right when it says: "The Soviet Union's goal is very clear: a communist nation run by administrators." Administration, yes, communist (in the sense of commune-ism), no; at least the "communism" claimed by the Soviets is never interrogated as a problem of construction but derived canonically from Lenin's own derivation of Marx (all thirty some volumes worth), as if Lenin was the best, or indeed, for Soviet purposes, *last* reader, after whom "dialectical materialism" is taught like physics or astronomy, without reference to its literary artifice. Communism is instead reduced to a body of conventional truths—"communism" being what Lenin meant Marx meant.

The Leninizing text tries to overcome the gap between a mirrored social nature and people's self-reproducing "fates," Marxist science differing from bourgeois science only in the adjective "dialectical," a principle of nature's unfolding for orthodox Marxists.[3] Both the Soviet and bourgeois texts suppress their own authorial perspectivity and thus the historicity of all texts in the interest of inducing a generalized muteness about the generic power of the social. Although for western science the master text is still being written in the busy work of discipline, Lenin in his version of Marx has already written the Marxist book; Soviet writing is simply canonical exegesis as distinct from ongoing research. Not that this is much of a difference especially where the results are the same—bureaucratic-technocratic administration as the epitome of reason. The posit of a last text has already been articulated within Marxism by Lenin in his defense of the vanguard party as the need for *textual/social control,* even if, as in capitalism, the last text is still an occasion for endless embellishments of it, the busy work of party savants and political educators. Although they do not collect data, like their western counterparts, Leninist scientists keep busy in hagiography.

> Marx thought the victory of the proletariat would end exploitation and that government would be replaced by an "administration of things." He hoped for a humane socialism and did not foresee the rise of totalitarianism as a more likely competitor to capitalist democracy. (Broom, Selznick, and Darroch 1981, 292)

Having lain Soviet Communism at the feet of Marx—as "administration" —sociology doubles back on itself and uses the Russification of Marxism to establish the failure of Marxism/Communism to "end exploitation," stressing the disproportion between Marx's antiquated "humane socialism" and the "totalitarianism" that ensued. This drives a wedge between good and bad Marxism now that Marx's own responsibility for the Soviet "experiment" has been established (lest the gulag be seen purely as an aberration). The text has it all ways here, rejecting Marxism as bad prophecy—no American socialism, the coping mechanisms of state capital having forestalled it—as well as undemocratic centralism. It also puts distance between Marx and the emergent "totalitarianism" to which his utopianizing unavoidably gave rise.

The text wants us to hear that the radical imagination risks the "central planning boards" and KGB by hoping for too much, to "end exploitation" rather than to achieve piecemeal, more presumably attainable goals of the kind encountered in the liberal textual politics of official sociology—godliness, decency, vegetables for the poor. In this surprising twist, it is suggested that Marx begat the gulag not so much because he wanted it, although the text just told us that he did ("central planning boards"), but because he could not avoid it once he turned over the revolution to the commissars who, given a selfish, brutish accumulativeness, arrested many of the acolytes and shipped them off to the biggest chill of all, distant Siberia.

If we know anything about Marxism, it is that Marx's route to "humane socialism" detoured around the procedural but otherwise frequently empty liberties allowing us technically to call capitalism "democratic," as the text does. Again, this splits Marxism into two halves that already coexist tenuously in Marx himself, the utopianized outcome—classlessness—set against the macabre means of achieving it, the millions of wasted lives deemed necessary casualties on the road to a socialist Damascus.

> Marxist ideology notwithstanding, snobbery reigns supreme in the Soviet Union. Those of the "intelligentsia" exhibit contempt for workers far beyond that normally encountered in the United States. (Popenoe 1980, excerpt from Shipler, 292)

As "snobs," the technicians and administrators of the socialist revolution are bound to perpetuate servitude without ever abolishing themselves as temporary servants of a purposeful history. True, but where does Marx, or why should Marxism, require this vanguardism? Again, one suspects that the text finds it already made to order in a Russified version of Marxism that simply repeats and reflects Soviet hierarchy as a generic revolutionary necessity, finding the Politburo, Drzezhinski Prison, and summer dachas for the elite somehow already present in Marx, concretizing phrases like "dictatorship of the proletariat" (but not "dictatorship *over* the proletariat," as Korsch called it). The text takes pains to indemnify Marxism against the "snobbery" found in the Soviet Union by saying "Marxist ideology notwithstanding" at the beginning of the passage, although by even mentioning Marxism the text constructs Marx's culpability for the gulag even if it appears to deny it. As well, Marxism is here "Marxist ideology," as if Marx knew all along that his call for "democracy" was only "ideological" window dressing concealing his (as it turns out correct) "prediction" that socialism would only be achieved on the broken backs of the peasants and proletariat. The text insinuates that Marxist words have always been inauthentic when compared to "Marxist" practice, including the "snobbery [that] reigns supreme everywhere in the Soviet Union."

Finally, to seal the case, it is established (but how?) that Soviet intellectuals are "far" more contemptuous of workers than are intellectuals in the United States, at least "normally." I doubt that this has ever been "studied," nor do I think it should be. But for the text to say this in the guise of indubitability ("normally encountered") as a way of deepening the case against (Russian) Marxism is at best a stretch, especially where this is designed to reflect the populism of American intellectuals.

We are left with the commissar communism Marx had perhaps hoped to avoid but could not, given the logic of his revolutionary politics propped by a dialectic fatefully turning the contingent particulars of revolutionary oppression into self-justifying expediency, in the long run only perpetuating itself. The existence of the Soviet Union is patent proof that Marxism is communism, that communism is the gulag, and that Marx, his "ideology notwithstanding," is inevitably stuck with the political liability of Siberia.

The text tames Marxism by contrasting American affluence and freedom with the horrors of the Soviet Union, a writing that goes beyond simple comparison; it disqualifies Marx's goal of ending alienated labor, the practice of which only seems to deepen it. In this way, the alleged "laws" of capitalism, the world reflected by sociology, are pitted victoriously against the "laws" of socialism proclaimed by Marx as the inevitability of the expropriation of the expropriators, repeated in Kruschev's notoriously misunderstood prophecy at the United Nations to the effect that "we will bury you," the demise of capitalism seemingly written into dialectical law. Marxism has the ambiguous, ambivalent status of being at once scientifically incorrect and correct; it falsely foretells an imminent revolution in the West that has since gone the route of tranquil *embourgeoisement;* and yet it successfully restores "conflict theory" and its attendant economism that sociology extracts from fallen Marxism. Lawlessness is thus turned into lawfulness. The outlaw science that leads to Leninism (not "humane socialism") is disqualified by a version that reserves a niche even for Marxism, albeit so ridiculously domesticated that it turns into anti-Marxism—the veneration of productivism, as we shall see shortly.

All sorts of western Marxists from Lukacs to Habermas have convincingly argued that Marx himself contained a moment of bourgeois scientism, effectively a weapon captured in war and now used against its own forces, where he described Marxism as a natural science of history. However this may be— for there are passages galore in Marx to sustain both scientistic and nonscientistic readings—subsequent Marxists have written representationality into him in a way that ironically facilitates his domestication by bourgeois scholars looking to put Marxism harmlessly to work in everyday sociology; Marxism acknowledges that the world harbors generic "conflict" as well as stasis. This construction of a self-vitiating Marxian scientism is so pedestrian in this Nietzschean age that most sociologists accept what they think is Marxism as legitimate scholarship—basically wrong on the evidence but constructively so, the counterpoint to mainstream truth and thereby, with Hegel, part of the truth itself. Marxian scientism, called "determinism" by the bourgeois text as if *it* were anything but that, extends later Hegel's dialectic of the *Science of Logic*. In their development of the apologetic catechism of dialectical "laws," Lenin and Stalin merely reflect the necessity of their own political privilege.

Western Marxism resists this concept of dialectical closure simply because the ontology of dialectic precludes free agency, essential for overthrowing the developmental "laws" of the dialectic as social nature. Located outside a history that thought would rupture, dialectic instead solicits obedience to an hypostatized master narrative that comes into being only as the illusion of its artifice; thus, revolution is not worth bringing about because it was mistakenly portrayed as an existential choice. The longer dialectical "synthesis" is postponed by a cunning history understood only by party savants, the less likely it is that the masses will be able to work around the vanguard who in the meantime have set themselves up as both teachers and leaders. The preordination of the revolution only precludes it by satisfying the heteronomized masses that the judgment day is bound to arrive, substituting a Marxian myth of progress for the capitalist one—with the same effect, socio-ontological servitude, induced textually.[4]

Marxian scientism legitimates a scientific politics that in Lenin's terms provides truth "from without," defending tight-fisted party rule, even terror, as historically expedient. Substitute the word "corporations" for "party," and the result is the same, as the text ironically realizes, attempting to discredit Marxism but thereby discrediting itself. "In actual practice, the socialist state can be as coercive as a group of stockholders, if not more so." A vanguard prepares the masses for their assigned roles as the revolution nears, deriving its political authority from textual author-ity found in an incontrovertible reading of *Capital*; power resides in epistemology as clearly as it does for positivist science.

But there are other versions of Marx that do not claim scientificity, albeit dialectically, and thereby prevent Marxist lawfulness from being turned into sociological absoluteness once (for whatever reason) the revolution fails, splitting and centering marginal intellectual/political projects and debunking Marxist lawfulness as failed prophecy.[5] As soon as Marx or later Marxists claim the sort of predictive power for their writing as postured by bourgeois science, they enter into contest with bourgeois science on its own turf, severing the theory-practice link so central to Marxism that would "prove" Marxism in the practice of a text prefiguring and thus bringing about a world. If left-wing scientism steps back from the fray and allows itself to be evaluated by criteria of correspondence to the reflected world, it abandons the ground in history that Marx felt would be the connecting wire between what in "Theses on Feuerbach" he called "philosophy" and the "world," again, the former intending both to understand and transform the latter. After all, for nonrepresentational Marxists synthesis is nothing more or less than the contingent advances we may make beyond the zero-point of domination and certainly not an absolute end or beginning of history.

Marxian scientism does not effectively oppose bourgeois science by announcing the inevitability of socialism or communism but, ironically, supports it, joining a common rhetoric of authorial disengagement deciding truth on past evidence and not by argument or practice rupturing the continuum of domination. This neutralizes Marxism that otherwise lives or dies not by prophecy or prediction, which at its most rigorous can only be trend analysis, but by the practice that either brings about socialism, or does not. *Marxism cannot name the socialist world of Marx's dreams (except as justification of Soviet practice) for that world does not exist*, unlike the bourgeois world that reproduces the disciplinary text as its completion. The more Marxism says "science," the more the disciplinary text will submit it to the test, invariably finding it wanting as an explanation of data that science is charged to reflect and thus enact. Marxism freezes nothing but the Siberian waste that is already frozen, offering itself for science's discipline as economism and conflict sociology, the "correction" of bourgeois sociology and thereby a part of it.

Although I would hope that Marx had a different sort of science in mind when he said that Marxism was a natural science of history—a science both understanding and celebrating its own investment in, indeed its constitution of, its object, contradictory capitalism—it is easy to read him otherwise, an Enlightenment determinist guaranteeing socialism in the concepts he used to analyze the imminent death throes of capitalism. When socialism does not arrive, except in Russified form, an enduring Marxian scientificity is integrated by the bourgeois text ecumenically borrowing lawfulness wherever it can find it, not the law of dialectical preordination to be sure—communism following capitalism as spring follows winter—but the law of economic "conflict." This is easily utilized by the main text as a telling stress on industrial-era productivism, the thin veneer of Marxism purged of its failed politics.

> It was inevitable, in Marx's theory, that the workers would become aware of their situation and act collectively to overthrow capitalism, if they did not allow themselves to feel hopeless, or to be duped into believing that they had a chance of moving up in the system, or to be misled by religious promises of a rich life in heaven. These were big *ifs*. Nevertheless, it was inevitable in the long run that the workers would become organized to fight their oppressors and to carry out their historic role in creating a new society. (Denisoff and Wahrman 1983, 312)

The text here undercuts its own "finding" of Marxist scientificity by acknowledging what it calls the "big ifs" standing in the way of socialist synthesis, notably the presence of class consciousness required to connect theory and practice. "In the long run" they would gain this consciousness, however blocked they might be in the shorter term by either the diverting enticements of personal betterment or an abject fatalism expecting little and hoping for less. The text overlooks its own recognition of the essential contingency of Marx's prophecy of socialism, forcing through the conclusion that Marx wrote laws and thus allowing for Marxism's disqualification and subsequent integration on the basis of its vitiation by evidence—history itself. Marxism is thus ironically accommodated as a latter-day version of eternal conflict, a twist on his alleged certainty that the dialectic would end conflict once and for all.

The bourgeois text here "finds" that Marxism is really lawless; yet it makes the Marxian search for invariant patterns of history, its scientificity, a common

ground on which eventually to engulf it in the cause of the world's iteration
—as if Marxism pursues ontology instead of history, a political practice vitiating community with science. The alleged dialectic supposedly guaranteeing
synthesis is flattened into the linear teleology of the bourgeois text, Marxism
upended—no empirical socialism—while its central "insights" into the relevance of economic conflict are retained. The text implies that Marxism can be
rehabilitated once its "predictions" are rendered invalid by history, revolutionary delay deflecting the high hopes, indeed prophecies, ascribed to Marx as
his eschatology.[6]

It is not hard to see that the text here constructs an infallible Marxism
only to scuttle it with the obvious "fact" that capitalism endures; yet as the
text avers, this is less because the elemental contradiction between capital
and labor has been solved than because the state and culture now intervene
to manage economic and psychic crisis respectively—a combination of fiscal
policy and fatalizing social texts. The construction of Marx as determinist or
voluntarist informs the "evaluation" of Marxism today; if the former, Marxism
is dead simply because "wrong," consumerism among other things abounding
to thwart his prophecy of deepening immiseration; and if the latter, Marxism
could be disciplined as a legitimate version unconstrained by the teleology of
dialectic as well as the antiteleology of negative dialectic, Adorno's critique
of positive thinking tending to take life as its own absolutist program.

By contrast, a negative dialectics recognizes that the negative exists in
counterpoint to the possible positive. Critique hopes as well as laments. This
is not a version of Aristotelian incrementalism but simply a recognition of
the undecidability of both writing and history. The text invents a scientific
Marxism precisely because it can that much more easily turn Marxism into
bourgeois text, almost as spies are "turned" from one allegiance to another.

> More than a century after the writing of Marx and Engels, we can see that the
> prediction of capitalism's development and downfall was not exact. Nevertheless,
> Marx's thinking provides many insights into the nature of class conflict and
> political struggles. (Popenoe 1980, 438)

The text exudes ecumenism as a veil for its biting judgment that Marxism
deserves a place on the intellectual scrapheap of history. The text vindicates its
disqualification of Marxism by characterizing its "prediction" as "not exact"
—which is to say the least. But this only reinforces the criteria of scientificity,
including predictiveness and exactitude, that imperil Marxism by disqualifying
its mix of science and politics. Marxism is instead reduced to yet another
version of the power of the social, stressing the inevitability of economic
conflict.

The text betrays its construction of Marxism as science where it praises
Marx's "insights into the nature of class conflict and political struggles." It

writes as if Marx were trying to announce the "nature" of anything at all and not, as I think he really did and in any case as *we* should do, showing that "nature" is intertwined with history and can thus be changed. Conflict was in the "nature" of "society" only for Weber and not for Marx, Weber's essentialism read back into Marx only retrospectively, after the revolution had failed. The text tames Marxism by ascribing to Marx a naturalism that like bourgeois sociology seeks to capture an enduring essence in a name, here "conflict." Marxism thus adds its voice to other versions together comprising the discourse of the power of the social—ever the textual practice of myth (of which religion, ideology, culture are simply versions).

> For Marx, dominant classes always try to stand in the way of inevitable change and in so doing cause conflicts, their own destruction, and changes in the make-up of society. (Orenstein 1985, 331)

The text is studded with *ontologemes,* a more explicitly philosophical version of what Jameson (1981, 76) calls ideologemes, freezing society's dialectical/ historical nature with words like "always" and "inevitable." Sociologized Marxism lacks history; science replaces a politicized version that suggests the world in order to change it. Critique opens nature—for example, "laws" of supply and demand, capital's dominance over labor—to history. Science stills versions of the world suggesting that science itself is a version helping constitute its seemingly naturelike object. "For Marx," dominant classes neither "always" nor never do anything decidably; and if truly "inevitable," changes would not require the resistance of "dominant classes" in order to spark the "conflicts" leading to new synthesis. Being inevitable, they would just happen, beyond the need of text's intervention.

> It is interesting to note that the communist revolutions, which Marx predicted would occur in industrialized societies, have in fact tended to occur in societies like Russia and China when they were going through the transition to industrialization. (Orenstein 1985, 369)

> Over the years Marxists have found certain facts hard to explain. Things simply have not turned out the way Marx predicted. Among these developments are the following.
>
> 1) The communist revolutions have not happened where and when Marx predicted that they would.
>
> 2) Modern corporations are owned by large numbers of stockholders who do not have any say in the management of their "capitalist" enterprises.
>
> 3) The workers in capitalist societies have become richer rather than poorer. (Spencer and Inkeles 1979, 443)

> [CAPTION] The Sandinista regime in Nicarauga illustrates Marx's miscalculations about where and why communist revolutions would occur. He thought the most industrialized capitalist nations such as Germany, Great Britain, and the

United States would be the first to have revolutions. Instead, Marxist revolutions have been restricted to less industrialized societies and have been based mainly on peasant support. (Stark 1985, 204)

Marxism as science is wrong because the "revolution" did not occur when or where Marx thought it would. Yet it is right where, as science once appropriately purged of polemic, it can be read as a set of "predictions," joining it in common cause with the bourgeois text to which it can be assimilated. More scandalous would be a marginal writing that did not make predictions at all (like feminism, which in this sense is harder to integrate, exhibiting too frequently the sentimental antimethodism of the women's movement, hard method being—some would say—male). Once the text exhausts its mockery of Marxism—"over the years Marxists have found certain facts hard to explain"—it restores Marxism by plumbing it for science. Lawless Marxism is legalized by a sanitizing sociology for, after all, Marx could so blatantly err in his so-called predictions because he was overcome with the zealot's passion, politics infecting science with wishful thinking that can be corrected.

Where the text first uses Marx's errors to disqualify the prospect of a classless society altogether, it now sets the stage for restoring Marxism as official sociology by discovering science in it, drawing on their common commitment to the Enlightenment's identity of knowledge and power—albeit weirdly reduced to science's suppression of itself as the will to power. Although the text's rejection of Marxist inaccuracy echoes loudly, at heart the text constructs a Marx who in a manly way sweated out the long hours of research in the British Museum as an exemplar of scholarship, a word used in bourgeois culture to signify the subtraction of the Dionysian from thought.

Marx wrote a natural science of history competing with the bourgeois version, if ultimately to lose (in a way integrating it). After the Cold War had thawed by the late 1960s, American sociology was big enough to make room for a Marxism languishing in the shadows of Stalin and his fellow travelers in the West. The disqualification of Communism opened the way for a Marxism written into the social text as an ontology of conflict, another disciplinary version of the power of the social.

Marx believed that conflict, revolution, and the overthrow of capitalism were inevitable. (Eshleman and Cashion 1985, 30)

All of them?

Lessons of History

Marxism chastised for Communism is Marxism chastened. The text sobers Marxism by disqualifying its prophecy of universal equality, vitiated by the gulag and commissars' privilege; it teaches tempering lessons of history on the basis of accumulated evidence where history is read and then projected into a determinate future. Accumulated capital does not result in crises precisely because accumulated evidence is marshaled to temper rebellion. The text infers not the imminence of communism from the fact that "all history has been hitherto the history of class-struggle" but only more of the same, inequality transformed into a universal rule, a generic requisite of all civilization. Marxism is tempered by being forced to confront its own data indicating the intractability of class structure and thus the folly of fighting it in a wholesale way (a fight, it is said, that inevitably leads to one form of authoritarianism or another). History's arrow points past socialism to a postindustrial capitalism reducing ideological differences to a common disciplinary argot. Marxism is misnamed conflict theory as an intermediate reflection failing to anticipate the Keynesian-primed welfare state along with the other cultural and psychic emoluments of post-WWII America intervening to protect capitalism from its demise.

The social text thus reduces the revolutionary advocacy of Marx to liberal conflict resolution derived from a version of teleological history, the avoidance of the socialist apocalypse requiring "Marxists" to conjure up yet more incremental political strategies. This was a project begun originally with Bernstein's *Evolutionary Socialism*,[7] the benchmark of subsequent social democracy now widely institutionalized from Scandinavia to Britain. Marxian science because it is scientific has the capacity to infer from evidence of the failed revolution that imagery of revolutionary transformation has to be scaled down to fit the facts of the new working class, middle class, technological advance, state and cultural intervention, and the travesty of the Soviet Union. Marxian politics is thus tamed with the proof of its own *scientific* failures to predict the future and yet redeemed by Marx's seeming affiliation to the disciplinary discourse of the power of the social modeled, with Comte among others, on natural science.

Another way of understanding the decline of revolutionary politics is simply in political terms, the opposition having defeated various left-wing margins and movements opposing it both because it was stronger to begin with and because left-wing sectarianism (e.g., 1914) too often precluded a united front.[8] I would argue that Marxian scientism itself helped defeat Marxist politics inasmuch as it contained a moment of socioontological fatalism. Where dialectic delivers world-historical guarantees and not simply negative thought, the faith in dialectic precluded spontaneous mass movements on the basis of socialist preordination, the dialectic defeating dialecticians as diversionary, wasteful mysticism.[9] Indeed, many Marxists today explain the failed revolution as a failure of Marxist science adequately to have understood both capitalism and *Capital*, an as yet infantile science producing the latter-day phenomenon of Marxist study groups poring over Marx's literal economic theory in search of the answer to history's riddle. This is as if economic theory stands apart from political and social theory, thus politics, one of the worst legacies of the mechanical Marxism of the Second International. Infantile science matures to deliver straightforward strategic advice on such things as the IMF, Third World "revolutions," or feminism; it kindles hope about the imminence of socialism.

When the bourgeois text pins the defeated revolution on the revealed inevitability of class inequality, Marxist scientism addresses the failure to read and understand *Capital* as essentially a political failure.[10] In both cases, political defeat defeats a new writing, instead submitting "Marxists" to an extended regime of study; where the one heralds "Marxist sociology," the "insights" of Marx integrated into the disciplinary text blending Marx, Weber, and micro-sociology, the other elaborates Marxology, the exegetical strategy eventually turning study groups into cells.

On the academic scene Marxist "scholars" march through the disciplines to offer each of them a Marxist antidote, thus ironically converging with the integration of Marxism as "insight" into the comprehensive social text. This is not to dismiss reading and writing only as the academic routinization of thought for they need not be, *in fact, they must not be*. Rather this is only to comment on the fetish of scientific Marxism, whether of the study groups or mainstream disciplines. Today many Marxists seek definitive interpretation extrapolated into correct politics; others pursue "Marxist" disciplinary work given license by the disciplines themselves to elaborate their "insights" in an atmosphere both of collegiality and fruitful intellectual crossfertilization, liberal academia exercising tolerance shrewdly by engulfing the margins.

The text requires Marxism to retreat into itself, giving up the grand sweep of its advocacy in favor of both a liberal textual politics and an intellectual ecumenism admitting its mistakes in light of "evidence." The text humbles Marxism with history in the process of its rehabilitation as officially tempered and temperate sociology; radicalism is rehabilitated with the lesson that radical social change is neither possible nor desirable, concluding, with liberal incrementalists since Karl Popper, that revolutionaries are inherently enemies of what he calls the "open society" (1963). The text wants Marxism to confront the gulag as the logic of its own misguided militancy, its confession to be a contribution to the therapeutic beginning of rehabilitation. Marxism is to be made safe by stripping it of its radical hubris (even periodized by Marxists like Althusser as Marx's adolescent phase, surpassed for his later mature science).[11]

The text deepens its case against Marx by submitting to him the bill of Stalinist terror that is generalized into the concept and practice of a generic "totalitarianism." Discipline educates the left to the perverse consequences of advocacy, ultimately integrating Marxism as centrist sociology into a liberalism minimizing if not abolishing inequality; conflict theory "functions" as the conscience of the discipline. The text tempers the passion of Marxian writing by reading into it the penchant for (indeed, necessity of) revolutionary violence, a charge valorizing nonviolence as the appropriately alternative textual-political stance, contrasting the "violence" of radical transformation with the gradualism of the immutable present, violence being virtually synonymous with ruptured history.

> Progressives and visionaries, who welcomed change, desired quick, decisive, large-scale modifications that would almost instantaneously create a higher form of society. Violence was viewed as the price of progress. Karl Marx, M. A. Bakunin, and countless lesser-known figures championed this view. (Denisoff and Warhman 1983, 541)

> As we have seen, the cost of revolution may be great. Revolutions are not merely romantic exercises. Much human misery and blood have been contributed in the name of social change. "Violence," wrote Karl Marx, "is the midwife of history." (Denisoff and Wahrman 1983, 559)

The text charges Marx with endorsing "violence" as a way to transvalue history "instantaneously," where Marx often wrote that the metamorphosis of full communism—statelessness and powerlessness—would take time. By quoting Marx's well-known passage on violence as the midwife of history the text conflates Marx's description with exhortation, giving the misleading impression that because he viewed the past as a period of virtually unrelieved inhumanity he therefore advocated violence seemingly for its own sake— more of the same. A way of leaping from quantity to quality, Marxism ends prehistory with a bang.

Marx is read not only to have endorsed violence as a strategic expedient but willfully to have glorified violence as a necessary physical/metaphysical rupture with the past, the text admonishing him that "revolutions are not merely romantic exercises" as if he, particularly in his discussion of the fate of the Paris Commune, was unaware of that. Science most clearly rejects politics (and thereby only endorses it) where it can show that politics by including violence in its tactical agenda offends the reasonableness that science wants to foster; Mill's marketplace of ideas is a paradigm of conflict-resolution replaced by a left Thermidor.

But a different reading would show that Marx favored no one strategy of transition, at times even discouraging violence; he precluded no strategy a priori, refusing to rule out of hand any political tactic simply because it offends bourgeois reasonableness. In denouncing the personal and constitutional violence of capital's degradation of labor—guns plus poverty—Marx *wrote* violently, bursting through bourgeois economics and morality precisely to denounce their violence against people falsely held in their sway. Far from celebrating violence or advocating death, as all sorts of protoanarchists (dressed up doctrinally as "terrorists") have done, Marxism abhors it, the phrase "violence . . . [as] the midwife of history" saying more about an insufferable history than about Marx's own strategic predilections, such as they were. In fighting violent practice with a violent text, recognizing both the identity and nonidentity of world and word, Marx would have agreed at least regulatively with Merleau-Ponty that even a single death condemns the revolution.[12]

Marxism's pretension to derail capitalist history, provoking horrible images of bloody discontinuity, demonstrates the general, indeed ontological, folly of radical thought and action. The text identifies Marx's defense of the necessity —even goodness—of violence with the tendencies to violence of many self-proclaimed radical and revolutionary movements.

> Revolutionaries want to control and direct massive changes in the system. They are usually willing to use force to win the necessary power. Frequently they also use force to bring their changes about once they are in power. (Rose, Glazer, and Glazer 1986, 534)

Marxism as a "revolutionary" movement aims "to use force" both to win and then consolidate power, rendering it prima facie illegitimate against the yardstick of liberal reasonableness. "Force" is abhorrent to the liberal committed to calm argumentation serviced by the dispassionate citation of "evidence"; science's textual politics allegedly negate "force" through its subtextual counterpoint between force and enlightenment. This construction of Marxism as ontological violence implies that Marxism resorts to "force" because it is unable scientifically to give reasons for its superiority over capitalism, the dialectic betraying positive/positivist common sense.

In addition, the liberal text is unforceful in its laissez faire objectivism, the "facts" settling disputes unmediately. But Marx does not condone force; indeed he would end force (power, politics, the state) with communism. Thus he refuses to dismiss "violence" altogether, recognizing that because world history has been, as Hegel said, the slaughter bench of individuals force is nearly ubiquitous, raising the deeper question of what we mean by "force" in the first place—welfare mothers stealing food for their children, female infanticide in China, Hiroshima, the American revolution?

Marxist writing makes problematic the meaning of force in a way that hears the voices of history's battered victims drowned out in general neglect. Yet Marxism refuses categorically to valorize or disqualify socialist violence as a commensurable response, especially in light of the near certainty that socialists will themselves be met with force. Marxism refuses to allow discipline to set its terms of disputation or dictate its textual-political strategies even if, unlike the liberal text, it absolutizes the values of life, peace, and love and thus endeavors not to betray them while working "toward" them—recognizing that product and process are necessarily entwined. Marxism reveals liberal reasonableness propped by science to be a form of violence itself in its imperviousness to the structural inhumanities often having no name, no one-to-one, victim-per-victim relationships, and thus no simple "solution" short of systemic changes. As such, violence is writing that pretends everyone can write (that is, make public their grievances); moreover, violence infers that because everyone does not write then everyone is not a victim.

This twist on the text's crude characterization of Marxism and indeed all radical movements as necessarily forceful shows that writing, in distancing itself from the reality it seeks to describe, does violence to the muted many by failing to take up their cause in a way that would help restore authorial voice to them. Even if justified by the professional norms of science bifurcating writer and reader in terms of differential intellectual competences, neglect is as forceful as the brutality of the prison guard, soldier, and terrorist. In recognizing its own historical complicity, Marxism does not pretend to be above or beyond advocacy or discount the constitutive impact of its own version on the present force field in which violence is both routinized and—thus—rationalized.

The text entrenches its construction of Marxist "violence" as a feature of all "revolutionary movements" in the way it discusses the inevitability of what it calls "revolutionary dictatorship" once the deed is done and history ruptured.

> Once in power, the radicals set up a revolutionary dictatorship. Step by step, all opposition is suppressed. Firmness and terror are the order of the day. (Broom, Selznick, and Darroch 1981, 475)

The text could easily, and accurately, be describing Soviet terror, although it refrains from thus historicizing itself. Instead it strains to reach a level of sociological universality—"the radicals": not particular ones, but all, presumably —on which it then implicitly vitiates radicalism by ascribing to it unnecessary but repugnant features. Here the gulag is an inevitable culmination of the radical imagination that cannot live within the strictures of the reasonable, only perpetuating a nightmare worse than the one we are now living. The text conflates monolithic Marxism and any number of other "revolutionary" theories before rehabilitating it as a version of conflict sociology endorsing welfare-state, even social-democratic, redistribution—American sociology politically coequal with the Democratic party. This eschews violence, terror, dictatorship as extravagances of the true believer.

The case against Marxism qua "revolutionary" theory is made to order once the identity between Marxism and the USSR has been established, the particulars of the Show Trials, KGB omnipotence, and the frozen gulag as presumably Marxist practices closely fitting the definition of "revolution" and revolutionary dictatorship as generic categories. Marxism is shamed into confessing its excesses and thus nudged in the direction of a textual liberalism wanting to make the world a better place to live, contributing money to the campaigns of favored political candidates, perhaps, but standing up for American "democracy" against Soviet "Marxism" as a refusal of radical thought and action; radicalism is ontologically identified with what the text calls "totalitarianism."

> After a revolution, a totalitarian government is created ostensibly to be the "caretaker" until things have calmed down and a democratic government can be formed. Karl Marx called this "interim" form of government "the dictatorship of the proletariat," which would cleanse society of the corrupting practices of the past. (Denisoff and Wahrman 1983, 553)

> *Radical Movement:* A social movement that is always nonlegitimate, accepts only its own ideology, works outside the usual political methods, and usually finds illegal methods such as violence to achieve its goals. (Denisoff and Wahrman 1983, 535)

The text ascribes "totalitarian government" directly to Marx in the first passage and then suggests disingenuousness on his part when he claims that the so-called dictatorship of the proletariat would be only a temporary measure required to eradicate the last vestiges of the past's "corrupting practices." No attention at all is given to the status or meaning of proletarian dictatorship in Marx inasmuch as the text is committed from the beginning to a version of Marx's political perversity.

First, Marx may not have required proletarian dictatorship per se as a transitional, "cleansing" stage, aware as he seemed to be of the heterogeneity of historical situations only one of which would seem to involve a fairly harsh period of defense against counterrevolutionary forces. Second, inasmuch as he was vague on the socio-organizational parameters of socialist transition and consolidation it is unclear that the Soviet Union in Marx's own terms is an authentic example of proletarian dictatorship—dictatorship, definitely, but not necessarily the kind advocated or implied by Marx. Yet the impression is virtually inescapable that the Soviet Union must be a Marxist dictatorship of the kind characterized by Marx as a "dictatorship of the proletariat," valorized by him, so the story goes, as a necessary vehicle for overcoming counterrevolutionary forces simply because the Soviets call themselves Marxist(-Leninist) and because the USSR is obviously a dictatorship.

Finally, the text makes this alleged Marxian necessity a universal requirement of all "radical movements," tautologically defined by the text "always [as] non-legitimate," thereby affixing to it the stigma of illegitimacy and marginality. The text loads onto "radical movements" the charge of monolithic commitment only to itself, "accepting only its own ideology," as if anyone accepts anyone else's except through the ruse of an intellectual relativism collapsing margins into center but not the other way around. Radicals "work outside the usual political methods," being by definition unusual, even resorting to "illegal methods such as violence." All sorts of "radical movements" eschew violence and illegality, either because they reject them out of hand as the oppressor's ways or simply because they are strategically inappropriate to the task at hand; what distinguishes many radicals from centrists is not simply means (guns versus ballots) but their envisaged goal, a component of which, for me and other western Marxists and socialist feminists, is precisely the "means" used to achieve them.

The text must marginalize the left, and it is usually talking about the left when it talks about "radical movements." The must split the left into safe and unsafe versions and silence possible radicalisms that in its terms are neither safe nor unsafe, neither against or for violence as a self-defining issue *and thereby are really unsafe*. The versions about which the text is silent threaten its duality, the either/or of bourgeois civilization. They cannot be reduced or contained by a single, simple reading; they resist discipline, especially their banalization. The text neither centers nor marginalizes them, neither assimilating them to science nor dismissing them as terrorism. Science above all fears "nonlegitimacy," existence beyond the sanction of the dominant authorities, tradition, literature, departments, journals, and conferences. And the only way the text can accommodate Marxism and other radical movements is to discipline them, assigning "radicals" to disciplines that contain them, thereby avoiding, it hopes, the extraparliamentary "force" marginalia threaten simply by being beyond the pale—noninstitutional and nonbureaucratic.[13]

For the discipline to mainstream Marxism and other radical movements requires that it debunk them as nonlegitimate for endorsing violence and requiring "totalitarianism"; it also requires their return to more centrist styles of dissent. Marxists and feminists employed in universities indicate a valuable ecumenism, exposing students to what the texts often call "multiple perspectives." This pluralism has its limit: one or two per department, one or two of each exotic species that are then expressly labeled—"the departmental Marxist or feminist"—so that both the department can be seen to be pluralistic and, like radioactive material, they carry a warning sign mediating their work and life. They are designated for others as ideologues, *political people,* thus constraining their intellectual and institutional impact.

My advocacy for or against job candidates in my own department along with my sponsorship of certain sorts of heterodox intellectual work by graduate students, as well as my own writing, is frequently understood through the filter of my "Marxism" or "feminism" (the latter especially outrageous as I seem to betray my gender). When job candidates come through, and if they are not likely to do my type of work, I am introduced to them jovially as "the Marxist," more recently as "the Marxist who has become a feminist!"—diminishing me, contextualizing my subsequent conversation as ideologically driven, and at once showing off our departmental (and disciplinary) tolerance of deviation. This discredits me as an ideologue who mechanically supports only "Marxists," tolerating my existence in the university *but not what I say or write* except as cant—although to the extent to which I remain a personable, helpful colleague as inoffensive cant. It also simultaneously constructs a departmental and disciplinary ecumenism serving the purpose of liberal legitimation.

Marxism is taught table manners at the knee of a civilizing history, disabused of its anarcho-syndicalist tendencies, its willful "totalitarianism" and radical "nonlegitimacy." Dressed in coat and tie, its renegade politics are tamed, truncating them from extraparliamentary ("violent") to parliamentary means in the name of a tactical expediency acknowledging the virtually ontological limits to social change, the generic priority of reformism over radicalism.

> Historically, most nonreformist movements have chosen absolute victory and have been reduced to small bands waiting for the glorious day when they are proved correct. In the U.S. only those movements with limited goals and a willingness to compromise have succeeded. Hundreds, if not thousands, of movements have failed. (Denisoff and Wahrman 1983, 521)

Marxism is headed on the road toward rehabilitation first by reforming its textual politics and (see next section) by disciplining it into an overarching conflict theory.

Inasmuch as Marxism's error has been largely political, exhorting violent revolution and proletarian dictatorship in western countries evolving steadily toward postindustrialism within a parliamentarist framework, Marx's radical politics are rewritten as social-democratic incrementalism in face of the virtually ontological unlikelihood of "nonreformist" political success. History dampens revolutionary ardor by defeating "hundreds, if not thousands" of radical movements, presumably the more the better. History in checking absolutism enforces on social movements both "limited goals and a willingness to compromise," opposing the constructed Marxism of the text, a radical movement "accepting its own ideology," as the text said above.

Liberal reasonableness meshes with Aristotelian balance in the attempt to rehabilitate Marxism as a gentle incrementalism shunning the absolutism of Marx the Father, along with his logic of totalitarian "force." The text proudly trumpets the American aversion to absolutist radicalism, "only those movements" that are tempered and tolerant "succeeding" in the United States, pragmatizing political purpose (as science would do) by operationalizing it; "absolute victory" is truncated into piecemeal gains. Marxism has the choice to either join the mainstream, deepening its doctrinal inwardness, or remain forever on the fringe, split into "small bands" awaiting the "glorious day" of judgment. In these terms, where the options are efficacy or isolation, the reasonable choice seems obvious lest Marxism sink into the oblivion of the "hundreds, if not thousands" of "failed" movements.

> The revolutionary movement believes man capable of living in some better social order that can be achieved only by the destruction of the existing order.

This is an absolute view of the world, with "good guys" and "bad guys" clearly identified in black-and-white terms. For Communists the "capitalists" are the villains and the "workers" the heroes. Most people oppose the radical's model of society. It seems unrealistic and oversimplified. (Denisoff and Wahrman 1983, 513–14)

"Most people" cannot be wrong. Radicals' construction of good and bad "guys" is tellingly "unrealistic and oversimplified"—the one a practical and the other an analytical concern. Radicalism is wrong because it cannot work where "most people" already oppose it. The judgment that it is also "over-simplified" is evoked to explain its inability to destroy "the existing order," especially where its simplicity is not elaborated but only announced, dismissing Marxism summarily as an "absolute view of the world." Radicalism is unrealistic today because it *is* unreal, unpopular, the text on this basis elaborating an argument against the radical simplification of good and bad guys, heroes and villains. The text ridicules Marxism as intellectual childishness where, in the subtext, it fears it will be found on the wrong side. Since as science it cannot advocate or exhort except in the innocent terms of liberal reasonableness, the text names nonabsolutist, reformist strategy as "realistic"; as the correct (because actual) preference of "most people," "most sociologists" earlier, consensus shadows marginality as its responsible conscience and thus disciplines "absolute views" into maturity.

Reformism is reflected in the actual "reforms" that allegedly disqualified Marxism in the first place (e.g., welfare state as unforeseen arbiter between capital and labor). The fact of reform ontologizes reformism both as the bane of Marxian prophecy and, here, as the untruth of "absolute" systems like Marxism. The welfare state that allegedly undid Marxian prophecy is now written as an exemplar of liberal-Democratic incrementalism endorsed by the social text as the will of the people. This in turn raises the timely question of how liberalism would accommodate the widespread hostility of Americans to the welfare state in a neoconservative age in light of its own epistemological consensualism. If Marxism is wrong because "most people" oppose it, preferring (in Sombart's terms) their roast beef and apple pie, this does not make an embittered, racist, sexist, and xenophobic neoconservatism correct; today American sociology imitatively regresses behind liberal conflict-theoretic textual politics towards Parsons's apology for the complacency of the Eisenhower years and even to Spencer's unrelieved Social Darwinism.[14]

On the one hand, the subterranean politics of the disciplinary text is more important, more *political,* than the surface politics taking the side of the victim, "social problems" analysis conceived under the sign of FDR's welfare state. On the other hand, it is noteworthy that the shifting public mood, both shifting and shifted by the social text—journalism, popular culture, sociology— is reflected in the recent neoconservative sociologies that both crusade against

Marxism and posit neoclassically mediated exchange relationships assuming cosmic balance or simply equity, bourgeois economic theory sociologized by Homans. The vogue of exchange theory predicating balanced reciprocity between actors as an ontological universal—everybody gets *some*thing—parallels supply-side economics and its valorization of inequality in support of "equity," with massive corporate profits allegedly "helping" the poor by promoting industrial growth. Although exchange theory was largely debunked during the politicization of sociology in the 1960s, it returns today as neoconservatism especially in the realm of family sociology. As such, it is made-to-order as an opponent of radical and socialist feminism bursting the myth of fair exchange among men, women, and children as patriarchal nonsense, bad science reproducing bad reproduction.

The text claims reformism on the basis of the post hoc success of "reforms" to "make the world a better place to live," forestalling proletarian insurrection by slightly leveling the apportionment of the economic pie, the classic redistributive route of the Robin Hood welfare state. The state as ever remains an "executive committee of the bourgeoisie" modestly redistributing wealth in order to salvage the appearance of its own bipartisan nature—government of "all the people," indeed an agent of progressive social reform. Even this patently procapitalist New Deal era populism recedes under sway of the Reaganomic reaction to welfare statism spurred by, and reinforcing, the resurgence of public selfishness blaming "victims" simply by ignoring them and the safety nets dismantled in favor of the apocryphal idealism of volunteerism—Christian capitalism at its most improbable. "Reform" proves not only that Marx was wrong to expect deepening immiseration but also that strictly in terms of instrumental criteria radicalism is not as "effective" as gradualism in making the world a better place to live. Effectiveness both reflects and is reflected in what the public has been trained to accept within the alleged limits of the power of the social: mitigating acid rain or lowering risk of heart attacks but not nuclear disarmament or the eradication of world poverty.

> Marx predicted capitalism would collapse as workers revolted and assumed control of industry. But Marx did not foresee the reforms brought by labor unions and the success of automation. In this century, Keynesian theory has improved capitalism's ability to cope with recessions and depressions. Inflation, structural unemployment, and distorted production goals remain problems for capitalist systems. (Popenoe 1980, 463)

> Founded originally on the doctrines of Marx and other nineteenth-century utopian thinkers, socialism over the years has moved away from a strict interpretation of Marxist ideology. Socialist parties are often more practical than ideological in their approach. Particularly since the end of World War II, the theory and practice of socialism have changed dramatically. (Popenoe 1980, 448)

Consequently, movements must "win the hearts and minds" of outsiders as well as maintain the commitment of the members. This is quite easy to do if the proposed change is a reformist one and the requirements for membership are minor. Reformers are not considered a menace to society. Police do not harass them. Employers do not fire them. Friends do not disavow them. (Denisoff and Wahrman 1983, 519)

The text acknowledges its role, here "Keynesian theory," in propping a cyclical capitalism, although it misleadingly attributes the endurance of capitalism to "reforms" such as unionization and, curiously, "the success of automation" (that so far has had the net effect of displacing workers from jobs). The case for the contribution of unionization to circumventing socialism interestingly shows not only that reform begets reformism, capitalism once saved requiring capitalism always to be saved, but also that labor purposely pushed for reform and not revolution, again ascribing the perpetuation of the world to the will of "most people." Here savvy workers allegedly realize that their fate lay in joining, not breaking, the capitalist economic system—big labor buying into a compromise of sorts with capital and the state that, like all sociology, defeats difference by swallowing it.[15] But the text lets the lid off its otherwise methodologically suppressed subtext where it acknowledges that "problems" remain in capitalism such as inflation, "structural" unemployment (that is, unemployment issuing from the same automation that the text just lauded) and what are called "distorted production goals," what Marx saw as the lack of articulation between production and consumption in capitalism. Although the text casually enumerates these three "problems" as future issues for welfare-state remediation, in fact these constitute the eruption of the basic capital/labor contradiction in the episodic destabilization—crises—that Marx felt imperiled capitalism over the long run.[16]

Qualifying unemployment with the adjective "structural" does not conceal the text's own recognition of the irrationality of capitalism that it tries to contain by *calling them* (and thus reliving them as) "social problems" where one "problem" is as bad as the next—pollution, prostitution, drugs, inflation, structural unemployment, nuclear accidents, "alienation," family, women, blacks, and so on. This word play crucially decenters their location at the center of capitalism, instead construing them to be only marginally dysfunctional episodes whose episodicity defuses their ultimate threat to the given order.

The text further claims reformism (and disqualifies Marxism as generic radicalism) by redefining Marxian socialism as in effect *capitalist* socialism, reform institutionalized through FDR's welfare state. This ironically demonstrates the elasticity of Marxism that, suitably split and then centered, is rehabilitated not as "strict interpretation of Marxist ideology" but rather as "practical . . . in [its] approach," fitting the facts as a presumably functional requisite of late-twentieth-century capitalism. This assimilates all possible socialisms, "originally . . . the doctrines of Marx," to what the text calls the "socialism" of the British and Scandinavian welfare states, a pastiche of nationalization, social welfare, and private ownership, the appropriately foreshortened socialism of nonideological proletarians and cooperative unions after World War II who settle for gradualist parliamentarist reform as "social democracy."

The text truncates socialism by calling it "practical" as against the doctrinally impassioned "ideological" socialism presumably measuring itself against the "original" writings of Marx, the term "originally" clearly connoting archaic. This is the text's shrewd way of broadening its own scientific synthesis to include an eclecticism of ameliorating strategies, borrowing the "practical" socialism of Democratic party policies as it borrows Marxian "conflict theory," recognizing FDR's debt to a version of socialist remediation expressed in common commitment to human betterment.

This is a curious twist on the text identifying socialism/Marxism with the Soviet Union, holding Marx responsible for the KGB.[17] Here socialism is modulated as social-democratic gradualism, modeled on the self-styled "socialist" parties of Europe and Britain and conflict-theoretic Democratic liberalism in the United States. It is all in a name, "socialism" filled with content by whoever claims it—the Bolsheviks, Mitterand, Harold Wilson, Bernstein, American sociology aping and informing American public opinion. This creates the unlikely impression of a text so comprehensive that on one page it decries Marxism as an agenda of the police state ("proletarian dictatorship") while on the next page it sanitizes socialism as a conflict-theoretic liberal-mindedness. Marxism "works within the system" safely ensconsed in universities and on the back bench of various national labor parties, young turks who keep the centrists honest in a selfish age; socialism is the text's surface political agenda reduced to a workable incrementalism.

I am not invoking a logic of consistency, for consistency can be deconstructed to belie a deeper inconsistency (indeed the necessity of inconsistency, or better, nonidentity). I am suggesting the recklessness of a text that splits Marxism into good and bad versions of itself thus reducing "Marx" to whatever and whomever he is said to "stand" for today, yesterday, tomorrow. This ultimately eviscerates socialism of content, both defying the text's liberal agenda and surfacing its deeper ontology. The text conceivably could defend its nominalism metatheoretically simply by referring the meaning of the term socialism to whoever uses it—for example, middle-class Scandinavians or the Nicaraguan Sandinistas. Yet the text does not learn from the perspectivity and intentionality of socialist writings. "Socialism" as a concept and practice can be defended contextually by those who argue for one version of socialism over another, with or without reference to Marx but certainly in light of socialist history during which these debates about revolution, reform, and agency have been going on since Kerensky and the Bolsheviks. Instead, the text uses the terms socialism, Marxism, and radicalism to make *a case against socialism as an axial transformation of capitalism and its accompanying scientism, sexism, and racism*, one minute denouncing Soviet socialism and the next valorizing the quasi-socialism of Johnson's War on Poverty. Indeed, I have a colleague who describes a local public swimming pool as an example of socialism.

Finally, the text resorts to its usual consensualism, epistemology by majority rule, in defending reformism as the people's choice, taking the route that the easiest socialism to sell is that which differs least from the extant social order —a truism that would become true in practice. This is very likely the same method used by the geniuses of Madison Avenue and network television who create markets through the miniscule variation of old products, surpassing them by calling the new product "new" yet realizing that people want it to be only somewhat different; after all, comfort is found in the cathexis of familiarity. Discipline constructs difference familiarly. Marxism is a next-door neighbor of Weber.

The text says that the hearts and minds of "outsiders" to social movements will best be won by this purposeful nominalism, the least radical reform being more attractive than a really radical one. In light of the disciplinary iteration of the laws of psychology and social psychology, freezing present-day audience manipulation into certain Nielsen "laws" of consumer choice in general, there is a certain case to be made for social movements that go slowly. And yet the text *admits* that "reforms are not considered a menace to society," portraying reformism as the safest strategy for avoiding censure, job loss, imprisonment, and self-isolation by going too fast too soon in the eyes of those to whom they must appeal for support; the people who have not yet read *Capital* or *The Second Sex* imagine a qualitatively different life for themselves.

But the connection is hazy between the claim that people are best won over by muted, reasonable advocacy and the observation that reformers are not considered menacing to society. The text implies that people join movements if they perceive the risks of sanction to be low. Even if that is granted, I would reverse the reification of this behaviorist psychology and suggest that the really compelling movements in this nearly totally administered world in which everything and every thought is made identical to every other—all noise, hucksterism, hype—offer imaginative resolutions of people's alienation in an imagery energizing people to break the bonds of their own naturelike existences. The more radical this imagery is and the more it can offer a real transvaluation of the present routines, the more energizing it will be precisely because it avoids the safe banalities of institutionalized politics reducing candidates' and parties' differences to Pepsi-Coke taste tests. Otherwise it will turn off an already jaded public inured to the insubstantial hype that only sells newspapers and advertising time on television and, elites hope, props the illusion that the United States is "democratic" as well as capitalist.[18]

Reformism taken for granted as the safest theory of social change misses the people's needs to be shown, and themselves to evaluate, the possibility of a qualitatively different "everyday life" no longer remote from the noneveryday life of the "social system" whose institutions, great leaders, and elites seem to inhabit a higher, inaccessible realm of existence, above their heads. Reformism only scratches the surface of the administered existence cutting us off from public space as we cede our constitutive agency to elites who make up these myths—"laws"—about the desirability of safe reform in the first place. The master myth of an intractable social world in which only minor adjustments can be made keeps us from walking on the wild side and busting out of "everyday life," a barless prison in which "choice" is reduced to delimited consumer preferences—what to watch on television, which car to buy, which candidate to vote for (or, more aptly, to root for).

The privatized public can be enlivened only by claiming our agency in all its literarily constitutive efficacy, thereby underlining the "risks" as well as opportunities we take in living differently. Routine existence seemingly inured to desperate limit situations accepts the administration of so-called everyday life as a fact of nature while freely choosing *itself* in light of the risky, unpredictable, even dangerous implications for people who eschew what Sartre (1961) calls "bad faith"—the pretense that our unfreedom makes others responsible for us. Sociology wants to demarcate everyday life as the humble horizon of the ritualized ever-the-same, the eternally reproductive, in order to dupe us to *stay there,* confined to our television sets, shopping malls, "careers," and the other junk with which we fill our lives and have them filled for us. The walk on the wild side, escaping the prison of *la vie quotidienne* toward a life risked and committed, is ruled out ahead of time by a text suggesting safety as normalcy, the "lifestyle" of the reasonably well adjusted.[19] The power of the social makes radicals seem mad. We respond that the discourse of the power of the social is madness itself, limiting imagination with words—and thus a world—connoting the irreversible modern.

The text labors to center socialism as the genteel politics of the liberal welfare state, compared glowingly to the Soviet gulag (to which it nonetheless bears a certain resemblance in its overbearing statism). It is crucial for the text to place the USSR and British Labour party on the same continuum so that the text can engulf "Marxism"—conflict-theoretic incrementalism—as a legitimate complement to a more self-serving political agenda. The text needs the mitigated Marxism of LBJ's War on Poverty as a safe politics looking out for the little person in the populist spirit of Jacksonian democracy, keeping faith with the pragmatic gradualism said to characterize the New World. The text has its cake, gulag Marxism, and eats it too, the safe social-Democratic parliamentarism of the official socialist and labor parties of Europe and, in a paler version, even the Democratic Party, at least in its Roosevelt incarnation. Atari Democrats like Carter and Hart who would scale back the redistributive activities of the state in favor of fiscal conservatism shun social democracy in step with a retrenching public mood reciprocally created by and creating the texts registering "public mood" as a significant historical factor. This tempers "doctrine" with a common sense that according to epistemological consensualists cannot be wrong.

> Socialism has taken many forms today. At one extreme [is] the Soviet Union and Eastern Europe. . . . A less extreme form of socialism is found in almost all Western European countries. (Hess, Markson, and Stein 1985, 298)

Although the logic of the text engulfs the "less extreme socialism," many American sociologists do not go even that far toward the "Marxism" of British Labour, Mitterand, or Papandreou. Indeed, technicians in a postpolitical age, mainstream sociologists do not indulge *any* surface textual politics, even the most banal kind urging a better world or progress, even if the socio-logic of their addresses to Marxism suggests a counterpoint between bad-Soviet and good-European versions.

Although claiming to notice the difference between Soviet and western European socialism in its catholic understanding of social diversity, the text virtually always conflates the Soviet Union and all of eastern Europe, presumably including Yugoslavia, Romania, and Hungary, in its construction of "extreme" or gulag socialism. A more acute version would take pains to acknowledge Tito's socialism, with its system of self-managing workers' councils, as a deviation from Leninist centralism as well as from the mere capitalist parliamentarianism of western Europe (Sher 1977). For all the disappointments of Titoism, continually confounded by Yugoslavia's territorial vulnerability midway between NATO and the Warsaw Pact, it represents something of a western Marxist variety of socialism eschewing both statism and parliamentarianism in favor of self-management, at least a stab at the communism Marx first envisaged.[20]

The text hides Yugoslavia because it wants to split Marxism, not diversely, into a myriad of possible and actual writings, but binomially, the gulag at one extreme ironically rehabilitating the safe socialism of the Scandinavians. Non-Soviet Marxism written in eastern as well as western Europe—the so-called Praxis group in Yugoslavia, the Frankfurt School, the Paris existential Marxists, Gramsci in Italy, maybe even Eurocommunism—threatens the social text with irreducible Marxes and Marxisms defying their caricature by Solzhenitsyn as well as the gentle parliamentarianism of Bernstein; instead, they claim their own autonomy as versions of socialism's undecidability and thus oppose both bourgeois and Soviet scientism and the practices they support.

Accordingly, the text ignores Marxism that does not fall neatly into the grid of dichotomous socialism, bad-Soviet and good-European. The less said the better about texts (for example, Sartre and Adorno) that seem to encourage their dismissal as virtually incomprehensible nonscience, refusing to speak plain English or propose a "positive" program of action yet instead prefiguring a world in which production and reproduction do not stand against each other but are versions of the same activity.[21] The texts mention Adorno only insofar as he was the senior author of *The Authoritarian Personality* (Adorno et al. 1950), a book about the administration of psyche in late capitalism egregiously misread as scientific social psychology, an impression to which Adorno unfortunately contributed in his short-lived attempt in postwar America to speak the "language" of positivist social science and thus to build bridges between himself and the dominant positivist center.

> Persuasion-centered movements tend to favor gradual change and compromise. They stress education, believe that people must be reached "where they are," and try to approach the public in terms that they can understand and accept. As a result, such movements often appear timid and self-restrained, but unlike power-centered movements they are more likely to respect the rights of others. (Broom, Selznick, and Darroch 1981, 471)

Good European socialism has the additional advantage of "respecting the rights of others," the catechism of liberalism, as if oppression or oppressors had "rights," willfully giving them license in the phony name of common humanity. So deep in the American subtext is the self-justifying belief in our own procedural decency that we condemn the decent to live indecently under regimes crushing decency. Like all liberalism, sociology conceals the hideous disfigurements of world history in the sanitized "explanations" of either (or both) functionalism—"necessary" inequality—or conflict theory—ontological struggle for scarce resources. Sociology suppresses the deeper barbarism of history with roots in the substratum of subjectivity, frustrated desire displaced in spurious gratifications, brutality a balm for lifelessness.

The text, in decency, cannot confront these motives, dismissing them as psychologism or satanism and thereby missing the fundamental link between biology and history, the sad reality that virtually nothing in the way of inhumanity is unknown to we humans. The text denounces "power-centered movements" in favor of "persuasion-centered" ones as if there were a necessary disjunction between the two; liberalism prefers "persuasion" and "education" to the Marxist will to power. The liberal text of science constructs a dichotomy of persuasion and power because it seeks to derive its own power from a consensus supposedly achieved on the basis of its demonstrated merit. But that is the empty circularity of liberalism, deriving its authority from what Habermas calls the power of the strongest argument. This ignores the possibility that the so-called power of the strongest argument is *power itself,* the public either beaten into submission or deceived to believe in the pretended scientificity of the text's claims, thus forfeiting their own reason and freedom.

Marxism is politically disqualified as totalitarian and then resuscitated as welfare-state reformism; socialism is split between the equally inauthentic versions of Soviet Marxism (Marcuse 1958) and social democracy, the one "extreme" and the other respectably respectful of the "rights of others." The rehabilitation of Marxism is notably contingent on its political reformulation, contrasting safe parliamentarianism with the gulag socialism sending people to oblivion at the far end of the Trans-Siberian Railway. The text's move in effect to make Marxism safe for democracy, Scandinavianizing it, promotes its disciplinary rehabilitation, thus integration. Marxism now opposes social problems, announces everlasting conflict and emphasizes the centrality of economic factors.

The text must first disqualify Marxism politically inasmuch as common sense fears its abundant authoritarianism. Once that has been accomplished, it is centered into the textual middle of the road, just another academic voice naming its own singular view of the world; Marxism suggests the "importance" of economics—disciplinary boundaries eased under pressure from *Capital*, if not Adam Smith and Keynes. The text mainstreams Marxism politically by "showing" that most Americans, including labor, resist the lunatic fringe, thus ontologizing incrementalism as the appropriately "pragmatic" route to a better world.

> Of course, there are defects in [Marx's] analysis of capitalism. The impoverishment of the laboring class has not occurred. Marx did not foresee that labor unions would become reform-minded, rather than revolution-oriented. (Popenoe 1980, 446)

The text boldly announces the end to class struggle as the triumph of reformism's inherently stronger argument, read in the emoluments doled out to certain segments of labor, at least unionized white male workers. The political failure constitutes a scientific failure, the "prediction" of "world wide class revolution" corrected only by a Marxism acknowledging the unexpected success of capital in raising wages. A liberal political text valorizing parliamentarian fine-tuning incorporates Marx into a disciplinary canon recognizing that Marx was wrong but that he can be accommodated anyway in a conflict-theoretic frame.

> Clearly, the worldwide class revolution that Marx predicted has not taken place, and most American social scientists have rejected the theory that it ever will. The workers of the world have not united, and it does not appear likely that they will do so in the near future. (Duberman and Hartjen 1979, 411)

Science comforts itself with the belief that Marx was wrong because capital was right, the latter's advances vitiating Marx's "prediction" of eventual socialism. The text on this basis—strangely, it would seem—recovers Marx's science not as the indubitability of socialism but the eternity of conflict, his "insight" integrated by a text squeezing all marginalia toward the center, their galvanizing appeal lost in the shuffle of academic sociology and/as Marx ology. The integration of Marxism is a hedge against the possibility that Marx was right after all and that capitalism is bound to self-destruct, or at least not to evolve painlessly into the final stage of prehistory. The political failure of Marxism—the gulag in the East and affluence in the West—is capitalized by the text as it uses the consensus of "most American social scientists" to allay its secret fear that Marx may have been right after all less in implying the inevitability of revolution than in addressing the logic of capital driving all wealth and truth toward the center.[22]

This ultimately poses a crisis of production's reproduction, the margins being so immiserated that they fail to stick to the rules after all, either turning on the center with a vengeance or just wandering off, looking for a winnable game with different rules. The text tries repressively to desublimate the margins—protest—in order to keep a lid on precisely this sort of insurgency, accommodating what passes for Marxism and feminism as reformist politics and normal science.

7

Mainstream Marxism

Weber's Marx

Once Marxism has been shown to be both failed prophecy and Siberian socialism, centered as Bernstein's, Mitterand's, and FDR's social democracy ("persuasion" triumphant over power, respecting the "rights of others"), the text easily ingests the left as conflict theory and economism. Marxism contributes logics of conflict and productivism to a pluralist discipline. Its integration marginalizes Soviet Marxism as the official renegade, enhancing the sociologized and parliamentarized Marx by comparison—science plus an appropriately reasonable textual politics. This is not to say that American sociology embraces even the neutralized Marx of conflict and economism with open arms, conflict theory in the text always constructed as a complement to its mainstream iteration but not a mainstream itself, only a current within a larger river. Ecumenism, after all, is phony; the leading scholarly journals and departments periodically prestige-ranked into a Top Ten do not declare Marxism a new center, a discourse replacing Durkheim's determinism and its liberalism. They simply use Marx to name what he patently opposed—the salience of economics.

The text's desire to identify, and thus engulf, all differences and thus the threat of difference itself, is only that, a desire, and not the real thing. Identity is resisted by the very intractability of objects resisting their penetration by concepts without leaving a remainder, Adorno's "indissoluble something." [1] This constrains conflict theory as addendum, complement, correction. As the banalization of Marxism, conflict theory must be addressed simply because it exists. Although not a dominant perspective, measured by its remoteness from the extant political and scholarly consensus in sociology, conflict theory endures, and thus commands attention, as the transvaluation of Marxism.

> The conflict perspective can be criticized for overemphasizing the importance of conflict and disregarding the prevalence of stability. In addition, while functionalists are often accused of being too conservative, some conflict theorists can be criticized for having a radical view that places too much emphasis on changing

society rather than trying to understand how order and stability can be maintained. Nevertheless, the conflict perspective helps us to understand the many ways in which conflict and the exercise of power are critical elements in social life. (Sullivan and Thompson 1984, 21)

The text's deceptive Aristotelianism, authoritarianism masquerading as pluralism, retains conflict theory with its standard "nevertheless" clause. Thus, conflict ontology completes the main ontology of the power of the social; conflict becomes "critical elements in social life"—conflict no less than order a disciplinary universal. But subtext strains against the superficial tolerance of conflict theory as another valid, or at least viable, perspective where the subtext, barely surfacing, says much more clearly than functionalism that conflict theory is political theory, a "radical view" putting "too much emphasis on changing society rather than trying to understand how."

Here the text crucially acknowledges the political nature of the conflict theory that used to be Marxism, now as before on guard against the eleventh thesis on Feuerbach. No matter how hard it tries, text cannot denature Marxism enough that it need not send up flares warning against conflict theory's, really Marxism's, penchant for politicizing science, elevating the "radical" emphasis on change over "understanding," ever the political agenda of positivism. It is noteworthy that the text does not explicitly accuse conflict theory of harboring a bias for change-oriented explanations against those emphasizing stability and equilibrium, although that is what the text wants to be read to say. Instead it decries the insufficient domestication of Marxism by the professional norms and practices of science, "explaining" and "understanding" instead of advocating. The "nevertheless" clause is too little and too late to repress the text's secret desire to marginalize conflict theory, not as inadequate explanation but really as bad politics; thus, "radicalism" becomes the bane of every liberalism.

I want to begin this last section on the disciplining of Marxism by resisting the text's identification of Marxism with the other "leading" sociological perspectives. At least I want to call attention to the incongruous sanitization of a version that is not representational science at all but a text that would become a life, a form of dialogical community at odds with the monologizing tenor of disciplinary discourse. In tension with its own subtext, text represses its desire to marginalize Marxism as it seems to center it, short of Soviet and prophetic excess baggage. Subtext threatens text's seemingly generous gesture of peace to Marxism, surfacing the fear of writing defying its identification with the textual project of science and thus the desire to silence Marxism just as it appears to welcome it to the disciplinary fold.

The subtext knows what the text will not admit: no matter how neutered, Marxism always threatens to break out of its disciplinary prison, particularly its assignment to the work detail of scientific sociology; it opposes not simply "functionalism," the least of Marxism's opponents, but the whole enterprise of the positivist social text (what Marx too crudely called ideology) pretending to be mere reflection as a constitutive or reconstitutive strategy—*science's politics the concealment of politics by science.* Although the text can easily center Marxism as conflict-theoretic economism in the sense that any pen can write anything, the text does not so readily succeed in concealing the tension within itself between its integration of a defused Marxism and subtext's timely warning that sociological socialism is a double agent; indeed, the text knows Marxism better to oppose it, the purpose of any text within academic life, reflected here as elsewhere. Text chooses not to heed subtext only at its peril; no ingestion of a denatured Marxism will ever expunge its insurgency entirely, the enemy within only appearing to be loyal opposition.

The Marxism centered by the text as conflict theory is no more Marxist than the familism centered by the text as feminism; marginalia are neutralized as they are simultaneously disqualified and rehabilitated. Even the text above admits that Marxism/conflict theory is too "radical," subtext taking control for a brief moment and then reverting to the phony ecumenism celebrating the differences-as-identities of functionalism, conflict theory, and all the rest. *The subtext does not lie* inasmuch as it contains the motives and desires informing positivist prose. Thus, we should take it seriously when it tells us that conflict theory wrongly proselytizes for radical social change while functionalism only seeks to "explain," the appropriate mission of a positivist discipline. Conflict theory is allowed into the realm of scientific discourse at all only on the text's sufferance, conditional on its well-mannered decorum submitting journal articles "instead" of engaging in political activity. Conflict theory is integrated as an immigrant to the land of science, refused full citizenship, and subjected to deportation depending on the ebb and flow of public and professional sentiment about communism, the Cold War, American labor, terrorism, and the like.

Today, after five or ten years of the explicit text's active pollination by Marxism, as well as the repressive desublimation of these Marxisms as responsible conflict theory, the return to the right in American politics does not bode well for the Marxist interlopers, no matter how academically respectable they appear to be. Giddens, Skocpol, even Habermas in places are typified by an ambivalence about the relationship between Marx and Weber. In times of retrenchment the center reserves the right to disqualify it once again, the pale conflict-theoretic sociologies thus far ingested by the text suddenly spit out as indigestible radicalism, Marxism, communism. The text's liberal accommodation of left-wing marginalia varies with the political context generally and, like all liberalism faced with a crisis, can be undone. Sociologized Marxism props the text's illusory pluralism, nothing more. The text does not seriously attempt to learn from Marxism that its generic world is, indeed, not *worth* ontologizing and can be reformulated. The discourse of the power of the social is not worth the social it conceals.

I want to trace the text's integration of what it takes to be Marxism, emphasizing the fraudulence of the "Marxism" it constructs as its desire not to adapt or adopt Marxism but to *discipline* it.

> The *conflict perspective* is based on *the idea that society consists of different groups who struggle with one another to attain the scarce resources that are considered valuable, be they money, power or prestige. Karl Marx* provided the foundation for the conflict perspective where he viewed society as consisting of different social classes. (Sullivan and Thompson 1984, 20)

Here the text establishes the Marxist "foundation" of so-called conflict theory and reduces Marxism to the idea that society is rooted in group conflicts over the disposition of "scarce resources." First, this covertly Weberianizes Marx where it was actually Weber who defined inequality as the differential attainment of "scarce resources" such as money, power, or prestige. Marxism opposes this construction of inequality for decentering the constitutive relevance of the social relations of production (and, with feminism, reproduction), a pluralist definition of "stratification" around Weber's three axes of class, power, and status.

The latter-day sociology of stratification, as it is called, replaces Marx's notion of the centrality of classes' (and with feminism, genders') differential relationships to the productive means in capitalism with Weber's decidedly non-Marxist attempt to relativize class stratification into a host of crosscutting and often countervailing generics. Although Weber and his epigones may describe inequality in any terms they choose, even using Marxist words like class, they are obliged to acknowledge Weber's own desire where he wrote in explicit opposition to a Marxism he felt simplified the complexity of capitalism and thus construed it to be more destructive and undesirable than it really is: not a world-historical struggle between capital and labor but a multilayered constellation of interacting, converging, and conflicting forces. This is reflected, hence reproduced, by "conflict theory" as a generic logos of the modern. As a critic of all socioontologizing discourse called ideology, Marx rarely talked about "society" at all but historicized social context into developmental/dialectical stages or epochs—social formations (Poulantzas)—refusing to view "[any] society [as] consisting of different social classes." The positivist version of Marxism abandons the utopian image of a classless world to be prefigured in a peaceful textual practice making all readers writers. Marxism is not about "society" but about history, where past, present, and future social orders are characterized by one or another modes of production and reproduction.

The text assimilates Marxism to a discourse naming American capitalism "society," thus incorporating what it construes to be Marx's own emphasis on the "struggle to attain scarce resources" when in fact that was Weber's subtext *against Marxism*. Conflict theory is not Marxism simply because it inflates the particular contradiction between capital and labor into the generic "societal" principle of conflict, utterly neglecting Marx's historicist understanding of human alienation and exploitation not as "conflict" but as *domination*—a self-reproducing acquiescence to the skewed conflicts of rich/poor, white/black, man/woman. Sociology's "conflict" and Marx's "domination" differ as form and content; the former is a trivial gloss of the dynamics constituting conflict in the first place, *ontologizing and thereby legitimating conflict*—merely one of Simmel's forms of "sociation."

I once had a colleague partial to a highly positivist symbolic interactionism who held that Marxism addresses "conflicts" between drunker interlocutors in bars, a "generic" sociology (as he tellingly called it) linking the similarities between Engels's analysis of factory misery and the pugilistic bravado of the barroom. (He also told me that "ideology"—selling ideas, to him—was like the time he spent selling encyclopedias, an Adornoian insight in spite of itself.) This sort of homology between domination and conflict identifies them in reducing domination to eternal brawling.

The text takes conflict from Marxism where Marx understood overt conflict as a very special case of maturing historical contradictions that he hoped one day would erupt in a transvaluing class conflict, opening to a new world. Marxists write the invisible history of domination precluding conflict by taking away the voices of the oppressed, the logos of world history to date not conflict at all but the dumb submission of slaves to masters—building the pyramids, dying in battle, sweating it out in the factories. *Conflict is precluded by social texts deepening the power of the social, hence of oppression.*

In this sense, a Marxist analysis of the text-fetish of conflict would emphasize science's stake in falsely empowering "disadvantaged" groups with the textual/material resources to fight back, to conflict, thus reinforcing the impression that capitalism at some level of group pluralism embodies equity; capitalism is at least open enough that the mutilated victims of Hegel's world-historical slaughter bench can fight back (an illusion similar to the idea that "consumers"—*not* producers?—can effectively "fight back").

> Conflict theorists do not see social conflict as a necessarily destructive force, although they admit that it may sometimes have that effect. They argue that conflict can often have positive results. (Robertson 1983, 19)

> Many sociologists and social theorists have followed the conflict tradition. Karl Marx, who assumed that all of history had been a constant series of changes and confrontations, was one of the major architects of conflict theory. (Smith and Preston 1979, 263)

> Conflict theorists assume that human beings are for the most part quite selfish and that chaos and strife are both common and natural. (Smith and Preston 1979, 262)

The text sanitizes conflict by showing off its "positive results," a standard American twist of conflict theory expressing the forward-looking exuberance of New World sociology no longer snared in the metaphysical gloom of the European founders. In the next section, I will return to this idea as an ontological expression of marketplace relativity, conflict analogous to robust economic competition; Marxism is conflict-theoretic economism, conflict thus curiously depoliticizing conflict. Marx's concept of domination is here named as the "positive" motive force of history, the engine of what the text calls a "constant series of changes"; Marx's dialectic is taken over as a sociological account of generic advance. In this sense American sociology unwittingly appropriates Engels's version of Marxism regarding history as a naturelike process governed by laws of dialectic involving thesis and negation of the thesis, its inevitable synthesis in turn breeding a new antithesis.

Marxists who follow Hegel's *Science of Logic* have always been challenged to live down the positivist predetermination of history implied by an essentially ontological construction of dialectic; after all, Marxism aims freely to rupture the continuum of domination. Marxists refuse to perpetuate an ontological dialectic leaving history to Hegel's cunning of reason or to the cult of personality required to speed up history when cunning either fails or detours. American sociology borrows this ontological-theological notion of dialectic, inevitable socialism, and simply retards it; antithesis ("conflict") replaces synthesis. Better, antithesis is said to enhance synthesis depicted, against Marx, as a functional capitalism, not socialism.

Conflict theory in the text's version of the Hegelian dialectic constructs group conflict/antithesis as a lawlike process of "society," issuing in synthesis mitigating conflict through the allocative and redistributive means of the advanced welfare state. Sociology makes conflict a law, pretending to imitate Marx but really duplicating the scientized/Hegelianized Marxism of the 2nd and 3rd Internationals reducing history to a pregiven unfolding. Order always triggers conflict (antithesis) that is then resolved in a higher, synthetic stage. The empiricist text would shudder at the Hegelian character of its own subtext: its Marxism is a version of dialectical determinism where group conflict produces the ontological antithesis of abstract "society."

The text purposely confuses this ontological conflict mouthed by its Marxism with a bourgeois "possessive individualism" (Macpherson)[2] that, like my former colleague, makes barroom brawling a "generic" feature of human nature, Hobbesian political theory ingested by the mainstream text through its Marxist back door. Nothing violates Marxism more dramatically than this conflict-theoretic valorization of human cupidity. In the text's decisive claim that "human beings are for the most part quite selfish," generic selfishness inevitably leads to a differential accumulation of "scarce resources," with "conflict" as the result. Marx historicized human nature precisely because he wanted to liberate it from the bondage of false history, "prehistory," dominating subjectivity with a preponderant objectivity. Domination is itself produced and reproduced *through* subjectivity and not simply in spite of or around it, giving rise to the analysis of discourses that discipline.

Marxism opposes the possessive individualism of Hobbes, Adam Smith, and American sociology underwriting a popular culture in which success is the best revenge—not getting mad but getting even, looking out for number one. A social product, selfishness is deepened in the name of Marxism, a twist of text rehabilitating "Marxism" as conflict theory. This selfishness suggests that "chaos and strife are both common and natural," Marxism complementing, completing, and correcting the harmonizing text of mainstream functionalism and its auxiliary, constructivist microsociology. The devilish subtext, threatening to surface, resists Marx's utopian imagery of "social freedom" or "collective subjectivity" (Sartre 1976; Gramsci 1971) as a direct threat to bourgeois heteronomy and thereby shrewdly ascribes the opposite to Marxism —the elaboration of human cupidity and volatility into perpetual "chaos and strife."

The text's Hobbesian human nature covertly supports conflict in the same way that the Hegelian-Marxist dialectic supposedly favored class struggle and the dictatorship of the proletariat; antithesis is celebrated as the order of things. Sociology needs Marxism to transform domination into conflict, eliminating the former by renaming it the latter. Hegemony is both cause *and* effect of "conflict," itself derived from generic selfishness. The text first neutralizes conflict as a way of defending its own frame of the power of the social— conflict, chaos, and strife the safe terms for domination and exploitation. It then valorizes competition as economism, teasing busy productivity out of the supposed universality of "conflict," intended as competition.

Thus, the text works from and through Marx's original critique of domination to its banalization as conflict in defense of universal inequality. This finally culminates in the deduction of healthy competition. Domination is thus identified with healthy marketplace vitality, sociology in this engulfing bourgeois economic theory. This is an ingenious move by the text, renaming domination in order to defend its universality and then construing healthy conflict as a "positive result," the give and take of scrapping interests said to essentialize American social life. The textual trajectory of the concept of domination could look like this:

Domination —▶ TEXT —▶ Conflict ———▶ TEXT —▶ Competition
         (inequality,   (economic activity,
         heteronomy)   productivity,
                     marketplace)

The text rewrites domination twice as it moves from Marxism to its opposition, bourgeois economic theory, deriving "conflict's" functionality as competition out of its version of Marxism as conflict theory. This is how text allies itself with conflict theory in spite of Marxism's historic negation of social texts in light of the world's indeterminate openness occasioning them. The text closes the world by ingesting a version of Marxism that after two mediations—domination into conflict and then competition—turns out to be a chamber-of-commerce paean to the private marketplace, "strife" construed as the dynamic of American capitalism. In this sense, the text's rehabilitation of Marxism is a sure route to capitalizing (the text's) "society" first as economic conflict and then as competition—topics of original Marxism and, thereby, through the text's egregious version of Marx, his endorsements. The text as much as says that Marx favored conflict/competition because he wrote *about* it; conflict theory thus names conflict as an essential societal "process" to be "explained" by a version not inimical to capitalism. *The text thus makes Marxism into its opposite by dehistoricizing it,* reading sociology into Marx that he would have attacked as disciplinary scientism.

The text casts the spell of sociology over Marxism by bleeding it of historicity, turning "society" into a "central power struggle," world conflict sanitizing world domination.

> Conflict theorists see social life as a continual power struggle that certain groups win and others lose. Each group in society has different interests, and each has different resources for protecting or maximizing them. (Goode 1984, 20)

The text betrays itself when it admits that "certain groups win and others lose" in the "critical power struggles" Marx supposedly considered endemic to history. Economic and social balance is threatened by the "fact" that some win and others lose. As Marx implied, this quickly becomes chronic, evolving into a highly skewed distribution of spoils rendering further "competition" inherently unfair, the outcome determined at the outset. Marx recognized that at a certain point it was futile for the dispossessed even to hope to engage in competition, struggle or striving, the future foreclosed in favor of those who formerly were "winners" (whether through effort or simply inheritance), a realization the bourgeois text suppresses in favor of the discourse of the power of the social. At a certain point—Auschwitz, the gulag, urban slums— "conflict" (competition, struggle) passes over into locked-in, chilled relations of hegemony/heteronomy losing their dynamism altogether; the voices of the oppressed are silenced; the marketplace of goods and ideas is rendered a sheer monopoly. That some lose and others win at their expense gives the lie to the text's Marxism where the inequality is so great that the losers simply give up and give in, by far the norm in world history.

As the text portrays it, conflict is a healthy economic and political cosmopolitanism. Here all shout to have their pitches heard and wares sold, without the more common malevolent muting of dissent. In spite of its poignant sympathy for the outsider, bourgeois writing sanitizes domination by calling it conflict; thereby it holds out hope in a pluralist America whose welcoming portal is Ellis Island. Losers can become winners given the right combination of hard work, lobbying, and luck—so-called upward mobility. This is not to say that Marx and Marxism do not too often share the same virtually entrepreneurial optimism, where winners and losers exchange places, history inverted by an apocalyptic rupture, indeed a Marxist myth of progress. Marx simply historicized all master-slave relations and thereby opened the door to new versions in which slaves/readers become masters/writers. Marxism certainly rejects the text's claims that "each group in society has different interests" and that each group can marshal "resources for protecting or maximizing their interests," an extravagant optimism.

Marxism addresses all center/margin disparities and the productive/reproductive relationships sustaining them. He opposed power, not all sorts of "group" differentiation—"different interests"—pluralizing an exotic urban existence. That was Weber, Marx's antagonist. Then again, Marxism is about classes and not groups in the sense that classes (sexes, races) are the objects of oppression and therefore possible agents of a new history, whereas groups are merely aggregates of people sharing an abstract interest or ephemeral common purpose. These interest groups are dear to American sociology and political science—the alleged plurality of interests demonstrating the openness of an entrepreneurial society in which the diligent can better themselves or effect other timely innovations: consumer protection, Tupperware, National Rifle Association, Jews for Jesus, triathletes.

It is emphatically not the case that "each group . . . has different interests," nor is it true that each group has "resources" available to it, especially in light of what the text just admitted about how winners produce losers and, Marx adds, the losses quickly mount up thus *preventing* groups from entering into competition with each other, stilling the happy hubbub of the New England town meeting. Marxism is crucially constructed as a forward looking theory of dynamic progress especially suited to the pragmatic American mien, no metaphysics allowed here.

> Karl Marx believed that radical change in capitalist society is both desirable and inevitable. *Conflict theory* is a perspective contending that the struggle for power and wealth in society should be the central concern of sociology. Unlike equilibrium theory, the conflict scheme emphasizes the occurrence of social change. (Doob 1985, 508)

> Societies attempt to remain stable, and although a stable one is usually better than a chaotic one, stability sometimes causes harsh conditions, injustice, and oppression. When this happens, conflicts arise and society is forced to change, perhaps for the better. (Eshleman and Cashion 1985, 600)

> Conflict theory argues that groups are inevitably organized to compete against each other. Change is a continuous element in conflict theory. Karl Marx's theory of class conflict is the foundation upon which modern conflict theory has been built. (Doob 1985, 17)

The bourgeois text appears to be conceding to Marxism in the name of functionalist "equilibrium theory," as it is sometimes called; it incorporates the alleged Marxist "emphasis [on] the occurrence of social change" when, in fact, the functionalist text already contains "social change" as its technological teleology, the end-of-history approached through disciplinary discourse. The text does not need a spurious Marxism to instruct it in the "inevitability" of social change, even if it is called "radical change." American sociology has always falsely read the sociological original literature as oblivious to "change" precisely in order to bring in the inevitability of the modern from the outside; Marxism names the progressivism of an order evolving toward a higher harmony in which seeming opposites are identified, conflict becoming consensus and change stability. The text recruits "change" as a means of improving a "society" that otherwise "attempts to remain stable" even when stability brings with it "harsh conditions, injustice and oppression." Applying one layer of ontology to another, the text suggests that societies court stability, that stability often brings with it injustice, that injustice makes "conflicts arise," and that finally "society is forced to change, perhaps for the better." This shrewdly integrates Marxism as the advocacy of "change" per se, as if the mainstream text did not also advocate change, albeit in Comte's terms the ordered progress of capitalism.

Marx did not believe that conflicts inevitably "arise," as the text suggests, serving invariably to confront "stable" society with its own episodic irrationality and thus paving the way for the balanced synthesis of redistributive welfare/warfare capitalism. But Marx felt the marginalization of what the text calls "conflict" would potentially rupture the historical continuum of domination, making the plight of the oppressed impossible to resolve in the system's own terms and thus deepening unlivable domination, starvation, repression. The text already contains a construed Marxist "emphasis" on conflict, the white blood cells of the social order curing episodic disease by raising the system's body temperature. Marx's "change," resolving "conflict," is utterly unlike that of the explicit text; the difference between radical change and incrementalist modifications separates Marx from the discourse of the power of the social.

Falsely speaking for Marxism, the text suggests conflict precisely to ensure its domestication, Marxism's politically terminal class struggle—the apocalypse bringing socialism in its wake—is scaled down to the healthy growing pains of a system whose exuberance occasionally is its undoing. For example, trickle-down economics rain wealth on the already wealthy and leave the poor desperate about their survival.

> Contemporary conflict theorists assume that conflict is a permanent feature of social life and that as a result societies are in a state of constant change. Unlike Marx, however, these theorists rarely assume that conflict is always based on class

or that it always reflects economic organization and ownership. (Eshleman and Cashion 1985, 42)

Sociology eschews the Marxian concept of synthesis as the prospect of a threateningly new history that would shatter the text's generic "social life" in favor of a new life joining peaceful writers in the nonidentical versions of a common humanity. Seeming to parrot Marx, the text makes conflict and the change into which it resolves a law of social nature. "Society's" ability to protect itself ironically against conflict (that Marx hoped would be its undoing) is born of structural contradictoriness and the resulting desperate necessity of the margin's survival, a conflict over life itself and not simply about a slice of this or that pie—federal funding for schools, the aged, AIDS victims.

The text remarks that Marx's fetish of class and "economic ownership" is too narrow, guarding against exactly the sort of "economic" synthesis Marx hoped for and expected as an *end* to (class) conflict. By relativizing conflict into any disagreement, struggle, or contest—barroom drinkers, again—the text disqualifies Marx's political synthesis, instead parading Marxism as a prisoner of war that, suitably acculturated, can play a role in the social text. Yet to more attentive readers the metaphysic of conflict is absolutely opposed to Marx's dream of synthesis—antithesis itself "sublated" (negated-preserved-transcended) into a new social order beyond structured conflict.

Conflict theory replaces Marxism while mouthing seemingly Marxist words: class struggle and domination are reduced to "conflict," particular inflated into general. Espousing an empty liberalism that would enslave humanity while respecting the rights of others, the text goes wild over its accommodation with Marxism, concealing its political agenda—more of the same—in the seemingly progressive claim that history is the history of group conflict, presumably Marx's insight.

> The conflict-oriented theorists argue that at a minimum conflict is as natural a process in society as stability and consensus and that it may be more natural and typical than stability. Stability may be an unusual and temporary state of society. (Denisoff and Wahrman 1983, 21)

But Marx was not writing against "stability and consensus," neither of which has predominated in world history, past or present. The text's deft construction of significant debate out of the stability/change contrast allows it to "resolve" it in a way that coopts Marx's seeming emphasis on conflict and thus preempts socialist synthesis, the historical *undoing* of the supposed "law" of conflict. The social nature of conflict does not lead to a more radical textual politics but rather depoliticizes conflict by relativizing it, precluding its dynamic-dialectical opportunity to put an end to itself by effecting a qualitative rupture in world history. Conflict theory only perpetuates conflict by according it a central role in history, thereby relativizing it; yet the text's version of conflict is no more tractable than the tides. Sociology's social nature is still nature (even if at some level it cannot be).

Marxism is disqualified by deceptively constructing "conflict" as "more . . . typical than stability"; in Hegelian terms antithesis becomes ontology.

> Dahrendorf attacks the basic premises of functionalism, regarding that perspective as based on a utopian view of society (1958). He directs attention to society's "ugly face"—that of conflict. In contrast to Marx, he sees conflict as more a struggle for power than a class conflict over economic resources. But like Marx, he views society as always verging on instability and change. (Popenoe 1980, 94)

The mantle of Marxism is passed over to American and European sociologists like Dahrendorf, Lenski, Coser, and Giddens who render conflict universal, "society . . . always verging on instability and change." To disqualify Marxian politics the text words hard to distance latter-day empirical sociology from original Marxism while premising its sociology on the ubiquity of conflict, instability, struggle, and change. Marxist sociology is thus Marxist only in name, not in political attitude; Marxism is deployed only to name capitalist disequilibrium as the dynamic openness of healthy American capitalism.

Marxist sociology is sociology but not Marxism. Marxism is not an ontology of any sort but an historical intervention that does not repress the deepest politics of its subtext, the one that really counts—a form of life that would reformulate life as we have known it. The text's capture of Marxism neutralizes it by allowing it to speak only through the representational voice of mainstream sociology, the world centered and thus enacted in writing dominating the reading it intends to provoke. Marxism in this way serves capitalism by checking capital's tendency toward disharmony, giving the welfare state a variety of topics that sociology calls "social problems" as objects of its redistributive remedy.

Marxist sociology deepens sociology's scientism, a few of Marx's "keen insights" blown into a system-serving metaphysic—much the same sort of reclamation that bourgeois psychology has made of psychoanalysis, reduced in its right to some of Freud's keen insights into the unconscious, sexuality, early childhood experience, and so on. In more responsible hands, for example those of Erik Olin Wright and his colleagues, "a growing number of studies . . . employ Marxist thinking," applying "a Marxist perspective" to the analysis of "data from a national sample." The text uses Marxism in this case literally to name the working class, said by these researchers to be the "largest of the classes," a certain percentage of the white and black population respectively.

It is a tremendous comfort both to have Marxism working for sociology and not, say, for the KGB or the radical-feminist wing of the women's movement and at the same time to be able to prove in this case that the size of the

American working class is much smaller—44 percent to be exact—than Marx in his apocalyptic zealotry had prophesied. A "Marxist" like Wright revised Marxism allegedly in its own name and thereby made a name for himself, a "Marxist" savvy enough to quantify Marxism, analyzing "national data" with sophisticated statistical methods and—thereby—publishing in the *American Sociological Review*.[3] Marxism practiced by sociologists like Wright is more respectable than the political Marxism scandalizing the academy with its unabashed, unscholarly advocacy, violating Weber's procedural separation of science and politics.

Many of the few Marxists in universities have been reviewed by departmental, faculty, and administrative tenure and promotion committees curious about the nature and extent of their politics. The central question is not simply the quality or amount of one's published scholarship (which is not to say that those should be, or are, self-evident criteria for "advancement" for such a discussion would have to rethink not only the tenure system but the whole world in which, about which, and through which judgments are made and our academic lives affected). Of primary concern is the kind of "Marxist" one is, the brick-throwing kind or the safe scholarly kind, as if *that* were an adequate construction of the left's polarity.[4] Collegial Marxists are read to be Marxologists, "students" or "scholars" of Marxism and not also or already politically engaged. Irascible ones, by contrast, are read to be political—their difficult personalities both producing and reproducing a doctrinal commitment held to be the antithesis of bourgeois academic values. If I am cooperative in my university, I am not really left; but if I am ornery, I am too left. My Marxism, thus, is *their* construction.

This is not to say that safe Marxists survive the scrutiny of these review committees simply because they are not overtly political in their intellectual work or interpersonal style but only to observe that unsafe Marxists inevitably, automatically bite the dust; safe Marxists still have to demonstrate such an extraordinary degree of disciplinary commitment reflected in "major" journal publications, citations, and supporting letters of reference from the discipline's big names that few will make the grade anyway. American academia overdetermines academic, personal, and textual politics.

There is no affirmative action for Marxists, who only occasionally manage to navigate through the stormy straits of what is so disingenuously called merit review (Lewis 1975, 1988). But if one aspires to do so, one must demonstrate a safe "Marxist" scholarship that, like Wright, both measures the size of the proletariat and then assures us that it is not threateningly large, at least with reference to Marx's original predictions. After all, Marx reminds us that contradictory capital seems to advance only by putting people out of work.

Some of his ideas have been misinterpreted, reformulated, or refined. Nonetheless, Marx's basic ideas have served as a guide to what things about stratification

are worth studying—a guide both for those who agree with his ideas and those
who vigorously disagree. (Denisoff and Wahrman 1983, 309)

We will discuss Marx's ideas much more extensively in other chapters of this
book. Here we simply want to point out his important influence on sociology.
(Light and Keller 1985, 11)

Marxism's reduction to a conflict-oriented sociology of stratification treats
Marx as a guide to what is "worth studying" but not what is worth doing,
writing, living; indeed, "political" concerns are deemed outside the purview of
the academy. His vaunted "influence on sociology" remains only that; society
has not been transformed in its relationship to the world discipline reflects
and thus only strengthens. "Marxism" as conflict theory freezes barroom
brawls and pork-barrel politics into virtually metaphysical features of scrappy
American life. It is as if the text only recently learned English and needed Marx
to name the "phenomena" of conflict for it, otherwise remaining a lopsided
paean to "equilibrium" and "stability"—a lopsidedness that, as I will argue in
the next section, inhabits the text's adulation of the vigorous entrepreneurship
etched in the subtext underlying the term conflict. Marxism not only names
what sociology calls "stratification" or inequality—the power of the social
justified in Marx's name for it, the utter political reversal of Marxism; it also
celebrates conflict's "positive functions," too.

The Generic Dialectic of Economism

The text works over Marxism twice: first, it reduces it to a conflict theory eternalizing group conflict and thus precluding the end of conflict or communism;
second, it makes a virtue of this necessity by explicating the economic and
socio-organizational utility of generic conflict. Thus, *Capital* is ingeniously
rewritten as business logic and conflict is valorized as a positive function.

Most sociologists agree that society is orderly and that social institutions function to maintain order. They also agree that conflicts may arise when the existing
social order causes hardship for the members of a society but that such conflicts
can be beneficial. (Eshleman and Cashion 1985, 616)

The text rarely explicates the utility of conflict and inequality with the same
degree of forthrightness as Davis and Moore (1945) who justified stratification on functionalist grounds, preferring passively to average truth instead of
arguing for the results of average truth. Here the text begins its subtle second
reduction of Marxism, restoring Marxism as a productivist economism that
would do the chamber of commerce proud—Marxism sealed in amber as the
epochal truth that economics *matters*. Consensualism again wins the day as
"most sociologists" believe that "society is orderly," conflict only episodically
throwing order into sharper relief as the normal state of affairs. The text mar-

ginalizes conflict as exceptional before integrating Marxism as the discourse of ontological conflicts. The text's economism suppresses Marxism by implying that existing conflict may actually be "beneficial," a signal that the ordinarily well-functioning social system only needs a little extra grease.

This second-order conflict theory is apologia, indeed celebration, where it extracts good news from the bad news of strife, struggle, and inequality. Sociology derives a born-again Marxism from the gloomy, worldly Marxism of the nineteenth century that seems too remote to us today. Although social problems are better addressed by liberal conflict theory than by a heartless Spencerian neoconservatism—FDR's welfare state versus trickle-down economics—it is possible to view these episodes of crisis in a "positive" light; conflict both facilitates and hinders the American dream. This case is made through economism, narrowing Marxism to a constitutive emphasis on economic production; it both *limits* Marxism to "economics" and *identifies* "conflict—a source of social problems" from the vantage of the liberal text—with competition, a manifestation of the healthy vitality of American capitalism. Inequality (Wright's 44 percent, plus the few percent of the population called the "structurally unemployed," as above in the text) becomes a veritable boon to initiative.

Now that the text has constructed conflict in Weber's sense of the ubiquitous struggle for "scarce resources" as a telling sign of tractable disequilibrium, it further translates this conflict-theoretic sociology into the primacy of economic production. It sanitizes the ontological antithesis addressed by official Marxism so that it tells the good news along with the bad and thus is repoliticized, becoming spokesperson for what Coolidge knew to be a business civilization.

Marxism once centered explicates the primacy of capital in this way, reinforcing its domination over the lives of people enwaged (and unwaged) to it. As "economic determinism" or economism Marxism reinforces the sway of capital over labor, men over women, and science over art in a way that the text calls "positive," supplementing official sociology as a "perspective . . . revolving around" economics. Conflict is made "beneficial" by being constructed less as inequality than competition—economic activity generally —thus giving sociology a ground in the disciplinary realm of economics and thereby further severing Marxism from politics. The text economizes Marxism both to depoliticize it and to address the dysfunctional effects of economic conflict (inequality) in economistic terms, liberally urging the redistribution of wealth as the central solution to "social problems" and valorizing capitalist business competition as the ontological cognate of (seemingly eternal) conflict.

> In the Marxian view, everything revolved about the production of goods and services and particularly who owned or controlled the means of production. At one time man lived off the land, no one owned the land, and supposedly no one exploited anyone else. (Denisoff and Wahrman 1983, 309)

While the text may occasionally snipe at Marx's economic determinism—determinism, after all, to determine an unavoidable socialism—it nonetheless incorporates what it takes to be Marxism's economism, the reduction of exploitation and inequality to distributive issues, glossing American political scientist Harold Lasswell's version of Weber, "Who gets what, when and how." [5] The construction of Marxism as economism has the enormous advantage of silencing Marx's politics; after all, he was writing in the tradition of political economy that addresses the interrelationship between economic accumulation and state intervention. At the same time such Marxism economizes social problems-analysis, construing their solution strictly in redistributive terms.

> To Marx, then, economics is at the heart of social life. Social stratification is a reflection of economics. Variations in systems of stratification among different societies are byproducts of different models of production (farming with horse and plow, a factory system, etc.). Politics and religion, science and art—even family life and personality—are reflections of economic relationships and material conditions. (Bassis, Gelles, and Levine 1984, 271)

> [Marx] asserted that all history was marked by *economic determinism,* the idea that all change, social conditions, and even society itself are based on economic factors and that economic inequality results in class struggles between the *bourgeoisie* or owners and rulers, and the *proletariat,* the industrial workers. (Eshleman and Cashion 1985, 29)

The text is ambivalent about Marx's seeming emphasis on economic factors, "economics . . . the heart of social life." It remains suspicious of what it construes as his determinism that is even more subordinating than bourgeois sociology and as such reduces consciousness altogether. This version of Marxism as natural science prevents text from eliciting compliance with "laws" in Marxist terms, leaving no room for a liberating ideology, only one deluding and thus determining. The text, albeit deterministically deriving behavior from the external constraints and conditioning of Durkheim's generic "society," postulates and cultivates a residual domain of freedom; subjectivity, required for societal reproduction, is not eclipsed altogether. The alleged Marxian portrait of a totally administered world disenchants the world too much; it ultimately extirpates the neo-Kantian "humanism" that micrologically carves out a place for the individual, whether in family or religion (two of the text's five "major institutions," the other three—economics, politics, education—affording people less free space). Determinism loses its own disciplinary reason for being; Marxism precludes writing *before* discourse has guaranteed social obedience. Thus, for the text's purpose Marxism as a distinctive theoretical version is too clearly antihumanist, too structuralist.

The text disqualifies Marx's alleged economic determinism as a violation of its own professed liberal individualism, all of social life, "even family life and personality," become mere "reflections" of economic forces. This utterly abandons the domain of the social, which the disempowering text pretends is a balanced reciprocity of objective and subjective regions of determination —economics and politics unfree, family and religion free. Although this is only pretense inasmuch as the Durkheimian world is no less an iron cage than Marx's or Adorno's administered society, sociology does not abide what it constructs as Marx's reductionism, an exemption science insists on so that it can transcendentally name necessity and thus necessitate it. The caricature of Marxian determinism depoliticizes Marx—no failsafe revolution—while preparing Marxism for rehabilitation not as economic determinism but as economism; the supposed influence of economic forces on "society" is a mode of causality, a way of monetarizing/economizing episodic social problems in a statist way.

Economics is important to sociology because it is the region of production that sociology's text would reproduce, the ground of a "world" that can be this way and no other, its reflection promoting its actualization as such. Although Marxism gets the region of economics wrong, reading it as inevitably self-contradictory, at least in claiming it for the map of sociology it opens the way for its own representation; capitalist economic laws are ground zero of the more superstructural laws of bureaucracy, division of labor, and patriarchy. Marxism is sociology's way of granting economic production and its attendant capitalist laws the constitutive reality sociology otherwise lacks, with bureaucracy and division of labor following from the compulsive logic of capital, as the text secretly recognizes.

Durkheim and Weber presupposed a market economy in transition to a stage-managed form; Marx sketched capitalist economic "laws" that enhance sociology as an account of generic "society." Bureaucracy revealed as capitalist bureaucracy loses its binding necessity when sociology becomes merely a version of social history. The text allows the rehabilitated Marxism of conflict theory to provide sociology with a constitutive bedrock of political-economic universals. Sociology's collective unconscious grants priority to economics without seeming to do so. Marxism, thus, is a reminder that the economic region *in capitalism* is the primary one, generically subordinating seemingly non- or reproductive activities from raising children to creating art.

> Sometimes conflict theory is merely a code term for Marxist sociology. Marxist sociologists, whose perspectives grow out of the work of Karl Marx, emphasize the importance of the economic system in societies, in contrast to functionalism's emphasis on shared cultural values. And they stress the constant struggle between economic classes of people. (Popenoe 1980, 93)

> Today's "mainstream" sociologists criticize Marxism most harshly for its concentration on economics. (Goode 1984, 222)

> Marx insisted that economic influences will be pervasive in all areas of social
> life in terms of how groups are organized and in terms of what ideas people hold.
> (Orenstein 1985, 272)

> According to Marxist theory, the defeat of the ruling class and the economic
> system it controls would create extensive change because economic systems sig-
> nificantly affect all other elements within any society. (Doob 1985, 17)

The text through its purported Marxism incorporates the primacy of economics into sociology, productivism underlying the sociologically constituted
"laws" of the original theorists. Economics is most constitutive in capitalism
according to Marx, utterly dominating the devalorized regions of the "merely"
reproductive. The text's subtext both *celebrates productive relations as "we"*
know them (capital subordinating labor) and *fine tunes what is purported to*
be primarily economic disequilibrium through statist redistributive strategies
inspired by the monetarization of social problems. This liberal reduction of
Marxism follows from Keynes and FDR's original sketches of the welfare
state and gains fuller form in LBJ's War on Poverty. Economics matters because, today, economics *matters:* capitalist productive relations subordinate
other social, political, cultural, sexual, and psychic relations that in turn reproduce the hegemony of productive relations through sociology, family, church,
education, entertainment, thus succumbing to their alleged ontological permanence.

The text cunningly uses Marxism to suggest the primacy of production,
rewriting Marxism virtually as apologia for economic dominance—the timeworn metaphysical confusion of what is and what ought to be. Marx, after
all, wanted to break the hold of production *over* social life, replacing its supposedly iron laws with the self-regulating process/product of workers control.
Marx wrote for a world in which all human activity is considered valuable
work, productive and reproductive at once.

The text through the voice of Marxism makes a virtue of (economic) necessity by acknowledging the primacy of production, shrewdly translating
the word "productive" (relations) into the word "productivity." Sociology's
Marx discovers the "beneficial" fact of competition in what might appear to be
deleterious conflict, the two entwining in a conflict-theoretic economism celebrating the helter-skelter pluralism of American frontier democracy in which
the ambition to garner a bigger share of the GNP is thought to be not only good
but also natural. Conflict is rewritten in "positive" terms by the text where
conflict is made to express the primacy of economic productive relations over
other (sociology hesitates to say epiphenomenal) social institutions freezing
the entrepreneurial marketplace in which buyers and sellers go head-to-head in
the struggle of self-interests. Of course, Marx did not laud the marketplace but
only noted its primacy as a lever over people's lives who had nothing else to

sell besides their labor power. But by accepting the metaphysical character of capitalist economic conflict (winners/losers, buyers/sellers, plural scrapping groups), economistic conflict theory restricts itself to economistic solutions only modifying allocation slightly and rendering the nature of the economic unchanged altogether; thereby the relations between the economy and other merely "reproductive" institutions like politics and sexuality remain basically the same. What is worse, this enables the disciplinary text to construct conflict (out of Marxism) as a veritable celebration of economics. Conflict is now described as competition—a neoconservatism advocating more competition as the solution to conflict construed as unequal competition.

The statist liberalism of the surface text is belied by the text's own valorization of conflict's "positive" functions in the context of a Marxian-inspired economism ontologizing the primacy of (capitalist) productive relations over the non- and reproductive. This limits remedies narrowly to allocative terms, whether statist intervention or, as the text implies at a deeper level (with Spencer, Reagan), enhanced competition unburdened of state constraints. By integrating Marxism in this way, sociology astonishingly becomes neoconservative, reducing Marxism to apologia for capitalist economic primacy and solving its allocative problems in these terms, either through the Keynesian welfare state or the unconstrained marketplace itself, "beneficial" conflict now a constitutive metaphor of capitalist business/busyness. This only reproduces the primacy of production no matter how vigorously the liberal text may advocate for the "victims" of an exuberant, if sometimes dysfunctionally skewed, capitalist "society." Through its version of Marxism the text names a pluralist society in which open avenues of opportunity and mobility exist for those hardy enough to set out on them, the word "pluralism"[6] replacing the word "capitalism" as conflict is softened and sanitized—and thus lived out by the acquiescent.

Finally, having settled its score with Marxism by centering it as the reflection of eternal inequality and productivist economism, conflict is transmogrified into healthy competition, the hallmark of a supposedly pluralist society. The text dismisses conflict theory as the survival of Marxism by reducing Marxism to conflict theory. And even conflict theory is denatured into an apologia for competition—capitalism. The margin centered, like the spy among us, always threatens its betrayal. Only apparently having been defused, defiant versions like Marxism really possess an explosive power insufficiently constrained by the metaphysical limits of the text.

Thus, sociology's seeming graciousness toward conflict theory—its neutralized Marxism, rewritten under the anti-Marxist aegis of Weber—is always in the end rescinded as the text ensures that the centered margin will still be seen as somewhat disreputable, a convert and not an original member of the faith. Despite Marxism's computerization, its conversation with mainstream sociology, its socialization in the ways of academe and the conference circuit, Marxism is still only *in* the text but not *of* it. The center ever retains its primacy, its constitutive power to name the margin and to take from it only as much as it needs to advocate a world in which it was originally an angry retort.

Center-margin relationships are above all power relationships, decided by a criterion of literal reading allowing one externally to adjudicate the correct balance between Marx and Weber or the exact size of the working class. The text, then, flexes its muscles when it thinks that the integrated margin— "Marxist sociology" in this case or "feminist sociology" in the next section— is being given too much play, overwhelming the center and becoming a center itself. Marxism is dangerous where it no longer only complements or corrects the main text but competes on an equal footing with it. Intellectual pluralism and liberalism are always illusions fostered by a text that wants to appear open to difference; in reality, Marxism is not a writing equal in the strength of its validity claims to functionalism but always defective, useful but never true.

The text's strategy of disqualifying Marxism a second time, no longer as Soviet practice but now as sociologized conflict theory or Marxist sociology, challenges the very economism it derived as a "keen insight" of Marx. This economism bridges between production and institutional reproduction in a disciplinary division of social-scientific labor otherwise bifurcating economics and sociology too cleanly.

> Marx nowhere gave empirical evidence that economic differences were the sole basis of other social differences such as power and respect (Dahrendorf, 1959). His claim, however, was an empirical one that could be tested by other social scientists. If power or prestige can be shown to vary independently of property, then Marx's statement is at least excessive and perhaps false. Indeed, the likelihood that the economic dimension of property does not govern all aspects of stratification made many sociologists who came after Marx very uneasy with his single-factor conception of class. Among them was Max Weber. (Stark 1985, 204)

The text's main challenge to a conflict theory constructing itself out of demonized Soviet Marxism rests on the explanatory status of economism, once held by the text as "keen insight" and now suspected of causal monism, exaggeration, being "excessive . . . perhaps even false." The instrumental rationality of science allows "other social scientists" to test Marx's presumably implied claim that "economic differences were the sole basis of other social differences such as power and respect," the usual Weberian truism.

Integrated as the primacy of economics and indeed of capital, Marx's economism is blunted by Weber's tripartite distinction among class, status, and power; the last two, as the text suggests, were reduced—empirically falsely— by Marx to epiphenomena of the social relations of production, obscuring the multidimensional, plural nature of capitalist stratification. For the Weberian discipline, the existence of crosscutting dimensions of inequality do not neatly resolve into two warring camps—prepotent capital and heteronomous labor. The multidimensionality of stratification deconstructively gives the lie not only to Marx's method of class analysis but also, even more important, to his apocalyptic projection of inevitable class warfare. It is impossible to guarantee increasing class polarization in a world in which a person can be ranked high on one dimension of stratification but low on another; for example, anti-Marxists trumpet Lenski's (1966) status inconsistency as an argument against Marx's alleged monism.

Thus, Weber's plural theory of stratification is used against a constructed Marxian economism to render that economism "empirically" excessive, maybe even false. This is another way of understanding conflict theory as a version of Weber in his opposition to Marxism and not, as the text hopes to convince readers, as an integration of a safe Marx *unless Marx and Weber are identified*. The Weber renaissance shortens the distance between Weber and Marx; today Marx was not a fringe radical after all but almost an official sociologist dedicated to disciplinary accumulation. Again, the idealizing impulse of capitalism holds sway over thought whose nature is distinction and differentiation. If conflict theory is Weberian, as it almost always is, then it is not Marxist. The text wants its cake and eats it, too, when it claims to integrate Marxism as economistic conflict theory but ends up Weberianizing Marx out of existence. Conflict theory gets its name (and thus its right to name) ostensibly only from Marx; in fact, Weber named conflict for sociology in his discussion of intersecting class, status, and power groups, the foundation of later interest-group theory in American social science with its ontology of pluralism.[7] Just as Marx is said to economize sociology appropriately, so Marx politicizes it if one traces the alleged pedigree of the concept of conflict back to Marx instead of Weber; thus, Marxism becomes not only productivism but also group pluralism, a fundamental voice of American capitalist democracy's good health. But all of this is Weber's text and not Marx's: Marx was not a metaphysicist of either the hegemony of economics or political pluralism; indeed, he was their opponent.

It is ingenious to impute these economic and political sentiments to Marx when they are owed to Weber's defense of the productivity and plurality of capitalist society *against* Marx. The conflation of Weber and Marx subordinates Marx to Weber. The Weber renaissance allows the text to integrate Marxism—economism and generic conflict—without losing the leverage to disqualify it again and again, first as the gulag itself and then as an overreaching conflict theory. Its three interrelated weaknesses are accordingly its economism and monism, the oversimplification of "complex" society and finally its conspiracy theory, all distortions. Once Marx is saddled with essentially Weberian sentiments about the eternity of conflict, and thereby sanitized, the text then hems in the resulting "conflict theory" by subjecting it to the same (yet different) disqualifications leveled originally at Marxism. The only difference is that the criticisms now take a more methodological form.

This twice removes the text from Marxism, banalizing it as "keen insight" into the importance of economics. Although disentangled from Soviet practice, Marxism is now made palatable for public consumption; it is still constructed as a monism either defying testing altogether or testing out to be false, alleged economism exaggerated (just as, politically, Marx exaggerated the ills of capitalism, as the text will tell us shortly).

> The most basic problem with the leftist perspective is that it borders on being a "monistic," or single-cause, theory. Must each and every feature of capitalist society serve the ruling class? The Marxists say that they must, and they prove it by dreaming up a "political economy" (that is, an analysis of how the ruling elite profits) of just any social institution. Thus, we get political economies of everything from sex, the family, education, medicine, religion, the state, work, cities, racism, crime, women's liberation, to the songs of Dionne Warwick. What the Marxists sometimes ignore is that it is equally possible to show how the ruling elite does not profit from certain social arrangements, behavior patterns, or institutions. The argument that society's noneconomic institutions (in Marxist terms, the "superstructure") are little more than a reflection of its economic "base" is one-sided and often mistaken. (Goode 1984, 445)

The text adopts Marxism but only as a set of heuristic emphases, suggestive but ultimately false economism. As the text itemizes the many topics allegedly or possibly addressed by Marxism, even (outrageously) including the songs of Dionne Warwick, it ridicules its alleged monism for taking its own "keen insights" too literally. What the text calls "political economy" operates in Marxist texts as a fiction replacing the nuances of empirical research probing the Marxian list of topics in a nonjudgmental way. Sociology's economics refuses Marxian overdetermination.

Here sociology jealously defends its territory from economics while it rejects the economism it earlier accepted if only as a complement to its own sociologism. "Economics" is a surrogate for Marx's threatening class analysis laying bare the power of the social as a deliberate historical construction—capitalism in fact and/as in text. Economism is fine as long as it only acknowledges the relevance of economic productive relations and conflicts for sociology, even twisting conflict as competition into healthy supply-side capitalism. But once Marxism elaborates an economic analysis showing the untoward domination of social and political life by the economizing imperatives of capital assigning everything a price, sociology rejects it as "monism," too much of a good thing. Marx's argument is taken too far with "noneconomic institutions" illegitimately derived as mere "reflections" of the economic base.

The text locates this sort of monistic determinism in Marxism for it can then easily reject Marxism as it would reject any seemingly unbalanced version wildly reducing the social totality to one or another expressive principles, whether economic interest or (in the case of feminism what the text constructs as) misogyny, women hating. It uses Aristotle against the sweeping presumptuousness of what it calls a "single-cause theory," averaging truth out of a variety of seemingly different framings together invalidating any single version as distortingly perspectival.

Marxism constructed as economism is rejected as economism. The text argues both that conflict is not the only social relation and that economic factors do not explain everything, a case seemingly strengthened by the ridicule of conflict-theoretic Marxism that "dreams up" a "political economy" to be applied to "just any social institution" from crime to music. Discipline vitiates this political economy, economistically constructed as "how the ruling elite profits"—and not in the broader sense of understanding the linkage between production and reproduction. This construction of Marxian economism decides against Marxism from the beginning, missing entirely the analytic strength of Marxism not in "explaining" profit per se but in addressing, and thereby attempting to overturn, not only profitable production but also the intellectual, sexual, and political reproductions, including science's text itself, perpetuating the world.

The text's dismissal of a protean, obsessive Marxism that cannot keep its hands off any topic is comprehensible only in this light. Yet it is difficult to take seriously the text's implied claim to noninclusiveness when it runs up just as long a serial list of topics for "explanation" as does its Marxism, probably longer at that—the twenty-five chapters/topics in most introductory and social-problems textbooks.

> Today's "mainstream" sociologists criticize Marxism most harshly for its concentration on economics. How does this Marxist perspective apply to ordinary men and women? How can we understand human behavior solely by knowing any person's relationship to the means of production? A tiny number of capitalists own these means, and everyone else owns practically none whatsoever—no income-producing land, no factories, no great wealth. This means that nearly all contemporary occupations—janitor, professor, lumberjack, doctor, mailcarrier, artist, and lawyer—are actually in the same social class, the proletariat, in that these workers do not own the means of production. (Goode 1984, 202)

The text again invokes a consensuality against Marxism where "today's 'mainstream' sociologists criticize Marxism most harshly for its concentration on economics." So what? Ten thousand American sociologists cannot be wrong, especially where they construct the same Marxism they dismiss as economism. The text rejects Marx's imputed reduction of people's behavior to their relationship with the means of production on grounds that that criterion alone fails to help us meaningfully distinguish among diverse occupations, from janitor to lawyer. If Marx used "solely" that criterion of relationship to productive means as an "explanation" of every aspect of social life, the text would be correct (assuming, of course, that Marx shared science's attempt to "explain" behavior at all).

But Marx was trying to make the point that, although individual "behavior" has all sorts of cultural, historical, and even psychological pivots (read his *18th Brumaire* along with his other historical writing), capitalism *reduces* differences among people who share the common experience of being waged; this tendency will eventually bifurcate capitalist society into inexorably opposed classes. Capital levels political, occupational, sexual, racial, ethnic, and religious differences in face of the myth of an indivisible bourgeois individuality regarding everyone as unique. Sociology vainly tries to halt the abstracting, depersonalizing process of identification it locates more in reductive naming than in totalizing capital—making out teachers no less than janitors to be servants of capital.

Marx was not oblivious to a degree of blurring between the two largest classes, capital and labor; and he wrote frequently about the distinctiveness of the petty bourgeoisie as well as of what Engels later called labor's aristocracy. However, he felt that the power of capital in eventually destroying the petty bourgeoisie would homogenize waged workers in a common, faceless sea of the powerless—a "prediction" the bourgeois text refutes only by innuendo. Indeed, the lion's share of bourgeois sociology is precisely an attempt to differentiate this large sea of the subordinated into the distinctions, levels, and ranks displaying the seeming heterogeneity, indeed healthy plurality, of capitalist society. This is further methodologized in the text's mathematical attempt to explain "variance"—assuming variance as typically characteristic of late capitalism.[8]

The bourgeois text cannot accept the proletarianization of its own labor; "professor" is included in the long list of occupations with the more menial labors of lumberjacks and janitors—of course, precisely Marx's point about neither owning nor controlling the process and products of one's work. I am not saying that academic labor or the professions are equally as degraded as janitorial work because in many cases they are not, at least for the tenured and partnered. But it is self-deluding to think that simply because some people have white collars, credentials on their walls, and work in pleasant environments they are in control of their work and lives. Academia and the professions are often nightmares for intellectually, politically, and socially marginal people who are all too often crushed by the weight of text, literature, mainstream, professional norms. As well, because white-collar professionals are enmeshed in a self-serving web of idealizations about the honor and integrity of that kind of work, professional workers are often unprotected by unions and experience the same (or *worse*) vulnerability as factory and office workers; their jobs are contingent on vague criteria of job performance secreted away in the minds of their beneficent employers.

Academics support the myth of their own unique merit and thereby reject Marx's understanding of their relative powerlessness as workers subject too often to the whim of management. Academics seek to join an elite only ambiguously granting them entry, using academic research when it is useful to them but otherwise disdaining the unworldliness and gentility of ivory-tower pedants. Marx hits too close to home for academics desperately in search of legitimacy and status, underlining their common cause with blue-collar and pink-collar laborers in terms of Marx's interdependent criteria of ownership-and-control of the production process.[9] The issue of whether academics and professionals truly control their work depends in large measure on the nature of the institution in which they work—an Ivy League institution, a small Jesuit school, a state university, an unusually progressive or politicized department. Class position, then, is not simply a function of the prerequisites of one's occupation in its relation to other occupations arranged vertically on the prestige ladders assembled by scholars in the so-called status-attainment tradition of Blau and Duncan (1967). Instead class, like sex and race, is nested in the social relations of production and reproduction in which whole groups are entwined.

Economism is abided by the text as long as it is constrained by a multivariate frame disqualifying supposedly "single-cause" theories. Multivariate analysis reflects and constitutes pluralist difference at once retaining the concept of causality while diversifying causality among a host of crosscutting "variables." Thus, multivariate analysis deconstructs the decenteredness and openness of "society" (of which the neo-Weberian status-attainment tradition in the study of stratification is among the foremost examples).

Sociology synthesizes the social sciences in the way it incorporates the "influences" of economic, political, cultural, religious, and geographic "variables" in its straightforward representation of the power of the social—behavior "caused" by an impinging social structure. Yet sociology is opposed to a monism that in reducing causality to a single variable points up the actual dominance of that "institution," for example capitalism (generically, economics), *over* the others. This gives the lie to a pluralism freezing multivariate causality as the essence of democracy. Marxism is fine as long as its alleged economism only implies the primacy of (capitalist) production intended as the virtues of competition and hard work; as text, however, Marxism exaggerates "economics" at the risk of closing the open society in which, as Weber saw, the trinity of class, status, and power is an artifact of a dynamic and complex opportunity structure. The person "low" on one of these "dimensions" is probably higher on another, or at least hopeful of moving up—Lenski's status inconsistency peculiarly proving that America is an open frontier in which everyone gets *some*thing, whether money, power, or prestige—occasionally, all at once. Exchange theory is thus an ontology.

This doubly disqualifies conflict theory as both "Marxism" and a monism failing to appreciate the ontological "complexity" of "society," the logos of conflict "only one piece in a very large puzzle."

> As with all other theories of deviant behavior, conflict theory provides only a part of the picture. Some forms of behavior are widely condemned, sometimes for reasons that reflect the interests and the views of many classes, not just the ruling class. Certain norms and laws do protect the members of the society at large— those that prohibit robbery, murder, and rape, for instance. In addition, conflict theory does not ask why certain individuals or categories engage in deviant or illegal behavior—only why that behavior is deviant or illegal in the first place. As a limited explanation, conflict theory has great value, but is only one piece in a very large puzzle. (Goode 1984, 191)

Again, the text invokes Aristotle against its own middled, mitigated version of Marx who "provides only a part of the picture." In its discussion of the limitations of Marxism in the analysis of crime and "deviant behavior," the text constructs conflict theory as a distorting perspectivity failing to appreciate the overall functional utility of certain universal prohibitions against "robbery, murder, and rape." Instead an overdetermining Marxism traces the criminalization of certain behaviors directly to the interests of the "ruling class."

A Marxist would argue that the seeming universalism issuing in universal taboos of robbery, murder, and rape only protects the production and reproduction of domination and reveals numerous inequities and inconsistencies in the arrest and prosecution of these crimes in capitalist and state-socialist societies. But the text in saying that conflict theory is "one piece in a very large puzzle" girds itself against an emboldening perspectivity by simultaneously disqualifying and then integrating the various official writings into a single disciplinary version. Once it has welcomed a version of Marxism as conflict theory to the fold, the text tellingly disqualifies it for a second time. *The double suppression of marginality remarginalizes it once a version of it has been centered,* indicting its simplistic perspectivity even as it is said to have "great value." Dissent once constructed and then disqualified again is that much less likely to infect the text with the extraneous passions of the political. Marxism once domesticated still misses the complexity, heterogeneity, and openness of multivariate capitalism—opened by the diversification of causality in a "differentiated" society replete with "countless factions and interest groups." But the factions are not countless, especially to a text that knows only what it can count, the urge to control a legacy of the Enlightenment inscribed in sociology as the methodological requirement that data must be encoded in the text as their quantity.

To wit, a colleague of mine voted against a job candidate who expressly emphasized an officially vouchsafed "qualitative methodology" combining participant-observation, archival work, and in-depth interviews in a study of major American corporate organizations simply—he said—because he had not developed "quantitative indicators" of the "variables" he was studying. This reveals the telling struggle between the will-to-count and a superficial ecumenism seemingly countenancing multiple methodologies elaborated under the sign of Aristotle, a clash inevitably resolved in favor of methodological monism. My colleague defended his vote by saying that the candidate's seeming imperviousness to the quantitative in the long run will make him untenurable because without quantification he could never hope to do "funded research," the latest operational criterion of meritorious scholarship imposed by the upper administration of our university and now gleefully aped by faculty who always wanted to be entrepreneurs anyway.

But the implied irreducible complexity of society missed by the dominant Marxist version of conflict theory is an empirical question, as it was for Marx, and thus it is incumbent on the text in its own terms actually to count the "significant" groups and classes that in conflict are said to produce social change and not just to assert that the number of these "factions" is "countless," an explicit vitiation of its own categorical imperative, the will-to-count. This would require not unmediated mathematization (the pages of the newspaper scoured for the names of topics, groups, and factions—air-traffic controllers, South African blacks, the Teamsters' Union) but a concept of significance to be constructed in much the same way that Marx defined class structurally in terms of groups' relations to the means of production (and, feminists would add, reproduction), a construction allowing the counting to begin.

The text assumes that because the "factions" are "countless" they cannot be orchestrated into an analytic totality intermediating race, age, religion, sex, and class, rejecting out of hand—unempirically—a Marxism or feminism that tries to think the complex mediations between and among levels and styles of domination. Instead the text shrinks from the "complexity of society"— "very large puzzle," "differentiation"—in assuming that complexity cannot be simplified by writing unraveling it in terms of the variously "significant" center-margin relationships comprising history; complexity is named as a crude datum, the "countlessness of factions" issuing in their pretheoretical assemblage. Thus multivariate analysis—the methodological response to Marxist monism—turns its back on interconstitutive relationships among variables except as these are to be correlated statistically.

But the so-called variables have to be constructed in a way that establishes their interconstitutive significance in terms of their location and function in the totality of the contemporary world, not simply itemized on a roster of quantitative variables to be manipulated through inferential statistics. If the "factions" are interconstitutively (and not only statistically) significant, they are real groups of people in struggle against their isolation and oppression, not abstract properties of individuals possessing no world-historical potential, *simply the products of their group affiliations but not also authors of them*. The text turns these affiliations into variables possessing an unreflectively constitutive equality (race = sex = religion = class, etc.) precisely because it refuses to simplify, and thereby further politicize, a world in which there are interconstitutive relationships among "factions" and in which members of some factions are struggling to be free. Such defiants resist reduction into their abstract membership in one or another marginal group but are now the universal people described by Marx, Sartre, and Gramsci as collective or social individuals. These self-totalizing people can no longer be studied multivariately as abstract products, not authors, of disempowered group affiliations; the so-called "variance" is reduced to zero in a reign of fundamental equality; variance is only a statistical artifact of domination and, particularly, of distributive inequality.

The alleged multivariate complexity of society allows it to be rendered unto text, science having a vested interest in abstracting people (in text and/as deed) as unequal bundles of affiliations and attributes. Freedom is freedom from methodological abstraction and statistical inference, the end of causality and thus sociology. This is scandalously utopian to the apparatchiks of social-science disciplines who live off abstraction as a reified social process, exactly what Lukacs (1971) called reification, oppression made (and remade) second nature. Conflict theory is lambasted as the politicization of these mutually reifying processes of abstraction, counting the "factions" that the text in its own defense (but ironically, given its quantitative fetish) contends are "countless." Although the text seems to drive for a cumulative glimpse of absolute causality, finally resolving the various correlations of variables into a seamless causal sequence, science's own rebellious authoriality prohibits this. At this juncture it only acknowledges that the complexity of society proliferates many "conflicts" irreducible (it is left unsaid) to conflict along a single dimension, be it economics, race, or sex, as "Marxist" conflict theory presumably tries to do.

This misses the nonexclusivity of so-called conflict theories (e.g., Marxism, feminism) that understand the range of interconstitutive relationships, as I have called them, among a host of "variables"—levels and forms of conflict, really of oppression—neither reducing causality to a single locus nor relativizing it into an endless series of coequal "conflicts" in its endlessness demonstrating the complexity, openness, and goodness of American pluralism. Marginal versions capturing the interconstitutiveness of concatenated yet nonidentical oppressions are disqualified by a text using multivariate analysis not to understand the totality but simply to reduce correlated variables to causal sequences; statistical manipulation enables the various variables one day to be connected

by identifying causal arrows. In the meantime, while the data are under accumulation, the conflict-theoretic search for causality is ironically rejected by the
text as simple-minded monism, apparently missing the genuine heterogeneity
of "society" divided among the scrapping "special interest groups" that seem
to contend today for a slice of the pie.

In this way the text obscures the difference between Marx's focus on the
proletariat, however problematic that may be today when read in his original historicizing terms, and the methodological (and thus political) pluralism
of competitive special interest groups looking out only for themselves. Marx
thought that the increasingly immiserated proletariat, constituted and at once
degraded by capital that lives off its surplus, embodied the universal interest
of humanity, not the special interest of this or that segment of one or another
national working class (dismissing the struggles of groups such as nonwhites
and women not literally tapped by him to carry the banner of transformative
struggle). And as the text diminishes Marxism into a speical interest economism it does exactly the same thing to feminism which, like Marxism, too
often leaves itself open to the caricature of a narrow economism.

Marx at least hoped for a world not torn apart by the turf battles among
various powerless groups, especially over which one has the best claim to a
nobility of suffering. The text's special interest pluralism reproduces a world
in which suffering has been differentiated in the spirit of divide and conquer.
Whether or not it took the literal form of Marx's original world-historical
male European proletariat, politically concerted dissent is shattered by a text
making "conflict" and its alleged ontological diversity an invariant feature of
the human condition. Thus, in the last analysis, the text seemingly redeems
a conflictual society—conflict valorized as pluck, the chosen form of life of
entrepreneurial personalities.

The text uses the diversity of dissent against marginal versions like Marxism
and feminism that, in what I regard as their best formulation, universalize the
"interest" of oppressed people and groups by providing accounts of the interconstitutive nature of plural oppression today. These defiant versions thereby
both create brotherhood/sisterhood and afford insights into the concerted character of the oppositional strategies thus required to dent the overdetermined
world. By saying, in effect, that Marxism is about male blue-collar workers,
feminism about women, and antiracist movements and writings about nonwhites, the text takes it to be so, especially when addressing an audience—reasonable American citizens—thus accustomed to seeing the world in Hobbesian
terms.

Finally, the text saddles reconstructed-Marxist conflict theory with an imputed conspiratorialism both reducing all human motivation to economic interest (following up on the "charge" of untoward economism, earlier) and
empowering capitalist elites with a concerted manipulativeness defying what

the text calls "reality." The most popular object of this second-order vitiation of Marxism is surely C. Wright Mills's (1956) *The Power Elite*, now commonly defended as a non-Marxist work by conflict theorists seeking to put more distance between conflict sociology and Marxism; they ironically do this by bringing Marx and Weber closer together—either removing Marxism from conflict theory or deradicalizing Marx. By his own admission in *The Marxists* Mills was a Marxist, albeit a "plain" nonintellectualizing one in the terms of his somewhat idiosyncratic typology of Marxisms. Mainstream sociology has always recognized this, especially in its opposition to *The Power Elite* as essentially Marxist conspiracy theory, empowering the "military-industrial complex" with more integrative efficacy than it really possesses. Here the text observes tellingly that capital is nonidentical to the state or other "dominant institutions of society" possessing what it calls "relative autonomy" (parroting without acknowledging a version of latter-day Marxism). Sociology's capitalism is not the seamless conspiracy suggested by Mills or by Marx and Engels in *The Manifesto*.

> The conflict approach draws our attention to the partisan nature of social institutions. Yet it is often difficult to determine from conflict literature, particularly its Marxist versions, which specific individuals and groups are covered by such phrases as "capitalist elites" and "governing classes." Indeed, one often gets the impression that the legal system and the state are instruments that can be manipulated at will by the capitalist class or segments of it. But this picture hardly conforms to reality. Many state policies do not advance the interests of capitalist groups. For instance, welfare legislation supports unemployed and nonproductive workers, and rent controls inhibit a landlord's ability to receive full market rates. In many situations the "state apparatus" in fact exercises a relative autonomy from the interests of outside groups. (Light and Keller 1985, 215)

Using the text's consensualism against it, it is difficult to imagine many Marxists today who do not agree with its claim that the capitalist elite is differentiated, does not pull strings like a puppeteer, and is propped by (but not identical to) a "relatively autonomous" state apparatus, sentiments found in Marx himself where he elaborates the role of the state characterized as an "executive committee of the bourgeoisie." Sociology makes Marxism a straw text by imputing to it a conspiratorially seamless view of capital-state functioning as a way of disqualifying its view of power-centeredness, a vitiation of the text's abiding liberal pluralism that hears all the voices of dissent.

The text sinks deeper into disingenuousness where it suggests that "many state policies do not advance the interest of capitalist groups" (could there be more than one capitalist group, on this interpretation?), using welfare as an example of the nonpartisan nature of social institutions. Of course the state doles out welfare to keep the poor in check, forestalling their open insurrection and keeping them in clothes, booze, and cars, without which economic reproduction would grind to a halt. In fact, state intervention is the key survival strategy of the original welfare state plotted by Keynes. It is a way of mediating capital and labor, appearing bipartisan (thereby enhancing democratic legitimation) and yet stoking the capitalist accumulation process through direct investment, fiscal policy, domestic social control, army, international imperialism, and the like.

In spite of the text, there need not be a simple conspiracy of capitalists and administrators of the state apparatus for Marx's critique of political economy to be credible as long as the structural mutuality of politics and economics is made clear, as surely it is today, with the profit system propped by all sorts of supporting "institutions" like politics, culture, family, church, and school.

> There is a serious flaw in this argument. Radicals generally, and Marxists especially, make the mistake of arguing from effects to causes. That is, they assume that when someone profits from a certain institution or form of behavior, the effect must be intentional. For instance, Marxists argue that the sensational nature of TV news diverts public attention from the "really important" issues—exploitation, oppression, racism, sexism, imperialism, etc. In fact, this is probably a real effect of the sensationalism of the TV news. Even so, it does not automatically follow that TV executives are even aware of the diversionary impact of sensationalism, are chiefly influenced by it, or even care about it. Marxists argue that we can reason from the status quo to what powerful people actually do to sustain it, but this is a step for which we need evidence, not mere unsupported claims. (Goode 1984, 444)

It is easy to refute Marx's analysis of structural mutuality by supposing that institutional elites should understand the structural contributions of their action to the reproduction of capital. Individuals need not understand structural mutuality at all—for example, television news as "diversionary"—for their actions to enhance that very mutuality, TV's portrayal of gore or sex diverting people from Reagan's sick joke about bombing the Soviets. Indeed, television executives sensationalize news to get better "ratings," sell advertising, and make more money for their networks and, thus, themselves. Marxism is not a social psychology of elite behavior (for that, see Pareto, Michels, Veblen, or Packard) but a theory of structural mutuality tracing "action" to the dominated lifeworlds produced by capital and reproduced by our limited, self-serving choices. This vitiates the notion that most people make "choices" at all but are simply led to cede their freedom to the alleged societal requisites of occupational and social reproduction. The dominance of capital takes place behind the backs of virtually everyone, including members of the elite; its dominance is scientized as "fate" and then/thus reproduced as we fulfill our various "role obligations" dictated by (what are taken to be) capital's imperatives, thereby becoming so.

Far from requiring network television executives to understand their own structural contribution to the reproduction process, Marxism says that they *do not,* inhabiting a lifeworld for all practical purposes decided for them by the structural mutuality between the media and capital. The "rational choice" model of bourgeois economics according to which people calculate their own benefits ("profit") from certain behavior is correct inasmuch as the rational-choice model has been constructed as the epitome of rationality today, both acted on and thereby acted out.

But Marxism does not add the additional requirement that insurgent people must look beyond their narrow self-interest, defined for them and by them in the various institutional settings in which they find themselves, where the only options are to go along or to succumb, defiance marginalized as, quite literally, nonsense. People in their resistance need not comprehend the objective interest of everyone in the world system—"all humanity." Instead, the hegemony of domination over our lives and leisure operates such that our "rational choices" are neither rational (for us, in the long run) nor choices but serve the world-historical interest of production and reproduction, keeping us spinning our wheels by going to work, getting married, having children, shopping, watching television. Marxism's point is that micrological "rationality"—reasonableness —that at least in the short term will not get us killed or imprisoned is defined for us as macrological reason, the system-serving lives that most of us lead in ignorance of qualitatively different alternatives.

Precisely in the nature of the modern, people both choose their oppression in the sense that they continue to play it out against their own true interest in liberation and at the same time do *not* choose it; it is merely imposed on them as the finite horizon of possibility, of reasonable expectations. Marx neither requires members of privileged groups to be fully aware of the systemic function of their behavior nor does he absolve them, or any of us for that matter, of culpability in producing and reproducing the given. Domination is not so much a conspiracy as an act of daily stupidity and cupidity, actualized in the host of miserable self-defeating, self-destructive choices we all make about our lives largely in ignorance of the enormous constitutive powers we possess; it is no longer (if it ever was) simply a problem of false consciousness but of false life—layer upon layer of self-negating routine promoted in and through our disempowering textual relationships reproducing themselves endlessly, without question. The text egregiously supposes that Marxism requires people to intend their behavior in the sense of understanding its full implications for themselves and others. It is just the opposite: virtually none of us does.

The text's last word on conflict theory asserts that it "fails to come to grips with . . . less controversial dimensions of social reality" such as "order" and "stability."

> The conflict perspective has the advantage of highlighting aspects of society that the functionalist perspective, with its emphasis on consensus and stability,

tends to ignore. But this fact also suggests an important criticism of the conflict perspective. By focusing so narrowly on issues of competition and change, it fails to come to grips with the more orderly, stable, and less controversial dimensions of social reality. (Robertson 1983, 20)

Integrated Marxism is still too political, willfully choosing controversy over consensus; its intellectual defiance exhibits an incorrigible infantilism. People and their "society" are not so bad after all; as "complex" bundles of aspiration, motivation, and attainment people are irreducible to the antagonistic framework of overdetermining class analysis. Sociology is at risk as long as it contains an enemy within, no matter how neutralized. Thus, it continues to invoke balance against the potentially wild discursive practices of a Marxism that, gratuitously, it seems, chooses controversy and thereby misses reality's assets. This means, of course, that the text never really centers Marxism at all but resists it shrewdly by appearing at times to speak a Marxist language, intoning "conflict" to name the generic conflicts raging (and silenced) all around us. When the chips are down, "most sociologists" reject the Marxism they have constructed as maniacal monism.

PART FOUR

Marginalia II

8

Straight Feminism

Splitting the Sisterhood

Once the text dispatches by integrating Marxism, it engages feminism, the other marginal text it seeks to ingest and thus defuse. As I demonstrated in the earlier Marxism section, the text splits marginal writing by constructing it as both a good and bad version of itself, integrating the safe version and outlawing the wild; scientificity proscribes the advocacy distinguishing Marxism and feminism from positivist representation. *Why* Marxism and feminism? The discipline's subtext recognizes without explicating the centrality of both the social relations of production and reproduction along with their attendant contradictions. As such it addresses Marxism and feminism as the texts of labor and women's dissent, the two central voices of defiance in late capitalism whose accomodation is vital for its functional equilibrium. Where Marxism is the battlecry of the group most exploited in the realm of production, feminism is the galvanizing discourse of those most entrapped in the seeming "privacy" of family and sexuality, the site of production's reproduction.[1]

Should the dam of insufferable alienation burst in either the realm of work or intimacy, the stability of the social system would be seriously compromised, thus provoking science's text to shore up the cracks seemingly by making peace with these two versions of dissent.[2] Most of the world's population are either male workers or women, indicating the enormity of the dampening, reifying task facing the text that would quell dissent. In this sense, *sociology takes on feminism as it attempts to reproduce reproduction,* the crucial contribution of the social relations of sexist family and bourgeois intimacy to reproducing the productive relations of capital and state-socialism. In this, feminism is read as the battlecry of underworkers in capitalism who refuse their bioontological "fate" as existential nurturers, unwaged at home and underwaged in the pink-collar sector of the labor force.

Feminism affords the text the crucial opportunity to generalize a biopolitics of reproduction propping the public realm of capitalist exchange relations. It ingeniously twists the women's movement from a movement at its most radical opposing the public/private split altogether, along with the devaluation of housework as nonproductive labor, into a version celebrating women's destiny as eternal caretakers of the realm of reproduction, privacy, family, sexuality, domesticity—all the while both ameliorating their burden in private and opening the traditionally male world of work to them through a liberal version of feminism. Although feminism is an opportunity to reproduce reproduction's subordination to production while keeping reproductive underworkers in check, it is moreover a sexual-political force opposing not only bad reproductive politics subordinating women to male productive labor but also bad productive politics subordinating labor to capital and, within labor, pink-collar to blue- and white-collar. The text shrewdly recognizes feminism's potentially global critique of the relationship *between* productive and reproductive relations in late capitalism and thus integrates it into the liberal mainstream; feminism is not the language game of angry women but a biopolitics celebrating the banality that "you've come a long way, baby."

The text domesticates feminism into what I call a HETEROTEXT—a version that reproduces its own subordination to the world it would provoke, of which a particular case is surely positivist science—freezing the subordination of writing to the world it props. As with Marxism, the text splits feminism into an incorrigibly wild version as against a safer politics accepting its status as one among any number of plural interest groups scrapping to be heard in the babel of the latter-day welfare state. Even more than Marxism, which in its unsavory version is made to resemble the totalitarian Soviet state, feminism is easy prey for its division; the safe feminism it constructs is contrasted with wild lesbian-separatism—inherently valorizing the majority mainstream feminism of Friedan, *Ms.* magazine, Geraldine Ferraro, responsible wives and mothers everywhere.

Wild feminism opposes not only the inequalities meted out to women as members of a so-called interest group clamoring for the various redistributive redresses of FDR liberalism but the whole infrastructure of "family" named by the text as a generic subordination of private/women to public/men, femininity, heterosexuality, and childrearing. Politically reprobate feminism is labeled a lesbian separatism, opting out of the malestream/mainstream altogether by refusing to work within "the system" alongside the other interests of labor, antinuclear, blacks, and even gays (where gayness is narrowly acceptable as an "alternative lifestyle" if not as a radical politics of the personal). The text works hard to construct bad political feminism as lesbian separatism while holding to a liberal surface agenda of prochoice and pluralist tolerance. Homosexuality is fine as long as it is only sexuality, not a thoroughgoing effort to revalue and relive "everyday life" as an existence subordinated to work, politics, and men. Sociology tellingly accepts feminism as a palliative political strategy of individual women who join groups in order to further their common interests but rejects it as an *anti-ontology,* a biopolitics, *working through the whole private/public split as a textual politics of domination.*

Sociology refuses to read feminism the way I do as only contingently a women's movement or women's theory but instead as a generic critique of the reproductive/productive relationships disempowering not only women but also poetry, nature, and mind—all use-value—under sway of a world-historical productivism assigning value only on the basis of commodity principles of fungibility and fetishism. Sociology does not really loathe lesbians, although lesbianism is perhaps interpersonally threatening to most middle-class liberals; it fears the political implications of radical and socialist feminisms addressing the subordination of private to public as a generative theme of a radical political otherness that would transvalue not only "everyday" life but *thereby* life itself —that is, in a structural way.

In this section I want to excavate this subtext from the liberal versions of a centered feminism serving the world both as a palliative politics—more communication between the sexes, husbands sharing housework, equal opportunity for women in the labor market, and so on—and as a version of the inferiority of private to public realms. No matter how good it sounds, no matter how studded with approbatory references to NOW feminism, the social text opposes the versions of feminism enacting a prefigurative politics by refusing the ontological differentiation between politics and personality. I want to work back and forth between the text's seemingly ecumenical progressivism on the one hand and its deeper and thus more telling agenda preserving the public/private split as a way of reproducing a male/capitalist/white productivism in much the same way that Parsons and colleagues (1955) intended when they suggested that women are functionally suited to play expressive roles while their husbands go out into the world and act instrumentally.[3] Although the text ostentatiously displays its tolerance of homosexuality, its subtext speaks louder than these words, disqualifying lesbianism as the wrong side of feminism subverting family, men, and children, indeed the whole ethos of romantic love. Responsible, reasonable, sociological feminism, like rehabilitated Marxism before it, walks down the middle of the road, balancing the costs and benefits of modern womanhood while eschewing the strident, sexually frustrated feminism of the fringe.

Beyond their obvious similarities as threateningly marginal writings, feminists can be dismissed as utterly unfit for heterosexual civilization where (male) Marxists at least retain their masculinity if not their political good sense. After all, spurred by its difficult education on the male-dominated New Left in response to which it developed a deep nonauthoritarianism and spontaneism,[4] American feminism stresses the inseparability of reproduction and production, private and public, the personal and political, thus living its own theorized politics prefiguratively in the here and now. As a result feminists court not just political disqualification but also their personal vitiation, notably the subtext that feminists are failed women.[5]

The text neatly splits the women's movement around the pivot of sexual politics, the "wrong" political choices—untoward, unreasonable radicalism—reflecting, even compounding, the wrong personal ones. Thus, the text easily constructs wild feminist women as saboteurs of the American way of life, their politics continuous with the psychopathology of inappropriately unfeminine womanhood.[6] Where Marxists are usually at least "men," living normative reproductive relations—Marx's philandering as an emblem—feminists are more easily neuroticized as their politics are thought to reflect underlying emotional and sexual maladaptation. Thus, because feminism's threat is deeper and more dangerous than that of traditional male Marxism, toward home and even beyond, to psyche and body, it must be more definitively vanquished. Wild feminists project their "own problems," as if "problems" were inherently only "personal" ones, the public-private dichotomy at the center of western thought. Feminism threatens male privilege in the realm of the private—what sociology calls "family"—by raising the question of the political character of what the male text desperately wants to retain as its privileged preserve of primacy. The private is the locale of what goes on behind closed doors, an outlet for surplus-repressed men, themselves dominated in the workplace, who expend their frustrated desire on women and children; privacy is an escape valve for the alienation suffered once in public.

Socialist feminism (Jaggar 1983) in particular suggests that women are victimized twice. They are denied access to work altogether or, if given access, relegated to underpaid and degrading pink-collar jobs usually unprotected by unions, thus playing out their alleged existential motherhood. As well, unwaged and sexually abused in the household, women are expected to reproduce men and children—and thus culture in general—as a bioontological responsibility, the text naming motherhood in the context of universal family as a functional requisite of social order.[7]

The public/private split is deeper than the dominion of capital or gender per se, although gender is almost always the basis for differentiating the public and private. The distinction between public/private and men/women is crucial. It is precisely one of the liberal text's ameliorating strategies to advocate companionate democracy in housework and childrearing as a way of *protecting* "family" against the reproductive revolt of women; men at times (or even solely: househusbands, as the up-to-date terminology goes) become "mothers," but they do not thereby really change the sexual division of labor central to the public/private split, separating the realms of production and reproduction as the realms of value and valuelessness in industrialized capitalism and state-socialism.

The figure of the lesbian who eschews the responsibilities of her femininity haunts mainstream sociology as it threatens mainstream life with the betrayal of heretofore natural reproductive relations. The patriarchal family is constructed as one of the five universal social institutions, along with religion, education, economics, and politics. Supposedly failed women who advocate politically for the end-of-family do not serve the majority of straight women seeking comfortably bourgeois work plus bourgeois family—love, husband, kids, legal marriage, if in these times also their own names, identity, and career. Liberalism is scandalized by what it constructs as radical feminism, albeit not necessarily the "radical" of radical feminism as a distinctive analytic and political contribution to feminist discourse, reflected in books by Firestone (1970) and Daly (1973) among others, and discussed in Jaggar's (1983) comprehensive socialist-feminist guide to the heterogeneous traditions of feminism.[8] In fact, feminism is scandalized by any radicalism that seems to exchange reasonableness for a dangerously unapologetic utopianism leaving too many bodies in its wake.

Yet liberalism is even more scandalized by lesbian feminism than by other radical versions intending "only" to modify one or more of the five basic institutions (e.g., Marxism viz. economics and, derivatively, politics) and not, like lesbian feminism, to *overthrow* one of them; "family" is reduced to lesbian love dyads, thus eroding intimate civilization. Wild feminism destroys personal life itself. Its subordination to the rigors of political duty thus overwhelms the all-too-human desire for intimacy, a haven in a heartless world. The liberal text's explicit political desideratum will be made possible by companionate marriage; see Edward Shorter's (1975) cynical *The Making of the Modern Family*, showing teleologically advancing egalitarianism between men and women accompanying industrialization.

Although it is imperative for science to disqualify feminism as well as Marxism, it is harder for the text at first blush to integrate feminism than Marxism simply because feminism is not intended as science, even a "dialectical" one, but as "study" and scholarship, even sensibility, facilitating political change and simultaneously celebrating women's distinctiveness. Like original Marxism (as I read Marx), but unlike later self-styled scientific Marxism, feminism is political theory and, as political practice, defies the text to intergrate it as a science, although eventually it does. What makes the assimilation of feminism by the text possible is the relatively incongruous politics of a familist feminism converging readily with the explicit politics of an ameliorating sociology: the democratic welfare-state plus ERA. Although Marxism claims greater scientificity than feminism, making it eminently susceptible to discipline, American feminism in fact is typically reformist and thus almost always compatible with the text's professed liberalism. Feminism is usually more politically homogeneous with the politics of "conflict" sociology than Marxism; and yet it claims less scientificity than most vulgar Marxisms, thus weirdly entering sociology initially as *familism* eventually disciplined into male science as yet another species of conflict theory embracing social psychologism and economism.

Initially, feminism in the text's terms has less to offer disciplinarily than politically; its science is read only as an interested species of male conflict theory where women form another plural group—"factions"—with its own axe to grind, therefore easily accommodated by the text's seeming political ecumenism. Feminism is most telling as a political version, challenging sociology to construct its agenda as familist and heterosexist, thereby silencing other feminist versions combining analysis and advocacy in struggle against heterotextuality. Beyond its mainstream progressivism—bourgeois work plus bourgeois family—official feminist sociology, unlike official Marxism cum conflict theory, inhabits the text less as a serious rival of functionalism than as a plural interest group propping the bourgeois family. *Feminism is thus first feminized as heterosexual politics and then masculinized as a rigorous account of family's universality.*

This version in rehabilitating a feminine feminism draws license from the mainstream women's movement itself, having allegedly embarked on what Friedan calls the "second stage" (1981)—beyond the posture of initial man-hating militancy.[9] Where Marxism contrasts with functionalism on its own terms, opposing Plato and Weber's epochal construction of eternal inequality and thus, once centered, emerging as a powerful disciplinary ally of the main text—Marxism reduced to an ontological version of economism and competition—feminism is treated by the male text as a marginal version even though the text welcomes the "feminist sociology" naming the universality of family, heterosexuality, marriage. The text's feminism importantly upholds family even from within its liberal politics, supporting (male) productivism with (female) reproductivism. In this way, feminism is centered by *remaining* ·disciplinarily marginal, not a serious sociological voice but, like blacks in the 1960s, a minority claim for thirty or forty pages in which safe feminism is allowed to argue for liberal androgyny while supporting the universality of the companionate marriage. Feminism unlike Marxism fails to march through the discipline—let alone beyond it—in transvaluing every so-called substantive area in sociology but remains localized, thus essentially muted.

Most soi-disant feminists in professional sociology accept their status as a special interest group seeking only to join (and thereby enlarge) the mainstream; they not only submit to but also forward their own feminization as nonlesbian women working shoulder to shoulder with men and their simultaneous masculinization as professional participants in discipline. Disciplinary feminism only reminds the male mainstream to make good on its own explicit liberalism in order to insure that women qua interest group receive their fair share of professional advancement. Feminist sociologists frequently accept their disciplinary trivialization just as many Marxists claim a scientificity that, twisted, allows the text to ingest them. Academic feminists frequently submit to their own masculinization when they demand supposedly equal professional status, gaining influence in the American Sociological Association, places on editorial boards of journals and jobs, eventually with tenure, in academic departments of sociology. Liberal feminist scholars willingly construe feminism as the struggle of individual women to become *like men* in the hierarchy of the established profession, androgynous "sex-blindness" being the moral-political manifestation of what it means to work and live as feminists. Just as Marxists hasten their own integration by calling their writing science, so feminists expedite their masculinization in accepting the professional apparatus of science on its own terms, thereby acquiescing to the text's familism as well as its regulative standards of science as the reproduction of production's hierarchy over reproduction. Women academics thus prop the bourgeois family originally opposed by feminism as the locale of women's domination, the universality-of-family reproducing universal motherhood and *thus* disempowering women in the domain of domesticity and intimacy as well as work.

Where liberal feminism seeks male status constituted by and for an elite it undoes itself. In enshrining androgyny as its political telos, liberal feminism fails to oppose the powerful structural and cultural forces making real androgyny impossible. This version of feminism protects unequal reproductive relations by naming universal family and thus reproducing women's oppression (even if, incrementally, men become mothers, thereby only postponing the family's demise as the key reproductive institution of this society). The social text encourages the professionalization of feminism as a way of ensuring the triumph of liberalism over lesbian separatism, reflected and reinforced in the drive toward masculine (i.e., elite) statuses among women sociologists. It is virtually inevitable in capitalism that minorities will clamor for dominant-group status no matter how much that status negates the distinctiveness and humanity of minority people. The text implicates feminist academics in a process of *both* feminization and masculinization together only reproducing the skewed reproductive relations of late capitalism and state socialism; this neuroticizes the "radical" margins and entrenches sexist family. Heterotextuality inexorably subordinates private to public, women to men, thus exploiting women who typically find themselves with greater responsibility for reproduction—and except for the lucky few who carry briefcases and publish articles, end up reproducing everyone but themselves.[10]

In this way feminism is split into feminine and lesbian halves and then rehabilitated through a process of disciplinary masculinization, professionalization, and centering encoding androgynous textual politics in scientific social psychologism and economism, reproducing women-centered reproduction by enacting it. Mitigated Marxism is rehabilitated simply by exchanging Marx for Weber, thus naming a logos of permanent conflict. Feminism undergoes a somewhat more arduous route from rejection to integration inasmuch as feminine feminism is too ladylike to enter the hurly burly of computers, statistics, and professional hard-ball without the masculinizing defense mechanisms afforded by a scientific education.

Aping Marx's valorized, mythified portrait as a hard-working reader in the British Museum, Marxists were always at least capable of hard work; indeed, academic Marxism is every bit as "demanding" as statistical sociology with numerous complex and convoluted literatures to conquer. Political feminists who began with no pretenses to be mainline scholars have to be professionally domesticated whether or not this takes place in the separate disciplines or in an isolated, struggling women's studies program. Although Marxists, mostly men, are pitiful when their political zealotry gets the better of their scientific mien, feminists are downright unstable, uncommitted to the life of the mind (not to mention to men).[11] This is not a contest, as vulgar feminists and Marxists often portray it (thus reproducing their own insular defensiveness), over which is the most dominated by the society it props but a way of understanding similarities and differences between the text's treatments of feminism and Marxism as challenging writings. Where Marxism can be integrated in a thoroughgoing way, reflecting its male centrality even as a marginal writing (hard work in the British Museum), feminism has a more limited utility for a text that virtually ignores its science and instead rewrites it largely as a local politics.

In this regard, the text is more threatened by the kind of "science" feminism would become, bonding political advocacy and analysis, the personal and the political. Science disqualifies writing that is intimately a perpetual questioning about why I find myself *here,* writing this, now; text transforms life by being itself and thus opens instead of closes possible history. Feminism, the text realizes, is closer to a textual practice (feminism's personal-as-political) inscribing life in writing by making itself its own topic, desire shedding light on desire's objects as an ultimate form of reason (not decorporealized in the epochal Cartesian dualism). As such, feminism does not separate science and life the way the text recommends, only secretly to prop (bad) life through its textual reproduction; it *lives the text* immediately as a modal writer-reader —thus political—relationship, heeding Marx's ("dialectical") unity of theory and practice as the equivalent of its own unity of the personal and political, a socialist feminism collecting the two texts and politics together.

Yet it is telling that science gives less credence to feminism than to Marxism, even though the sanitized feminist account of family as the universal locale of reproduction is clearly an enduring part of the discipline's text, crucially palliating lesbianism as the possibility of a nonheterotextual world. Marxist sociology occupies a more central place in science's text than does feminism precisely because the social relations of production that it props (e.g., importance of economics, conflict/competition, etc.) are more important to the productive text than the social relations of reproduction, which have always been more or less taken for granted; the universality of male superiority has never been historically problematic.

Only with the recent threat of antifamily feminism, as the text hysterically reads it, a disciplined feminism can be granted a chapter in the disciplinary text, vitiating the wild feminism calling bourgeois family into question in the first place.[12] A male/productive Marxism is more credible to the text because it was never as unruly as a feminism driving to open "private" life to the harsh light of political criticism and thus transformation. Marxism conceals the subordination of private/reproductive to public/productive "because" it is a male text routinized to the seeming inexorability of the patriarchal family. Although Marxism differs with the main text on the nature and possibilities of the public sphere, it shares with science the notion that public is public and private private. This relegates feminism to a realm of sub- or metapolitics not half as important as the male politics defining both its differences from and similarities to the mainstream text; in the end, left-wing males have more in common with their right-wing brethren than with their feminist sisters who, if left unbridled, in addressing their so-called private lives as a crucial political transmission belt between self and society would bring Marxism itself into question.

As my version demonstrates, not all male Marxists are inured to the seemingly bioontological plight of women (that Marxism too frequently only deepens);[13] Marxism becomes socialist-feminist once it thinks through and beyond the apparent depoliticization of privacy and domesticity *as a textual mode of reproduction itself,* silence speaking louder than words. Nor is sexism necessarily written into every Marxism, a theory of universal human liberation at best. But the disciplinary text either suppresses this feminist Marxism altogether or is unaware of it, instead construing safe Marxism as the economism and conflict theory of the preceding section. Not every Marxism is inevitably sexist, where sexism is simply an inattention to the valueless realm of reproduction historically assigned to women on spuriously bioontological grounds. Certain Marxisms assign the "superstructure" (politics, culture, family, sexuality, psyche) all sorts of "productive"—that is, constitutive—efficacy (for example, see Max Horkheimer's (1972) "Traditional and Critical Theory" in which he sets the agenda of a critical theory refusing to accept the vulgar Marxist subordination of superstructure to base). Rather, the text chooses to affiliate itself with a disciplinary Marxism sharing science's valorization of valued over valueless activity, thus neuroticizing feminism where it disqualifies Marxism on abstractly intellectual grounds.

The text splits feminism into familist and lesbian separatist halves in order to integrate the former as the ironic announcement of family's universality and hence—subtext—the inherent inferiority of reproduction to production, the deepest theme of the bourgeois text's version of a feminism that works against itself. Although the text acknowledges, indeed insists, that family is universally necessary, this discussion is more a way of depoliticizing feminism by prohibiting inquiries into what the text constitutes as the private sphere; family is tellingly universal because it is closed off from public/political scrutiny.

All in all, family is only one of the text's five major institutions. It achieves primacy because feminists have made it a political battleground, insisting in effect that reproduction is a form of production and not secondary, as the epochal subtext of patriarchy suggests. Feminism insists that privacy, especially housework, produces value and should be waged as well as politically empowered. The text produces "family" because it wants to keep reproduction hidden from political view, thus vitiating the allegedly antifamily currents of political feminism. Thus, reproduction is *itself* reproduced by science—the liberal familist/"feminist" defense of the democratic family as haven-in-a-heartless world—*in order to keep its bioontological status as a natural fact intact*. Privacy's politics are to be invisible and the voices of its actors muted except where surplus-repressed males frenetically discharge their workplace alienation and pummel the female Other—a problem of "family" that then becomes a topic of liberal textual politics no less than of the interventionist "helping" professions. Thus, made-for-television movies galvanize opposition to wife- and child-abuse while raising ratings, and sociology sells by seeming to care.

Although sociology gives feminism voice as protest against the strife emanating from the otherwise happy homestead not to be invaded by political eyes, it tellingly does not raise this protest to the level of totality in addressing the essentially public nature of what the text contends (and most of us believe) is a private institution, linking the family's reproductive politics to the productive politics and economics historically dominating them and thus dominating all of us. The text induces us to continue to live family as if it were really the apolitical practice it is supposed to be.

Marxist feminism rewrites and relives *re*production—intimacy, childbirth, education, culture: *text*—as productive in its own right, exploding the hegemony of men/science/politics/economics in capitalism and state socialism over women/literature/privacy/housework. Feminism seeks to liberate desire from its bondage to the imperatives of capital and state capital in the *deeconomization* of human experience; in this, feminism threatens both vulgar Marxism and the main text that uses Marxism to write the importance of the productivist order restricting text only to iteration. Feminism challenges productivism as the deepest layer of sexism/textism inasmuch as it traps women—historically, as existential mothers—in merely reproductive, that is, essentially unmeaningful, unwaged activity. Discipline rips the world into public and private parts, thus readily enforcing a sexual division of labor in which women reproduce everyone but themselves.[14] Marxism-feminism opposes this productivism in the same sense it opposes the reduction of all human relations to relations between things (Lukacs's "reification"), joining Marx's original critique of the alienation and exploitation of human labor to the feminist critique of the public/private split entrenching women's unremunerated nurturance and thus subordination.

Feminism does not oppose production as a domain of irremediable maleness or, with liberal feminism, enters that domain essentially as men; rather it seeks to unhinge production, regarded as any expressive activity, from the wage relationship. In this way, human worth would no longer be equated with the performance of wage labor, an equation excluding many women and otherwise denigrating the so-called realm of reproduction as ontologically devalorized in comparison to valuable production—a sleight of text inevitably working against women both publicly and privately.

By regarding waged work performance as the only legitimate basis of social worth, productivism inevitably marginalizes the reproductive as *non*productive, making allegedly nonproductive people objects of social disapprobation as well as economic shortfall. Marxist feminism informs traditional Marxism with the feminist critique of productivism (paralleling the Frankfurt critique of instrumental rationality, a connection virtually no one makes). This both negates the notion that "family" is reproductive but not productive and points politics beyond the epochal productivist definition of social worth toward a new order in which the barrier between reproduction and production (female/male, labor/capital, text/world) is broken down. Heterotextuality subordinating the seemingly non- and reproductive to male productivism is negated in a world in which poetry, childrearing, industrial labor, daydreaming are all equally worthy and "output" is no longer the measure of human dignity.

Vulgar Marxism and vulgar feminism alike misplace their own potentially powerful critique of productivism as they separate themselves, respectively, into the study of production as against reproduction. Marxism and feminist economisms together accept the capitalist standard of worth as output. Vulgar Marxism clamors for state production so vast it eventually obviates human work, bourgeois sociology's postindustrialism; vulgar feminism lobbies for the androgynous treatment of women (as men) in the bourgeois labor market, following the so-called income gap between men and women as a barometer of feminist progress. These are not wrong, only incomplete, for they miss their own disjuncture as a topic for their conjoined study. The primacy of production in capitalism and state socialism is addressed in terms of its victims, *both* those who "lose out" in the marketplace and those excluded from the market altogether. This version of production and reproduction illuminates their inexorable connection. Whether Marxist or feminist, economism only capitulates to production's primacy, thus denigrating the allegedly nonproductive, whether labor or women.

It is easy for oppositional movements to fetishize the texts that reproduce reproduction, production, and their buried relationship in such a way that their own utopian agenda merely duplicates the present power hierarchy, albeit with new elites, whether corporate women or proletarian dictators. *Social facts become social nature once enacted for the second time:* the first time they are unconscious servitude yet the second time they enact the text's myths as unalterably "factual"—hence politically unavoidable. Feminists and Marxists too frequently learn their marginal natures from the bourgeois text that disqualifies them and then restores them to science's text as pale images of themselves, in service perversely to the very realities they originally opposed. As readers learn feminism and Marxism from discipline, identifying with one or the other, they only reproduce the neutralized versions of themselves opposing their wild, political versions, just as black people learn blackness from white people and women learn true womanhood from men. No wonder feminists and Marxists talk at cross purposes when the bourgeois text pits them against each other as it pits production against reproduction, public against private, hard science against soft method; Marxists view the household and sexuality as "unproductive," and feminists celebrate feminism as "expressive" and reject Marxism as "science."

Economism is learned, not inherited; it can be undone as long as the text's mitigation of marginal writings is confronted by people on the fringe who risk adopting the oppressor's identification of themselves—Marxist/conflict, feminist/family. It is unusual in this day and age for either feminists or Marxists to escape the pull of the text's own self-serving constructions of them in a way that they can generate a more total, less fragmented textual practice that understands *everything* in terms of its transvaluation by the dominion of capital, patriarchy, racism, and state socialism. Often in spite of themselves, the marginal writings of the left accede to the text's interest-group pluralism dividing them against each other and then artificially coalescing them into the encylopedic version seemingly affording everyone air time. "Marxism" and "feminism" are reduced to particularisms, perspectives, excluding everything but themselves. Thus, in the isolation enforced on them by the text they fail to grasp the totality. I am not saying that totality, whatever that might mean, can be grasped in one version (or that it is accumulatively equivalent to a thousand writings, or all disciplined writings, as the bourgeois subtext contends) but that totality can be addressed by the concerted opposition of margins that resist their own constructed isolation and particularism. They thus accept their own intrinsic complementarity with other radical writings that, together, all address the same oppressive object: (nearly) totally administered society.

The Lesbian Other

The text splits the women's movement by threatening family with the specter of lesbian feminism, accompanied by the demise of women's love of men and children. The disqualification of lesbian feminism takes place on a deeper level than that on which the text disingenuously seems to embrace "gay rights" as one among numerous different interest groups or "factions." Surface science is careful not to engage in overt antilocution against gay women lest it appear to vitiate its own liberalism. But in subtext lesbian feminism is neuroticized both to defuse radical and socialist-feminist politics and to reinforce the apparent reasonableness of the androgynous feminism seeking nothing more than bourgeois work alongside bourgeois family; privacy's subordination to the public/productive is carefully sustained. The text props appropriately straight feminism by playing it off against an unnamed Other—I call it lesbian separatism.

By asserting the political nature of the ostensibly "private," as Jean Elshtain (1981) suggests, political feminism bursts out of its domesticity and defies its domestication by the bourgeois text. This opens reproduction as a topic for different political versions. The text deftly sidesteps this oncoming feminism, socialist feminism in the current vernacular, constructing forbidding political feminism as a maladapted lesbian attack on heterosexuality, men, straight women, and children—on *family*. Thus, the text clears the way for a straight feminism usefully supplementing the pluralist politics of sociology as well as naming the universality of "family," thus reproducing the epochal subordination of reproduction to production. Feminism is first feminized as familism and then masculinized as rigorous science.

The lesbian Other is played off against this appropriate feminism as the inferiority of politics to science. Mainstream "feminist" sociologists proudly trumpet their heterosexuality as evidence that they are successful as women. A colleague once decried our local women's studies program as a hotbed of "international lesbianism," just as she defended the norms whereby men list family and marital status on their curriculum vitae and women do not; after all, as she told me, she was "proud" to have a husband and sons, implying that those who do not are less than fully disciplined sociologists. Mainstream sociologists in this way reject the central feminist tenet that "the personal is political."

Where feminists have resisted the productivist text as a monopoly of valued humanity, they are often oblivious to the perils of scientization where science has turned their feminism officially into a bioontologizing account of family. This "family" is regarded by most American women as the appropriately centrist position on sexuality, refusing to alienate average women and men in return for a certain legitimacy, a place in the cacaphony of American pluralism

as another voice to be heard. Sexuality scandalizes science, now as in fin de
siècle Vienna.

> Those totally committed to a program of women's rights may see little wrong
> with this [lesbian] sexual preference, but they must consider the reactions of those
> outside the movement. This consideration requires compromising the "is" with
> the "ought to be." The success of a movement hinges upon its ability to avoid
> a split over the "art of the possible" versus "absolute victory." (Denisoff and
> Wahrman 1983, 521)

The liberal text "allows" gay rights, indeed celebrates its tolerance of what are
euphemistically called alternative lifestyles, but only out of an Aristotelian reasonableness drawing the line at political homosexuality as a singular vitiation
of "marriage and parenthood . . . as important goals for all Americans."

Although it is convenient to dismiss lesbianism as bad strategy in a world
in which "compromise" is said to be necessary, a deeper plunge into subtext
reveals that lesbianism is intended by the text as an instance of inappropriate
feminist advocacy, the failure of women to act womanly. Gayness is irrepressible womanhood; the upsurge of passion into science threatens not only
scientists' manhood but also their middling science. The text *needs* political
feminism in order to play off its own reasonableness against a writing bound
to scandalize. The text disqualifies supposedly lesbian feminism as uncompro-
mising "total commitment" to the cause, necessarily flawed when compared
to liberal reasonableness that, tellingly, in light of the text's consensualism, is
gauged against public opinion, "the reactions of those outside the movement."
This public opnion has a binding force "requir[ing] compromise," neglect of
which dooms the social movement in question. Science disqualifies radicalism
simply because in mainstream terms it radically departs from the normative;
as such, it uses (its construction of a thoughtless) common sense as an argument for itself against the scandalous utopianism of those women who, being
"totally committed" to a (lesbian) politics of the personal, reject compromise
as a betrayal of doctrine.

The text that formerly grounded its own validity as a break with the perspectivity of common sense now enlists that very common sense—"reactions of
those outside the movement"—to disqualify the feminism that, with Marxism,
falsifies common sense as a false consciousness imposed by both habit and
choice. In this way reproduction reproduces the distorted lifeworlds of average
Americans who reject a nonsexist politics of everyday life as an outrage to
their occupancy in the seeming haven of bourgeois family.[15] Thus, *the text
constructs lesbian feminism,* a politics of the personal willfully rejecting the
split between public and private, production and reproduction, *as an intrusion
into the naturalistically reproduced lifeworlds seeming to shelter us from the*

ravages of the public sphere. Thus, so-called family is at least a temporary reprieve from capitalist and state-socialist economic manipulation. This version of lesbian feminism is *any* politics of the personal, challenging readers who have been taught to act out the reproductive institutions of bourgeois "privacy" even if that privacy is not private at all but itself a crucial circuitry of the (re)production of production's primacy.

Although it is no surprise that men who benefit from "family" would want to protect it against sexual-political attacks, it is arresting at first glance that women would also support "family" as the privatization oppressing them. The text elicits this self-contradictorily false consciousness on the part of liberal-feminist (let alone more "traditional") women by constructing any politicization of the personal, any critique of the necessity of the subordination of reproduction to production (and thus women to men), *as lesbianism*, [16] the desire not to procreate and nurture (*men*). This political sexuality challenges both Friedan's 1981 argument about the mature familist feminism of the "second stage" and the outright masculinism and misogyny of Phyllis Schlafly.[17]

It is ingenuous for the text to construe any historicization of reproductive relations as lesbianism, as if to unravel the thread surreptitiously joining work, home, self, body, and text is to oppose biological reproduction altogether as generically antimale, antichild, antilove. This powerfully obscures the fact that feminism at best addresses all the reproductive relations enmeshing us, cultural as well as bioontological; it is not simply a social movement of and for women. Feminism's universalism desires to liberate *all* reproduction from the obscurity of its natural repetition of extant productive relations. Women prepare husband and children for the public sphere. Now they even reproduce themselves as superwomen who both work and mother and, as pink-collar workers, labor as existential mothers to their bosses and customers.

Feminism is about women only because women have been contingently burdened with domestic and now increasingly public mothering, not an accident of nature at all but a design of artifice: privatization aids men's public lives and their relations to dominant capital and the whole productive apparatus. Men are the enemy neither simply because they do not help "parent" or do housework nor because they make more money than women; these are but symptoms of the deeper subordination of text to world and, with it for most of human history, the subordination of women to men in the sexual division of labor, the oldest excuse for oppression. Women who eschew their domestication per se, taking to the offices and factories to work alongside men, are less threatening than women and men who question the subordination of privacy to publicity and with it a sexual divison of labor requiring women (and now men in second-stage feminism) to nurture male exchange-value producers. Thus, the text constructs this sort of reproductive politics as bioontologically inappropriate—unwomanly—and scandalizes readers taught now more than ever to fear and hate homosexuality as the most indulgent betrayal.

To be a lesbian in this light is to refuse one's assignment to appropriate reproductive responsibilities—motherhood, mothering, love of men. Interestingly, male homosexuality gets off easier at the hands of the text simply because gay men's liberation seems unable to address the sexual division of labor and its familism. After all, gay men can still be real men, living out alternative "lifestyles" and not politics, although the text self-consciously embraces the politics *of* gay rights as another legitimate interest group trying admirably to secure full constitutional freedoms of expression. This recognizes that lesbianism is inherently political because, in Rita Mae Brown's terms, it is "women-identified," embracing an ensemble of women-to-women bonds that far surpass the sexual and thus threaten men all the more with the specter of a biocultural separatism; these women do not need men to make them whole. Gay men's male identification is culturally appropriate, reproducing the male bonds that, allegedly "by nature," exlude women—bars, sports, cars. American male homosexuals by and large have not joined the women's movement in its common cause against the *occlusion* of the politics of reproduction but instead have mainstreamed themselves as advocates of just another lifestyle, a "social problem" only to the extent to which certain right-wing politicians attack their right to be sexually different, especially now that AIDS shocks straight America.

Although this is neither to exaggerate the overall tolerance of male homosexuality in either text or society [18] nor to suggest that many male homosexuals do not "support" the women's movement in its quest for group and individual liberties, I suspect that the public outcry would be even greater if women homosexuals were victims and carriers of AIDS or its equivalent. This would call forth the epochal witch-hunts typifying the way men historically have dealt with wild women. As it stands, AIDS has been problematized largely where *heterosexuals* are shown to be its targets.

The text disqualifies lesbianism by showing it to be an infantile disorder, in the process, as I have suggested, disqualifying all political feminisms addressing the public/private link.

> Radical feminists oppose any form of leadership, viewing it as a play for personal power. As a result their meetings are often disorderly, with participants interrupting each other and expressing their feelings whenever they want to. (Spencer and Inkeles 1979, 130)

In a text written by a woman, lesbian infantilism, couched as "radical feminism," is revealed as the abnegation of even the most rudimentary interpersonal *politesse,* "participants interrupting each other" and thus giving the lie to the nonauthoritarian New Left consciousness building that is supposedly the inspiration of feminist *process;* instead political women act out their failed sexuality. Moreover, as existential women unable to master their emotions, they express "their feelings whenever they want to," further diminishing the prospect of orderly consensus formation.

The text's subtext is about not only "radical feminists" but all women who refuse their assigned (or now, in liberalism, negotiated) place in the sexual division of labor, refusing or simply failing to achieve "femininity": women should accept their own wildness as a scar of nature only mitigated by certain ladylike behavior—listening when spoken to, not acting out ("expressing their feelings"), and so on. Moreover, the text construes what it calls radical feminism as instrumentally irrational, "their meetings" blocked, and subverted, by the dippy, driven enactment of their failed femininity. Their out-of-control desire fails to accept "any form of leadership," meaning male or masculine; alternatively, men know where to draw the line at free-floating emotion, or, in my Marxist-feminist terms, liberation. Patriarchy as subtext valorizes generically male "leadership" in text.

As lesbian-feminist resistance to "leadership" is constructed in the empirically descriptive language of science, so is "society's" prohibition of "alternative" modes of personality, the empirical generalization tantalizingly becoming a moral imperative, warning women who do not do their reproductive duties. Under the influence of the text's dehistoricizing gaze, the reader is misled to believe that "society" is *right* to "view parenthood as compulsory for almost everyone," and then to taboo "alternative" roles, particularly, the text broadly implies, homosexuality.

> Since society views parenthood as compulsory for almost everyone, it follows that any alternative roles are either looked down upon or prohibited. Alternatives are subject to sanctions, punishments, and criticisms. (Ritzer, Kammeyer, and Yetman 1982, 187)

Again, consensualism wins the day as the reader is scared straight under the influence of "society's" compulsions. Instead of understanding these compulsions as human constructions given the natural appearance of binding necessity, the text stays on the surface; in naming heteronomy the text only provokes heteronomy, "attitudes subject to sanctions, punishments, and criticisms." The very construction "society" bestows universality on the merely contingent, reflecting the generic lawfulness of the given and encouraging people to live through the "laws" and—thus, fatefully—to give them binding power. That "society" does not condone noncompulsory parenthood says more about history than about the ontological power of the social and, as such, does not preclude new social texts of sexuality.

Where the text addresses homosexuality directly, again it scientizes it as ego developmental failure, the psychic equivalent of the "radical feminist" political chaos named above.

> Homosexuals are rarely able to maintain stable relationships with partners for long periods. Many homosexuals would like to have monogamous unions but few actually do. (Spencer and Inkeles 1979, 344)

Here empirical sociology gives the lie to its own surface liberalism embracing "alternative," as well as mainstream, lifestyles, all equally deserving of First Amendment protection. Heterosexism valorizes straight over gay relationships for, presumably, they last longer, a curious imputation when read against the text's own worry about threats to the haven of bourgeois family—high divorce rates, sexual promiscuity, television, fast food.

The tragedy for gays is compounded where the text "finds" that, just like straights, they would like to have "monogamous unions," even though "few actually do." The text subtly twists its first claim about gay unions' stability *into* the second claim that gays sleep around (in spite of their natural preference for monogamy), precluding the quite plausible interpretation that in this world gays, like straights, tend to have *serially* monogamous relationships, one partner at a time. And the text fails to distinguish between male and female homosexuality in a way that would shed light on their telling differences: gays are less monogamous than lesbians because of serious differences between constructed masculinity and femininity today.[19] Instead, homosexuality is construed as an ego developmental failure manifested in the inability to work out viable monogamous relationships.

> To become fully adult, the adolescent must outgrow her or his dependence on the family of childhood and be prepared to engage in close emotional relationships with members of the opposite sex. (Hess, Markson, and Stein 1985, 266)

In a book coauthored by two women (and a man) heterosexuality is the supposedly essential terminus of adolescent development, the break between one's family of origin and emergent family of adulthood. Homosexuality is degraded by implication, and normative/normal heterosexuality is constructed as a developmental requirement stipulating "close emotional relationships with members of the opposite sex." The text is coy, not admitting that these "close emotional relationships" are sexual ones; after all, if they are not, what is the point? Gays, of course, can have close emotional relationships, strictly speaking, with the "opposite sex." The text's indirection softens the blow of its heterosexist absolutism where it is said to be imperative only that men and women learn to snuggle, not to go all the way, thus perhaps enhancing the impression of the text's open-mindedness, when in fact those passages indicate that it is anything but.

Finally, science decides the issue once and for all where it assures straights of the presumably biological limits to homosexuality in the population, pegged at an "estimated 5 percent of exclusive homosexuals," the language of quantity winning the day as a definitive version; this presumption occurs in spite of the widely-proclaimed estimate that already one of every ten Americans is gay.

> Despite the new gay activism, greater public tolerance, and attempts to ensure basic civil liberties, it is unlikely that the homosexual lifestyle will attract more than the estimated five percent of exclusive homosexuals and another, smaller group drifting in and out of the subculture. (Hess, Markson, and Stein 1985, 286)

Like Lysenkoism, the text forges the new man and woman, enforcing this safe rate of gayness and thus assuring that the heterosexual family will survive the episodic upsurge of interest in gayness, as the text says "despite the new gay activism." Facile science predicts, and thus helps enact, "trends" on the basis of who knows what epistemological/philosophical authority. Text assures readers that gay rights will only be a marginal, if liberally espoused, cause, fundamentally unthreatening to the nuclear family of heterosexual love. The text sounds reasonably guarded where it quantifies the gay threat—5 percent —a number low enough not to shock and precise enough to have scientific verisimilitude. How can the smug text be so certain about the homosexual Other? The text encourages its readership to choose family, marginalizing homosexuality as the 5 percent–exception. This holds open the door of "deviance" and "alternative lifestyles" for the few readers who are gay, including them the same way the text includes other minority and interest groups. But the writing in normalizing heterosexuality (and neuroticizing homosexuality) leaves little doubt that gayness is virtually self-limiting and therefore unhealthy, marginal, wrong.

Couched elegantly in a quantitative scientism knowingly naming the ("5 percent") marginality of homosexuality, the text homophobically disqualifies political feminism cunningly reduced to lesbian separatism; such feminism is rejected as any advocacy of new public/private, political/personal relationships. Feminist politics is beyond the pale of a discipline that gets the facts (and, it hopes, the readers) straight and then makes informed policy recommendations, the so-called "roles" of science and political advocacy kept separate. The liberal text is sociological first and feminist second (or at least separately, which amounts to the same thing), contradictorily chilling the heterosexist/ sexist world it then tries to thaw. Mainstream liberal feminists seek bourgeois work along with—and *separately*—bourgeois family.[20]

Liberal feminists are threatened by women's homosexuality both on a surface level where lesbian otherness disconfirms their own heterosexuality, family, children and on a deeper level where lesbianism is a wild politics of the personal addressing "personal life" as a sticky web of social determination mediated by existential choice. Liberals fear homosexuality mainly when it breaks the conceptual straitjacket of "alternative lifestyle" and interest group, instead prefiguring a whole new relationship between the social relations of production and reproduction, insisting on its own constitutive role and refusing to view itself merely as unmediated sexuality. *Instead it makes its own desire thematic as a topic of the interpenetration of preponderant objectivity and historically heteronomous subjectivity.*

This scandalizes liberal scientism for it reads, writes, and lives *everything as political,* the intimate as well as the overtly institutional. It also (contradictorily, for straight-ahead linear science) reads desire as impervious at some level to its socialization, what I have called in the language of critical theory an "inner second dimension" resisting total administration and thus affording at least a modicum of hope that people can resist.[21] Even if it is self-consciously apolitical, lesbian sexuality is written by liberal science as a scandalous intrusion of politics into the sacred domain of intimacy, privacy, family, emotion; as such, it seriously threatens the pluralist textual politics of sociology seeking to hold its opposition down to a meager 5 percent. The textual stance toward homosexuality reflects its discomfort with any version that both reveals desire's administration and historicizes desire's ineluctable irreducibility to those forces, enabling political opposition literally beginning at home, indeed from within.

While the text is discomfited by radicalism challenging writing to thaw the seemingly frozen world, it is even more troubled by sexual politics addressing desire's interest in reproducing its own subordination to the realm of male value, refusing to allow science the posture of disinterestedness crucial for enhancing its own occluded role in this reproduction: *heterosexuality born of heterotextuality.* Science denies its literariness in concealing its wild authorial desire to create a gentle community out of mutually supportive reader-writer relations, writing directly a form of liberating textual politics that resists its (and sexuality's) subordination to real (men's, science's) work. Where production produces things, reproduction produces humans, surely a happier, more joyous version. In tracing constructions like "5 percent homosexuality" to writerly desire, I link such desire to the surface text understanding it in that light.

My writing chases the hidden politics of writing in pursuit of its desire to disqualify political texts and lives, like those of feminists, *because* they surface their own desire and thus—it is said—distort science with the extraneous, inadmissible constructions of not only self-consciousness but also advocacy. After all, good science not only independently reflects imbeddedness in desire —contingency, body, place, motive—but also *argues unembarrassedly for* that subtext. I want to know why sociology disqualifies political sexuality and yet sinks its own desire for conjoined family and work so deep that it is only tortuously excavated, its occlusion empowering its natural account of the social. Sociology's desire in this sense is *familism,* extravagantly buried and surfaced in a host of telling ways, beginning with a consensualist account of familied life:

> In spite of the stresses and strains of married life, most people still want to marry, and most remain married. (Ritzer, Kammeyer, and Yetman 1982, 333)

Appropriate Womanhood: Getting Started on Male Careers

Sociology's version of the normative family takes a variety of twists and turns, as we shall see. But it is to be read continually against the backdrop of the disqualified lesbian Other; familism is simply the text's desire to protect family *against* a political feminism that the text weirdly coopts as a defense of family. Liberal feminism accepts and enacts family's supposed universality. This is second-stage feminism, in Friedan's terms, or bourgeois feminism that would do no more than androgynize the labor market and share household "duties," if not remunerate housework. Yet it is never clear exactly how involved the husband would be in the realm of domesticity—doing the dishes, perhaps, but not so surely taking major responsibility for nurturance.[22] Sociology's feminism announces the universality of family as a way of further separating public and private spheres. "Family" occupies the allegedly nonpolitical realm of privacy to be untouched by a radical rethinking opposing the continued subordination of reproduction to production as a degradation of the unpaid work women usually do. *This defense of the bourgeois family coopts feminism as an opponent of feminism,* bourgeois feminists besting (with evidence) the wild feminism the text falsely constructs as man- and family-hating.

It does not matter much whether these versions have been written by women or men; in fact, some of the most twisted, tricky texts are those written by women. Authorial sex does not matter because most professional sociologists, to *be* professional, condone the women's movement only as a legitimate interest group. *The scientific text remains a male text by appearing to be feminist, thus only coopting feminism for a defense of bourgeois family.* To the extent to which women sociologists are responsible professionals, they suppress their own authorship as an ideal to which women as disciplinary outsiders and latecomers must conform. Political capitulation is the cost of male professionalization.

Appropriately feminine women are to reject political feminism in favor of a familism that is then masculinized and scientized in the discipline's ready integration of feminism as a version of conflict-theoretic economism. The defiance of lesbian separatism celebrates "family values" in a way that further subordinates reproduction to production. Real women who appropriately acquire husband and children gain access to essentially degendered academic careers as the women's movement is integrated by sociology, eschewing the politics of the personal. By being good women, would-be professional sociologists feminize themselves in refusing lesbianism as a separatism vitiating biological destiny. Good women as degendered academics can then be masculinized as appropriately nonpolitical scientists, subordinating feminism to (male) conflict theory of which it becomes simply a version, a chapter, an article. Once familied and masculinized, feminism is then further degendered, thus engendered, by reducing sexist exploitation conceptually to social-psychological "role strains" and "conflicts" that become topics of a text in favor of greater domestic equity, workplace androgyny, and male-female care—the cosmetic stuff of "second stage" gender relations cooled into meaningful communication and mutual role taking. Disciplined feminism suggests a truncated political agenda, that is, capitalist patriarchy.[23]

Feminine feminism is welcomed by the text both as the depoliticization of feminism and as the addition of women's interests to the laundry list of the pluralist text's favored conflict groups. Disciplined women sociologists make good colleagues and, potentially, wives, feminism cunningly chilling "family" as a universal institution. The text's feminism thus freezes its subordination to the primacy of production that for all intents and purposes remains a man's world. Women continue to experience underemployment, unemployment, and sexual harassment at work, only extending their allegedly existential nurturance to the workplace and thus providing a new sex-class fraction for a male labor aristocracy to exploit. By opening its ranks and pages to feminists, sociology expediently silences its version of radical feminism and then elaborates a safe heterotextuality toning down radical and socialist feminisms and enhancing the text's liberal legitimacy.

The text wants women to be scientists who reproduce a world in which they are appropriately heterosexual, pursuing husbands, children, and an otherwise solid "private" life. Feminine women, like men as professional sociologists, fulfill their female destiny in the opportunity both to do bourgeois work and enact bourgeois womanhood, carved into public and private. To be feminine in these terms is to reject a politics of the personal in favor of familied life or, if marriage is not the choice, then simply heterosexuality as serially monogamous *apolitical sexuality*. Familied practice does not require one to be married, only to separate public and private existence. To be masculine is *not* to be feminine for a portion of the working day, maleness tellingly constructed as the absence or negation of femaleness and not the other way around, thus showing the power—both attraction and threat—that women hold for the text. Masculine women implicitly accept the mission of dispassionate science as appropriately socialized professionals, while they revert to (emotional, nurturant, expressive) womanhood after work, eschewing political feminism both as bad science and bad life—that is, life without men, or at least without their hegemony over them.

In this sense, although both healthy public and private lives are available to some women, men have only their "careers," a subtext that would seem to construct womanhood—work plus domestic destiny—as an ideal, more rounded than the emotionally straitjacketed lives men lead. As a result, men become overstressed by their macho single-mindedness (unless, of course, as new-age men they learn to cry and raise babies, thus enjoying the dual lives led by real women). But the version that women have it better than men in that they have a foot in both public and private worlds is precisely what the text wants women to believe so that they continue to be existential mothers—housewives, mothers, secretaries, filing clerks, even lawyers who specialize in family law, and sociologists of family, gender, sex-roles.[24] We can view the simultaneously public/private nature of women's experience either as a wonderful emotional complementarity or as double jeopardy—unpaid labor at home, poorly paid and often harassed labor at work. This heterotextual politics of familism pretends that women are *winning* on both fronts, "progress" reduced to role sharing, emotional flexibility, and the expanding availability of work outside the home.[25]

Media and academic social science increasingly portray men as losers in the so-called battle of the sexes, their lack of emotional versatility reducing their overall well-being, victims of badly diseased hearts caused by overstress and of broken hearts caused by insensitivity. This is a recent version of the notion that white people are not as musical, athletic, or sexual as blacks as an argument seemingly *for* black pride—an argument made by white people who want to afford blacks some solace. Men devour books like Ehrenreich's (1983) *The Hearts of Men*[26] as proof that women have always been better off, thus precluding the need for social change. Although many men do "lose," dominated by capital and other forms of sociocultural administration, it is a civilizational constant that women have lost more, and more often; their precious "femininity" is nothing but a millstone in the name of which their subordination has been excused, even celebrated.

The text constructs a straw woman where it endorses a second-generation feminism appropriately modulating the strident man-hating of galvanizing New Left feminism. Of course, lesbian otherness did not dominate the New Left stage of the women's movement at all; it is a more recent evolution of original liberal feminism in a radical/cultural direction, giving the lie to an imputed evolutionary maturation toward reasonable, responsible heterosexuality that the text suggests feminists have undergone. To be sure, lesbianism per se is no more a political strategy than heterosexuality. Yet the text conflates strident political feminism (recall from the preceding sections how those dykes could not run a rational meeting for they would all talk at once) with lesbian sexuality. This sets the (second) stage of a familist feminism that does its duty at home while setting out in Yuppie attire for the allegedly degendered battles of the work world; the crazy lesbians are left to their own fractious, futile devices. Indeed, feminine feminists who *have it all* are now to be "helped" by the destressed husband undergoing his own "feminization," an image about as likely as Charles Reich's prophecy that American corporate leaders would get "greened" by wearing bell-bottom jeans and growing long hair.

It is not that the women's movement has eclipsed lesbian separatism, for it has never been particularly separatist. Rather, the text constructs a maturing feminism moving away from strident man-hating toward cooperation with self-sensitizing men, thus ensuring its own mainstream legitimacy. But this picture neglects the fact that American feminism has always been at best liberal and cultural.

> From the mid-1970s on . . . these [radical vs. reformist] strands have lost their distinctiveness, as movement organizations turned to interest-group politics centered on passage of the Equal Rights Amendment and the protection of reproductive rights. (Hess, Markson, and Stein 1985, 550)

The text here cites coalition between radical and liberal-familist "strands," although the subtext constructs coalition as an episode of disciplinary centering, doctrinal dispute having given way to hard-headed "interest-group politics." This apparent centrism in the American women's movement is no change at all because it has virtually always been centrist, concentrating on suffrage, reproductive rights, equal opportunity, and domestic equity. The subtext's implication that the women's movement has finally gotten down to business is only a way of putting distance between the pragmatic coalitionism of NOW-feminists and the doctrinal squabbling of lesbians, radicals, and socialists, marginal women all.

> Like many social movements, NOW split into several factions in the late 1960s. Today, there is evidence of institutionalization, and in many ways the movement has become an integral part of society. There is widespread sensitivity towards sexist language in textbooks and the media. Affirmative action programs encourage the employment of women, and they are moving into roles formerly considered the province of men. This is not to say that the movement has met all its goals. Many would argue that institutionalization will not be achieved until an equal rights amendment is added to the Constitution. (Eshleman and Cashion 1985, 539)

The text has no trouble with the women's movement's incipient "institutionalization" it names as fact, especially where it trumpets this centering as progress, "widespread sensitivity towards sexist language" and successful

"Affirmative action programs," leaving only ERA to be ratified. As I will elaborate later, this optimism imbued with a sense of self-congratulation is especially dissonant today when the New Right has buried ERA and is attempting to roll back abortion rights and a host of other (*modest*) feminist gains of the past fifteen years.

Finally, the text's "preliminary research" is marshalled to indicate the convergence of the sexes themselves: radical feminist separatism has been vanquished by sensitizing men and freeing women for men's work in the public sphere. Again, subtext suggests that radical feminists were wrong to have given up on men who needed only a little encouragement and emotional care to become like women themselves in that they "become more involved in domestic activities than they traditionally have been."

> According to preliminary research, Friedan reported, many equality-minded women are consciously and effectively implementing two ideologies that most people consider contradictory. One ideology is the woman-as-individual, often enhanced through a career that women pursue part time or on different shifts from their husbands. The other ideology is woman-serving-her-family, and wives receive support in this area when husbands become more involved in domestic activities than they traditionally have been. (Doob 1985, 271–72)

The text fails to conceal its sexist, and for women, self-hating, desire where it talks about synthesizing two "ideologies that most people consider contradictory"; the contradiction is resolved not through negation-preservation-transcendence but by a rude averaging. Although women are free in public time to "pursue" careers, this public time is only "part time or on different shifts from their husbands"; what about the possibility of daycare, an obvious agenda item of the liberal text? In private they continue to "serve [their] family." [27] Grounding a second-stage feminism where women are both feminine and masculine, private and public, *and thereby really feminine* (in that their maleness is only a coping strategy in a masculinized work world), the subtext surfaces as plain sexism, women in service to men and children. The text conditions women to accept less-than-freedom in the guise of compromise with themselves and their own powerful desire to be fully functioning public adults as well as with "supportive" men not confronting the dilemma of the public/private split, having always "belonged" in the workplace and having always been serviced at home.

Women's liberation in this writing is compromise, adjustment, gradualism, defined in reference to the bioontologically fixed public/private relationship constructed and maintained by male producers. And this whole second-stage synthesis, women's existential subservience viewed as historical progress, is given the patina of scientificity as a real social trend—therefore one to be applauded and furthered. The very first phrase, "according to preliminary research," tellingly strengthens itself by ascribing the report of such research to Friedan herself—after all, the leading feminist would not get this wrong. "Preliminary" research points the way toward scientific validity, promising harder confirmation as the alleged social facts are appropriately enacted by millions of readers trying to work through a surface textual politics in the framework of oppressive productive and reproductive relations. In answer to Kant's question, "What can we hope for?" the subtext answers, "at least *this*."

The Universal Family

Like Marxism, feminism, once disciplined, is a candidate for incorporation into the centering text. Although feminism as an interest-group particularism, a women's study, is not as crucial to the main text as is "Marxian" conflict theory valorizing both competition and productivism, as science the text can at least throw it the bone of becoming a chapter, a subfield, a journal, a new faculty member, whether as the sociology of gender, family, or sex-roles. And "feminist sociologists" themselves are invited to join the mainstream once they become real women and real scholars.

Disciplinary feminism both integrates safe women and then in their name announces the universality of bourgeois family along with its subordination to the requirements of capitalist productive relations. Feminism is perversely rewritten as a familism defended against wild feminist women neuroticized as failed personalities—women who cannot make it with men, radicals who just don't know when to quit.[28] Most Marxist males at least accept their own status within the eclectic academy, where they have any status at all, with the appropriate gratitude, doing their version of science and otherwise leading appropriate lifestyles: I am more dangerous to my colleagues and university as a male feminist than as a Marxist, for at least I might be familied with a woman subordinate to me. As a feminist, I threaten a dangerous erotic politics making me a traitor to my sex.

As women prepare for professional careers in male/mainstream sociology, they are taught variously to accept their masculinization as sober scientists (thus keeping department meetings decorous), to be potential marriage partners for academic men, to provide role models for professionally-aspiring women students, and, finally, to show the ecumenism of the institution that risks harboring the enemy within. The professional masculinization of already-feminized women requires the reformulation of feminism as an egalitarian familism reflecting, thus reproducing, family's universality as a way of eliciting its enactment. Heterotextuality reproduces the subordination of its reproduction to production.

> Indeed, far from being "dead," marriage and parenthood continue to be important goals for all Americans. (Hess, Markson, and Stein 1985, 266)

The family may be the only institution that is found in all human societies. If it actually is universal, this would suggest that no society could survive without families. (Spencer and Inkeles 1979, 349)

If the nuclear family is universal, it may be pointless to try to find alternatives to it. (Broom, Selznick, and Darroch 1981, 325)

The modern family has many imperfections. Many families abuse or neglect their children. Arrest statistics show that family fights are common and that homocides frequently occur within families. Perhaps half of today's marriages will end in divorce. Yet these problems do not demonstrate that family life is deteriorating or that the family is less able to fulfill its functions. We have seen what the good old days were like, and as far as family is concerned, they should be called the "miserable old days." (Stark 1985, 303)

Paeans to the universality of family, these writings contain explosive, if repressed, material valorizing heterosexuality and childbearing as well as con-flating "family" as a generic social unit with the bourgeois nuclear families that are culturally if no longer statistically normative in western societies today. This blur has the tremendous advantage of putting the debate over "family" between lesbian feminists and familist-feminist sociologists into context, the profamily version winning hands down simply because family is identified with the privatized social units that we call "home" today. Like the concept of the universality of inequality in the hands of functionalists, family is universal simply because world history has been the history of family. It is even more so today now that the intimate social unit of reproduction seemingly has been increasingly privatized, protected as a sheltered harbor for the restoration of alienated personality stressed in the ubiquitous wars of the marketplace and office. Although the public and private are at some level nonidentical, luck-ily so for emancipatory theory regarding identity as hierarchy, the social text universalizes not simply ego autonomy or intimacy per se but the particular mode of intimacy represented by the bourgeois nuclear family.[29] No matter how much the text may iterate the variety of possible family structures, the text clearly intends the nuclear family as the essentially normal/normative form of which the others (extended, childless, etc.) are only versions, tolerated by the text as long as they are statistically and normatively marginal.

The first passage, above, as subtext suddenly surfaces where the second is only text, designed to conceal precisely what the former reveals. The second passage speaks the hesitant, skeptical language of scientific empiricism where it says that family "may" be a universal institution which, if true, "would suggest that no society could survive without" it. The text here occludes its own deceptive attempt to fill formal "family" with the content of the here-and-now, thus blurring the necessity of some universal reproductive unit with the alleged necessity of the Parsonian (Parsons et al. 1955) family surviving relatively unmodified to the present at least as the text's idealization of reproductive intimacy.

Sociology here fatefully reproduces the social fact of which it pretends to be a disinterested iteration, the universality of *some* family, some reproductive unit or institution nonidentical to the public sphere, equated with the alleged universality of western patriarchal "family," albeit with some minor historical and cultural variations. This conflation of the generic social organization of reproduction and the particular sexist family oppressing women and children by exacting unpaid housework and cloistering them away from the public sphere is not *argued;* it is not developed reflexively out of its own passionate subtext as what text really wants to say but is instead to be read and thus lived immediately in a dehistoricizing way.[30] Family sociology families its readers.

The text conflates the universal subordination of reproduction and that of women out of anxiety that family otherwise would be politicized, the threat of an implosively personal politics betraying men, children, domestic responsibility. "Family" is a nearly universally accepted western value insinuating itself into liberal-left writing as well as that of the center and right, promising a safe retreat from the sullying influences of marketplace and polity. The women's movement was initially so galvanizing because it criticized the externally administering forces threatening genuine intimacy *as a way of* protecting that intimacy, historicizing and politicizing the analysis of reproductive relations thus occasioning the liberation of the ensemble of relations comprising privacy—desire, affect, sexuality. In this regard, the representation of universal family is an invitation to marry, reproduce, and nurture and thus to keep desire hidden away in the golden locket of the apolitical.

Masculine sociology names family as the most universal of social institutions, carefully avoiding shrill advocacy in favor of cautious generalization from evidence—as the text has it, "the family may be the only institution that is found in all human societies." Does this mean that the family "may" be found in all human societies or that the family is the "only institution" to be found everywhere? The universality of family is not boldly asserted but suggested in a way that vouchsafes the methodical version seemingly used to arrive at this inference, protecting the text against the charge of advocacy or interest in reproducing that particular state of affairs. The text does the same thing with the alleged inevitability of inequality (*pace* Marxism), not rejoicing in it but appearing to arrive at it cautiously, history having yielded no significant examples of destratified social orders. The text packs more punch when it delivers its definitive conclusions in the reserved tone of skepticism, concealing and thus reinforcing its subtext of driven heterosexism. It is far more convincing to say that homosexuality probably will crest at 5 percent than to argue against homosexuality on either ethical or normative grounds;

the discipline suppresses any speculativeness opening the door to dedisciplined knowledges and practices that shamelessly *advocate*.

Sociology generalizes the alleged ubiquity of sexist nuclear family in the sober world-weariness of science. It admits that "modern family has many imperfections," seemingly a major concession, and yet the liberal text is unashamed to admit episodes of "imperfection," using them as a counterpoint to what it constructs as the basically healthy nature of this social system. It enumerates a list of domestic dysfunctions from child abuse and teen suicide to divorce before it concludes cautiously that "these problems do not demonstrate that family life is deteriorating or that the family is less able to fulfill its functions." Indeed, the family, by being privatized, is thus shielded from the glare of the cameras and thus can "fulfill its function" in reproducing men and children, even if that reproduction dysfunctionally ranges into the perverse as men occasionally expend their frustrations by beating up the wife and kids.[31]

As for the deterioration of "family life," the text correctly suggests that the past was no better, although this is not the ringing celebration of family that it might like to be. The text's cautiousness is precisely what makes its announcement of universal family so powerful; the numerous caveats to its argument make its conclusion appear the more considered, the more reasonable. A seemingly inviolate sphere of reproduction in which nature holds sway, "family" conceals the domination of private domesticity by the external imperatives of the logic of production and admnistration. I agree that there should be private spaces in which people can recover from the hurly-burly of public life. But the family today is neither private nor restorative, instead oppressing women, children, and men under sway of the primacy of production (to which the sphere of reproduction is made auxiliary). The text understands the invasion of domesticity by the forces of television, permissive sexuality, and the apparent erosion of authority only as a despoiling of family's natural haven for unproblematic domestic relations, to be fine-tuned occasionally by having males share housework and nurturance and by allowing females to hit the corporate trail. The text occludes the commodification and administration of *all* activity better to commodify and to administer.

This imagery of invasion implies that, uninvaded, the family as such would be restoratively insulating, thus failing to address the structural-functional linkage between capitalist and state-socialist production and the reproductive relations of the sexist nuclear family (as well as culture and personality generally). In this light, family cannot be reprivatized without transforming the realm of production overwhelming family with the functional imperatives of biological reproduction, socialization, nurturance. The text's fashionable familist retreatism that would solve family by cutting it off from disruptive external forces is as ineffective and ultimately counterproductive as the humanism ameliorating public alienation with touchy-feely psychologism, especially where the text itself shows its hand by valorizing the family's fulfillment of its "functions," which tellingly remain unexplicated. The text pretends to defend the universal primacy of family when in fact it really defends family's subordination to the imperatives of a productive logic turning people into use- and exchange-values and thus subordinating family to itself. Feminism in its radical/cultural and socialist versions addresses the public-private relationship in a way that threatens this version of the family's destructive colonization by the sullying forces of the public. A political feminism dangerously politicizes the category of femininity, no longer "allowing" women to shave their legs or get married without serious political circumspection.

But the wild feminism targeted by the text is named lesbian in a way that understands lesbianism as *any* version of the politics of the personal, a politics prefiguratively transforming "everyday life," regardless of whether its literal advocacy is lesbian or lesbian-separatist. This opens the way for a *feminist familism that keeps family sheltered from its imbeddedness in a logic of production/reproduction* commodifying and degrading household activity. The text's feminism supports family as a universal need and essential function while it contradictorily decries its invasion by the colonizing forces of total administration. What the text will not say is that family has *already* been invaded and cannot latterly become a snug harbor of nonalienated sensibility until the totality ensnaring it is transformed—the agenda of a feminist critical theory recognizing the public nature of the personal without advocating for their simple identity (lest the personal be sacrificed covertly for the movement, world-history, whatever passes for the greater good).

Heterotextual sociology announces universal family on more than the grounds of family's seeming ubiquity across cultural time and place, that is then equated to its universality—past projected scientifically into future *and thus ensured*. It also uses a disciplining method (here, interestingly marshalled by a woman) to show that normal/normative families have to be heterosexual and not monosexual. What is masculine about empirical method here is not quantitativeness or abstraction, for that construction would relegate feminist method to the idealism of empathy and participant observation, thus precluding a political grasp of the complex totality. What is masculine about disciplinary science is simply that its text suppresses its own interest in reproducing male supremacy.

> The psychologist Eleanor Maccoby . . . expresses concern that the rise in single-parent families (especially those headed by women) may pose problems for the socialization of children. A father, she feels, is more effective at commanding obedience than a mother; he is usually adept at engaging the children in play; he can take over child care when the mother is unable to cope for any reason; and

he is able to provide important emotional support for his wife. (Light and Keller 1985, 348)

The prose of a woman scientist here is rehearsed to support the necessity of heterosexual family, notably on grounds of the father's special ability to "command obedience," a vestige of a medical version of psychoanalysis informing all sorts of politically conflicting traditions from mainstream child psychology to bad derivatives of the Frankfurt School (from which Lasch [1977] draws in his *Haven in a Heartless World*, a central text of left-wing familism). Of course, the father today commands obedience *because* women have been rendered obedient, their survival requiring adaptation to "given" male prepotency. To conclude that family needs men because men are the most appropriate leaders and role models would simply be zany if it were not so perverse. Women do not command obedience because they do not enjoy the status and charisma accompanying power; let a woman run the family, and she quickly becomes as prepotent and thus as likely to "command obedience" as the absent father. As for the notion that men are "adept at engaging the children in play" (is the mother not?), one wonders how the authors could have missed the fact that women for the past two thousand years have been primarily responsible for organizing reproductive activities, including entertainment and play. Presumably the text is referring to the Saturday afternoon fatherhood when dutiful dad takes the kids to the park while mom cleans house or does the shopping.

Finally, the notion that men are essential because they "can take over child care when the mother is unable to cope" presumes that other women could not do it just as well, if not better, and—subtext tellingly surfacing—that nurturance is primarily the woman's responsibility; the indispensable man takes over when the woman cannot cope "for any reason"—having her period, out with the girls, or simply gone off the deep end. These wondrous extrapolations from what "is" to what (the text says) "must be"—patriarchy reproducing itself through the enactment of this kind of writing—are given a definitive disciplinary imprimatur where they allegedly have been replicated or duplicated by other male scientists.

A study conducted by the Kettering Foundation and the National Association of Elementary School Principals lends support to Maccoby's concern. (Light and Keller 1985, 348)

Science eternalizes the heterosexual family, which it cunningly claims is all possible families by attributing its dysfunctions to its incompleteness, a product of male abandonment, separation, divorce.

Since society views parenthood as compulsory for almost everyone, it follows that any alternative roles are either looked down upon or prohibited. Alternatives are subject to sanctions, punishments, and criticisms. (Ritzer, Kammeyer, and Yetman 1982, 187)

It is useless to try to brook family's generic necessity since "society" fulfills its own prophecy of marital failure attendant on inadequate enactment of the "compulsory" role responsibilities by turning fact into fate; "alternative" arrangements are doomed by the sanctions sure to be visited upon them.

Family fails simply because it is not acted out in socially validated ways, deciding the text's claim that abnormal family will produce abnormal people, heterosexism reproducing itself heterotextually in the reproduction of concepts —and thus as practices—of the normal/normative. Although it is contingently true that deviants by definition will be sanctioned, the text ontologizes the sanction of people who refuse to live out appropriate "family" by stating that "society views parenthood as compulsory for almost everyone," *thus freezing a particular world by promoting its enactment.*

Sociology vitiates its own pluralist politics by portraying a generic world —"society"—in which deviation from its logic of administered production/ reproduction will be punished, implicitly counseling an adaptive reasonableness that toes the line of submissive motherhood and dominant fatherhood.

> However pleasant it is for small children to spend time together in nursery school, collective child rearing cannot take the place of family living. (Spencer and Inkeles 1979, 344)

The text goes further by denying the developmental appropriateness of "collective child rearing," as if the only nondisruptive alternative is "family living." Heterosexual privatization is said to be better for kids than daycare and the kibbutz, again reproducing the given by assessing developmental well-being in terms of normal/normative standards of development against which deviation will automatically be found wanting. And this is justified in the name of what is now called "tough love," stoic, nonindulgent principles of "parenting" that give the children what they need, if not necessarily what they want: a stern father and hectoring-but-loving mother.

"However pleasant it is for small children to spend time together in nursery school" sooner or later they have to grow up and learn to obey father and mother, developing an obedience best inculcated in the bosom of the privatized family, challenging the gravitational pull of school, peer group, and media over the hearts and minds of children. That family is "good" for children is a recurrent theme circularly formulated in the observation that the adjustment problems invariably experienced by people who have not been familied, successfully taught reasonably to fit in and knuckle under, are effects of having not been familied. This disqualifies alternative families tautologically with reference to their inability to service the developmental needs of people who must learn to fulfill—"carry forward"—their public and private duties.

Many adults get along fairly well without permanent partners, but a child
without a family is at a serious disadvantage. (Spencer and Inkeles 1979, 344)

The family's basic purpose is to create offspring who will become useful members of the society in adulthood, carrying the human species forward. (Spencer
and Inkeles 1979, 342)

But you may not know that being divorced or separated is about as harmful to
your health as smoking. Loneliness kills. (Spencer and Inkeles 1979, 346)

The text that just above acknowledged hesitatingly that the unmarried could
actually survive two pages later recants and suggests, with implicit reference to
research data, that "loneliness kills," as if the unmarried are necessarily lonely
and the married necessarily connected. That failure to accept imposed social
responsibilities results in dis-ease is virtually a truism, although the text intends
the claim as a counterintuitive finding buttressed by the piles of research results
accumulated by child psychologists and family therapists. The prospects of
spending Christmas alone or going to a restaurant alone are forbidding because
they have been constructed as rituals of family togetherness, both excluding
nonfamily and requiring that one have a family of one's own. Necessarily
people acculturated to obtain intimacy from the heterosexual family will be at
sea when confronted with a world seemingly made up only of families, where
all the good men are taken and single or childless people are marginalized.

This becomes an ontological state of affairs only where the text fails to
historicize the intimacy that other types of family could conceivably afford.[32]
The "findings" that loneliness kills and that broken families wreck children are
named by the text not to historicize a world that could be different—in which
absence of family need not preclude other types of intimate belonging—but
perversely to freeze the suffering of those who have lost out, or simply failed,
in the marriage market; scientific sociology thus elicits appropriate behavior
by underlining the striking perils of noncompliance.

The text makes a rule of privatized bourgeois family by declaring the perils
of being single or divorced even when, on the surface, it seems plurally
to accommodate the occasional alternative lifestyle. Seeming to deliver the
facts presuppositionlessly, sociology conceals its subtext heterotextually in a
version that recites the surface of the given ameliorated by a cloying familism
advocating plural (hetero)sexual practices. The masculinization of feminism
(endorsed, too, by many women who, as oppressed everywhere, mimic the
lives of the oppressors) scientizes feminism as a paean to "family" via its
allegedly theoryless description, affording women sociologists a denatured,
degendered role in the university and defusing Marxist-feminist advocacy of a
reconstructed public/private relationship.

The disciplining of feminism aims to make it responsible male sociology,
value-free "women sociologists" integrated into the fold of the profession

much as Marxists have been, with their own ASA sections, meetings, and even journals. The subtext is here given the aura of disciplinary respectability and reasonableness, science's text extrapolating present trends into a vouchsafed future, assuring readers that extant reproductive relations are here to stay.

> The existence of patterns such as these does not mean, however, that the nuclear family is about to disappear. Some 96 percent of all Americans get married at some point in their lives, and even the divorced are still deeply committed to marriage—their marriage rate at all ages is higher than that for single or widowed persons. What is more likely is that the United States, a pluralist society with an extraordinary range of subcultures and a strong emphasis on individualism and freedom of choice, will increasingly tolerate a variety of alternative marriage and family styles. No other society has ever endorsed more than one family form at a time, but no other society has been both as heterogeneous and as rapidly changing. (Robertson 1983, 370)

Science clinches its argument with the construction "96 percent" ("of all Americans get married at some point in their lives"), deriving certainty from both quantity and the enormity of the proportion itself. We are assured, on the evidence, that "even the divorced are still deeply committed to marriage," more a commentary on false consciousness in service of social reproduction and self-reproduction than on the continued viability of the bourgeois family. Tacked onto the comforting sound of the familist text is the prophetic assurance that an extraordinarily "pluralist" America will "increasingly tolerate a variety of alternative marriage and family styles." The text ends on the ringing declaration that only in "heterogeneous" and "rapidly changing" America can we finally hope to see the flowering of "more than one family form at a time," a version of the myth of progress in the meantime eliciting duty—here obedient enactment of the necessary roles of heterosexuality.

Feminist sociology heralds androgyny just as it further entrenches the family scientifically, saving family by democratizing it, predicting that it will be "new and different, but not unrecognizable." Indeed, we are assured that "some form of marriage and the family will survive."

> For the foreseeable future, most men and women will seek and find more-or-less monogamous relationships with people of the opposite sex. A high proportion of these relationships will culminate in conventional marriage. A high proportion of them will produce children. The experience of divorce will not deter most of the men and women who pass through it from remarrying. The increasing numbers of divorced parents who marry each other will result in a new and broader definition of family relations. Greater sexual equality will redefine and restructure the family, not destroy it. The constantly increasing number of working wives and mothers will produce new sex roles, and new definitions of right and wrong. New and different, but not unrecognizable. Some form of marriage and the family will survive. (Goode 1984, 348)

What is striking here is not simply the prophecy that family will outlast its current turbulence but the certainty with which science projects the future from past and present. Although the writing seems to be cautiously circumspect at the start—"for the foreseeble future"—this hesitancy is thrown to the wind by the end ("we will seek . . . will culminate . . . will produce . . . will not deter . . . will result . . . will redefine . . . will produce . . . will survive"). Scientificity overhauls feminist advocacy that above all gathers its energy from the inevitable nonidentity of present and future, the fact that the world in its contingency is subject to new authorship, an ineradicable basis of hope.

The text reduces this fragile hope, whose only certainty is that anything can be made possible, to the universal reproduction of reproductive relations currently subordinated to the male/capitalist/racist logic of production and administration. Sociology tries to ensure that "the family will survive" simply by predicting it. When compared to ridiculed political advocacy science turns out to be the more idealist, conjuring what is-not-yet out of the facticity of the present, a magic trick turned by science's seemingly neutralized/normalized text.

> Whichever view is correct, the American family is hardly in danger of extinction. Although there are more single people, unmarried couples living together, and single-parent families, these arrangements remain for most individuals merely stopping-off points in their lives. Frequently, they are life styles for particular stages in a person's life. Most individuals will continue to live some part of their lives as a spouse in a nuclear family. Although Americans may be disappointed in their marriage partner, they are not disappointed with marriage itself. If their marriage does not measure up, they are inclined to end it and look for something better. In sum, humankind's most basic and oldest social unit, the family, has taken on many forms and undergone many changes over history, and it will probably continue to change in the future. Increasing diversity in family arrangements will very probably be its hallmark. (Light and Keller 1985, 366)

The text does not inquire into the social construction of family, notably people's commitment to the ideal of marriage no matter how lousy their marriages; it simply reflects the given mood of the moment thus covertly contributing to the formation of that mood. The 96 percent of Americans who eventually get married cannot be wrong, even if 99 percent of that 96 percent fall into marriage as the only seeming option, or the only moral one, or the only essential one. That "humankind's most basic and oldest social unit" is "the family" does not decide the politics of intimacy, no matter how the text constructs marriage as an essential fragment of social nature. Nor does the text's spirited projection of "increasing diversity in family arrangements" imply that future versions of intimacy will seriously modify the heterosexual family of today; it only assures those presently without partners that there is still hope.

9

Androgyny: "Beyond" Misogyny and Patriarchy

Masculinizing Feminism

Beyond its masculinization as centered science—the self-reproducing prophecy that marriage is here to stay—feminism is further assimilated to male conflict theory for which so-called gender conflict is only one episode among many. In the same way that Marxism is reduced to Weberian conflict theory, thus betraying Marx's dialectical vision of an end of history, feminism is transformed from a politics addressing the public/private split into interest-group particularism standing shoulder-to-shoulder with the other interests of class, culture, and race as it tries to "get theirs." This both blunts its utopianism —a nonsexist, nontextist world in which value is not determined simply by activity's waged or unwaged status—and reduces sexism to group conflict thus failing to make the public/private connection that could unfold sexism in deeply psychological/political forms.

Conflict theory masculinizes feminism in the frame of gender conflict, reducing male misogyny to unthreatening terms, "private" space kept private as "conflict" is conceptually restricted to the public sphere. This contains a grain of truth for indeed men and women, just as classes and races, do collide in the public sphere. But it conceals the interest of men in conceptually restricting sex conflict to the public sphere, thus healing its episodic dysfunctions without changing the underlying sexual division of labor subordinating unwaged/ private to waged/public activity.

The conflict-theoretic version of deep collisions between structurally contradictory people and groups in late capitalism allows them to be resolved redistributively; for example, women are now said to enjoy something approaching equity at both work and home to the extent that new-age men increasingly "share" income, parenting, housework. The text buries sexual-political contradictions crystallizing in men and women's differential connection to the means and relations of reproduction in the supposedly generic "conflicts" of heterogeneous, not hierarchized, subgroups.

Conflict theory is a male version of feminism covering over the sexual-political depth of women's oppression, the dominance of public productive politics over personal reproductive politics, just as text covers subtext where really they feed off each other. The text integrates feminism through the blunted Marxism of conflict theory, playing out the absurdist drama of a domesticated male left domesticating a female left, art following life—mitigated Marxism swallowing heterotextual feminism in the text's centering.

> In conflict theory, sexual stratification has the same basis as any other form of inequality: unequal access to the means of production (tools, knowledge, land), and to its products (goods and services). (Hess, Markson, and Stein 1985, 195)

The text suppresses the basis of sexism in unequal access to the means of reproduction, thus compounding women's restriction from, as well as exploitation in, the public productive sphere. It does so to defeminize—*to masculinize*—sex conflict so that it can continue to keep the closed doors of "family" closed. If opened, the text would find itself under siege by a feminist version not only acknowledging but also celebrating its roots in the subtext of desire as the resource of its transvaluing energy.

> The underlying source of sexual inequality, in the view of conflict theorists, is the economic inequality between men and women. . . . [W]ealth is a prime source of social status; moreover, it can readily be converted into power and prestige as well. It follows that if men make a greater economic contribution to the family and the society than women, then men are likely to have superior social status in both. (Robertson 1983, 318)

The alleged causality traced between "wealth" and "sexual inequality" exactly reverses the socialist-feminist portrayal of women's economic exploitation as a function of a sexual division of labor (that is, a skewed public/private relationship) turning women into existential mothers and either keeping them home doing unpaid work or deskilling and impoverishing their waged jobs by assigning them auxiliary pink-collar labor.[1] The mechanical causality drawn by disciplined feminists from "wealth" to "power and prestige as well" is inspired by the neo-Weberian status-attainment tradition[2] separating these components of hegemony and heteronomy as if it were meaningful to draw causal arrows among them. The text's causality between men's "greater economic contribution to the family and the society" and "their superior social status" accepts the capitalist allocative principle allegedly rewarding people justly for their "economic contribution." This assumes that men do indeed make a "greater economic contribution" to "family and . . . society" than women, presumably accepting women's unwaged work in and outside the household as a natural fact, the only "variable" being the extent of women's *waged* contribution. But women *in social terms* frequently do not make a so-called economic contribution simply because men do not pay them (or pay them well enough) for being mothers, wives, secretaries, and bank tellers; women's exploitation is a moment of their millennial subordination to productivist rationality circularly degrading unwaged activity.[3]

Conflict theory conceals the real source of women's exploitation in the heteronomy of "women's work," any unwaged activity. The depoliticization of domesticity and sexuality economizes women's oppression much as the conflict-theoretic text economized the Marxist concepts of alienation and domination.[4]

> While functional and conflict theorists are sharply opposed to each other, some points of agreement do exist. Many functional theorists recognize that extreme gender inequalities are no longer functional in the modern world— such inequalities lead to discontent, conflict, and the massive loss of potential female talent for an array of occupations. An up-to-date functional perspective will allow for women's greater involvement in occupations and men's increased participation in domestic tasks. On the other hand, conflict theorists, though critical of traditional gender roles, will recognize that these roles were often highly functional in the past. (Doob 1985, 136)

The text here reveals its deeper nature by putting its own words to what I have just been describing. It blurs functionalism and conflict theory by addressing conflict theory's roots in a superficial textual politics of feminist economism ("women's greater involvement in occupations") and familism ("men's increased participation in domestic tasks") that an "up-to-date" functionalism endorses in its reasonableness. And conflict theory, already narrowed from a political feminism to a perspective merely "critical of traditional gender roles," amazingly concedes to functionalism "that these roles were highly functional in the past," much as if Marx were made absurdly to confess the functional indispensability of Plato's "republic" or the monarchy. Just as it integrates the male left, the text engulfs feminism as an "up-to-date" perspective "on the modern world," recognizing the dysfunctionality of "discontent, conflict and the massive loss of potential female talent." A masculine feminism is enlisted by sociology to offer the labor force a cadre of smart women, just as it is called on to demonstrate the text's nondoctrinal ecumenism; women's rights are a "point of agreement" between the two allegedly opposed writings, conflict theory and functionalism.

In this way, feminism's integration ironically brings the two seemingly warring male camps together; women serve their time-worn role of mediation. At least the two parts of the text can agree on women's rights, the greater opportunity for women to work, along with the call for men to share the unenviable domain of domesticity, thus in the long run benefitting *everyone*—business, labor, even women.

> Conflict and functionalist theories are not as contradictory on this issue as they might initially seem to be. Many conflict theorists accept that sex inequalities

may have arisen because they were functional, even if they are functional no longer. Many functionalist theorists would also accept that traditional sex roles are becoming dysfunctional in the modern world. More important, both agree on one point: existing gender characteristics are primarily social in origin, not biological. (Robertson 1983, 320)

The text rehearses the concessions made by both sides: conflict theorists concede the historical function of sexism, and functionalists acknowledge the anachronistic nature of sexism "in the modern world" (although, of course, the text does not use the term sexism but "sex inequalities" in order to depathologize sexism along with the racism and rapaciousness of capitalism).

Not only does the text reduce sexism to "sexual inequalities" but it does so under the aegis of a male conflict theory, feminism tempered by Weber's version of Marx.[5]

> In her book, *Sexual Politics*, Kate Millett (1970) has emphasized that men traditionally have dominated women in all institutions and activities. The conflict perspective on gender roles makes the same point. Randall Collins concluded that gender inequality, like any other inequality, involves a conflict for scarce resources between a dominant group (males) and a subordinate group (females). In order for men to have superior political, social, and economic status, women must have inferior status in all respects. (Doob 1985, 136)

The text in two sentences tellingly moves all the way from Millett's committed writing making "sexual politics" thematic for feminist thought and life to the male feminism of sociology. The text banalizes Millett's radical feminism by prising from it the sentiment that "men have traditionally dominated women in all institutions and activities." Millett says much more than that when confronting the way male writing entwines both men and women in the sticky web of text reproducing reproductive relations dominated by male-dominated relations of production. Even as early as 1970, it was a truism for the women's movement that "men dominated women"; the more pressing issues were *how*, and especially how women acquiesced to and thus deepened their own unnatural subordination. The text extracts conflict theory from Millett only disingenuously where it conceals the deeper, more pressing issue of how sexism is reproduced in terms of its apparently natural necessity.

> Conflict theorists such as Jetse Sprey agree with the functionalists' position that the family institution is essential to the survival of human beings and their societies. (Light and Keller 1985, 335)

Yes, they do, but radical and socialist feminists do not reduce sexism to the collision of men and women in the public sphere; instead, with Marx, they envision an end to sex conflict as a historical possibility (more so among socialist feminists). For their part, radical feminists foresee women's transcendence of the whole "male world" in which groups eternally lock horns and act out the various male-dominant rituals of territoriality and virility. The text's enormous leap from the likes of Millett or even Friedan to conflict-theoretic "feminism" is driven by its ambition to scientize feminism in its own version of deconstructive reading, people like Millett and Friedan buttressing Randall Collins (1971, 1975), whose writing is a gloss on the Weberian version of Marxism.

There is no agreement among feminists "that the family institution is essential to the survival of human beings and their societies" as long as "family" is the heterosexual marriage bond, as the subtext intends. No amount of wordplay will make political feminism read like a conflict sociology reinforcing the public/private split and thus ensuring that sexuality, indeed reproduction generally, is subordinated to visible politics and economics.

Finally, conflict theory as an economism identifying freedom and resource attainment, a standard Weberianism, pronounces an optimism about women's standing.

> Conflict theory suggests that the structure of domination shifts as resources shift. Thus, women today have a better bargaining position because they hold jobs and are economically independent and because they are free from unwanted pregnancies and childbirth. (Eshleman and Cashion 1985, 341)

This assumes that "resources" have actually "shifted" away from men and toward women. Even in economistic terms this is largely mistaken; American women continue to earn just over half of men's salaries. And it misses the socialist-feminist argument that the issue is not simply "resources" but the *social relations* of the production *and* reproduction of those "resources," including human beings and human feelings. Economism fails to understand the relational and organizational dimensions of simple wealth; thus, it does not understand that women's workforce entry per se (reflected in "resource shifts") means little if, degraded at work, they remain responsible for the unwaged labor of the household, including the affective reproduction of men and children as well as the actual reproduction of biological offspring. Economism virtually guarantees that "progress" can be squeezed out of the hardscrabble world of today's feminized poverty encompassing male desertion, neglected alimony payments, threatened repeal of abortion laws and affirmative action, and more stringent control of the dissemination of contraceptives. The text's grandiose claims that "women have a better bargaining position," "are economically independent," and "are freer from unwanted pregnancies and childbirth" [6] are no longer compelling in light of the New Right's ascendancy. In fact, they were probably wrong all along—simply wishful thinking.

In any case, the economization of feminism accepts the definition of value as exchange value prevailing in contemporary capitalism where "resources" are the market rewards assigned to public labor. This economism refuses to valorize "private" labor (reproduction) in a way that "solves" women's oppression only by having them enter the labor force, leaving the split between work and home in place and thus reproducing women's unwaged responsibility for reproduction, childrearing, sex, and nurturance. Economism only reinforces a heterosexism oppressing women *no matter how seemingly emancipated they are in the labor force.* Instead work is precisely the balm for their "private" wounds. But this solution rarely has its intended effect because occupationally "liberated" women still confront a deeply destructive world of domestic obligations, compulsory motherhood, and sexual abuse.[7] Democratizing "resources," as economistic feminism recommends, only deepens the illusion that women are best off when, briefcase or lunchpail in hand, they emulate men who, themselves oppressed in the public sphere, are as such an inappropriate model for the new socialist-feminist personality.

The social text disciplines feminism as a conflict theory and thereby reproduces the depoliticization of the private sphere—a realm of experience in which the oppression of women arises and thus in which a permanent end to sexism must originate as a politics of the personal. Rewriting feminism as a male scientism searching for universal social laws, sociology thereby intends to bring them into being. Feminism is further masculinized, professionalized, and scientized by the text that, in all reasonableness, announces the universal's inherence in the merely episodic, ultimately giving up a lot of ground claimed by feminists to a distinctly antifeminist text. In particular, beyond its translation of feminism into conflict theory, *the text undercuts feminism with a dehistoricizing construction of the destiny of anatomy,* a project all the more amazing given its sociological, and thus officially nonbiologistic, auspices.

Sociology seeks universal bases of women's submission to the power of the social as a "reasonable" way of foreshortening the political goals of what it takes to be radical feminism; science in effect defends sexism with reference to a past and present fatefully bioontologized as women's generic fate. In this way not only is feminism to live up to masculine standards of high science and responsible professional comportment;[8] it is also to negate itself with "findings" frozen into a destiny only reproducing women's subordination. The supposedly liberal-feminist text turns out to be as sexist as the misogynies from which it claims to have broken; women's inferiority is now validated, albeit usually only in subtle, subtextual ways.

> The science of sociology moves such issues as sexual inequality out of the muddy waters of philosophical or common-sense debate onto the solid ground of objective inquiry. (Bassis, Gelles, and Levine 1980, 30)

However, "objective inquiry" into contemporary social arrangements fails to evoke their possible dialectical motion; subjectivity is imprisoned and distorted in the shell of the unalterably given. The disciplinary representation of "sexual inequality" can only show the modalities or "function" of such inequalities in masking the subjectivity perversely *promoting* such inequalities *both* on the parts of victim and oppressor. The text constructs these "objective inequalities" as the inert facticity that in itself is either natural and necessary or unnatural and superfluous; thus, it fails to address the human roots of sexism, reproducing it generation after generation.

Only if we examine the core of sexism as a discursive practice can it be undone, even if this requires us to confront our own complicity in perpetuating unnatural suffering. Objective inquiry, in the text's parlance, neither excavates the subjective mechanisms of domination—real men screwing over real women and *why*—nor as such imagines a different future. The text suppresses subjectivity here lest the public/private relationship itself becomes an "object" of critical scrutiny, addressing the reproductiveness that, through a billion everyday lives, lives and relives sexual-political domination as a natural fact. Science accomplishes this suppression in disqualifying "philosophical or common sense debate" as writings that swim in "muddy waters," contraposing philosophy to science as a contrast between *doxa* and *episteme,* a convincing construct of science's superiority since the Enlightenment. Naming nonscientific writing philosophy is really to call it political; science suppresses politics as a mode of inquiry in transcending advocacy toward a grasp of the unalterably objective. So-called "objective inquiry," as the text says, is a "solid ground" only because politics/philosophy is considered an insubstantial, oozing swamp of perspectivity and militant commitment, thus obscuring the *nature* of "sexual inequality" as if it could be named as such, ahistorically. This conceals the contribution writing itself makes to doing or undoing what otherwise passes for social fate—in the case of feminism, women's oppression. Sexist writing provokes its own subordination to the world to which it already bears a disempowered relationship; Marx's false consciousness is reformulated in terms of constitutive authorial practices.

Although the text seems to want to purify the "muddy waters" of politics/ philosophy by allowing people to know the true nature of sexual inequality in order to change it, at a deeper level it defends such aspects of sexual inequality impervious to historicization and hence change. Disciplined feminist writing names purportedly eternal bases of women's subordination to men as text balances biological and social oppression, thereby accommodating explanations accounting for women's oppression as an unalterable fact of nature —as the text says, "functional." The suppression of philosophy forces the text (to be a "man," implacable in the face of danger) to come to grips with the unmuddy truth that women's oppression in social terms is nature's way in biological terms, an argument prohibited only in the most outrageously illiberal case of sociobiology. Indeed, sociological feminism is a tame version of sexist sociobiology, excusing women's oppression on grounds of biological differentiation.[9]

In short, the real basis for traditional sex roles was not simply culture, or beliefs about what men and women ought to be like, but reality. When the tasks that could be assigned to women were no longer subject to women's fertility and strength, cultural patterns began to shift. (Stark 1985, 146)

Feminism will give up something to get something, the right to occupy the liberal text's surface, the women's movement mainstreamed as a central interest group of the time, in exchange for disciplining women's oppression as a necessary accomodation to "reality." This version argues against interpretations of sexism presumably reducing it to "culture" (for example, to "beliefs about what men and women ought to be like") and thus, the subtext fears, blames men who have always been the main authors of culture, preferring instead to coopt angry women as potentially reasonable masculine sociologists. This in turn promotes a balanced view of sexism that in effect both exonerates oppressive men and justifies their social (because biological) inequality.

Feminist science defends a version of sexism with all the paraphernalia of method, a methodical *lack of argument* the essence of appropriate validity claims. The text defers to Kuhnian normal science as a way of validating its own subtext, reproducing the public/private split and with it women's oppression. The text does not advocate a sexual division of labor, turning women into eternal mothers; its advocacy is concealed in the deauthored text of presuppositionless representation only entrenching male superiority as obdurate "reality."

A number of studies indicate several well-established differences between the sexes in task performance—in particular, that females score higher on tasks involving verbal ability and males higher on visual-spatial tasks and mathematical skills (Maccoby and Jacklin, 1974; McManus and Mascie-Taylor, 1983; Newcombe, Bandura and Taylor, 1983). While these differences appear to be biologically based, it should be emphasized that cultural patterns, which often affect sex role development in both a profound and subtle way, might be exerting a simultaneous impact. (Doob 1985, 130)

The text tries to freeze male-female differences in "verbal ability . . . and visual-spatial tasks and mathematical skills" simply by documenting them, as if their description were enough to entrench them as accounts of an essential human nature; sex difference here are only an instance of more far-reaching differences destining women for nurturance and men for what Parsons (1955) called "instrumental" roles. The power of the text's adjectives makes an argument concealing its own hortatory nature. The writing begins by talking about a "number of studies" that "indicate several well-established differences between the sexes in task performance." How are those studies (of which there have been a certain "number") different from studies showing "well-established" sex differences in task performance and, thus, innate ability? If they are different (confirmations, repetitions, different methodologies, more recent?), then how could the other studies have already "established" sex differences as a natural fact? If they are not different, why does the text bother to repeat what is already known, except for effect? I suspect the truth is that the differences between women and men are neither well-established nor "indicated" by the new studies but artifacts *both* of culture (that tracks boys into visual-spatial and math courses and girls into verbal-poetic studies) and of texts purporting to establish, *thus establishing,* this natural fact. For effect, the text places three "studies" in parentheses in the cryptic American Psychological Association style dispensing with specific footnote references, accumulating the effect of names strung together in authority chains, their seriality establishing scientific consensus or at least a preponderance of expert testimony.

Finally, the text allows subtext—sexism dressed up as science—to surface, mingling it with a superficial agnosticism about nature/nurture preserving the text's seeming avoidance of nonessentialist, in this case, biological, explanations. This gives the initially confusing impression of a catholicism about whether sex differences are biological or social, although the text has already decided the issue, supported by numerous studies, in favor of biologism.[10] *The very notion of male/female differences as a research topic valorizes differential treatment of public men and private women,* and when it allows women to go public ensures that their work largely duplicates their biologically-destined reproductiveness. Although it may be useful to understand women's deficiencies in skills like math and engineering usually reserved for men, these can only be understood in a way that does not freeze them into the hard patterns only reproducing themselves in choices feeling they have no choice, that is, fatefully. The only credible text of these differences would account for the way *writing itself* reproduces these differences unwittingly by using the words "male" and "female" as an axis around which allegedly differential skills pivot.

By setting itself the agenda of explanation, writing immediately becomes justification if it does not thematize its interest in using the oppressor's own terms to address the problem. As soon as sex differences become a topic sui generis, without reference to the discursive practices that create a notion of difference in the first place, differentiation all too quickly becomes hierarchy; nonidentity takes the form of a margin heteronomously distinguished from (that is, subordinated to) a center or mainstream. As Irigaray (1985) and Kristeva (1974) suggest, female is only a term for the not-male; as such it cannot be accepted by women as an adequate identity without a struggle interrogating the male/not-male differentiation in the first place as a piece of political history, of textual artifice.

It is obvious that the oppressor is smarter and more facile in the ways of the world than the oppressed because he has more education and perhaps motivation and because he constructs the sense of intelligence and facility not simply as their measurement (IQ tests, sexist usage) but as the exemplification of successful knowledge—smart being tautologically the ability to control. As women mother (Chodorow 1978), and thereby reproduce motherhood by teaching girls to mother, so men *make,* and thereby reproduce the male monopoly of productiveness. The most central male/female difference is the ability of men to make both material things and a language through which "female" stands for the incompetently not-male.[11]

The discipline's text by failing to question the word difference only reproduces differences that lie as much in language as in the inanimate world, purporting that male/female differences as a researchable topic can be explained *differentially;* that is, they can be explained beyond the inescapable fact that men control knowledge by not only running universities but also personifying what is meant by intelligence, capability, efficiency, maleness only another word for performance. For the text to open up the question of male/female differences to differential explanation—biology versus culture—decides in favor of biology, refusing to understand sex in any but biological terms and not, alternatively as I do, in light of the social production and reproduction of sex as simply the power difference between men and women, woman being anyone man is not—margin to his center. Thus, where gender is its social articulation, sex is not biological, as the text repeatedly tells us. Rather it is an artifact of text itself, another way of producing hierarchy.

As long as the text understands sexuality in biological terms, it will inevitably biologize whatever performative differences between men and women it "finds" in its research, no matter how equivocal it is about the decidability of the nature/nurture controversy. The text's subtext in scientizing women's oppression intends a feminism seeking narrowly to upgrade women's bourgeois life-chances to those of men. In this way, a free woman is one who has transcended her not-maleness and become a man in the sense of acquiring male intelligence and aptitude. This inevitably reproduces a biological notion of sex forever imprisoning women in the less-than-personhood of being not simply sexed people but deficient men, however multidimensionally these so-called differences are "explained." The closest the text comes to admitting its purpose is this:

> The issue, then, is not whether males and females differ biologically, but the extent to which these differences have social significance. For example, if women do more poorly on tests of mathematical ability because of biological differences, then women will always be underrepresented in science and engineering—fields that have great influence. On the other hand, if men excel in math only because of socialization differences, then male dominance in science and engineering will probably soon disappear. There has been heated debate on whether sex differences in math aptitude scores are biological or the result of socialization (Benbow and Stanley 1980), but the issue remains unsettled. (Stark 1985, 142)

The text suggests that the issue for sociology is not biological differentiation per se but the "social significance" of this differentiation—if any. It concludes that the "issue remains unsettled" whether men and women innately have different cognitive abilities. But if "socialization" explains all performative differences, then we could expect that "male dominance in science and engineering will probably soon disappear," indeed a low probability. The text anticipates a biologistic outcome simply "because" men will likely continue to dominate women and control the language in which we reproduce masculinity and femininity hierarchically. So in spite of its ameliorating intentions, the text essentially sides with a biological account of women's inferiority—their not-maleness—at least giving biology enough credence to suggest that "the issue remains unsettled."

The bite is taken off this sort of argument inasmuch as the text *seems* to compensate women for math and science deficiencies by suggesting their superiority in "verbal skills," art and poetry, empathy and sensibility.[12] Jensen's stupid blacks are just stupid, where the social text's women are more skilled than men at the socially necessary tasks of "expressiveness," raising kids and helping husband with loving concern, while husband performs the "instrumental" chores required by the family—making money, fixing the roof, defending the family home against burglars. The text in decrying radical feminists as traitors to family rehearses the argument of some radical feminists themselves that men are cursed with a death-wish compelling them to oppress women and make war, whereas women are blessed with a serenity preventing them from acting out all of their unresolved infantile anxieties.

A general sort of equality in the text's acknowledgment of women's and men's special talents (empathy versus instrumentality) seems to mitigate the subtle effects of the text's familism. This at least postpones judgment on these ultimate questions until all the "data" are in, as if research would decide the issue (and not simply reflect, as I suggest, an issue already decided).

> As we have seen, some uncertainty currently exists on the issue of whether sex-linked abilities and psychological attributes are principally biological or culturally determined. (Doob 1985, 134)

> Gilligan's (1982) research on how women make moral judgments showed that they did indeed bring a different set of values into their reasoning. (Hess, Markson, and Stein 1985, 128)

Even a book coauthored by two women trumpets (a woman's) "research" as testament to implied biological difference; Gilligan's (1982) well-known critique of Kohlberg's theory of moral development is read to demonstrate that women *are* elementally different in cognitive and emotional ways. The text wants to find this true in order to arrive at a certain equity in the distribution of biological aptitudes. Gilligan's research intensifies the text's sexist subtext inasmuch as she did not simply report male/female math scores but looked at what we commonly hold to be a deeper, more profound level of "reasoning," more elemental than different ratios of body fat that may result in differential marathon performances. If many women reason morally in a way different from men, it is because the oppressed view moral priorities differently from their oppressors. But again, the text peculiarly misses this patent "social" explanation of differences in moral reasoning between men and women because it wants to find innate differences as well that can then become the basis for the differential treatment of men and women and their enactment of that difference.

> The primary cause of females entering the labor force was modernization and its impact on the biological basis for the traditional sexual division of labor. . . . [A] major consequence of the rise of modern industrial societies was a major decline in fertility. Not much more than a century ago, the average American women was pregnant more than seven times during her lifetime. Today on the average, American women bear slightly fewer than two children each. Moreover, the modern woman need not stay close to an infant in order to nurse it—baby bottles and formulas can take her place. Since the average American woman has her last child by age 27, when she is in her early 30s her last child is already in school, and she can expect to live for at least another 40 years. Thus, women have been freed of the limits imposed on them by their reproductive biology, which had been the basis of traditional sex roles. (Stark 1985, 146)

The text dramatizes the burden imposed on women by their biology where it suggests that a hundred years ago the "average American woman was pregnant more than seven times during her lifetime" while in this century the birth rate has fallen to fewer than two children per woman. Stark interprets this as women's liberation from "the limits imposed on them by their reproductive biology," as if continually being pregnant had nothing to do with the men who impregnated them.

The text reconstructs what it calls "traditional sex roles" (which it rarely defines except by implication) as biologically necessary, "modernization"—presumably contraception—being their undoing. This is extremely problematic from at least two points of view. First, in effect it exonerates men from oppressing women in these "traditional sex roles," as if women's reproductive biology itself was enough to keep women confined to the home (when, in fact, many women in premodern societies overcame their biological infirmities and worked in the fields). Second, it implies that these traditional sex roles typified by the treatment of women as chattels have largely disappeared.

> It is . . . evident, however, that most societies have adopted a fairly consistent pattern in their sex roles. Why? The answer seems to lie in the fact that originally it was highly functional in traditional, preindustrial societies for men and women to play very different roles. A society is more efficient if tasks and responsibilities

are allocated to particular people, and if the members are socialized to fill specific roles. This division of labor need not necessarily be along sex lines, but sexual differences do offer an obvious and convenient means of achieving it. (Robertson 1983, 317)

This sort of functionalism dominating American sociology conflates sexual differentiation ("very different roles") with sexual inequality—or, boldly, sexism—as well as traces this differentiation/stratification to the originary functional necessity of a division of labor between men and women (and, more deeply, public and private). The text's global pronouncement that "a society is more efficient if tasks and responsibilites are allocated to particular people" reflects the deep Durkheimian-Weberian undercurrent in American sociology naming division of labor and an accompanying bureaucratic hierarchy as virtually self-evident requirements of modernization, arguably the most "efficient," "obvious," and "convenient" ways of organizing human activity.

But even if I grant that the industrial division of labor does not inevitably imply a high degree of structured inequality but is in a sense theoretically reward neutral, the sexual division of labor between men and women has been the ruination of women in the way it has excluded them from the public sphere, impoverished them in "private," and degraded them into appendages of men and children, mothers to the world reproducing everyone but themselves. That women mother is entirely a social product; that women nearly exclusively mother in "modern" societies reproduces the pattern chilled by science into a universal law that women *should* mother. And sociology effects this reproduction as it defends the assignment of mothering to women on scientific grounds, occluding the historicity of public/private relations.

Finally, the text resolves a variety of other sexist practices with the hesitant circumspection of disciplined investigation and not the inflamed advocacy of the personal-as-political.

> Pornography violates many values in a society like ours: the dignity of the person; the emotional components of sexual attraction; ideas about morality. But does it produce sexual harm? The evidence says no. On the contrary, legalized pornography has benefited certain societies, as measured by decreases in sex-related crimes. Sociology and other disciplines have the ability to demonstrate things that many people do not want to believe. (Rose, Glazer, and Glazer 1986, 7)

> Many people see a positive value in prostitution, although official morality opposes it. Others view prostitution as not only immoral but criminal. Feminists object to its exploitation of women (Mercer 1977). But social historians claim that many poor women have found the profession superior to factory work. (Hess, Markson, and Stein 1985, 141–42)

The text here extracts the latent familism of legalized pornography ("decreases in sex-related crimes") and then constructs prostitution as a viable career move for "poor women" otherwise destined for "factory work." The writings self-consciously distance themselves from "official morality" as well as political advocacy in defending unpopular truths on grounds of evidence, research, data, even a version of what sociology calls "social history." The text does not simply defend practices unpopular with middle-class liberals and all feminists (if not with many men) but defends them on grounds of unalterable objectivity.

Feminist writing that is tough enough not to flinch at the facts is man enough to be disciplined, even if it betrays itself politically by endorsing misogynist practices. This only repeats within disciplinary sociology an old story of how minority people must outdo members of the dominant center in emulating their values and behavior. The text thus reinforces sexist second nature and further integrates feminism into itself as an apolitical version of alleged social necessity, creating the ironic reality of an originally oppositional writing so beaten down that it ultimately mouths the truth of its captors—again, a common story. As the text says, "sociology and other disciplines have the ability to demonstrate things that many people do not want to believe," such as the inevitability of their own objectification as a healthy social release for men.

Sanitizing Women's Oppression

Once appropriately disciplined, feminism is invited into the world of the text as a version mature enough to transcend its own special status. It is fully translated into a genderless language game suggested as a reasonable strategem of cooperation, compromise, and (thus) cooptation—the peace overture of a second-stage feminism making an effort to live with men within the framework of bourgeois family and workplace.

After being feminized and then masculinized, feminism barely makes waves in the larger discipline as a sociology of gender or sex roles, virtually a marriage manual for straight couples trying to resolve combat in the erogenous zone.[13] *Official feminist sociology reconstructs sexism as corrigible instances of faulty socialization that can be resolved within bourgeois family and workplace.* The text of a feminist sociology pivots around the redefinition of sexism simply as a problem of women's role conflict, the confused role of men in the egalitarian family, and finally the prophesied androgyny of a sex-blind labor market; together these suggest incrementalist strategies of reform in matters of gender. Once disciplined, the sociology of gender, sex-roles, and family constructs a view of domesticity and work echoing the earlier sentiment that feminism is only a special case of conflict theory and, as a result, that women's lot can be improved largely through conflict resolution, compromise, cooperation.

A disciplinary feminism translates sexism into the notion of women's role strain and role conflict, reducing sexist exploitation essentially to social psychology. Sociology as a cleanly dualist text denies that sexism has both structural and personal dimensions interprenetrating in a complexly overdetermining way. By renaming women's oppression, the text hopes to relieve it, going "beyond" patriarchy and misogyny by narrowing them to terms of family maladaptation and job discrimination. It is not that women do not suffer role overload and role contradiction or that the bourgeois labor market is not deeply sexist but that the text reduces the deep structure of interlocking productive and reproductive relations together oppressing women (largely by privatizing them) to dysfunctions of bourgeois sexual relations to be remedied in these terms. The text moves beyond sexism by sanitizing it conceptually—women's experience of too much to do, too little time to do it, to be relieved by hiring help and getting father to pitch in. Of course, these adjustments are possible within the bourgeois family that, as such, continues to appear sundered from the public world. The structural exploitation of women is here narrowed to banal terms of family reform that in spite of political feminism save "family" by reducing the frictions within it—women with so much expected of them that they freak out in exactly the ways originally described by Friedan (1963) in *The Feminine Mystique*.

The text cleans up the persistent ugliness of sexism and turns it into an episode of social-psychological dysfunction, thereby occluding its real location in a sexual division of labor propping both capitalist and state-socialist relations of production; reproduction is ever subordinated to the alleged requirements of male-dominated capital accumulation. A domesticated feminism sanitizes/ scientizes the oppression of women in researchable, reformable terms, taking the blame off both men and a productive/reproductive system turning men against women as well as capital against labor and white against colored.[14] Sociology eschews a structural understanding of the relation between production and reproduction because that would strike too close to home, threatening the privatization of domesticity and its reproductive relations with a political unmasking. It would dangerously confront not only women's unwaged status but also their imposed existential motherhood as merely contingent particulars of historical domination that are heterotextually reproduced. Once feminized as familist and then masculinized as professional science, feminism ameliorates the social-psychological dysfunctions of the family in order to *save* and not undo the privatization of domesticity.

Thus, a disciplining feminism restricts itself to diagnosis within the confines of the male-feminism of universal family and conflict theory and thus destructures sexism in micrological terms; it is no longer patriarchy and misogyny but episodic destabilization, strain, and conflict of so-called gender roles. This addresses almost phenomenologically the negotiations undertaken by heterosexual couples to keep the family intact without utterly sacrificing women's well-being in the process.[15] Seen this way, feminist sociology as marriage counseling conceptually destructures patriarchy into role playing. As such, it suppresses a political interest in structured productive/reproductive relations as these condition the quality of intimate life for women and men in favor of a focus on social-psychological disequilibrium within the interpersonal circuitry of bourgeois family *which it assumes as the normal/normative mode of reproductive intimacy.*

Feminist sociology asks how "family" can be salvaged in a way that redresses some of the grievances of women. It is compelled within these terms to ameliorate women's suffering through a combination of heightened self-awareness, a more democratized division of household labor between wife and husband (while wife retains her primary responsibility for that work), and finally increasing support for women's labor force entry. These three reforms follow from a feminist disciplining that reduces structured sexism to role ruptures between men and women.

At the outset, women are induced to bear the burden of sexism more cheerfully simply by rewriting their plight not as a limit situation in which they risk the loss of sanity and limb but as a melange of costs and benefits; this understanding will surely help them accommodate.

> Women are treated and institutionalized for certain types of mental illness, such as depression, more often than men are. Perhaps this is because women must repress their hostile and assertive feelings more, because housework does not provide many rewards for educated women, because the housewife feels that hers is an inferior status, and because the role of housewife is unstructured and unsung, leaving much time for brooding—especially when the children have grown up and left home. (Light and Keller 1985, 145)

With all the hesitating skepticism of science, the text wonders why women are more depressed than men, as well as treated more frequently for it. "Perhaps," it says, it is because they are more emotionally repressed than men and find housework to be a drag, "leaving much time for brooding." This misses entirely that inasmuch as housework is nearly universally unpaid women are depressed/oppressed about having to do it while their husbands get paid for their public work. In addition, women are "treated and institutionalized for certain types of mental illness" more than men because men as psychiatric professionals diagnose and treat them.[16] That a disciplinary version could favor a vacuous psychologism ameliorating women's "depression" with a little more role flexibility, a part-time job, and some positive thinking is no less awe-inspiring than that the text just quoted was coauthored by a woman.

Simply by addressing women's complaints, such as "brooding," the text thinks it makes serious steps toward resolving the social problem of "sexual (or gender) inequality." Disciplinary feminism hopes against hope that women can be induced to stick with family as long as their "benefits" rise and "costs" diminish—an economization of suffering informing all sorts of currents within mainstream sociology flowing from bourgeois economic theory via Bentham's utilitarianism and Weber's accounting rationality.

> Each of these sets of beliefs [traditional sex-role expectations] has certain costs and benefits for each of the sexes, and each involves role conflicts. (Light and Keller 1985, 154)

> *The Benefits of the Traditional Female Role*
> Although increasingly large numbers of women are entering the work force all the time, many women are not obliged to work thirty-five or forty hours a week all their lives to provide for others. Furthermore, they have the legal right to claim support from their husbands. In many states, a man is liable for his wife's debts, but she is not responsible for his. Until recently, men could not sue for alimony or child support (in the rare case where a divorced man was awarded the custody of his children), but women could. Of course, women do work; but employment, though often an economic necessity and a personal choice, is not yet a *moral* duty for most women. (Light and Keller 1985, 144)

> Under these circumstances, roles in the marriage are subject to *negotiation*, and the partners bring different resources and aspects of power into their struggle to define the relationship. . . . If marriage is stressful for some women, it is profoundly satisfying to others. (Hess, Markson, and Stein 1985, 271)

The text asserts that sex roles have "certain costs and benefits for each of the sexes," where costs include giving up the independence to work and benefits include being "kept." The notion that the obligation to work is "not yet a *moral* duty for most women" incredibly misses the fact that many women *have to* work, either (or both) because their family requires two incomes in order to survive or their husbands have divorced or deserted them.

That women can sue for alimony or child support and "are not obliged to work thirty-five or forty hours a week all their lives to provide for them" is in no sense a "benefit" of what the text ironically calls the "traditional female role." It is only oppression. The irony in the text's usage of "traditional female role" is that it reveals both the text's ambivalence about whether these are good or bad for women and its desire to cash in on the rightward shift valorizing "tradition," notably the golden age when men could oppress women (and whites blacks) without apology. The disciplinary text would have us believe that "traditional sex-role" is a technical usage devoid of these echoes of ambivalence, although even a cursory reading gives the lie to this. Oppression is not good for anyone, least of all the victim. Science refrains from naming oppression lest it seem to be advocacy, instead couching its own advocacy in scaling down the domination of women to a cost-benefit analysis, balancing women's "gloominess" against the security of being kept by men. Liberal science cannot name oppression without equivocation; indeed, it sanitizes oppression as a version of necessity, eliciting enactment of allegedly universal family with the promise that participation in it will not be all bad.[17]

Furthermore, women are not depleted of "resources and aspects of power" by which to meet their needs in negotiated contest with men. The unconstrained marketplace assumption, in which buyer and seller both benefit by exchanging goods and services, enters mainstream sociology via either Homans's (1950) unvarnished exchange theory or the constructivisms like symbolic interactionism and ethnomethodology underlining the actively negotiated nature of social-exchange relationships—marriage somehow inherently "subject to negotiation." [18]

It is wishful thinking to suppose that all women possess "resources and aspects of power" enabling them to negotiate with men as if so-called gender relations were processes and products of bargaining between essentially equal partners; this ideal increasingly informs the micrological text naming the essentially balanced nature of social life. Sociology conceives of people as social "actors" already freighted with "resources and aspects of power" they then deal strategically for what they want. Often people do not negotiate because one party has such a preponderance of power that he or she can dominate the other into a cowed silence, suggesting the inappropriateness of exchange metaphors to characterize a whole host of muted "relationships." This is true of relations between individuals and the huge institutions controlling them as well as between individuals who dominate each other in relations based not on dialogic mutuality or reciprocity but on monologue, power, and coercion.[19] This exchange ontology echoes an essentially middle-class optimism about communicative reason, assuming that people do in fact manage to negotiate a shared reality and make themselves understood. Yet history frequently shows otherwise.

Finally, women are not only ahistorically empowered to "negotiate" with men in the give-and-take of the companionate marriage; they are also often "profoundly satisfied" by the married state (again, this written by two women). While they acknowledge that marriage is "stressful for some women," they redeem their optimism about "family" by ending on the upbeat note that many women are fulfilled by marriage. Like all social statuses, marriage is both stressful and unstressful, undesirable and desirable; the balance between the two is determined by the woman's negotiating skills plus her "resources and aspects of power." This tells the old story of how marital quality rests on the woman's shoulders in the sense that it is her responsibility to "negotiate" a good deal with her spouse, failing which she will be "stressed" and forced to visit a marriage counselor or, worse, a psychiatrist. Marital quality is ultimately the woman's responsibility inasmuch as she is obliged to *get* her recalcitrant husband to be less slothful about doing his occasional stint of housework or "parenting," to listen to her "problems" more often, and to be a more skilled, more sensitive "lover." Although perhaps this expresses the useful, if pedestrian, hope that victims ought not simply succumb to their lot with abject pessimism, it perpetuates the responsibility that the text wants women to bear for the "success" of their marriage *inasmuch as they are to be in charge of the private sphere.*

Replete with the middle-class purposiveness of the tenured academic woman more or less in control of her own life, this misses the nearly intractable powerlessness of most of the world's women. The text's positive thinking embodied in a felicific calculus toting up happiness on a scale of costs and benefits reduces domination to the profundity, "stress."

> With the typical employed wife spending between seventy and eighty-three hours a week working both outside and inside the home, *role overload* is a major problem. Her lack of time for companionship with her husband will cause some stress in the marriage, which is only partly compensated for by the extra money that the couple have for raising their standard of living. In this situation, role negotiation takes place (Hood 1980, Hiller 1980, Spitze and Waite 1981). Those couples who cannot make a satisfactory adjustment will eventually experience extreme tension. If the wife leaves the labor force, she may become resentful; if she remains employed, her husband may be unhappy. Most marriages overcome these problems, however. (Hess, Markson, and Stein 1985, 283)

The text proposes "role negotiation" between marital partners; failing that "extreme tension" will result. The seemingly easy way out for women— simply quitting the job that seems to aggrieve their husbands, thus exposing themselves to the angst of role overload and role conflict—is not an ideal solution; it might make the woman "resentful," perhaps even gloomy (as the text earlier said), proving dysfunctional to marital harmony. On the other hand, by remaining in the labor force, as if she were there for quite frivolous reasons of self-expression and not also to make money to facilitate her and her family's survival, she might make "her husband unhappy," another trigger of marital disharmony. Faced with what appears to be a no-win situation—gloomy, displaced wife or jealous, underattended husband—the only viable solution is "role negotiation" that, we are assured, usually succeeds; after all, "most marriages overcome these problems." The text thus offers something for everyone: social-psychological wordplay, a conflict analysis of reciprocal felicity and infelicity, and finally some sober empirical science, quieting the fear that disequilibrium—that is, role overload, that is, stress, that is, oppression—is indeed the normal/normative case in the bourgeois family.

The text delves even deeper into the casuistry of a functionalist social psychology turning oppression into a virtue, a destresser.

American values have typically not placed the same pressures on women to achieve that have been placed on men. Although a woman may strive to reach the top of her profession, there is less shame in failure or in achieving only moderate success. Consequently, women may be less prone to fall victim to the career syndrome, which entails almost total devotion to the workplace, often to the exclusion of outside interests and solid interpersonal relationships. (Light and Keller 1985, 144–45)

Even if occasionally depressed and resentful, kept women at least are not exposed to the risks of the "career syndrome," compulsive devotion to paid work to the "exclusion of outside interests and solid interpersonal relationships." The conventional wisdom that women as essentially sensitive beings are not as brittle and blocked as men, unashamed to show emotional vulnerability, informs the text's account of the fortunate benefit of their psychic well-being traded off (reasonably, it would seem: subtext) against a "career"—a virtue thus made of sexist necessity.

Optimally, women would have it both ways, both bourgeois work and bourgeois home, even if they do not enjoy full equality in either arena. Women recognize that even if they cannot have it all at least they can make the best of an imperfect world, utilizing one or another of the coping strategies of middle-class feminism, from daycare and flex-time to emergent male sensitivity.

More and more working wives are in the "double bind," facing urgent demands both from family and job. The double bind puts great stress on the mother and, as a result, on her marriage and on her whole family, too. Three possible ways of relieving the burden are now emerging: first, child-care services; second, a more active role in child care by the father; and third, more flexible working conditions for working mothers. (Goode 1984, 343)

Clearly, this is a functionalist text inasmuch as the so-called "double bind" —being oppressed both at home and work—"puts great stress [not only] on the mother [but also] on her marriage and on her whole family, too." Women's stress is dysfunctional only when it sabotages the marriage with her gloom and anxiety and therefore must be contained if the family is not to go under. This strategy of deriving functional and dysfunctional consequences from women's alleged psychic states—role overload, role conflict, stress, gloom and the like—is remarkably similar to the neo-Weberian tradition in the sociologies of stratification and work addressing the disequilibrating effects of workers' "job satisfaction," termed "alienation" by the functionalist text (e.g., Blauner 1964).

This purposely confuses Weber's alienation with the Marxian sense of workers' oppression that is simultaneously (see Richard Centers 1949) subjective and objective; a reduction through psychologism transforms ameliorating strategy into psychic enhancement and not a wholesale transformation of the mode and relations of production leading workers to be "dissatisfied" with their work. The feminization of sociology as a social psychologism reducing oppression to stress, the so-called double bind, similarly narrows and idealizes women's oppression. Although the text tries to temper the disadvantages of oppressed labor—low job satisfaction—to check the motivation crises of advanced capitalism, it also attempts to cool out the rage of "stressed" women to prevent insuperable crises in the reproductive relations underlying capitalist production. Just as capital is propped by male workers' reproduction of it, so it is also reproduced in reproductive relations willingly enacted by women adapted to their "destiny" as eternal facilitators, compromisers.

Should either job satisfaction or women's psychic well-being fall too low, the cycle between production and reproduction—the reproduction *of* reproduction —will unravel, leading to all sorts of systemic disturbances, even cataclysm. Sexism props capitalism that in turn (through its modest "rewards" to both men and women) makes sexism seem bearable, especially where people's expectations have been so reduced that they express "satisfaction" with meager offerings—a benign boss, a sensitive husband, a day or two off each week, the occasional vacation. The text foreshortens our imaginations by reducing the realm of the ontologically unnecessary, thereby turning any "gain" or "reward" into a public relations coup. The text would reduce the pain of social nature through superficial coping strategies—hire a maid, cajole your husband to pitch in, ask your boss for time off—thereby deepening the intractability of pain as a social fact.

The Hearts of Men

The text's version of women's oppression reduces her oppression to the computation of costs and benefits and thus suggests incremental strategies for dealing with the stresses of existential motherhood coupled with exploited work in the public sphere; the so-called double bind leads to an essentially conciliatory posture toward men that would negotiate with them for a few more benefits and a few fewer costs. The assumption that people necessarily derive benefits from exchange—and thus that women always have some power, some modicum of "resources," as the text calls them—only reproduces women's heteronomy by making her think both that she is more powerful with regard to men than she really is and that her husband is not an enemy but an ally, even a victim himself of what are described as rigid or "traditional" sex roles, as such deserving compassion in his own right.

I am not against conciliation or cooperation; but meeting half-way, where one party, class, race, gender is inordinately powerful, either invites disaster, a charge of the light brigade against inevitably victorious opposing forces, or preserves the illusion that consensus between opposing parties is both possible and actual, equally self-destructive in the long run. And the notion that men are victims—strictly true in the sense that all oppressing and oppressive humans live distorted, alienated lives—psychologizes very real forces of oppression and subordination and diverts attention from women to the male structures ensnaring them. I do not call for a *lex talionis,* enacted as a judicial principle in the so-called war between the sexes, for it is less a war with a more or less clearly defined goal than a grinding daily struggle for psychic and material survival in which each side scrambles around trying to avoid yet more misery. It is profoundly true that because sociology falsifies the real source of people's suffering most men and virtually all women who lead powerless, degraded lives are thus diverted from attacking the forces of administration and accumulation; instead they release their pent-up fury on weaker, even more pitiful "others"—Jews, blacks, women, gays, the list is endless, shifting from one historic contingency to another. Scapegoats appear wherever needed as targets of displaced rage.[20]

Powerless men "read" texts—*Penthouse*, the Bible, sociology—that name the natural responsibility of women for the private sphere and thus suggest to them that women are as much chattels as house, car, golf clubs. The issue is not to affix "blame" to either texts or their readers, for neither women who unnecessarily submit nor men who accept women's inferiority as second nature are blameless. The issue instead is to understand and then to resist the diversion of critical attention from women's, indeed *privacy's,* heteronomy to the broken hearts of men in the arena of reproductive politics. This is not to forget that most men and many women are already oppressed in the public realm of waged work but only to resist the identity of any and all oppression as distortion. Moreover, to resist the masculinization of women's suffering is a way of opposing men's oppression in the productive sphere, a nearly inevitable tendency once the dam bursts and women are forced to share the malaise of "stress" and role confusion with men. Domination, although nearly universal, is nonidentical.

The text's concern for the sensibilities of men suggests that men, victims of "traditional" gender roles as well as of the women's movement mounting an unsparing, bitchy attack on them, are increasingly sensitive to both women's needs and their own matters of the heart. The image inescapably emerges of new-age men in emotional crisis yearning not to be John Wayne but unsure of how best to soften themselves without giving away too much to the women's movement or appearing gay, ever a threat to heterotextuality.

> There is a growing "men's movement" among those who feel that typical male roles are limiting and even destructive of supportive relationships with women, children, and other men (Pleck 1983, Stein 1984). (Hess, Markson, and Stein 1985, 208)

It is notable that the text sees men yearning only for "supportive relationships" with women and not also egalitarian ones; supportiveness is the prerogative of the superordinate offered to the subordinate much as the state offers handouts to the poor—a token and not a substantial transfer of power. Disciplined feminism drinks deeply of third-force psychiatry, stressing self-actualization over liberation, recognizing that men care about sexual politics when they feel "limited," not when they perceive great injustice, and then addressing their own part in it. Men would prefer to self-actualize, avoiding alienating and even "destructive" gender roles as long as posttraditional roles do not strip them of the primacy allowing them the luxury of being "supportive" of women. Liberal feminism is as much liberal masculinism in the way it aggrandizes men on the backs of a women's movement, substituting patronizing male "supportiveness" for the real thing.

Liberalism, as always, seeks to improve the quality of personal life and of "relationships" without transvaluing social structure today dominating the personal in a way that stymies the standard existentialist remedies of care and concern. Kierkegaard wrecks on the shoals of contradictions that cannot be resolved without more radical interventions. At least in the short term these contradictions will be more painful to hegemonic groups than the hopeful text's sweet reasonableness would have us believe.[21]

> Given the contradictions inherent in the traditional male role, many men welcome the changes in the female role as a liberation from the burdens of traditional masculinity. These men seek a new male ideal, less geared toward competition and dominance. Men will be better off, they argue, if they can learn to acknowledge their human vulnerability and limitations and escape the posturing and pretense of the male role. (Light and Keller 1985, 149)

It is not at all clear what the "contradictions inherent in the traditional male role" are, although the text indicates that new-age men seek to lessen the pull of "competition and dominance" over their lives (and wives) and welcome women's liberation as an easing of the "burdens of traditional masculinity." This straightforward construction on its face appears to contain no hidden demons in its nether regions. Yet the notion that free women will help free men's "human vulnerability and limitations" suggests that men do not oppress women today but preexisting roles lock us all in, implying that men and women ought to share their common victimhood *and thus exonerate (some) men from sex-political crimes against women and children.* After all, the liberal text does not encourage the notion that basically good people willfully do bad things to each other or that they do not mean what they say or say what they mean, unschooled in the subtext of desire that is a force in all our lives, whether for good or ill.

Although it is true that most people experience their lives as degradation, locked into the realm of reproduction as it interacts with, and is dominated by, the productive sphere, everyday life is mediated by desire, by choice.

However unlikely that men habituated by the heterotext to oppress women as the weaker sex will spontaneously change themselves, the literal account of this habituation as unfortunate-but-unintended denies men and women any responsibility for reproducing reproduction and essentially closes the door of social change (even though it advocates modest changes like men's lib). As before, liberalism is contradicted by an underlying version of science undercutting its power of positive thinking as a ruse of unreason. Men brought up to be "men" will continue to act like "men" as long as the power of the social over choice remains unchecked, reproduced heterotextually under the sign of implacable "social facts" lived out speciously as species fate. The liberal wishes only for wish fulfillment, small comfort in a world in which the "roles" stifling us are reproduced thoughtlessly. Although men and women are responsible for what they do to each other, accepting that responsibility risks undoing what has for centuries passed for a natural fact, thus reproducing itself. Reproduction becomes production; rather, the distinction fades.

Costs of the Traditional Male Role

The responsibilities attached to the male role in America can be a source of great stress and anxiety as well as a source of satisfaction and pride. Being in a position to make decisions is fine for people who are confident of what they are doing, but it seems less of a privilege to those who are uncertain of themselves. Complicating matters is the fact that men are supposed to maintain the impression of strength and courage at all times. Fear of inadequacy and failure is the dark side of the pressure on men to achieve. What is more, the emphasis men place on strength, toughness, initiative and superiority can have unintended consequences, including the requirement to test and prove these attributes by engaging in violent exchanges with other men. (Light and Keller 1985, 147)

The text spells out the "contradictions inherent in the traditional male role" as the clash of authority and "fear of inadequacy and failure," men engaging in "violent exchanges with other men" as a way of resolving the contradictions. Presumably men unsuccessful at work take it home and find release in dominating wife and children, "acknowledging [their human] vulnerability" by exploiting the vulnerability of women. Although is it undeniable that much hu-man history can be read correctly as a barroom brawl in search of prepotent masculine identity, this can be reckoned a "cost of the traditional male role" only at the risk of relativizing the violence women have always experienced at the whim of men.

Susan Brownmiller's (1975) epochal book on rape, *Against Our Will*, shows the utter wantonness of male domination of women's bodies, absolutizing men's plunder of women as a uniquely perverse relationship, far more sinister than the mano-a-mano combats in the male spheres of war and sports in that the combatants in the former case have unequal social as well as physical power.

A total theory of domination comprehends the interlocking variety of oppressions, refuses to identify them, and finally acknowledges that some forms of inhumanity—the Holocaust, rape—are more deeply perverse than others. Although men have been trapped in self-destructive patterns of comportment, at least most have trapped themselves. Women have had little choice.

> Women also have more emotional freedom than men; they are permitted to express their doubts and vulnerabilities, and they have more outlets for tension and anxiety. The sphere of intimacy and close human contact is more accessible to women. The expression of nurturance, warmth, and sympathy, qualities which to some extent are denied men in our society, can be most rewarding. (Light and Keller 1985, 145)

Not only are women said by the discipline's feminism to "have more emotional freedom than men," women are to be envied by men for the emotionally "rewarding" lives they are said to lead. The text reproduces conventional wisdom—apologia—in suggesting that women are less emotionally blocked than men, "permitted to express their doubts and vulnerabilities" and enjoying greater access to the "sphere of intimacy and close human contact": close human contact, indeed, means being bludgeoned by men physically and verbally. Not only are men disadvantaged compared to women, but women are also positively blessed compared to men as the text announces their "expression of nurturance" as "most rewarding." This powerful construction deprives men of the alienated activity imposed on women as their birthright, namely "nurturance, warmth, and sympathy"; these qualities, of course, benefit men as recipients of this nurturance.

Although the text suggests that men are disadvantaged with respect to women's seeming monopoly of nurturant sympathy, it suggests that the women's movement has increased the emotional equity between the sexes by unleashing women's power drive, thereby further disempowering *men.*

> [T]he women's liberation movement has also affected the sex life of married couples. The effect has been two-fold. First, the movement has encouraged women to foresake passivity and to take a more active part in all aspects of living, including sex. Second, as many women struggle openly to gain more power in their marriages, the struggle often extends to the bedroom. Many husbands who strongly support a tradition of male sexual dominance are unable to cope with wives' sexual assertiveness. It appears that one symptom of this failure has been a sharp increase in the incidence of impotence (Hunt, 1983). (Doob 1985, 142)

The old caricature of the castrating women acting in "masculine" ways is resurrected scientifically to cast doubt on the move to uproot "traditional" sex roles, with potent men going out to work and nurturant women at home to receive their husbands' sexual advances.

This construction belongs to the text's secret effort to defend traditional—

that is, sexist—sex roles against their reversal, with women becoming men and vice versa. It is interesting that the text depicts sex-political change in this way as a process of the threatening sexual masculinization of women, as if masculinity were the sought-after status and femininity only an unwanted residual outcome—resulting here in male impotence. The text understands women's liberation as a usurpation of masculinity, before which usurped men lose their potent manhood, instead of understanding it quite differently as an appropriation of femininity—or simply humanness. The scientization of inappropriate female "assertiveness" as the cause of "a sharp increase in the incidence of impotence" only confirms the text's (and, it hopes, readers') suspicion that women ought not act like biologically licentious men *in private* lest the sacred family fail because men can no longer get it up.

Finally, as a way of defending "traditional" sex roles against horny, castrating women, the text more discursively elaborates the reasons why so-called traditional sex roles function to preserve the bourgeois family. As it defends the male against broken hearts as well as the unremitting sexual assault of aggressive women, so it suggests the allegedly functional utility of the traditional male "role," further vitiating the seeming feminist assault on traditional men.

> All this does not mean that mothers and fathers are interchangeable; rather, each seems to make a unique and vital contribution to the child's development. For instance, American fathers play with babies more than do mothers, encouraging them in the development of curiosity and motor activities. In contrast, American mothers tend to restrict their infants more and to play more verbal games with them. . . . As the children grow older, a positive relationship with their father (especially for sons) seems to facilitate their development of well-internalized moral standards and to promote their academic achievement. (Light and Keller 1985, 365)

Even on the text's surface, its argument that men are unfortunately denied the nurturing roles of women contradicts its claim that "American fathers play with babies more than do mothers," although the contradiction is eased if we understand that women are usually responsible for the child's primary care; thus, men, only marginally involved in child care, would be less encumbered by the child and as a result could spend more time in directed play (that the text goes on to say stimulates "the development of curiosity and motor activities"). The father is clearly charged with the allegedly more important contribution to the child's cognitive formation, priming the "development of well-internalized moral standards and [the promotion of] . . . academic achievement," echoing Parsons's distinction between male instrumentality and female expressiveness. Liberal textual politics aside, sociology is deeply committed to patriarchal domestic relations hinging on male intellectual superiority; women function best as teachers of language and emotional expressivity.

The text continues that the traditional male role is not only invaluable for the child's development but also essential for the adult male's further development.

> In sum, researchers are increasingly finding that fathers make a difference. They are also finding that being a father frequently improves a man's self-concept, well-being, and life satisfaction. (Light and Keller 1985, 366)

Undoubtedly fathering in the patriarchal family would improve his "well-being" and "self-concept" in granting him an even broader primacy than the one he enjoys with respect to his hegemony over his wife. Male destiny is reproduced by men as fathers who seek to reproduce little men in their own image and girl children who embody the cherished femininity of the adored if subjugated wife.

Where the father can afford to be only a part-time parent, bouncing children on his knees after they have been fed and bathed, he certainly might derive a sense of his own continuity from generation to generation, even his eternity, where the favored son can duplicate his own efforts and bring pride to the family (that is, father's) name. The text only further ontologizes patriarchy where it suggests on evidence that neither can children survive well without father nor men without children to enhance their sense of well-being. It is a truism that men do better than women in the married state (Bernard 1981) just as it is clear that children do better in this heterosexist society, acquiring a systematic morality and, perhaps most important, a relation to authority enabling them later to survive a difficult public world. Men do better in theory because they do better in practice even if, as today, according to the up-to-date text, men feel overshadowed by the dark demands of bitchy women, the rug pulled out from under them after all these years of habituated obedience.

The text builds in an arresting escape valve for men who, stifled by traditional marriage, are either dulled into a dreary routine or overdemanded on by women whose time seems to have come. The text puts a fine point on its versions of the bilateral nature of sex-political trouble where, citing current "research," it defends the man's right to philander.

> As Kingsley Davis (1932) points out, prostitution is functional. Many men, it seems, desire a variety of sexual outlets. Prostitution meets this need without undermining the family system in the way that more affectionate extramarital relationships would. (Robertson 1983, 29)

Davis's argument, endorsed uncritically by the text, is the more equivocal where it defends prostitution on grounds that (given essential male promiscuity) "more affectionate extramarital relationships" would "undermine the family system."

Not a word is said about the violation of the prostitute's humanity, betrayal of the wife's trust, or the essential biologization of men's alleged tendency to wander. This defense of prostitution suggests that women recently (perhaps eternally, I suspect) have been too hard on men who, after all, must ungrudgingly bear the onus of responsibility for keeping the family intact. This reduction of the personal to function gives the lie to the text's surface account of family as a realm apart, unsullied by political concerns. One might force a reading of the text on Davis defending the destruction of the privatization of family on grounds that, he quite explicitly says, prostitution is a covert but essentially public practice; by its very nature it saves the family. And yet the notion of public functions designed to protect private freedom misses the obvious connection between public and private in the practice of prostitution, which fatefully affects all sorts of supposedly "private" lives. There is no such thing as an escape valve for public alienation that is not itself firmly anchored in the public sphere, thus bearing with it all kinds of what the text calls "costs."

The text ringingly announces that the judgment day of full equality between the sexes is at hand; the workplace has been androgynized and the family democratized, or at least made a site of "equity." The text trumpets the inevitability of women's progress as evidence of the world's openness to a diverse array of interest groups. Just as the *embourgeoisement* of American labor further vitiates apocalyptic Marxism, with its alleged prediction of an unavoidable socialist revolution, so the text incorporates feminism both as a contribution to scientific sociology and *as a liberal practice that must be right because (allegedly) it works,* enabling women to overcome the episodes of role strain, conflict, and depression to which it has already reduced the experience of women's oppression.

As the text, along with many pundits in the 1960s and 1970s, tried to placate American blacks by describing their imminent integration into the mainstream of American life, now it cools out feminists with what has become an advertising slogan, "You've come a long way, baby"—less a dampening of further civic activism than self-congratulation about the correctness of a liberal reasonableness that, with evidence, the text suggests has borne (and will continue to bear) fruit. The construction of feminism's successes is less a suggestion that the fight is over, for the text plainly acknowledges that the road ahead is still long, than approval of the middle-range strategies valorized as sensible alternatives to the wild feminism hastening the break-up of the family, among other things. The notion of an inevitable feminism validates the safe feminism the text has constructed as an alternative to a radical version of purported lesbian separatism.

But in the more advanced industrial nations, the picture begins to change. Women play an increasing role in the labor force, and as they do so, they gradually gain more and more equality with men. In 1940, for example, only 27.4 percent of the American labor force was female; by 1981, the proportion had risen to 42.8

percent. During this period, the sexes have grown steadily more equal; and as women come to play an even greater part in the economic life of the nation, full sexual equality will become a reality. (Robertson 1983, 319–20)

The text clearly bases its optimism about the right road taken not on sentiment, for science as a masculine text is avowedly unsentimental, but on "hard" evidence that rings true simply because it is expressed quantitatively, studded with dates, percentages, and figure. That "women play an increasing role in the labor force" does not mean that "they gradually gain more and more equality with men" even on the text's face, let alone that this is a warrant for announcing that "full sexual equality will become a reality." Against both bourgeois and Marxist economisms, women's entry into the work force does not indicate "more equality with men," only, perhaps, more equity—victims' acquiescence to the power of the social. Most women are still unwaged and otherwise oppressed in the so-called private sphere of "family"; also, women are paid less and do more degraded jobs than men. As the rates of divorce, desertion, unpaid alimony, and child support continue to rise or remain high, poverty is increasingly feminized. Women are coerced to enter the menial, deskilled, often pink-collar labor force simply to try to replace the income formerly obtained by their husbands, a struggle that almost always fails *because* women do not share "equality with men" in the workplace. The percentage game that can be used to "show" that women are becoming "more equal" simply because they increasingly work outside the home can be turned against the text when things like desertion, divorce, and unpaid alimony are taken into account as well as the so-called income gap between men and women; the gap itself is distorted by almost always ignoring the huge discrepancy between women and men in nonsalary earnings in the form of investment and inheritance. As before, the source of women's oppression is patriarchy in its manifold sense, notably the structuring of public and private lives around a sexual division of labor restricting women to domesticity—and not labor force participation per se.

The sexual division of labor oppresses women not simply because it prevents them from entering the public sphere; rather, as the text's own data show, women are in fact increasingly entering the work force *because, however many exceptions it may allow, the public sphere is a man's world and the private sphere a woman's world*. Thus, women who find themselves in public (at work, in politics, whatever) are compelled to become men, undergoing what the liberal text deceptively calls androgyny, a term connoting in subtext what the text intends as *masculinization* rather than the whole degendering of sexuality.

There are small but definite causes for optimism. Couple by couple, household by household, office by office, company by company, profession by profession, women are winning equality with men. Full sexual equality will not be achieved in this century, but milestones in that direction will be detectable each day, month, and year. The signs are unmistakable; progress, though slow, is inevitable. Sex roles have changed more in this century than in the previous 10,000 years. The glass is half full, not half empty. (Goode 1985, 302)

The text authoritatively guarantees a positive outcome based on what it calls "unmistakable signs." It closes with a metaphor popularized by presidential wishful-thinker Ronald Reagan that in the fashion of all idealism chooses self-consciously to see domination as freedom, or at least as the "unmistakable" harbinger of a teleologically vouchsafed future. The argument pivots on the construction "winning equality with men," the text intending equality-within-domination, within a patriarchal sexual division of labor making women compulsory and unwaged or underwaged mothers. Tradition is softened by more companionate marriages and greater occupational opportunity for women.[22]

A different sense of "equality" would demolish patriarchal reproductive relations reproducing capitalist and state-socialist modes of production; indeed, *real* androgyny refuses to assimilate images of women's success to performative images of male conquest and thinks new concepts and practices of sexuality unhinging it from the production/reproduction of the authoritarian state. It is easy to announce increasing "equality" if the spoils are constructed as *a bourgeois life,* replete with 9-to-5 subordination, modest leisure time in which to consume symbolically-mediated goods and services and "family" riding on the backs of women whose fate is said to be reproduction.[23] If equality is masculine-capitalist equality of this sort, still oppressing those situated structurally nearer the bottom than the top of the opportunity pyramid, recent slight gains for primarily middle-class white women do not spell the sort of *embourgeoisement* that the text in another context uses to vitiate Marxism. There are certainly more bourgeois, feminine, disciplined women than fifty years ago (or, even more certainly, than "10,000 years" ago, as the text suggests), just as there are more white-collar and modestly well-off blue-collar workers than half a century ago.

If equality is defined narrowly, unimaginatively, unhopefully as the ingress of women to the public sphere, no matter how economically exploited they may be at work, and as the democratization of some household chores, even "parenting"—despite women's continued responsibility for "family"— then it is easy to find evidence of women's advance, even its imminence. However, if equality is construed differently as the very subversion of the constellation of bourgeois work and family authorizing the narrower concept of equality, then women are no closer to the actuality than they were hundreds of years ago, and in some sense they are even further away.[24]

The assumption of a self-reproducing progress is no less metaphysical than the postulate of innate male superiority or, for that matter, nurturant female

superiority. Even the most obstinately cautious empiricist would be forced
to acknowledge the recent ideological, legal, and emotional retrenchment of
modest women's advances made in the past twenty years under sway of the
New Right and its virulent evangelical Christianity opposing every effort to
uncouple biology and destiny. Even in its own liberal terms the text vastly
overstates the gains of women, failing to understand the growing backlash
against women in properly depth-psychological and structural terms. It is prevented from doing so by its own occlusion of the interpenetration of public and
private, objective and subjective, long the topic of renegade western Marxism
(Agger 1979a) and, lately, of some of the more Marxist versions of feminism
—all commonly grounded in a liberatory version of psychoanalysis.

The text's resistance to the politics of sexuality is not just a "political"
resistance, assuming (as we cannot) that resistance could be only political,
productive, or public and not also deeply anchored in psyche and body. The
text shares a constitutional inability to understand the bridge between desire
and society that it in turn constitutes, thus reproducing, reproductive and
productive relations suppressing their own connection—both as a topic and/as
a reality fatally lived and relived by people who (*want* to) believe that their
minds and bodies are inviolate territory off limits to the invading tentacles of
total administration.[25]

> Social change is likely to be slow and fitful. Fathers will continue to resist
> child-care responsibilities. But the pressures upon them to become equal parents
> will surely mount. The more important a woman's career becomes, and the more
> her income approaches her husband's, the more husbands will be forced to accept
> child-care responsibilities. It is just a question of time. (Goode 1984, 343)

The text acknowledges that the inevitability of equality will only be reached
on a long road; the certainty of its arrival does not diminish the travail in getting
there. The writing has almost a conflict-theoretic tone, announcing struggle
bound to ensue between men and women over "child-care responsibilities" and
acknowledging the intergender frictions this will provoke. It is revealing that
the text allows its subtext to surface where it suggests with seeming certainty
that "fathers will continue to resist" these new domestic "responsibilities,"
all but admitting the interest men have in oppressing women—not that that
interest is at all opaque to anyone in touch with the politics of reproduction.
The text says something new and yet contradictory when it suggests that
change is inevitable, "just a question of time," and that men who have a
stake in perpetuating the status quo by virtue of their inevitable "resistance"
will force change to be "slow and fitful," opening the Pandora's Box of
social meteorology: By simultaneously suggesting the inevitability of women's
progress along with the gradualism allegedly necessary to attain it, the text has
it both ways; it blunts the present imperative for a new and different world with

the guarantee of an eventual Judgment Day and thus cumulates all the interim small steps into a finality—the inevitable dawn of a world without privations.

Even within its own liberal economism, it is a construction of faith to suggest that the woman's "income approaches her husband's," inexorably so. The text's optimistic gradualism runs so deep that *in its own terms* it forgets to prop its deep assumptions about the inevitability of progress with cogent references to the here-and-now, a contradiction made to seem even more glaring by the text's own postured scientificity. All sorts of studies show that women's incomes are not converging with men's, just as blacks' are not rising to meet whites'. A cabalist might even find some significance in the oft-declared data that women and blacks make about 60 percent of male and white salaries, respectively, a "coincidence" merely compounded in its cosmic meaning when it is remembered that blacks were deemed three-fifths of whites in the original apportionment by the U.S. Constitution.

A less cosmic interpretation would clearly suggest a common *rate of exploitation* among the peripheral, marginal fractions of waged and unwaged labor on which the political-economic system depends. In fact, though, the text's metaphysical progressivism does not require a logic of strict economic convergence between women and men; it is probably enough in its own terms that women "enter the work force in increasing numbers," no matter how subordinate, unskilled, and deskilled. The text flows freely from the obvious reality of increasing numbers of women in the labor force to the conclusion that "in general [they] have formed a more equal partnership with men in society."

> In the intervening years [since 1963] women have entered the work force in increasing numbers, finding more careers open to them, and in general, have formed a more equal partnership with men in society. (Light and Keller 1985, 131)

It is a huge, and false, leap from women's growing participation in the work force, required by economic necessities such as systemic capitalist crisis often intensified by male desertion, divorce, and unpaid alimony, to their "more equal partnership with men in society." Wishing it so does not make it so, even if the subtext of bourgeois economism on which the text rests is raised to view and the proposition defended that women's bourgeois work is their ticket to equality with men. Only a writing that relates public to private oppression through a concept of the sexual division of labor reproducing capitalist productive relations can give the lie to the tempting identification of modest, largely economistic, gains of middle-class feminism with the overall emancipation of women—emancipation which, in any case, as Marx understood, must be general for it also to be particular, free humanity a condition and simultaneously a component of free women.

The text declares the inevitability of gradualist convergence between men and women both in work and family, a case it tries to make by describing parallel "progress" in both realms (yet without relating them structurally). When women are inexorably advancing in the workplace, they are also enjoying the fruits of more companionate, democratic marriages. The text claims that there is a connection between workplace androgyny and family democracy, although it merely asserts but does not explicate it.

> American families have traditionally been patriarchal, but a gradual movement toward the egalitarian form has been encouraged by women's steadily improving educational and occupational status in the society at large. (Doob 1985, 298)

> In the long run, however, American marriages will become more fully egalitarian as the incomes of the spouses become more equal. (Robertson 1983, 366–67)

> Given the trend toward wives' empoyment, and the attitude shifts among young adults, it is safe to predict more egalitarian relationships in marriage, with a more flexible division of labor both in and outside the home than in our recent past. (Hess, Markson, and Stein 1985, 284)

> There seems to be a major trend, at least in the more industrialized nations, toward greater equality between the sexes both within and outside of marriage and the family. (Eshleman and Cashion 1985, 341)

> Generally, the modern family is characterized by reduced power differences between husband and wife and between parents and children. This trend, called *egalitarianism*, is largely the result of the many liberating currents in Western civilization, stemming from the Enlightenment. It is difficult to maintain a commitment to freedom and equality in the general society while denying its exercise in the most intimate unit of the social system. Furthermore, affection is more likely between equals than between superior and inferior. (Hess, Markson, and Stein 1985, 265)

The text is definite about the positive relationship between women's economic advances and the democratization of the formerly "patriarchal" family; this is one of the few times it calls the "traditional" family what it really is— run by men. "American marriages will become more fully egalitarian as the incomes of the spouses become more equal": it is initially unclear why this should be so, leaving the reader to probe a deeply repressed subtext. Finally, the text ascribes overall advances for women to the "many liberating currents in Western civilization, stemming from the Enlightenment," essentially suggesting that women both at work and home have advanced on the basis of *male goodwill,* a construction already implied in its argument that men, too, suffer from confining "sex roles."

Although I do not dispute that alienation alienates everyone, it does not do so equally (domination, as I suggested, being nonidentical in the structural totality of the concatenated world system). This undercuts the text's implication that alienated men will liberate alienated women (that they themselves alienate) on the basis of self-interest. As self-interest is today a distortion of true "interest"—true human needs—men's and women's self-interests are structurally as well as phenomenologically unequal. Thus, because the text's men ease women's burden on grounds other than self-interest, it appeals to the hallowed liberal concept of "enlightenment," male goodwill. As the writing suggests, "it is difficult to maintain a commitment to freedom and equality in the general society while denying its existence in the most intimate unit of the social system." An enlightened society seemingly tends toward its total enlightenment; male concessions in the public sphere are matched by their concessions in private lest it become "difficult to maintain a commitment to freedom and inequality in the general society." The embarrassment of private oppression amidst public enlightenment vitiates the system's legitimacy.

This assumes that an enlightened male goodwill already effects public changes and then follows them up in private. This construction bears the imprint of the text's social psychologism in reducing sexist oppression to in-appropriate gender relations, to be addressed in the companionable marital dyad. The text's story of an imbedded logic of enlightened good will, although enticingly comforting, is a spurious way out of the text's (and world's) con-tradiction between public androgyny and private oppression. This postulate of a deus ex machina in effect extends liberation to "the most intimate unit of the social system" even in face of massive evidence of rape, spouse and child beating, and a still-skewed division of household labor thus disregarding the fact that most women do not enjoy anything approaching "freedom and equality in the general society."

The text twists itself inside out in order to buttress its claim that "the modern family is characterized by reduced power differences between husband and wife," a fragment of which in another context is called modernization theory. But *where* is the universal telos of modernization allegedly bringing with it the impulse toward equality and democracy? The supposed law of progress is only a *text* intending to solicit its enactment and, thus, to explain away contemporary inequality as a vestige of the premodern and thus, through this periodization, to make it bearable—a progressive, if ephemeral, "stage" today holding us captive to the various "laws" of hierarchy, bureaucracy, division of labor, and here patriarchy. There is no stigma attached to the past: patriarchy was a golden age. Premodern families are simply "traditional," evolving toward the companionate marital dyads the text says sprout like mushrooms across the contemporary American landscape.

Nonetheless, there is a serious difficulty with this view of the family, for it confuses the specific practices of various societies with the more general concept of the family as an institution. The fact that women have been subordinate in all family systems in the past does not necessarily mean that there is something inherently wrong with the whole idea, for it is entirely possible that utterly different family forms might emerge in the future. In some of the advanced industrial societies, in fact, there is already a strong trend toward equality between the spouses. (Robertson 1983, 352)

It is telling that the text emphasizes its critique of a stridently biological sexism and then offers the allegedly "strong trend toward equality between the spouses" as evidence to support its criticism. It invokes what it calls the "more general concept of the family as an institution" against the confusion of particular (patriarchy) and general (family qua "institution") that, it implies, disqualifies "utterly different family forms . . . in the future." Although I agree that this has happened, I do not think the text's denunciation of biologism is sufficient to absolve it of exactly the same charge of false universalism, especially where it talks of "family as an institution." The text opposes the most egregious types of "sexual inequality." But it accepts and thus accelerates the privatization of family in a way that fails to address the deep structure of "family's" perversity in the cycle of bourgeois production/sexist reproduction. The text tries to save "family" as the possibility of bourgeois privatization by "modernizing" it, subjecting it to the sort of democratization supposedly occuring in the public sphere.

The notion that "family" is worth saving, if not the excesses of the "traditional" family, is not obvious. How can we decide the essence of "family" only with reference to family *today* thus, in effect, duplicating the oppressive subordination of private to public spheres by giving what we take to be ideal the name of the real, "democracy" becoming *this* democracy, "family" becoming *this* family? The text slips by us this confusion of generic and actual, as if it is possible to hold in mind a Platonic essence of family apart from its historical manifestations.

The text diverts attention from its subtle conflation of generic "family" and actual family, thus only reinforcing the hegemony of the historical by eliciting its enactment. The assumption that all societies require "family" is false if family means a privatized social unit cut off from public relationships, as the subtext intends. Heartfelt liberalism cannot conceal the text's interest in privatizing "family," hence only reproducing the subordination of reproduction to the productive relations it reproduces in turn. Glaring "sexual inequality" only disequilibrates the privatization of desire that holds women captive, (the text's version of) sexual equality a way of maintaining the more deeply structured inequality.

Finally, as one would expect, the text's familism emerges in a cooperativeness between men and women not only as a reasonable strategy but as a feminist one, Friedan cited as an authority in this.

According to Betty Friedan, the most effective way to accomplish both goals is to have wives and husbands cooperate. In recent years, Friedan reported, many equality-minded women are consciously and effectively implementing two ideologies often believed contradictory. One is the woman-as-individual ideology, often involving careers pursued part-time or on different shifts from their husbands; the other is the woman-serving-her-family ideology, ideally supported by husbands willing to assume much more extensive domestic roles than they did in the past. (Doob 1985, 145–46)

While at some level the truth of liberalism is that some*one* must be free for *any*one to be free, feminist cooperativeness takes the edge off an overly adversarial feminism disqualified as lesbian separatism. The effort of women to save men's souls is here called women "serving-her-family," the counterpart of the androgynized careerism supposedly available to women outside the home in these enlightened times. Women are to ease men's psychic burden of manliness just as men are to lend a hand in the household. Yet women retain primary responsibility for reproduction and men primacy in the productive sphere. The text ascribes this view to liberal feminists like Friedan in order to defuse a more radical feminism regarding this sort of cooperativeness as capitulation, the standard acquiescence of slaves to masters throughout the long tradition of idealism.

In recent years Betty Friedan (1981) has suggested that women and men would do well to cooperate more fully. Often, compromise is possible, in the realm of couples' careers and domestic responsibility for example. (Doob 1985, 271)

The notion that women have a choice in cooperating or refusing to cooperate with men in social change is exactly the illusion typically promulgated by idealists who suggest that slaves have the authority to recognize masters and thereby in an ironic way hold the balance of power. Although Hegel (1910) in the *Phenomenology of Mind* was certainly right to suggest that the powerless are never entirely without recourse—liberation at a deep level being an act of will and desire—thus vitiating mechanistic models of revolution and setting the stage in this for subsequent western Marxism, the slave is not in a position to cooperate or refuse to cooperate with masters, as the text implies with regard to women.

Men cede to women certain communicative opportunities precisely in order to diminish their own opportunities to initiate speech that may prove challenging to male hegemony. Although women, as victims everywhere, can seize political chances, it is not in their power to grant men the same opportunities *for they already have them*. The text is gratuitous where it suggests in Friedan's voice that "women and men would do well to cooperate more fully," as if a certain stubbornness or arrogance on women's part has prevented them from arriving with men at a negotiated peace. The text constructs the possibility of sex-political accommodation to convince women to lower their sights from, in its own terms, a full glass to a glass half full. Heterotextuality, thus, reproduces itself.

In this section I have examined ways in which sociology defuses tradition-ally Marxist and feminist opposition. Although in large measure successful, sociology as one among many latter-day ideologies is nevertheless susceptible to different versions that it cannot so readily constrain. In the next two chapters I will suggest such a version, drawing on the Marxism and feminism the text only thinks it has swallowed whole.

PART FIVE

Sociology as a Literary Production

10

The Argument Revisited

A Single Social Text

Let me briefly review my argument so far in a way that I can suggest a mode of literary resistance as a new form of life—negative dialectics (Adorno), new science (Marcuse), ideal-speech situation (Habermas) together breaking through the weighty texts of a discipline only provoking our passivity. It should be clear that I am not going to propose "new" versions of sociology as if a different discipline would make any difference. Discipline as such is the problem. Rather in this chapter and the next I want to work toward and thus exemplify a notion of writing that effectively refuses to reproduce the present under the sign of ontological unalterability, thus freezing it into fate enacted as such—laws emerging because they are called "laws."

Moreover, without the risk or shame of being either blissfully cheerful about the linearity of history or absolutely certain that the positive can be constructed in writing—or in reality—in an unambiguous way, I want to speculate about what an alternative textual practice, indeed life "itself," could entail.[1] Although we are what we write, so we write what we are, engulfing the negative in a text that turns the world in a different, less destructive direction. I can conceive of writing as an activity dialectically criticizing and constructing once I refuse to separate the two entirely; a concept of the negative makes way for a possible future. My version addresses the damaged present without sentimentality lest advocacy become simply idle utopianizing.[2] Writing, then, transpires in the space between author and topic, bearing the imprint of each. The writer kindles hope, however remote it may be, the more a version delves into the topic of social criticism, the near-totality of darkness, setting off a realm beyond in which darkness turns to light, echoing Plato. Thus, I can claim that my critique of sociology is not Luddite destruction so much as a deconstruction that, by its nature, reconstructs—at least in a prefigurative way.

I criticize sociological writing done under the sign of Durkheim in the passionate conviction that new writing turns on a different, nondominating relationship between world and text through which writing becomes an elemental mode of nonauthoritarian social organization as well as creative self-expression —Marx's *praxis,* seeking its own humanity in a world it appropriates without dominating. And Durkheim's disciplining is characteristic of all disciplining today. Writing is free as long as the version is self-conscious of its own ground in interest, desire, body, and locale *and celebrates that groundedness as the resource of its energy, heterogeneity, openness, and invitation to dialogue.* As such, discursive practice is inherently political in the way it understands itself understand. Andy Warhol caricatures Hollywood instantaneity where he envisages a world in which everyone could be famous for fifteen minutes; and yet a free world could be imagined in Habermas's (1984, 1987) version as one in which people appropriate communicative competence such that they all write books, letters, articles, art as a way of authorizing the world. As Habermas suggests, every speech act intends consensus, as any writing in provoking response and correction constitutes a society of unconstrained but gentle writers not struck dumb by scientisms cleansing the text of the traces of authorial artifice and thereby fatefully reproducing the world writing originally opposes. Writing must be more than a way of giving the given.

In developing a critical theory of the text I assimilate science to fiction as writing aware of and committed to its own authorial corrigible literariness, a topic to which I will return later. Suffice it to say here that theory confronts science with the excavated proof of its own construction, thus vitiating science's claim to be an unmediated reflection of an inanimate world. In laying bare sociology as a version of sweaty work that somehow pretends not to be constitutional—through *method*—I have tried to prefigure a world in which writer and reader are not suppressed by a text subordinating itself to the regime of productivism. A different version of writing, call it critical theory, demonstrates the possibility of itself and thus of an open world not reproduced iteratively by a text that would end itself in a last paroxysm of cumulated data—text swallowing whole the world finally reduced to the tracelessness of number, signification failing to signify. Otherwise thought dissolves into the whir and hum of computers.

As such, then, I am not particularly interested in the actual organization of the existing discipline of sociology—who's who—but in the social text that Marx originally called ideology to which scientific sociology is a disciplinary contribution. Ideology is merely a local example of discipline, the generic case of writing provoking the world whose indubitability it already discloses. This is not to say that professional sociology and its text count for very much but only that *they count,* adding a voice to the overall text disqualifying radical action metaphysically as impossible. I agree with Althusser and the Frankfurt School that ideology today is not "out there," suspended in a superstructural ether, but is continually produced and reproduced in the interstitial pockets of "everyday life" encoded in advertising, media, culture, education as well as religion and politics. Ideology's literary practice both provokes system-serving conformity and discourages wild action breaking the cycle of production and reproduction in undoing the latter's subordination to the former. This helps uncouple a heretofore automatized/mediatized everyday life from the structural imperatives imposed on it by capitalist and state-socialist political economies. The disciplinary text in this light is the ensemble of codes and practices enveloping and enveloped by the various lifeworlds in which people carry on the struggle for survival, too frequently convinced to be powerless before what is named an unalterable social nature.

Sociology as such belongs to this "text" as do the other social sciences along with the diverse variety of cultural props of bourgeois lifeworlds. Sociology is a *Zeitgeist,* discipline—a thought and text of our time enticing social obedience out of the seeming necessities it reads into the "facts" littering its page. Sociology is not the most important social text. Yet some people are taught sociology as part of their cultural formation where others learn it indirectly through its cultural assimilation in the discourse of the power of the social. Sociology stands alongside the other academic discourses as well as the codes of news and entertainment together comprising a formative discourse keeping us deaf and dumb to our own reconstitutive role in bringing about what the text hopes will be our future—*amor fati,* less love than resigned acceptance of the given. Although it is hubris to think that a single academic discipline is world-constitutive, it is occluding to think it is not. Sociology offers an exemplary account of the power of the social, thus in its own small way bringing it about. In any case, reading sociology helps us read discipline in its other varities, a task to which I turn in *Fast Capitalism* (1989).

The totally administered society, as Adorno called it, administers itself in every nook and cranny of ordinary and extraordinary experience, leaving no social practice inviolate nor any psychic space uninvaded. As an employee of a state university who works in a sociology department, I am no more or less exempt from the general principle of capitalist administration—*discipline*—than workers on the automobile assembly line or office managers in large corporations. Bending Mao to the New Left through Marcuse, Rudi Dutschke in the 1960s called for a long march through the institutions breaking through social reproduction on every level of experience, together comprising the administered totality.

None is more important in the large scheme of things than any other, Marxian economism and productivism notwithstanding, for culture is productive as well as reproductive. And work reproduces as well as produces, making the Althusserian (1969, 1971) version of Marx's notion of economic determinativeness "in the last instance" a betrayal of his own decentered concept of ideology as interstitial textual practice. The social text can only be "read," thus lived, hermeneutically, *at once* line-by-line and text-by-text and yet simultaneously as a complex totality disclosing itself only in its emergent wholeness.[3] In this light, the critique of disciplinary sociology's suppressed literary ontology presupposes and is presupposed by a critique of current economic theory, politics, media, religion, and sexuality—a useful starting point inasmuch as everything is a starting point, leading to the center as well as away from it toward the margins.

I began this book with the contention that all versions of positivist sociology homogeneously repeat the natural story of alleged laws of social necessity, thus subordinating people to the overarching hegemony of what Durkheim took to be the generic power of the social. For sociology, people are and must remain metaphysically unfree. Social facts congeal into ontology through discipline's ironic provocation of them as inevitable excrescences of the modern. When discipline writes this, people believe and thus relive it, text becoming a mode of life "itself." I have tried to say that the discipline disciplines, its texts having a clear but methodically suppressed politicality. That sociological versions share a common subtext of assumptions about the virtually ontological permanence of the surrounding surface world is no accident for the authors of these versions are also their readers, whether as manuscript referees, consulting editors, or teachers. Writing socializes readers and produces other writers. No byzantine conspiracy theory is needed to explain how discipline imitates itself: its iterations participate in the same text that uses what is claimed as science in order to reproduce a scientized reality, bringing it forth by portraying it as a frozen horizon of timeless social nature. The texts' concatenated reproduction of each other transpires under the sign of epistemological accumulativeness authorizing disciplinary productivism. In effect, intellectual as social reproduction is taken to be a commitment to rigor; the piecemeal iteration of a disciplinary "literature" makes intellectual innovation an incremental process at best. This version of a presuppositionlessly representational science repeats itself as a measure of its own scientificity, thus proving what it knew all along.

For this reason, it is unsurprising that textbooks like journal articles, yet more discursively and more pedagogically, virtually without exception rehearse the same ontology, epistemology, theory, textual politics, and a version of marginal writing—what one version called characteristics of "standard American sociology." This is the kind written and taught in most North American sociology departments, whether as texts, if they are assigned directly to students, or as subtexts in the cases where teachers do not "use" textbooks as such but still participate in the world they espouse and thus reproduce—mainstream intellectuality.

Although these versions may differ in nuance, form, and style, the striking degree of their homogeneity cannot be ascribed simply to the manipulations of major publishers scrambling to secure a profit by creating a market in its image; of course that surely happens. The textbook business is energized by quest for profit, and publishers will publish virtually anything authors write as long as it is given a disciplinary imprimatur and thus sells. Academic textbook publishing is structurally anomalous in that authors are also consumers ("adopters") and are thus empowered through the manuscript review process to manage the content of the writing quite independent of external editorial scrutiny. Editing amounts to a combination of market research and technical improvement of prose style along with the vital collation of referee reports from other academics suggesting profitable paths for authorial revision. And academic journals proceed in exactly the same way, where referees promote writing that in effect *they* have already done and would thus see reproduced.

Academic sociologists, then, reproduce a monolithic and hegemonic scientificity out of a disciplinary imbeddedness, taking for granted the parameters and substance of normal science. It is difficult to overemphasize the sameness of professional perceptions of the common core of sociology reflected in the textbooks as well as in the journals, conferences, and curricula of most American departments—in spite of the conventional wisdom afoot that the discipline has never boasted as much "diversity," Marxists here, interactionists there. What passes for diversity is really only a growing consensus about the scientizing mission of sociology, precisely the opposite of diversity in fact: a monolithic homogeneity utterly oppressing the disciplinarily apostate as nonscience and thus nonsense.

Normally this would be an occasion for pride in disciplinary maturity, the more principles and practices held in common the more advanced the discipline, at least by the standards of the natural sciences. But I have suggested that the canon's replicability in the case of human studies like sociology purposely dampens innovation, conversation, and thus community building in both text and the world enmeshing text. The more consensual the definition of discipline, the less science is deconstructible as a literary production fundamentally nonidentical to the world it addresses. Yet consensus is not in and of itself a bad thing (e.g., if a consensus existed that human studies ought not to proceed on the basis of positivist strictures). The quest for a version of science authorized by an original literature setting its boundaries and defining its problems prohibits sociology from entering the dialectic of theory and practice, instead forcing it to side with a version of the power of the social only to be described and thus fatefully reproduced.

In this sense, normal science accumulated in the overarching disciplinary text reproduces both sociologists in its image (and they, it) and a world in which sociology allows itself heteronomously to be imbedded; intellectual and social reproduction perversely become identical as actual texts provoke just what they already describe as timeless. By pretending to be outside politics, disciplines act politically in the name of a postured representationality. The only way to penetrate and thus reverse this is to read texts not as lifeless pieces of nature but as corrigible products of authorial artifice—as *literature*—even if this scandalizes the notion that science ought not to be fiction. In turn this is to understand literary work as any constructive reconstitution of the world in letter and figure, a generic form of expressive human labor provoking more labor—reading a social practice in its own right. Thus, a mechanical model of the derivation of so-called ideology from social and economic interest is misleadingly monistic. Social reproduction as discourse elicits readerly acquiescence; text, a moment of intellectual reproduction, adds new iterations to the central canon—the world's reproduction crucially requiring the reproduction of writers who write the texts that provoke, in turn, social reproduction. Orthodox Marxism has failed to understand ideology as both reproduction and new production, not simply a mechanical reflex of the economic base—Marx and Engels's "ruling ideas as the ideas of the ruling class."

Although religion can be said to be ideology in the sense of collective delusion, the complexly mediated writing of religious texts both conditions and is conditioned by the writers' place in religious community, their relationship to church elders and to tradition generally and their doctrinal investments. Thus, religious writing must be understood as a thoroughly constitutive and constituted process, not mindlessly accomplished above the heads of people simply to fulfill a functional requirement of the social order's own projection of other-worldly salvation. Ideology is written and lived—reproduced—in a version nonidentical to the social reproduction it hopes to occasion, ever so slightly opening the door of new writing and thus new community.

My account of the discipline's seamlessness is not meant to imply authors' mechanical thoughtlessness. There is no guarantee either that the printing presses, microcomputers, telephones, televisions, movies, and radios will not suddenly fail to function, thus short-circuiting the endless repetition of the text, or that readers will always receive their encoded imperatives of acquiescence and adjustment without critical mediations, interpretation, questioning. To write is to hope, even if, as Walter Benjamin suggested, every piece of culture is an act of barbarism or, with Adorno, poetry is impossible after Auschwitz. There is nothing dialectically inconsistent between the conception of writing's complicity in a world sucking in most writing—after all, writing is a luxury while people continue to be killed—and the claim of writing's necessity in a world that can only be undone discursively. The first step toward an undisciplined world is a critique of disciplines methodically concealing their own interest in social reproduction. I read sociology as a discourse of the power of the social, as such affording insights into the disciplinary nature of discourse generally.

Although the contribution of any ontology-critical version is miniscule in the larger scheme of things—in light of totality—I would agree that a long march through the institutions necessarily passes through the various lifeworlds including academic sociology together comprising totality. No discursive practice is inherently more or less important than any other; no version can be determinative in the last instance without insisting on and enacting its authority over seemingly lesser versions. The nonidentity of world and text, in spite of text's identitarian—that is, self-negating—impulse closing the gap to nothing, is an occasion of more literary work, not a lament for the bygone role of writing's traditional estrangement from the world. Science's text nearly monolithically closes the world by constructing it as generically unalterable even if it allows the possibility of cosmetic reforms; yet critique need not apologize for its own apparent lack of engagement. As writing formulated the world so can it reformulate it, no matter how vast the task. But to do so writing must be read simultaneously as a constitutive and constituted process, a potent force of social reproduction as well as a construction flowing from people's pens and typewriters *and thus that can be undone*. The text's literariness always promises new literature; indeed, new versions are necessary given the insufficiency of history.

A so-called Marxian analysis of religion as an ideology, for example, could examine not only the doctrinal and institutional role of religion but also its textuality, reading and thus raising the possibility of its reformulation as a social accomplishment. Without understanding religion in this case as a literary version mystifying essentially oppressive aspects of a particular form of social existence, and instead viewing it simply as a mechanically imposed deception, we get nowhere in trying to strengthen people's resistance to it, let alone reformulating a new version addressing ultimate issues of mortal existence. But orthodox Marxism and some of its Hegelian-Marxist critics have left the unfortunate legacy of a criticism that treats the cultural universe as an automated one. In that universe writing is either mechanically adequate to the functional requirements of capitalist domination or endlessly spewed out of a monolithic "culture industry," and thus equally debased and defused. The Adornoian ban on poetry after Auschwitz contradicts Adorno's own aesthetic-critical oeuvre (1982) that both explicitly and implicitly takes writing seriously as a world-constitutive activity, thus ironically making Adorno's own criticism a version of the transformative art it addresses immanently. The tendency to mechanize the concept of culture is fatal to critics of its actual mechanization. It leaves them with no medium of dissent if all words are drowned in the babel of banality.

The more monolithic the disciplinary text, the more imaginative the excavation process must be in bringing the silenced voice of the author to the surface as a way of restoring the constitutive powers of a disempowered authorial subjectivity. This is much the same effort as a critical phenomenology tracing all objectifications back to the pretheoretical lifeworld (itself a problematic conceptual reification, to be sure), thus provoking awareness of constitution's possibility today concealed by domination.[4] And yet a process of simple deconstruction is overly optimistic about the ease of reformulating a world already written as a self-sufficient version. Reformulation is systematically defied by the sort of posttext a presuppositionlessly representational version of science aspires to be. Excavation of the author's constituting intentionality must be set against the permanent nonidentity between social objects (albeit traced back to an originally constituting consciousness or intersubjectivity) and the texts/ practices producing and reproducing them. Writing always runs the risk of being read to say more or less than it intends, just as the institutions we would design in fullest freedom may somewhat hinder us as they sediment themselves inertly in history; the intention of any writing, in other words, is doomed by its publication.[5]

Although there is a temptation to try to reverse the monolithic text by writing absolutely without ground (Barthes 1967), it is crucial to recognize the irrevocable distance between author and topic both as a way of retaining our humanity in times of near-total administration and of tempering our reconstructive ambitions—the recognition of eternal nonidentity serving to deflate the otherwise destructive idealism that would remake the whole world in the image of the imperial subject. Precisely as opposition to scientism's pretension to say everything—that is, to bring it under its rule of discipline (thereby itself succumbing in the end)—a different version refuses to purge itself of what science regards as a tarnishing subjectivity, the stain of authorial fingerprints on it. The excavation of science's authorship, then, does not aid a version that more successfully suppresses its intentional roots—ultimate objectivity attained, for example, in a definitive Marxist or feminist version—but restores subject to its properly dialectical nonidentity with objects, whether world, text, topic, or reader.

The temptation is nearly irresistible to replace sociology books with other books better reflecting the chilled world when the goal ought not be disciplined representation at all but nonauthoritarian discourse practices breaking out of the library in reconstituting all versions—work, home, the inner life—as *perpetual texts*. Within the logic of my version of textual practice it is impossible to suggest new versions of writing only exchanging positivist absoluteness for a new set of certainties; writing is a social relationship invariably provoking new texts, new challenges to a notion of the last word. Instead, closure is resisted in a way that one balances the universe's ineluctable ambiguity against our innate, if historically distorted, capacity to think a different world.

I oppose a scientific sociology following Durkheim in teasing fateful subordination out of the generic power of the social with a literary version deconstructing discipline as disciplining. Unlike the former, the latter treats the nonidentity of subject and object as a vital source of its energy and not as a drag on so-called objectivity. Marxist or feminist scientism is scientism none-theless.[6] In our opposition to the monolithic we end up no further ahead—or deeper—if we oppose opposition with the inevitably authoritarian certitudes of a representational version of science. I will return to the issue of a text—and thus life—avoiding closure. I want to emphasize here that discipline repro-duces itself along with the world to which it wants to become identical, driven quixotically by the impulse toward intellectual self-destruction. Paradoxically discipline remains monolithic only if it is continually rewritten, retaught, relived. Admittedly, the momentum of intellectual/social reproduction is in-credibly powerful, a deep vein of imbedded habits and second nature taking courage and stamina to challenge. The risk in writing against discipline is more than intellectual or political disreputability but rather the disqualification of one's version, and thus life, as nonscience, a rupture with reasonableness trailing off into Nietzschean raving in a self-destructive parody of what Weber called science as a "vocation."[7]

Nonscience is so marginal that it can belong to no "literature," denied an academic home. And who anymore thinks of himself or herself as an intellectual, however exalted the academy might be? Like the world of which it is a part as its essential self-understanding, writing does not write *itself*. For that reason alone there is hope that eventually the web of textuality mirroring and thus undergirding the web of administered social relationships can be broken, if in the first instance only in the marginal versions Adorno (1973b) in *Philosophy of Modern Music* characterized as the message of despair from the shipwrecked.[8] The positivist text's apparent seamlessness is no excuse not to write, especially where it is only a version—one that deceptively proclaims its own versionlessness.

Social Facts and Social Fate: Text as a Mode of Discipline

My argument is that the disciplinary text by reproducing allegedly eternal "facts" of people's subordination to the unalterable social thereby reproduces the social—capitalism, sexism, racism—under the guise of lawfulness. This does not read science as straightforward advocacy inasmuch as science eschews the bald partisanship it disqualifies as wild politics. Instead it traces the power of science's intellectual and thus social reproduction of the given to its methodical disinterestedness; its suppression of argument is exactly the sort of presuppositionlessness argued by Vienna Circle positivism.

Durkheim drew the disciplinary boundaries of sociology as the study of social causality, pursuing "social facts" described by him as episodes of deter-mined behavior within an impinging social structure dominating it.[9] The text of social science, and in a larger sense the whole social text of culture reproducing itself discursively, witnesses the eternity of the power of the social as a way of provoking it. Durkheim may not have intended this outcome as such; he as a liberal enjoined social science to resolve the "social problems" of early capitalist industrialization, urbanization, and secularization. Yet he founded sociology as a discourse of discipline where in *Rules of Sociological Method* he modeled the iterative work dominating the discipline for the next century —this in spite of the seeming ecumenism of a discipline coopting marginal versions like Marxism and feminism by claiming to admit them to the status of disciplinary legitimacy. It is crucial not to confuse apparent authorial intention with textual outcome precisely because positivism suppresses its own desire to reproduce the world, thus occupying a privileged place within it. It does so for reasons quite inaccessible even to the closest readings or the most imaginative reconstructions. Why, after all, do people seem to desire a dominant order oppressing them? Utilitarianism cannot answer.

Although the emoluments of the academic role are sometimes significant, especially in a hard-scrabble world in which many mental workers are unemployed or underemployed, it is difficult to understand why what Arendt (1960) called the life of the mind would increasingly subordinate itself to a world engulfing it; Weber's objectivity issuing in what Adorno called the preponderance of objectivity (1973a) now penetrates into the deep psychic substratum— as deep as the text's own subtext. The ascription of motive[10] is less important than an understanding of how science's text suppresses speculation about motive, as if writing leaps full blown onto the page with no mediation between pen and paper, a construction only guaranteeing the world's mimicry in a text that has neither heart nor mind. This is what Weber described as a "calling," using the language of religious predestination to explain why we become what we are, even as writers.

After a time science reproduces itself so routinely that it seems disciplinary writing could not undo itself even if it wanted. This is strictly false inasmuch as writing is always open to its own reformulation as is the host of other disciplinarily reproductive choices made about book adoptions, course content, and curriculum structure—everyday life. Indeed, since reading must always rewrite what it reads, no version can guarantee its reception. Yet writers already integrated into the sticky web of discipline are unlikely to think twice about the words they write or the lectures they give in support of the so-called advancement of science as socially reconstitutive practices. The machine of science grinds on relentlessly; its iterative logic penetrates the various levels of academic production and reproduction, from textbook and journal to teaching and conference. The reproduction of the world as data out of which laws are to be adduced only encourages the life of the mind to become a business and coopts political efforts by sanitizing them. Almost inevitably science casts its spell over the "reality" it names as eternity, succumbing to (its version of) the world as the logic of scientific accumulation drives out thought—*mediation*—from the text. As such, discipline presages a world so inert that writing no longer *needs* to bridge between alleged laws and the nonidentical behavior they purport to decide and thus provoke. The domain of science reproducing itself in conformity with disciplinary norms set fatefully by Durkheim models the automatic reproduction of social fate the text seeks to inculcate.

Inasmuch as the motives of the scientist count for so little in face of the bureaucratic apparatus of science's production, science succumbs to the same hegemony subordinating other practices. Even though science has a special role in hastening this automation, it is not spared the same fate as other practices; there is no exemption principle elevating science above the fray. At least many people in their various lifeworlds manifest all sorts of resistance—ineradicable nonidentity to the world they suffer—thus making their absorption into the administered totality at least problematic. Science quickly loses the capacity for resistance as it seeks identification with a totality swallowing it. Although this is not preordained because there are any number of versions, the positivist version of science renounces its own autonomy as an unwanted blemish of a vestigial subjectivity standing in the way of an account reconciling differences by mastering them.

This is not to suggest that scientists today foresee their own self-transcendence. Like nonauthoritarian socialism, science is faced with a long march of its own for which the authorizing metaphor remains the slowly approaching light at the end of Plato's cave. Meantime, like the industry it models and tries to rationalize, science eschews contemplation of first and final things, a subject left professionally to philosophers, theologians, perhaps even theoretical sociologists. This sort of self-understanding is simply not attempted by the typical hard-working sociologist, making it next to impossible for world-historical self-consciousness to be gained. Young sociologists are trained to solve methodological, not metaphysical, problems.

Thus, sociology as a definitive version exhausts all possible knowledges in the name of a version modeled on what it takes to be the presuppositionless reflection of nature.[11] But, as I demonstrate here, a possible version of science refuses its role in social reproduction, instead celebrating its own literariness in prefiguring nonmonologic writer/reader relationships as a paradigm of all social relationships in which the powerless are gradually empowered (and empower themselves) to speak. The disciplinary text escapes and usurps the possibilities of what Nietzsche called playful sciences in submitting itself to the ever-increasing discipline of the preponderant social, concealing the historical authorship of history and of itself as a historical project in order to conceal the possibility of any authorship, inevitably including its own. Yet other versions may not conceal the imbeddedness of text in subtext methodologically but celebrate authorial desire as the occasion of new, ever-innovating versions—

community. As long as science understands that action cannot be predicted, it can both celebrate and oppose the world bringing it forth. This version of versions insists on its own productivity without forgetting its inevitable continuity with the subtexts of interest, passsion, and desire that Adorno (1978d) called objective subjectivity.

A writing aware of its own literariness challenges the discipline's claimed monopoly of validity by exposing its own unacknowledged vulnerability, even utter subordination, to the "world" science constructs as the inhuman fiction of identitarian causality. The power of the social can be reversed, notably by discourses refusing to empower it. Nonidentical writing refuses to identify with power because it knows at some level it *cannot,* even though (or better, *as*) it acknowledges its own power to think differently.[12]

Although most mainstream sociologists admit that science is conditioned, even partly "biased," they do so as a gambit they hope to recoup in the reproduction of a readership largely impervious to science's literary nature as one version among many. I returned from a talk on this book where I was roundly criticized by an audience of academic sociologists who think they do not work within disciplinary boundaries but are critical of a ruthless economic order.[13] They claim not only to be free of presuppositionlessness and to take stands; they also use high-tone collections of essays, articles, and monographs in their classes and not the banal textbooks that one audience member dismissed as mere "commodities," not the "cultural products" I seemed to say they were. Thus, they reflect precisely the economism, the mitigated Marxism, somehow bifurcating commodity and culture. And another sociologist told me that he was basically a "qualitative" sociologist even though he had written two "quantitative" articles (using techniques of so-called multiple regression analysis) *in order to prove to himself and others that he could.*

Having "values" and admitting them means nothing if these ethical-evaluative constructions are preparatory to, and thus to be inexorably engulfed by, the chilling version of the power of the social. It is not enough to oppose human suffering, even to work for its amelioration, if science cleaves from one's explicit politics, the public/private, productive/reproductive, valuable/valueless distinction fatefully preserved and relived. Rather, the private predilection for a world without oppression must inform public science not only as a guide to research (topic selection, disposition of research results, etc.), without objectivist imperatives taking over the research once "guiding" has concluded, but throughout the literary artifice of science versions. Texts that dissect the "phenomena" of oppression inevitably chill them into generics no matter how much they may protest that "we have to understand the problem before we change it." There is no "before," just as there is no instant punctuating the gap between the process and product of social change. Criticism flows into reconstruction, self-awareness of the intentionality of one's own advocacy prefiguring a world peacefully transacted between versions respecting each other.[14]

The two cannot be separated as analysis and advocacy because the implicit notion of an analysis not charged with subjectivity leads to a version of weak advocacy only shadowing the surface of the argument. The temporal separation of knowledge and desire inevitably gives analysis the upper hand, according it a centrality enfeebling advocacy as either a preface or a postscript. Scientism overwhelms the good intentions "using" science for good human purposes in chilling the world of which science is an inextricable part. The world science freezes engulfs science and freezes it, too, reducing it to a voiceless witness to domination but nothing more; its method turns against itself in reducing even negation to affirmation.

This is not to call for a version eschewing analysis; this book analyzes in order to oppose. Rather I refuse to separate discipline and desire even for heuristic purposes. Such a separation takes for granted analytic terms (e.g., power, conflict, oppression, inequality) that must be *argued* in a way that blurs the distinction between description and exhortation. Social criticism is written into the concepts we use to understand society because concepts reproduce or vitiate the given simply by being written. This is not to empower writing unduly but to argue against the exemption of writing from its own principle of social determination, a textual practice schizophrenically torn between the recognition and repression of its own artifice as imaginative fictions. Advocacy cannot begin and end, nor can analysis, as if passion and dispassion were sequential episodes in the life of the text, indeed in any life.[15]

Instead, a literary version of science continually makes thematic its choice-of-themes as a piece of artifice not only informing its argument but also *being* the argument; for example, a text about poverty is simultaneously a text about its own motive in writing against poverty, the express link between advocacy and analysis constituting the nature of its version. A text that for the sake of "objectivity" brackets out its own motive in writing only *invites its own subor-dination to a preponderant object-world using all texts against themselves;* they are sucked into a monolithic master version seeming to have a place for every grievance yet turning them into the second nature of discipline.[16] The prolif-eration of surface social criticism sundered from analysis undermines criticism by averaging it with other superficially different versions; in sociology con-flict theory and functionalism "explain" the same "thing" differently, agreeing on everything but the nature of "explanation"—its ontological coordinates assumed a matter of substantial agreement. Because epistemological pluralism assumes a single, simple world named differently, it misses the constitutive-ness of writing entwining a theory of being and explanation. By accepting the scientistic distance between subjects and objects—in this case, text and world,

author and writing, advocacy and analysis—so-called critical sociology represses its own analytical constitution as a self-constitution. It thus acquiesces
to the hegemonic epistemologies of the time revealing a single "world" transparent except for its naming by one or another regional version of unfreedom
—"conflict," "function," whatever.

But to forget the relationship between subject and object only allows objectivity, that is, the historically given, surreptitiously to infiltrate the subject
by cancelling the necessary critical distance between subject and object, their
nonidentity making criticism possible in the first place. Any construction accepting the world's own self-understanding as adequate—only to criticize that
world through it—is doomed to its centering by a text displaying its own pluralism in domesticating marginal writings simply as different, albeit deficient,
versions of the same disciplinary story.

Critical sociologists who believe that positivist "tools" can be used to criticize the dominant social order—surveys, computers, hypothesis testing, tables
—only become tools themselves when they are integrated into the disciplinary
world reducing them to different, deficient Durkheimians.[17] No matter how
"critical," critical sociology is still sociology; it is ensconced within a web
of assumptions, suppressions, and practices reproducing a disciplinary version
disqualifying mediating thought as nonreproductive, useless. Real criticism
would interrogate the meaning and practice of the word "tool," not simply
"use" tools as if they are already preontologically available to *be used*. Critical sociology employing positivist method only legitimates the hegemonic
positivism further marginalizing criticism as inappropriate advocacy.[18]

The allegedly critical text cannot bridge mute analysis and its surface political agenda, the two voices of a version schizophrenically divided between
representation on the one hand and exhortation on the other. Although it would
seem plausible to advocate an alternative state of affairs *once* that state of
affairs had been described, the deplorable state of affairs in the nearly totally
administered society distorts writing in a way that makes purely analytical
language in effect an advocacy of the described states of affairs based on its
own scientization; or to put this differently, language that refuses to condemn
implicitly goes along. *Nothing* today says what it means and means what it
says. No criticism devised as straightforward analysis can survive its own version as an affirmative, apologetic text; the seeming display of a possible, albeit
"critical," version reinforces the main text's monolithic self-confidence as the
averaging of all possible versions, making "critical sociology" ironically a
genuflection to an *uncritical* discipline. By affirming the validity of a positivist version of science, critical sociology constructs the existence of "critical
sociology" as a symptom of the discipline's, and hence world's, openness. By
failing to disentangle itself from what it takes to be value-free methods, critical sociology is no less subjugated by those very methods secretly holding

it under their socioontological spell. Dispassionate analysis is the passionate subordination of advocacy to analysis, knowledge to desire, driving to bring knowledge into being.

The Weber renaissance not only construes Weber to be a profound social critic but also subtly valorizes his strictures on the necessary separation of science and politics, diminishing Marx's critique of the contradictory capital-labor relationship and also tempering the engagement of Marxism in favor of a more analytic-sociologic Marxism working with scholarly journals, data, computers. The text's abiding liberalism swallows Marxism where it reduces it to a positivist version of science. It usurps Marxism's political struggles as the province of a radical liberalism buttressed by "conflict theory." This leavens a revolutionary Marxism by parliamentarizing the political program of socialism. Liberalism is the surface of science to which it is bonded sentimentally, appended to show that neither science nor scientists are heartless. Once the world is analytically chilled, the only available politics is a maudlin longing for a victimless world, a "better place to live," as the text calls it. Once frozen, the world can be warmed only by an insufficient, ineffectual liberalism treating "social problems" piecemeal in the hope that their individual solutions, like the text's data, can be accumulated into an exhaustive world-historical tableau, every interest group's inequality corrected through the intervention of a beneficent state propped by the well-intentioned policy sciences.

Indeed, Weber is increasingly both the scientific and political icon of a discipline that showcases its critical rump—conflict theory, even a quantitative Marxism—as proof of its ecumenism. With Weber you get the cake and eat it, too, inasmuch as his encyclopedic corpus can be plundered for any number of stabilizing or critical resources, from *Economy and Society* and musicology to cultural criticism and the sociology of religion.[19] A man for all seasons, Weber in his Nietzschean mood rails against the rationalization of the world where, in his Enlightenment reasonableness, he heralds double-entry accounting as the harbinger of social progress. And the best thing is that Weber is not a Marxist, a revolutionary of any kind, even though his version of conflict theory can swallow the text's Marxism without taking on its rude tone of advocacy, a violation of Weber's liberal gentility as well as scientism. The hagiography of Weber amounts to the extirpation of Marxism, indeed of any and all marginal writings bringing passion and position to the surface and eschewing the studied reasonableness typical of the age—commitment avoided in favor of free-floating equivocation, even disinterest. Ask any Enlightenment-era academic to take sides and you get endless waffling that tends toward the self-evident center: "it seems reasonable to . . . ," a style epitomized by Weber.

Liberalism is the ethic of the Enlightenment, good faith and feeling appended to a discourse of the power of the social taking us along for the ride;

Weber's rationalization is really a simpering moralism. The alternative, however, is not a version rejecting morality as a flinch of intellectual courage in face of eternal ambiguity. That is a construction of liberal scientism making its opponent seem satanic, a nonchoice in an already horrified world. Instead, a rationalism in touch with its own primordial roots in desire and thus girded to some extent against its own self-importance and thus authoritarianism might better oppose both liberal scientism and nihilism. Liberalism is only superficially a form of rationalism, empowering the subject with the ability to make world-constitutive decisions, both theoretical and practical. In fact, it is captive of a subtext that would use it only to deflect attention from itself—its passion and perspectivity—by assigning it the ingenuous mission of "making the world a better place to live." Divided from a subtext it suppresses, this surface agenda fails to do much beyond pay lip service to abstract ethical ideals shattering when exposed to the world frozen with the aid of a silenced desire, the absent author.

The paradox of liberal scientism is that the writer is both self-confident in resolving social problems and utterly ineffectual to facilitate change, inasmuch as his or her text is preponderant. Since C. Wright Mills, the pragmatic social engineering of policy-oriented American sociology conceals its own impotence in the bravado of world making, pretending a reformism nearly completely denied by the science in which it invests. No matter how appealing to social critics who enjoin us to "know the enemy," as long as analysis is cleaved from and subordinates advocacy, the enemy will remain an enemy within, a nest of debilitating assumptions about the hegemony of social structure canceling the prospect of free agency on ontological, not empirical, grounds.

Centering the Margins

By defeating social criticism residing at the episodic surface of the social text, a hopelessly last-ditch effort to tame the concatenated world denying any of us agency, the text covers itself with a patina of heartfulness seemingly mitigating its harsh hegemony. By showing that resistance movements actually exist in the world, the text legitimates its own liberalism *as if* that liberalism was the adequate voice of this extant defiance.

At the talk I gave recently about this book, I provoked audience members who felt that I ignored the attempts within sociology to further the "causes" of various oppressed groups, instead indulging the cynical view that everything we do ends up wrong, defeated, even turned against us. But no matter how seemingly committed to women's liberation, the Third World, or the environment, disciplinary sociology is overwhelmed by the disqualifying forces dividing politics and science allegedly in order to protect their "analysis" from the corrupting advocacy properly reserved for a scholar's second life.

This splitting of scholarship into dispassion and passion allows science to integrate passion as the guiding framework within which everyday research is conducted. Acknowledging that politics/passion is fundamentally extraneous to science, the text nonetheless makes room for it as the liberal orientation to problem and topic choice thought to animate most social movements today.

As a sign of the text's hubris it takes on the world's burdens—those of women, minorities, Third World, the poor—as if its measured reason provides a world-historical standard with which to assess the depth of suffering and the route beyond it. The sociologist's skepticism is here united with a conviction that the world ought to be less unjust, providing a text on the surface advocating an end to such things yet underneath naming them virtually as our social fate, to be mitigated but not avoided. Thus, liberal ethics centers justice the same way it centers the truth, avoiding extremism. But the text's liberalism is usually inadequate to describe, let alone take the side of, those who illiberally rage against their oppression. The world is all too often so unbearably tragic that the cheerfulness of the text is not only inadequate to address it but also deepens it.

There is so much beneath the text's own surface in the way of badly repressed demons—self-hate, self-love, neither in awareness of the other—it is little wonder it fails to understand the world's demons except as straightforward obstacles to the forward march of Enlightenment. Through what it contends is science, sociology surfaces its own predilections for small changes and nonstrident speech. In appropriating the struggles and voices of others, liberal sociology engages in the worst kind of arrogance, speaking out for those it has helped to render voiceless under sway of scientism. All inequality is coopted by a text that denies the margins a validity sui generis but makes them over into acceptable versions of itself and its own moralism. First Marxism and then feminism are subjected to reconstruction, defusing their political marginality by incorporating them into the text both scientifically and politically, thus simultaneously ontologizing the oppression they oppose and mainstreaming their politics that now serve the purpose of *policy*.

The ultimate outrage of this centering is not that it distorts marginal writing; there are no self-evident criteria of correct reading, only versions. But it presumes to present liberal Marxism and feminism as good alternatives to bad political versions, thus intruding its own suppressed subtext—adjustment —into the very real suffering of others. It is not that their cries of oppression are either unique or privileged, as many Marxists and feminists would claim in their quest for theoretical primacy, but that liberalism as the iceberg tip of scientism suppresses its own interest in perspectivity, thus perpetuating the oppression it opposes on its surface. Incrementalism seems to reverse the chill of socioontologizing description. It is not that sociologists themselves oppose social reconstruction but that they remain captive of a discipline obliterating the prospect of social change under sway of the chillingly reproductive text of a representational version of science. In the beginning, biographic contingencies led many of them to a discipline seeming to address fundamental social problems. An ineffectual liberalism divides the text sharply between scientific and political missions and thus deactivates politics merely as sentiment.

The text collects a lot of mongrels in this way, assimilating all sorts of Marxists and feminists, if not Marxisms and feminisms. By muting their anger, the text appears to remain intellectually eclectic in a way covertly defusing any desire that eschews eclecticism, thus absolutizing electicism in opposition to what it takes to be other absolutisms. This fragments analytic-political discourse as it silences advocacy appearing unnuanced. But relativism is absolutist precisely because it suppresses its latent authoritarianism underneath the glossy surface of texts, proliferating pictures of oppressed people and dealing in the dulcet tones of sweet reasonableness and forward-looking optimism. The texts are not only cheerful in this way. They also rub off the rough edges of advocacy in a way that only further suppresses their political interest. It is in the nature of the text claiming scientificity to portray oppression as a mechanical social process admitting of piecemeal resolution, in this imposing a kind of liberal order on it.

Liberalism centers the margins because it secretly fears that they oppose liberalism itself and not only the world centering them. The liberal text fears the margins more than it does the world that science props; marginal writings would unmask and undo precisely that reproductive relationship between the text's depth and surface, the latter seemingly humanizing the former with the aura of concern. Adorno (1970) in a different context called this the jargon of authenticity. The text sunnily chatters on about the remediability of discrete social problems while disciplining marginal versions otherwise disqualifying liberalism as simple-minded nostalgia.[20] In effect, then, the discipline disqualifies marginal writing before marginal writing disqualifies it. Its text cheerfully props a somber science, freezing our subordination into fatalizing concepts enticing their own slavish enactment.[21] At their best Marxism and feminism resist the text's bifurcation into description on the one hand and incrementalism on the other; they insist instead on the inseparability, if nonidentity, of text and subtext and thus make thematic their own political interest in a different state of affairs. Writing about it hastens its arrival because writing crucially prefigures qualitatively different human relationships. Peaceful text welcoming other writers constitutes peaceful social relationships.

The more sociology is apparently ideologized, with "Marxist" subgroups proliferating as official versions of discipline, the less it is really ideologized in the sense that it addresses its own scientism as a political issue.[22] By integrating marginal writings, the main text turns the objects of their concern —economic exploitation, the primacy of public over private—into virtually inevitable features of the social terrain to which "Marxist sociology" or "feminist sociology" bear witness, resolving the "social problem" of particular interest groups each writing is said to represent.[23]

By disqualifying wild Marxism and feminism the text is really denying versions defying their truncation into purely local causes, instead demonstrating a universality that would set everyone free. By regionalizing marginal writing and matching up assigned "social problems"—Marxism/exploited workers, feminism/exploited women—the text denies a version resisting the text's synthesis of all differences, the world ingested by the word and thus ingesting it in turn. The text allows "Marxist sociology" only if it respects the paradigmatic practices of science instead of clamoring for the unity of theory and practice, text and world, duly respecting the text's diremption of text and subtext or politics and science.[24] In this way, the text's Marxism or feminism is not the Marxism or feminism of nonscience; the text's disciplined version not only stays off the streets but also respects both the institutional practices and the overarching mission of science in its trivially iterative work. Sociology depoliticizes the margins that now stand against it only as methodological caveats. Marxism reminds mainstream sociology to attend to issues of class as well as status.

Seeming intellectual diversity is trumpeted as the healthy maturation of a pluralist discipline that has come to terms with its former narrowness, "bias" for "equilibrium" and analytic mechanism.[25] Voices from Skocpol (no matter her initially unsuccessful tenure fight at Harvard) to Giddens and Wallerstein are invoked to demonstrate a mainstream so secure it can tolerate and even embrace such "critics," even if only as luminaries. For every Giddens embraced, there are a dozen renegades dismissed, disqualified, defanged by a discipline supporting difference only when surrounded by a protective layer of identity. Giddens is turned into merely a "name" by a discipline that does not read him let alone the deeper traditions he plumbs. As Marcuse said (1966), tolerance is repressive where, I would add, it is required at all.[26]

A recent comment by a well-known sociologist addresses what he calls the seeming "smorgasbord" of theoretical approaches, a comment otherwise defending " 'doctrinaire eclecticism' " guided by a centering functionalism.

> [S]ociology, from the outset, has been "multi-paradigmatic," to use today's Kuhnian jargon—Comte versus Tarde, Spencer versus Marx, Ward and Cooley versus Sumner and Giddings, MacIver versus Lynd, Lundberg versus Blumer, Homans versus anti-reductionists, defenders of the scientific faith versus "humanists" and so on. In recent years, sociologists could select from a theoretical and methodological smorgasbord: neo-positivism, structural functionalism, exchange theory, systems theory, symbolic interactionism, dramaturgy, several varieties of American phenomenology, critical theory, and more. Perhaps we have been faced with an over-abundance of perspectives, but competing approaches are endemic in the study of social life and human behavior. Would we wish it otherwise?[27]

Just listing the many names of these "perspectives" makes them seem equal in the weight they bear in the current discipline, showing off its eclecticism to best advantage. But the author himself is writing in defense of a functionalism that he claims dominates the American tradition and needs no apology by those who like Jeffrey Alexander (1985) neologize functionalism into neofunctionalism. According to the author, eclecticism embraces even "the longtime trinity of Marx, Durkheim and Weber." *The margins are ingested by the centrifugal pull of a center so powerful it ceases to need the name functionalism as long as it is scientism,* doctrinal disputation blending into the sweet harmony of businesslike empiricism. Thus, theories survive only as the interim names given to eternity's essences. Like an intergalactic being in a science fiction movie, the center is strengthened the more it ingests intellectual traditions on the margin; the process of ingestion both depoliticizes and rehabilitates them.

All aforementioned "perspectives" are acceptable as long as they are shorn of the self-consciousness of deeper motive making them unabashedly political, where politics is understood as the temerity to write even in the face of one's own constituted, as well as constituting, humanity. Advocacy is not only exhortation to action but an authorial self-consciousness objectifying itself without the fear of authority requiring most scientists to invest their writing not unashamedly in desire but comfortably in tradition, canon, discipline. The more the text can swallow in the way of authentic writing turned inauthentic, the more enticing it becomes as the basis of all validity claims, building on itself to provide a reference point (Kuhn would say "paradigm") for all disciplinarily appropriate work. The main text of scientific sociology arrogates to itself the right to integrate these marginal versions as disciplinary "perspectives" as Page, above, calls them; they are not simply other versions sharing the bookshelf if not necessarily guiding assumptions. I would rather understand the question of what it means to be a sociologist as the question what it means to be a writer—that is, to think publicly. Sociology today is exhausted by its positivist version, a discourse of the power of the social it would reproduce through its own version. Disciplinary work adds value to discipline, an untheorized totality of unmediated particulars.

In the next section, I want to suggest what writing can do to deconstruct this conventionalizing wisdom, followed in my final chapter by a discussion of nonpositivist discourse. I intend this book as an example of better discourse as well as the breakout from within a disciplinary text discarding versions such as this out of hand, leveling at it the charges of distortion, overdetermination, and the like with which I began. It is important to understand my insistence that *this* is not sociology in the larger political context in which I locate any such discussion about the literary nature of discipline. Yet as Adorno said that epistemology is politics, so disciplines discipline—perversely, in a heterotextual way, that is, *through* the language games reproducing them dumbly and unnecessarily.[28] Thus, for me to claim not to be a sociologist pretends a distance from my topic greater than the degree of my desire's investment in it would suggest possible. I am concerned not about what it means to "be" a sociologist but about sociology's implications for social being.

Resistance, or the Critique of Socioontology

A different writing would in effect bore from within the social text—culture, science, media—freezing the present into an eternal ice age by raising the world we currently suffer into a universal, "fate," *and thereby universalizing it.* Discourse disciplines people to rehearse their victimhood as fate. This boring from within pits version against version in a struggle for autonomy, a struggle best waged squarely on the battleground of science's text and not in a merely esoteric transcendence of it. That is why I am writing this book. Laissez faire always ends up in favor of the strongest party; or to put this more sharply, only the center can afford to tolerate the margin, has the choice of doing so. For itself, oppositional writing can only save its life by confronting the central text in terms that challenge its suasion over virtually all public discourse, refusing to indulge the illusion that it can exist in its own rhetorical framework without being tainted by an imperial text usurping it, turning its language of negation into the chatter of affirmation.

The critique of ideology begins with ideology precisely because ideology threatens to engulf it before it can make any strategic headway. The positive only emerges from the negation of the negation—not because we can guarantee a dialectical metaphysics but simply because the disciplinary text drives to turn the negative into a piece of affirmation; for example, mainstream sociology gobbles up the latest critical writings as soon as they hit the bookstores. Criticism devolves from what orthodox Marxism calls "practice" in mouthing the dominant discourses of the administered society—television, religion, movies, sociology, psychology. Critique tries to show its political desire imbedded as scientism in its tentacular subtext entwining negation. Critical writing announces itself politically by working through the allegedly nonpolitical text of science, thus exposing its inherence in authorial desire.

The marginal text tries to remain marginal, that is uncoopted, in order one day to become central—or, better, to destroy the distinction between center and margin—by addressing, and trying to break out from within, a central text otherwise swallowing it, recognizing a potential enemy when it sees it. This is indeed an intellectual-political struggle between mainstream sociology and the version rejecting the postulate of binding "laws," and thus the laws enacted on that basis, as socioontological deception, occluding the literary possibility of a different version of versions—hence, of history. Writings that think they can avoid the fray do not recognize their own imbeddedness in a desire yearning, and therefore writing, to be free.

Writing either avowedly or supposedly political is in any case always political in the way desire informs its relation to the world, either totalizing it in its seeming unmediatedness or reliving it as the nonidentical yet bonded relation of free subject and topic. The politics of texts are not simply "what" is said in the way of exhortation but more in the relation of writing to itself, its desire surfacing in the text's indeterminate openness and thus prefiguring an open world in which writing is the endless process of self-revelation, transvaluation, and correction—political epistemology. Ultimately, text is liberating when it understands the boundary between itself and the world as permeable, thus actualizing its own ability to change the world; text is a form of society, if not all society a text.[29]

Writing writes against writing, pretending only to reproduce and reflect, thus providing the imaginative alternative of communication constituting and mediating as much as representing. Strong writing acknowledges its indeterminate nonidentity to the world while weak writing seems to be rigorous reflection, really only explication or revisionism. Rigor impossibly attempts to suppress desire's subtext, the eclipse of authorial interest in enlivening a version that can never be a simple reflection but is always imaginative construction, the authentic commitment to one's own sense-giving speech acts and text acts.[30] The text *acts* when authorial interest is refracted prismlike in a writing dancing with enlivening marks of subjectivity, not simply first-person familiarity but an overlapping, spiraling interweaving of depth and surface eventually preventing any clear distinction between text and subtext, reproduction and production. My disciplinary reading is an imaginative resistance that cannot be trivialized merely as criticism or exegesis. Confident of its voice, marginal writing gives primacy to its critical object in order to reclaim a primacy the main text would deny it. Criticism is diminished only if it is carried out on the model of unmediating exegesis preferred by the discipline in order to disempower it.

This is exactly what the text hopes to achieve when it swallows Marxism and feminism as captives of the social objects they oppose, writings that so merge with their topics that they lose the ability to say anything, instead taking derivative life from their remoralike attachment to the tradition to which they are inextricably suckered. The text constructs marginal writing merely as criticism in order to diminish and subordinate it. But it need not succeed in reformulating formulation simply as derivation. Discipline fails to discipline texts of resistance where they oppose it through *a deconstructive reading turning the text into a political voice in spite of itself,* showing author where before only figure had been.

This undoes the text in order to redo it, excavating it as an authorial version that, reconstructed, becomes the counter model of a dedisciplinary version.[31] This idea is the most subversive: science is descientized as a text act of literary, hence political, desire and thus in a curious sense fulfills the otherwise empty promise of its surface politics that would make the world a better place in which to live. The text's superficial liberalism is authenticated by the surfacing of subtext that, once brought to light, no longer vitiates the progressive promise of sociology heretofore canceled by the positivist diremption of text and subtext. A social text is undone and rewritten in the same version, offering a new version as the excavation and contestation of the old. This is why I do not call for "new" textbooks, journal articles, or scholarly monographs that better grasp the social object but write a different version as the undoing of a text that, turned against itself, becomes other than itself—an emancipatory glimpse always latent in the desire of its craft. It is irrelevant whether we call readings of sociology sociologies in their own right. Better to call sociology a reading —thus prompting other versions to oppose discipline.

The notion of disciplined writing is exactly what the spongelike main text would have us pursue to claim it as its own. Discipline is only an illusion that an improved representation can better grasp the totality, precisely the ethic of commodities' inherent obsolescence as an occasion for the manufacture of false needs that are really only replicas of the old ones, in different packages. In any event, even the notion of a new disciplinary version supports discipline's political project by trying to outdo it. The notion of better disciplinary books holds constant the idea of presuppositionless representation attempting to complete the imputed lawfulness of what it describes, only different from the extant discipline in its surface substance, the words seeming to make it different but that can be said by anyone—exploitation, alienation, discrimination. Thus, it is folly to try to make a new discipline as if there were already general agreement on its topic, its method, its relationship to the world. The most politically apposite writing criticizes present versions as a way of showing the ubiquity of desire as well as its connection to writing in such a way that the ossified world can be seen to flow freely back and forth between topic and the world. This opens the way for new formulations of subject-object relations, the object less preponderant because it is traced back, as well as down, to the constitutive/constituting experiences of subtext, lifeworld, imagination—what makes us write.

The main text, thus in effect melted, shows its own humanity and as a result is opened to new versions of itself. This accords it a potential comprehensiveness that at least raises many of the right questions so that the process of excavation can turn these epochal issues—freedom, equality, justice—in a new direction, refracted to give off a new light. Sociology is closer to the truths of social life than, say, physics, microbiology, or even economics by virtue of its engagement with the nature of subject-object relations that it perversely wants to turn further in favor of the already preponderant object. A new version of sociology would resemble the old disciplinary text so little it makes no sense to call it sociology. If we retain the same name, we confuse a nomothetic version with one vitiating it in the direction of thawed subject-object relations; yet without introducing a new absolutism or identity-theory, we merely invert the old. It must be utterly clear that sociology since Comte has intended to suppress its subtext *as a political act*. Whether or not we could still "practice" sociology hinges on the nature of the version intended. A genuinely different text would make its own intentionality a topic, moving back and forth between analysis and its commitment to that analytical account.

Writing unashamed by its authorial subtext frees writers from their trained incapacity to comprehend the totality in mediating analysis and advocacy, thus detotalizing itself without being idiosyncratic, a text connecting with no other. A discipline strangling thought can be broken by rewriting it from the point of view of *possible authorship,* thus deconstructing the encyclopedic canon as a necessarily contingent product of authorial artifice—the *nth* draft of an original version that has been greatly worked over in the meantime. This does not mean that official sociology can be saved by tracing it back to the constituting minds and bodies that wrote it in the first place; the version embodying this plumbing of text to subtext will be entirely different from the echoless prose of representation. Desire cannot be controlled for, bracketed, or cleansed. Method always reveals its politics, poetry, and passion to a reading working underneath its suppressions. The text that listens to itself is not at all the same text repressing the scratch-scratch of its pen, effacing the authorial fingerprints that, it is thought, besmirch surface constructions.

Although the sociologist can be taught to allow subjectivity to inform the text without ever becoming one with it, sociology is ended as the dispassionate representation of social facts as they are thought to dominate human action in a generic sense, not only historically. Sociology is imploded by a writing refusing to rewrite it as an allegedly improved version of itself. This rewriting restores to authors the capacity to essay the social world in full awareness of the impact of their desire, advocacy, and interest on their version *as an archetype of free subject-object relations* reinforced by this posture toward one's own writing— or, better, since "posture" and "text" are now inseparable, by writing itself as a modal public activity opening mind to community.

Undoing sociology undoes texts oppressing their writers and readers with the indubitability of the social as it now discouragingly exhausts hope. It is a text opened to its own passions, however self-contradictory they may be. This difficult process requires the disciplinary epigone heretofore thoughtlessly employed in emulating appropriate norms governing the iteration of research to confront his or her reason for having done so;[32] liberation confronts one's own life and death instincts, the demiurges animating one's version of a life.

Writers who have heretofore ceded their constitutive authority to a text calling the shots are liberated by both understanding their own motives, however misguided, and then reformulating their practice in developing a nonantagonistic relation to it. Writers who willingly abandon their power instead write in ways fatefully organized by a world taking advantage of this self-denial. Emancipation inspects one's own participation in blocking out this suppression of motive as a methodical requirement of disciplinarily accredited membership.[33]

It is not simply that motive is suppressed by the sociologist but that the suppression of motive is defended as a condition of professional dispassion. Over the course of a life the writer engages in a process of increasingly rigorous suppression of desire in a way that we say he or she has developed a "professional career"—professionalism a methodic disinterestedness in one's own drive to do literary work. This cultivation of disciplined careers is defended as a universalism transcending the contrasting insufferable particularism and localism of scholars who do not publish, otherwise mired in the minutiae of university politics. Disinterestedness reflected in the suppression of desire as method is seen to be an antidote to a suffocating provincialism making everything "subject," utterly collapsing the distinction between subtext and text in relativizing the concerns of writing into purely local, even personal, terms. But this construction so central to Weberian sociology misses a third option neither suppressing subtext entirely, for no writing can succeed in doing that, nor inflating it to be all literary practice, the personal losing its creative tension with the general. It is possible to write in a way that neither pretends disinterestedness nor revels in interest but instead makes thematic the nonidentical relationship between interest and argument and thus illumines both of them.

Today disciplines find in favor of a universalism that, in the interest of disinterestedness, disdains involvement in the world and thus defends its own suppression of literary desire on grounds of professional maturity. This is called methodology, the twentieth-century version of metaphysics. The world is supposedly shunned by this universalism when in fact it is embraced by the text describing it; indeed, desire itself is really shunned, buried in the name of an appropriate technical competence. But this assumes that the contaminating influences of world and desire are equivalent when in fact the world so overwhelms the writer's solitary subjectivity that its preponderance is not guaranteed. Although professional disinterest is supposed to be a way of bracketing out the muddying effects of authorial desire, there is no corresponding process through which the historical preponderance of the world's objectivity can be easily controlled; seeming universalism is ironically particularized by an allegiance to *this* world, this state of affairs, in the *name* of the suppression of local desire, especially the desire of liberation. This is like a defense of cosmopolitanism, constructing it not as a genuine internationalism but as the absence or negation of localism, failing to articulate it as anything other than escape from the parochial prison house of the close at hand.

Universalism, then, refuses the world, as if to accept the world would be irresponsibly immature, a conceit of particularism. But the attack on the parochial need not abandon the world; all versions are worldly, whether or not they admit it. *A different version of versions can accept its roots in motive without losing sight of the expanse of things lying far beyond the region of self, instead recognizing that the notions of particular and general are only implied in each other and inevitably belong together.* Particularisms lose the oppressive weight of the parochial in being informed by broader, but for other writers no less local, concerns. As well, the general loses its emptiness by committing itself, otherwise only embracing this-world as the seeming epitome of a cosmopolitan disinterestedness. This is to say that science's version exercises a peculiar kind of closure that in appearing unparochial is thereby all the more so in allowing its unacknowledged desire covertly to inform the text's surface with the patina of the transcendental and timeless. This is largely why sociology talk today so closely resembles natural science prose, assuming historical invariance and thus allowing the writing to name the "world"—this-world—without historicizing it. "Society" takes the place of "nature" as writing's topic, hence becoming nature.

The undoing of sociology would restore desire to writing not only as an account of why it is what it is but as a qualitatively different version that did not dehistoricize itself in freezing its topic ("society"), instead accepting and acting upon its own inherence in the world it addresses. Committed literature refuses the distinction between cosmopolitan disinterest and parochial perspective for ironically (at least among the "educated" classes) finding in favor of the incorruptible universal—nothing more than another literary construction from *someone's* pen or typewriter.

Committed literature not only eschews this universalism as impossible but reveals it for the intellectually and socially reproductive practice it is, gaining a purchase on readers and other writers precisely by virtue of its seeming Archimedean disinterest only concealing an ontogenetically universal desire that is the fount of writing. Committed literature commits itself to a version of the world that it self-consciously *brings into being through its own craftspersonship,* both understanding and announcing itself as a *transformative practice* taking license from the irresolvable nonidentity between what Adorno called concept and things. Writing, then, transforms the world simply by understanding itself as *advocacy* for one or another state of affairs, even if that advocacy is subtle and not surface ("I recommend . . ."). The bridge this sort of writing acknowledges between its own desire and text allows text in turn to connect with the world, writing listening to itself, better its subtext; writing is the central constitutive practice of literary production. What I prefer to call fiction gains voice through its alternation between a nonidentical writerly subjectivity and the objectivities of text and social world.

This understands text as both a constitutive and constituted part of the world, not a mirror or eye somehow, like Archimedes, standing outside it. Indeed, the confidence I have in a sociological version not just debunked and opposed but opened to its own desire is inspired in large measure by the likelihood that more than other writings, perhaps, it understands its version in light of this worldliness. Writing is worldly not simply in the institutional "uses" of its knowledge (via universities, journals, consulting) but through its self-conscious inherence in history as the possibility of its transformation. Sociology is conceived as the reflexivity of any writing *plumbing the depth of text for animating desire without reducing one to the other*.

This disestablishes sociology in wrenching it out of the academic division of labor as it becomes a more general literary reflexivity, tying text to subtext without subordinating one to the other. This self-consciousness engages in self-psychoanalysis, trying to remember why it says what it does in light of methodical self-examination, analysand's dialogue with oneself freeing oneself for more public conversations. The problem with these metaphors is that they all stand for something else today, especially a sociology that is virtually identical to the voiceless textual practice of disinterested, often mathematizing representation. Calling programmatically for new writing vested with sociological self-consciousness runs the enormous risk of raising an old standard—Durkheim's discourse of the power of the social—to describe a new practice. The nonrepresentational mutuality within writing between text and subtext, practice and desire, remains the single best hope of a demythified social world now open to all sorts of previously muted readers and writers. In undoing sociology it may not be worth saving the word "sociology" to cover this sort of self-politicizing version of literature; it may lead to too many confusions. Yet my aim here is not to reinvent a discipline but to interrogate the way the discipline disciplines through its own suppression of literary reflexivity—both as a contribution to what Marxists call ideology critique and directly as a version of critical theory. Although sociologists understandably care about their discipline, my interest here is in opposing the extant disciplinary version politically as well as in understanding, and thus opposing, how all disciplining happens. Whether or not this would leave room for the rectification of sociology sometime in the future, or at least to allow us to use the word "sociology" again, is quite irrelevant today, given the imperativeness of the emancipatory agenda (including, locally, the various disciplines only adding to oppression by naming it).

Another way to understand the sort of writing I am both proposing and exemplifying here as a new form of subject-object relations is to return to Marx's central notion of accumulation, describing primarily the process of the centralization and concentration of capital as mechanisms of labor's oppression. It is clear by now that domination pivots around both economic and intellectual accumulation—Gramsci's hegemony, Lukacs's reification, Frankfurt domination, my heterotextuality—as power increasingly is vested in the various texts reducing people's apparent freedom of action. Discipline proffers a version of social nature to be lived out in fulfillment of the text's seemingly disinterested "description" of these allegedly binding patterns. I want to understand the accumulated constructions of the discipline's text as fragments of writing *belonging to someone else* in the sense that the text coopts marginal versions both to defuse them and to reinforce the impression of its own impartiality, even tolerance. Although it is perilous to be heard to imply that writing belongs to anyone (except in the sense of copyright, itself an artifact of bourgeois society in which words are bought and sold), I want to offer this sort of construction heuristically, suggesting a discursive practice burrowing from within the entrapping scientism by engaging in a process of textual decentering, breaking the hold of the discipline on these oppositional versions.

This is to pursue a theory and practice of literary heterogeneity resisting the centering pull of the main text by rejecting its claims to disciplinary autonomy on grounds that all texts are created equal inasmuch as they are equally created. Decentering slows the text's swallow of the margins, even reversing it by eroding its hegemony, intellectual decentering both auguring and animating the decentering of wealth and power in general. This is to argue for a *decentering, disaccumulating* version of political life that resists the text's disciplining hegemony by refusing its integration as official science, insisting on its incommensurability with the main text's socioontologizing project. This sort of writing undoes the text that would usurp Marxism and feminism; it argues against their usurpation less on grounds of distortion, presupposing a singularly valid reading accessible to a determinate community of scholars, than on grounds of unacceptable conflation toward the goal of total administration, a last text saying so much it says nothing.

A decentering writing frees the margins from the center by refusing their bland reduction to terms of present discourse and instead preserving their angry response to the present version of the world. The goal is not so much to produce inviolate readings of writings that shine through transparently but to break the hold of the discipline on playful, poetic, oppositional versions "central" in their own right.[34] This is emphatically not to argue for an eclecticism adjudging every text equally valid or valuable; that only makes way for their centering at the hands of an Archimedean version pretending to mediate all differences. Rather the resistance to texts' disciplining is only a way of engaging the ideal speech situation between and among writings addressing each other as legitimately irreducible voices.

Textual disaccumulation is less the repetition of the main text's mock relativism than a thoroughgoing rethinking of some fundamental epistemological-political issues, particularly the usefulness or even necessity of distinguishing between a main text and more marginal versions it brings into an ecumenical fold where they are disciplined—disqualified and then rehabilitated. Although the absolutism of disciplinary cooptation is clearly authoritarian, the absolutism of marginality fetishizing its estrangement courts the solipsizing danger of private language as well as a certain authoritarianism rooted in the labored hagiography-hermeneutics of esoteric texts. Both ecumenical and closet centrisms of fetishized marginalia stifle free literary practice, describing the world of possible texts in terms of themselves. Neither manages to escape the deeply corrupting hubris of the Enlightenment asserting possible knowledge around a model of a knowing subject which has the power to center, and thus master, all things external to it.[35] A nonsubjective epistemology in the relations it prefigures between subjects and objects, texts and topics, is deeply democratic inasmuch as it does not define possible knowledge only in terms of itself. Rather it frames and fosters the nondominating alternation between subjecthood and objectivity particularly in its creative mediation of an empowering desire and the surrounding object world. As such, it opposes the accumulation of wealth and power through the ontologizing impact text has on world, turning description in effect into ice—if not stone.

The promise of a disaccumulating version of writing lies in its inherent nonidentity with the disciplinary version splitting it in two, good and bad versions subject simultaneously to centering and then further marginalization. This decentering neither holds out for a new center—itself—nor abandons the notion of definitive text altogether; instead, it respects every version as marginal and thus it relativizes writing vis-à-vis other social practices. I want to defend writing neither as aspiring center nor perpetual margin but as a definitive practice making sense of life by listening to itself live, opening itself both to what it is in essence and to what other writers might have to say to it in the back-and-forth of an intertextual community. In this way I want to think a version of left deconstruction directly as political practice. Disaccumulation is not privatization indulging its own uniqueness but an invitation to respond to it without collecting partial versions into a new truth, literature, discipline. The modern has trouble accepting the possibility of decentering prose liberating itself from an octopus text denying it a life of its own and then opening up lines of communication with other decentered versions. The critique of discipline need not succumb to the temptation of a new discipline made up of margins now pulled centrifugally toward the center. There are not only two options but three. Text can be other than either a fragment risking private language or the accumulation of fragments into a new totality, albeit one in-diversity, as a Derridean Marxist might say. Or it can open itself to other versions without being swallowed by them, letting itself be corrected as well as correcting without collapsing the boundaries between itself and these other voices together comprising an ideal speech situation. Center/margin dualism allows an entity to be either subject or object but not both or neither. Thus, it is difficult to think a text so confident of its own imperviousness to discipline that it can let itself be interrogated by other versions without either assimilating them or risking its own assimilation. Texts in a better world refuse to legislate the truth but instead enjoy the dialectic of dialogue for its own sake, the concerns of epistemology—subject knowing an object outside itself—subordinated to the concerns of aesthetic politics (Agger 1976a). The portrayal of a decent, happy world springs discursively from its nonantagonistic relation to other versions and is not simply reflected or projected by it. Writing can both oppose discipline and create a new order of value in the way it relates to its own practice as well as its readership.

As it turns out, the dichotomy of absolutism/relativism does not exhaust the possibility of a writing that writes for an audience to which it accords equal dialogue chances and yet is satisfied not to conquer or join forces with other versions. Disaccumulation does not look to new accumulation, albeit recentered around formerly opposing traditions. It realizes that as soon as it constructs its own centrality it sets up tensions with margins inevitably arising to oppose it. But writing that loves its marginality too much concedes the center and thus is always threatened by it.

The most progressive posture is to treat all versions as centers without endorsing a relativism silencing one's own voice in a sense of hopelessness about saying or doing anything special. The hegemony of the center today does not mean that all self-confident writing must accumulate other versions as part of its own story. Once we overcome writing's self-suppression, allowing it to derive meaning only from what it swallows of other people's worlds, we can eliminate the center/margin distinction altogether. The disaccumulation of the main text sets text free to play freely with its own subtext and with other versions neither threatening it nor presenting themselves as subjects of integration. Decentered writing is only decentered with respect to the disciplinary version dominating it. It works out its own center in the interplay of subtext and surface as a process of endless self-clarification *without* having to ingest other writings filling up its own emptiness.

Lest this sound like another idealism,[36] as monadic as it is illusory, let me reflect on the notion of substance. Scientism seeking to capture the world in amber transcribes this history into all histories, exhausting the range of sociopolitical possibilities in what exists today and existed yesterday. The notion that discipline is on solid footing simply because it borrows the best from a variety of analytic literatures is typical of a culture afraid to speak for itself without buttressing from authorities and yet unafraid to announce itself as a singularly legitimate mainstream once it has swallowed other versions.

This is an epistemological social contract theory of sorts, forestalling the nastiness, brutality, and brevity of human life in the supposed state of nature by forming a compact among competing versions pivoting around a Leviathan-like canon centering the different versions. But this contract theory erodes where the Leviathan-like text only ingests marginal writings in order to strengthen itself but thereby violates their *resistance* to just such a contract that would be their undoing. Like bourgeois political theory, science's mainstream constructs its own alleged state of nature—nonscience—out of which mature science emerges as the resolution of warring factions. But the state of nature is a fiction designed to contrast our present security in a centering literature to the demons of nature that would otherwise imperil any writing, much as barbarism threatened "civilization" in early Europe.

The epistemological state of nature is constructed to be the prehistory of science, that lawless, dangerous time when no central text could collect the piecemeal scribblings that, left atomized, only bespeak the cosmic terror of a world without a center. Science is simply the supposed contract among writings agreeing to cede their constitutive power to it in order to hold back the godlessness announced by Nietzsche (1956) as the modern circumstance. The more the disciplinary text can swallow in order to display it in the elaborate ritual of references, tables, graphs—the world in effect reconstituted spatially and figurally inside the covers—the less it has to attend to its own suppressed motive and thus the more comfortable it will be with a version utterly lacking the boldness of imagination.

Writing lacking meaning does not obtain it simply by citing authorities and sources in the Taylorist mode of academic production today; footnote and bibliography proliferation intends but fails to fill the text's emptiness, an effect of its own diremption of depth and surface. The former emerges only as the soulless reliance on others that—no quid pro quo—sucks them under as they are mastered. The spell of accumulation is so general that we have come to equate it not only with material worth but with truth itself; the more fungible units are acquired (references, grants, data), the more impregnable the version. One of the most common questions asked of teachers who assign essays to their students is whether they "*have* to use outside references," as if this were more a question of normative usage, even morality, than of the logic of presentation. Academic discourse mandates the use of the scholastic apparatus propping iterative writing becoming simply the sum of what it integrates under the rubric of dispassionate citation.

It is clear that the intellectual accumulation process serves to domesticate political advocacy; otherwise it would not need to mediate a world it pretends merely to reflect. Opposition affords writing an energy putting it to the task of disqualifying and then rehabilitating the opposition, living off that energy like capital lives off the surplus labor of its wage slaves. The sparks given off in the hierarchical confrontation of marginalia by discipline afford its text the appearance of a thoughtful mediation transcending mere mimesis in turn serving its deeper purpose as the discourse of the power of the social.

No matter how falsifying, integration is perversely the motive force of the text's power over writers and readers allowing integration to occur in the first place. Marginal writing is domesticated into mere "contribution" and thus gives the text an intellectual problematic. Without the scholastic apparatus and all its implications about the intellectual/social accumulation process, science's text would have no fuel for what in the end is merely a reflection of the given dressed up as intellectual achievement. The discipline is made up of all of what it has swallowed, although in this—by swallowing some things and not others—it *politically disciplines*.

It is a mistake to think of the sort of disaccumulation I propose and am doing here as criticism but not also construction, a negativism only reacting to the agenda set by the main text, which exercises power simply because it commands our deconstructive attention. But like it or not, *the agenda has already been set* and cannot be dissolved with resort to a cheerful pragmatism getting down to the task at hand of rebuilding the lousy world. The sway of a disabling scientism extends to the webs of thought and text enmeshing us in discipline simply by the power of texts, culture, ideology, everyday life over us—and thus *through* us. We cannot think except through the modalities of possible/impossible, freedom/necessity, private/public reinforced in us millions of times as language games that Marx in an unfortunate mechanism called superstructure or ideology. We live ideology, and in turn it lives us, its self-reproducing discipline leaving us no alternative but to unravel it from within. Construction can only proceed deconstructively in a textually deep and overdetermined world.

No apology is required for textual-critical writing *against discipline* inasmuch as a more direct approach is incredibly difficult after so many years of our powerlessness. The axiological assumptions we "make" about human and social nature are really made for us in the language games in Jung's terms inhabiting our collective unconscious. They seem to be simply fragments of nature and not also social products or processes burying the so-called binary oppositions of domination deep in mind. We cannot rethink before we learn how to think beyond the aegis of texts precluding the possibility of thought, prose, speech—the liberating mediation of the world. Kant was wrong: the categories of the understanding are not a priori but rather social products, the entwining writing "given" to us so that the world they name may also be given, accepted, and enacted for what the texts say it "is"—*must be*. Discipline reproduces disciplined lives through the discourse of the power of the social. Sociology as the name of this discourse only deepens discipline.

11

Open Text, Open World

Writing Difference

Negative writing turns toward the positive where it dislodges the accumulated text from its preponderant place in the center and instead models a discursive practice eschewing all center/periphery dichotomies, encouraging every writing to decenter and yet refusing an utter relativism only inviting the intrusion of a new textual accumulativeness, a new disciplining. This is to return to my earlier notion, from Wittgenstein in his *Philosophical Investigations* (1953) through Habermas (1984, 1987), that writing is a "form of life," a mode of association itself, and not simply an instrumental means of what is now typically called "communication." Where Wittgenstein and Habermas focus on talk, I concentrate on the literary bases of domination, offering what might be read as a Marxist version of communication theory (if that self-understanding refuses affiliation with Marx's overly reductive concept of ideology).

I want to understand writing as a social and political relationship both reflecting and constituting the ensemble of social relationships describing experience in a highly differentiated world. The permeable boundary between text and world requires a double reflection at once addressing the preponderant objectivity of the world dominating the disempowered subject and, from the other direction, interrogating writing that remakes a world infiltrating writing as its bounteous, unavoidable subtext (much deeper than mere "subject matter"). Aware of its own literary ground in authorial desire, a new version undoes the entrapping discourse of the power of the social by approaching the world in a confident way yet beholden to its own motives of advocacy. This undoing is not the same "topic" simply handled differently but a breathing of motive into the purposely dehumanized text of science as ways of both getting scientism off our backs and showing the possibility of subject-object, text-world, human-human rapprochement, if not their full identity.

By uncovering the buried motive of a representational version of science, a different science resists its sway over thought and action. It no longer accepts the heteronomy it would impose on us as fate, idealist freedom said to lie in a hoped-for region beyond seeming necessity, instead exemplifying and at once constituting a world comprising a new relationship between itself and texts. Criticism designed to break the umbilical link with a discipline threatening to swallow marginal writing as one or another contribution to official sociology models a textual practice (a) refusing *intellectual closure,* (b) regarding itself as creative *self-expression* (not only "communication"), and (c) inviting others to address it *dialogically* as it addresses other versions in self-confidently incomplete prose.

With Wittgenstein, the original Frankfurt School, a variety of poststructuralists, and particularly Habermas, writing is a form of social life crucially empowering or disempowering us in our relationships to the internal and external world. Texts are not only socially situated, as the sociology of literature would hold, or politically partisan but social relationships of construction and reconstruction joining writer, reader, world, and text in a complexly nonidentical relationship. This is not to forget the so-called meaning of the text but rather to locate the problem of meaning in the context of the world to which it is a response and of which it is a manifestation; writing's social character lies in the worldliness of text and the textuality of world and not reductively in the "influence" of the social "on" it or of it "on" the social.

The text concretizes ideation in the power of words, symbols, codes *that provoke practice out of us.* Today, in service of the disabling forces of hegemony, writing, like sexuality—the heterotext—transcends sheer reproduction, even though my reading has shown that reproduction is also fatefully a new production inasmuch as the productive can never subsist entirely on its own without being reformulated. Deconstruction reveals the productiveness of reproduction as it tries to demolish the distinction between the productive and reproductive or valuable and valueless as realms of superior and inferior being.[1] Writing as a form of life aims to make this productiveness thematic to dislodge versions (like bourgeois science) that (re)produce by appearing only to represent. Writing against discipline exemplifies a world-constitutive practice creating a world based on its own intertextual concatenation of writer, reader, text, and world through the three principles of opposition to closure, thematic self-expression, and a dialogical orientation to otherness. Writing recreates the world in its image where it decenters disempowering discipline by reflecting our extant powerlessness in an apparently unalterable realm of social nature and instead offers its own openness, playfulness, and inherently voluble democracy as constitutive principles of a better social order.

This transformative notion of textual practice draws on a long tradition of both cultural and political criticism all deriving in one way or another from Marx's concept of ideology as the mystification of people's lived oppression, fostered to prevent both their enraged revolt and their imagination of different, better modes of existence. Ideology has been broadened and deepened since early capitalism to become a variety of social texts insinuating themselves into nearly every nook and cranny of our lived experience. The ingenious text in all its concatenated varieties elaborates a "world" governed by a social nature it hopes/hypes to bring about through readerly practices regarded, as I do here, as forms of life, establishing for analytic purposes a continuity between how and what one reads and how and what one enacts of the professed version in question. The continuity between text and world mirrors Marx's relationship between superstructure and base and, like it, eludes reduction of one to the other. The scientific text's claimed presuppositionless representationality occludes its deeply constitutive role in producing the power of the social, which in Marxist terms is already a reproduction. To put this differently, it shows how false the sharp distinction is between production and reproduction as an adequate account of the social today. Although production dominates, it could not do so without the prop of reproduction, routing domination through the reproductive circuitry of psyche, body, family, and culture to which it allegedly stands in a relation of the valuable to the valueless.

I imagine freedom to reverse the priority of text-world, superstructure-base, and production-reproduction as these all manifest the epochal subordination of inferior to superior being, valueless to valuable activity. Writing both deconstructs the object-world's present preponderance as nonidentically dependent on the representational texts silencing rebellion socioontologically and prefigures a new world shaped by a playful and dialogical text. Like ideology for Althusser and the Frankfurt School, ontology is lived and relived through the reproductive circuitry of desire, taking shape in the simultaneously overdetermining and underdetermining codes of our various lifeworlds, from science to religion to sexuality.

The continuity between this version and the iterative version of positivist science is not the presence or absence of advocacy; science's text is as programmatic as any call to arms, even if science falsely foreswears this programmatism as the vitiation of objective scholarship. Writing comfortable with its literariness discloses its motive in both admitting its world-constitutiveness as well as its inherence in the world, thus celebrating it as the possibility of a dialogic community *that it begins to create through its very practice*. By recognizing simultaneously its world-constitutive character and its foundation in worldly interest, this version of versions breaks the cycle of a science hiding its own constitutionality in order to be all the more effective in getting it done.

I am not proposing a new version of Enlightenment object mastery substituting one imperialism for another. That only introduces a socialist scientism that, since Engels and the Bolsheviks, has duplicated the bourgeois iteration of authoritarian social arrangements. Instead my version of science can afford to acknowledge, even celebrate, its subtext of desire, motive, and worldly interest without abandoning the claim to veracity, modeling all sorts of lifeworlds through which people produce and reproduce themselves and the larger social order. Writing that refuses merely to reflect the world engages in textual practice, transforming the world without failing to see that it is thus itself transformed; the nexus between subject and object is dialectical, that is, a relation both of identity and nonidentity.

Nonviolent textual practices embrace and embody *nonauthoritarian nonidentity,* the organizing principle of an entire social order once production loses its sway over reproduction, men over women, capital over labor, world over text. Relations patterned on subject-object dynamics comprise the ensemble of meaningful relationships—production-reproduction, public-private, world-text, text-subtext, person-person, writer-reader. Although each of these relationships' terms is imbedded in its counterpart term, they overlap and leave what Adorno called a "remainder," a piece or trace of brute facticity resistant to socialization or identification. Whether inanimate nature or the volcanic nature within us that Freud originally understood as life instincts, id, Eros, Adorno's (1973a) "indissoluble something" is the recalcitrant piece of objectivity unavailable for the subject's mastery. The original Frankfurt School (and now Derridean deconstruction) has consistently argued that the Enlightenment bequeathed to later industrial-era generations the dangerous, arrogant impulse to master this inner and outer nature fully. Camus (1955) described this as the "myth of Sisyphus," a Promethean urge to submit the object-world to human will as a sort of political-economic solution to the original Cartesian dualism —object either mined or simply named.

Adorno, Horkheimer, and Marcuse along with a variety of French Marxists and critics from Sartre and Merleau-Ponty to Derrida and Foucault indict Descartes's dualism of passive-aggressive subject and mute, inert object for simply reproducing the extant power of the social. People are today dominated by their prideful objectifications in capitalism and state socialism—history inflated into ontology only deepening history. By the same token, though, postmodernist philosophical anthropology, deeply indebted to psychoanalysis as a critical theory and not clinical practice, constructs the subject-object duality clearly abundant in history as a virtually invariant tendency; it issues in subjects' domination of objects (and, indeed, other subjects) and, in turn, the boomerang of preponderant objectivity seeming to take on a life of its own. What for the Greeks and Descartes is ontology, for many postmodernists is a history that by subsisting so long virtually turns into ontology—fact into an apparent fate. The only solution for postmodernism is the abandonment of solutions—not a solution, either. Nietzsche is not an adequate basis for cultural and social theory.

A way around divided subject-object relations is to understand them in a relationship of fluctuating nonidentity, making possible a nonauthoritarian attitude of subjects toward other subjects, objects like nature and themselves. This refuses the arrogant project of a conquering identity-theory—where object-world becomes simply an ingested part of subject—as well as the idealist consolation of *Innerlichkeit* (interiority, private "freedom" in thought alone) disengaging entirely from the threatening object-world—as if that were even a possibility. The theory and practice of nonidentity enacts the objectivity of subjectivity (reason, production, text) in the organon of "forms of life," linking base and superstructure and production and reproduction through the lifeworlds mediating personal and public existence.

Like the writing I describe and do here, nonidentical prose refuses to forget its grounds in desire as well as in the external world through which we are bound in what Merleau-Ponty (1962) called our body-subjecthood, resisting the temptation of the destructive and self-destructive search for final identity between one's practice and the world it would misguidedly overwhelm. So the first, most important, principle of a literary, hence social, nonidentity is the refusal to *identify* that which is inherently nonidentical, although dialectically entwined.

Nonidentical writing allows itself to alternate between text and celebration of text's inherence in subject as a way of preventing the suppression of objectivity that otherwise, if allowed to surface, humbles the text by keeping it grounded in desire, body, nature, community, and history. The seemingly passive text professing only to reflect is the one most heedless of its own productive activity and thus ends up cutting itself off from its own basis of motive and interest, thereby neutralizing itself in face of a preponderant world utterly overwhelming it with the unalterable power of the social. The more text's underlying desire is acknowledged and celebrated as the ineradicable bond of knowledge and interest, the more writing can resist its own identification with a nearly hegemonic object-world dominating versions lacking self-conscious foundation in their own volcanic, irrepressible, and, above all, insurgent objectivity of motive, interest, passion, and need. It is a question here of opposing the writerly subject-object to the ossified object of the external world needing to be (made) *less* identical than it already is.

Nonidentical discursive practice accepts the nonidentity of its text and subtext as the inevitable failure of words to "say" all of what is meant, felt, desired. However, the prison house of language is liberated once we understand, and enact, the nonidentity of desire and text as a further impulse to write and live free, the inexhaustibility of desire somehow compensating for its insatiability and, sometimes, its ineffability. That each sign does not attach to a simple or single object in the world only encourages more talk and text, indeed *community,* not less. After all, nonidentity is dialectical, as are all subject-object relations, inasmuch as it contains a moment of identity, of connection, when suddenly words do grasp and thus convey the "meant." Indeed, the meant is said precisely to the extent to which the usual nonidentity of text and world (including desire) is acknowledged as the rule, not the exception. Nonantagonistic relations between subject and object, although possible, are less frequent than their diremption; their dialectical relationship—interpenetration or overlap—always tends to undo itself in the inability of desire to make itself known and felt in a text *both* giving desire its due (often as advocacy) and gently opening itself to other versions.

Closure in this sense is possible only as the possibility of nonidentical identity. This version of freedom marks a free society made up of free subjects in touch with their sensuous objectivity, the contact of desire, text, world, and other subjects in the serendipitous moment of mutual comprehension —surely an interregnum in the moral drama of history. Western Marxism has been primarily concerned with the perilous necessities of a notion of totality in Hegel's sense as well as with the issue of part-whole relationships as a fundament of socialist political theory. In general terms most western Marxists like Adorno and Merleau-Ponty reject the "socialist" conflation of individual and group, inescapably emerging in one form of terror or another. Although Marxism differs from liberal individualism in the way it understands the concatenated levels and interrelationships of capitalism, represented by the Hegelian concept of a totality irreducible to mere actors or interests, nonauthoritarian Marxists do not condone the sacrifice of particular to general —people to the state apparatus, movement, or party—because, like early Hegel of the *Phenomenology*, they regard history and society as essentially characterized by what Hegel called negation or nonidentity.

Unfortunately, the later Hegel of *Science of Logic* who resolved negation in negation of the negation, a new positive or totality, sacrificed particular to general and in a philosophical sense only paved the way for scientific Marxism and eventually Stalinism; the Siberian camps are a "socialist" version of Hitler's absolute state obliterating nonidentity in a more intensive, if not qualitatively different, way. Western Marxism's project since 1923 has been precisely to retain the notion of totality as a crucial improvement over liberal atomism and individualism while decentering it in such a way that it does not reproduce its own version of capitalist, fascist, and state-socialist center/ periphery distinctions; the juggernaut of history's allegedly cunning reason sweeps away every instance of the nonidentical under the sign (or so it believes) of historical necessity. Ultimately, this notion of decentered totality would provide for textual/social practices embodying the indeterminacy of text-world relationships *both* as nonidentical *and* constitutive, avoiding monologic terror on the one hand and a fatalizing heteronomy on the other—which in history, of course, end up being exactly the same thing, albeit flying different flags. Discipline is discipline; only the discourses are different.

Given the enormous power of ideology, culture, author, and text since Marx's time, it is just as well to elaborate a socialist imagery in terms of textuality, a project begun most self-consciously by Habermas (1984, 1987) in his communication theory with its political ethic of the ideal speech situation, a dialogic practice unconstrained by mystification or manipulation. But (Agger 1976b, 1981, 1985) Habermas's communication theory is too rationalistic, closer in crucial respects to John Stuart Mill than to Marx, especially in Marx's Freudian reformulation by the original Frankfurt School (who Habermas dismisses as "mystics" for their sweeping imagery of reconstructed subject-object, particularly subject-nature, relations).[2] Habermas privileges speech over writing by displaying a fundamentally rationalist optimism about the ability to understand and be understood, seemingly ignoring the claim of desire (reduced by him (1971) to the more rationalist/capitalist concept of interest) on surface text and speech. Nevertheless, Habermas at least constructs his image of socialist "process"—ideal speech situation—in discursive terms. He thus crucially addresses the enormous hold of scientism over mind in late capitalism, an argument he presaged in his earlier essay (1970) "Technology and Science as 'Ideology,' " making way for my claim that positivist science disciplines through its literary self-occlusion. While Habermas understands discipline as the incursion of system into lifeworld, his version of an alternative in privileging lifeworld over systems fails to address power.

As Adorno and Horkheimer (1972) suggested in the *Dialectic of Enlightenment*, the frame of liberation and oppression is the ontological relationship between subject and object, as well as the way epistemologically we think and write about, and therefore politically enact, it. Text *becomes* world by seeming to accept the preponderance of social objects where actually it asserts its own autonomy by *transferring* it to the object. This suggests a version of ideology as the dispersal of textuality into naturelike objects defying reconstitutive reading and rewriting. Reproduction under sway of scientism would reproduce extant domination by reflecting its unalterability in a text that seems to have no author and thus requires no active reader, ironically encouraging reading practice to extend beyond the confines of study, classroom, and theater to work, politics, and home. The fatalism taught by science is transvalued into political acquiescence by being acted out unthinkingly.

The text is not set apart from the world transcendentally in order to purify itself of motive in its iteration of a seeming social nature (that it knows is only a version of necessity, one among many possible constructions). Text anchored in the world both produces and reproduces it. Every sentence changes the planet in some way or other, from "A specter is haunting Europe . . ." to "You've come a long way, baby." Nonidentical literary practice only acknowledges what the text conceals in the worldliness of its apodictic version of itself. The choice is not to raise a text above or beyond the world but only to acknowledge its constitutiveness as a way of opening writing to the possibility of its own *difference* from the reality it otherwise reproduces. One is either for or against discipline. No discourse fails to take a stand, especially those eschewing politics in this postmodern age. Postmodernism is the decisive stance of stancelessness supporting discipline surreptitiously.

Nonidentity is dialectical because it is not *simply* difference but the alternation between text and world varying between the self-confidence of strong writing and the circumspection of that surface construction in light of an implacable subtext, its worldliness it cannot efface. Writing tries to overcome the plenitude of its own contexts in desire and the extant world otherwise threatening to engulf it in the oceanic feelings of infantile emotion from the inside or utter determination from the outside—disciplinary literature merely iterating the imposed, the imperative, the given-to-hand. Text can most effectively elude its objectification, and thus silencing, where it addresses its own reproduction in the interest of social reproduction and not simply by proclaiming its methodical "value-freedom" as if textual practice could be cut loose of the gravity grounding it in an engaged/enraged authorial subtext.

No amount of method can free the text from the pull of desire turning text toward an intentional object—generically, history (O'Neill 1972). The only way to address the worldliness of writing is directly, engaging writing's worldly effort to work free of the gravitational pull of the object, flesh, time, death. Although Heidegger's existentialism falsely resolves historical domination through authenticity, at least he understands the historicity of the *ego cogito* in a way that allows for all sorts of non-Cartesian versions of good existence, especially Marxist and feminist ones replacing private authenticity with political struggle. Existentialism's recognition of the historicity of the subject too frequently precludes the transformation of history itself—of what is falsely hypostatized as eternal "throwness" or "useless passion." Postmodernism, the contemporary existentialism, suppresses the prospect of new historicities making possible different versions of Heideggerian authenticity shorn of his tragically privatized overtones. As the subject's generic form of life, its self-expression externalized, text is enmeshed in the simultaneous sameness and difference of its relationship to the world bringing it forth as its self-consciousness, indeed its Marxist transformation. Science mythically pretends to float above the concreteness of Heidegger's *Dasein,* the person "thrown" into the historical maelstrom confronted with the certainty of meaningless death, the only address to which is a resolute commitment to one's universalizing, immortalizing projects. In failing to challenge the identity of modernity and the power of the social, postmodernism like Heidegger before it becomes its discourse. Durkheim ironically converges with Derrida.

Science dehistoricizes itself in the ultimate illusion that it alone can outlast or outlive mortality, time, body, and other people. Yet other versions of science accept the subject-object engagement in the dialectically nonidentical terms calling forth not method but essay—text's acceptance of itself as another *literary project,* another discourse, poetry, and pamphlet no more or less apodictic than the other scribblings marking our difference/sameness from the world. A version of writing as a form of life embodying intellectual openness, playful self-expression, and the desire to listen as well as talk, essay prefigures a good political community and is, strategically, the most propitious way to get there. Marcuse (1969) in the tradition of western Marxism has called this the project of a "new science," a political-cognitive form of life exemplifying a better world just as it deconstructs the old world as a reification of positivist representationality dispersed into the naturelike prose of what I (1989) call a fast capitalism. Positivist text hides its own nonidentical constitutionality behind the posture of a methodical disinterestedness; criticism and construction merge in the prophetic engagement of text with the world it would herald in its own nonauthoritarian intertextuality.

Text's politics, then, are characterized by heterogeneity, openness, self-expression, and dialogue brought forth in a voice not only recognizing but also accepting, even flaunting, its own infiltration by worldly interest, history, and mortal embodiment. Its existence as a form of life, not above life, makes possible its own contribution to thawing out the patterns of reproduction that have long since become second nature. This acceptance of historicity forces the text to relinquish the apodictic claims of virtually every mode of self-styled science since the Enlightenment (as well as religion before and after it); its purchase on history was gained only at the expense of admitting its own subtextuality, contextuality, and animation by authorial motive: the desire to change the world by writing (it).

The new text prefigures a politics of decentered centering, *of dedisciplining,* refusing to impose certainties on others because it is uncertain about its own objective-subjective desire—yet not so uncertain it refrains from writing altogether. After all, not to essay a version of the actual and possible world is to succumb to the preponderant objectivity only entrenched by what passes for writing today but is really only duplication. Text apes a world it secretly knows is not as clear as the text's copy makes it out to be—science air-brushing a two-dimensional world nonidentical to its own version. Merleau-Ponty's ineluctable ambiguity connotes the present absence between things and people that eludes final understanding yet cannot be breached entirely by a Promethean pen or politics. By respecting the mysteries within itself, nonidentical discursive practice—essay—respects others and nature without sacrificing itself to them; reproduction reproduces its own subordination to the discipline of this history—productivism/capitalism/sexism/racism, *scientism.* Willing to celebrate its own literariness as its constitutive ingress to the world, essay exemplifies communicative as well as productive/reproductive ethics defining a host of our relationships with nature, other people, and our own worldly interiority.

Where text models the future world in this sense, it changes the present one, introducing a practice both deconstructing and constructing at once, breathing life into lifeless texts and thereby reducing their implacable hold on us. Writing is a social relationship as well as a text "about" such relationships; the former is nonidentical to the latter and yet connected. The page is the tissue opening one version to other possible versions, telling them something—here, the world has been unnecessarily frozen—in a way eschewing closure and monologue, thus also essaying the nature of the possible. Writing thus becomes the kind of community it wants to be, either hierarchical or dialogic.

Reclaiming Science in the Name of Essay

If my version here is both an interplay of my critique of sociology and an open writing grounded in its own reflexivity about its subtext—relationships modeling the openness, self-expression, and dialogic nature of a good polity —I want to rethink the name ordinarily given to texts purporting to describe the social as well as nature. This reclaims "science" for a literary version carried out under the aegis of dialectical difference; I call it essay. Throughout, I have been straining against a version of science blurring all differences and thus tending to lose its own crucial difference from the world. My problem is that this critique of scientism all too easily becomes a critique of any and all liberating abstraction. The charge of nonscience made by scientism against rival writings is so definitive I do not want to relinquish science altogether as a literary project different from fiction only in that it claims validity. A positivist version of science only thinks it overcomes the caprice of the purely poetic, the nonrepresentational. Although I refuse the distinction between science and nonscience as a prop of scientistic society, divided as much between knowers and known as rulers and ruled, I nonetheless confront its reality at a time in the history of knowledge when scientism is ascending and poetry declining; the 1960s were the watershed of aesthetic sensibility after which it is time to return to business as usual.

Science can be reclaimed from the disciplinary text as not only a kind of prose but also as a form of life refusing to live science's thoughtless reproduction of the power of the social. Essay instead understands itself as a world-constitutive mode of production. In this, my science's goal is not simply "cultural transmission" but criticism, play, talk, and self-insight, the intertextual building of community. *Science can be understood as the perpetual posture of subject toward its own, and the world's, objectivity as a mode of its transformative nonidentity with that objectivity,* freeing text from a mindless duplication of things at the same time as writing understands itself as a thing, as well as a form of thing-ification. Instead of accepting science as the prevailing institutional practice cleansing texts and suppressing authors, a different science, no less disciplined, is intimate with and unembarrassed by its own literariness and thus liberates discourse from practices texts currently support. Against the disciplining of the dominant order, my notion of discipline retains a moment of aesthetic and political self-expression. This is perhaps nothing more than an imagery of a humane society beyond (or simply apart from) economic and political metaphors (e.g., socialism, democracy), portraying free subjects intertextually in touch with inner and outer objectivity—desire and nature—about which they write as topics of universal concern.

The *telos* of the species is not narrowly labor in the sense of waged male activity but all constitutive practice, the self-creation and self-expression that Marx (1961) in 1844 regarded as the full potential of dealienated labor. After all, Marx and Engels first imagined socialism as a society of writers where they addressed the "all-around individual" in *German Ideology* (1949) as one who "criticized," as well as fished and hunted, without adopting the lifelong imprint of any of these singular roles. Marx's original notion of socialism as a literary society only modifies Plato's early notion of the Good as philosophy, although Plato understood philosophy as pedagogic talk, a Socratic preference Derrida rightly regards as a modern prejudice for dialectic speech over evocative text. Since Marx, the notion of writing as imagery of the good polity is found in a number of versions of non-Soviet Marxism, notably in Sartre, Gramsci, Marcuse, Adorno, and Habermas, although Adorno said art and Habermas communication or what he calls "communicative competence."

The notion of labor as text has not been better developed largely, I suspect, because modern Marxists in one way or another are almost exclusively concerned with explaining domination and not, as well, with projecting a future prefiguratively linked to the present by their own literary practices. Marxist criticism since Lukacs is instead focused mainly on the reproductive role of texts and not also on their prefigurativeness as a qualitatively different, de-reifying relationship among writer, reader, and world—utopianizing largely scorned in these times of "mature" Marxism deriving science from fiction (e.g., Lukacs on Balzac, Sartre on Flaubert, Adorno on Schoenberg) rather than fiction from science, as I am trying to do. I am trying to correct this by reformulating a Marxist version of deconstruction as a different version of imagination *including* science, a relationship between criticism and construction that cannot be severed lest criticism itself so ape its topic it becomes merely a moment of it, its integrated margin only strengthening the center's claim to universality. It is important to overcome the Marxist tendency to concentrate only on the economically and ideologically reproductive roles of culture, science, intimacy—text. Instead I theorize socialism as a world in which superstructure does more than merely reflect the requirements of material production but in (re)formulating those requirements becomes a constitutive medium of human freedom. A better metaphor of generic human activity, including labor, is text; this risks idealism only if we forget that texts have constitutive power themselves—forms of life.

Once the so-called superstructure has become merely an appendage of capital, it seems to lose its analytic relevance for Marxists except inasmuch as they can chart its empirical utility for the economy. A golden opportunity is thus missed to elaborate a galvanizing imagery not only of cultural resistance but of free cultural constitution transplanting its logic of essay to the entire social order. Ideology-critique in classical Marxist terms gives rise to *a new concept of the ideational and expressive* thus remaking the whole relationship between production and reproduction, public and private. The end of capital is the freedom from capital, as well as from its cultural supports—sexism, racism, scientism.

A new science reformulated as essay uses the opportunity to destroy capital's dominance of the seemingly only ideational as an occasion to rework all relationships between what has been taken to be the dichotomy of material and ideal, a rethinking that would reverse the order of priority of base and superstructure, with the latter now superordinate. This is not a version of idealism for it does not dismiss or ignore productive relations but submits them to what Marcuse (1955) called a "rationality of gratification" or (1964) "pacification." This version of science suggests discourse that submits the social to a literary will without pretending to transcend the ultimate nonidentity of subject and object. Text is an image of a free world in which determinative primacy falls to writing and not to the world it passively represents (even if, as I have said, reflection is far from passive or nonconstitutive). Writing is what we do to release ourselves from the tyranny of capital making writing only a device for distortion or the deepening of discipline—heterotextuality.

Text opposes the muteness imposed on us by capital ironically using writing only to complete its own prematurely reported version of totality. Muteness is required lest writing expose the near-totality as not-yet-totality on which writing as the exemplification of a new form of life could capitalize as the antithesis of capital's logic of total control. Although it could be said that the preoccupation with texts reflects only the sad fact that the only Marxists in the West are employed in universities and so deal with writing as their primary product, this is a preoccupation only if the very subordination of writing to the alleged requirements of material/social reproduction is ignored in favor of yet another version of transcendentalism. The denigration of the textual floats text above the world from which text struggles to disengage, yet another perpetually idealist subject whose imbeddedness in flesh and world is suppressed through what scientists love to call rigor, only intellectual Taylorism.

The mechanical Marxist legacy survives, even thrives, in an economistic society. At best, base-superstructure relations, if not decided explicitly in favor of the supremacy of the base (Engels and Althusser), are frozen by

Marxist "method" into unalterable modalities to be continued, it is implied, in socialism where, as in capitalism, ideation takes a back seat to production. Just to *distinguish* material and ideal methodically accepts the primacy of the material in a time and place when, indeed, the material enjoys primacy over ideas. The ideal distinction of ideal and material only reproduces the real distinction—one of hegemony—between them today. By contrast, essay is both a metaphor and practice of a nonauthoritarian politics of nonidentity, recognizing text's imbeddedness (Marx's "social being") and yet refusing the alleged primacy of production; the material or economy is a condition of text's existence. A worldly discourse can nonetheless rule the world where what has been millennially degraded as mere reproduction (writing, culture, thought) ascends over production in constituting the various forms of life from home to work. Marxist economism is infected by the general economism of the Enlightenment making instrumentality and machination veritable rules of reason—the sense of Horkheimer and Adorno's (1972) claim in *Dialectic of Enlightenment* that "enlightenment behaves towards things like a dictator toward people," perceiving their value only in their manipulability.[3]

The rule of production can only be broken by a new rule of gratification or here, of text, making self-expression the acknowledged motive of authorial desire and thus unhinging writing from the virtually Taylorist productivism of discipline. Today under the regime of representationality authorial minds and bodies are sacrificed to the relentless accumulation process only diverting thought and pen from their proper engagement with the power of the social. This is not to say one can simply "oppose" writing that takes its bearings from dominant literatures for criticism also attaches to the discipline disciplining it in its effort to excavate its suppressed desire as a way of exemplifying the possibility of reflexive versions. Rather, I want to confront mainstream writing's suppression of motive as a way of vitiating its dominance over other versions, unashamed to link advocacy with analysis in a text enacting qualitatively different subject-object relations from within text's own form of life. The first step is not simply referenceless writing purporting to be "new and different" in the tone of Madison Avenue hucksters but one offering a different version of the dominant social texts enmeshing us in their total administration.

Like art for the original Frankfurt theorists, particularly Adorno, writing is both a refuge from the absorbing ideational forces only streamlining the logic of capital and a life beyond the productivism reducing reason to an adaptive reasonableness through detextualizing method. I would choose essay over art as metaphors today because domination more frequently takes a textual form, thus requiring textual/political criticism directly confronting these disciplines with their own complicity in reproducing their frozen topics. Although art is surely an important part of the "text" of popular culture and, like science, deceives and diverts us, today it is less relevant to political reproduction than is science. This is precisely why Adorno pursued aesthetic resistance in the totally administered stage of capitalism. But it is not enough for self-expression to escape the reductive maw of culture/capital's main text; the center does not have to deal with margins so remote as to be unthreatening. This is not to reject Adorno and Derrida's attempts to shatter the reasonable sensibility of the modern but rather to incorporate it in a concept of writing resisting its own absorption by managing to live differently and yet also addressing the entrapping distortions of a representational version of science.

Although aesthetic opposition in a culturally commodified society threatens to lose its prefigurative, transformative moment, psychic survival, however it is obtained, is to be fostered. I say this in response to the crude insensitivities of an orthodox left that dismisses Adorno's aesthetic theory as treason "because" it lacks political blueprints—which buildings to capture, its economic plan? See Phil Slater's (1975) *Origin and Significance of the Frankfurt School* for an example of this political tendency. Text is at once resistance and new life nonidentically linked in the region between the surface version criticizing other versions for their self-suppression and demonstrating their real motives and its own self-understanding in light of subtext; thus, text suggests a writing that is both itself and an understanding of itself as something other—its carnal core.

Text is both identical and nonidentical to itself; its animation derives from its dual character in this respect. Writing suggests meaning not only in its constructions but also in ineffable echoes in these constructions from deep within the text, from its otherness, its nonidentity to itself—driving to live differently through words (that words alone cannot fulfill). I am suggesting a political *telos* of writing resembling but extending beyond Habermas's assertion that every speech act intends a consensus; differently, *every text intends a new world* it would bring into being through its own essay, reception, reworking. Text prefigures a community, ontology intending political theory—the more so that ontology is concealed in the sham of presuppositionless representationality.

The positivist version of science, too, intends a world, yet one it anchors inertly in being. It would improve on its version of being only by enhancing its own methodological being, thus enforcing a general conformity to it that, ironically, brings it to fruition. Science is a text uniquely eschewing its own otherness, its poetry and fiction, driving toward a future world only latent in the shape of the present. Positivist representationality thereby only courts the vengeful return of the repressed, the upsurge of demons from within eventually destroying science; world engulfs discipline in the epiphany of history when "social problems" finally resolve through the divine intervention of policy science (Diesing 1982). But science accepts its own impermanence even when it seems to refuse historicity in its enactment of the iterative logic eventually concentrating *everything* at a single center, text in its distance from the world no longer having a role to play, a version to write.

Having no death-wish of this sort, rather a *depth* wish, text could incorporate its self-understanding as a motivated writing; after all, commitment in Sartre's (1965b) sense only accepts one's authorial impulses without shame. Writing is essay, an attempt to live. Life lives between words, discourse its form. The writing contains a double surface of its argument—complexity arising from Merleau-Ponty's ambiguity—plunging simultaneously outward, into the world, and downward, into its own desires tellingly disclosed in its surface engagements. I have struggled with disciplinary sociology as a discourse of the power of the social provoking the version of the social characterized by deep inequalities. Sociology truncates the modern by concealing stratification in differentiation, the projects of Durkheim and Weber. This is not only my malaise, an existential problem one might say, but also a glimpse of the machinations of intellectual (re)production overwhelming thought—critique, anger, hope, love—with discipline. I write against sociology not in sorrow for a version somehow gone astray but in conviction that a betrayed intellectuality is somehow worth saving. My interest in sociology as a topic is not simply a reflection, in Marx or Mannheim's sense, of my vocation as a person paid to teach and write in sociology but reflects a political involvement in the critique of all socioontologizing texts of which sociology is an exemplary one, and in any case one that I know. This book would be useless exposition if it only dealt with its topic in a way severing that engagement from political desires to reveal this sort of methodical disciplining as deceptive and enmeshing, moving the world "forward" but not questioning the meaning of either world or forward.

This alternation between topic and my own desire only gaining momentum the more it is set loose on the topic—or as scientists would say, the more my argument is confirmed by evidence—is not simply an occasion for autobiography but is written into the fabric of the text as a search for the question appropriate to the answer with which I started, research in the literal sense of the word. In this way, writing works backward from the known to that which motivated the search in the first place, as always a *political* desire. I say that writing is inevitably political inasmuch as all text is animated by its desire to become a world, a constellation of dialogic sense and sentience.

This notion of the textual world returns me to the way I began, where I suggested that the power of a representational version of science is to blur fact into fate by calling forth certain enactments of it. Science disperses its sense into text-objects appearing to be pieces of nature, thus failing to call forth constitutive work acknowledging the nonidentity of reading and writing or text and world. All writing intends itself as transformation into certain social relations of it to itself, to nature, to others, and to history. Science is unique not in its inhabitance of the membrane between itself and the world but only in the way it veils this inhabitance methodically in the illusions of the transcendental subject that has no interest whatsoever in writing. This disciplinary text is only divination and not the rough work of what Lévi-Strauss (1966) called *bricolage,* putting the pieces together in a way that when finished it is no longer possible clearly to distinguish between part and whole, phrase and whole text, from which the notion of the hermeneutic circle or my version of writing as a decentered totality emerges.

Accepting its own nonidentity to itself, essay can more easily acknowledge the permeable boundary between itself and the world; the object to which it is nonidentical is the worldliness of our own bodies, drives, desire. Writing accepts its nonidentity in this way because it feels the pull of its own internal worldliness—pen, paper, days too short or too long, readers, criticism. This pull of history threatens to identify writing with the world and thus threatens its autonomy. The continuity between text and world is the rule and their rupture the exception, only present where the writing can accept its own mortality *and writes in its light,* forging mediation, thought, critique—nonidentity— where before there was only dumb immediacy. Subtext and text appear one and the same where either naively, unselfconscious of their own mutuality, or purposely science conceals its desire to return to the primal identity with the world to which it would return through its own deception that Marx earlier called ideology.

The future of sociology cannot be addressed independent of this or other meditations on the relationship between writing and the world. Such a project from within sociology has already begun, albeit hesitatingly, in the reflexive sociologies since the 1960s—Gouldner (1970), especially O'Neill (1972), whose work inspires much of my sense of the textual-political enterprise. But the time for those studies seems to have passed under pressure to hasten the development of disciplinary professionalism. In any case, the so-called sociology of sociology (Friedrichs 1970) is hampered by its very sociologism reducing text to context and yet giving itself a reprieve in the vaunted transcendentalism of all idealism up to Mannheim, intellectuals exempted from the interest and motive thought to muddy their account of the rest of the world.

I doubt that American sociology in its own terms would afford the pause to think, let alone rethink, its own textuality as a mode of being-in-the-world, propelled as is almost everything else in this productivist society by the drive to accumulate. What is called professionalism in emulation of the latter-day guilds with their own inclusion/exclusion principles stands in the way of the dedisciplining I advocate here, too comfortable with itself as a version that has finally arrived—professional association, stars, newsletters, conferences, journals. Sociology is so deeply infiltrated by scientism that it is not about to give up its purchase on institutional respectability or its somewhat distant but nonetheless prestigious relationship to the state in a process of thorough-going transvaluation. Indeed, such rethinking would be only proof of the discipline's postured multifariousness and not the invitation to disaccumulation that I intend

—the shattering of scientism and with it the discipline's collective identity ("at least we are all sociologists . . ."). This is why it is important to avoid the agenda-setting urging a new or better discipline; that only refurbishes the old with a brief period of self-scrutiny, invigorating precisely because it is only an *interregnum*. Sociology hinders its own transvaluation in the circular way that all such discussions must begin and end in identification with the disciplinary mission, however that may be defined on the surface. Agenda-setting only postpones a reckoning with the essentially affirmative role of science, its proclamations about sociology's service to humanity notwithstanding.

Even the language "what is needed is . . ." intends to be a first-construction necessarily forgetting the history of occlusion that has only facilitated domination. There is truly no before or after, only writing—in Adorno's sense, writing *from within*, trying to wriggle out by rewriting the main text in light of itself. Far from leaving the edifice intact, this subverts science's transcendental claims by showing the dirty work of artifice that, like the slave labors in Egypt, has consumed so many lives and minds. No sociology is possible after deconstruction, triggering a jealous rage on the part of those who have insisted on it as their contribution to social advancement, albeit one highly diluted through the deauthorizations of method. Commitment to the disciplinary norms of extant sociology as the discourse of the power of the social will invariably lead to a scientism rooted deeply in the comfort of professional identity refusing to think its approach to writing as disciplinarily *extraneous*, a concern to be more appropriately addressed in the philosophy of science or literary theory.

This misses the nonidentity of the text/world relationship that sociology shares with other social and natural sciences as well as with literature. At least until quantity and figure drive out all prose, the text of science will be a literary version that ought to be challenged to disclose its own imbeddedness in the desire to create a world that will never be entirely identical to itself and thus subject to the playful conversations of humanity. Writing that confronts its literariness is not conceding to insatiable subject but using that mark of its inherent worldliness as ingress to a world in which it particularly participates through the various forms of life joining subject and object. By denying its literariness in this sense, science rejects its own worldliness in a puritan gesture. The desire for identification, text melting into world, reflects its insecurity about its own world-constitutive status as well as its ineluctable carnality. Essay plays itself out in writing that both accepts its motivation by desire and yet employs that desire to distance itself from the present world in the mediation called thought, profoundly understood by all idealism as the basis of both hope and imagination.[4]

That people write attests to the identical nonidentity forever haunting writing as the awareness of its own necessary incompleteness—necessary both because it has to be (text never being entirely world) and because we should *want* it to be. Essay accepts writing's political purpose as the circuitry flowing back and forth between text and topic, the attempt to create a world with "mere" words. Avoiding programmatic pleas or mandates to which the text would only pay lip-service, one might hope that captives of the main text would, confronting the literariness of their versions, thus enable themselves to appropriate their own desire in an authorizing way. Disciplinary decentering begins when the falsely accumulated margins resist the eternity of their servitude to the official canon.[5]

It is not enough for the main text to acknowledge its human foundation (values, theory-ladenness), for that acknowledgment, if isolated from the literary practice of everyday journal science, will itself be integrated into the intellectual production process. The text cannot change without already being different from what it is in reality, namely a decentering version eschewing absolutism and recognizing that the center should be at the margins, no writing claiming other writings as its own. So a new sociology must be decentered by renegade texts it has captured that burst out of its force field and thus gain lives of their own as both critiques of the center and constitutive forms of life in their own right—intellectual and political life beyond the compass of the enmeshing, deadening discipline. It is impossible to disentangle a "new" sociology from the positivist legacy of the discipline to now. Yet it is not too much to hope that some sociologists may address—are already addressing—their own authoriality and thus political practice as an opening to a new version of versions not only envisaging but constituting a nonheteronomous, nonidentical world in which writing is valuable praxis as well as communication, exemplification as much as explanation.

It is hard to know what to call a decentered, disciplined version shorn of the mock certainties of reflection and thus reproduction. "Discipline" would no longer refer to its institutionalized organization and oppression but to an authorial confrontation with the worldliness of text, a generic form of free labor. Whether or not people would still practice "sociology" in the university matters less than whether they would write beyond the coordinates of science's/society's suppression of motive only neutralizing transformative forms of life by encoding text with the ontologized surface appearances of the power of the social. When I advocate dialectical writing, I recognize that mainstream sociology only integrates dialectic as a necessitarian logic of productivism and economism paralleling the logic of capital. It also integrates advocacy as the insufficiency of good intentions. Indeed this proclivity for integration is why I despair of programmatic manifestos within the aegis of the extant discipline.[6] *Thought drives not to identify but to disaffiliate,* a tendency that should not be explained reductively in terms of individual psychopathology but understood as an invariant feature of literary mind. It is not that bad things have happened to me within my home discipline but that my home discipline disciplines—

that is, it purges thought of the Dionysian as scholarship. In this, of course, sociology is only one among a million practices that reproduce and thereby sustain.

Although sociology counts for little organizationally, unbeknownst to itself it has (hetero)textual significance for the modal version of metaphysics it provides, stemming originally from Durkheim's statement of method where he charged sociology with a depiction of the power of the social. Since Durkheim, sociology has added to the general text reproducing history by scientizing it, eliciting subordination by entrenching it in social nature—the contingency of action on lawful social processes defying their textual/political transvaluation. New sociology intending novelty primarily as hurried but largely insubstantial modification of a mainstream literature and disciplinary practice, regarding "novelty" as yet another legitimation of its own hold over the center, is not only illusory but downright intellectually degrading. Beyond keeping faculty and publishers employed, endless iterations of the same basic text only affirm the original literature and disqualify other versions as disciplinary subversions. American sociology will not undo itself; it is a center of intellectual/social power; it weakly colonizes writings it has ripped out of their own contexts of desire. The reality of power cannot be overcome by any text in itself, although text is a component of power. Base and superstructure are dialectically nonidentical. Like Marx's ideology-critique, disciplinary decentering would spark the revolt of illegitimate knowledges struggling to attain dialogical and thus political mutuality.

To freight writing—culture, superstructure, intimacy, desire—with expectations about its likelihood of overthrowing the very power invading texts with the imperatives of total administration only diminishes the likelihood that textual practice will be politically transvaluing. Writing is an adequate lifeworld only to the extent to which it invites, and reciprocates, *other versions;* without that it remains private language, deluded that the world will heel to its advocacy. Text is not omnipotent because no one, thing, or principle is omnipotent in a world characterized essentially by heterogeneity, complexity, and nonidentity. Writing is not ancillary to other seemingly more productivist practices; that is a formulation of text's heteronomy, hence insufficiency, typically subordinating subject to object. But defiant writing does risk monologue and thus its own lack of social efficacy. No amount of communication theory will change the fact that theory communicates to very few today, this book included. Of course, that is reason to write, not to succumb. In spite of Habermas's contention that speech always intends consensus, this consensus is often not achieved, nor are the nonauthoritarian subject-object relations remaining the global goal of critical theory. The world frustrates any version that risks falling on uncomprehending ears, either suppressing the text in question (dismissed as nonscience, propaganda, or the like) or integrating it in a way that inverts its meaning and further ecumenizes the main text in its relentless accumulation process.

The assurance of friendly readings and thus other versions can only be derived from education, that is, from writing that has already been understood as a legitimate voice. But this describes an infinite regress where one writing must always prepare the way for another en route. *Programmatic foundation setting that builds new writing on the architecture of critique goes beyond itself by writing in the voice it recommends,* refusing or simply being unable to separate process and product. Writing circularly seeks a readership that must be present already, the timeworn dilemma of educating the educator. Perhaps this is to say nothing more than that the quest for a readership is as problematic as the search for a new world. Indeed, they are one and the same process, effected only in the serendipitous play of history, politics, and language overdetermining the present only as we can retrospectively understand it as a more or less linear product of the past. But life cannot be lived backward anymore than it can be lived without looking backward in retrieving the play of concatenated circumstances bringing us to where we are. Although perhaps a certain version will prove more effectively transvaluing in the long run, like the surprise bestseller it cannot be predicted.

"Communication" is deception raised to the level of technique. It aspires to presage the audience that must already exist in order for writing to be understood, the fateful necessity of works that no longer bear the blurry imprint of their own craft and thus are received uncritically. Communication as ideology is a means of political reproduction, a standard of writing against which critique is always found wanting—failure to speak clearly, offer a definite blueprint of social change, or play fair with its topics. Indeed a critique of communication risks its own dismissal as a nihilistic rejection of lucidity when in fact the possibility of clear language is problematic in an age of socially structured mystification. Ironically mystification takes place under the very banner of its seeming opposite, communication.

Although writing is no less blameless for the falling rate of intelligence than any practice, it is no more so either. The most truthful writing is frequently the least accessible if access involves surface familiarity with the jargons interposed by texts between readers and writers in order to deceive. Lucidity itself is a deception where it pretends that the truth is an object, the world flat and without historical depth, and that words only represent the unalterably given— thus covering over the constitutiveness of writing as a material practice. Dialectical prose neither attempts to simplify the complexly overdetermined world nor conveys its sense of this complexity in a language purposely simplified into the world's naming of *itself*—for example, democracy is what American leaders say it is. We can learn something from the way reality names itself. But we cannot simply use its words for things in a way that would tell the world differently. We must make language exhume the meanings it secretly suppresses.

The text is reduced in the name of communication precisely in order to deny the possibility of a version that could contain the contradictions eluding "common sense" without itself pretending a new closure. The issue is not decipherment, for nonidentical writing is not a code underneath which the world can be reduced to identity, ever the false hope of scientism. Rather reading works hard to follow the alternatives, interpretations, and shadows of a text necessarily engaging an overdetermined world shrouding itself in identity that therefore must be uncovered. Its intentionality must be traced downward to desire and then outward to the world to which its desire belongs and to which it wants to return as transformative energy. Text is no one-way street —concept "to" world—but the play of itself and its own motive, *freedom,* against the occlusions that are its topics. Nonidentical prose tries to overcome identity in a way that would provoke readers to do the same in their own practices.[7]

The insufficiency of earlier Frankfurt images of a demystifying discursive practice is that they do not transcend the monadology of an idealism forced in the sheer isolation of consciousness to address directly the communicative tissue of texts and readings reproducing the current subordination of reproduction —here, text—to production. Habermas's communication theory corrects early critical theory with this dialogical focus, although I am uncertain whether he sufficiently surpasses the framework of liberal communication regarding writing and reading merely as the production and consumption of representational images—information, ideas, whatever. In any case, literary practice is crucial today because so much of what we know and are is lived through the various texts of the time especially where writing is dispersed into the built and figural environment, thus in effect preempting any mediating reception, an issue to which I will return below.

The admonition to speak plain English—to communicate—centers defiant voices within the orbit of discipline's comprehensibility. Critical theory is dismissed by sociology not because it fails to get its facts straight but because it does not even try; instead, it addresses the possible dialectical motion of those frozen pieces of history, unthawing them by revealing them to be constructions of literary artifice. As much as science would assail critical theory for its isolation, even an infantile inability to "speak clearly," at least critical theory accepts its permeation by worldly interest, not suppressing it as a distortion of its lucidity. It even abandons lucidity as a prop of the obscuring, enmeshing project of scientism that writes linearly precisely in order to preclude the possibility of a nonlinear literariness—a self-conscious transformation of the positivist form of life. Clarity constrains writing from evoking and thus enacting the complex nonidentity of subject and object that is the primary hope of a version refusing to be disciplined into sheer reproduction. Common sense is commonly oppressed by its own abandonment of the desire within that could otherwise allow it to burst forth both as a worldly form of life and, vitally, the preservation of a critical distance from it.

Nonidentical writing rejects linearity because it cannot penetrate the surface of its own imbeddedness in the world, thus failing to understand itself in an irreducible relationship to the given. But it does not simply exchange a studied complexity for the linear in a way that fetishizes obscurity or a precious aestheticism. Instead, it tries to make itself understood within the constraints of the oppressive reduction of language to the superficial—simple reflection—without taking responsibility for its comprehension or distortion by other versions, acknowledging the dilemma of comprehension in a world that does not understand itself (let alone understands itself understanding). Such a text hopes to be understood, tries its best to be, but without obscuring the enormous dilemma of bridging between knowledge and the known, writer and reader, which cannot be crossed a priori or through a conventionalized "communication" only translating old banalities into "new."

This was Wittgenstein's problem at the end of *Tractatus-Logico Philosophicus* where he concluded that language is an imperfect vehicle for what is now facilely called "communication" simply because one cannot speak directly or read of what one does not yet know. Luckily, the knowledge/ignorance relationship is itself dialectical, suggesting bridging practices that somewhat ease the relationship between (dialectical) writer and (linear) reader, ever acknowledging the impediments to unproblematic understanding. After all, although socially situated (Sapir-Whorff), language borrows from what one might call universal presentiments, archetypes, or structures allowing for linguistic differentiation and variation within some common frameworks or, as Kant called them, categories of understanding. These shared frameworks of meaning that ultimately must exist for community to be possible have been the basis of western rationalism from Descartes and Kant through structural linguistics (Saussure and Chomsky), anthropology (Lévi-Strauss) and, most recently, the "universal pragmatics" or communication theory of Habermas (building on Searle and Apel).[8]

Critical writing surpasses idealism in the nature of its political self-understanding as a text advocating (even when it appears only to be analyzing) a certain relationship between subject and object, itself and its own subtext, other people, nature, the world at large. Politics here is nothing more than the self-consciousness of one's posture toward one's own desire, notably about how it is formative and thus inescapable—and thereby can be reformulated, if only incompletely. Viewed this way, politics requires a commitment to its own transformative literariness in order to address the relationship between its motives and what it declares in the way of advocacy. Similarly, theory implies a kind of politics in the way it directs its self-understanding as committed literature to the task of further, deepened commitment, enlightening its advocacy by instructing it about the nature and context of the advocate herself/himself.

All writing intends a certain subject-object relationship even if it is only the one it strikes to itself and the world; in the case of science politics is merely exemplification. Description solicits acquiescence by acquiescing to the supposedly inert. In this way, all writing has an audience for which it is (and advocates) one or another version of the world. Again—all writing is political in its constitutive relationship to the social world, intending to change the world in every utterance. Science acts politically precisely when it suppresses its own political nature and thus gives the lie to the reasons it offers for its own rejection of a more overt political rhetoric either as intellectually disreputable or simply as private language—rage the failure to "communicate." Cleansing or bracketing procedures will neither eliminate the worldliness of writing nor guarantee it an audience. The science/nonscience distinction fails where readers cannot be uplifted out of interest in a text that must on that basis speak to them in their own tongue. Writing necessarily faces the dilemma of seeking a competent readership without which it cannot be received and yet that would by definition obviate the necessity for writing altogether; readerly competence is only a euphemism for preunderstanding.[9] Unlike a representational version of science, of discipline, we cannot simply ignore this dilemma of educating the educator. Instead we confront it as the central challenge of politics—to create intersubjectivity out of subjectivity, form consensus, reach agreement, a "process" that, as I have argued, is also a "product," a form of life simultaneously strategy and outcome. Yet it does not presume that a fully intersubjective text is possible beyond the heterodox versions fragilely comprising it.

In a better world there would be no margins or centers but only different degrees of authorial consensus, depending on the historical character of subject-object relations or simply politics. Essay would self-consciously seek this identity within the guiding axiology of nonidentity in which every writing is deemed worthy or at least irreducible to any other or to a singular center —tradition, literature, or regime. This version celebrates its own literariness as the artificelike nature of a version unashamed to become a world, simultaneously belonging to and remaining separate from the world bringing it forth. Science is not superior to fiction; fiction includes science as one of its literary possibilities, simply another version of authorial self-consciousness, albeit one that, unlike poetry, explicitly claims validity—a way of being-in-the-world with other people, nature, and one's own mortality. Center/margin is a construction imbued with the historicity of domination, a category of political understanding if not of all possible understanding. Every text intends itself as a new center but fails to attain it because there are both internal and external barriers—desire plus other people—that shatter identity before it congeals into the inertness of a social glacier, thawing as soon as it hits the air. I want to build a good polity around this alternation of identity and nonidentity, a literariness that is nothing less than a political "strategy."

The art of the political, then, is in elaborating a world literarily without expecting it will be everyone's world, or even anyone's. Nonetheless we may arrive eventually at a semblance of a decent community in which the epochal question of center and margin has finally been put to rest; the quest for apodicticity has been abandoned as yet another motive of domination, science's laws stilling writing's resistance altogether. Stalwart materialists will respond by saying that writing is an insufficient model of human practice, probably opting for imagery of labor from Marx, Smith, or Ricardo. Yet its seeming insufficiency is itself an artifact of a certain history in which intellection and self-expression are subordinated to the production of exchange-value. Writing is "only" writing in a world in which writing writes representationally to become a world that would have no use for different versions, anymore than capital has use for labor that does not expend itself in the creation of surplus value. But it is politically important to insist on the value of seemingly valueless activity lest we fail to undo the order of value making it so.

If this notion of a textual politics seems inadequate to those weaned on more traditional concepts of politics, whether liberal or Marxist, then so much the worse for politics. Politics today is what it has to be, not what we want it to be in a better world. The hegemony of text today in a world in which reproduction must be provoked requires us to interrogate the self-subordination of writing to discipline. Marx took ideology seriously because ideology abounded to suppress recognition of the structural possibilities of the emancipation of labor. In other words, he wanted to open ontology to the light of historical becoming. He wrote ideology-critique because he recognized that the only way around was through.

Doing New Science: Construction, Deconstruction, Reconstruction

Just as Marx did more than criticize bourgeois political economy, opening a vision of nonalienated labor while opposing alienated labor, I want to extend my critique of a discipline in a way showing the possibility of nonalienated literary activity—call it science, fiction, or essay. Deconstruction overcomes its own postmodernist skepticism about objective knowledge—hence reason—in a reflexive version of science. The crude caricature of positivism embraced by many American social scientists has been untrue to natural science's own self-understanding at least since relativity theory. Indeed, Heisenberg's principle of indeterminacy in suggesting that measurement necessarily changes its object is a Derridean notion par excellence. That a positivist version of science prevails does not mean that we must abandon objective knowledge, thus speculative reason, in favor of the decentered play of an infinity of signifiers. Essaying a nonpositivist version of science is itself a way of doing science in a mode of dialogical democracy. The only shame attached to the word "science" today is prompted by our inability to think why we are under its spell. It is not only that science can liberate but also that science, literarily self-understood as a mode of happy, humble community-building, *already liberates*.

Let me amplify this by relating something I heard on the news. A broadcaster announced that 69 percent of all Americans supported President Reagan's actions in bombing Libya for their alleged involvement in terrorism directed against Americans abroad. This is bad science *not* because it is or was untrue; I am not concerned with science's validity per se but only with the ground of its validity claims—again, understanding science as literature, rhetoric, argument. We are unsure of the protocol used in generating what it claims to be knowledge. Were people asked, Do you support the President? Do you support dropping bombs on Tripoli? Do you support the killing of Libyans, including infants? The science in question did not even understand the basis of its *own* validity claims. Thus, the very term "to support" is a construction; as such, it could be varied to produce the number of, say, 22 percent if, alternatively, Americans were asked whether they supported killing Libyan children.

I am not saying that the number 22 is any truer than the number 69 but only that the newscast did not stipulate the conditions of validity when it suggested that Americans supported the president's actions. Even more important, the science in question *did not argue for one construction of validity over another,* showing the political interest behind one or another attempt to construct the generic notion of support in certain protocol statements. Good science here would not only understand its own version of the term "support the president" as a construction but would argue *for* that construction in a committed way, that is, with the intent to persuade. As Habermas said, all speech acts intend consensus—they intend to persuade, provoke empathy, change the world, science no less than *King Lear*, *Portnoy's Complaint*, or the *Communist Manifesto*.

So the problem with the Libyan question as science is both that we do not know what 69 percent signifies and we do not hear and thus cannot rebut the argument for that signification in terms of authorial desire—that is, in light of political aims. Good science would *both* exhume its own construction of the word "support"—in other words, here, what question the sample was asked—and *then* it would defend this construction in terms of its impact on text itself, science a fiction in the sense it listens to itself write and makes this echo of authoriality directly a topic. In the case of Libya, deconstructive reading would probably conclude tellingly that many Americans wanted to *drop* bombs over Libya but self-contradictorily did not want them to *land* on unspecified civilians.

The concept of good science implies a concept of good politics as well as a

constitutive means to achieve it. Deconstruction strengthened with the emancipatory agenda of critical theory suggests that the best world is optimally
heterogeneous, displaying the text's inherence in a subtext of indomitable desire that writing makes a topic in the back-and-forth of its own reflection and
self-reflection. Where the representational model of text wants only to "communicate," a one-way process of production and reception, a deconstructive
text builds community out of discourses self-understood as necessarily decentering and undecidable. In this it models an intertextual politics that does not
short-circuit the dialectic of product and process—a humane society *and at
once* the route to achieve it.

Adorno for his part suggested that the only credible textual politics in an
era when language has been almost totally divested of its power to refuse,
to negate, works through the world's contradictions "from within," undoing
the secret affinity of text with a world to which it would unhesitatingly attach
itself as its source of meaning. This notion of negation is an explicit contrast
to Lenin's claim that the early twentieth-century Russian proletariat required
texts "from without," from a vanguard, thus sealing the subsequent history of
socialism as a dictatorship over the proletariat buttressed by a Marxist-Leninist
scientism—faith in dialectic—no less disempowering than the scientism of the
western countries. This version of Adorno in turn suggests a more explicitly
political deconstruction reading the objectivist texts of science and culture
against themselves as the real fictions that they are—where "fiction," unlike
science, does not connote falsehood but alternatively writing's openness to
its own desire as the foundation of a dialogical community of many writers,
what Habermas calls the ideal speech situation.[10] Science subordinates fiction
to itself as escapist illusion, affording spiritual uplift in an otherwise implosive
bourgeois culture. Yet deconstruction shows the untruth of a version of science
that represses its own purposeful construction of a signified world; as such, it
is a political strategy of sorts, if a somewhat unusual one in these times when
writing is at once everywhere and nowhere.

In the fashion of Derrida where he declares that the margins are really at
the center, I would add that fiction is not inadequate science but rather generic
discourse where science is a discursive version unprivileged with respect to
other discourses. This helps us address the timeworn problem of educating the
educator or, in different terms, of a vanguard or new class. The very construction of a science/fiction contrast is science's way of gaining primacy over the
merely conversational, common sense, everyday, and literary, basing political
authority on epistemological privilege deriving from the derogation of nonscience. This allows me to return to my earlier critique of Marx's physicalist
notion of ideology as a *camera obscura,* false consciousness simply inverting
the world in order to sustain it. Let me continue with some observations
about what a different conception of science's ideology means for a canoni-

cal Marxism still haunted by the Soviet experience sustained by a heritage of Marxism, mechanism, and scientism. In rethinking and, thus, I hope, reliving ideology as a textual practice intermediating writer and reader in a gentle political community, I am moving away from Marx's notion of ideology simply as an inversion of the real, to be made right in a future social order. Instead, ideology is writing that in concealing its own artifice reproduces a readership that lives out its own unfreedom—freely, as it were, ever the irony of oppression.

Although I agree with Sartre that Marxism is the thought of our time in the sense that human practice cannot be understood without some reference to the immensity of the world that capital so inexorably colonizes, most extant Marxisms continue to fixate on the male proletariat, the supposed necessity of a dialectic of nature as an adequate model of history and a quite reductive understanding of relations between so-called base and superstructure or world and text. More sharply, Marxism, like representational versions of science, continues to fetishize the productive, the realm of largely male wage labor, ignoring the allegedly nonproductive as a concern of merely superstructural analysis, whether sociology of art, feminism, or literary criticism. As such Marxism disciplines nonproductivist versions and practices, entrenching the masculinist/productivist subordination of reproduction, whether housework or text, to male wage labor and its positivist iteration.

A more adequate understanding of ideology as a disempowering writer-reader relationship is achieved not through this version of Marxism but rather in thematizing the relationship *between* production and reproduction as the central problematic of the age, addressing how and why people continue to acquiesce to their own victimhood. Like sexuality and housework, texts seemingly belong to the realm of the nonvalorized and nonpolitical millennially reserved for women, a segregation Marxism too often perpetuates in its denigration of the realm of domesticity, culture, and science merely as superstructure. On this reading feminism is not simply "about women" except as women have had the historic responsibility for reproduction. More globally it is about the subordination of reproduction to production, private to public, fiction to science, women to men, and unpaid to paid labor.[11] If feminism is understood as a critique of all reproductive relations, then a critical theory of the text is a feminist topic even if the text in question is not ostensibly about or written and read by women.

It is increasingly obvious that Marxism is incomplete without feminism and feminism incomplete without Marxism, each comprehending the fractured halves of a world split between outside and inside, ever the epochal theme of western dualism that the Frankfurt School contends is the deepest subtext of oppression. Yet Marxism like mainstream social science continues to deepen the subordination of reproduction—women, texts, the unwaged—by treating their subordination somehow as derivative from labor's domination by capital, a notion frequently wrong and in any case politically arrogant. And through science, whether left, right, or center, this conceptual hierarchy reproduces the world it mistakes for being itself. This is not to say, in Marxist language, that contradictions have been mechanically displaced from the economic to socio-cultural and sexual spheres as if the more fundamental contradictions were ever originally economic in nature. It is rather to suggest that *any* distinction between production and reproduction, world and text, science and culture, work and household inevitably redounds to the advantage of production, the world, science, and work, respectively. The oldest form of domination is the split between center and margin, the useful and unuseful; this is only further amplified in the subsequent dualities of capital/labor, man/woman, and white/black. Deconstruction crucially suggests a politics blurring the reproduction/production contrast, margin always center and vice versa, each equally worthy.

What we need, then, to risk agenda-setting even if I offend doctrinal de-constructionists who think they can avoid construction altogether, is a version resisting its own subordination to the seemingly more significant practice of production. This is to subsume the critique of sexual politics under a more global critique of textual politics—of what I have called *heterotextuality*—that reads and thus resists the various discourses of discipline from television to textbooks generically subordinating us to the power of the social. It is no longer adequate and *probably never was* to combat bourgeois positivism with a socialist version of it, thus only perpetuating people's self-subordination to expertise, texts seeming to require no reading and thus rewriting.

To the extent to which Marxism has become another oppressive canon against the effort to relive it in the permanent revisionisms of deconstructive essay and ethics, it is no less oppressive than the bourgeois science it dismisses simply as a world upside down, waiting to be put right by politically correct scientists. As all reproduction, writing will only become worthy, an archetype of free society, when practice is not split into the productive and merely reproductive; that choice is the essence of politics today. Perhaps it is virtually impossible in these times to distinguish between the camera reflecting an upside down world and the world itself, no longer possible to separate the discourses hemming us in and the world to which they would bind us in a thoughtless enactment of what they purport to freeze in one-dimensional description.

This is not to conclude by saying that text would replace labor or for that matter gender or race as a postmodernist fetish, each "age" embracing its own supposedly unique logos, but only to acknowledge the thoroughgoing over-determination of oppression by discourses disqualifying our possible author-ship. Whatever space remains open for self-emancipation in an incredibly administered world must be cultivated and thereby enlarged first in writing since our lifeworlds are already saturated with the enmeshing signifiers of family, politics, science, religion, and entertainment. As yesterday's ideologies, today's texts defy their ready demystification by a literary mode of resistance, defining their falseness with reference to unambiguous standards of evidence.

Although the deconstruction of positivist social science is not a substantial contribution to overall emancipation, one insight of a decentering version of science written under the sign of poststructuralism is that every contribution addressing local problems is as necessary as every other simply because people are dying everywhere. The discourse of the power of the social extends beyond sociology, defining the decentered variety of a positivist culture. The first sociologists were perhaps only especially sensitive to the emerging nature of discipline in mid-capitalism. Likewise, I do not mean to concoct a new master text—a new social science, new Marxism, new feminism, new literary criticism—measuring up to the logocentric standards of closure better than science does itself; that is precisely how Marxism got itself into trouble in the first place, thinking itself as what Marx called a natural science of history —another unfortunate formulation of discipline. Indeed, the deconstruction of deconstruction too frequently reveals a groundless Nietzschean resignation rejecting the prospect of the negation of negation as yet another mythic version of the gullibly, cheerfully positive—an advertising slogan promising a whole new world, a whole new text, thus only subordinating readers anew.

The notion of negation's negation need not falsely promise totality. Instead it might simply offer a glimpse of the *not-negative,* as appropriate an imagery of utopia as I can imagine in a world in which politics is so often terror and thought mindlessness. Intellect today is debased into the cliches of popular culture or an academic productivism measuring thought in dollar signs and citations. Deconstruction as an interpretive methodology in English departments betrays its allegiance to the marginal, the non-negative, a world that does not close or totalize. An embarrassingly minimalist political agenda would urge writing to hold out against what Sartre called its own institutionalization, its own reduction to method, as a way of retaining at least a modicum of autonomy. Accordingly, Marxist, feminist, and poststructuralist would frequently need to take up the pen against those who, by calling themselves Marxist, feminist, and poststructuralist, like sociologists, thereby entrench a new center whose implacability precludes dialogue.

Whether art or science, essay is inadequate politics. Yet we must interrogate the notion of adequacy as part of the political process. Otherwise, the texts inspiring us will be our tombstones.

Slowing Down Fast Capitalism

By this point the critical reader might say that I talk *about* good or new science listening to itself write but I fail to listen to my own account, thus disciplining anew. Let me try to check that tendency here. The only way to avoid the degeneration of insight into method is to avoid it—working out an argument taking itself to a higher plane of understanding from which dialogical practice can proceed. Essays are not planned to the last detail; like this book, they have their own logic. We can either learn from the serendipity of nonpositivist writing, thus inviting other versions, or simply conclude, as too many postmodernists do, that reason is yet another bourgeois chimera. If I really thought it was, I would hardly bother to write. To some extent, essay opposes the eclipse of reason; it does not welcome it. I write "about" writing; but I do not forget that in doing so I am *already* writing. In this last section, I want to recoup my heuristic attempt to put my own argument at one remove from itself, even though I realize that concluding is not method quieting metaphysical doubts but only dialectical circularity.

I consider the political and methodological implications of my critical theory of discipline for an overall critical theory moving from agenda-setting to new intellectual/political constitution itself. The distinction between writing "about" and writing "beyond" fades the more we think deconstructively about the mutuality of texts and their topics. It is fair to say that I have *already* presented a version of an analytically and politically more relevant critical theory in the way I have read sociology. Engaged by sociology as a discourse of discipline, my account reduces discipline through a different version of discourse. I read sociology not as a sociologist but as an opponent of discipline; sociology for its part usually refuses to read critical theory. Here I will make critical theory itself my topic, having presupposed all of what has gone before. This does not marginalize my earlier argument as prolegomenon any more than it renders what I am about to write an exemplary appendix or programmatic research design. I am not calling "for" new theory but writing it directly, keeping in mind, indeed exemplifying, the principles of dialogical self-interrogation, of essay, I drew out of my extended deconstruction of sociology. My strong critique of disciplinary sociology as a literary practice purposely losing its mind in method gives me the momentum to write more positively a version of critical theory shedding light on the impasses and possibilities of the historical present. Yet against methodical deconstruction (and with Marx) I refuse to allow sociology to arrogate empirical analysis to itself. Disciplinary reading can illuminate the world concealed in it.

My disciplinary reading has opened the way for a more general formulation of the nature of ideology. Books have outcomes; of course, for critical theory and deconstruction that is the wrong way to pose the question of their worldliness. Yet my reading of sociology contributes to a more empirically and politically relevant critical theory. Indeed, these two aims are inseparable; the one exemplifies the other. A disciplinary critique suggests an overall critical theory of texts helping us understand and then overcome the ways in which history decides writing for us and not writing history. In my rethinking of an adequate account of the nature of ideology as a way of reading a discipline, I have employed some recent insights from poststructuralist literary theory and feminist theory, notably in the way Derrida and others conceive of the relationship between writing and the reality writing purports to represent, or in feminist terms between reproduction and production. This admittedly courts the further academization of critical theory. On the surface, at least, deconstruction and even French feminism seem to offer little of empirical and political value. At the outset, let me only assert and then try to develop the empirical and thus political significance of poststructuralist feminist literary theory for my version of critical theory.

Although left theorists rightly resist intellectual trendiness for its own sake, developments in poststructuralism and feminism significantly advance the analytic and thus political task of opposition, notably in the way they help us think more deeply about the nature of ideological reproduction. For Marx originally, texts like Adam Smith's *Wealth of Nations* and the Bible stood apart from the reality they attempted to reflect. Marx held that ideology modeled on bourgeois economic theory or religion essentially *falsifies* an otherwise straightforward reality, thus serving the instrumental interests of class domination. For Marx falsification only entrenches people's false servitude to the allegedly intractable institutions of the time by convincing them that the world cannot be changed. Marx on the basis of his historical materialism claims a validity for his own *repudiation* of representationally falsifying claims as distortions of the real—untruths that he contends serve functionally the interest of domination by inculcating a love of fate among their readers. For Marx ideological texts misrepresent the real in eternalizing domination, whether capitalist economic patterns portrayed as laws or earthly suffering excused by the promise of eventual salvation in an afterlife. Thus, for Marx the *critique of ideology* would show these falsifying and disempowering ideological constructions to be misrepresentations designed to both justify and thus perpetuate the existing social order.

The second distinctive approach to the conceptualization of ideology emerged in the 1920s first with Lukacs and Korsch's Hegelian Marxism and then with the critical theory of the Frankfurt School. In no way do these so-called western Marxists retract or recant Marx's understanding of ideology as a falsifying and thus self-reproducing claim. Rather they attempt to deepen Marx's straightforward search for a version of science that could penetrate ideological illusions. In particular they contend that even the *language* of truth or science has been *mystified* such that we find it virtually impossible to think or talk about the world in terms readily capturing the possibility of a different future. Words mean *both* themselves *and* their opposites. For example, the word "pacification" comes to describe an aggressive military maneuver in

Vietnam, and the term "freedom" signifies the ability to choose among trivially different political parties or brand names.

Marcuse's (1964) notion of one-dimensionality suggests that ideology-critical texts themselves tend to fall victim to the dominant currencies of power and thus only reproduce that power. Even the classical argot of original Marxism succumbs to its mystification as notions like Marxism and socialism are used to describe and exhort thoroughly non-Marxist practices in eastern Europe and elsewhere. For the Frankfurt School, Marxism does not have privileged access to a presuppositionlessly Archimedean language of critique positively penetrating the falsehoods of classical political economy and Judeo-Christian religion with respect to a self-evident criterion of validity. Instead Marxism itself too frequently fails to reflect on the grounds of its own validity claims, thus ironically reinforcing a disempowering representationality, precisely Habermas's point in *Knowledge and Human Interests* (1971).

Where Marx wrote ideology critique to right an upside down world seen through the camera obscura of bourgeois thought and culture, the Frankfurt School attempts to *rectify language* by disengaging it from the world it so thoughtlessly reflects. Far from being antiscience, the Frankfurt School's critical theory would invigorate science but only by disentangling it from pregiven meanings preventing us from grasping the historicity of the social world and thus projecting the possibility of a dialectically different future. In particular, Frankfurt theory empirically shows the duplicitous ironies of mystifying languages that conceal their own subtexts of political desire—namely, to reproduce by reflecting the given order of things; critical theory methodically *makes falsehood speak the truth,* where putatively value-free claims are historicized and thus read to be accurate if context-bound evocations of the given. For example, Parsons and colleagues' (1955) naming of universal patriarchal family, once historicized as the disciplinary text it is, tells a powerful truth about the way men and women are differentially assigned to the realms of waged instrumentality and unwaged expression. Critical theory reads Parsons and Bales as the ironic authors of dialectical critique—the *suppression* of their text's historicity *revealing* its ideological drive and force. We must understand that Parsons attempted to *prove* "family" by provoking familied practices, the nature of all disciplining suggesting itself as naturelike necessity.

Unfortunately neither Marx nor the Frankfurt School adequately addresses the nature of ideology in what I have called a fast or late capitalism. Whether there were intrinsic weaknesses in their original formulations is irrelevant; our responsibility is to improve on them. Let hagiophiles go back to the original texts. Both Marx and western Marxists assume the autonomy of texts, of writing, sufficiently standing apart from the material world that they can understand their own complicity in reproducing it. Although Adorno in his *Negative Dialectics* (1973a) and *Minima Moralia* (1974) despairs of writing clearly about a labrynthine late capitalism, he and after him Derrida, Foucault, and others working within the broad current of poststructuralism recognize that this representational model of writing's subservience to a world external to it is empirically false; in fast capitalism the lines between text or ideology and reality blur to such an extent that ideology oozes out from between the covers of books into the world itself, thus making true/false distinctions enormously problematic.

Texts are displaced into the object world such that *they cannot be read as purposeful, authored constructions at all and thus they cannot be rewritten.* This only extends the logic of commodification originally understood by Marx to freeze all social relations, indeed all intellection, into intractably natural patterns. Thus, Lukacs's concept of reification, Marx's commodity fetishism, and my own notion of dispersed texts are essentially the same, although I tease out its meaning through theories of interpretation ostensibly outside the ambit of Marxist discourse.

Ideology in fast capitalism increasingly is encoded in methodology, edifice, figure, and money. The authorship of these "texts" is suppressed, making them difficult to read at a distance. Instead the worlds they covertly recommend are read instantaneously—thus enacted. Texts today are less between covers than out in the streets, in public spaces, buildings, homes, movies, and talk itself. Writing has been dispersed precisely so that it cannot be read, criticized, reformulated. Writing no longer enjoys an autonomy from the reality it addresses but is now deceptively part of it, although deconstruction can reveal the dispersed texts—the buildings, movies, and sciences—to have *once* been written (my effort here in reading sociology). *The postmodern era in this regard virtually dispenses with textuality as such, although its encoded textuality speaks more powerfully for all that.* In fast capitalism image and reality blur to such an extent that reality seems elusive and ephemeral, hard to grasp in the representational categories of science. In addition, images take on a reality of their own as they become displaced texts lived only as they are read, like Parsons's family, above. Our ability to read and thus rewrite our public environments is diminished to the extent to which the authorship of material practices is concealed in the naturelike appearances of buildings, textbooks, television that seem to emanate from no intelligence, no artifice. Ideology has become the world itself; ideological texts—like texts generally—are passe.

Ideology cannot be pierced as readily as before: Marx debunked bourgeois political economy in the Promethean labor of *Capital*; the Frankfurt School interrogated a mystifying language for ironic dialectical truths. Today writing leaks all over the place as ideological claims are deauthorized—indeed, truth is not claimed at all but simply objectified. Texts are lived, not read. Disciplinary discourse directly disciplines, provoking the power of the social inscribed in it as sufficient being. We play out the functional imperatives of capital, patriarchy, racism, and the domination of nature as if these were not historical choices that could be made differently. Validity is unproblematic in a world in which texts do not stand at one remove from the world but are frozen into the seemingly inert patterns of bourgeois experience. Thus, to read is to possess an adaptiveness allowing one to negotiate the lousy routines of work and family experienced ontologically as degradations—as practices with no author. This is especially disabling where discourses like sociology formulate our subordination to structure into a generic feature of the modern, disciplining versions conceiving of social being differently.

Ideology-critique in fast capitalism addresses this deauthorization of validity claims by reconstructing social structure undecidably and dialogically. That is, in *reading* prisons, office buildings, science, math, and money as texts, we immediately strip away their bureaucratic inertness and open them to reformulation as essayed versions. This is not to say that all life is a text, a Nietzschean extravagance of an apolitical version of deconstruction, but only to observe that all text today is a life, a mode of vitally productive and reproductive social relations between writer and readers. Where ideology in Marx's era was more or less clearly explicated in economics and religion, today it is displaced into the built, textual, and figural environments carefully cleansed of the traces of authorial subjectivity so that they cannot be reformulated in different forms of life.

The falling rate of profit is checked by a falling rate of intelligence. Writing's eclipse by techno-rhetorics of quantity, space, and body is a crucial political topic for an emancipatory theory that does not enjoy the luxury of addressing ideologizing validity claims in unironic terms of simple reflection. Marxism is not, and has never been, simply a shelf full of books; it is a literary practice prising open the dispersed texts of capitalism—the giant disciplining institutions of public and private life—precisely in order to engage their secret authors in dialogue. Developments in poststructuralism and feminism inform critical theory otherwise relying uncritically on Marx's representational notion of ideology as falsehood. The false today does not reside in discursive constructions of corrigible authors but in what Sartre (1976) called the practico-inert, the objectified environment that looks like anything but a text yet conceals powerful claims about the nature of being. The world suggests itself as a final version of the social. No one reads at one remove from reality; books are lives themselves.

Our critical challenge, then, is to crack the codes of figure, quantity, and design as I have tried to do with sociology in order to show how in Foucault's terms institutions discipline. This version of reading reauthorizes social structure and thus opens up dialogue about ultimate social purposes—precisely the desideratum of Habermas's attempt to reconstruct historical materialism along the lines of communication theory. In the meantime it is locally useful to deconstruct Marxism itself as a discipline investing too heavily in the protocol of natural science. Few read Marxism anymore. Ideology is not only a *camera obscura* inverting the real but also the ensembles of "everyday" discursive practices enacting political codes without ever interpreting a line of prose. The everyday is precisely that region of experience in which people do not read or think; action is the embodied intelligence of the postmodern. Although now as before the disciplinary texts are still false, our problem today is that *we cannot even recognize our public environment, including the academic disciplines, as the authored construction it is*. Thus, we cannot interrogate the grounds of its validity; or, to put this differently, we cannot ask the world for its reason *because* the world is not conceived as reasonable. Social nature resists our interrogation of it. The eclipse of reason (Horkheimer 1974b) is hastened by the dispersal of textuality into lifeless book-things. Considered reflection provoking its reformulation in the spirit of gentle dialogue belongs to an obsolete intellectual world.

My notion of a fast capitalism in which images blur with the reality they come to embody is not a turn away from Marx's original notion of ideology as a cultural practice disciplining imagination. It is instead to refresh Marxism's tired economisms with perspectives from outside of political economy, thus restoring Marx's distinctive grasp on the nature of deception. Ideology falsifies the more effectively where we cannot even recognize the built, textual, and figural environment as the text it has become. Even if we could, we have a hard time making ourselves understood without trading on slogans like socialism and communism. Although any theory written under the shadow of Adorno ought to be reluctant to invite its own administration by setting out a research agenda, it seems to me that this notion of a fast capitalism might occasion a number of lines of interesting literary work—science—assuming, of course, that this work is not narrowly positivist but broadly includes all kinds of discursive methodologies understanding themselves as essay, speculative reason.

Urban social science pursues the dispersal of texts into the built environment, into edifice, in some of the work of Harvey (1973, 1985) and Castells (1983) as well as in Walter Benjamin's (1970) discussion of Paris. A critical perspective on communication and media could trace dispersed cultural messages back to their concealed authors as an active strategy of reauthorization, a project begun in different ways by Leiss (1976), Habermas (1984), and Foucault (1976, 1977). A critical perspective on the politics of sexuality and gender understands sexual objectification in the continuity between violence and figural objectification. Pornography, for example, is read and thus opposed in a way that builds on some of the work of the French feminists (Irigaray 1985; Kristeva 1974, 1980). Finally, this notion of fast capitalism can be turned against the disciplines themselves as a way of exhuming the literary roots of discipline, notably with respect to the incursion of positivism into the human sciences. Foucault leads the way in his books *Archaelogy of Knowledge* (1976) and *Discipline and Punish* (1977). Here I have tried to read the discipline of sociology as a process and practice of deauthorization, adding critical theory and deconstruction to what we used to call the sociology of sociology.

The appropriate method for studying fast capitalism is any interrogation excavating authorial presence as a way of engaging objectlike institutions and disciplines in their own reformulation. Good method in this regard is any version that can hear the echo of its own voice without being driven to silence it; indeed, the less we fear the buried subtexts of our desire, the evidence we have written, the more we peacefully invite our readers to become writers themselves. If readers can see the evidence of authorial artifice, they will be empowered to write, that is, to take control of social processes heretofore chilled into the intractable patterns of domination. Thus, weirdly, perhaps, to positivists, method can become a political strategy as it busts out of the covers of the books and journals by encouraging people to read with an eye to rewriting. That will seem an insufficient notion of political strategy to some only if we are unsuccessful in making the point that textuality is political in fast capitalism. Books today are often hard to read, concealing the dense work of literary artifice. For that reason, they must be read and reformulated.

My disciplinary critique opens into and is itself informed by a larger notion of a fast capitalism in which writing disperses hurriedly into the built and figural environment, shiny sociology textbooks and impenetrable journal articles standing alongside the billboards and office buildings encoding meaning and thus provoking practice today. It is not simply that social objects can be read textually; that has always been the case. What is new in fast capitalism is that textuality in the more traditional form, standing at one remove from the reality it addresses, is eclipsed as texts are dispersed into the built and figural environment in a way that precludes other versions of themselves and further disempowers readers who do not labor at interpretation. Thus, texts increasingly discipline as they are no longer read as such; their obdurate facticity provokes their reliving as fate, Marx's traditional category of ideology now phenomenologized into a nearly self-reproducing everyday life.

The extension of my argument against sociology into a full-blown theory of fast capitalism is another book, although here, before closing, I want to comment on the auspices under which my disciplinary critique has proceeded. Readers who have stayed with me this far may worry that I have overdrawn my portrait of a discipline subtracting desire from thought, the literary from its own text. For what it is worth, given the enormous complexity of dominations today (to which disciplinary sociology adds only a little in the way of its sustenance), I am convinced that what I have said about sociology as a discourse of the power of the social extends to other textual practices. Thus my reading points the way toward a more comprehensive understanding of the dispersal of texts in administered society. Where Marx developed Marxism by rewriting bourgeois political economy, I am trying to develop a better version of critical theory within which Marxism is a central voice by rewriting academic sociology. Thus, I am trying to be clear about how my disciplinary critique trades on a more substantial notion of fast capitalism in which discipline is dumbly self-generated—what I called heterotextuality.

Toward a Critical Theory of Significance

Sociology disciplines by presenting an incontrovertible world that it would then have us enact. It does not read like old-fashioned texts at one remove from the world but presents itself as a hardened piece of nature. In reading it as a text, I have tried politically to open it to different versions not only as ideology-critique in Marx's sense but also directly as a way of building good community among equal speakers. I suppose this has political utility in the sense that others may read it. It also bears on the way we radicalize our pedagogy as we go about training human capital in the universities and colleges. My own department teaches more than two thousand students each year in our introductory course. Many of these students will work in the professions and business, and thus their political formation is systemically important.

In any case, sociology is a discursive practice that can be prised open deconstructively for traces of its desire suppressed by method. To sociologize is not only to chart unfreedom; it also reproduces it if its mapping pretends to proceed ontologically. The power of the social rests on power (to which value is added by disciplinary discourse). The discipline does not think of itself in these terms; that would deprivilege its version as against other versions refusing to use methodology as an excuse not to be heard to think and talk. But there is hope: sociology reveals the world's need to be disciplined. In the meantime, *because* Durkheimians continue to iterate the power of the social, *we* can resist.

I have begun to suggest a way of building a critical discourse theory that in crucial respects both converges with and diverges from those of Habermas and Foucault. My emphases are different, and yet we are all trying to understand the structural significance of *signification,* of textuality as a material force. Habermas manages to retain at least a tenuous connection to a Marxism relentlessly historicizing, thus remaining hopeful. Indeed to get too close to Marxism today means to abandon critique under sway of cant as well as a mathematizing economism. For its part too much of deconstruction, and Foucault, too, wherever one locates him, is only an intellectual fad blocking Derrida's most political insight; differentiation almost inevitably becomes hierarchy, an insight theorized more systematically by Adorno. Yet as a historical materialist I agree with Habermas and Marx that people can achieve just social relationships through what Habermas calls a communicative ethics. The way we think and speak about freedom is inseparable from freedom. I have tried to develop that ethic in literary terms largely to suggest a version of science eschewing the presuppositionless representationality of positivism. It is not that positivist disciplines like sociology count for much in the overall calculus of domination but only that they count. It is more that they reflect the power of the social than that they constitute it; no—sociology constitutes authorlessly. It is secret writing. That is how it adds power to power.

Disciplines do not have inalienable rights. Like an obdurate history that remains a nightmare on the brains of the living, disciplines *exist*. As such, they are engaging only to the extent to which they dominate or liberate. Durkheim's axial version of sociology as a text of the power of the social adds value to that power, albeit in its small role in the complex circuitry of world history. I write against sociology here because I know it. And also because the power of the social it reproduces is an axial principle of domination today. Sociology joins everyday life thoughtlessly. It would be disingenuous for me to urge a new better discipline arising out of an act of sheer intellectual will. Like Marx's original notion of the critique of ideology, my disciplinary reading fully intends to be more than that—negation constructing a better version of the world, prefiguring a new order of value in which textuality is no longer denigrated as the merely ideational or superstructural. Foucault said that historians make history; similarly, in their local way, people who write under Durkheim's aegis —and sociologists do—reproduce subordination by reflecting it as unalterable.

The text of science is inherently political in the stance it strikes to itself and its readers. Good science narratively understands itself as a version of versions, inviting its gentle community as a way of making community. By contrast the positivist version suppresses its artifice in order to still other writings, the purpose of every ideology. In this way, Durkheim intended to bring about a certain order of social being. To read his discipline this way confronts positivism with its own literary nature—better, with its political desire that sociology methodologically foreswears. Innovations in theories of interpretation all the way from deconstruction to left feminism (through Frankfurt) have made my reading possible. The more writing claims a freedom from desire, as scientific sociology does, the more we must read deeply into its political nature. Otherwise, we will continue to be disciplined and thus discipline in turn.

Notes

Every writing can be made to speak the truth as long as we listen to it in a way that pits its authorial desire against the whole methodizing apparatus suppressing author falsely in the name of science. Thus, endnotes in a book like this that treats authority simply as author-ity—corrigible validity claims traced downward to political and ontological motive—bring to light the suppressed desire of numerous versions. All sorts of voices inform this version of the truth, this book, and I acknowledge them not as authorities upon whom I rely to achieve closure but as referents that help orient my own sense of things. In this regard, these endnotes do not establish validity or pedigree. Instead they try to view certain ostensibly wrong-headed versions from the point of view of their possible redemption. That is, I try to join them in a genuinely nonauthoritarian political community, something I dare say they would not easily do for me. But one of my themes here is that the left must assiduously avoid setting up new center/margin distinctions that are really only hierarchies; thus, it is prefiguratively important for me to be more generous to politically errant versions than they would be to me by excavating the libertarian desire within them making anyone write. Otherwise, I develop yet another version of discipline.

I want these endnotes to be read as my discussions and acknowledgments of my interlocutors. Authority can only be established in the play of texts off other texts and cannot be claimed definitively. No amount of citation of Marx or Derrida will strengthen (or weaken) my argument which must be heard to refer simultaneously to itself—its own subtext of driving desire seeking to bring about a certain state of affairs —and to other writings joining me in the conversation of humanity.

I want to get positivism off the backs of those of us who claim science for ourselves, albeit not a presuppositionlessly representational version of it. That is my political purpose posed in the negative; in the positive, I want to build a new political community out of versions claiming truth passionately but understanding themselves as corrigible, perspectival versions making way for other versions. In this way I maintain that the function of science, to use a Parsonian turn of phrase, is not the establishment of truth but through it the institution of good community; I facilitate that aim by rewriting Marxism through a variety of heterodox intellectual traditions like critical theory, deconstruction, and feminism as a theory of textuality. Words are inescapably self-limiting. My difference from literal Marx is one of emphasis, that is, of critical and political priority.

There are some genres from which I repeatedly draw in my disciplinary reading, specifically addressed in particular endnotes. First, I read some sociology textbooks. References to the books cited parenthetically at the ends of quoted passages will be found in the Bibliography. Second, I read some of the discipline's discussions of itself, which I will sketch below. Third, I read Frankfurt critical theory. Fourth, I read deconstruction. Fifth, I read different feminisms. I will generally outline readings in critical theory and deconstruction below especially for those unfamiliar with them. My bibliographic discussion of feminism is best found in quite extensive endnotes to section four. I exclude feminism from this introductory ground breaking simply because it is less doctrinal, less canonical. Apart from Beauvoir's *Second Sex* (1953) feminist theory has developed in inseparable relation with feminist research.

Methodologists may be concerned that my "sample" of textbooks plundered here for quotes is unrandom or otherwise ideologically jaundiced. Mea culpa. Adorno and Horkheimer do not read Homer in their *Dialectic of Enlightenment* as a typical Greek writer but as a telling voice of western enlightenment. By the same token, I have tried not to sample recent American sociology textbooks in a purposely methodical way but simply to read in the variety of books that come across my desk for possible adoption. I have tried to stick to some of the biggest selling and thus most prestigious ones, although there are some notable exceptions.

As for the anticipated charge that I do not sample the textbooks correctly and thus read them too monolithically (let alone the whole discipline that many, even on the left, will insist is far more ecumenical than I allow), let other writers respond with counter examples in a way joining intellectual community. Or let people proud to be professional sociologists respond by demonstrating that I misread a diverse discipline. In any case, I attempt here a symptomatic reading, much like the reading given Homer by Adorno and Horkheimer or Hegel and Rousseau by Derrida. I duly acknowledge the irony that the early Frankfurt thinkers read works of high culture to resonate a civilization where I read only college textbooks. But cultural critique as it intends a larger political theory cannot ignore what it finds out there. Discipline has reduced high culture to academic discourse.

For a historical overview of trends in the writing of American introductory sociology textbooks, see E. Doyle McCarthy and Robin Das, "American Sociology's Idea of Itself: A Review of the Textbook Literature from the Turn of the Century to the Present," *The History of Sociology* 5, no. 2 (1985): 21–43. For other discussions of introductory textbooks, also see Ian Gomme, "First Light, A Review of Five Introductory Sociology Texts," *Canadian Review of Sociology and Anthropology* 22, no. 1 (1985): 146–53; J. Graham Morgan, "Courses and Texts in Sociology," *The Journal of the History of Sociology* 5, no. 1 (1983): 42–65; Henrika Kulick, "Sociology's Past and Future: Prescriptive Implications of Historical Self-Consciousness in the School of Social Sciences," *Research in Sociology of Knowledge, Sciences and Art* 2 (1979): 73–85; Jack Nusan Porter, "Radical Sociology Textbooks: A Review Essay," *Humboldt Journal of Social Relations* 9, no. 1 (1981–82): 198–206; Warren R. Papp, "The Concept of Power: Treatment in 50 Introductory Sociology Textbooks," *Teaching Sociology* 9, no. 1 (1981): 57–68; William D. Maslow, "Academic Sociology as a 'Classist' Discipline: An Empirical Inquiry into the Treatment of Marx in the Textbooks of North American Sociology, 1890–1965," *Humanity and Society* 5, no. 3

(1981): 256–75; Wayne J. Villemez, "Explaining Inequality: A Survey of Perspectives Represented in Introductory Sociology Textbooks," *Contemporary Sociology* 9, no. 1 (1981): 35–39; Robert L. Herrick, "Nineteen Pictures of a Discipline: A Review of Recent Introductory Sociology Textbooks," *Contemporary Sociology* 9, no. 5 (1980): 617–26; Helen Fein, "Is Sociology Aware of Genocide?: Recognition of Genocide in Introductory Sociology Texts in the United States, 1947–1977," *Humanity in Society* 3, no. 3 (1979): 177–93; Alan Wells, "Conflict Theory and Functionalism: Introductory Sociology Textbooks, 1928–1976," *Teaching Sociology* 6, no. 4 (1979): 429–37.

For a discussion of disciplinary sociology from the point of view of trends in journal and monograph publishing see Patricia Wilner, "The Main Drift of Sociology Between 1936 and 1984," *The History of Sociology* 5, no. 2 (1985): 1–20. For a view opposing my claim that textbooks represent current research and the state of the discipline generally, see Robert Perucci, "Sociology and the Introductory Textbooks," *The American Sociologist* 15, no. 1 (1980): 39–49. Inasmuch as his work extends only up to 1977, he misses the many recent attempts by textbook authors and publishers to be more synthetic and eclectic. Until 1977, few books gave much (if any) coverage to Marxism or feminism; the situation has since reversed itself, thus buttressing my argument that for better or worse the texts represent the false diversity of the discipline today.

For a good, brief introduction to some of these recent developments in literary theory, especially of the kind called poststructuralism, on which I draw heavily, see Terry Eagleton's excellent *Literary Theory* (Minneapolis: University of Minnesota Press, 1983); also see Michael Ryan's *Marxism and Deconstruction* (Baltimore: Johns Hopkins University Press, 1982) for an appreciation of the convergence and tension between "deconstruction" and (especially Adorno's) Marxism. For a sensitive introduction to poststructuralism per se, albeit more from the point of view of literary criticism than social theory, see Jonathan Culler, *On Deconstruction* (Ithaca: Cornell University Press, 1982). For a more general exemplification of the way I use the term "text" and "social text" throughout this book, see the journal called *Social Text*, and in particular see the recent work of one of its coeditors, Fredric Jameson, who has contributed much to the development of what one might call a deconstructionist Marxism. See his earlier *Marxism and Form* (Princeton: Princeton University Press, 1972) and, more recently, *The Political Unconscious* (Ithaca: Cornell University Press, 1981). For commentary on Jameson see William Dowling, *Jameson, Althusser, Marx* (Ithaca: Cornell University Press, 1984). For some of the many original works comprising poststructuralism, one might read Roland Barthes (although it is unclear whether he is structuralist or poststructuralist): *The Pleasure of the Text* (New York: Hill and Wang, 1974); *S/Z* (New York: Hill and Wang, 1974); and *Writing Degree Zero* (New York: Hill and Wang, 1967). See also Jacques Derrida, *Speech and Phenomena* (Evanston, Ill.: Northwestern University Press, 1973); *Of Grammatology* (Baltimore: Johns Hopkins University Press, 1976), and *Writing and Difference*, London: Routledge and Kegan Paul, 1978); and Julia Kristeva, *Desire in Language* (New York: Columbia University Press, 1980) and *Polylogue* (Paris: Seuil, 1977).

Finally, for a general overview of critical theory, see my *Western Marxism* (Santa Monica: Goodyear, 1979) as well as David Held's *Introduction to Critical Theory*

(Berkeley: University of California Press, 1980). Also see Martin Jay's *The Dialectical Imagination* (Boston: Little Brown, 1973) for historical background. Among original Frankfurt works, see Max Horkheimer and Theodor W. Adorno, *Dialectic of Enlightenment* (New York: Herder and Herder, 1972); Theodor Adorno, *Negative Dialectics* (New York: Seabury, 1973); Max Horkheimer, *Eclipse of Reason* (New York: Seabury, 1974), and *Critical Theory* (New York: Herder and Herder, 1972); Herbert Marcuse, *One-Dimensional Man* (Boston: Beacon, 1964), *An Essay on Liberation* (Harmondsworth: Penguin, 1972), and *Eros and Civilization* (New York: Vintage, 1955); Jürgen Habermas, *Knowledge and Human Interests* (Boston: Beacon, 1971), *Legitimation Crisis* (Boston: Beacon, 1975) and *The Theory of Communicative Action*, Vol. One and Two (Boston: Beacon, 1984 and 1987).

Here I am working toward a *postmodernism* that accepts neither the willful centerlessness (and, therefore, ironically, centeredness) of an apolitical version of deconstruction nor the utterly centering tendencies of a Promethean Marxism portraying the proletariat as a world-historical collective subject. I am postmodernist as a way of being authentically modernist—that is, recognizing the original resistance of modernism to the banalized, routinized status quo. In the same way, but differently, I am postmodernist as a way of being Marxist. The names do not matter *and yet they do* as signifiers of earlier politics and practices. That is, naming is inherently political in a world in which difference betokens hierarchy. Ultimately, the end-of-ideology will end the identity of difference and hierarchy. I am not sure whether names will return rightfully to the things they are essentially meant to describe or whether they will be said and heard dialectically, as ironically both themselves and their differences. This is the sense of my concluding discussion in Chapter 11 about what it can mean to use the name "sociology" to describe writing.

There are a number of ways to understand, and thus advocate, a detotalized, decentered, deconstructed—essentially postmodernist—world. One can argue with Jean-Francois Lyotard in this *The Postmodern Condition: A Report of Knowledge* (Minneapolis: University of Minnesota Press, 1984) that all we can hope for is a contemporary world construed as "heteromorphous language games," pushing aside all "metanarratives" of History, whether liberal-Enlightenment or Marxist; or one can agree with Habermas that a "postmodern condition" might still have to be confronted with the epochal radical-democratic appeal for communicative openness and the democratization of our various lifeworlds. See a Habermasian critique of Lyotard in Selya Benhabib, "Epistemologies of Postmodernism: A Rejoinder to Jean-Francois Lyotard," *New German Critique* 3 (1984): 103–26. Although I agree with Habermas that postmodernism is essentially politically empty as method, if not downright neoconservative, Habermas's communication theory does not adequately address the deeply entwining ideologies reducing our communicative/transformative opportunities virtually to nil. My own version of a (call it) deconstructive Marxism hopes to be an alternative.

INTRODUCTION

1. This notion of the palliation of workers' alienation through the enhancement of leisure time spans a broad neo-Weberian literature from Robert Blauner, *Alienation and Freedom* (Chicago: University of Chicago Press, 1964) to Daniel Bell, *The Coming of Post-Industrial Society* (New York: Basic, 1973).

2. See Irving Zeitlin, *Ideology and the Development of Sociological Theory* (Englewood Cliffs, N.J.: Prentice-Hall, 1968) for a similar, but not identical, argument about the rise of sociology. Also see Alvin Gouldner's trilogy *The Dialectic of Ideology and Technology* (New York: Seabury, 1976); *The Future of the Intellectuals and the Rise of the New Class* (New York: Seabury, 1979); *The Two Marxisms: Contradictions and Anomalies in the Development of Theory* (New York: Seabury, 1980), as well as his earlier *The Coming Crisis of Western Sociology* (New York: Basic, 1970) initiating the efforts of "reflexive" sociology to comprehend sociology's own political interests.

3. I develop this argument about the roots of early sociology in the transition of market to state-managed capitalism in my *Social Problems Through Conflict and Order*, coauthored with S. A. McDaniel (Toronto: Addison-Wesley, 1983), especially 29–34.

4. For a parallel appreciation of Weber's ambivalence about western rationalization see Hans Gerth and C. Wright Mills's introduction to Weber's collected essays, *From Max Weber* (New York: Oxford University Press, 1976), especially their apt characterization of Weber as a "nostalgic liberal," 50. Also see Lewis Coser's similar reading of Weber in his chapter on Weber in his *Masters of Sociological Thought* (New York: Harcourt Brace Jovanovich, 1977). Both Gerth-Mills and Coser as "conflict theorists" belong to an American tradition of Weber scholarship resisting the cheerful Parsonian reading of Weber simply as a father of functionalism untroubled by the aporias (if not—Marxian—"contradictions") of capitalist industrialization. What this conflict-theoretic construction of Weber lacks, however, is a thoroughgoing understanding of the ultimately apologetic thrust of Weber's ontology of "rationality," only sugar-coated by his ambivalence about the "iron cage" he nonetheless takes to be eternal, inexorable. Although it is sometimes said incorrectly that the original Frankfurt theorists, notably Adorno, Horkheimer, and Marcuse, were more Weberian than Marxist (or at least as much), in fact the pivot of the Frankfurt Marxism was their critique of the Weberianization/rationalization of late or state capitalism, the extension of the logic of capital into a deeply "instrumental rationality" named by Weber as the essence of modern reason. See Marcuse's 1964 essay on "Industrialization and Capitalism in the Work of Max Weber," in his *Negations* (Boston: Beacon, 1968). For a more circumspect perspective on Weber's apologia for instrumentally rational capitalism from the point of view of second-generation critical theory, see Jürgen Habermas's essay on "Technology and Science as 'Ideology' " in his *Toward a Rational Society* (Boston: Beacon, 1970), and his later *The Theory of Communicative Action* in which he devotes much space to discussions of both Weber and Parsons. Weber was critical of the emerging capitalist-statist juggernaut; yet he did not theorize this criticism in a way that undid his overall version of the modern but only added it to his main text in a wistful, parenthetical way. Although Weber is not the cheerful optimist, neither is he an adequate critic.

5. See Horkheimer's *Eclipse of Reason* and particularly the "The Revolt of Nature" chapter for an elaboration of what is an essential theme of Frankfurt critical theory, addressed in other ways in the coauthored *Dialectic of Enlightenment*.

6. For a discussion of the concept of "everyday life" as an historical (and not generic) reality, see Henri Lefebvre, *Everday Life in the Modern World* (New York: Harper and Row, 1971). As well, see work in the tradition of critical phenomenology such as Enzo Paci, *The Function of Modern Science and the Meaning of Man* (Evanston, Ill.: Northwestern University Press, 1972), and John O'Neill, *Sociology as a Skin Trade*

(New York: Harper and Row, 1972), especially the "Can Phenomenology Be Critical?" chapter, 221–36. Also see Herbert Marcuse's *One-Dimensional Man*, especially 123–99.

7. For a pertinent discussion of similarities between Frankfurt critical theory, especially that of Adorno, and poststructuralist deconstruction, see Martin Jay's *Adorno* (Cambridge: Harvard University Press, 1984).

8. See Theodor W. Adorno, *Negative Dialectics*. "Dialectics is the self-consciousness of the objective context of delusion; it does not mean to have escaped from that context. Its objective goal is to break out of the context from within"(406).

9. See Marcuse, *One-Dimensional Man*, 257.

10. For an example of Lukacs's aesthetic criticism, see his *Studies in European Realism* (New York: Grosset and Dunlop, 1964), as well as his *The Historical Novel* (Boston: Beacon, 1962).

11. See Sigmund Freud, *Civilization and its Discontents* (New York: Norton, 1962), especially 92.

12. See Daniel Bell, *The Coming of Post-Industrial Society*.

13. Although suffocated in the stale air of political cliches oft-repeated, a fresh reading of *The Communist Manifesto* (New York: Washington Square Press, 1964) reveals it to be an amazingly self-conscious text, straining against its hermetic enclosure by its own covers in order to *become* veritably a new world. Indeed, Marx and Engels were acutely aware of the historicity of their own writing where in the preface to the German edition of 1872 they referred to the *Manifesto* as a "historical document" (121), not apologizing for its inaccuracies but acknowledging (their) text's deep inherence in the history of which it was a part.

14. My point is that all of these discourses, including sociology, reproduce dominant productive and reproductive relations (indeed, the subordination of the latter to the former) and thus they are all "ideological." For an intelligent rethinking of the topic of political-literary criticism in general, see 194–217 of Eagleton's *Literary Theory*.

15. Kingsley Davis and W. E. Moore's defense of inequality on functionalist grounds is found in their 1945 article, "Some Principles of Stratification," *American Sociological Review* 10 (1945): 242–49.

16. See John O'Neill, *Five Bodies* (Ithaca: Cornell University Press, 1986).

17. See C. Wright Mills's *The Sociological Imagination* (New York: Oxford University Press, 1959), especially 3–24.

CHAPTER ONE

1. For a discussion of the different versions of the personal/political relationship in feminist theory, see Alison Jaggar, *Feminist Politics and Human Nature* (Totowa, N.J.: Roman and Allenheld, 1983); also see Jean Elshtain's *Public Man, Private Woman* (Princeton: Princeton University Press, 1981).

2. See Max Horkheimer's 1937 essay "Traditional and Critical Theory," in his *Critical Theory*.

3. See my "Dialectical Sensibility I: Critical Theory, Scientism and Empiricism," *Canadian Journal of Political and Social Theory* 1, no. 1 (1977): 1–30.

4. See Nietzsche's *The Gay Science* and Marcuse's discussion of the "new science and technology" to be practiced by a "new sensibility," as he calls it in his *An Essay*

on Liberation. This notion of a noninstrumental, eroticized cognition and technique scandalizes a sober Marxist tradition in which science belongs to the realm of "necessity." Even Habermas in his *Knowledge and Human Interests* lambasts Marcuse, Horkheimer, and Adorno (32–33) for their alleged "mysticism" about the possible redemption/eroticization/liberation of science under socialism.

5. For a discussion of the politics of speech and communication, see my "A Critical Theory of Dialogue," *Humanities in Society* 4, no. 1 (Winter 1981): 7–30.

6. See Karl Popper, *The Logic of Scientific Discovery* (New York: Science Edition, 1961). Although Popper says he is not a positivist but a "critical rationalist," he presents a sophisticated version of positivism resonating throughout mainstream social science. For the 1961 dispute between Popper and the Frankfurt School, see *The Positivist Dispute in German Sociology*, Theodor W. Adorno, Hans Albert, Ralf Dahrendorf, Jürgen Habermas, Harold Pilot, and Karl R. Popper (London: Heinemann, 1976). Also see Herbert Marcuse's "Karl Popper and the Problem of Historical Laws," in his *Studies in Critical Philosophy* (Boston: Beacon, 1973).

7. See, for example, Maurice Merleau-Ponty, *Sense and Non-Sense* (Evanston, Ill.: Northwestern University Press, 1964), and his *Signs* (Evanston, Ill.: Northwestern University Press, 1964); Jean-Paul Sartre, *Critique of Dialectical Reason* (London: New Left Books, 1976); and John O'Neill, *Sociology as a Skin Trade* (New York: Harper and Row, 1972) and his *Making Sense Together: An Introduction to Wild Sociology* (New York: Harper and Row, 1974).

8. See the appendix to his *Knowledge and Human Interests*, "Knowledge and Human Interests: A General Perspective," 301–17. "[T]he positivist self-understanding of the *nomological sciences* lends countenance to the substitution of technology for enlightened action. It diverts the utilization of scientific information from an illusory viewpoint, namely that the practical mastery of history can be reduced to technical control of objectified processes" (316).

9. Although not directly a contribution to the science/humanism debate, see Theodor Adorno's "Subject and Object," in *The Essential Frankfurt School Reader*, ed. by Andrew Arato and Eike Gebhardt (New York: Urizen, 1978), 497–511, for an important reflection on what I later call the dialectical nonidentity of subject and object (text/world, woman/man, labor/capital), a way of reformulating the science/ humanism construction neither relinquishing subject to preponderant object world nor dissolving object into the melt-down of which Marx speaks in the *Manifesto*. For other perspectives on problems of constitution from within a more disciplinarily defined attempt to address issues raised in neo-Kantianism, see, for example, Peter Berger and Thomas Luckmann, *The Social Construction of Reality* (New York: Doubleday, 1967), and Burkart Holzner, *Reality Construction in Society* (Cambridge: Schenckman, 1968).

10. See John O'Neill's "Marxism and the Two Sciences," *Philosophy of the Social Sciences* 11 (1981): 281–302. Also see Karl-Otto Apel, *Understanding and Explanation* (Cambridge: MIT Press, 1984).

11. See Walter Benjamin's essay, "Art in the Age of Mechanical Reproduction," in his *Illuminations* (New York: Schocken, 1969). For Adorno's critical response, see his "On the Fetish-Character of Music and the Regression of History," 270–99, as well as his "Commitment," 300–18, both in *The Essential Frankfurt School Reader*, ed. by Andrew Arato and Eike Gebhardt (New York: Urizen, 1978). For a

discussion of the relation between literature and politics, see Jean-Paul Sartre's *What is Literature?* (New York: Harper and Row, 1965), a work from which I borrow the term committed literature, keeping in mind the sense of Adorno's objection to the seeming valorization of a superficial political committedness over "autonomous" art in his essay "Commitment," in *The Essential Frankfurt School Reader*. Although I agree with Adorno that art and writing must not slavishly pander to "political" concerns, it seems to me that there is another sense of commitment exemplified by Sartre at least in his literature; this notion of advocacy advocates without losing touch with one's foundation in desire, interest, body, and history. I think Adorno, too, shares this sense of commitment, if not Brecht or Benjamin's often crude politico-pragmatism (the target of his criticism). Adorno disentangles himself from appartchik art at one extreme only to hypostatize the "autonomy" of art at the other, thus desubjectivizing art too much. Perhaps this is only to say that I am more existentialist in a certain way than was Adorno, although, again, I think the distance among Sartre, Adorno, and me is less than Adorno (for good, if sometimes overdrawn, political reasons) admits. It all depends on the reading of the term commitment and, thus, on what one means by literature—for me, *any writing* essaying its own ground in the not-I (desire, time, etc.). Language here strains against its own assimilation to conventional usage *as a mode of political resistance*.

12. This "free will," allowed by a degree of unavoidable systemic openness or non-identity, occasions the state steering mechanisms and policies depicted in John Kenneth Galbraith's *The New Industrial State* (Boston: Houghton Mifflin, 1967) in order to keep capitalism solvent, stoked by at least a modicum of psyche diverted from the sociopolitical implications of that openness—the indeterminacy of history. Sociology conceals these implications by inducing a love of fate; the modern precludes both submission to the power of the social plus the emoluments of advanced-capitalist status attainment. The undoing of discipline would capitalize on the essential indeterminacy of the world but not in support of a state management merely plugging systemic gaps.

13. See Roland Barthes, "The Death of the Author," in *Image-Music-Text: Roland Barthes* ed. Stephen Heath (London: Fontana, 1977).

14. I use the term subtext no more elegantly or technically than I use the term reproduction, trading off a kind of psychoanalytic "subtext" of both deconstruction and critical theory representing a text's unconscious. This does not revert explicitly to Lacan. See, for example, his *Écrits* (London: Tavistock, 1977). See Eagleton, *Literary Theory*, 178. "In reading *Sons and Lovers* with an eye to these aspects of the novel, we are constructing what may be called a "sub-text" for the work—a text which runs within it, visible at certain 'symptomatic' points of ambiguity, evasion or emphasis, and which we as readers are able to 'write' even if the novel itself does not. All literary works contain one or more such sub-texts, and there is a sense in which they may be spoken of as the 'unconscious' of the work itself. The work's insights, as with all writing, are deeply related to its blindnesses: what it does not say, and *how* it does not say it, may be as important as what it articulates; what seems absent, marginal or ambivalent about it may provide a central clue to its meanings." I use the term in this way to connote a *double text*, a *text that makes its own subtext a topic* and thus opens itself to its own openness, energizing writing with the glimpse of its own foundational desire—its drive to be (as to make) a new world. Subtext can never be completely

exhausted by methodology; a nonpositivist version of writing celebrates literary motive in an apparently motiveless world. This does not solve objectivity with subjectivity but simply understands object as a formulation—and thus possibly a reformulation—of the subject.

15. I want to understand the notion of "reproduction" throughout this book as a complex of biological, psychological, cultural, economic and, at bottom, epistemological activities—discourses. *Text* reproduces the world productively, a world in which representation is ironically devalued. For various understandings of the term reproduction, see Mary O'Brien, *The Politics of Reproduction* (London: Routledge and Kegan Paul, 1981); Karl Marx, *Grundrisse* (London: Allen Lane, 1973); and Nancy Chodorow, *The Reproduction of Mothering* (Berkeley: University of California Press, 1978). Any aim at a unified usage of reproduction is not in pursuit of elegance or what the textbooks call "rigor" but trades off the important concatenation of biological, cultural, economic, and textual reproductiveness that, literally, reproduces the world. Finally, I want to reject by working through the subordination of reproductive to productive (woman to man, nonscience to science, the cultural to the economic) in a way that eventually liberates us from their differentiation altogether—one of the central insights of a feminism that thematizes the masculinist/positivist valorization of production as man's work.

CHAPTER TWO

1. For a Marxist discussion of the problem of the subject, see Rosalind Coward and John Ellis, *Language and Materialism: Developments in Semiology and the Theory of the Subject* (London: Routledge and Kegan Paul, 1977). See especially 61–92 for reflections on both the nature of ideology and subjectivity.

2. For an Adornoian perspective on defeat, see Russell Jacoby's *The Dialectic of Defeat* (New York: Cambridge University Press, 1983).

3. See Philip Wexler, *Critical Social Psychology* (London: Routledge and Kegan Paul, 1984), for a systematic critique of mainstream social psychology as well as for an Adornoian reconstitution of it.

4. For a different, neo-Heideggerian version of the activity of making or writing theory, see Alan Blum, *Theorizing* (London: Heinemann, 1975).

5. Where I borrow the term "committed literature" from Sartre, I use it somewhat differently, as I discussed above, when I acknowledged Adorno's critique of Sartre's notion of commitment. Sartre is more existentialist, thus subjectivist, than I am, less prone to understand an originary, even objectlike, commitment located in a depth of desire—the yearnings for freedom, beauty, justice—that is not simply or evidently political. Commitment in my terms is the activity of desire, orienting the project of a psychoanalytically-informed Marxism. For what I regard as a relevant reflection on this ineradicable but all-too-frequently distorted substratum of objective subjectivity, see Joel Kovel's *The Age of Desire: Case Histories of a Radical Psychoanalyst* (New York: Pantheon, 1981).

6. This notion of nonidentity, so central to my work, derives from Adorno, in particular his *Negative Dialectics*. Also see Harold Bloom, *The Anxiety of Influence: A Theory of Poetry* (New York: Oxford University Press, 1973). In this vein, see his later *A Map of Misreading* (New York: Oxford University Press, 1975).

7. See my "The Dialectic of Desire: The Holocaust, Monopoly Capitalism and

Radical Anamnesis," *Dialectical Anthropology* 8, nos. 1–2 (1983): 75–86.

8. And I have written such a book—(on) "my" Marx and Marxism—called *Western Marxism: An Introduction.*

9. In other words, we essay science as a literary production (see ch. 5). See John O'Neill, "The Literary Production of Natural and Social Science Inquiry," *The Canadian Journal of Sociology* 6 (1981): 105–20.

10. I am not convinced that deconstruction as a methodology of literary criticism (e.g., Yale School) is worth the huge amount of ink spilled in its name. And as metaphysics deconstruction turns from politics, ontologizing seriality, difference, marginality as orders of being. As such, these versions of deconstruction are versions of what Adorno called the "jargon of authenticity," referring to existentialism. See his *The Jargon of Authenticity* (Evanston, Ill.: Northwestern University Press, 1973). Again, I use deconstruction as a kind of literary prop, as *revealing words,* but not as a canon in which I invest, treating its writers as people to be engaged who have addressed the duplicity of metaphysical dualism but not as adequate critical-political thinkers. So much of literary theory is aestheticism and, as such, precious, avoiding the realm of the social and political like the plague, the epochal stance of idealism. For its part, Marxist aesthetics is often crudely reductionist, little better than the bourgeois mechanism it opposes.

11. I say "apparent" because all writing is committed, even if in a way hidden from itself. Positivism closes the world, reproduces the given, tends toward the monologic, and—the ultimate irony—aims at its own exhaustion by a world it would freeze into being.

CHAPTER THREE

1. "Hard" science is not really passionless, either; it only pretends to be in order to establish its validity. See, for example, Ernest Nagel, *The Structure of Science* (New York: Harcourt Brace and World, 1961) or Abraham Kaplan, *The Conduct of Inquiry* (San Francisco: Chandler, 1964). Biology and physics are as much "texts" as sociology. One might say that sociology reproduces a world where physics only reproduces the physicist. See Karin D. Knorr, "Producing and Reproducing Knowledge: Descriptive or Constructive? Toward a Model of Research Production," *Social Science Information* 16 (1977): 969–96; also see her *From Scenes to Scripts: On the Relationship Between Laboratory Research and Published Papers in Science,* Research Monograph No. 132 (Vienna, 1978).

2. Christopher Lasch remains an important chronicler of the vicissitudes of "selfhood" in the modern age, first in *The Culture of Narcissism* (New York: Norton, 1979), and then in *The Minimal Self* (New York: Norton, 1984). Although Lasch can be criticized for superficiality in places, he is among the few, with Kovel and Jacoby, who have managed to wed psychic and social analysis without either sacrificing one to the other or portraying them in bland harmony—what sociology generically calls the "micro" and "macro." This is not to deny the sexism of Lasch's work on the family.

3. For a non-Marxist reflection on the meaning of the public sphere, see Hannah Arendt, *The Human Condition* (Chicago: University of Chicago Press, 1960); for more critical perspectives see John O'Neill, "Public and Private Space," in his *Sociology as a Skin Trade* and Richard Sennett, *The Fall of Public Man* (New York: Vintage, 1974).

4. For critiques of neo-Freudian and humanist/third-force psychologies see Russell

Jacoby, *Social Amnesia* (Boston: Beacon, 1975), especially the essay "The Politics of Subjectivity," and Herbert Marcuse's *Eros and Civilization*, especially the epilogue "Critique of Neo-Freudian Revisionism," 217–51.

5. For an incisive discussion of Freudian-Marxism, particularly that of Marcuse, see Gad Horowitz, *Repression: Basic and Surplus Repression in Psychoanalytic Theory* (Toronto: University of Toronto Press, 1977).

6. Herbert Marcuse, *An Essay on Liberation*, particularly "The New Sensibility" chapter, 31–54.

7. Adorno in *Philosophy of Modern Music* (New York: Seabury, 1973) characterizes critical theory as the message in the bottle tossed out to sea by the shipwrecked, underlining the lack of strategic political purchase of Marxism today, if not the importance, indeed now intensified, of negative thought, the less "identical" the better.

8. See Chodorow, *The Reproduction of Mothering*, and Juliet Mitchell, *Psychoanalysis and Feminism* (New York: Vintage, 1975). Chodorow succeeds better than Mitchell in blending psychoanalysis with feminism through a version of socialism; Mitchell essentially exonerates doctrinal psychoanalysis from Freud's personal foibles as a fin-de-siècle middle European sexist, thus accepting clinical psychoanalysis more or less uncritically. Although I talk here about, and urge, a Freudian version of Marxism and cite people like Marcuse and Jacoby in support of it, such a version rests on a reading of Freud taking liberties with the canonical texts and their usual interpretation. With Jacoby, I want to save the critical theory in psychoanalysis—that is, I read psychoanalysis as a version of critical theory, what Jacoby calls "negative psychoanalysis"—rejecting much (if not all: Kovel) of its medical model of psychopathology. Yet there is little explicit critical theory in surface Freud. Thus, in either interpolating or constructing it (e.g., Marcuse's brilliant *Eros and Civilization*) I run the risk of offending most feminists and Marxists by using a depth-psychological rhetoric oppressive in its metaphysic of psychic structure. Where sociology is the discourse of the power of the social, psychology risks being the discourse of the powerlessness of the personal. Nonetheless, given my view of reading and writing as inherently political, I believe we ought to take the plunge and talk about the value of a depth-psychological version of critical theory, especially at a time when domination has sunk so deep into desire that surface sciences like Marxism and sociology simply cannot plumb it; indeed, they too often occlude it. Also see Gilles Deleuze and Felix Guattari, *The Anti-Oedipus* (Minneapolis: University of Minnesota Press, 1983).

9. See Emile Durkheim, *Suicide* (New York: Free Press, 1966).

10. For this debate about science, see my "Marcuse and Habermas on New Science," *Polity* 14, no. 2 (Winter 1976): 158–81. Also see Jürgen Habermas, "Technology and Science as 'Ideology' " in his *Toward a Rational Society*, and Herbert Marcuse's *An Essay on Liberation*, especially "The New Sensibility" chapter.

11. See John O'Neill, ed., *Modes of Individualism and Collectivism* (London: Routledge and Kegan Paul, 1973), for expressions of the science/humanism debate. Also see Peter Winch, *The Idea of a Social Science* (London: Routledge and Kegan Paul, 1969). Finally, see Edmund Mokrzycki, *Philosophy of Science and Sociology* (London: Routledge and Kegan Paul, 1983).

12. See Randall Collins, "On the Microfoundations of Macrosociology," *American Journal of Sociology* 86 (1981): 984–1014.

13. See, for example, Herbert Blumer, *Symbolic Interaction: Perspective and Method*

(Englewood Cliffs: Prentice-Hall, 1969); also "Comments on Parsons as a Symbolic Interactionist," *Sociological Inquiry* 45 (1975): 59–62.

14. For further consideration of the parallel themes of Adorno and Derrida, see Michael Ryan, *Marxism and Deconstruction*, especially 65–81.

15. For a critical perspective on Habermas's notion of the "ideal speech situation," see Paul Connerton's *The Tragedy of Enlightenment* (Cambridge: Cambridge University Press, 1980), especially 91–108.

16. See Susan Buck-Morss's *The Origin of Negative Dialectics* (New York: Free Press, 1977), for a discussion of Adorno-Benjamin debates.

17. For a discussion of "repressive desublimation," see Herbert Marcuse's *One-Dimensional Man*, 56–83.

CHAPTER FOUR

1. For some representative (as well as constitutive) statements of recent positivism, see Ernest Nagel, *The Structure of Science*, and Carl G. Hempel's *Philosophy of Natural Science* (Englewood Cliffs, N.J.: Prentice-Hall, 1966). For a comprehensive critique of various critiques of positivism, see Norman Stockman, *Antipositivist Theories of the Sciences* (Dordrecht: Reidel, 1984).

2. This cry of the (feminist) victim is emphasized in Carol Gilligan's *In a Different Voice* (Cambridge: Harvard University Press, 1982), valorizing women's alleged biological/emotional "differences" from men, thus only reinforcing their *power* differences—the cruel irony of a heterotext written by women aping a disciplinary version of science.

3. For a discussion of a radicalized hermeneutics, see Dieter Misgeld's "Critical Theory and Hermeneutics: The Debate Between Habermas and Gadamer," in John O'Neill, ed., *On Critical Theory*, 164–83.

4. See Derek Phillips's *Knowledge from What? Theories and Methods in Social Research* (Chicago: Rand McNally, 1971). Also see Robert K. Merton, "Priorities in Scientific Discovery: A Chapter in the Sociology of Science," *American Sociological Review* 22 (December 1957): 655–59; also see his *The Sociology of Science* (Chicago: University of Chicago Press, 1973).

5. See Bertrand Russell and A. N. Whitehead, *Principia Mathematica*, 3 vols. (Cambridge: Cambridge University Press, 1910, 1912, and 1913).

6. Artificial negativity is a concept developed by Paul Piccone. See his "The Crisis of One-Dimensionality," *Telos* no. 35 (Spring 1978): 43–54. Also see his "Labriola and the Roots of Eurocommunism," *Berkeley Journal of Sociology* 22 (1977–78): 3–44, and his "The Changing Function of Critical Theory," *New German Critique* 12 (Fall 1977): 29–38.

7. In this I explicitly oppose Habermas's essentially Kantian dualism of instrumental and rational/communicative modes of cognition, ceding science to the scientists and restricting communicative disputation and consensus formation only to the circumscribed realm of politics. See his *Knowledge and Human Interests* and my "Work and Authority in Marcuse and Habermas," *Human Studies* 2 (1979): 191–208.

8. See Robert Merton, *On the Shoulders of Giants* (New York: Free Press, 1965).

9. This notion of a good dialogic community as developed in different terms by Habermas is the main topic of John Forester's edited *Critical Theory and Public Life*

(Cambridge: MIT Press, 1985). See particularly John O'Neill's "Decolonization and the Ideal Speech Community: Some Issues in the Theory and Practice of Communicative Competence," 57–76, and my own "The Dialectic of Deindustrialization: An Essay on Advanced Capitalism," 3–21.

CHAPTER FIVE

1. *The Chronicle of Higher Education*, July 9, 1986, acknowledges the upsurge of academic Marxism as a legitimate, if marginal, voice of its own.

2. This obdurateness in the body politic is, as ever, Marxism's article of faith, evidenced minimally by its own existence. See, for example, John O'Neill's essay "Public and Private Space," in his *Sociology as a Skin Trade*, 20–37.

3. Although written in a different vein, Habermas's *Legitimation Crisis* gives the lie to the notion, either Parsonian or Adornoian, that capitalism is beyond crisis, whether economic, political, or what Habermas calls "motivational."

4. An exemplary statement of this "position" (such as it is) is Phil Slater's *Origin and Significance of the Frankfurt School* (London: Routledge and Kegan Paul, 1975). See my response, "Marxism 'or' the Frankfurt School?" in *Philosophy of the Social Sciences* 14 (March 1983): 347–65.

5. See Paulo Freire's *Pedagogy of the Oppressed* (New York: Seabury, 1973).

6. Much of deconstruction in its ingrown fetish of textuality is an instance of this repressive desublimation. Critical theory largely avoids this fetishism in its articulation of an admittedly peculiar version of historical materialism. If anything, critical theory in its Habermas-era formulation is too materialist, too rationalist, too disciplinary, notably with Habermas's extraordinary effort to integrate the conceptual apparatuses of Parsons, Weber, microsociology, and systems theory, risking what amounts to a Frankfurt encyclopedism. See Habermas, *The Theory of Communicative Action*.

7. See Lewis Coser, *The Functions of Social Conflict* (New York: Free Press, 1966).

8. Marxist scientism abounds. Both Marxists and positivists canonize his so-called economic theory as a set of researchable, testable propositions, thus tailor-made for incorporation into sociology alongside the other languages of causal interpretation. See, for example, Tom Bottomore's *Marxist Sociology* (New York: Holmes and Meier, 1975). Also see John O'Neill's critique of this scientism in his *For Marx Against Althusser* (Washington, D.C.: University Press of America, 1984).

9. This unfortunate notion of *theoria* as a life apart, what Hannah Arendt calls the "vita contemplativa," is the risk of any approach to theory as a practice, implying its self-sufficiency. The left is obviously not immune. How much difference can this (or any) book make in an era when, as Horkheimer once said, books are obsolete? Not much—yet that is not *nothing*. See, for example, Hannah Arendt's *The Human Condition* (Chicago: University of Chicago Press, 1960).

10. This construction of the power of textuality avoids the overvalorization of language by situating textual practice squarely in the political practices of domination and resistance. Contributions to this political/critical theory of language include my "A Critical Theory of Dialogue"; Claus Mueller, *The Politics of Communication* (New York: Oxford University Press, 1973), and Habermas's own *oeuvre*, notably including his *The Theory of Communicative Action*.

11. For a different, more critical discussion of needs see William Leiss, "Needs,

Exchanges and the Fetishism of Objects," *Canadian Journal of Political and Social Theory* 2, no. 3 (Fall 1978): 27–48.

CHAPTER SIX

1. For an incisive account of Marxism-Leninism both as theory and practice, see Herbert Marcuse's *Soviet Marxism* (New York: Vintage, 1958).

2. Nevertheless, party Marxists still keep faith with the Leninist "experiment." See, for example, Al Szymanski's *Is the Red Flag Flying Over Russia?* (London: Red Press, 1979).

3. For Lenin's conflation of dialectical materialism and positivism, see his *Materialism and Empirio-Criticism* (Moscow: Foreign Languages Publishing House, 1952).

4. Robert Tucker elaborates this argument in his *Philosophy and Myth in Karl Marx*, 2d ed. (Cambridge: Cambridge University Press, 1972), especially 218–32.

5. For an excellent example of nonpositivist Marxism see Maurice Merleau-Ponty's *Adventures of the Dialectic* (Evanston, Ill.: Northwestern University Press, 1973).

6. For an interesting discussion and critique of scientific Marxism, see Stanley Aronowitz's *The Crisis in Historical Materialism* (New York: Praeger, 1981), especially "The End of Political Economy" chapter, 139–200.

7. Eduard Bernstein, *Evolutionary Socialism* (New York: Schocken, 1961).

8. See, for example, Karl Korsch's *Revolutionary Theory*, ed. by Douglas Kellner (Austin: University of Texas Press, 1977).

9. Much the same argument is made by Russell Jacoby in his *The Dialectic of Defeat*.

10. An example of this tendency is found in Louis Althusser and Étienne Balibar, *Reading Capital* (London: New Left Books, 1970).

11. A counter to Althusser here is Kostas Axelos's *Alienation and Techne in the Thought of Karl Marx* (Austin: University of Texas Press, 1976).

12. See Maurice Merleau-Ponty's *Humanism and Terror* (Boston: Beacon, 1972).

13. This type of Marxism is often said to be in effect anarchist (as if that were automatically bad), a criticism explicitly conflating critical theory, deconstruction, and Nietzsche. For an example of good anarchism, see Murray Bookchin's *Post-Scarcity Anarchism* (Berkeley: Ramparts Press, 1971).

14. See, for example, Robert Burgess and Ted Huston, *Social Exchange in Developing Relationships* (New York: Academic Press, 1979); also see Elaine Walster, *Equity: Theory and Research* (Boston: Allyn and Bacon, 1978).

15. See Stanley Aronowitz's "The Question of Class" in his *The Crisis in Historical Materialism*, 73–112.

16. See, for example, James O'Connor, *The Fiscal Crisis of the State* (New York: St. Martin's 1972).

17. The so-called French new philosophers have elaborated this conflation. See Bernhard-Henri Levi, *Barbarism with a Human Face* (New York: Harper and Row, 1978).

18. See Stanley Aronowitz's "Culture and Politics" and his "History as Disruption: On Benjamin and Foucault" in his *The Crisis in Historical Materialism*, 225–300 and 301–21, respectively. Also see Horkheimer and Adorno's *Dialectic of Enlightenment*, especially "The Culture Industry: Enlightenment as Mass Deception" chapter, 120–

67. Finally, see my "On Happiness and the Damaged Life," in John O'Neill, ed., *On Critical Theory*, 12–33.

19. Guy Debord explores *la vie quotidienne* as a discursive practice in his *Society of the Spectacle* (Detroit: Black and Red Press, 1972). Also see Henri Lefebvre, *Everyday Life in the Modern World*.

20. For a discussion of Yugoslav social theory and practice, see Gerson Sher, *Praxis: Marxist Criticism and Dissent in Socialist Yugoslavia* (Bloomington: Indiana University Press, 1977); also see Sharon Zukin, *Beyond Marx and Tito* (New York: Cambridge University Press, 1975).

21. And the text ignores not only critical theory in its focus on culture, consumerism, and desire but even the more engaged but nonvanguardist statements like Andre Gorz's *Strategy for Labor* (Boston: Beacon, 1967).

22. See Alfred Sohn Rethel's *Intellectual and Manual Labor* (London: Macmillan, 1978) for a discussion of the viability of Marxism in an essentially post-Marxist age.

CHAPTER SEVEN

1. Gilles Deleuze and Felix Guatteri in their *The Anti-Oedipus* extend the critique of identity theory to Marxism and psychoanalysis themselves.

2. See C. B. Macpherson, *The Political Theory of Possessive Individualism* (Oxford: Oxford University Press, 1962).

3. Of course, this eternalized conflict is also found in the scientific Marxism inspired by Engels, Kautsky, and the Austro-Marxists. See my *Western Marxism*, especially 75–115.

4. For a discussion of the politics of (Marxist) academia, see my paper, coauthored with Allan Rachlin, "Left-Wing Scholarship: Current Contradictions of Academic Production." *Humanities in Society* 6, nos. 2–3 (1983): 241–56.

5. For a discussion and exemplification of this approach to power structure research, see Robert Dahl's *Who Governs?* (New Haven: Yale University Press, 1959).

6. See the development of Robert Dahl's concept of polyarchy in various works by him including *A Preface to Democratic Theory* (Chicago: University of Chicago Press, 1956) and *Modern Political Analysis* (Englewood Cliffs, N.J.: Prentice-Hall, 1963). For a discussion of pluralist theory in general see Robert E. Agger, Daniel Goldrich, and Bert Swanson's *The Rulers and the Ruled*, abridged ed. (Belmont: Wadsworth, 1972), especially 46–50.

7. For a development of this notion of "democracy" see Gabriel Almond and Stanley Verba's *The Civic Culture* (Palo Alto: Stanford University Press, 1966).

8. A signal example of this neo-Weberian attempt to differentiate the various "classes" in advanced capitalism is D. W. Rossides's *The American Class System* (Boston: Houghton Mifflin, 1976), where he elaborates at least six "classes."

9. For a discussion of working-class academics, see Jake Ryan and Charles Sackray, *Strangers in Paradise: Academics from the Working-Class* (Boston: South End, 1984).

CHAPTER EIGHT

1. For a discussion of reproductive politics by a radical feminist, see Mary O'Brien's *The Politics of Reproduction*.

2. Habermas in his recent *The Theory of Communicative Action* examines what he

calls system-lifeworld penetration in much the same terms, albeit without going deep enough into the textuality/sexuality of desire in advanced capitalism, foreswearing what he takes to be the untoward mysticism of Marcuse, Horkheimer, and Adorno's Freudianism. He criticizes this alleged "mysticism" in his *Knowledge and Human Interests*, 32–33.

3. See, for example, Talcott Parsons, et al., *Family, Socialization and Interaction Process* (Glencoe, Ill.: Free Press, 1955); also see Talcott Parsons "The Social Ambience of the Family," in *Family: Its Function and Destiny*, ed. by Ruth Nanda Anshen (New York: Harper, 1949).

4. See Sara Evans, *Personal Politics: The Roots of Women's Liberation in the Civil Rights Movement and the New Left* (New York: Vintage, 1980).

5. For the classic discussion of the notion that women are constitutionally inferior to men, see Simone de Beauvoir, *The Second Sex* (New York: Knopf, 1953). Also see Dorothy Dinnerstein, *The Mermaid and the Minotaur* (New York: Harper and Row, 1976).

6. See Jill Johnston, *Lesbian Nation: The Feminist Solution* (New York: Simon and Schuster, 1974). Also see Del Martin and Phyllis Lyn, *Lesbian/Woman* (New York: Pantheon, 1972).

7. See Susan Strasser, *Never Done: A History of American Homework* (New York: Pantheon, 1982); also see Donald Treiman and Heidi Hartmann, *Women, Work and Wages: Equal Pay for Jobs of Equal Value* (Washington, D.C.: National Academy Press, 1981); also see Louise Kapp Howe, *Pink-Collar Workers* (New York: Putman, 1972).

8. Shulamith Firestone, *The Dialectic of Sex* (New York: William Morrow, 1970). Also see Mary Daly, *Beyond God the Father: Toward a Philosophy of Women's Liberation* (Boston: Beacon, 1973). Finally, see Alison Jaggar's *Feminist Politics and Human Nature* for a discussion of the range of feminisms.

9. See Betty Friedan, *The Second Stage* (New York: Summit Books, 1982).

10. On the subordination of woman/private to man/public, see Jean Elshtain, *Public Man, Private Woman*. As well, see Mark Kelly, *Private Woman, Public Stage* (New York: Oxford University Press, 1984).

11. For a classic "scientific" defense of feminist neurosis, see Ferdinand Lundberg and Marynia F. Farnham, "The Psychopathology of Feminism," from their *Modern Women: The Lost Sex* (New York: Harper and Row, 1947), 69–75.

12. For expression of a lesbian-feminist problematic, see the Boston Gay Collective, "In Amerika They Call Us Dykes," in *Our Bodies, Ourselves* (New York: Simon and Schuster, 1971), 57–59; also see Vivian Gornick, "Lesbians and Women's Liberation," in *Essays in Feminism* (New York: Harper and Row, 1978), 69–75.

13. Beginning with Engels's *The Origins of the Family, Private Property and the State* (Moscow: Progress Publishers, 1948), in which he argues that the "question" of women will be resolved (like all problems of exploitation) by setting them free to enter the collectively organized and owned productive sphere. Marx and Engels obviously regard women's oppression in the household and sexuality as essentially private matters giving rise, later, to the domestic-labor debate. Is housework productive work? Yes. It is therefore an item on the political agenda, as socialist feminists know (see Jaggar 1983).

14. See Nancy Chodorow, *The Reproduction of Mothering*, and Adrienne Rich, *Of Woman Born: Motherhood as Experience and Institution* (New York: Norton, 1976).

15. Christopher Lasch's *Haven in a Heartless World: The Family Besieged* (New York: Norton, 1977), argues for the inviolability of bourgeois family and so-called patriarchal authority as a check against the administering forces of the "helping" professions in Habermas's terms increasingly colonizing the private sphere. Although he is right to worry about the invasive forces of the state and culture, his defense of "family" as a private sphere is unfortunate especially in light of the socialist-feminist critique of Marxist sexism in general and the domestic-labor debate in particular. Lasch unwittingly reads like Parsons et al. (1955). This is especially unfortunate because it further distances critical theory from feminism when in fact their critiques of the politics of personality could be made virtually identical, as I do here, thus vitally joining them in intellectual and political cause.

16. Most lesbian feminists support this conflation, only further marginalizing *themselves*. See Jill Johnston, *Lesbian Nation*. Also for a critique, see Vivian Gornick, "Lesbians and Women's Liberation," in *Essays in Feminism*, 69–75.

17. See Phyllis Schlafly's remarks against the passage of the ERA in *The Congressional Digest*, June–July 1977.

18. After all, I am writing this footnote on the morning after the Supreme Court upheld the state of Georgia's law prohibiting "sodomy" between consenting adults, a serious blow to the gay movement and gays generally. Straight tolerance of gays is as episodic as white tolerance of blacks, men of women, gentiles of Jews.

19. See Judith Long Laws and Pepper Schwartz, *Sexual Scripts: The Social Construction of Female Sexuality* (Hinsdale, Ill.: Dryden, 1977). Also see John Money and Anke Ehrhardt, *Man and Woman, Boy and Girl: The Differentiation and Dimorphism of Gender Identity from Conception to Maturity* (Baltimore: Johns Hopkins University Press, 1972).

20. This liberal feminism is resonated by two of its most popular statements, Friedan's *The Feminine Mystique* (New York: Norton, 1963), and Rosabeth Moss Kanter's *Men and Women of the Corporation* (New York: Basic, 1977). For a critique of this strain of liberalism feminism, see Suzanne Gordon, "The New Corporate Feminism," *The Nation*, Feb. 5, 1983, 129.

21. See Marcuse's vibrant argument for a new sensibility capable of throwing off the yoke of domination in the here-and-now. This is a way of ensuring that socialism/feminism will not be in Karl Korsch's terms a dictatorship *over* the oppressed. See Herbert Marcuse, *An Essay on Liberation*, and Karl Korsch, *Marxism and Philosophy* (New York: Monthly Review Press, 1970). Also see Bruce Brown, *Marx, Freud and the Critique of Everyday Life* (New York: Monthly Review Press, 1973).

22. On housework, see Ann Oakley, *The Sociology of Housework* (New York: Pantheon, 1974). Also see Susan Strasser, *Never Done*. For a more historical perspective on family and work, see Winifred D. Wandersee, *Women's Work and Family Values, 1920–1940* (Cambridge: Harvard University Press, 1981).

23. See Zillah Eisenstein's *Capitalist Patriarchy and the Case for Socialist Feminism* (New York: Monthly Review Press, 1979). Also see her *The Radical Future of Liberal Feminism* (New York: Longman, 1981).

24. This notion that women ironically are better off than men is reinforced by books

like Nancy Chodorow's *The Reproduction of Mothering*, and Carol Gilligan's *In a Different Voice*. Also see Ashley Montagu's *The Natural Superiority of Women* (New York: Macmillan, 1962).

25. See, for example, John G. Richardson, "Wife Occupational Superiority and Marital Trouble: An Examination of the Hypothesis," *Journal of Marriage and the Family* 41, no. 1 (1979): 63–72. He concludes (on the evidence) that women's working, even in higher status jobs than their husbands, does not necessarily improve the family.

26. See Barbara Ehrenreich's *The Hearts of Men* (New York: Doubleday, 1983).

27. This double-bind/double-opportunity argument is amplified in Myra Marx Ferree's "The Confused American Housewife," *Psychology Today* 10 (September 1976): 76–78, 80.

28. See Phyllis Chesler's *Women and Madness* (New York: Avon, 1973) for a discussion of the psychiatrization of feminism.

29. See Morton Hunt, "The Future of Marriage," in Harold M. Hodges, ed., *Conflict and Consensus* (New York: Harper and Row, 1973), 264–74.

30. For a discussion of the emerging feminist resistance to the sexual division of labor subordinating private/women to public/men, see Rosalind Rosenberg, *Beyond Separate Spheres: The Roots of Modern Feminism* (New Haven: Yale University Press, 1982).

31. Of course, this is not to suggest that violence of men against women and children is not a "problem." Rather the problem is nested in a concatenated, overdetermined web of perverse desire and structure, making it futile to try to isolate it as a singularly remediable "phenomenon." See Judith Gingold, "Battered Wives," *Ms.*, August 1976, 51–54.

32. A telling example of the extraordinary force of sociology's text is found in the national media hoopla over a study of demographic barriers to the search of women in their thirties for marriageable men. That "all the good men are taken" is valorized by high science and thus (through the pages of *Newsweek* and on the Donahue show) is *enacted* by women made frantic by their looming spinsterhood.

CHAPTER NINE

1. See Louise Kapp Howe, *Pink-Collar Workers*. Also see David M. Katzman, *Seven Days a Week: Women and Domestic Service in Industrializing America* (New York: Oxford University Press, 1978). And Nancy Seifer, ed., *Nobody Speaks for Me!: Self-Portraits of American Working Class Women* (New York: Simon and Schuster, 1971).

2. See Peter Blau and Otis Dudley Duncan, *The American Occupational Structure* (New York: Wiley, 1967).

3. See Louis Scharf, *To Work and to Wed: Female Employment, Feminism, and the Great Depression* (Westport, Conn.: Greenwood, 1980). Also see Louise Tilly and Joan Scott, *Women, Work and Family* (New Haven: Holt, Rinehart and Winston, 1978).

4. Male identity is equivalent to the exchange value of his labor power; women's worth is only derived from her unwaged housework. Thus, women's worth is shrouded in sentiment and romance, inherently less accessible than worth quantified in fungible units of currency. See Jessie Bernard, *The Female World* (New York: Free Press, 1981); Lois Banner, *American Beauty* (New York: Knopf, 1983).

5. See Linda Gordon, *Woman's Body, Woman's Right: A Social History of Birth Control in America* (New York: Grossman, 1976).

6. See Catharine A. MacKinnon, *Sexual Harassment of Working Women: A Case of Sex Discrimination* (New Haven: Yale University Press, 1979). Also see Mark Bularzik, "Sexual Harrassment at the Workplace: Historical Notes," *Radical America* 12 (1978): 25–43.

7. See Judith Stacey, Susan Bereaud, and Joan Daniels, eds., *And Jill Came Tumbling After: Sexism in American Education* (New York: Dell, 1974).

8. See Edmund Wilson, *Sociobiology: The New Synthesis* (Cambridge: Harvard University Press, 1975) and his *On Human Nature* (Cambridge: Harvard University Press, 1978).

9. See, for example, Eleanor E. Maccoby and C. N. Jacklin, *The Psychology of Sex Differences* (Palo Alto: Stanford University Press, 1974).

10. See Dale Spender, *Man Made Language* (London: Routledge and Kegan Paul, 1980).

11. See Arthur B. Jensen, *Educability and Group Differences* (New York: Harper and Row, 1973).

12. As illustrative examples, see Irene H. Frieze, *Women and Sex Roles: A Social Psychological Perspective* (New York: Norton, 1978), and see Leslie Friedman, *Sex Role Stereotyping in the Mass Media: An Annotated Bibliography* (New York: Garland, 1977).

13. See Angela Davis, *Women, Race and Class* (New York: Random House, 1981); Regina Green, *Native American Women: A Bibliography* (Bloomington: Indiana University Press, 1983); Gloria Hull, Patricia Bell Scott, and Barbara Smith, eds., *All the Women are White, All the Blacks are Men, But Some of Us are Brave: Black Women's Studies* (Old Westbury, N.Y.: The Feminist Press, 1982).

14. For an early statement of this feminist position, see Gloria Steinem, "What it Would Be Like if Women Win," *Time*, August 21, 1970, 22–23.

15. See Betty Friedan, *The Feminine Mystique*, especially 13–29.

16. For an excellent and wide-ranging critique of the "sociology of family," see Jane Flax, "Tragedy or Emancipation?: On the 'Decline' of Contemporary American Families," in Mark E. Kann, ed., *The Future of American Democracy* (Philadelphia: Temple University Press, 1983), 83–115.

17. See the versions of an exchange-theoretic sociology of family in this regard, particularly Wesley Burr's *Contemporary Theories about the Family* (New York: Free Press, 1974).

18. For a discussion of dialogue and power, see Bruce Ackerman's *Social Justice in the Welfare State* (New Haven: Yale University Press, 1980), and my counterpoint and critique, "A Critical Theory of Dialogue." I read Habermas against Ackerman and then try to transcend them both in what amounts to a version of a more comprehensive critical discourse theory.

19. See Habermas's *Legitimation Crisis*.

20. For the classic discussion of scapegoating and its psychopolitical dynamic, see Theodor W. Adorno et al., *The Authoritarian Personality* (New York: Harper, 1950).

21. For a striking critique of this sort of existentialism, see Adorno's *The Jargon of Authenticity*.

22. This bourgeois optimism is elaborated in Edward Shorter's *The Making of the Modern Family* (New York: Basic, 1975). Although Shorter convincingly argues that the "traditional" family was a hell-hole for women and children, he idealizes contemporary "companionate" marriages as the epitome of intergender democracy.

23. For an innovative discussion of the modalities of this "bourgeois life" as it is expressed and experienced by women today, see Bonnie Allesi's "Women and Shopping: A Sociological Perspective," Ph.D. diss., department of sociology, SUNY-Buffalo, 1986. Allessi blends socialist-feminist and Frankfurt perspectives on women's shopping, arguing that shopping is dialectically both unwaged labor and a trivial compensation for a beleaguered existence.

24. For a suggestive socialist-feminist perspective on work and family, see Eli Zaretsky's *Capitalism, The Family and Personal Life* (New York: Monthly Review Press, 1976).

25. The most important elaboration of a psychoanalytically informed Marxist-feminism comprehending the politics of desire remains Joel Kovel's *The Age of Desire: Case Histories of a Radical Psychoanalyst*. Kovel blends case studies drawn from his own clinical work with dialectical/deconstructive disussions of how these psychopathologies refract and reproduce larger systemic dynamics. His facility in moving back and forth between desire and its capitalist-sexist subject/object exemplifies deconstructive practice without sacrificing the insights afforded by discourse analysis to their usual methodological fetishes. Kovel dramatically demonstrates how the "texts" of experience and dream can be read (and thus reformulated) politically.

CHAPTER TEN

1. I attempted this rethinking, albeit without the buttress of either feminism or deconstruction, in my "Dialectical Sensibility II: Towards a New Intellectuality," *Canadian Journal of Political and Social Theory* 1, no. 2 (Spring–Summer 1977): 47–57. Also see my "Marxism, Feminism, Deconstruction: Reading Sociology," in Christine Gailey and Viana Muller, eds., *Critical Anthropology*, forthcoming.

2. I read Adorno's *Negative Dialectics* not as gloomy nihilism, a reading imposed on him both by Marxists and positivists who freight criticism with the expectation that it arrive at precise blueprints of an imminent future. But negative dialectics aims at the positive, at new construction, *indirectly,* working through the aporias of the past and present as the prehistory of possible freedom.

3. For a critical perspective on this and other approaches to hermeneutics, see Dieter Misgeld's "Critical Theory and Hermeneutics: The Debate Between Habermas and Gadamer," in John O'Neill, ed., *On Critical Theory*, 164–83. Also see James Schmidt's "Reification and Recollection: Emancipatory Interests and the Sociology of Knowledge," *Canadian Journal of Political and Social Theory* 2, no. 1 (Winter 1978): 89–111.

4. An analogue of this excavation process is found in Michel Foucault's *The Archaeology of Knowledge* (New York: Harper and Row, 1976).

5. I have reflected on the ontological constraints of the social object world in the last chapter of my *Social Problems Through Conflict and Order*, "Ecology, Growth and Social Futures," 243–68.

6. See John O'Neill's "Merleau-Ponty's Critique of Marxist Scientism," *Canadian*

Journal of Political and Social Theory 2, no. 1 (1978): 33–62; also see Herbert Reid, "Totality, Temporality and Praxis: Existential Phenomenology and Critical Political Theory," *Canadian Journal of Political and Social Theory* 2, no. 1 (Winter 1978): 113–35.

7. See Max Weber's essay "Science as a Vocation," in Gerth and Mills, eds., *From Max Weber*, 129–56.

8. See Theodor Adorno, *Philosophy of Modern Music*. For a more comprehensive view of his aesthetic/social theory, see his *Aesthetic Theory* (London: Routledge and Kegan Paul, 1982).

9. See Steven Lukes, *Emile Durkheim: His Life and Work* (New York: Harper and Row, 1977) for a more general discussion of the intellectual and political problematics addressed by Durkheim.

10. See Alan Blum and Peter McHugh, "The Social Ascription of Motive," *American Sociological Review* 36 (1971): 98–109.

11. For a different sort of discussion of ideology/text, see Fredric Jameson's "Ideology of the Text," *Salmagundi* 31 (1975–76): 204–46.

12. For a programmatic blend of Marxism and deconstruction, see Andrew Parker's "Of Politics and Limits: Derrida Re-Marx," *SCE Reports* 8 (1980): 83–104.

13. For an earlier example of this sort of positivist conflict theory, see, for example, J. David Colfax and Jack L. Roach, *Radical Sociology* (New York: Basic, 1971); also see Paul Connerton, ed., *Critical Sociology* (Harmondsworth: Penguin, 1976), for a version of critical sociology more heavily indebted to the Frankfurt School.

14. See, for example, Peter Rabinowitz, "Truth in Fiction: A Reexamination of Audiences," *Critical Inquiry* 4 (1977): 121–42.

15. See Harold Bloom, *The Anxiety of Influence: A Theory of Poetry*.

16. For a further discussion of the importance of the concept of canons for "normal science," see Margaret Masterna, "The Nature of a Paradigm," in *Criticism and the Growth of Knowledge*, ed. by Imre Lakatos and Alain Musgrove (Cambridge: Cambridge University Press, 1970), 59–89.

17. See Derek Phillips, "Paradigms and Incommensurability," *Theory and Society* 2 (1975): 37–62.

18. On the relation between critique and science, see John J. Sewart, "Critical Theory and the Critique of Conservative Method," *American Sociologist* 13 (1978): 15–22.

19. This ecumenism is resonated throughout the discipline. See, for example, Pierre van den Berghe, "Dialectic and Functionalism: Toward Reconciliation," *American Sociological Review* 28 (1963): 695–705; and Jonathan Turner, "A Strategy for Reformulating the Dialectical and Functional Theories of Conflict," *Social Forces* 53 (1975): 433–44.

20. See Alexander D. Blumensteil, "The Sociology of Hard Times," in George Psathas, ed., *Phenomenological Sociology: Issues and Applications* (New York: Wiley, 1973), 187–215. Also see Dusky Lee Smith, "Sociology and the Sunshine Boys," 18–44.

21. For a cogent critique of liberalism, see Alan Wolfe, *The Limits of Legitimacy* (New York: Free Press, 1977); also see Christian Bay, *Strategies of Political Emancipation* (Notre Dame, Ind.: University of Notre Dame Press, 1981).

22. For a discussion of the seeming ecumenism of the main text and mainstream, see Nicholas Mullins, *Theories and Theory Groups in Contemporary American Sociology* (New York: Harper and Row, 1973).

23. This integration of diverse theories into a single concatenated voice is exemplified in George Ritzer's *Sociology: A Multiple Paradigm Science* (rev. ed. Boston: Allyn and Bacon, 1980) and also in his *Toward an Integrated Sociological Paradigm: The Search for an Exemplar and an Image of the Subject Matter* (Boston: Allyn and Bacon, 1981).

24. An example of this depoliticization of dialectic is found in Louis Schneider's "Dialectic in Sociology," *American Sociological Review* 36 (1971): 667–78.

25. See, for example, Whitney Pope's "Classic on Classic: Parsons' Interpretation of Durkheim," *American Sociological Review* 38 (1973): 399–415; also see Whitney Pope, Jere Cohen, and Lawrence E. Hazelrigg, "On the Divergence of Weber and Durkheim: A Critique of Parsons' Convergence Thesis," *American Sociological Review* 40 (1975): 417–27. Also see Jere Cohen, Lawrence Hazelrigg, and Whitney Pope, "DeParsonizing Weber: A Critique of Parsons' Interpretation of Weber's Sociology," *American Sociological Review* 40 (1975): 229–41.

26. Herbert Marcuse, Robert Paul Wolff, and Barrington Moore, Jr., *A Critique of Pure Tolerance* (Boston: Beacon, 1966).

27. Charles Page, correspondence, *ASA Footnotes*, October 1985, 10.

28. For a discussion of speech-act theory, see John Searle's *Speech Acts* (London: Cambridge University Press, 1969) and J. L. Austin's *How to Do Things With Words* (Oxford: Oxford University Press, 1962). For a critical discussion of speech-act theory, see Jurgen Habermas's *The Theory of Communicative Action*, especially 273–337.

29. See Jacques Derrida, "Living On: Border Lines," in *Deconstruction and Criticism*, ed. by Harold Bloom et al. (New York: Seabury, 1979), 75–175.

30. See Aaron Cicourel, *Method and Measurement in Sociology* (Glencoe, Ill.: Free Press, 1964); also see Peter McHugh et al., *On the Beginning of Social Inquiry* (London: Routledge and Kegan Paul, 1974).

31. See Richard Rorty's "Philosophy as a Kind of Writing: An Essay on Derrida," *New Literary History* 10 (1978): 141–60. Also see John Brenkman's *Culture and Domination* (Ithaca: Cornell University Press, forthcoming).

32. See Janice B. Lodahl and Gerald Gordon, "The Structure of Scientific Fields and the Funding of University Graduate Departments," *American Sociological Review* 37 (1972): 57–72.

33. John O'Neill has sharply addressed the requirement of methodical self-restraint as an ethic of sociological professionalization in his essay "Sociology as a Skin Trade" in his book of the same name, 3–10.

34. An evocative example of this decentering writing is Adorno's aphoristic, epigrammatic "presentation" of critical theory in his tellingly post-World War II *Minima Moralia: Reflections from Damaged Life* (London: New Left Books, 1974). Also see Gillian Rose, *The Melancholy Science: An Introduction to the Thought of Theodor Adorno* (London: Macmillan, 1978).

35. Habermas offers a cogent critique of this bourgeois monadology in his *The Theory of Communicative Action*, especially 366–99.

36. Charles Rachlis has criticized an earlier version of this aesthetic politics (not

yet a full-blown discourse theory) for its alleged idealism. See his "Marcuse and the Problem of Happiness," *Canadian Journal of Political and Social Theory* 2, no. 1 (1978): 63–88.

CHAPTER ELEVEN

1. See Julia Kristeva, "La Femme, ce n'est pas jamais ca," *Tel Quel* 59 (1974): 19–24. Also see Shoshana Felman, "Rereading Feminism," *Yale French Studies* 62 (1981): 19–44.

2. Jürgen Habermas, *Knowledge and Human Interests*, 32–33.

3. I have reflected on the science embracing and exemplifying this role of reason in my "On Science as Domination," in *Domination*, ed. by Alkis Kontos (Toronto: University of Toronto Press, 1975), 185–200.

4. See, for example, Geoffrey Hartman, *Saving the Text: Literature/Derrida/Philosophy* (Baltimore: Johns Hopkins University Press, 1981).

5. See Gerald Graff, *Literature Against Itself: Literary Ideas in Modern Society* (Chicago: University of Chicago Press, 1977).

6. See Robert Friedrichs, "Dialectical Sociology: Towards a Resolution of Current 'Crises' in Western Sociology," *British Journal of Sociology* 13 (1972): 263–74.

7. See Herbert Marcuse, "A Note on Dialectic," second preface to *Reason and Revolution* (Boston: Beacon, 1960); also see Theodor Adorno's *Negative Dialectics*.

8. Habermas in his own terms summarizes this tradition in his *The Theory of Communicative Action*, especially 273–337.

9. For an account of reader-response theory, see Steven Mailloux, *Interpretive Conventions: The Reader in the Study of American Fiction* (Ithaca: Cornell University Press, 1982).

10. See Peter Rabinowitz, "Truth in Fiction: A Reexamination of Audiences," *Critical Inquiry* 4 (1977): 121–42.

11. See, for example, Luce Irigaray, *This Sex Which Is Not One* (Ithaca: Cornell University Press, 1985) on the modalities of femininity and thus feminism.

Bibliography.

Abott, Walter J.. *Foundations of Modern Sociology: Study Guide and Workbook*. 4th ed. Englewood Cliffs, N.J.: Prentice Hall, 1985.

Ackerman, Bruce. *Social Justice in the Welfare State*. New Haven: Yale University Press, 1980.

Adorno, Theodor. *Aesthetic Theory*. London: Routledge and Kegan Paul, 1982.

———. "Commitment." In Andrew Arato and Eike Gebhardt, eds., *The Essential Frankfurt School Reader*. New York: Urizen, 1978a. 300–318.

———. *The Jargon of Authenticity*. Evanston, Ill.: Northwestern University Press, 1970.

———. *Minima Moralia: Reflections from Damaged Life*. London: New Left Books, 1974.

———. *Negative Dialectics*. New York: Seabury, 1973a.

———. "On the Fetish-Character of Music and the Regression of History." In Andrew Arato and Eike Gebhardt, eds., *The Essential Frankfurt School Reader*. New York: Urizen, 1978b. 270–99.

———. *Philosophy of Modern Music*. New York: Seabury, 1973b.

———. "Society." *Salmagundi*, nos. 11–12 (1969–70): 144–53.

———. "The Stars Down to Earth: The *Los Angeles Times* Astrology Column: A Study in Secondary Synthesis." *Telos*, no. 19 (Spring 1974): 13–90.

———. "The Sociology of Knowledge and its Consciousness." In Andrew Arato and Eike Gebhardt, eds., *The Essential Frankfurt School Reader*. New York: Urizen, 1978c. 452–65.

———. "Sociology and Psychology." *New Left Review*, nos. 46–47 (1967–68): 67–80, 79–90.

———. "Subject and Object." In Andrew Arato and Eike Gebhardt, eds., *The Essential Frankfurt School Reader*. New York: Urizen, 1978d. 497–511.

Adorno, Theodor W., et al. *The Authoritarian Personality*. New York: Harper, 1950.

Adorno Theodor W., Hans Albert, Ralf Dahrendorf, Jürgen Habermas, Harold Pilot, and Karl R. Popper. *The Positivist Dispute in German Sociology*. London: Heinemann, 1976.

Agger, Ben. "A Critical Theory of Dialogue." *Humanities in Society* 4, no. 1 (Winter 1981): 7–30.

———. "The Dialectic of Deindustrialization: An Essay on Advanced Capitalism." In John Forester, ed., *Critical Theory and Public Life*. Cambridge: MIT Press, 1985.

——. "The Dialectic of Desire: The Holocaust, Monopoly Capitalism and Radical Anamnesis." *Dialectical Anthropology* 8, nos. 1–2 (1983a): 75–86.

——. "Dialectical Sensibility I: Critical Theory, Scientism and Empiricism." *Canadian Journal of Political and Social Theory* 1, no. 1 (1977a): 3–34.

——. "Dialectical Sensibility II: Towards a New Intellectuality." *Canadian Journal of Political and Social Theory* 1, no. 2 (1977b): 47–57.

——. *Fast Capitalism: A Critical Theory of Significance.* Urbana: University of Illinois Press, 1989.

——. "On Happiness and the Damaged Life." In John O'Neill, ed., *On Critical Theory*. New York: Seabury, 1976a.

——. "Marcuse's Aesthetic Politics: Ideology-Critique and Socialist Ontology." *Dialectical Anthropology.* Forthcoming.

——. "Marcuse's Freudian Marxism." *Dialectical Anthropology* 8, no. 4 (1982): 319–36.

——. "Marcuse and Habermas on New Science." *Polity* 14, no. 2 (Winter 1976b): 158–81.

——. "Marxism, Feminism, Deconstruction." In Christine Gailey and Viana Muller, eds., *Critical Anthropology: The Critical Ethnology of Stanley Diamond.* Forthcoming.

——. "Marxism 'or' the Frankfurt School?" *Philosophy of the Social Sciences* 14 (March 1983b): 347–65.

——. "On Science as Domination." In Alkis Kontos, ed., *Domination.* Toronto: University of Toronto Press, 1975.

——. *Reading Science: A Literary and Political Analysis*, forthcoming.

——. *Western Marxism: An Introduction.* Santa Monica: Goodyear, 1979a.

——. "Work and Authority in Marcuse and Habermas." *Human Studies* 2 (1979b): 191–208.

Agger, Ben, and S. A. McDaniel. *Social Problems Through Conflict and Order.* Toronto: Addison-Wesley, 1983.

Agger, Ben, and Allan Rachlin. "Left-Wing Scholarship: Current Contradictions of Academic Production." *Humanities in Society* 6, nos. 2–3 (1983): 241–56.

Agger, Robert E., Daniel Goldrich, and Bert Swanson. *The Rulers and the Ruled.* Belmont: Wadsworth, 1972.

Alexander, Jeffrey. *Theoretical Logic in Sociology.* Berkeley: University of California Press, 1982.

——. *Neofunctionalism.* Beverley Hills: Sage, 1985.

Allesi, Bonnie. "Women and Shopping: A Sociological Perspective." Ph.D. diss., department of sociology, SUNY-Buffalo, 1986.

Almond, Gabriel, and Stanley Verba. *The Civic Culture.* Palo Alto, Calif.: Stanford University Press, 1966.

Althusser, Louis. *For Marx.* London: Allen Lane, 1969.

——. "Ideology and Ideological State Apparatuses." In his *Lenin and Philosophy.* London: New Left Books, 1971.

Althusser, Louis, and Étienne Balibar. *Reading Capital.* London: New Left Books, 1970.

Amin, Samir. *L'Accumulation à l'échelle mondial*. Paris: Anthropos, 1970.

Apel, Karl-Otto. *Hermeneutik und Ideologie-kritik*. Frankfurt: Suhrkamp, 1971.

————. "Szientismus oder transzendentale Hermeneutik?" In R. Bubner et al., eds., *Hermeneutik und Dialektik*. Vol. 1. Tubingen: J.C.B. Mohr, 1970.

————. *Towards a Transformation of Philosophy*. London: Routledge and Kegan Paul, 1980.

————. *Understanding and Explanation*. Cambridge: MIT Press, 1984.

Arendt, Hannah. *The Human Condition*. Chicago: University of Chicago Press, 1960.

Arnold, Matthew. *Literature and Dogma*. New York: A. L. Burt, 1903.

Aron, Raymond. *Main Currents of Sociological Thought*. Vols. 1 and 2. Harmondsworth: Pelican, 1968 and 1970.

Aronowitz, Stanley. *The Crisis in Historical Materialism*. New York: Praeger, 1981.

Austin, J. L.. *How to Do Things with Words*. Oxford: Oxford University Press, 1962.

Axelos, Kostas. *Alienation and Techne in the Thought of Karl Marx*. Austin: University of Texas Press, 1976.

Balch, Stephen H., et al. "The Politicization of Scholarship." *Society* 23, no. 3 (1986): 3–13.

Banner, Lois. *American Beauty*. New York: Knopf, 1983.

Baran, Paul, and Paul Sweezy. *Monopoly Capital*. New York: Monthly Review Press, 1966.

Barthes, Roland. "The Death of the Author." In Stephen Heath, ed., *Image-Music-Text: Roland Barthes*. London: Fontana, 1977.

————. *The Pleasure of the Text*. New York: Hill and Wang, 1974.

————. *S/Z*. New York: Hill and Wang, 1974.

————. *Writing Degree Zero*. New York: Hill and Wang, 1967.

Bassis, Michael S., Richard J. Gelles, and Ann Levine. *Sociology: An Introduction*, New York: Random House, 1980.

————. *Sociology: An Introduction*. 2d ed. New York: Random House, 1984.

Baudrillard, Jean. *The Mirror of Production*. St. Louis: Telos Press, 1975.

Bauman, Zygmunt. *Towards a Critical Sociology: An Essay on Commonsense and Emancipation*. London: Routledge and Kegan Paul, 1976.

Baxandall, Rosalyn, Linda Gordon, and Susan Riverby. eds. *America's Working Women: A Documentary History, 1600–Present*. New York: Vintage, 1976.

Bay, Christian. *Strategies of Political Emancipation*. Notre Dame, Ind.: University of Notre Dame Press, 1981.

————. *The Structure of Freedom*. Palo Alto, Calif: Stanford University Press, 1956.

Bell, Daniel. *The Coming of Post-Industrial Society*. New York: Basic, 1973.

————. *The Cultural Contradictions of Capitalism*. New York: Basic, 1976.

————. *The End of Ideology*. New York: Basic, 1976.

Bendix, Reinhard. *Work and Authority in Industry*. Berkeley: University of California Press, 1974.

Benhabib, Selya. "Epistemologies of Postmodernism: A Rejoinder to Jean-Francois Lyotard." *New German Critique*, no. 3 (1984): 103–26.

Benjamin, Walter. "Art in the Age of Mechanical Reproduction." In his *Illuminations*. New York: Schocken, 1969.

Bennis, Ingrid. *Combat in the Erogenous Zone*. New York: Knopf, 1972.

Berch, Bettina. *The Endless Day: The Political Economy of Women and Work*. New York: Harcourt Brace Jovanovich, 1982.

Berger, Peter. *An Invitation to Sociology: A Humanistic Perspective*. Garden City: Doubleday, 1963.

Berger, Peter, Brigitte Berger, and Hansfried Kellner. *The Homeless Mind*. New York: Random House, 1974.

Berger, Peter, and Thomas Luckmann. *The Social Construction of Reality*. Garden City: Doubleday, 1967.

Berghe, Pierre L. van den. "Dialectic and Functionalism: Toward Reconciliation." *American Sociological Review* 28 (1963): 695–705.

Berle, A., Jr., and G. Means. *The Modern Corporation and Private Property*. New York: Macmillan, 1933.

Bernard, Jessie. *The Female World*. New York: Free Press, 1981.

Bernstein, Basil. *Class, Codes and Control*. London: Routledge and Kegan Paul, 1971.

Bernstein, Eduard. *Evolutionary Socialism*. New York: Schocken, 1961.

Bernstein, I. N., and H. E. Freeman. *Academic and Entrepreneurial Research*. New York: Russell Sage, 1975.

Blackburn, Robin, ed. *Ideology in Social Science*. London: Fontana, 1972.

Blau, Peter. *Exchange and Power in Social Life*. New York: Wiley, 1964.

Blau, Peter, and Otis Dudley Duncan. *The American Occupational Structure*. New York: Wiley, 1967.

Blauner, Robert. *Alienation and Freedom*. Chicago: University of Chicago Press, 1964.

Bloch, Ernst. *Philosophy of Hope*. New York: Herder and Herder, 1970.

Bloom, Harold. *The Anxiety of Influence: A Theory of Poetry*. New York: Oxford University Press, 1973.

————. *A Map of Misreading*. New York: Oxford University Press, 1975.

Blum, Alan. *Theorizing*. London: Heinemann, 1975.

Blum, Alan, and Peter McHugh. "The Social Ascription of Motive." *American Sociological Review* 36 (1971): 98–109.

Blumensteil, Alexander D. "The Sociology of Hard Times." In George Psathas, ed., *Phenomenological Sociology: Issues and Applications*. New York: Wiley, 1973.

Blumer, Herbert. "Comments on Parsons as a Symbolic Interactionist." *Sociological Inquiry* 45 (1975): 59–62.

————. *Symbolic Interaction: Perspective and Method*. Englewood Cliffs, N.J.: Prentice-Hall, 1969.

Bookchin, Murray. *Post-Scarcity Anarchism*. Berkeley: Ramparts Press, 1971.

Boston Gay Collective. "In Amerika They Call Us Dykes." In *Our Bodies, Ourselves*. New York: Simon and Schuster, 1971. 57–59.

Bottomore, Tom, ed. *Austro-Marxism*. Oxford: Clarendon Press, 1978.

————. *Marxist Sociology*. New York: Holmes and Meier, 1975.

Bowles, Samuel, and Herbert Gintis. *Schooling in Capitalist America*. New York: Basic, 1976.

Braverman, Stanley. *Labor and Monopoly Capital: The Degredation of Work in the 20th Century*. New York: Monthly Review Press, 1974.

Breines, Paul. "Redeeming Redemption." *Telos* 65 (Fall 1985): 152–58.

Brenkman, John. *Culture and Domination*. Ithaca: Cornell University Press. Forthcoming.

Brinkerhoff, David B., and Lynn K. White. *Sociology*. St. Paul: West, 1985.

Broom, Leonard, Philip Seznick, and Dorothy Broom Darroch. *Sociology*. 7th ed. New York: Harper and Row, 1981.

Brown, Bruce. *Marx, Freud and the Critique of Everyday Life*. New York: Monthly Review Press, 1973.

Brownmiller, Susan. *Against Our Will: Men, Women and Rape*. New York: Bantam, 1975.

Buck-Morss, Susan. *The Origin of Negative Dialectics*. New York: Free Press, 1977.

Bularzik, Mark. "Sexual Harrassment at the Workplace: Historical Notes." *Radical America* 12 (1978): 25–43.

Burgess, Robert, and Ted Huston. *Social Exchange in Developing Relationships*. New York: Academic Press, 1979.

Burr, Welsey. *Contemporary Theories About the Family*. New York: Free Press, 1979.

Camus, Albert. *The Myth of Sisyphus*. New York: Knopf, 1955.

Cargan, Ballatine. *Sociological Footprints: Introduction Readings in Sociology*. 3rd ed. Belmont: Wadsworth, 1984.

Castells, Manuel. *The City and the Grass Roots*. Berkeley: University of California Press, 1983.

Centers, Richard. *The Psychology of Social Classes*. Princeton: Princeton University Press, 1949.

Carchedi, Guillermo. *On the Economic Identification of Social Classes*. London: Routledge and Kegan Paul, 1978.

Chambliss, William. *Whose Law? What Order?* New York: Wiley, 1976.

Champion, Dean J., et al. *Introduction to Sociology*. New York: Holt, Rinehart and Winston, 1984.

Chesler, Phyllis. *Women and Madness*. New York: Avon, 1973.

Chodorow, Nancy. *The Reproduction of Mothering*. Berkeley: University of California Press, 1978.

Cicourel, Aaron. *Method and Measurement in Sociology*. Glencoe, Ill.: Free Press, 1964.

Cohen, Jere, Lawrence Hazelrigg, and Whitney Pope. "DeParsonizing Weber: A Critique of Parsons' Interpretation of Weber's Sociology." *American Sociological Review* 40 (1975): 229–41.

Coleman, James S.. *The Evaluation of the Equality of Education Office*. Santa Monica: Rand, 1969.

Colfax, J. David, and Jack L. Roach, eds. *Radical Sociology*. New York: Basic, 1971.

Collins, Randall. *Conflict Sociology*. New York: Academic Press, 1975.

———. "A Conflict Theory of Sexual Stratification." *Social Problems* 12 (1971): 3–12.

———. "On the Microfoundations of Macrosociology." *American Journal of Sociology* 86 (1981): 984–1014.

———. *Three Sociological Traditions*. New York: Oxford University Press, 1985.

Conklin, John E. *Sociology: An Introduction*. New York: Macmillan, 1984.

Connerton, Paul, ed. *Critical Sociology*. Harmondsworth: Penguin, 1976.

————. *The Tragedy of Enlightenment*. Cambridge: Cambridge University Press, 1980.

Coser, Lewis. *The Functions of Social Conflict*. New York: Free Press, 1966.

————. *Masters of Sociological Thought*. New York: Harcourt Brace Jovanovich, 1977.

Coward, Rosalind, and John Ellis. *Language and Materialism: Developments in Semiology and the Theory of the Subject*. London: Routledge and Kegan Paul, 1977.

Culler, Jonathan. *On Deconstruction*. Ithaca: Cornell University Press, 1982.

————. *Ferdinand de Saussure*. London: Fontana, 1976.

Dahl, Robert. *Modern Political Analysis*. Englewood Cliffs, N.J.: Prentice-Hall, 1963.

————. *A Preface to Democratic Theory*. Chicago: University of Chicago Press, 1956.

————. *Who Governs?* New Haven: Yale University Press, 1959.

Dahrendorf, Ralf. *Class and Class Conflict in Industrial Society*. Palo Alto, Calif.: Stanford University Press, 1969.

————. "Homo Sociologicus." In his *Essays in the Theory of Society*. Palo Alto, Calif.: Stanford University Press, 1968.

————. *Life-Chances*. Chicago: University of Chicago Press, 1979.

Daly, Mary. *Beyond God the Father: Toward a Philosophy of Woman's Liberation*. Boston: Beacon, 1973.

Davis, Angela. *Women, Race and Class*. New York: Random House, 1981.

Davis, Kingsley, and W. E. Moore. "Some Principles of Stratification." *American Sociological Review* 10 (1945): 242–49.

de Beauvoir, Simone. *The Second Sex*. New York: Knopf, 1953.

Debord, Guy. *Society of the Spectacle*. Detroit: Black and Red Press, 1972.

DeFleur, Melvin L., and William D'Antonio. *Sociology: Human Society*. 4th ed. New York: Random House, 1984.

Deleuze, Gilles, and Felix Guattari. *The Anti-Oedipus*. Minneapolis: University of Minnesota Press, 1983.

Denisoff, R. Serge, and Ralph Wahrman. *An Introduction to Sociology*. New York: Macmillan, 1983.

Derrida, Jacques. *Of Grammatology*. Baltimore: Johns Hopkins University Press, 1976.

————. "Living On: Border Lines." In Harold Bloom et al., eds., *Deconstruction and Criticism*. New York: Seabury, 1979.

————. *Speech and Phenomena*. Evanston, Ill. Northwestern University Press, 1973.

————. *Writing and Difference*. Chicago: University of Chicago Press, 1978.

Diesing, Paul. *Science and Ideology in the Policy Sciences*. New York: Aldine, 1982.

Dinnerstein, Dorothy. *The Mermaid and the Minotaur*. New York: Harper and Row, 1976.

Doob, Christopher Bates. *Sociology: An Introduction*. New York: Holt, Rinehart and Winston, 1985.

Douglas, Jack, et al., eds. *Introduction to the Sociologies of Everyday Life*. Boston: Allyn and Bacon, 1980.

Duberman, Lucile, and Clayton Hartjen. *Sociology: Focus on Society*. Glenview, Ill.: Scott-Foresman, 1979.

Dowling, William. *Jameson, Althusser, Marx*. Ithaca: Cornell University Press, 1984.

Dunayevskaya, Raya. *Marxism and Freedom*. New York: Bookman Associates, 1977.

Durkheim, Emile. *The Division of Labor in Society*. New York: Free Press, 1964.

————. *The Rules of Sociological Method*. Glencoe, Ill.: Free Press, 1950.

————. *Suicide*. New York: Free Press, 1966.

Eagleton, Terry. *Literary Theory*. Minneapolis: University of Minnesota Press, 1983.

————. *Marxism and Literary Criticism*. London: Methuen, 1976.

Eco, Umberto. *The Role of the Reader: Explanation in the Semiotics of Texts*. Bloomington: Indiana University Press, 1979.

Ehrenreich, Barbara. *The Hearts of Men*. New York: Doubleday, 1983.

Eisenstein, Zillah, ed. *Capitalist Patriarchy and the Case for Socialist Feminism*. New York: Monthly Review Press, 1979.

————. *The Radical Future of Liberal Feminism*. New York: Longman, 1981.

Eitzen, D. Stanley. *In Conflict and Order: Understanding Society*. 3rd ed. Boston: Allyn and Bacon, 1985.

Elshtain, Jean. *Public Man, Private Woman*. Princeton: Princeton University Press, 1981.

Engels, Friedrich. *The Origins of the Family, Private Property and the State*. Moscow: Progress Publishers, 1948.

Eshleman, J. Ross, and Barbara G. Cashion. *Sociology: An Introduction*. Boston: Little, Brown, 1985.

Evans, Sara. *Personal Politics: The Roots of Women's Liberation in the Civil Rights Movement and the New Left*. New York: Vintage, 1980.

Fein, Helen. "Is Sociology Aware of Genocide?: Recognition of Genocide in Introductory Sociology Texts in the United States, 1947–1977." *Humanity and Society* 3, no. 3 (1979): 177–93.

Fekete, John. *The Critical Twilight*. London: Routledge and Kegan Paul, 1978.

Felman, Shoshana. "Rereading Femininity." *Yale French Studies* 62 (1981): 19–44.

Ferree, Myra Marx. "The Confused American Housewife." *Psychology Today* 10 (September 1976): 76–78, 80.

Firestone, Shulamith. *The Dialectic of Sex*. New York: Morrow, 1970.

Fish, Stanley. *Is There a Text in the Class?* Cambridge: Harvard University Press, 1980.

Flax, Jane. "Tragedy or Emancipation?: On the 'Decline' of Contemporary American Families." In Mark E. Kann, ed., *The Future of American Democracy*. Philadelphia: Temple University Press, 1983.

Forester, John, ed. *Critical Theory and Public Life*. Cambridge: MIT Press, 1985.

Foucault, Michel. *The Archaeology of Knowledge*. New York: Harper and Row, 1976.

————. *Discipline and Punish*. London: Allen Lane, 1977.

Frank, Andre Gunder. *Dependent Accumulation and Underdevelopment*. New York: Monthly Review Press, 1979.

————. *Latin America: Underdevelopment or Revolution*. New York: Monthly Review Press, 1969.

————. *World Accumulation, 1492–1759*. New York: Monthly Review Press, 1978.

Fraser, Nancy. "The French Derrideans: Politicizing Deconstruction or Deconstructing the Political?" *New German Critique*, no. 33 (1984): 127–54.

Freire, Paulo. *Pedagogy of the Oppressed*. New York: Seabury, 1973.

Freud, Sigmund. *Civilization and its Discontents*. New York: Norton, 1981.

Friedan, Betty. *The Feminine Mystique*. New York: Norton, 1963.

———. *The Second Stage*. New York: Summit Books, 1981.

Friedman, Leslie. *Sex Role Stereotyping in the Mass Media: An Annotated Bibliography*. New York: Garland, 1977.

Friedrichs, Robert. "Dialectical Sociology: Towards a Resolution of Current 'Crises' in Western Sociology." *British Journal of Sociology* 13 (1972): 263–74.

———. *A Sociology of Sociology*. New York: Free Press, 1970.

Frieze, Irene H. *Women and Sex Roles: A Social Psychological Perspective*. New York: Norton, 1978.

Frye, Northrop. *Anatomy of Criticism*. Princeton: Princeton University Press, 1957.

Gadamer, Hans-Georg. *Hegel's Dialectic: Five Hermeneutical Studies*. New Haven: Yale University Press, 1976.

———. *Truth and Method*. New York: Seabury, 1975.

Galbraith, John Kenneth. *The New Industrial State*. Boston: Houghton Mifflin, 1967.

Gans, Herbert. "The Uses of Poverty: The Poor Pay All." *Social Policy* (July–August 1971): 20–24.

Garfinkel, Harold. *Studies in Ethnomethodology*. Englewood Cliffs, N.J.: Prentice-Hall, 1967.

Hartman, Geoffrey. *Saving the Text: Literature/Derrida/Philosophy*. Baltimore: Johns Hopkins University Press, 1981.

Gerth, Hans, and C. Wright Mills, eds. *From Max Weber*. New York: Oxford University Press, 1976.

Giddens, Anthony. *Central Problems in Social Theory*. Berkeley: University of California Press, 1979.

———. *The Class-Structure of the Advanced Societies*. London: Hutchinson, 1973.

———. *New Rules of Sociological Method: A Positive Critique of Interpretive Sociologies*. New York: Basic, 1976.

———. *Social Theory and Modern Sociology*. London: Polity, 1987.

Gilligan, Carol. *In a Different Voice*. Cambridge: Harvard University Press, 1982.

Gingold, Judith. "Battered Wives." *Ms.*, August 1976, 51–54.

Goffman, Erving. *Frame Analysis*. New York: Basic, 1974.

Gomme, Ian, "First Light, A Review of Five Introductory Sociology Texts." *Canadian Review of Sociology and Anthropology* 22, 1 (1985): 146–53.

Goode, Erich. *Sociology*. Englewood Cliffs, N.J.: Prentice-Hall, 1984.

Gordon, Linda. *Woman's Body, Woman's Right: A Social History of Birth Control in America*. New York: Grossman, 1976.

Gordon, Suzanne. "The New Corporate Feminism." *The Nation*, February 5, 1983, 129.

Gornick, Vivian. "Lesbians and Women's Liberation." In *Essays in Feminism*. New York: Harper and Row, 1978.

Gorz, Andre. *Strategy for Labor*. Boston: Beacon, 1967.

Gouldner, Alvin. *The Coming Crisis of Western Sociology*. New York: Basic, 1970.

———. *The Dialectic of Ideology and Technology*. New York: Seabury, 1976.

———. *The Future of the Intellectuals and the Rise of the New Class*. New York: Seabury, 1979.

———. *The Two Marxisms: Contradictions and Anomalies in the Development of Theory*. New York: Seabury, 1980.

Graff, Gerald. *Literature Against Itself: Literary Ideas in Modern Society*. Chicago: University of Chicago Press, 1977.

Gramsci, Antonio. *Selections from the Prison Notebooks*. London: Lawrence and Wishart, 1971.

Green, Regina. *Native American Women: A Bibliography*. Bloomington: Indiana University Press, 1983.

Greer, Scott. *The Logic of Social Inquiry*. Chicago: Aldine, 1969.

Habermas, Jürgen. *Communication and the Evolution of Society*. Boston: Beacon, 1979.

———. *Knowledge and Human Interests*. Boston: Beacon, 1971.

———. *Legitimation Crisis*. Boston: Beacon, 1975.

———. "Modernity versus Postmodernity." *New German Critique*, no. 22 (1981): 3–14.

———. "Technology and Science as 'Ideology.'" In his *Toward a Rational Society*. Boston: Beacon, 1970.

———. *The Theory of Communicative Action*. Vol. 1. Boston: Beacon, 1984.

———. *The Theory of Communicative Action*. Vol. 2. Boston: Beacon, 1987.

———. *Toward a Rational Society*. Boston: Beacon, 1970.

Haralambos, Michael. *Sociology: New Directions*. Dobbs Ferry: Sheridan House, 1985.

Harvey, David. *Consciousness and the Urban Experience*. Baltimore: Johns Hopkins University Press, 1985.

———. *Social Justice and the City*. Baltimore: Johns Hopkins University Press, 1973.

Hauser, Arnold. *The Sociology of Art*. Chicago: University of Chicago Press, 1982.

Hegel, G. W. F. *Phenomenology of Mind*. New York: Macmillan, 1910.

Heidegger, Martin. *What is a Thing?* Chicago: H. Regnery, 1969.

Heisenberg, Werner. *Philosophical Problems of Quantum Physics*. Woodbridge, Conn.: Ox Bow Press, 1979.

———. *Philosophy and Physics*. New York: Harper, 1958.

Held, David. *An Introduction to Critical Theory*. Berkeley: University of California Press, 1980.

Heller, Agnes. *The Theory of Needs in Marx*. London: Allison and Busby, 1975.

Hempel, Carl G. *Philosophy of Natural Science*. Englewood Cliffs, N.J.: Prentice-Hall, 1966.

Henschel, Richard. *Reacting to Social Problems*. Don Mills, Ont.: Longman Canada, 1976.

Henslin, James M. *Down to Earth Sociology: Introductory Readings*. 4th ed. New York: Free Press, 1985.

Herrick, Robert. "Nineteen Pictures of a Discipline: A Review of Recent Introductory Sociology Textbooks." *Contemporary Sociology* 9, no.5 (1980): 617–26.

Hess, Beth B., Elizabeth W. Markson, and Peter J. Stein. *Sociology*. 2d ed. New York: Macmillan, 1985.

Hesse, Mary. *Revolutions and Reconstructions in the Philosophy of Science*. Bloomington: Indiana University Press, 1980.

Hewitt, John P., and Myrna L. Hewitt. *Introductory Sociology: A Symbolic Interactionist Perspective*. Englewood Cliffs, N.J.: Prentice-Hall, 1986.

Hirsch, E. D. *Validity in Interpretation*. New Haven: Yale University Press, 1967.

Holzner, Burkhardt. *Reality Construction in Society*. Cambridge: Schenckmann, 1968.

Homans, George. *The Human Group*. New York: Harcourt Brace, 1950.

———. "Social Behavior as Exchange." *American Journal of Sociology* 62 (May 1939): 595–660.

Honneth, Axel. "An Aversion Against the Universal: A Commentary on Lyotard's *Postmodern Condition*." *Theory, Culture and Society* 2, no. 3 (1985): 147–56.

Honneth, Axel, Eberhard Knodler-Bunte, and Arno Widmann. "The Dialectics of Rationalization: An Interview with Jurgen Habermas." *Telos* 49 (1981): 5–31.

Horkheimer, Max. *Critical Theory*. New York: Herder and Herder, 1972.

———. *Critique of Instrumental Reason*. New York: Seabury, 1974d.

———. *Eclipse of Reason*. New York: Seabury, 1974b.

———. "Traditional and Critical Theory." In his *Critical Theory*. New York: Herder and Herder, 1972.

Horkheimer, Max, and Theodor W. Adorno. *Dialectic of Enlightenment*. New York: Herder and Herder, 1972.

Horowitz, Gad. *Repression: Basic and Surplus Repression in Psychoanalytic Theory*. Toronto: University of Toronto Press, 1977.

Horton, Paul B., and Chester L. Hunt. *Sociology*. 6th ed. New York: McGraw-Hill, 1984.

Howe, Louise Kapp. *Pink-Collar Workers*. New York: Putnam, 1972.

Hull, Gloria, Patricia Bell Scott, and Barbara Smith, eds. *All the Women are White, All the Blacks are Men, But Some of Us are Brave: Black Women's Studies*. Old Westbury, N.Y.: The Feminist Press, 1982.

Hunt, Morton. "The Future of Marriage." In Harold M. Hodges, ed., *Conflict and Consensus*. New York: Harper and Row, 1973.

Husserl, Edmund. *The Crisis of the European Sciences and Transcendental Phenomenology*. Evanston, Ill.: Northwestern University Press, 1970.

Huyssen, Andreas. "Mapping the Postmodern." *New German Critique* 33 (1984): 5–52.

Hyppolite, Jean. *Studies on Marx and Hegel*. New York: Basic, 1969.

Institute for Social Research. *Aspects of Sociology*. Boston: Beacon, 1972.

Irigaray, Luce. *This Sex Which Is Not One*. Ithaca: Cornell University Press, 1985.

Iser, Wolfgang. *The Act of Reading: A Theory of Aesthetic Response*. Baltimore: Johns Hopkins University Press, 1978.

Jacoby, Russell. *The Dialectic of Defeat*. New York: Cambridge University Press, 1983.

———. "Falling Rate of Intelligence?" *Telos* 27 (1976): 141–46.

———. *The Repression of Psychoanalysis*. New York: Basic, 1983.

———. *Social Amnesia*. Boston: Beacon, 1975.

Jaggar, Alison. *Feminist Politics and Human Nature*. Totawa, N.J.: Roman and Allanheld, 1983.

Jakobsen, Roman. *Selections Writings*. 4 vol. The Hague: Martinus Nijhoff, 1962.

Jameson, Fredric. "Ideology of the Text." *Salmagundi* 31 (1975–76): 204–46.

———. *Marxism and Form*. Princeton: Princeton University Press, 1972.

———. "Science Versus Ideology." *Humanities in Society* 6 nos. 2–3 (1983): 283–302.

———. *The Political Unconscious*. Ithaca: Cornell University Press, 1981.

Jay, Martin. *Adorno*. Cambridge: Harvard University Press, 1984a.

——. "The Concept of Totality in Lukacs and Adorno." *Telos* 32 (1977): 117–37.

——. *The Dialectical Imagination*. Boston: Little Brown, 1973.

——. "Habermas and Modernism." *Praxis International* 4, no. 1 (1984b): 1–14.

Jencks, Christopher. *Inequality: A Reassessment of the Effect of Family and Schooling in America*. New York: Basic, 1972.

Jensen, Arthur B.. *Educability and Group Differences*. New York: Harper and Row, 1973.

Johnston, Jill. *Lesbian Nationa: The Feminist Solution*. New York: Simon and Schuster, 1974.

Kann, Mark. *The American Left*. New York: Praeger, 1982.

Kant, Immanuel, *Critique of Judgment*. New York: Hafner, 1972.

——. *Critique of Practical Reason*. Indianapolis: Bobbs-Merrill, 1956.

——. *Critique of Pure Reason*. London: Macmillan, 1968.

Kanter, Rosabeth Moss. *Men and Women of the Corporation*. New York: Basic, 1977.

Kaplan, Abraham. *The Conduct of Inquiry*. San Francisco: Chandler, 1964.

Karp, David A., and William Yoels. *Sociology and Everyday Life*. New York: Peacock, 1985.

Katzman, David M.. *Seven Days a Week: Women and Domestic Service in Industrializing America*. New York: Oxford University Press, 1978.

Kelly, Mary. *Private Woman, Public Stage*. New York: Oxford University Press, 1984.

Kirkpatrick, George R., and George N. Katsiaficas. *Introduction to Critical Sociology*. New York: Irvington Publishers, 1985.

Knorr, Karin D. *From Scenes to Scripts: On the Relationship Between Laboratory Research and Published Papers in Science*. Research Monograph No. 132, Vienna, 1978.

——. "Producing and Reproducing Knowledge: Descriptive or Constructive? Toward a Model of Research Production." *Social Science Information* 16 (1977): 969–96.

Kolodny, Annette. "Dancing Through the Minefield: Some Observations on the Theory, Practice and Politics of a Feminist Literary Criticism." *Feminist Studies* 6, no. 1 (Spring 1980): 1–25.

——. *The Lay of the Land*. Chapel Hill: University of North Carolina Press, 1975.

Korsch, Karl. *Marxism and Philosophy*. New York: Monthly Review Press, 1970.

——. *Revolutionary Theory*. Edited by Douglas Kellner. Austin: University of Texas Press, 1977.

Kovel, Joel. *The Age of Desire: Case Histories of a Radical Psychoanalyst*. New York: Pantheon, 1981.

Kristeva, Julia. *Desire in Language*. New York: Columbia University Press, 1980.

——. "La Femme, c'n'est jamais ca." *Tel Quel* 59 (1974): 19–24.

——. *Polylogue*. Paris: Seuil, 1977.

Kulick, Henrika. "Sociology's Past and Future: Prescriptive Implications of Historical Self-Consciousness in the School of Social Sciences." *Research in Sociology of Knowledge, Sciences and Art* 2 (1979): 73–85.

Lacan, Jacques. *Écrits*. London: Tavistock, 1977.

Lakatos, Imre, and Alan Musgrove, eds. *Criticism and the Growth of Knowledge*. Cambridge: Cambridge University Press, 1970.

Lasch, Christopher. *The Culture of Narcissism*. New York: Norton, 1979.

———. *Haven in a Heartless World: The Family Besieged*. New York: Norton, 1977.

———. *The Minimal Self*. New York: Norton, 1984.

Laws, Judith Lang, and Pepper Schwartz. *Sexual Scripts: The Social Construction of Female Sexuality*. Hinsdale, Ill.: Dryden, 1977.

Leavis, F. R. *The Great Tradition*. London: Chatto and Windus, 1948.

———. *The Living Principle*. New York: Oxford University Press, 1975.

———. *New Bearings in English Poetry*. Ann Arbor: University of Michigan Press, 1964.

Lefebvre, Henri. *Everyday Life in the Modern World*. New York: Harper and Row, 1971.

Leiss, William. *The Domination of Nature*. New York: Braziller, 1972.

———. *The Limits to Satisfaction*. Toronto: University of Toronto Press, 1976.

———. "Needs, Exchanges and the Fetishism of Objects." *Canadian Journal of Political and Social Theory* 2, no. 3 (Fall 1978): 27–48.

Lenhardt, Christian. "The Wanderings of Enlightenment." In John O'Neill, ed., *On Critical Theory*. New York: Seabury, 1976.

Lenin, V. *Materialism and Empirio-Criticism*. Moscow: Foreign Languages Publishing House, 1952.

Lenski, Gerhard. *Power and Privilege: A Theory of Stratification*. New York: McGraw-Hill, 1966.

Lentricchia, Frank. *After the New Criticism*. Chicago: University of Chicago Press, 1980.

Levi, Bernhard-Henri. *Barbarism with a Human Face*. New York: Harper and Row, 1978.

Lévi-Strauss, Claude. *The Savage Mind*. Chicago: University of Chicago Press, 1966.

Levin, William C. *Sociological Ideas: Concepts and Applications*. Belmont: Wadsworth, 1984.

Lewis, Lionel S. *The Cold War on Campus*. New Brunswick, N.J.: Transaction, 1988.

———. *Scaling the Ivory Tower*. Baltimore: Johns Hopkins University Press, 1975.

Lewis, Lionel S., and Dennis D. Brisett. "Sex as Work: A Study of Avocational Counseling." *Social Problems* 15, no. 1 (1967): 8–18.

———. "Working at Leisure." *Society* 19, no. 15 (1982): 27–32.

Light, Donald Jr., and Suzanne Keller. *Sociology*. 4th ed. New York: Knopf, 1985.

Lodahl, Janice B., and Gerald Gordon. "The Structure of Scientific Fields and the Funding of University Graduate Departments." *American Sociological Review* 37 (1972): 57–72.

Lukacs, Georg. *The Historical Novel*. Boston: Beacon, 1962.

———. *History and Class Consciousness*. London: Merlin, 1971.

———. *Studies in European Realism*. New York: Gosset and Dunlop, 1964.

Lukes, Steven. *Emile Durkheim: His Life and Work*. New York: Harper and Row, 1977.

Lundberg, Ferdinand, and Marynia F. Farnham. "The Psychopathology of Feminism." In their *Modern Women: The Lost Sex*. New York: Harper and Row, 1947.

Lyotard, Jean-Francois. *Economie Libidinale*. Paris: Minuit, 1974.

————. *The Postmodern Condition: A Report of Knowledge*. Minneapolis: University of Minnesota Press, 1984.

McCarthy, E. Doyle, and Robin Das. "American Sociology's Idea of Itself: A Review of the Textbook Literature from the Turn of the Century to the Present." *The History of Sociology* 5, no. 2 (1985): 21–43.

McCarthy, Thomas. *The Critical Theory of Jurgen Habermas*. Cambridge: MIT Press, 1978.

Maccoby, Eleanor E., and C. N. Jacklin. *The Psychology of Sex Differences*. Palo Alto, Calif.: Stanford University Press, 1974.

McDaniel, S. A., and Ben Agger. *Social Problems Through Conflict and Order*. Toronto: Addison-Wesley, 1983.

McHugh, Peter, et al. *On the Beginning of Social Inquiry*. London: Routledge and Kegan Paul, 1974.

MacKinnon, Catharine A. *Sexual Harassment of Working Women: A Case of Sex Discrimination*. New Haven: Yale University Press, 1979.

Macpherson, C. B. *The Political Theory of Possessive Individualism*. Oxford: Oxford University Press, 1962.

Mailloux, Steven. *Interpretive Conventions: The Reader in the Study of American Fiction*. Ithaca: Cornell University Press, 1982.

Mandel, Ernest. *Marxist Economic Theory*. London: Merlin, 1968.

————. *Late Capitalism*. London: Verso, 1978.

Mannheim, Karl. *Man and Society in an Age of Reconstruction*. London: Routledge and Kegan Paul, 1954.

Marcuse, Herbert. *The Aesthetic Dimension*. Boston: Beacon, 1978.

————. *Counterrevolution and Revolt*. Boston: Beacon, 1973.

————. *Eros and Civilization*. New York: Vintage, 1955.

————. *An Essay on Liberation*. Boston: Beacon, 1969.

————. *Five Lectures*. Boston: Beacon, 1970.

————. "Karl Popper and the Problem of Historical Laws." In his *Studies in Critical Philosophy*. Boston: Beacon, 1973.

————. *Negations*. Boston: Beacon, 1968.

————. "A Note on Dialectic." Second Preface to *Reason and Revolution*. Boston: Beacon, 1960.

————. *One-Dimensional Man*. Boston: Beacon, 1964.

————. *Reason and Revolution*. Boston: Beacon, 1960.

————. *Soviet Marxism*. New York: Vintage, 1958.

Marcuse, Herbert, Robert Paul Wolff, and Barrington Moore, Jr. *A Critique of Pure Tolerance*. Boston: Beacon, 1966.

Martin, Del, and Phyllis Lin. *Lesbian/Woman*. New York: Pantheon, 1972.

Martindale, Donald. *The Nature and Types of Sociological Theory*. 2d ed. Boston: Houghton Mifflin, 1981.

Marx, Karl. *Capital*. Vol. 1. Moscow: Progress Publishers, n. d.

————. *Economic and Philosophic Manuscripts*. Moscow: Foreign Languages Publishing House, 1961.

————. *Grundrisse*. London: Allen Lane, 1973.

Marx, Karl, and Friedrich Engels. *Basic Writings on Politics and Philosophy*. Garden City: Doubleday, 1959.

————. *The Communist Manifesto*. New York: Washington Square Press, 1964.

————. *The German Ideology*. New York: International Publishers, 1949.

Maslow, William D. "Academic Sociology as a 'Classist' Discipline: An Empirical Inquiry into the Treatment of Marx in the Textbooks of North American Sociology, 1890–1965." *Humanity and Society* 5, no. 3 (1981): 256–75.

Masterna, Margaret. "The Nature of a Paradigm." In Imre Lakatos and Alain Musgrove, eds., *Criticism and the Growth of Knowledge*. Cambridge: Cambridge University Press, 1970.

Medvedev, Pavel Nikolaevich. *The Formal Method in Literary Scholarship: A Critical Introduction to Sociological Poetics*. Baltimore: Johns Hopkins University Press, 1978.

Mehan, Hugh, and Houston Wood. *The Reality of Ethnomethodology*. New York: Wiley, 1975.

Merleau-Ponty, Maurice. *Adventures of the Dialectic*. Evanston, Ill.: Northwestern University Press, 1973.

————. "Hegel's Existentialism." In his *Sense and Non-Sense*. Evanston, Ill.: Northwestern University Press, 1964a.

————. *Humanism and Terror*. Boston: Beacon, 1972.

————. *The Phenomenology of Perception*. London: Routledge and Kegan Paul, 1962.

————. *Sense and Non-Sense*. Evanston, Ill.: Northwestern University Press, 1964a.

————. *Signs*. Evanston, Ill.: Northwestern University Press, 1964b.

Merton, Robert K. "Paradigm for the Sociology of Knowledge." In Norman W. Storer, ed., *The Sociology of Science: Theoretical and Empirical Investigations*. Chicago: University of Chicago Press, 1973.

————. "Priorities in Scientific Discovery: A Chapter in the Sociology of Science." *American Sociological Review* 22 (December 1957): 655–59.

————. *On the Shoulders of Giants*. New York: Free Press, 1965.

————. *Social Theory and Social Structure*. Glencoe, Ill.: Free Press, 1957.

————. "On Sociological Theories of the Middle Range." In his *On Theoretical Sociology*. New York: Free Press, 1967.

————. *The Sociology of Science*. Chicago: University of Chicago Press, 1973.

Millet, Kate. *Sexual Politics*. Garden City: Doubleday, 1970.

Mills, C. Wright. *The Power Elite*. New York: Oxford University Press, 1956.

————. *The Sociological Imagination*. New York: Oxford University Press, 1959.

Misgeld, Dieter. "Critical Theory and Hermeneutics: The Debate Between Habermas and Gadamer." In John O'Neill, ed., *On Critical Theory*. New York: Seabury, 1976.

————. "Education and Cultural Invasion: Critical Social Theory, Education as Institution and *Pedagogy of the Oppressed*." In John Forester, ed., *Critical Theory and Public Life*. Cambridge: MIT Press, 1985.

Mitchell, Juliet. *Psychoanalysis and Feminism*. New York: Vintage, 1975.

Mitzman, Arthur. *The Iron Cage*. New York: Grosset and Dunlop, 1971.

Mokrzycki, Edmund. *Philosophy of Science and Sociology*. London: Routledge and Kegan Paul, 1983.

Money, John. *Sexual Signatures*. Boston: Little Brown, 1975.

Money, John, and Anke Ehrhardt. *Man and Woman, Boy and Girl: The Differentiation and Dimorphism of Gender Identity from Conception to Maturity.* Baltimore: Johns Hopkins University Press, 1972.

Montagu, Ashley. *The Natural Superiority of Women.* New York: Macmillan, 1962.

Morgan, J. Graham. "Courses and Texts in Sociology." *The Journal of the History of Sociology* 5, no. 1 (1983): 42–65.

Morgan, Marabel. *The Total Woman.* New York: Fleming H. Revell, 1973.

Mueller, Claus. *The Politics of Communication.* New York: Oxford University Press, 1973.

Mulkay, Michael. *The Word and the World: Explorations in the Form of Sociological Analysis.* Winchester: Allen and Unwin, 1985.

Mullins, Nicholas. *Theories and Theory Groups in Contemporary American Sociology.* New York: Harper and Row, 1973.

Nagel, Ernest. *The Structure of Science.* New York: Harcourt Brace and World, 1961.

Nietzsche, Friedrich. *The Birth of Tragedy.* Garden City: Doubleday, 1956.

———. *The Gay Science.* New York: Random House, 1974.

———. *The Uses and Abuses of History.* Indianapolis: Bobbs-Merrill, 1957.

Nisbet, Robert. *Social Change and History: Aspects of the Western Theory of Development.* New York: Oxford University Press, 1969.

Norton, Theodore Mills, and Bertell Ollman, eds. *Studies in Socialist Pedagogy.* New York: Monthly Review Press, 1978.

Oakley, Ann. *The Sociology of Housework.* New York: Pantheon, 1974.

O'Brien, Mary. *The Politics of Reproduction.* London: Routledge and Kegan Paul, 1981.

O'Connor, James. *The Fiscal Crisis of the State.* New York: St. Martin's, 1972.

O'Kane, John. "Marxism, Deconstruction and Ideology: Notes towards an Articulation." *New German Critique* no. 33 (1984): 219–47.

Ollman, Bertell. *Alienation.* New York: Cambridge University Press, 1971.

O'Neill, John, ed. *On Critical Theory.* New York: Seabury, 1976.

———. "Decolonization and the Ideal Speech Community: Some Issues in the Theory and Practice of Communicative Competence." In John Forester, ed., *Critical Theory and Public Life.* Cambridge: MIT Press, 1985.

———. *For Marx Against Althusser.* Washington, D.C.: University Press of America, 1984.

———. "The Literary Production of Natural and Social Science Inquiry." *The Canadian Journal of Sociology* 6 (1981): 105–20.

———. *Making Sense Together: An Introduction to Wild Sociology.* New York: Harper and Row, 1974.

———. "Marxism and Mythology: Psychologizing *Capital*." In his *For Marx Against Althusser.* Washington, D.C.: University Press of America, 1984.

———. "Marxism and the Two Sciences." *Philosophy of the Social Sciences* 11 (1981): 281–302.

———. "Merleau-Ponty's Critique of Marxist Scientism." *Canadian Journal of Political and Social Theory* 2, no. 1 (Winter 1978): 33–62.

———. ed. *Modes of Individualism and Collectivism.* London: Routledge and Kegan Paul, 1973.

————. *Perception, Expression and History: The Social Phenomenology of Maurice Merleau-Ponty*. Evanston, Ill.: Northwestern University Press, 1970.

————. *Sociology as a Skin Trade*. New York: Harper and Row, 1972.

Orenstein, David M. *The Sociological Quest: Principles of Sociology*. St. Paul: West, 1985.

Paci, Enzo. *The Function of Modern Science and the Meaning of Man*. Evanston, Ill.: Northwestern University Press, 1972.

Page, Charles. Correspondence, *ASA Footnotes*. October 1985, 10.

Palmer, Richard E. *Hermeneutics*. Evanston, Ill.: Northwestern University Press, 1969.

Papp, Warren R. "The Concept of Power: Treatment in 50 Introductory Sociology Textbooks." *Teaching Sociology* 9, no. 1 (1981): 57–68.

Parekh, Bhikhu. *Marx's Theory of Ideology*. Baltimore: Johns Hopkins University Press, 1982.

Parker, Andrew. "Of Politics and Limits: Derrida Re-Marx." *SCE Reports* 8 (1980): 83–104.

Parsons, Talcott. "The Social Ambience of the Family." In Ruth Nanda Anshen, ed., *Family: Its Function and Destiny*. New York: Harper, 1949.

————. *The Social System*. New York: Free Press, 1951.

————. *The Structure of Social Action*. New York: McGraw-Hill, 1937.

Parsons, Talcott, et al. *Family, Socialization and Interaction Process*. Glencoe, Ill.: Free Press, 1955.

Pascal, Rory. "Georg Lukacs: The Concept of Totality." In G. H. R. Parkinson, ed., *George Lukacs: The Man, His Work and His Ideas*. New York: Random House, 1970.

Persell, Caroline Hodges. *Understanding Society: An Introduction to Sociology*. New York: Harper and Row, 1984.

Perucci, Robert. "Sociology and the Introductory Textbooks." *The American Sociologist* 15, no. 1 (1980): 39–49.

Phillips, Derek. *Knowledge From What? Theories and Methods in Social Research*. Chicago: Rand McNally, 1971.

————. "Paradigms and Incommensurability." *Theory and Society* 2 (1975): 37–62.

Piccone, Paul. "Beyond Identity Theory." In John O'Neill, ed., *On Critical Theory*. New York: Seabury, 1976.

————. "The Changing Function of Critical Theory." *New German Critique* 12 (Fall 1977): 29–38.

————. "The Crisis of One-Dimensionality." *Telos* 35 (Spring 1978): 43–54.

————. "Labriola and the Roots of Eurocommunism." *Berkeley Journal of Sociology* 22 (1977–78): 3–44.

Pope, Whitney. "Classic on Classic: Parsons' Interpretation of Durkheim." *American Sociological Review* 38 (1973): 399–415.

Pope, Whitney, Jere Cohen, and Lawrence E. Hazelrigg. "On the Divergence of Weber and Durkheim: A Critique of Parsons' Convergence Thesis." *American Sociological Review* 40 (1975): 417–27.

Popenoe, David. *Sociology*. 4th ed. Englewood Cliffs, N.J.: Prentice-Hall, 1980.

Popper, Karl. *The Logic of Scientific Discovery*. New York: Science Edition, 1961.

————. *The Poverty of Historicism*. 2d ed. London: Routledge and Kegan Paul, 1960.

————. *The Open Society and its Enemies.* Vols. 1 and 2. 4th ed. New York: Harper and Row, 1963.

Porter, Jack Nusan. "Radical Sociology Textbooks: A Review Essay." *Humboldt Journal of Social Relations* 9, no. 1 (1981–82): 198–206.

Poulantzas, Nicos. *Political Power and Social Classes.* London: New Left Books and Sheed and Ward, 1973.

————. *State, Power, Socialism.* London: New Left Books, 1978.

Rabinowitz, Peter. "Truth in Fiction: A Reexamination of Audiences." *Critical Inquiry* 4 (1977): 121–42.

Rachlis, Charles. "Marcuse and the Problem of Happiness." *Canadian Journal of Political and Social Theory* 2, no. 1 (Winter 1978): 63–88.

Ransom, John Crowe. *The New Criticism.* Norfolk, Conn.: New Directions, 1941.

Rawls, John. *A Theory of Justice.* Cambridge: Harvard University Press, 1970.

Reid, Herbert. "Totality, Temporality and Praxis: Existential Phenomenology and Critical Political Theory." *Canadian Journal of Political and Social Theory* 2, no. 1 (Winter 1978): 113–35.

Rethel, Alfred Sohn. *Intellectual and Manual Labor.* London: Macmillan, 1978.

Reuter, Edward B. *Handbook of Sociology.* Philadelphia: Century Bookbindery, 1984.

Rich, Adrienne. *Of Woman Born: Motherhood as Experience and Institution.* New York: Norton, 1976.

Richardson, John G. "Wife Occupational Superiority and Marital Trouble: An Examination of the Hypothesis." *Journal of Marriage and the Family* 41, no. 1 (February 1979): 63–72.

Ricoeur, Paul. *Hermeneutics and the Human Sciences.* Cambridge: Cambridge University Press, 1981.

————. "The Model of the Text: Meaningful Action Considered as a Text." *Social Research* 38 (1970): 529–62.

Rieff, Philip. *Freud: The Mind of the Moralist.* Garden City: Doubleday, 1961.

Ritzer, George. *Sociology: A Multiple Paradigm Science.* Rev. ed. Boston: Allyn and Bacon, 1980.

————. *Sociological Theory.* New York: Knopf, 1983.

————. *Toward an Integrated Sociological Paradigm: The Search for an Exemplar and an Image of the Subject Matter.* Boston: Allyn and Bacon, 1981.

Ritzer, George, Kenneth C. W. Kammeyer, and Norman P. Yetman. *Society.* 2d ed. Boston: Allyn and Bacon, 1982.

Robertson, Ian. *Sociology.* 2d ed. New York: Worth, 1983.

Rorty, Richard. "Philosophy as a Kind of Writing: An Essay on Derrida." *New Literary History* 10 (1978): 141–60.

Rose, Gillian. *The Melancholy Science: An Introduction to the Thought of Theodor Adorno.* London: Macmillan, 1978.

Rose, Peter I., Myron Glazer, and Penina Migdal Glazer. *Sociology: Inquiring into Society.* Scranton: Canfield Press, 1986.

Rosenberg, Rosalind. *Beyond Separate Spheres: The Roots of Modern Feminism.* New Haven: Yale University Press, 1982.

Rosenfeld, Jeffrey P. *Sociology.* 2d ed. New York: Macmillan, 1985.

Rule, James. *Insight and Social Betterment.* New York: Oxford University Press, 1978.

Russell, Bertrand, and A. N. Whitehead. *Principia Mathematica*. 3 Vols. Cambridge: Cambridge University Press, 1910, 1912, and 1913.

Ryan, Michael. *Marxism and Deconstruction*. Baltimore: Johns Hopkins University Press, 1982.

Ryan, William. *Blaming the Victim*. New York: Vintage, 1971.

Sartre, Jean-Paul. *Being and Nothingness*. New York: Washington Square, 1961.

—————. *Critique of Dialectical Reason*. London: New Left Books, 1976.

—————. *Situations*. Greenwich, Conn.: Fawcett, 1965a.

—————. *What is Literature?* New York: Harper and Row, 1965b.

Saussure, Ferdinand de. *Course in General Linguistics*. London: Peter Owen, 1960.

Schaefer, R. T. *Sociology*. 2d ed. New York: McGraw-Hill, 1986.

Scharf, Louis. *To Work and to Wed: Female Employment, Feminism and the Great Depression*. Westport, Conn.: Greenwood, 1980.

Schlafly, Phyllis. "The Question of Ratification of the Equal Rights Amendment." *The Congressional Digest*, June–July 1977.

Schmidt, Alfred. *The Concept of Nature in Marx*. London: New Left Books, 1971.

Schmidt, James. "Reification and Recollection: Emancipatory Interests and the Sociology of Knowledge." *Canadian Journal of Political and Social Theory* 2, no. 1 (Winter 1978): 89–111.

Schneider, Louis. "Dialectic in Sociology." *American Sociological Review* 36 (1971): 667–78.

Schutz, Alfred. *The Phenomenology of the Social World*. Evanston, Ill.: Northwestern University Press, 1967.

Schwartz, Bill, ed. *On Ideology*. London: Hutchinson, 1971.

Searle, John. *Speech Acts*. Cambridge: Cambridge University Press, 1969.

Seifer, Nancy, ed. *Nobody Speaks for Me!: Self-Portraits of American Working Class Women*. New York: Simon and Schuster, 1971.

Sennett, Richard. *The Fall of Public Man*. New York: Vintage, 1974.

Sewart, John J. "Critical Theory and the Critique of Conservative Method." *The American Sociologist* 13 (1978): 15–22.

Sher, Gerson. *Praxis: Marxist Criticism and Dissent in Socialist Yugoslavia*. Bloomington: Indiana University Press, 1977.

Shils, Edward. *Tradition*. Chicago: University of Chicago Press, 1981.

Shorter, Edward. *The Making of the Modern Family*. New York: Basic, 1975.

Slater, Phil. *Origin and Significance of the Frankfurt School*. London: Routledge and Kegan Paul, 1975.

Smelser, Neil J. *Sociology*. Englewood Cliffs, N.J.: Prentice-Hall, 1984.

Smith, Dusky Lee. "Sociology and the Sunshine Boys." In J. David Colfax and Jack L. Roach, eds., *Radical Sociology*. New York: Basic, 1971.

Smith, Ronald W., and Frederick W. Preston. *Sociology: An Introduction*. New York: St. Martin's Press, 1979.

Soberano, Rawlein G., ed. *Sociology in Action*. Vienna: Alive Associates, 1984.

Spencer, Metta, and Alex Inkeles. *Foundations of Modern Society*. 2d ed. Englewood Cliffs: Prentice-Hall, 1979.

Spender, Dale. *Man Made Language*. London: Routledge and Kegan Paul, 1980.

Stacey, Judith, Susan Bereaud, and Joan Daniels, eds. *And Jill Came Tumbling After: Sexism in American Education*. New York: Dell, 1974.

Stark, Rodney. *Sociology*. Belmont: Wadsworth, 1985.

Steinem, Gloria. "What It Would Be Like if Women Win." *Time*, August 21, 1970, 22–23.

Stewart, E. W., and J. A. Glynn. *Introduction to Sociology*. 4th ed. New York: McGraw-Hill, 1985.

Stockman, Norman. *Antipositivist Theories of the Sciences*. Dordrecht: D. Reidel, 1984.

Stokes, Randall G. *Introduction to Sociology*. Dubuque: Wm. C. Brown, 1984.

Strasser, Hermann. *The Normative Structure of Sociology*. London: Routledge and Kegan Paul, 1976.

Strasser, Susan. *Never Done: A History of American Homework*. New York: Pantheon, 1982.

Straus, Roger A., ed. *Using Sociology: An Introduction from the Clinical Perspective*. Bayside: Clinical Sociology Association, 1985.

Sullivan, Thomas J., and Kenrick S. Thompson. *Sociology: Concepts, Issues and Applications*. New York: John Wiley, 1984.

Szymanski, Al. *Is the Red Flag Flying Over Russia?* London: Red Press, 1979.

Taylor, Ian, Paul Walton, and Jock Young. *Towards a New Criminology*. London: Routledge and Kegan Paul, 1970.

Thompson, John B. *Critical Hermeneutics: A Study in the Thought of Paul Piccone and Jurgen Habermas*. Cambridge: Cambridge University Press, 1981.

———. *Studies in the Theory of Ideology*. Berkeley: University of California Press, 1984.

Tilly, Louise, and Joan Scott. *Women, Work and Family*. New York: Holt, Rinehart and Winston, 1978.

Treiman, Donald, and Heidi Hartmann. *Women, Work and Wages: Equal Pay for Jobs of Equal Value*. Washington, D.C.: National Academy Press, 1981.

Tuchman, Gaye, Arlene Kaplan Daniels, and Jane Back. *Heart and Home: Images of Women in the Mass Media*. New York: Oxford University Press, 1978.

Tucker, Robert. *Philosophy and Myth in Karl Marx*. 2d ed. Cambridge: Cambridge University Press, 1972.

Tudor, Henry. *Political Myth*. London: Macmillan, 1972.

Turner, Jonathan. *Sociology: A Student Handbook*. New York: Random House, 1984.

———. "A Strategy for Reformulating the Dialectical and Functional Theories of Conflict." *Social Forces* 53 (1975): 433–44.

Vander Zanden, James. *Sociology: The Core*. New York: Random House, 1986.

Vickers, Geoffrey. *Value Systems and Social Process*. London: Tavistock, 1968.

Villemez, Wayne J. "Explaining Inequality: A Survey of Perspectives Represented in Introductory Sociology Textbooks." *Contemporary Sociology* 9, no. 1 (1980): 35–39.

Walster, Elaine. *Equity: Theory and Research*. Boston: Allyn and Bacon, 1978.

Wandersee, Winifred D. *Women's Work and Family Values, 1920–1940*. Cambridge: Harvard University Press, 1981.

Weber, Max. *The Theory of Social and Economic Organization*. Glencoe, Ill.: Free Press, 1947.

Wellmer, Albrecht W. "Communications and Emancipation: Reflections on the Linguistic Turn in Critical Theory." In John O'Neill, ed., *On Critical Theory*. New York: Seabury, 1976.

Wells, Alan. "Conflict Theory and Functionalism: Introductory Sociology Textbooks, 1928–1976." *Teaching Sociology* 6, no. 4 (1979): 429–37.

Wexler, Philip. *Critical Social Psychology*. London: Routledge and Kegan Paul, 1984.

Wild, Ronald. *An Introduction to Sociological Perspectives: Theory and Research in the Australian Context*. Winchester: Allen and Unwin, 1985.

Wilner, Patricia. "The Main Drift of Sociology Between 1936 and 1984." *The History of Sociology* 5, no. 2 (1985): 1–20.

Wilson, Edmund. *On Human Nature*. Cambridge: Harvard University Press, 1978.

————. *Sociobiology: The New Synthesis*. Cambridge: Harvard University Press, 1975.

Wilson, H. T. *The American Ideology*. London: Routledge and Kegan Paul, 1977.

Winch, Peter. *The Idea of a Social Science*. London: Routledge and Kegan Paul, 1969.

Wittgenstein, Ludwig. *Philosophical Investigations*. Oxford: Basil Blackwell, 1953.

Wolfe, Alan. *The Limits of Legitimacy*. New York: Free Press, 1977.

Wright, Erik Olin. *Class Structure and Income Determination*. New York: Academic Press, 1979.

Yahiel, N. *Sociology and Social Practice*. Elmsford: Pergamon Press, 1984.

Yorburg, Betty. *Introduction to Sociology*. New York: Harper and Row, 1982.

Zaretsky, Eli. *Capitalism, The Family and Personal Life*. New York: Monthly Review Press, 1976.

Zeitlin, Irving. *Ideology and the Development of Sociological Theory*. Englewood Cliffs, N.J.: Prentice-Hall, 1968.

Zukin, Sharon. *Beyond Marx and Tito*. New York: Cambridge University Press, 1975.

Index

Academe, age of, 1, 3
Administration, 1, 75–76, 166–67, 257, 285,
  305, 369, 371; of existence, 209, 256; of
  things, 16; total, 36, 44, 48, 58, 76–77, 81,
  138, 187, 208, 240, 305, 316, 347, 353
Adorno, Theodor, 2–3, 5, 9–10, 12, 22, 28,
  32, 44–48, 54, 58–60, 64, 74, 77–79,
  81–82, 86, 91, 93, 96, 103, 127, 140–43,
  145, 172, 190, 193, 197, 209, 303, 305,
  308–9, 311–12, 314, 320, 322, 328, 338,
  340–41, 345, 347–48, 351, 360, 366–367,
  369, 372
Agger, Ben, 77, 83, 248, 294, 332, 341
Alexander, Jeffrey, 322
Alienation, 4, 84, 148, 150, 153–54, 187,
  258, 266, 283, 291
Althusser, Louis, 16, 46, 79, 144, 176,
  304–5, 337, 346
Anarcho-syndicalism, 182
Androgyny, 234–35, 250, 262, 264, 291–93,
  296–97
Antimethod, 47, 82; and women's movement,
  174
Apel, Karl-Otto, 356
Arendt, Hannah, 122
Aristotle, 106, 194, 215, 218; and incremen-
  talism, 182
Auratization, 32
Auschwitz, 45, 47, 158, 200, 308
Austin, John, 25
Authenticity, jargon of, 342
Author, death of, 43
Authorial: aura, 53, 304; constitution, 1, 53,
  110–11; presence, 26, 31, 66, 145, 310,
  370
Authoriality, 27, 41, 99; possible, 326

Authority, 2, 8, 18, 27, 30, 34, 49, 51, 63,
  72, 111, 150, 257
Autobibliography, 3

Bachelard, Gaston, 46
Bacon, Francis, 95, 110,
Bad faith, 188
Bales, Robert, 231, 255, 366
Barthes, Roland, 21, 48, 310
Base-superstructure model, 10, 22, 24, 50,
  66, 237, 337, 339, 346, 353
Beckett, Thomas, 141
Bell, Daniel, 36
Benjamin, Walter, 30, 32, 47, 96, 111, 308,
  369
Bentham, Jeremy, 280
Berger, Peter, 88
Berle, Adolf, Jr., 152
Bernard, Jesse, 290
Bernstein, Edward, 175, 189, 193
Bible, 38, 51, 55, 285, 365
Biologism, 273, 298
Biopolitics, 229, 231
Blau, Peter, 154, 217
Bloom, Allan, 160
Bloom, Harold, 7
Blumer, Herbert, 8, 88
Body politic, 140
Bolsheviks, 186–87, 337
Bricolage, 93, 350
Brown, Rita Mae, 244
Brownmiller, Susan, 287

Camus, Albert, 338
Capital, 6, 8, 18, 23, 30, 65, 155, 185, 196,
  207, 214, 216, 223, 240, 330, 352; human,

80, 216; iron laws of, 57, 156; rising organic composition of, 15

Capitalism, 1, 4–5, 27, 41–44, 47, 57, 72–73, 89, 100, 149, 152, 162, 167, 175, 185, 200, 214, 216; administered, 66, 75, 78; entrepreneurial, 11; fast, 1, 8, 16, 23–24, 76, 98, 106, 120, 363, 366, 369–71; late, 16, 18, 41–44, 57–58, 76–77, 97, 229–30, 235, 341, 366–67; liberal, 46, 168; monopoly/monologue, 72; multivariate, 217, 220

Castells, Manuel, 369

Castro, Fidel, 166

Causality, 36, 87, 215, 217, 221, 265

Center-margin relationships, 45, 54–56, 137–38, 140–41, 151, 201, 212, 272, 320, 331, 335, 362

Centers, Richard, 283

Centralism, democratic, 167, 189

Chodorow, Nancy, 273

Chomsky, Noam, 356

Cicourel, Aaron, 88

Class: and group affiliations, 175; struggle, 145, 154, 175, 202–3, 213

Cold War, 174, 195

Collins, Randall, 88, 116, 268

Command economy, 166

Commodity fetishism, 367

Communication: as deception, 28, 354; paradigm of, 150–51; theory, 10, 22, 25, 62, 335, 341, 353, 355

Communicative: competence, 8, 121, 304, 345; rationalism, 28, 50–51

Communism, 16, 145, 147, 153, 157–58, 161–62, 166, 174–75, 189, 195, 206; commissar, 163, 167–68; Eurocommunism, 155, 189; Soviet, 154, 157, 164, 167

Community, 2, 4, 8, 10, 23, 27, 30, 71, 132, 143, 314, 339, 360; dialogic, 63, 66, 125; good, 8, 18, 31, 37, 41, 63, 71

Comte, Auguste, 4–5, 11, 15, 33, 36, 52–53, 59, 85, 326

Concepts, 2, 7–8, 34, 94

Condorcet, Marquis de, 10, 12, 17, 106

Conflict: as competition, 145, 173, 192, 196–98, 200, 203–4, 207, 210–11; theory, 6, 13, 125–26, 137–38, 145, 153, 161, 165, 169, 171, 176, 186, 188, 190–91, 193–200, 203–4, 206–7, 211, 215, 218–22, 224, 237, 264–67, 317

Consciousness: false, 4, 46, 54, 114, 153, 165, 224, 242–43, 270; paradigm of, 150–51; true, 46, 54

Coser, Lewis, 145, 204

Counterhegemony, 71

Crisis: psychic, 16, 65; tendential laws of, 15

Critical theory, 2–5, 7, 9–10, 22, 24, 28, 42, 77–78, 81, 89, 91–93, 96, 123, 138, 144, 237, 248, 304, 329, 353, 355, 364–65, 370–71; of significance, 371–72; of text, 22, 130, 304, 361, 364

Critique, 1, 3, 22, 24, 48, 55, 59; of discipline, 2, 358; of ideology, 323, 329, 346, 365, 372

Culler, Jonathan, 7

Culture, 4, 65; high, 76; mass, 33; popular, 11, 65, 91, 183; positivist, 1

Czarism, 162–63

Dahrendorf, Ralf, 204

Daly, Mary, 233

Darwin, Charles, 52

Davis, Kingsley, 290–91

Davis-Moore thesis, 17, 79–80, 206

Deauratization, 32–34

Deauthorization, 30–31, 41, 370

Deconstruction, 3, 8–10, 25, 38, 48–49, 55, 57, 59, 61–62, 75, 78, 81–82, 92, 99, 110–11, 119–20, 125, 138, 145, 303, 336, 338, 351, 358, 360, 362–64, 368, 370–72; and excavation, 129

Dedisciplining, 61, 72, 257, 343

Deindustrialization, 128

Depth wish, 349

Derrida, Jacques, 2–3, 21–22, 25, 27–28, 30, 38, 46–49, 59–60, 64–65, 71, 79, 81–82, 91, 93, 96, 127, 137, 139, 145, 338, 342, 345, 348, 358, 360, 365, 367, 371

Descartes, Rene, 64, 236, 338, 356

Desire, 9, 14, 16, 26, 31–32, 46, 87, 98, 113, 121, 141, 150, 236, 248, 294, 324, 327, 343, 351, 357

Determinism, 66, 74, 198; economic, 169, 207–8, 214–15, 305

Dialectic, 175; of myth and enlightenment, 86; of nature, 84, 162; nonidealist, 58; of theory and practice, 307, 321

Dickens, Charles, 21

Diesing, Paul, 348

Difference, 12, 50, 72–73, 108, 127, 139–40, 142–43, 273, 341
Differentiation, 274, 276, 371
Dilthey, Wilhelm, 13
Disciplinary: canon, 112, 191; desublimation, 99; differentiation, 79–81; reading, 1, 14, 324, 364, 370; writing, 111, 139, 312, 325
Discipline, 2–4, 6, 15, 36, 39–40, 42, 47, 49, 71, 73–74, 90, 95, 100, 111–12, 114, 126, 133, 138, 150, 303, 306, 311–13, 345–46, 364, 370, 372; and disciplining, 4, 8, 11, 18, 41, 71, 83, 372; rights of, 372
Discourse: disciplinary, 1, 3, 11; theory, 10, 21–22, 62, 371
Division of labor, 4–5, 11, 14, 16, 79, 163, 209, 276, 297; sexual, 87, 232, 239, 243–44, 271, 276, 292
Domination, 1–6, 8, 11–13, 15–18, 24, 27, 41, 61–63, 74–75, 81, 107, 118, 142, 170, 197, 199–200, 203, 214, 219, 224, 266, 270, 285, 288, 293, 310, 347, 357, 362, 372; of nature, 12, 23, 77, 368
Dualism, 13, 24–25, 37, 50, 66, 108, 236, 278, 361
Duncan, Otis Dudley, 154, 217
Durkheim, Emile, 3–6, 11–13, 15, 17–18, 22, 27, 33–34, 36, 38–39, 41, 52–53, 59, 66–67, 71, 73–74, 76, 79–80, 85–86, 90, 94, 109, 115, 130, 140, 144, 193, 207, 209, 276, 303–04, 306, 310–13, 316, 322, 329, 342, 371–72; and methodology, 3, 6, 39, 66, 74, 92, 353; study of suicide, 81, 90
Dutschke, Rudi, 305

Eagleton, Terry, 7, 21
Economics: salience of, 206, 208, 210, 212; supply-side, 184; trickle-down, 206
Economism, 65, 137, 149–50, 153, 165, 171, 193, 195, 198, 206, 212–15, 217, 221, 235, 237, 239–40, 266, 268–69, 292, 347; productivist, 170, 199, 206
Écriture, 10
Edison, Thomas, 114
Educating the educator, 45–46, 354, 360
Ehrenreich, Barbara, 251
Einstein, Albert, 26
Eisenhower, President Dwight, 5, 58, 127, 183
Elshtain, Jean, 241

Engels, Friedrich, 16, 84, 144–45, 152, 216, 222, 337, 346
Enlightenment, 5, 10, 24, 64, 86, 107, 110, 128, 138, 165, 171, 174, 218, 270, 296, 317, 319, 337, 343, 347
Epistemology: nonsubjective, 331; political, 90, 322
Equity: and equality, 283; marital, 283
Essay, 344, 349–52, 357, 362, 363–64, 369
Ethnomethodology, 6, 8, 14, 27–29, 84–85, 88–89, 124, 281
Everyday life, 1, 4, 6, 23–24, 32, 41–43, 51, 88, 91, 116, 128, 188, 231, 242, 258, 304–5, 334, 369–70
Exchange theory, 149, 184, 218, 281
Existentialism, 4, 342
Expropriation of the expropriators, 153, 169

Facticity, 270
Familism, 36, 234, 237, 244, 249, 251, 258–59, 298; and retreatism, 257
Family, 4–5, 16, 31, 230, 238, 247; attack on 241; companionate, 232, 281, 296–97; defense of bourgeois, 141, 255; negotiated, 281–82; as universal locus of reproduction, 229–30, 232, 234–35, 249, 254–58, 278; as western value, 255–56
Fate, love of (*amor fati*), 4, 17, 22, 55
Feagin, Joe, 195
Femininity, 108, 233, 250–53, 258, 289–90
Feminism, 4, 10, 22–23, 65, 103, 107, 130, 229; and conflict theory, 89, 234, 254, 264–65, 269, 277–78; economistic, 295; and lesbian separatism, 147, 230–31, 237, 241–43, 255, 291, 299; liberal, 108, 147, 230, 235, 247, 251–52, 269, 286; as marriage counseling, 279; masculinized, 249–50, 254, 261, 264, 266, 269, 278; and New Right, 253, 268; as political theory, 249; and poststructuralism, 7; as psychopathology, 232, 254; radical, 245–46, 250, 251–53, 258, 267, 269, 274; safe and unsafe, 148, 230, 235, 321; second-stage, 234, 243, 249–50, 252–53; socialist, 42, 153, 181, 233, 237–39, 241, 250, 258, 261, 265, 267, 372; sociological, 133, 147, 231, 270, 277; and third-force psychiatry, 286
Feminist method, 107–8, 110, 258
Feuerbach, Ludwig, 194

Fiction as generic discourse, 22, 96, 119, 357
Firestone, Shulamith, 233
Forms of life, 335–36, 347, 349, 351, 356–57
Foucault, Michel, 2, 39, 41, 43, 64, 74, 338, 368–72
Frankfurt School, 3–4, 7, 10, 16, 28, 42, 48–49, 84, 140–41, 146, 189, 259, 304, 336–38, 341, 347, 361, 365–67, 372
Freedom: existential, 118; theory, 76
Freire, Paulo, 27
Freud, Sigmund, 5, 12, 62, 77, 119, 142, 338
Friedan, Betty, 230, 234, 243, 249, 254, 268, 278, 298–99
Friedman, Milton, 160
Friedrichs, Robert, 350
Functionalism. *See* Structural functionalism

Gadamer, Hans-Georg, 63, 112
Galbraith, John Kenneth, 36
Garfinkel, Harold, 6, 27–28, 35, 62, 88–89
Gay rights, 241–42, 244, 247
Gellner, Ernest, 27
Gender, differences in performative abilities, 150
Giddens, Anthony, 40, 116, 195, 204, 321
Gilligan, Carol, 274
Gouldner, Alvin, 350
Gramsci, Antonio, 138, 162, 189, 199, 220, 329
Grand Hotel Abyss, 141
Greene, Graham, 119

Habermas, Jurgen, 2, 7–10, 17, 22, 24–25, 28–29, 41, 43, 47–48, 50, 62–65, 73, 78, 80, 83, 91–92, 96, 112, 119, 131, 150, 169, 190, 195, 303–4, 335–36, 341, 345, 348, 353, 355–56, 359–60, 366, 368–69, 371–72
Harvey, David, 369
Haven in a heartless world, 259
Hayek, Friedrich, 83
Hegel, G. W. F., 5, 11, 39, 46, 65, 79, 81, 116, 128, 137, 169, 197–98, 340; master-slave relation, 138, 197, 299
Hegemony, 30, 65, 89, 108, 122, 127, 132, 153, 200, 224, 313, 330, 332; of text, 358
Heidegger, Martin, 131, 142, 342
Heisenberg, Werner, 26, 130, 358
Hermeneutic circle, 129

Hermeneutics, 7, 39, 51, 112–13, 305; radical, 112
Heteronomy, 47, 65, 80, 85, 108, 200, 335, 353
Heterosexism, 234, 246, 256, 260, 269
Heterotextuality, 107, 230, 235, 248, 254, 258, 260–61, 287, 300, 322, 346, 371
Hierarchy, 4, 6, 11, 23, 105, 126, 163, 272, 297, 371–72
History, 6, 9–11, 13–16, 18, 21, 24, 55, 57–58, 83, 85, 102, 104, 123, 131–32, 148, 172; philosophy of, 12, 18, 130, 156
Hobbes, Thomas, 88–89, 198–99, 221; problem of order, 88–89, 116
Homans, George, 184, 281
Homophobia, 247
Homosexuality, 230–31, 244, 247–48; construction of, 246; empirical incidence of, 247, 256
Horkheimer, Max, 10, 23–24, 48, 65–66, 74, 78, 86, 237, 338, 341, 347, 369
Horowitz, Gad, 77
Housework, 230, 256, 265, 279, 361; disposition of, 243, 281–82, 297; and surplus value, 238
Humanism, 8, 15, 77, 83–84, 89, 104, 108, 127, 129, 208, 257
Husserl, Edmund, 34, 64, 89

Ideal speech situation, 2, 8, 48, 62, 65, 91, 119, 131, 303, 332, 360
Idealism, 15, 23–24, 39, 48, 65, 74, 76, 84–85, 88, 94, 116, 128, 142, 149, 258, 332, 351
Identity theory, 5, 13, 48, 58, 126, 339
Ideology, 2, 6, 16, 17, 22, 25, 27–28, 32, 42, 54, 56, 60, 65–66, 159, 195, 300, 304, 334, 336–37, 341, 358, 361, 365; and clarity, 369; critique, 15, 38, 45, 55, 366, 369, 371; critique of, 4; end of, 133, 147; and literary practice, 23, 196, 305, 308; secular, 165
Imagination, dialectical, 161
Income gap, 268, 295
Indeterminacy, 130, 358
Industrial Revolution, 4, 15
Intelligence, falling rate of, 354, 368
Intentionality, 51, 114, 355
Interest groups, 201, 221, 230, 234, 240, 248, 271

Intermediation, 128, 139
International: Second, 51, 176, 198; Third, 162, 198
Intersubjectivity, 30, 38, 50, 73–74, 109, 113, 357
Intertextuality, 7, 9, 33, 38, 41, 50, 62, 71, 113–14, 124, 128, 150, 166
Irigaray, Luce, 272, 369
Iron cage, 15, 17, 58, 61, 209
Irony, 60, 85, 366

Jacoby, Russell, 77
Jaggar, Alison, 233
Jakobsen, Roman, 71
Jameson, Fredric, 42, 88, 173
Jay, Martin, 28
Johnson, President Lyndon, War on Poverty, 187–88

Kant, Immanuel, 41, 94, 106, 118, 133, 254, 334, 356
Keynes, John Maynard, 16, 185, 191
Kierkegaard, Martin, 286
Knowledge, 45, 55, 59, 174; constitution, productive principles of, 110
Kohlberg, Lawrence, 274
Korsch, Karl, 4, 84, 365
Kristeva, Julia, 7, 21, 272, 369
Kuhn, Thomas, 83, 111, 271, 322

L'art pour l'art, 127
Labor: alienation of, 149, 153, 155, 169, 177, 239, 345, 362; nonproductive, 230, 240, 252; parties, 154–55, 186, 188–89; pink-collar, 229, 243, 292; power, 211; wage, and social worth, 42, 239, 268–69, 361
Lacan, Jacques, 64
Language: games, 8, 10, 22, 26, 30, 53, 93, 277; ordinary, 26, 28–29, 51
Lasch, Christopher, 75, 259
Lasswell, Harold, 208
Left: New, 83, 231, 245, 251, 305; Old, 23
Legitimation, 17, 83, 182; crisis, 65
Leiss, William, 369
Lenin, V. I., 46–47, 147, 155, 161–63, 166, 169
Leninism, 77, 162, 169, 189; and van-guardism, 77, 147, 162, 168
Lenski, Gerhard, 204, 213, 217–18

Lesbianism, 231–32, 236, 242, 244, 247, 252, 258 and otherness, 232–33, 241, 247, 250; and separatism, 147, 230–31, 235, 241, 250
Lévi-Strauss, Claude, 93, 350, 356
Lewis, Lionel S., 205
Liberalism, 47–48, 50, 61, 72, 83, 108, 176, 178–79, 182, 190, 193–94, 212, 222, 230, 233, 235, 241, 246, 248, 281, 287, 298–99, 317, 319–20, 325
Life-chances, 11, 273
Life instincts, 77, 326, 338
Lifeworld, 22–23, 25, 84, 88–89, 224, 242, 305, 309–10, 337–39, 353, 362; colonization of, 7, 8, 24–25; and system, 50
Literary: corrigibility, 9, 95; criticism, 7, 62, 71, 79, 145, 361; version of science, 9
Literature, 21, 34, 151; committed, 48, 54, 56, 129, 328; original, 52, 112, 114–15, 125, 202, 307
Locke, John, 26
Logocentrism, 55, 65, 96, 363
Luckmann, Thomas, 88
Luddism, 303
Lukacs, Georg, 4, 28, 84, 141, 169, 220, 239, 329, 345, 365, 367
Luther, Martin, 11, 128
Lysenkoism, 247

Macpherson, C. B., 198
Macrosociology, 88
Male, method, 107
Mannheim, Karl, 37, 55, 349–50
Marcuse, Herbert, 2, 6, 10, 22, 28, 42, 44, 48, 65, 77–78, 83, 97–98, 115, 119, 130, 140, 142, 191, 303, 305, 321, 338, 343, 345, 366
Marginalia, 32, 47, 49, 125, 138–39, 142, 144, 146, 148, 151, 154, 218, 334
Marginality, 95, 103, 108–9, 112, 139–40, 142, 144, 323, 331–32
Margins, splitting, 153–54
Marx, Karl, 1, 2, 4, 12, 15–16, 25, 33, 43, 46, 48–49, 52, 55, 78, 139; as determinist or voluntarist, 172, 305; his prophecy of socialism, 2, 172
Marxism, 13–14, 22–24, 65, 76, 93, 103, 130, 205; Derridean, 331; disciplining of, 89, 133, 144, 191; and existential

phenomenology, 28; Freudian, 77, 97, 119, 349; Hegelian, 4, 22, 198–99, 309, 365; lawless, 35, 174; and Leninism, 162, 166, 180, 360; mainstreaming, 193, 211–12; mechanical, 25, 55, 62; monolithic, 66; monopoly/monologue, 183; as natural science of history, 162, 174; neo-Marxism, 10; as ontology of conflict, 145, 147, 152, 161–62, 174, 199, 207; orthodox, 7, 23, 25, 59, 66, 167; Paris existential, 189, 338; and poststructuralism, 21; proving, 149; quantitative, 154; repressive desublimation of, 195; Russification of, 162–67; safe and unsafe, 137, 146, 148–49, 151, 181, 205, 225, 321; its scientific failures, 13, 144–45, 152, 156–58, 161, 170, 172, 174, 191–93; sociologized, 54, 89, 99, 138, 141, 145, 148, 152, 163, 174, 195; as sociology of stratification, 153; Soviet, 82, 146, 154, 163–64, 180, 191, 193, 212, 214; and violence, 165, 177; western, 3–4, 24, 84, 162, 169, 181, 294, 299, 340, 366

Materialism: dialectical, 51; historical, 22, 51, 365, 368; interdisciplinary, 78, 80; intertextual, 79

Matriarchy, 56

Mead, George Herbert, 88

Means, Gordon, 152

Mehan, Hugh, 29, 88

Men: hearts of, 251, 283–85, 289; women, and child care, 259–60, 289

Merleau-Ponty, Maurice, 28, 49, 71, 338–40, 343, 349

Merton, Robert, 159

Metaphysics, 23, 49, 64–65, 81, 99, 141, 201, 313, 327

Methodology, 2–3, 8–9, 14, 27, 32, 40, 49, 51, 54, 64, 84, 94, 99, 106–7, 109–10, 114–15, 119, 122, 125, 129–30, 132, 145, 219, 313, 327, 371; Derridean, 64, 363

Michels, Robert, 223

Microsociology, 84, 88–89, 108, 128, 199

Mill, John Stuart, 43, 47–48, 341; marketplace of ideas, 47, 128

Millett, Kate, 267–68

Mills, C. Wright, 17, 222, 318

Misogyny, 65, 87, 108, 150, 215, 264, 269, 278

Mitterand, Francois, 186, 189, 193

Mobility, upward, 201

Modernism, 2

Modernity, 12, 58, 60, 61, 65, 73, 90, 100, 224

Modernization, 5, 11, 161, 275, 297

Monogamy, 246

Motherhood, eternal, 232, 238, 244, 251, 265, 269, 276, 284

Motive: ascription of, 312; suppression of, 312, 315, 327

Movements, radical, 180–82

Narrative, 1, 6, 17, 21, 26, 30, 40, 61, 82, 101, 166

Narrativeness, 37, 71, 82, 91, 94, 96, 117

Necessity, regime of, 82

Negation of negation, 48, 56, 81–82, 323

Negative, dialectics, 5, 9, 45, 48–49, 59, 172, 303

Negativity, artificial, 125

Neoconservatism, 154, 159, 163, 183, 211

Neofunctionalism, 8, 322

Neo-Kantian, 13, 15, 17, 28–29, 37, 78–79, 83–84, 87, 104, 107, 110, 140, 142, 208

New Criticism, 7, 51

New sensibility, 65, 77, 303

Newton, Isaac, 26, 36, 114

Nietzsche, Friedrich, 4, 9, 17, 22, 64, 81, 98, 115, 311, 313, 317, 333, 338, 368

Nihilism, 130, 149

Nonidentity, 9–10, 32, 34–36, 50, 55, 59, 64, 66, 103, 109, 118, 120, 124–26, 132, 137–38, 141–43, 150, 185, 220, 309, 328, 339–40, 344, 347, 350–51, 357; dialectical, 59, 338–39, 341; of subject and object, 91, 178, 311, 316, 355

Nonscience, 2, 39, 45, 71, 82–83, 85–89, 94, 96, 99, 103, 105, 125–26, 130, 138, 144, 146–47, 165, 311, 321, 333, 353, 357

Nonsociological, 67, 73–74, 82, 125

Nozick, Robert, 160

Objectivity, 2, 30–31, 39, 58, 63, 66, 90, 95–98, 100–101, 277, 315; preponderance of, 11, 46, 58, 75, 77, 199, 248, 312, 325–26, 335; of subjectivity, 31, 62, 314, 339

One-dimensionality, 42, 44, 362, 366

O'Neill, John, 28, 342, 350

Ontologemes, 173
Ontology, 5–6, 10, 12, 14, 16, 18, 21, 24, 31, 35, 56, 58, 66, 81, 82–83, 85, 104, 159, 172, 194, 218, 306
Otherness, 10, 48, 55, 58, 72, 103, 109, 133, 138, 144–45, 147, 231
Overdetermination, 22–23, 25, 63, 221

Pacification, 55
Packard, Vance, 223
Page, Charles, 322
Parenthood, compulsory, 245
Pareto, Vilfredo, 223
Paris Commune, 158, 177
Parliamentarianism, 189, 191, 317
Parsons, Talcott, 5, 13, 15, 22, 51–53, 57–58, 60, 75, 88–89, 125, 127, 139, 183, 231, 255, 271, 289, 366–67; and American common values, 57–58, 74
Particular and general, 40, 49, 86, 328
Patriarchy, 3–6, 14, 23, 30, 90, 107, 209, 233, 240, 245, 250, 264, 278–79, 290, 292, 368; and child development, 259, 290
Personal and political, 231–32, 236, 242–43, 247–48, 258, 276
Phenomenology, 4, 7, 34; critical, 14, 28, 309
Philosophy, analytic, 27, 51
Plato's cave, 118, 313
Platonism, 52, 131, 234
Pluralism, 213, 216, 221–22, 240, 315
Poetry after Auschwitz, 308–9
Political, 30, 86, 106; art of, 358; conformity, 2; economy, 22, 25, 55, 214–15, 223, 305, 358, 371; theory, 51, 90, 176, 198, 233, 333; unconscious, 42
Politics: good, 345, 359; of otherness, 146
Polity, moral, 45
Popper, Karl, 37, 176
Pornography, 276, 369
Positivism, 3, 5, 7, 9, 13, 15–17, 24, 26, 28–29, 33, 35, 37, 42, 55–60, 63, 73, 84, 94, 118–20, 129, 132, 139, 147, 150, 190, 194, 316, 372; and interpretation, 7; logical, 109, 120, 124, 311
Possessive individualism, 16, 198–99
Postindustrialism, 15, 36, 152, 239
Postmodernism, 2, 23, 50, 147, 342, 358, 362, 364, 367, 369
Poststructuralism, 4, 7, 12, 21–22, 25, 47, 64–65, 336, 363, 367–68; and discourse theory, 22, 62; and literary criticism, 365
Poulantzas, Nicos, 196
Poverty, 152, 159, 164, 184, 202
Practico-inert, 112, 368
Praxis, 9, 28, 92, 94, 96, 189, 304
Production, 22, 24, 49, 151, 190; primacy of, 55, 210–11, 239, 243; its reproduction, 192, 229, 235; social relations of, 29, 153, 212, 229, 236–37, 268
Progress: myth of, 170, 201
Proletarianization, 216
Proletariat, dictatorship of, 168, 180
Promesse de bonheur, 16
Prostitution, 276, 290–91
Psychoanalysis: negative, 77, 81–82, 97, 294; neo-Freudian, 62, 74
Psychologism, 74–76, 137, 258, 279, 283
Psychology: and sociology, 66, 73, 75–76, 80; third-force, 78, 98
Public/private split, 24, 237
Pythagoras, 52

Quantification, 53, 88, 108, 125, 154, 219, 247, 314

Racism, 3, 18, 23, 42–43, 57, 73, 100, 102, 137, 183, 187, 240, 368
Rape, 287–88
Rationalism, 12, 24, 28, 224, 317
Reading, 3, 22–23, 29, 31, 38, 43–44, 50, 55–56, 58–59, 72, 308; aporetic, 61; close, 51; deconstructive, 4–5, 7, 56, 60, 324, 359; disciplinary, 3, 6, 8, 21, 25, 58, 61
Reagan, President Ronald, 133, 158–59, 164, 223, 293, 359
Realism, photographic, 91
Reason: eclipse of, 128, 369; instrumental, 83, 143; nonlogocentric concept of, 65; speculative, 97, 104, 106, 110, 117, 127, 369; technical, 10, 12, 94
Reception theory, 7, 66
Reformism and radicalism, 188
Reich, Charles, 252
Reification, 28, 41, 220, 239, 330, 367
Relativism, 4, 47–48, 71, 81, 114, 125–26, 149, 320
Relativity, 48, 81

Religion, civil, 17
Representation, 1, 6, 10, 14, 22, 30, 36, 47–48, 59, 63, 90, 103, 108, 121, 124, 129, 132, 148–49, 151, 159, 229, 326, 367; presuppositionless, 10, 18, 21, 26, 29, 35, 56, 61, 113, 271, 310, 372
Repressive desublimation, 98
Repressive tolerance, 321
Reproduction, 8, 16–17, 24, 41, 49, 55, 109, 126, 128–29, 139, 151, 190, 223–24, 230, 287, 308, 341, 352, 356, 362; biopolitics of, 230; intellectual and social, 114, 307–8, 311; mechanical, 32–33, 105, 111; social relations of, 237, 268; subordination to production, 23, 42, 107, 141, 238, 254, 361
Ricardo, David, 358
Rickert, Heinrich, 13
Rigor, 97, 99–100, 103, 105, 107–8, 324
Role: conflict, 277–78, 291; negotiation, 251, 277–79, 281–82; strain, 150, 278, 291
Romanticism, 52
Roosevelt, President Franklin Delano, 16, 183, 185–86, 189, 207, 230
Rousseau, Jean-Jacques, 64, 114
Russian revolution, 138, 158, 162

Sandinistas, 186
Sartre-Jean-Paul, 28, 48–49, 112, 188, 190, 199, 220, 338, 345, 349, 363, 368
Saussure, Ferdinand de, 26, 356
Schlafly, Phyllis, 243
Schoenberg, Arnold, 141–43, 345
Scholarship, 3, 62, 66, 94, 130, 174, 205, 319, 353
Schutz, Alfred, 88–89
Science, 5, 8–9, 11, 14, 16, 18, 21, 24, 26–30, 32, 35, 37–38, 40, 43, 45, 52, 55, 58, 72, 84, 97–98, 100, 104, 130, 150, 159; good, 9, 248, 359, 372; and humanism contrast, 78, 87, 104, 107; new, 77, 83, 95, 108, 343; normal, 83, 111, 192, 271, 307; playful, 77, 98, 104
Scientificity/scientism, 2, 14, 23, 26, 30–31, 34, 36, 47, 51–52, 54, 61, 66, 84–87, 89–90, 95–99, 101, 104, 105, 107–8, 110, 112, 121, 125, 128–30, 142, 144–45, 156, 170, 187, 200, 204, 229, 233, 236, 247–48, 253, 263, 269, 306, 310, 315,

318–19, 322–23, 332, 341, 344, 350, 355; Marxian, 169–70, 175, 189, 311, 337, 360
Searle, John, 356
Self, 5, 75–77, 98, 328
Sex: and gender, 266, 273; roles, 251, 266, 277, 289, 296; roles, traditional, 275, 280, 284–85, 289
Sexuality, 4, 204, 229–30, 242, 273, 292, 361; apolitical, 256, 369; political, 248
Sher, Gerson, 189
Shorter, Edward, 233
Show Trials, 157, 179
Signification, 26, 54, 371
Simmel, Georg, 5, 197
Skocpol, Theda, 195, 321
Slater, Phil, 348
Smith, Adam, 51–52, 191, 199, 358, 365
Social: historicity of, 56–57; power of, 3, 10, 13, 17–18, 27, 36, 41, 43, 53, 56–57, 61, 67, 72–78, 80–82, 85–87, 90–91, 95, 100, 120, 124, 130, 138–40, 145, 148–49, 158, 194–95, 199, 202, 206, 269, 306, 310, 312, 314, 329, 334, 339, 351–53, 363, 370–72
Social being, 55, 87, 119, 323, 347, 372
Social change, inevitability of, 13–14, 48, 188, 202
Social class, 25
Social control, 109
Social criticism, 303, 315
Social Darwinism, 183
Social democracy, 154, 182, 186, 188–89, 193
Social facts, 1, 3, 6, 13, 18, 39, 48, 83, 90, 94, 97, 103, 115, 127, 240, 256, 284, 306, 311
Social fate, 3, 11, 100
Social formations, 196
Social freedom, 199
Social laws, 4, 7, 11, 14, 48, 60, 90, 103, 117, 149, 269, 306
Social nature, 1, 12, 31, 38, 57–58, 203–4, 240, 284
Social phenomenology, 8
Social physics, 5
Social problems, 13–15, 137, 146, 159, 185, 204, 207–8, 279, 320–21, 348
Social psychologism, 235, 284
Social psychology, 6, 50, 74, 278, 282

Social science, mainstream, 1, 5, 13, 35, 78
Social text, 8, 16–17, 29, 41, 49, 53, 55–56, 82, 91, 172, 195, 200, 231, 274, 303–4, 311, 325, 337
Social theory, 3, 21–22, 28, 50, 76, 93, 176
Socialism, 2, 9, 16, 18, 25, 65, 83, 131, 155–56, 162, 166–67, 186, 188, 192, 208; capitalist, 185; democratic, 37; evolutionary, 175; humane, 155, 168–69; nonauthoritarian, 50–51, 313; state, 57, 163, 218, 235, 240; western European, 154–55, 186, 189–90; Yugoslavian, 189
Socialist parties, 154
Socialization, 109, 257, 274, 277
Sociology: American, 1, 5, 11, 36, 43, 52, 65–66, 72, 74, 83, 137, 179, 193, 198–99, 201–2, 276, 318, 350; critical, 15, 146, 316–17; disciplinary, 1–3, 7, 22, 27, 47, 71, 98; of gender, sex roles, and family, 31, 73, 134, 138, 230, 250, 277; of knowledge, 3, 6, 40–41; of literature, 303, 336; mainstream, 1–4, 8, 11–12, 57, 113, 134, 148, 162, 204, 314, 321, 323; and Marxism, 89, 127, 134, 146–48, 151, 161, 169, 176, 192, 204, 210, 225, 233; masculine, 254, 256; middle-range, 85, 123; new, 353; positivist, 1, 4, 18; reflexive, 329, 350; of sociology, 350, 370; Standard American, 1, 306; its symptomatic silences, 67; textbooks, 7, 14, 16, 31, 52, 66, 80, 306–7, 314, 370; undoing of, 95, 326, 328; and value, 100; western, 4
Socioontology, 18, 94, 98, 115, 175, 196, 319, 323, 349
Sombart, Werner, 183
Sontag, Susan, 157
Soviet: gulag, 137, 147–48, 154, 163, 167–68, 179, 188–89, 200; terror, 157, 179; Union, 82, 140, 146, 155–57, 161, 163, 165–69, 180, 186, 189
Speech act theory, 25, 64, 304, 348, 359
Spencer, Herbert, 33, 183
Stalin, Joseph, 48, 82, 146, 154–55, 161–62, 164, 166, 169, 174, 176, 340
Stark, Rodney, 275
State: intervention, 24, 65, 137, 184, 223; police, 78, 161, 165; relative autonomy of, 65, 184, 222

Statism, and redistributive strategies, 210
Status: attainment, 23; attainment research, 6, 217, 265; inconsistency, 213, 217–18
Stratification, 163, 196, 206, 212–13, 217
Structural functionalism, 5, 27, 52, 54, 84, 123–26, 190, 194–95, 199, 202, 234, 255, 266–67, 276, 282, 321–22
Structuralism, 7, 154
Subjectivity, 6, 11, 26, 31, 38, 49, 63, 66, 76–78, 81, 97, 110, 114, 127, 133, 248, 270, 326; Archimedean, 45, 47; collective, 46
Subtext, 18, 31–32, 34, 37, 40, 42–43, 62–63, 66, 73, 81–82, 86, 90, 96, 98, 100–101, 105, 113, 116–17, 119, 122–23, 126, 128–29, 151, 183, 194–95, 248, 262, 317, 325, 335, 350, 360
Surplus repression, 65, 77, 97–98, 101, 232
Surplus value, 77, 149–50
Symbolic interactionism, 29, 84, 125–26, 281

Taylorism, 333, 346–47
Technology, high, 16
Text, 1, 6–9, 16–17, 23, 25, 30–33, 35, 60, 92, 101, 128, 348; last, 36, 118–20, 129, 139–40, 159; play, 56, 64; as tombstones, 363
Textual politics, 146–47, 160, 176, 178, 203, 231, 238, 306, 358
Textuality, 22–23, 25–26, 43, 50, 54, 61, 96, 98, 120, 123, 127, 133, 367, 370
Theoretical practice, 123, 236
Theory: construction, 52–53, 93, 116; grounded, 116; and utility, 125
Tito, Josef Broz, 189
Toennies, Ferdinand, 5
Totalitarianism, 176, 180, 182, 191
Totalization, 8, 39, 49, 60, 81, 123
Tradition, 63, 112, 114
Transcendental ego, 30

Undecidability, 8, 25–26, 58, 62, 86, 139, 141, 172
Underconsumption, 15
Unemployment, structural, 15, 185
Universal pragmatics, 73
Universalism, 43, 327–28
Utilitarianism, 280, 312

Validity, 32, 34, 121–22, 126, 130, 157, 242;
claims, 21, 26, 91–92, 124, 129
Value-freedom, 38, 100–101, 130, 261, 316
Variance, explanation of, 74, 219–21
Veblen, Thorstein, 223
Vienna Circle, 37, 120, 311

Wallerstein, Immanuel, 321
Warsaw Pact, 189
Weber, Max, 4–5, 10–12, 15, 17, 22, 33,
36, 43, 52–53, 55, 58, 60–61, 74, 83,
85, 115, 127, 144, 154, 205, 207–9, 212,
234, 241, 276, 280, 311–12, 318, 322,
327; on class, power, and status, 13, 79,
196; and Marxism, 14, 147, 161, 173, 187,
193, 211, 222, 267–68, 283; plural theory
of stratification, 153, 196, 212–13, 217;
renaissance, 213, 317
Welfare state, 183, 185–86, 191, 233;
capitalist, 13, 184, 207; Keynesian, 175,
211
Wilson, Harold, 186
Windelband, Wilhelm, 13

Wittgenstein, Ludwig, 5, 8, 335–36, 356
Women: advantages of, 251, 274–75; and
careerism, 249, 283; disciplined, 286, 293;
failed, 232; good, 249–50; movement, 229,
232, 234, 241, 244, 249–52, 286; real,
249; straight, 233, 249; and stress, 251,
283–84; studies, 144, 147, 236; wild, 232;
workforce participation, 42, 231, 268–69,
292
Wood, Houston, 29, 88
World: Second, 166; Third, 166, 318–19
Wright, Erik Olin, 154, 204–5, 207
Writing, 1, 7, 9, 16, 22, 26, 31, 35, 37,
43–44, 49–50, 53, 57, 72, 81, 94, 106,
129, 132, 139, 324, 348; degree zero, 48;
and desire, 16, 40, 122, 372; dialectical,
9, 26, 303, 354; different, 303, 335;
dispersal of, 367, 369, 371; nonidentical,
314, 339, 355–56; nonpositivist, 54,
149; oppositional, 141; positivist, 3, 8;
unmediated, 130; wild, 40, 114, 145

Zhdanovism, 10

Note on the Author

Ben Agger, associate professor of sociology at SUNY-Buffalo, is the author of many articles on critical theory, Marxism, feminism, and discourse theory. He has published several related books, including *Western Marxism: An Introduction, Social Problems through Conflict and Order* (with S. A. McDaniel), *Fast Capitalism: A Critical Theory of Significance*, and *Reading Science: A Literary and Political Analysis*. He is working on *The Decline of Discourse: Textual Politics in the Postmodern Age*, a book about what writers write today.